York Deeds, Volume 6

You are holding a reproduction of an original work that is in the public domain in the United States of America, and possibly other countries. You may freely copy and distribute this work as no entity (individual or corporate) has a copyright on the body of the work. This book may contain prior copyright references, and library stamps (as most of these works were scanned from library copies). These have been scanned and retained as part of the historical artifact.

This book may have occasional imperfections such as missing or blurred pages, poor pictures, errant marks, etc. that were either part of the original artifact, or were introduced by the scanning process. We believe this work is culturally important, and despite the imperfections, have elected to bring it back into print as part of our continuing commitment to the preservation of printed works worldwide. We appreciate your understanding of the imperfections in the preservation process, and hope you enjoy this valuable book.

YORK DEEDS

BOOK VI

EDITED BY
WILLIAM M. SARGENT, A. M.
MEMBER OF THE MAINE HISTORICAL SOCIETY, OF THE MAINE GENEALOGICAL
SOCIETY, AND OF THE GORGES SOCIETY

PORTLAND
BROWN THURSTON & COMPANY
1889

PRINTED BY B. THURSTON & CO.

CONTENTS.

PREFACE	Page	5
REGISTER'S CERTIFICATE	Page	9
ERRATA	Page	10
YORK DEEDS,	Folios	1—177
INDEX,		
I. Grantors	Pages	2— 49
II. Grantees	Pages	50— 99
III. Other Persons	Pages	100—110
IV. Places	Pages	111—114
V. General	Pages	115—130

PREFACE.

THIS book was opened February 26, 1686 [i.e. 1687][1] by Thomas Scottow, the Deputy Register for Maine under Edward Randolph, who was sole register in New England under the Andros government.[2]

He had continued the record of deeds of his predecessors in the fourth book. It is probable that that fourth book was abandoned by him, while only half filled, in consequence of the orders of the Andros government, and that in further compliance therewith, the fourth book was taken with the earlier books to Boston in May, 1687. He continued the record of deeds herein until April 14, 1689[3], only four days before the revolution in Boston. This sixth book was not again resumed till August 26, 1699[4] by the elder Joseph Hammond, after he had filled the blank spaces left in books four and five. He continued them quite regularly until the last of May, 1700[5]: and being in June, 1700, appointed a judge of the County Court of Common Pleas, he was succeeded in the office of Register of Deeds by his son Joseph Hammond, junior. The younger Hammond recorded the balance of this book; his last regular entry being apparently in August 1703[6], although there are scattered entries of later dates apparently inserted as marginal notes.[7]

Though mainly a record of deeds, this book embraces records of historical importance contemporaneous with the so-called Usurpation of Andros, and preserves to posterity the names of many of the officials of "his Majesty's Territory and Dominion of New England"; there is a recital by President Danforth of his authority to make legal confirmation to the Inhabitants of Maine of their holdings

---

[1] Infra fol. 1. [2] See his commission 27 Mass. Hist. Soc. Coll. 161.
[3] Infra fol. 37. [4] Infra fol. 38. [5] Infra fol. 56 and 57. [6] Infra fol. 173.
[7] Compare fol. 106, 163 and 165.

under Gorges, from the Governor and Company of the Massachusetts Colony, " the now Ld Propriet^r of ye above named Province of Maine[1]"; a cautious expectancy by some of these "inhabitants" that in time to come " there [might] happen a Chief Ld Proprietor"[2] to revive dormant claims; some scattering references to General Assemblies of the Province; and others to various acts of the General Court of Massachusetts.

The completion of this book fills the gaps in the printed records of registered deeds for the whole of the seventeenth century. Besides filling those gaps chronologically, it is further especially valuable by supplying conveyances, necessary to connect the chain of titles to large and important tracts, that in some cases did not find their way upon record for many years after their dates; among these may be cited the conveyance by the Agamenticus colony in 1638 to Henry Simpson of a large and important tract in York[3]; of George Cleeve in 1651 to Nicholas Bartlett of the hundred acres now the heart of Portland[4]; of other grants by Cleeve in 1658 to the two Mittens at Portland[5]; of Francis Champernown in 1669 to Walter Barefoot in Kittery[6]; of Roger Hill in 1671 to John Hellson at Saco[7]; and many others.

Quite as noticeable is one omission to which it directs attention; in folio 175 may be read the recital of a conveyance of forty-five square miles along the Newichewannock River by Sir Ferdinando Gorges to Capt. John Mason of London in 1635. This should have gone on record; but there being then no place for a record, and Capt. Mason having died before Gorges' establishment of his court and registry, it was overlooked. A certified copy of the original was lately discovered with other muniments of the Mason titles and is now deposited in the Collections of the Maine Historical Society[8].

The recurrence at fol. 120 of the double share or portion of an

[1] Infra fol. 78.   [2] Infra fol. 91.   [3] Infra fol. 74.   [4] Fol. 139.
[5] Fol. 3 and 8.   [6] Fol. 158.   [7] Fol. 6.
[8] See the Portland Advertiser of April 11, 1887, for a description of these papers.

estate belonging to an eldest son by the Laws of this Province, as there stated, and its occurrence elsewhere previously in these books,[1] seems to call for a brief abstract of the legislation establishing so important a change in the law of inheritance. So far as has been disclosed in these books, prior to the purchase of the District of Maine in 1676 by Massachusetts, the property of intestates was equally distributed among all the children, but after that date the laws of that Colony then in force governed the descent; of which the following are abstracts, viz: —

"CHAPTER IV. (Enacted Dec. 10, 1641.)
"*Of the Right of Inheritance.*

"§ 5. Inheritances are to descend naturally to the next of kin, according to the law of nature, delivered by God.

"§ 6. Observe, if a man have more sons than one, then *a double portion* to be assigned and bequeathed to the eldest son, according to the law of nature; unless his own demerit do deprive him of the dignity of his birthright."

"PROVINCE LAWS, 1692-3
"Chapter 14: Passed November 1st.
"*An Act for the Settling and Distribution of the Estate of Intestates.*

"One third part of the personal estate to the wife of the intestate forever, besides her dower or thirds in the houses and lands during life . . . . and all the residue of the real and personal estate, by equal portions, to and among his children, and such as shall legally represent them (if any of them be dead) . . . . . except the eldest son then surviving (where there is no issue of the first-born or of any other elder son,) who shall have two shares, or a double portion of the whole; and where there are no sons, the daughters shall inherit as co-parceners."

This law was continued by the Act of March 9, 1784, in full force as regards the provision under consideration; it was repealed by the Act of June 8, 1789, and a new enactment passed, that all the

[1] York Deeds III., 137.

Preface.

children should share alike after the 1st of January 1790. This law was continued by the Act of March 12, 1806, until the Separation of 1820, and was in substance re-encacted by the first Maine Legislature and approved March 20, 1821.

The few errors discovered after seven distinct readings of this text, shows the care of the committee, the zeal of the publishers and their employés, and its general excellence and handsome appearance reflect credit upon all concerned.

The contractions and abreviations are those used throughout and explained in the Preface to Book I.

WM. M. SARGENT.

REGISTER'S CERTIFICATE.

State of Maine.

COUNTY OF YORK, ss:

This may certify that the following printed volume is a true copy of the sixth book of records of the Registry of Deeds for this County; that I have read and compared the same with the original records; and that all accidental variations that have been detected are noted in the table of errata on the following page.

Attest:

Justin M. Leavitt
Register of Deeds for York County.

ERRATA.

Folio 35, line 49, *for* Clearb *read* Clarke.
" 37, " 5, " iiij " iij.
" 92, " 14, *expunge* the second d in andd, and *add* I, to read And I.
" 112. " 2, *for* Jobnson *read* Johnson.
" 134, " 21, " odle " pole.

ADDENDA.

In the Index of Grantees, Joseph Hill and John Morrell are printed out of place, next after Rowland Young.

YORK DEEDS.

Know all men by these presents that they John John Ingersoll, and George Ingersoll Junr both of Casco Bay in the Province of Main in New England for & in Consideration of the Summ of seventy five pounds to them in hand before the Ensealing and Delivery hereof well and truly paid, by John Phillips of Charlestown, Syllvanus Davis, James English and John Endicott of Boston in the Massachusetts Colony of New England, the Receipt whereof as a valuable summ of money, they do hereby Acknowledge, and thereof, and of every part and parcell thereof, do exonerate acquitt and Discharge, the s^d John Phillips Syllvanus Davis, James English, & John Endicott, them & either of them their heires Exec^rs Adm^rs & Assignes forever by these presents, Have granted bargained sould & confirmed, and

<small>John & Georg Ingersoll to John Phillips &c</small> by these presents do fully & absolutely grant bargain sell enfeofe & confirme unto the s^d John Phillips, Syllvanus Davis, James English and John Endicott in equall parts and proportion, One full moiety of all that their Saw Mill, and the River on which it stands commonly called Mill River, scituate and being at Fallmoth in Casco Bay aboves^d within the Province of Main, granted to us by the President of the s^d Province, with the Priveledge of the Falls and Timber, and one half of the Land on both sides of the Falls sufficient for accomodation to the said Mill, which s^d Land is bounded by marked Trees, with the Wood Trees and timber standing lying and growing thereupon. To have & to hold the s^d granted premises with all waters, dams, utensills, Liberties and priveledges, accomodations and appurtenances thereto belonging unto them the s^d John Phillips, Syllvanus Davis, James English & John Endicott their heires and Assignes in equall Parts, and proportion, and to their only proper use and be-

Book VI, Fol. 1.

hoof forever, And wee the s^d John Ingersoll and George Ingersoll do hereby avouch o^r Selves, at the time of the Ensealing, & untill the delivery of these presents to be the true and Lawfull Owners of all the above bargained premises, Freely and clearly acquitted and discharged from all former, and other barguines, Sales, Titles & Incumbrances, And do bind our Selves, our Heires Exec^rs and Adm^rs to Warrant and Defend all the said Premises and appurtenances, unto the s^d John Phillips, Syllvanus Davis, James English and John Endicott their heires and Assignes forever against all persons whomsoever lawfully claiming the Same or any part thereof. Witnesse our hands and Seales hereunto sett this thirteenth day of March, Anno Domini sixteen hundred eighty three four

Sealed & Delivered in
  presence of   John Ingersoll (seal)
  Anthony Brackett,   George Ingersoll, (seal)
  Sarah Baker.

The abovesaid John and George Ingersoll do for themselves their Heires Exec^rs Adm^rs warrant the above Bill of Sale no further, then the grant of the President of the Province of Main will Beare/

John Ingersoll and George Ingersoll Junr appeared before me and owned the within mentioned Instrument to be their Act and Deed this 13th March 168¾

                Before me Edw: Tynge Just P.

Deborah Ingersoll the wife of John Ingersoll, and Katterne Ingersoll the wife of George Ingersoll Junr appeared before me, and owned their free Consent to the within mentioned Bill of Sale the 13th of March 168¾

Jno & George Ingersall to John Phillips &c

                Edw: Tynge Just Pea

A true Copy of the Originall Instrument Transcribed and and compared this 2^d of ffebruary 1686   Attest^r

              Tho: Scottow: Dep^t Reg^tr

Book VI, Fol. 2.

Know all men by these presents that I Isaack Davis of Casco Bay in the Province of Main in New England for and in Consideration of the Summ of Six Poundes to me in hand before the ensealing and delivery hereof well and truly paid by Syllvanus Davis of s^d Casco Bay the Receipt whereof as a valuable Summ of money I do hereby Acknowledge, and thereof and of every part and parcell thereof, do exonerate acquitt and discharge the s^d Syllvanus Davis, his heires, Exec^{rs} Administrators & Assignes forever by these presents, Have granted bargained, sould and Confirmed, and by these presents do fully absolutely, grant, bargain, Sell enfeofe and confirm unto the s^d Syllvanus Davis, a Certain [2] parcell of fresh Marsh or Meadow to the full Quantity of ten acres lying scituate in the Towneship of Blackpoynt, alias Scarborough within the Province of Main at a Place there commonly called Nonsuch Marshes, lying near the head of the s^d marshes, which s^d marsh or meadow, I the said Isaack Davis purchased of John Skillin of afores^d Fallmoth, To have and to hold the afores^d ten Acres of marsh or meadow however butted or bounded or reputed to be butted and bounded with all its Rights Priveledges and appurtenances thereunto belonging, unto him the fores^d Syllvanus Davis, his Heires, Exec^{rs} Adm^{rs} & Assignes, and to his and there proper use forever, and I the s^d Isaack Davis do Avouch my self at the time of the ensealing and untill the delivery of these presents, to be the true and lawfull owner of the above granted and bargained premises, five acres of the aboves^d Marsh or Meadow was measured, bounded and delivered unto s^d Syllvanus Davis the twenty six day of May in the year sixteen hundred eighty and four, and lyes in fors^d meadow betwixt a parcell of Marsh that did then belong to William Burrage, and a parcell of Marsh that did then belong to George Ingersoll Junr and I the s^d Isaack Davis do by these presents bind myself my heires, Exec^{rs} Adminis^{rs} & Assignes

<small>Isaack Davis
to
Syll Davis</small>

to measure lay out bound and deliver unto the s^d Syllvanus Davis the remaining part of sd ten Acres of meadow upon all demands, or to the s^d Syllvanus Davis his heires or Assignes/ And for the true performance of the fore dementioned bargaind premises, without any fraud deceit or mentall Reservation whatsoever, I the said Isaack Davis with the free Consent of my wife Lydia Davis in full Relinquishment of Right of Dowry or thirds, have hereunto sett o^r handes and Seales this twenty second Day of December sixteen hundred eighty & six and in the Second year of the Reign of our soveraign Lord James the Second by the Grace of of God of England Scottland, France & Ireland King defender of Faith,

Sealed, Signed & delivered in presence of us
Jonathan Clarke }
Elizabeth Tynge }

Issaack CC Davis (seal)
his signe,
Lydia ⅄ Davis (seal)
her signe

Fallmoth Province of Main December the 22th 1686
Isauck Davis and Lydia Davis his wife appeared before me the Subscriber being one of the Council for this his Majesty Territory and Dominion of New England and Acknowledged this Instrument to which they have signed and sealed to be their Actuall & voluntary their Act and Deed.

           Edward Tynge.

A true Copy of the Originall Instrument transcribed and compared this 2^d of ffebruary 1686 Attest^r
        Th^o: Scottow Dep^t Regist^r

These Presents witnesseth that I George Cleave of Casco Gentleman have given granted, bargained and sould & by these presents do give, grant, sell and confirm, unto Nathaniell Mitten my Grand Child one hundred Acres of Land in Casco Bay in manner and form following That is fivety Acres of Land in the Back Cove, and next adjoyning to the fivety Acres formerly granted to his father Michaell Mitten, towards the South west side and so to go towards the North East by the water side home to the Lott of Humphrey Durram being fivety Poles by the Waters side or thereaboutes and so into the Woodes upon a strait Line eight score Poles till fivety Acres be Ended, together with fivety Acres of Upland or Marsh, to begin at the Narrow of the Neck, and up the River above the Now dwelling house of Michaell Mittten, to begin at the Eastward side of a little Round Marsh of mine excepted out of this grant, and redound a little Gutt that runneth toward the Long Marsh, and from thence up the River to the next Gutt Southerly or thereaboutes, and to Run from that Gutt Northwesterly into the Woods home to the side of the Long Marsh, but not to have any Part of the s^d Marsh, untill fivety Acres be ended according to the true meaning hereof/ To have and to hold all the s^d Lands & present premises of timber and Woods, & all other Immunityes to him the s^d Nathaniell Mittten of and from the s^d George Cleaves, and his heires forever, yealding & paying yearly, & every year, two shillings and one dayes work for one man, the Rent to be payd [3] at Michaell mass every year, and the two dayes Worke to be payd at any time when they shall be demanded by the s^d George Cleaves his Heires and Assignes for all services and demands, and this Grant to be Inrolled according to Constitution, and the Land measured marked & bounded with all Convenient Speed/ In Testimony hereof I

Geo Cleave to Nath: Mitten

have hereunto sett my hand & Seale this twentieth of May 1658.

Witnesse us   George Cleave (seale)
  George Munjoy,
  Phenik Rider,
  Francis Neale

George Cleeve
to
Nathanll Mitton

Boston November the 8th 1686, Francis Neale appeared before us underwritten, both of his Majestyes Councill for his Territory and Dominion of New England, and made Oath that he saw George Cleaves signe seale and deliver the abovewritten Instrum^t as his act and Deed, and that he saw George Munjoy sett his hand to it, as a Witnesse, and that he sett his hand to it as a Witnesse himself allso.   Wait Winthrope.
                                            Edwd Tynge.

A true Copy of the Originall deed of Sale transcribed & compared this 2^d of ffebruary 1686
                    Attest^r Tho : Scottow Dep^t Registr

Denis Morrough
to
James ffrees

To all Christian People to whom these presents shall come Know yee, that I Dennis Morough of Fallmoth in the Province of Main yeoman, in the County of Yorshire in America, sendeth greeting, Know yee that I the said Dennis Morough for diverse good Causes and Considerations me thereunto moving, but especially for the Summ of ten Poundes received to Content before the Signing Sealing and delivering hereof by James Frees of Fallmoth Shipwright, the Receipt whereof, I do Acknowledge & for myself, my heires, Exec^{rs} Adminis^{rs} & Assignes for every part and parcell thereof, have given granted, and by these presents, do fully freely and absolutely, give grant bargain sell, aliene, assigne and sett over unto James Frees, his heirs Exec[n] administ[rs] or assignes thirty Acres of Land, on the South side of Casco River, & to begin at a Red Oake Tree which is the Eastern Bounds by the Waters Side, & so to Run by the Waters Side thirty Poles in breadth West, or as the River runs to a Stake their Pitcht down, which is the west bounds with all the Marsh lying within the s[d] bounds, & so to Runn into the Woods the same breadth as is above exprest, namely thirty Poles, till thirty Acres be accomplished & made up and as it is layd out & bounded, by the Town Surveyors and Layers out of Landes, allwayes allowing to M[r] Thadeus Clarke and to his Heires the old foot Path over the Marsh to the Falls for Water, with all my Right, Title & Intrest that I now have or ought to have at the Time of the Sealing of these presents, with all the Woods underwoodes, Mines, Minerells, Commonages, profitts, priveledges & appurtenances thereunto belonging as it was given me by the Select men of the Town of Fallmoth as the Records will plainly make appear, to have and to hold all & Singular the above granted & bargained premises to every Part & parcell, with all & singular other priveledges, and to every part & parcell unto me belonging, with all my Right, Title and Interest thereof unto the s[d] James Frees his Heires Exec[rs] Adm[rs] & Assignes to his or their own proper use & benefitt & behooff forever. Before the Signing & Sealing hereof Jane Morough the wife of Dennis Morough doth make over all her Right & Title, Interest in the above bargained premises/ In witnesse we have hereunto sett our handes & Seales this 7th of December 1686,

Den: Morough
to
James Frees

Signed Sealed & delivered
in the presence of us.
    Richard ⊤ Pousland,
      his Marke/
Elizabeth Tynge.

Dennis ✝ Morough
  his marke/   (seal)
Jane ⌒ Morough
  her marke.   (seal)

Book VI, Fol. 4.

Dennis Morrough and Jane Morrough his wife personally appeared before me underwritten one of his Majestyes Councill for this his Territory in New England, & Acknowledged the Instrument on the other side to be their Act and Deed in Fallmoth in the Province of Main this 7th of Decemb^r 1686,

p Edward Tynge.

A true Copy of the Originall Deed of Sale transcribed and compared this 6th ffebruary 1686 Attest^r

Tho : Scottow : Dep^t Regist^r

[4] This Indenture made the twenty fifeth day of October in the second year of the Reign of our Soveraign Lord James the Second by the Grace of God King of England, Scotland, France & Ireland Defender of the faith &c Anno Domini, 1686/ Between Thomas Parkes of Barwick, in Kittery in the Province of Main in New England on the one Part, & Henry Child of ye same Towne & Province afores^d on the other Part. Wittnesseth, That the said Thomas Parkes for diverse good Causes & considerations him moving hereunto, more especially for & in consideration of Henry Childs keeping him the s^d Parkes, & finding of him the s^d Parkes sufficient meat, drinke, washing & Lodging, and all other things necsessrary for his comfortable Subsistence, both in sicknesse & in health, all the time during his naturall life, the s^d Parkes allso doing what worke he is capable to do not to wrong his Body to do it for the said Henry Child, or his Order, when it shall be required of him, at all tyme as long as the s^d Parkes shall live, with s^d Child & is capable of working, The s^d Thomas Parkes hath given granted, bar-

Tho: Parkes
to
Hen: Child

gained sould, aliened enfeofed & Confirmed, & by these presents do absolutely, give, grant, bargain, sell, aliene, Enfeofe & Confirme unto

BOOK VI, FOL. 4.

the above named Henry Child his Heires, and Assignes forever, a peice or parcell of Land being by Measure forty Acres, lying & being in Barwick in the Towneship of Kittery afores^d lying near a certain place, commonly called & knowne by the name of Postwigwam, being one hundred and twenty Poles in length from Newitchawanick River North East & by North, & in breadth fivety three Rods & half, North East & by East, & South west and by west bounded on the South west with the Land of Abraham Lord, & on the South East with the River, on the North East, with the Land of Mr Cutts, and on the Northwest with the Commons, with four Pole in breadth at the Northwest end of s^d Land, in leiu of the high way passing through it, with the houses, fences, wood & timber that is either standing or lying upon the Land aforesaid excepting the Pine timber belonging to Mr Leader grant of timber/ To have and to hold, the above given & granted Landes, houses, fences, with all the woodes and tymber standing or lying upon the Land (not excepted) to him the s^d Henry Child his Heires & Assignes forever and to his & their own proper use, benefitt, & behoof forever/ The s^d Henry Child yeilding & finding the said Thomas Parkes comfortable maintenance for victualls & Cloaths & lodging, both in sicknesse, and in health during his naturall life as above, And the s^d Thomas Parkes doth further Covenant and promise & grant to & with the s^d Henry Child his Heires & Assignes that he hath in him self good Right, full power, and lawfull Authority the above granted & given premises, and to sell & dispose off and that the same, and every part thereof, is free & clear and freely and clearly acquitted, exonerated & dischargd off & from all & all manner of former Gifts, grants, Leases Morgages, Wills, Entailes, Judgem^{ts} Executions, and power of thirds, and all other Incumbrances, of what nature and kind soever, had, made, done, acknowledged, committed or suffered to be done or committed, whereby the s^d Henry Child or his Assignes, shall or may be any wayes molested in, evicted, or ejected out of the above granted premises, or any part or parcell thereof, by any person or persons whatsoever, having claiming, or pretending to have or claime, any Legall Right, Title, Interest, claime or demand of in or to the above granted premises And the Thomas Parkes doth for himself, his heires, Executors & Adm^rs covenant & promise to & with the s^d Henry Child, his Heires, Exec^rs & Assignes, the above given & granted Land & houses with all the appurtenances and priveledges above mentioned to Warrant & Defend from all persons from by, or under him by these presents/ In witnesse whereof the Partyes hereto, have Interchangeably sett their handes & Seales, the day & year first above written

Thomas Parkes
to
Henry Child

Signed Sealed & delivered
 in presence of us,
 George Broughton }
 Joseph Barnerd }

Thomas ⟨mark⟩ Parkes (seale)
the marke of/

Thomas Parkes came before me this 28th day of October 1686 & acknowledged this Deed or Writing to be his Act or Deed before me

John Hinckes of the Counc^ll

A true Copy of the Originall Deed of Sale transcribed and compared this 6th of ffebruary 1686. Attesta^r

Tho: Scottow: Dep^t Regis^tr

[5] Be it Knowne to all men by these presents that I William Frost, of the Towne of Wells in the Province of Main in New England Cordwinder, with the Consent of Mary my wife severall good Causes & Consideratiō me thereunto mooving, and especially for & in Consideration, of sixty & two Poundes, and some other Considerations to

me in hand payd performed, and well assured to be performed, by Lues Allin of the fore said Town & Province, wherewith I do Acknowledge my Self to be fully payd, satisfyed and contented/ Have given granted Infeofed & confirmed, and by these presents do give grant make over Infeofe and Confirm freely, fully, & absolutely, unto ye aboves^d Lues Allin, from me my Heires, Exec^{rs} Adm^{rs} & Assignes, my sole Right Title & Interest of one hund Acres of Upland, as it is granted to me, by the Inhabitants of the Towne of Wells at the Little River in the Towneship aboves^d together with my dwelling house on the s^d

Will: Frost
to
Lues Allen

Land, with all the profitts priveledges, Commones, Commonages, with all the singular appurtenances in any wise appertayning or belonging, allso one third part of that Saw Mill, now built at the aboves^d Little River, with all the appurtenances that is thereunto belonging, as it is expresd in the Towne grant to my self & Jonathan Hamond together with one third part of one hundred Acres of Upland & ten Acres of Medow granted to the s^d Mill, allso my part of Iron Worke, belonging to the s^d Mill freely & Quietly to have & to hold all the aboves^d Premises, without any matter of Challenge, claime, or demand of me the aboves^d William Frost, or any person or persons either from by or under me, my Heires, Exec^{rs} Adm^{rs} & Assignes forever, he the s^d Lues Allen, & his Heires Executors Adm^{rs} & Assignes, I do hereby declare to be rightly & truly possessed of each & every part & parcell of the premises, abovementioned, and that he the said Lues Allen his Heires, Exec^{rs} Adm^{rs} & Assignes, shall peaceably, have hold & Injoy all & every part & parcell thereof of the premises above granted, & Sould to them forever, and I here promise & Covenant to & with the said Lues Allin, that all & every part of the Estate granted & sould are free & Clear, from all former gifts grants, bargaines, Sales, Leases, Leageses, Judgments, Mortgag^e Executions, & all other Incumbrances whatsoever, & do promise to Warrant & Defend the Title & Intrest of the premises from me, my Heires, Exec^rs Adm^rs & Assignes or from any other person or persons under me, or by my meanes or procurement/ In wittnesse whereunto I William Frost & Mary Frost have sett o^r handes & seales this nineth day of September, one thousand six hundred & eighty five, 1685

<small>William ffrost
to
Lewes Allen</small> Signed Sealed & deliv- · William Frost (seal)
ered in presence of us Mary /┌┐/ Frost. (seal)
Nicholas Coale, her marke/
William Sayer.

William Frost acknowledged this above Instrum^t to be his Act & Deed this 9th day of Septemb^r 1685 before me/

Samuell Wheelright Just Pea

A true Copy of the Originall Deed of Sale transcribed & compared this 8th of ffebruary 1686 Attest^r

Tho: Scottow Depu^t Regis^tr

To all to whom these presents shall come, I Samuell Storer of Wells in New England in the Province of Main <small>Samuel Storer
to
Lues Allen</small> Marriner, Owner and Master of the Good Brigandine Indeavour of Wells aforesaid, lying in the afores^d Wells, builded by Sam^ll Bankes, burdend about fourty five Tunns, send greeting/ Know yee that I the s^d Samuell Storer for and in Consideration of thirty five Poundes of Currant lawfull money of New England to me in hand payd by Lues Allen of Wells, in the afores^d Province of Mayne whereof I the s^d Samuell Storer, doe hereby Acknowledge my self therewith satisfyed, have for my self and heires, given, granted, bargained, and sould and confirmed, and by these presents do fully freely give grant bargain, sell, and, deliver, confirm unto the said Lues Allen, his heires, Exec^ts Adm^r, and [6] Assignes, the one half part of the aboves⁴ Brigandine Indeavour, with all the half part belonging to the s⁴ Brigandine Indeavour now belonging or in any wise appertayning/ To have and to hold the one half part of s⁴ Brigandine & premises hereby bargained for & sould to s⁴ Lues Allin, his Heires, Execⁿ Admⁿ and assignes, as his proper Right forever, and I the s⁴ Samᵘ Storer for my Self, my Execⁿ Admⁿ & every of them do covenant & promise, grant to and with the s⁴ Lues Allen, his Executores, Administⁿ & Assignes p these presents that I the s⁴ Samuell Storer, Marriner and Master of the s⁴ Brigandine, have good Right & lawfull Authority, to sell and deliver, & confirm the half part of the s⁴ Brigandine bargained & Sould to the s⁴ Lues Allyn, his Execⁿ Administⁿ & Assigns forever, in manner & form afores⁴ & the s⁴ Lues Allin his Heires, Execⁿ Admⁿ & Assignes shall lawfully from time to time hereafter peaceably and quietly have hold, use & Injoy the half part of the s⁴ Brigandine hereby bargained for & sould, without any manner of Suite, trouble & molestation, Claimes denialls or demands whatsoever of or by me the s⁴ Samuell Storer my Execⁿ Administⁿ & Assignes or any of them or off, or by any other person whatsoever from by or under mee, my Act or Title, In witnesse hereof I have hereunto sett my hand & Seale

Samll Storer to Lues Allen

   Testes   Samᵘ Storer (sigill)
   John Wheelright
   Samᵘ Wheelright
    Junʳ

Samuell Storer Acknowledged this Instrument to be his Act & Deed this 6ᵗʰ August 1685 Before me
        Samᵘ Wheelright Just Pᶜᵉ

A true Copy of the Originall Instrument transcribed & compared this 8ᵗʰ of ffebruary 1686, Attestatʳ
        Tho : Scottow Depᵗ Registʳ

Be it Knowne to all men by these presents that I Roger Hill of Saco in the County of Yorke & Collony of the Massachusetts Planter, for due and full consideration of ten Poundes Contented & paid, the Receipt, whereof I do Acknowledge, & of the same do discharge & acquitt all & every person of the same, do bargain sell, alienate & demise, Ratify & Confirm the Sale, Bargain & alienatiō of a Certain Tract of Land, formerly disposed of bargained for sould & possesion given by my father Peter Hill in his life time unto John Hellson Senior of the County & Town afores^d ffisherman, The s^d tract of Land being & lying on the on the Western side of the River of Saco to the Quantity of one hundred Acres, to Runn along by the River Side, upwards unto the fresh Water next adjoining unto the Land that Richard Sealy hath in possesion, & doth Inhabitt on, & so downward upon the River Side to the Poynt, just upon the Southern side of the Dock, that is made for the Laying and Securing of Boates, from which Poynt to Run up upon West South West, as farr as right against the present footway out of the present feild of John Hellsons, unto the feild of the afores^d Roger Hill & at the upper end of the afores^d Roger Hill feild the aforesaid West South west Line, to Begin again & so to Runn up into the Woodes, And from the River side, on the Northern side of the afores^d Tract, upon a West South west Line up into the Woodes, until it butt with the West Southwest Line on the Southern side, & that the End Line may Include the Tract of one hundred Acres, except what is excepted in a writing given p the s^d John Hellson Senr unto the afores^d Roger Hill, concerning a Small peice of Land that the s^d Roger Hill house standeth upon, the which Instrument beareth date with this present writing. To have, and to hold the afores^d Tract of Land to him the s^d Hellson, his heires Executores Adminis^r & Assignes, hereby warrantising the s^d Land from any Claim of any person

Roger Hill
to
John Hellson
Senr

Book VI, Fol. 7.

directly or Indirectly by from or under him, And for the true performance hereof, to all true Intents and meanings, the s⁴ Roger Hill bindeth himself his Heires, Exec^r Adm^r In wittnesse hereof he doth hereunto Sett his hand & Seale this twenty Sixth [7] day of December, one thousand six hundred seventy & one, with the Consent of his wife

Signed Sealed & Delivered
  in presence of/   Roger 〆 Hill (seale)
  Seth Fletcher/   marke/
  Mary 𝓜 Griffin/   Mary 𝓜 Hill (seale)
      her Marke.   her marke/

This Instrument was Acknowledged by Roger Hill to be his Act & Deed this 24th of January 1672 before me
                       Brian Pendleton Ascosi

This Instrument was Acknowledged by Mary Hill this eighteen day of September 1672 to be her free Act & Deed with her husband/
          Before me.   Brian Pendleton Ascosiate

A true Copy of this Originall Instrument transcribed & compared this 8th ffebruary 1686 as Attests,
                 Tho : Scottow, Dep^t Regist

---

*Joana Hellson
to
Will Dicer*

Be it known unto all men by these presents that whereas John Hellson deceased, did in his life time make Sale of the above mentioned Tract Land unto William Dicer, & Received pay in Part for the same, & by his Last Will & Testament Ordered that the Remaining due of that Purchase frō William Dicer should be Improved in the bringing up of his Children, I Joana Ellson widow, Executrix of the last Will & Testament of the s⁴ John Hellson deceased, having now Received Security in Law for the payment of what Remained due of

the afores^d Purchase of the abovesaid Tract of Land/ Have given, granted, aliened, assigned over and & Confirmed, & doe by these presents Ratify & confirm the s^d Bargain, & alienation made by my s^d Husband in his life tyme/ Moreover I do Assigne unto the s^d William Dicer his Heires and Assignes forever, this above written Deed of Sale William Dicer, To have and to hold, the Tract of Land therein mentioned, as it was by Roger Hill conveyed, Butted & Bounded, with all the Appurtenances and Priveledges thereunto belonging, to himself, his heires, Exec^r, & Adminis^r, Assignes forever, without any Lett Deniall Molestation, and Hinderance from me the s^d Joana Executrix & from all and every person whatsoever claiming the same from, by or under me/ In wittnesse whereof, I have hereunto Sett my hand & Seale this twenty eight day of July 1686
Signed Sealed & delivered
  in presence of us/   Joanna ———— Hellson (seale)
  Benjamin Ashby ⎫   the marke of.
  Benjamin Stone ⎭

Joanna Hellson Widow Executrix of the last Will & Testament of John Hellson deceased, and Samuell and Ephraim Hellson Acknowledged this Instrument whereunto

Joanna Hellson to William Dicer

their handes & Seales are affixed to be their Act & Deed this twenty eight day of July 1686 before me.

                  Bartholomew Gidney one of his
                  Majestyes Councill for his Territory & Dominion of New England

Samuell Hellson and Ephraim Hellson Sons of John Hellson do hereby manifest their free Consent to the above written Sale of Land unto William Dicer, & Release & Quitt claim unto the said Dicer for themselves & their Heires forever, whatsoever Right Title or Interest, they

have or might have had in, or unto the said Land therein conveyed the s^d Dicer, to have & to hold the Same for himself & his Heires forever/ In witnesse whereof they have hereunto Sett their handes and Seales this 28th day of July 1686 Samuell Hellson : (seale)
Ephraim Hellson (seale)

A true Copy of the Originall Instrument transcribed & compared this 8th ffebruary 1686
as Attests,

Tho Scottow : Dep^t Regist

[8] These Presents, shall witnesse that I George Cleave of Casco Gentleman, doe bargain, Sell & confirme, & absolutely confirm, Sell Assigne and sett over unto Michaell Mitten, his heires and Assignes forever, all that tract of Land lying upon the Northeast side of Casco River, to begin at the now dwelling house of the s^d Michaell Mitten & from thence down the River to the Boundes of Richard Tucker, that is to Say, to the marked Tree at the great Poynt of Rocks, & from thence up the River by the Water Side Southwesternly to the great standing Pine Tree, marked this day, & from the both marked Trees upon a direct Line Northwesternly or thereaboutes, home to the Back Cove/ For & in Consideration of a competent Summ of money to me in hand payd before the Sealing and delivery hereof/

Geo: Cleaves
to
Michael Mitten

All which Landes with either Uplands & Marshes, Trees and Underwoodes, with what other Just Priveledges Soever contained within the s^d Bounderie, are to be proper and properly the Sole right of the s^d Michaell Mitten his heires & Assignes forever/ To have and to hold, all the s^d Landes & priveledges unto him the said Michaell, his heires & Assignes of & frō the s^d George Cleave & his aforesaides forever doing fealty

Book VI, Fol. 8.

to him or them, & in Consideration of the Rents Reserved, that is to say one farthing an Acre Reserved in the Grant to the Lord Proprietor thereof for all Services & Demands and this Grant to be Inrolled, according to the Constitutions Confirmed by the Authority of the Supremacy of England/ In witnesse whereof I the s^d George Cleave, have hereunto sett my hand & Seale, this first day of May 1658

Sealed, Signed & Delivered   George Cleave : (sigll)
  in presence of us/

   George ⊣ Lewes by his marke
   Richard Tucker

A true Copy of the Originall Instrument transcribed & Compared this 6th Aprill 1687 as Attests.
          Tho : Scottow Dep^t Reg^{tr}

Attested by Mr George Cleave this 9th of May 1660 before us to be his Act by me
   Vera Copia/   Robt Jordan Ascosiate/
         Francis Neale Com^{ner}

To all Christian People to whom this Writing shall Come/ Know yee, that I Ephraim Crockett of Kittery for diverse good Causes & valuable Considerations, me hereunto moving and for & in Consideration of the Summ of twenty eight Poundes in hand Received of Richard White of Kittery afores^d do Acknowledge & confesse my self to be fully contented and satisfyed for a parcell of Land, & accordingly

Ephrm Crockett   Have given granted bargained, Sold, Aliened,
to   Enfeofed, and confirmed, & do by these pres-
Richd White   ents, give, grant bargain, sell, unto the s^d
Richard White, his heirs Exec^r, Adm^m & Assignes, fifety Acres of Upland lying at the head of Broad boate harbour, and bounded on the Eastern side, with Yorke Boundes

which is to Run from thence fifety Rod in breadth as the Land was formerly layd out by Capt Wincoll/ and so to Run back untill the fivety Acres be fully compleated, according to Coarse, & from thence to run out by Coarse, to the Water Side as layd out by Captain Wincoll to me the said Crockett, as allso allowing to the said White all the Marsh as far as the Land Runneth in breadth forever/ To have & to hold the said Land and Marsh, with all Trees Woodes, priveledges, profitts with appurtenances thereunto belonging to the only use & behoof of the s^d Richard White, his heires Exec^{rs} Adm^{rs} and, Assignes forever/ And I the s^d Ephraim Crockett for my self, my heires Executores, Adm^{rs} and [9] Assignes do Covenant to and with the s^d Richard White, his heires Exec^{rs} Adm^{rs} and Assignes and to every of them by these presents that all the aforementioned Land & Marshes at the sealing hereof, shall remaine clearly Acquitted exonerated, and discharged, or otherwise saved & kept harmlesse, from all & all former Gifts bargaines, & sales whatsoever/ And that the s^d Crockett the afores^d premises, have sould against him the said Crockett, his heires and Assignes, & against all & every other person or persons whatsoever claiming any Right or Interest into or out of the premises, or any part thereof, shall and will warrant and forever defend by these presents according to the true Intent & meaning of these presents & to no other Intent, use or Purpose whatsoever In witnesse whereof, I have hereunto sett my hand and Seale this tenth day of ffebruary in the year of o^r Lord one thousand, six hundred seventy & eight/ 1678.

Ephraim Crockett to Richard White

Signed, Sealed, & delivered
  in the presence of   the marke of
    Francis Hooke/   Ephraim *E* Crocket (sigl)
    Mary Hooke.

Book VI, Fol. 9.

Ephraim Crockett owned this Instrument to be his Act and Deed to Richard White this tenth of ffebruary 1678 before me

       Francis Hooke Just Peace

A true Copy of the Originall Instrument transcribed & compared this 6th of Aprill 1687 as attests

       Tho : Scottow : Dept Regist

At a Generall Court held at Boston by the Governour & Company of the Massachusetts Bay, the 27th of May 1685

Whereas in Answer to the Petition of Capt Joshua Scottow for the payment of two hundred & odd Poundes claimed by him, on Acco of his disbursemts by him made in the last Indian Warr The Generall Court in the year 1684 granted him in full of all his demands, five hundred Acres of Land to be layd out in the Province of Main, in any free place, which Vote not being entred, said Scottow is uncapable of Receiving benefitt thereby This Court doth hereby confirme the abovesd Grant of five hundred Acres to him, his heires & Assignes forever, And Capt Edward Tynge & Mr Dominicus Jordan are Impowred to lay out the abovesd Grant

This is a true Copy taken out of the Court Booke of Records as Attests/

       Edward Rawson Secret

Merekuneeg Neck to Joshua Scotto͠

I do desire and Appoynt Capt Syllvanus Davis to Officiate and perform the trust desired of me in my Place and Stead, wittnesse my hand/

       Dominicus Jordan.

ffallmoth the 6th of Aprill 1686/ Whereas we the Subscribers were appoynted by the Governr & Company of the Massachusetts to lay out for Capt Joshua Scottow five hundred Acres of Land on any free Place in the Province of Main.

These are to Certify that we layd out on a Neck of Land, Commonly called Merrikoneag Neck in Casco Bay the aboves^d Tract bounded as followeth, Beginning at a Red Oake Tree marked on the four sides, bearing Northeast Northernly from Pullpitt Island, coming in at Newdamaras Cove Sound and allso to Run from the abovesaid Marked Tree Northwest and by North, to run over the first Creek unto a Little River commonly called Little or Croocked Lane. Allso to Run from the first s^d Red Oake marked Tree Northeast up by the Water Side up the Bayward to Come up to Sandy Poynt taking in all that small Poynt of Marsh or Meadow [10] further to Run up from the head of Little River or Crooked Lane Northeast into the Woodes, and so far up along fronting to the Bay at Sandy Poynt to run on a Paralell Line, untill two hundred Acres be expired, being added to the aboves^d Parcell, to make up the aboves^d Summ or Quantity, In wittnesse hereof we have hereunto sett o^r handes/

Edward Tynge
Syllvanus Davis

I underwritten one of his Majestyes Councill in the Territory and Dominion of New England, doe assert my name to this writing above to be my subscription, & that Syllvanus Davis did in my presence Subscribe his/ Witnesse my hand. Blackp^t the 6th of July 1686

Edward Tynge/

A true Copy of the Originall Instrument transcribed & compared this 16th Aprill 1687   Attests/

Tho : Scottow Dep^t Regis^{tr}

Book VI, Fol. 10.

Jon Start
to
Tho: Scottow:

To all Christian People, to whom this present writing shall Come, greeting/ Know yee, that I John Start of Scarborough in this Province of Main ferryman, have of my own free will and Consent for and in Consideration of fifeteen Poundes Currant Money to me in hand well and Truly paid at the Ensealing hereof by Thomas Scottow now Resident at Scarborough, doe hereby Acknowledge my Self to be Content and Satisfyed, and thereof and every part thereof doe fully Acquitt and discharge the s^d Scottow, his heires, Executors Adm^{rs} forever by these presents/ Have given granted, bargained, Sould, Aliened, Enfeofed and confirmed, and by these presents bargain, sell, aliene, Enfeofe, and Confirm, thirty Acres of marsh, lying and being in the Towne of Scarborough in the Province of Main, being formerly the Land and Marsh of George Taylor deceased namely the Marsh lying and being on Pigsgutt River, butted and bounded on the Northernmost & Eastern side with the Land of Henry Watts, allso with the Southern Side bounded with the abovesaid River, on the Western Side with the Marsh now called Mr Houghton Marsh/ To have hold & possesse the s^d thirty Acres of Land be it more or lesse, butting, bounding as abovesaid with all the profitts, priviledges, and Imunityes belonging of Right or in any wise appertayning to him, the s^d Thomas Scottow, his heires, Admininistratores, and Assignes forever, And that I John Start for

Jon Start
to
Tho: Scottow

my self, my heires Exec^{rs} Adm^{rs} & Assignes, do Covenant and grant to and with him the s^d Thomas Scottow, his heires Exec^{rs} Adminis^{rs} and Assignes, shall or may Quietly and peceably Injoy Possesse and Improve all the s^d Marsh, containing and bounded as aboves^d with all the priveledges and profitts thereunto belonging, or in any wise appertayning, without any Lett, Suite, Molestation or Interuption from me the s^d John Start, my heires, Executors, Administrators, and Assignes from by or under me, or from any other person laying claim thereunto, And at the Bargain and Sale of the Premises, I was the true and lawfull Owner thereof, And that I have full power in my own Right, to sell and dispose the s^d Land as aforesaid And that it is free from all Sales, Gifts, Mortgages whatsoever/ And that I will doe or Cause to be done any other Act or Acts, that may be for the full and Legall Confirmation of the hereby granted Premises/ In wittnesse to all and Singular within mentioned premises, I the s^d John Start have hereunto sett my hand, and Seale this twenty [11] fifth day of ffebruary 1685, And in the Second year of the Reign of o^r Soveraign Lord James the Second King of Great Brittan &c Testes/

Andrew Johnson

George *A* Adams
marke/

Henry *HH* Ellkins
marke/

John *ES* Start his Mark & Seale/ (sigil)

Province of Main, Scarborough 11th Aprill 1687. Henry Ellkins and andrew Johnson appeared the day as above before me, being one of his Majestyes Councill, for this his Territory and Dominion in New England, and made Oath that they Saw the late John Start, Signe, Seale and deliver the within written Instrument unto Thomas Scottow as his Act and Deed free & voluntary and they putt their hand, and Mark to the s^d Deed as Wittnesses, and that at the same time George Adams sett his marke to the s^d Deed of Sale as a Wittnesse/ Taken before me   Edward Tynge

Hen Ellkins
&
Andrew Johnsons
Oath

A true Copy of the Originall Deed of Sale transcribed and compared this 16th April 1687 attests,

Tho: Scottow Dep^t Regis^t

Book VI, Fol. 11.

To all People unto whom this present Deed of Sale shall come, Sampson Sheafe of Boston within his Maj[ties] Territory and Dominion of New England Merchant sendeth greeting

Sampson Sheaf
to
Samll Walker

Know yee, that I the s[d] Sampson Sheafe, for and in Consideration of the Summ of Eighty Poundes Currant Money of New England, to me in hand well and truly paid, before the delivery and ensealing of these presents by Samuell Wallker of Boston afores[d] Marriner, the receipt whereof I do hereby Acknowledge to full Content and satisfaction, and thereof and of every part thereof, do Acquitt exonerate and discharge the s[d] Samuell Wallker his Heires Executo[rs] and administ[r] forever by these presents/ Have, given granted bargained, sold, aliened and Enfeofed Assigned, sett over and Confirmed, and by these presents, Do fully freely clearly, and absolutely, give, grant, bargain, Sell, Aliene, Enfeofe, Assigne, sett over and Confirm unto the s[d] Samuell Wallker his Heires and Assignes forever, all the Estate, Right, Title, Interest, Use Possesion Reversion Remainder or Property, claime, and demand whatsoever, which I the s[d] Sampson Sheafe

Samps Sheaf
to
Samll Wallker

have or had, or that I my heires or assignes or any of us at any tyme or times hereafter, shall have, may, might should or to ought to have or claim of in and to One third part of a certain Tract or parcell of Land scituate lying and being in Saco within the Province of Main in New England afores[d] sold unto me s[d] Sampson Sheafe by Benjamin Blakeman of Saco by Deed under his hand and seale bearing date the 9th of March 168$\frac{4}{5}$ and by him purchased of James Gibbens and John Bonighton Containing by estimation six thousand Acres, and be the Same more or lesse, being bounded with a Brooke Southeasterly, commonly called Nicholes Brooke, Northeasterly with two Miles from the great River, and Northwesternly with the Extent of three Miles and one half and eighteen Poles above the Saco Mill ffalls and Southwesternly with the great River/ As allso of in and to the Herbage, commonage for timber, and all other things standing lyeing and growing upon four thousand five hundred Acres more of Land or thereaboutes lying upon the Northeast side of the Land abouesaid/ As allso of in & to the one third part of a Saw Mill and one third part of a Grist Mill standing upon and near Saco River ffalls afores^d built by me the said [12] Sampson Sheafe. Samuell Wallker and Benjamin Blackman in equall thirds/ Together will all my right and Interest of in and to one third part of all the Soile whereon the s^d Mills stand and belong thereto, and of in and to One third part of all the Going geares Utensills, Damms, Ponds, headwares streams woods, timber, profitts priveledges, rights Commodityes herediments and appurtenances whatsoever to the premises or any part or parcell thereof belonging or in anywise appertayning, or therewith now used occupied or Injoyed, with one third part of twelve Oxen formerly purchased in thirds, and belonging to the premises with all Deeds writtings and Evedences touching and concerning the premises To have and to hold all the above granted premises with their appurtenances,

Samps Sheafe
to
Samll Walker

and every part and parcell thereof unto the s^d Samuell Wallker his heires and assignes forever, to the only proper use, benefitt and behoof of him the s^d Samuell Wallker, his heires & assignes forever^{mr} And I the s^d Sampson Sheafe for me my heires Exec^{rs}, and Administ^{rs} doe hereby Covenant promise and grant to and with the s^d Sam^{ll} Wallker his heires and assignes in manner following (that is to say) that att the time of the ensealing hereof and untill the delivery of these presents, I do avouch my self to be the true sole and lawfull owner of all the afore bargained premises, and have in my self full power good right and lawfull authority to sell and dispose of the same in manner aboves^d and y^t the s^d Samuell Wallker his heires and Assignes shall and may by force and vertue of these presents from time to time and all times forever hereafter lawfully peaceably and quietly, have hold use occupy possesse and Injoy the abovegranted premises, and every part thereof free & clear, and clearly acquitted and discharged of and from all, and all manner of former and other Gifts, grants, bargaines, sales leases, mortgages, Joynters, dowers, Judgements Executions, Intailes, forfeitures, and of and from all other Titlles, troubles charges and incumbrances whatsoever had made Committed, done or suffred to be done by me the s^d Sampson Sheafe or my heirs or assignes at any time or times before the ensealing hereof, and further that I the s^d Sampson Sheafe my heires Exec^rs, and Adm^rs shall and will from henceforth and forever hereafter warrant and defend the abovegranted premises with the appurtenances thereof unto the said Samuell Walker his heires and assignes, against all and every person or persons whomsoever any wayes lawfully claiming or demanding the

<small>Samps Sheaf to Samll Walker</small> same or any part thereof by from or under me my heirs or Assignes, And at any time or times hereafter on reasonable Request and at the Costs and charges of the s^d Samuell Wallker his heirs and assignes shall give and pass unto him or them such further assurance and Confirmation of the premises as in Law or Equity can be reasonably desired or required according to the true Intent and Meaning of these presents/ In wittnesse. whereof I the s^d Sampson Sheafe have hereunto sett my hand and Seale the twenty sixth day of March anno Domini/ One thousand six hundred and eighty seven Annoq RR^s Jacobi Secundi Angliæ &c Tertio

Signed Sealed and delivered   Sampson Sheafe (sigilm)
  in the presence of us.
  James Barton
  Eliazer Moody.

Mr Sampson Seafe personally appearing before me underwritten being one of his Majestyes Councill acknowledged

BOOK VI, FOL. 13.

this Instrument to be his act and Deed the day and year above written

William Stoughton

A true Copy of this Instrument transcribed, [13] out of the Originall this 24th day of May 1687 as attests

Tho Scottow Deput Regist^r

Know all men by these presents that I Benjamin Blakeman of Strattford, now resident in Saco in the Province of Main, upon good Considerations mee moving, especially a Valuable Summ to be in hand paid, the receipt whereof and my self therewith fully satisfyed I do by these presents acknowledge, have given granted, aliened, Enfeofed and Confirmd and by these presents do give, grant, alien, Enfeof and Confirm unto Mr Sampson Sheafe of Boston Merchant one third part of a tract of Land by me bought of James Gibbens and John Bonighton as by their Bills of Sale Anno Dom 1683 the twelfth day of December may more perticularly appear, being Six thousand Acres more or Lesse, being bounded Southeasterly with a Brooke commonly called Nicolls Brook, North eastwardly with two Miles from the great River and Northwestwardly with the Extent of three Miles and half & eighteen Poles above the Saw Mill falls & Southwestwardly by the great River, as allso the herbage commonage for timber, and all other things growing upon four thousand five hundred Acres of Land or thereabouts, lying upon the Northeast Side of the Land abovesaid, as allso one third part of a Saw Mill standing upon Saco River ffalls built by s^d Blakeman upon the proper Acc^o of Mr Sampson Sheafe afors^d Merchant To have and to hold the s^d third part of Land Saw Mill, with all Woods, Trees, tymber herbage with all priveledges of Rights, Streams, and Con-

Benjn Blakeman
to
Samps Sheafe:

veniences whatsoever to him the s^d Mr Sampson Sheafe, his heires, Exec^rs administ^rs and Assignes by these presents, further the s^d Blackman for himself, heires, Exec^rs, and administ^rs, doth promise and Covenant to and with the s^d Mr Sampson Sheafe his heires and assignes from all person or persons whatever by or under him laying claim to any part of s^d Land or Saw Mill or above mentioned priveledges will forever defend by these presents/ Allso that he hath full

<small>B Blakeman
to
Samps Sheafe</small>
power & lawfull authority in his own proper Right at Signing and Sealing hereof, to Bargain alienate Sell and Confirme the abovementioned premises and will do or cause to be done all and every such thing and things, act or acts, devise or devises in the Law for the more full Confirmation of the s^d Land, Mill, and all the above mentioned priveledges to him the s^d Mr Sampson Sheafe his heires, Exec^rs, adm^rs, and Assignes according to Law and Custom of this Province In wittnesse have sett to my hand and Seale 9th of March 168⅔

        Benjamin Blakeman (sigill)

Matthew Middleton/

 Mr Benjamin Blakeman Acknowledged this Instrument above to be his Act and Deed, this 9th of March 168⅔ before me/   Samuell Wheelright Just Pea

 A true Copy of the originall Deed of Sale transcribed and compared this 24th of May 1687 as attests/

        Tho : Scottow Dep^t Regist^r

[14] To all unto whom these presents shall Come I Arthur Bragdon Senr of York in the Province of Main in New England, for and in Considera^t of the Summ of Six Poundes of Currant pay of New England to me in hand payd by Alexander Maxell of Yorke aforesaid, In the behalf of James Grant, likewise resident in the s^d Town many yeares before

Book VI, Fol. 14.

the ensealing and Delivery of these presents, the Receipt whereof I said Arthur Bragdon do hereby Acknowledge, and therewith do owne my Self to be fully satisfyed and payd, have given granted, sold delivered & confirmed unto s^d Alexander Maxell in the behalf of James Grant, and by these presents, fully and do absolutely, give, grant, sell, de-

Arthur Bragdon to James Grant

liver and confirm unto the s^d James Grant, his heires Exec^{rs}, administ^{rs}, and Assignes a Certain tract of Upland, lying in the Precincts of the Towne of Yorke, contayning the Quantity of forty Acres of Upland be it more or lesse, upon wch Land, the house, Barne, and out houses of the afores^d Grant now standeth and are built/ The Boundes whereof by a full perpetuall and mutuall agreement, are to Run by a standing fence as it now standeth between s^d Maxell and Grant according to their own free and Irrevocable consents on the lower Boundes of the said Lott the fence running towards the Southeast near to the Marsh of Jeremyah Molton, and the upper part of s^d forty Acres or thereaboutes to Run back into the Woods exactly as the fence now standeth between James Grant and Robert Jinkins without any alteration till it attain the end of the fence, and from thence to Run on a due Northeast Line as the rest of those other Lotts there do, till about forty Acres be compleated, which land lyeth next adjoyning to a parcell of Land formerly granted unto the s^d James Grant by the Town of Yorke, with all and singular Woods underwoods, priveledges & all other appurtenances belonging unto the afores^d forty Acres of Land, sold unto Alexander Maxell for and in the behalf of the aforenamed James Grant, unto the s^d Grant his heires Exec^{rs} administ^{rs} and assignes forever, for his and their own proper use and behoof/ And further I the s^d Arthur Bragdon do Covenant and promise to and with the s^d Maxell in

Arthur Bragdon
to
James Grant

behalf of the s^d James Grant, his heires, Exec^{rs} Adm^{rs} and Assignes, that at the time and delivery hereof and ensealing by these presents, that I the s^d Arthur Bragdon in my self have full power & good Right Lawfull Authority to sell, give grant and Lawfully to Confirm and dispose of the s^d bargained premises of about forty Acres of Land, unto the S^d alexander Maxell for and in the behalf of James Grant his heires, Exec^{rs}, Adm^{rs}, and assignes forever and y^t s^d Land is free and clear, from all Leases Sales, Titles Judgements, Mortgages, Executions and all other Incumbrances whatsoever and that the s^d Grant his heires and assignes, shall or may from time to time, and at all times hereafter, have, hold, use, possesse, occupy and Injoy the s^d Land above specifyed, without any manner of Lett, Suite, trouble, and molestation challenge and deniall whatsoever, and do hereby warrant the same, against all person or [15] persons whatsoever claiming or pretending any claime from by or under me, or any other by my procurement either my heires, Exec^{rs} Adm^{rs} or assignes/ In wittnesse whereof I have hereunto affixed my hand and seal In the third year of the Reign of o^r Soveraign Lord James the Second of England, Scotland, france and Ireland King fidei defenssor/ ffebruary the 14th One thousand six hundred eighty six.

Signed Sealed and,   Arthur Bragdon (sigil)

Arthur Braggindon
to
James Grant

delivered in presence of
John Saywood }
Mary Saywood }

John Saywood and Mary his wife being Wittnesses, do attest upon their Oaths that this Instrument above written is the act and Deed of Arthur Bragdon Senr to Alexander Maxell in for the behalf of James Grant, taken upon Oath before March 16, 168$\frac{6}{7}$

                                 Edward Rusworth Just

Book VI, Fol. 15.

A true Copy of the Originall Instruments transcribed and compared this 24th May 1687 as attests.

Tho : Scottow Dep^t Regis^{tr}

Alex: Maxell to James Grant

Whereas I Alexander Maxell of Yorke in the Province of Main by order of James Grant of s^d Town received a Certain Summ of him to the value of Six Poundes in s^d Grants behalf to purchase a certain tract of Upland in his behoof, and for his only proper use and benefitt containing about forty Acres more lesse, which Land I bought and payd for to Arthur Bragdon severall yeares past, and in s^d Bragdon behalf gave James Grant Possesion thereof, of which ever since the s^d Grant hath quietly and peaceably Injoyd without any Lett or molestation and by these presents I said Maxell Declare that I never had, nor have any Title or Interest in the s^d Land or premises, but do from our selves, our heires Exec^{rs}, administ^{rs}, and assigns renounce and disclaime all our Rights or pretence of Right unto s^d forty Acres of Land or thereaboutes and do make a full Resignation of every part of the premises according to the Bill of Sale on the other Side as his true and proper Right unto s^d James Grant his heires Exec^{rs} administ^{rs} and assingnes forever, as wittnesse my hand and Seale at the day and date hereof the fourteenth of

Alexd Maxell to James Grant

ffebruary one thousand six hundred and eighty six

Signed Sealed and delivered in the presence of
John Saywood/
Mary Saywood

Alexander ⟨mark⟩ Maxell
his Mark & (sigil)

John Saywood and Mary his wife being wittnesses do attest upon their Oaths that this Instrument of Resignation

BOOK VI, FOL. 16.

above written is the act & Deed of Alexander Maxell to James Grant taken upon Oath before me this 16th March 1686
       Edward Rushworth Just Peac
A true Copy of the Originall Instrument transcribed and compared this 24th of May 1687 as attests/
      Tho: Scottow/ Dep^t Regis^{tr}

Know all men, by these presents that I Alexander Maxell of Yorke in the Province of Main in New England Planter, with [16] the free consent of my wife Annis, upon good & valuable Considerations thereunto me moving & more especially for & in Consideration of a Mare and Colt sold unto me & delivered by James Grant of Yorke afores^d the Receipt whereof I do hereby acknowledge, & wherewith I do acknoledge my self to be fully payd Contented, and Satisfyed and do upon the Considerations afores^d in the behalf of my self my heires, Exec^{rs}, administ^{rs} and assignes acquitt and discharge the s^d Jams Grant from all or any Sum, or Summs of money or any other pay due for the premises, his heires Exc^{rs}, adm^{rs}, & assignes forever, have given granted bargained Sold Enfeofed and confirmed and do by these presents, give, grant, bargain sell and Confirm from me my heires, Exec^{rs}, Adm^{rs}, and assignes, unto the above named James Grant his heires, Exec^{rs}, administ^{rs}, and Assignes a certain Tract or parcell of fresh Marsh, lying and next adjoyning to my own fresh Marsh at or near the head of the Northwest branch of Yorke River, bounded on the North side of ye Crick running up to an Elm Tree lying on the South east side of John Twisden Marsh about four or five Acres more or lesse, allso about half an Acre of Upland whereon James Grant his Barn now standeth, be it more or lesse/ To have & to hold the afores^d

Alexander Maxell to James Grant

Tracts of Upland and Marshes as above bounded, with all the profitts, libertyes priveledges Commons, with all other & Singular the appurtenances thereunto belonging, or any wise appertayning from me, my heires Execut^{rs} administ^{rs} and assignes forever, unto the said James Grant his heires, Exec^{rs}, administ^{rs} and assignes forever/ And I the s^d Alexander Maxell do own my self to be the true and lawfull Owner of the above named premises & that I in my self have full right & power and authority to make sufficient sale of s^d Land and that it is clear from all Titles, Mortgages Judgements, alienations and all other Incumbraces whatsoever, and further I do Covenant and promise in behalf of my self my heires and assignes to Warrant and defend the Title and Interest thereof, unto the before named James Grant his heires and Assignes forever, from all person or persons whatsoever claiming or pretending any claim title or Interest thereunto from by or under me, or any other by my procurement In Testimony whereof I have hereunto affixed my hand & Seale this 10th day of June in the three & thirteth year of o^r Soveraign Lord Charles the Second, of England Scotland ffrance & Ireland King, fidei defensor 1681

Alex: Maxell
to
James Grant

Signed Sealed & delivered
in the presence of   & due self Interlined
Edward Rushworth   before Signing &
                    Sealing hereof/

Tho ・ Harris
marke   Alexander ⌒ Maxell

Alexander Maxell & Annis his wife came before me & owned this Instrument to be their Act & Deed at the date herof/   Edw: Rushworth Just Peace

A true Copy of the Originall Instrument compared, and transcribed this 24th May 1687 as attests

Tho: Scottow, Dep^t Regis^{tr}

BOOK VI, FOL. 17.

Jno Prichett
John Burrell &
his wife
to
Henry Emms

To all Christian People to whom this present Deed of Sale shall Come John Prichett of Boston in New England Marriner, John Burrell of Rumny Marsh in the County of Suffolk in New England afores^d and Ann his wife send greeting/ Know yee, that the s^d John Prichett, Jonn Burrell and Ann his wife, for and in the Consideration [17] of the Summ of fivety Poundes of Currant money of New England to them in hand payd at and before the Ensealing and Delivery of these presents by Henry Emms of Boston aforesaid Baker, the Receipt whereof they doe hereby acknowledge, and themselves therewth fully Satisfyed, and Contented and thereof and every part thereof, do Acquitt, Exonerate and Discharge the s^d Henry Emns, his heires, Execu^{rs}, Admin^{rs} and Assignes and every of them forever by these presents, Have given granted, bargained, sold Aliened Enfeofed and Confirmed, and by these presents Doe fully freely clearly and Absolutely give grant bargain sell aliene Enfeofe and Confirm unto the s^d Henry Emms his heirs and Assignes forever, all that their Tract or parcell of Land, Scituate lying and being at Sagadehoc in the Province of

Jno Prichet
Jno Burel
& his wife
to
Henry Ems

Main in New England aforesaid on the Northern side of a Certain place, there commonly called and known by the name of the Mill Pooll being butted and bounded, as followeth, viz, beginning at the great Rock at the upper End of the late Thomas atkins feild and Close, and from thence to the stepping stones, and from thence upon a strait line, to the head of all the Marshes, as far as the Salt water Runneth at Small Poynt Side, with all the Land and Marsh on the Northern Side of the Main Crick there, and all the s^d Landes and Marsh so far as the Northern Crick Runneth on Small Poynt Side as the Same was first Purchased by the said John Prichett of Thomas Atkins of S^d Sagadehoc Planter, and perticularly mentioned in a Deed of Sale or

Book VI, Fol. 18.

grant, under the hand and Seale of y{e} s{d} Thomas Atkins bearing date the 15{th} day of April 1660 together with all Landes, Meadows and Marshes, Rivers, fishings fowlings Cricks Coves Beeches Flatts, Trees, Woods, Underwoods, Swamps, Rights, profitts, priveledges Commodityes hereditam{ts} immoluments and appurtenances whatsoever to the s{d} Tract or parcell of Land belonging or in any wise appertayning/ To have and to hold the s{d} Tract or parcell of Land, being butted and bounded as afores{d}, with all other the above granted premises, and every part thereof, unto y{e} s{d} Henry Emms, his heires or Assignes, unto the only proper use benefitt and behoof of the Said Henry Emms his heires and Assignes forever and the s{d} John Prichett, John Burrell and Ann his wife for themselves, their heires, Execut{r} and Adm{rs} do hereby Covenant, Promise and grant to and with the s{d} Henry Emms, his heires and Assignes, in manner and form following/ That is to say that at the Time of the Ensealing hereof they are the true sole and lawfull owners of all the afore bargained premises and

<small>Jno Pritchet Jno Burrell and his wife to Henry Emms</small> have in themselves full power, good Right and lawfull Authority, to grant Sell Convey Assure the Same unto the s{d} Henry Emms as a full firm perfect and absolute Estate of Inheritance without any manner of Condition Reversion or Limitation whatsoever, so as to Alter Chang defeate or make Void the same, and that the s{d} Henry Emms his Heirs and Assignes, shall and may by force and vertue of these presents from time to tyme and at all tymes forever hereafter lawfull peaceably and quietly have hold Use Occupy Possesse and Injoy all the above granted premises with their appurtenances and every part thereof free and Clear and Clearly acquitted and discharged of and from all and all manner of former and other gifts grants bargains, Sales, Leases Mortgages Joynters Dowers, Judgements Executions, Intailes [18] forfeitures, and of and from all other Titles Troubles Charges and Incum-

brances whatsoever had made Committed done or suffred to be done by them the s^d John Prichett, John Burrell and Ann his wife, or either or any of them their or either or any of their Heires and Assig^n at any time or times before the Ensealing hereof, and further that the s^d John Prichett John Burrell and Ann his wife, their heirs Exec^r Adm^n and Assignes shall and will from time to Time and at all Times forever hereafter Warrant and Defend the above granted premises with their appurtenances and every part thereof unto the said Henry Emms his heirs and Assigns against all

<small>Jno Prichet Jno Burel & his wife to Henry Emms</small> and every person and persons whatsoever any wayes lawfully claiming or demanding ye same or any part thereof/ In wittnesse whereof the s^d John Prichett John Burrell and Ann his wife, have hereunto Sett their handes and Seales, the tenth day of November Anno Domini, 1686 Annoq, RR^s Jacobi Secundi Angliæ &c Secundo.

Signed Sealed and delivered   John Prichett   (seale)
by s^d John Prichett on the day   John Burrell   (seale)
of the date within written in
the presence of us.   Ann M Burrell (Seale)
John Hayward Not^r Pub^ls marke
Zachariah Suite/ Servt.

Signed Sealed and Delivered by John Burrell and Ann his wife the 19th November 1686 in the presence of us/
John Hayward Not^rs Pub^ls

John Prichett personally appearing before me underwritten, being one of his Majestyes Councill in his Territory and Dominion in New England in America, and Acknowledged the within written Instrument to be his Act and Deed, the 10th November 1686
                         Edward Tynge.

John Burrell and Ann his wife personally appearing before me underwritten being one of his Majestys Councill in

Book VI, Fol. 19.

Jno Burel & his wifes acknowledgment

his Territory and Dominions in New England, and acknowledged the within written Instrument to be their Act & Deed, the 19th November 1686 before

Edward Randolph/

A true Copy of the Originall Instrument transcribed and Compared this 24th May 1686 as attests

Tho: Scottow Dep Regis^t

Humphrey Chadbourne to ffrancis Champnown

To all Christian People to whom these presents shall Come/ Know yee, That whereas Maj^r Nicholas Shapleigh of Kittery in New England, did in the year of our Lord one thousand six hundred and sixty three Convey and make over unto me Humphrey Chadborn my heires and Assignes, a Tract of Land and a parcell of Marsh, lying and being Scituate in or about Sturgeon Crick, within the precincts of Kittery afores^d, and accordingly did give and [19] make unto me the s^d Humphrey a Bill of Sale bearing date the eleventh day of Septem^{br} 1663/ The bounds of which Land and Marsh are in the s^d Bill of Sale are at large expressed. Now Know all men by these/ That I the s^d Humphrey Chaborne for diverse and sundry Causes and Considerations me thereunto moving but more especially for & in Consideration of a valuable Summ in hand Received have and do by these, give, grant Enfeofe convey and Confirm, unto my trusty and well beloved freind Capt Francis Champernoon all that parcell of Land or Marsh which I so bought of him the s^d Nicholas Shapleigh lying and scituate at Sturgeon Crick aforesaid wth all the appurtenances thereunto belonging and all the priveledges and Immunityes thereto in any wise appertayning/ To have and to hold unto

Book VI, Fol. 19.

Humphrey Chadbourn
to
ffran: Champernown

him the said Francis Champernoon in manner and form, and to the Intent and purposes hereafter in these presents Limited and Appoynted, and to nor for no other use, Intention or Purpose whatsoever (that is to say) to and for the Sole and proper use and behoofe of my Loving wife Lucy Chadborn, and her Exec^n and Assignes for and during the Term of her Naturall life, And after the decease. of my s^d Wife to and for the sole and proper use, benefitt and behoof of my Children that I now have or hereafter may have by her according as she see cause or Reason to dispose of the same, or any part of thereof amongst them   And that the s^d Francis Champernoon shall not nor may dispose of the afores^d Premises or any part thereof to any other person or persons whatsoever, to no other use or uses without the free and full Consent of her my said wife any thing herein Contayned to the Contrary, Notwithstanding. And if I the s^d Francis Champernoon shall happen to die or depart this Country before the Death of my s^d Wife, that then it shall and may. be lawfull for her to make choise of another freind whom she shall think fitt, who may be a feofee in Trust for the afores^d Premises, for the Uses Intents and Purposes before Expressed/ And I the s^d Humphrey do for my self my heires Exec^n and Adm^n, convey and make over the afores^d Premises in like Manner hereby unto whomsoever she shall so make Choice of after him to the Uses Intents and purposes before expressed, and to and for no other Uses Intents and purposes whatsoever, any thing herein Contained to the Contrary notwithstanding/ In wittnesse

Book VI, Fol. 20.

Humphrey Chadbourne
to
ffrancis Champernowne

hereof I have hereunto sett my hand and seale this Twelth day of Aprill in the Year of our Lord one thousand six hundred sixty and three/ 1663.

      Humphrey Chadborn (seale)

Signed Sealed and delivered
 in the presence of us/
 Thomas Kemble
 John Shapleigh.

Mr John Shapleigh came before me as as a Wittnesse doth Attest upon his Oath that this was the Act and Deed of Mr Humphrey Chadborn by him subscribed and signed

      Edw Rushworth Jus^t p

Thomas Kemble came before me one of the Councill, and made Oath that he did see Humphrey Chadborn Sign Seale and deliver the above Instrument as his Act and Deed/

 Boston 9th August 1686

      Jn° Usher/

[20] A true Copy of the Originall Instrument as on the other side written transcribed & Compared this 24th May 1687 As attests/

    Tho : Scottow Dep^t Reg^tr

Jno Hole
to
George Harris

Know all men by these presents that I John Hole of Kittery yeoman for and in Consideration of the Summ of fivety Pounds in fish or goods equivolent to be paid in four yeares from the Date hereof in equall proportion yearly untill the s^d Summ be paid, hath unto Farm Letten, and by these presents doth unto Farm lett, all that his dwelling house, and Quarter of an Acre of Land more or lesse, scituate lying and being on the south side of Thomas ffirnalls Island, unto George Harris Shipwright or

Book VI, Fol. 20.

his Assignes from the day of the date hereof untill the eight day of March one thousand six hundred eighty & eight, he the s^d George Harris to have, hold Occupy and peacebly to Injoy the s^d House and Quarter of an Acre of Land, with all the right Title and Interest, priviledges and appurtenances thereunto belonging or in any wise appertayning according to a Grant of the s^d Land from Thomas ffurnall unto me ye s^d John Hole/ In wittnesse whereof I the s^d John Hole have hereunto sett my hand and Seale the fourth day of May one thousand six hundred, seventy and five/
Signed Sealed and Delivered   John Hole (seale)
  in presence of
Elias Stileman

Great Island the 4th of May 1675 Mr John Hole came before me and Acknowledged the above written to be his free Act and Deed

                              Elias Stileman Com^ner

A true Copy of the Originall Instrument transcribed and compared this 24th June 1687 as Attests/
                              Tho : Scottow Dep^t Reg^tr

Know all men by these presents that I George Harris Junr, and Johanna my wife for and in Consideration of the Summ of twenty Poundes in Currant pay of New England in hand Received, have bargained and sold and do hereby bargain and sell unto Thomas ffirnald of Kittery Shipwright to him and to his heires and Assignes all my Right Title &

George Harris to Tho: ffernald

Interest in and unto the dwelling house and Quarter of an Acre of Land mentioned in the the Deed above written, with all the priveledges and appurtenances thereunto appertayning. To have and to hold the house and Quarter of an Acre of Land with the Appurtenances to him the s^d Thomas ffirnald his heires & As-

BOOK VI, FOL. 21.

August 7 °1683
Recd of mr Thom-
as ffernald twenty
pounds in full
Satisfaction for
be house & land
I Say Received
by me.
George Harris
A true Copie
Transcribed out
of ye origenall
and compared
Jan 28: 1695-6
p Jos Hamond
Regr

signes forever free, clear, and clearly acquitted for all Dowryes or other Incubrances what soever In Wittnesse whereof we have hereunto sett o^r handes & Seales this 28th August 1682 Signed Sealed & Delivered in presence of
Elias Stileman

George   mke
       R   Harris (seale)
Johanna   Harris (seale)

     Great Island Province of New Hampshire, the 28th of August, George Harris Junr & Johanna his wife came & Acknowledged this Instrument to be their free Act & Deed before me
Elias Stileman Dep^t Pres^{dt}

A true Copy of the Originall Instrument transcribed and Compared this 24th June 1687 as Attests
Tho Scottow Dep^t Reg^{tr}/

Jonth Mendum
to
John Fennick

[21] Know all men by these Presents that we Jonathan Mendum and Mary Mendum in the County of York hath sold and delivered unto John Fennick of the same Towne and Place a Tract of Land lying on the North side of Spurce Crick in the Towneship of Kittery, which said Land is Sixteen Rods or Poles in breadth by ye Water side, and begins at a Red Oake marked Tree, on the East side/ And a Small Round Rock on the West Side and goes back into the Woodes upon a Northeast line upon the aforesaid breadth untill twelve Acres be Accomplished with all Appurtenances thereunto belonging. to the only proper use and behoof of the s^d John Fennick, his heires Exec^{rs}, Adm^{rs} or Assignes forever from the afores^d Jonathan and Mary Mendum, their Heires, Exec^{rs} Adm^{rs} and Assignes forever, promising the

said Fennick the s^d Bargained Land to be clear from all former Sales Gifts grants Mortgages or Incumbrances of any kind whatsoever, and allso doe hereby own our selves fully paid & satisfyed for the same, and wittnesse o^r hands and seales this second Day of March in the year one thousand six hundred seventy and two

Wittnesse Jo^n Willson   Jonathan Mendum (seale)

     Joseph *J W* Willson   Mary *M* Mendum (seale)

Jonathan Mendum came and Acknowledged this Instrument to be his Act & Deed to John Phenix the 2^d of June 1684 he owned to have delivered Land aboves^d by Twigg & Turfe/

Before me/

                         Francis Hooke Just Peace

A true Copy of the Originall Instrument transcribed and Compared this 29th July 1687 as Attests

                         Tho : Scottow Dep^t Regis^tr

To all whom these Presents shall Come/ Whereas upon the sixth of December, In the year of our Lord, one thousand six hundred sixty & two, John Wincoll formerly of Watertown, now of Kittery did give, grant Mortgage bargain & sell unto Capt Thos Clark of Boston all y^t his Grant in the Sallmon ffalls upon great Nechawannick River, with Mill or Mills &c, as in the s^d Deed more fully Appeareth upon Consideration of the s^d Capt Thos Clarke Joyning in security with the s^d John Wincoll for the paying and satisfying six hundred Poundes unto Mr Richard Russell, Maj^r John Leverett, and Capt Thos Lake & John Hull, which

Tho Clarke to Roger Plaisted   said summs not being payd, some of them at all, nor none of them according to Time by the s^d John Wincoll/ And in y^t Respect are forfeited to the s^d Capt Thos Clarke his heires and Assignes/ Now Know all men That whereas Roger Plaisted of Kittery Yeoman & John Hull of Boston Goldsmith, have this day Obliged & beCome bound unto the s^d Thos Clarke for the payment of the Summ of four hundred Poundes owing by the s^d Wincoll unto the said Clarke, and for the securing & paying or Causing to be payd that former Debt due from Mr Thos Broughton unto s^d Clark, which is now seven hundred Poundes, to be payd according to the Terms of the s^d Ingagement Annually/ The s^d Capt Thomas Clarke Merch^t of Boston hath Given Granted, bargained, Sold, assigned, sett over and fully Confirmed, unto the s^d Roger Plaisted yeomā and unto the s^d John Hull Goldsmith, and unto their Heires, Exec^rs Adminis^rs, and Assigns the [22] above mentioned Premises of the Sallmon ffalls Grant both of River & Timber, and all manner of Right and Priveledges belonging thereunto/ As allso with the two Mills, dwelling house, Barns, Stables Oxen Carts, Carriages, Geares, & all manner of Utensills in any sort belonging or appertayning to the s^d Mills with Damm, fflumes, Timber allready Cutt whether Sawn or Unsawn, or whatsoever doth in any kind belong unto the whole Premises/ And that the same is, and shall be free and Clear for the s^d Roger & John, their Heires, Exec^rs, Adm^rs, and Assignes from henceforth/ To have, hold, Use Occupy and Injoy in as full and ample Manner in every Respect, as the s^d Thos Clark might or Could Doe/

Tho Clarke
to
Roger Plaisted

And allso whatsoever shall be Judged Necessary, for the more effectuall making over, and Conveyance of the Premises, the s^d Thos Clarke Obligeth himself to Sign, Seale, Do, or perform according to Law, that the s^d Roger Plaisted and John Hull may quietly and peceably Injoy the Same/ Unto the Premises the s^d Capt Thos Clark hath hereunto putt his hand and seale this sixth day of Aprill in the year of our Lord one thousand, six hundred, seventy one, Annoq RR^s Caroli Secundi xxiij.

BOOK VI, FOL. 22.

It is declared by Cap⁺ Tho Clarke, that he will Assigne the Originall Deed, and in signing to this, he only Conveyeth Over to the s⁴ Roger & John, what was by the s⁴ Deed Conveyed over unto him

Signed Sealed & Delivered in   Tho⁵ Clarke. (sigillm)
  the presence of.   Maj⁺ Thomas Clark acknowledged
  Jabez Fox   this Instrument to be his Act
  Tho Lake   & Deed this 13ᵗʰ day of ffebru-
  George Broughton   ary 1679 before me Symon
                                   Bradstreet Governer

A true Copy of this Originall Instrument transcribed & Compared this 28ᵗʰ day of September. 1687/ Attests/
                       Tho : Scottow Dep⁺ Regist⁺

Know all men by these presents that I Samuell Knight of Kittery for & in the Consideration of the Summ of Nine Poundes Sterling, allready satisfyed me by Samuell Spinny of Kittery aboves⁴ whereof and wherewᵗʰ I doe Acknowledge my self to be fully satisfyed and Contented for a parcell of Land which I have bargained and Sold and Delivered unto the afores⁴ Samuell Spinny/ And doe by These Presents give grant, bargain, Aliene, Enfeofe & Sell and Confirm unto the s⁴ Samuell Spinny, his heires Execut⁺ˢ

Samll Knight
to
Samll Spinny

Administ⁺ˢ, and Assignes the aboves⁴ Land containing six Acres of Upland, lying in the Towne of Kittery and is part of a Towne grant formerly given me by my father in Law Richard Kirle, as may fully Appear by an Instrument under his hand bearing date the 27ᵗʰ July 1676, which said six Acres of Land is near to the dwelling house of the s⁴ Kirle, and beginneth at the great Cove and so to Runne Sixty Eight Pole next to the Land, that now is Cristian Ramocks Land, with such bredth as may make up the aforementioned six Acres of

Land. To have and to hold all and Singular the s⁴ six Acres of Land, to the s⁴ Spinney, his heirs Execⁿ, Admⁿ, and Assignes forever to his Own proper use and behoof, freely, peceably and Quietly to Injoy, without Challenge, Claime or Demand of me s⁴ Knight, or of any person or persons whatsoever for me, in my name, by my Cause or proCurement And I the s⁴ Knight the s⁴ Premises doe hereby give grant, bargain and sell, and every part and parcell thereof with the Appurtenances, against me the [23] s⁴ Knight, my Heires Execⁿ, Admⁿ, and Assignes and agaynst all and every other person or persons whatsoever clayming any Right or Interest in to or out of the Premises, or any part thereof, shall and will Warrant and forever Defend by these presents In wittnesse whereof, I have hereunto sett my hand and seale this twenty fourth day of August Anno Dom¹ One thousand six hundred eighty and six/

Signed Sealed and Delivered   Samuell Knight (sigillum)
  in the presence of us.
  Francis Hooke
    Ephraim *E* Crockett
      the mark of

Samˡˡ Knight to Samˡˡ Spinny   Samuell Knight came before me and Acknowledged the above Writing to be his Act and Deed this 24ᵗʰ August 1686

                          John Hinkes of the Councill

Samuell Knight gave Possesion by Twigg and Turf according to Law, unto Samuell Spinny this 6ᵗʰ Novembʳ 1686, of the Six Acres of Land withinmentioned before us Wittnesses

    Thomas Spinny   Samˡˡ Knight
    John Fearnuld   John Spinny
    Richᵈ ⌒ Karter   Richᵈ Kerle
        marke

BOOK VI, FOL. 23.

A true Copy of the Originall Instrument transcribed and Compared this 10th, October 1686, Attests.
                                    Tho : Scottow Dept Registr

Know all men, by these Presents/ That I Richard Carle of Kittery in the Province of Main Planter with the Consent of Amie my wife, for and in Consideration of three Pounds and fiveteen Shillings, in good provisions in hand to me allready payd to full Content and satisfaction have given granted Bargained, Sold Enfeofed and Confirmed, and do by These presents for my self, my Heirs, Execrs, Admrs, Give Grant bargain sell Infeofe and Confirm unto Samuell Spinnye of the Towne and Province aforesaid a certain parcell of Land scituate and being in the Town of Kittery aforesd containing three Acres by Measure lying on the North side of the Great Cove, bounded on the West with a Country high Way, and on the South West with the Land of Thomas Spinney, on the East with the Land of Christian Ramock, & on the North with the Land of the sd Richard Kirle, it being part of a Lott of fiveteen Acres formerly granted to me by the Town of Kittery, and now by me the said Richard Carle

Rich Karle
    to
Samll Spinney

sold unto the sd Samuell Spinney To have and to hold the above bargained three Acres of Land all and Singular the Appurtenances and priveledges thereto belonging, to him the sd Samuell Spinney, his heires Execrs, Admrs or Assignes forever, clearly acquitted from all former Mortguges, Sales, Gifts, Dowries or titles of Dowries done by me or suffered to be done by any other person or persons by from or under me or my Assignes/ In Confirmation of the truth hereof, I the sd Richard Carle and Amie my wife have hereunto sett our handes and seales this three and twentyth day of March in the Year of our Lord One thousand, six hundred eighty one, eighty two/

Signed, Sealed & delivered   Richard Carle (sigll)
  in the presence of us/   Amie ⁓ Carle (sigll)
John Furnald   her Marke
John Wincoll

Richard Carle and Amie his wife appeared before me and Acknowledged the above written Deed of Sale to be their free Act and Deed 23ᵈ March 168½

[24] A true Copy of the Originall Instrument transcribed and Compared this 10ᵗʰ day of October 1687   Attests/
T

Be it Knowne unto all men by these Presents that I John Buckland of the Towne of Wells in the Province of Maine In New England Planter, severall good Causes and Considerations me thereunto Moving and more especially for and in Consideration of a Certain Tract of Land & Meadow containing one hundred and seventy four Acres, with a Dwelling house and Barn upon the sayd Place to me in Possesion delivered by the the abovesayd James Littlefeild of the abovesayd Town and Province, wherewith I do acknowledge my self to be fully satisfyed and Contented/ Have bargained sold Granted and Exchanged, and by these Presents do grant, Bargain, make Over Infeofe and Confirm fully freely

Jon Buckland   and Absolutely, unto the abovesayd Jams Lit-
to   tlefeild, from me, my Heires, Executors, Ad-
Jas Littlefeild   minisʳˢ and Assignes my now Dwelling house, with my Upland and Meadow Containing six hundred Acres scituate and being in the Towneship of Wells at a Place known by the Name of Kennebunck, and bounded as follow: eth/ The Lower End next to the sea, beginneth at the Rivers Mouth at Kennebunck, on the South east side & so up to

Run as the River Runs, and from the sayd River Kennebunck to run Westward till it Comes to the South west End of the Second Sands, from the afores^d River Kennebunck, and from thence to Run up into the Countrey till Six hundred Acres be fully compleated, with all the Singular Appurtenances and Priveledges, thereunto belonging or in any wise appertayning, as all Woodes and Underwoodes Commons and Commonages, with all Brookes and Water Courses Ponds Swamps, heathy Land, with all Meadows and Meadow Land made or to be Made within the Boundes aforementioned, freely and Quietly to have and to hold without any matter of Challenge Claime or Demand of me the said John Buckland or any Person or Persons either from by or under me my heires Exec^{rs} Adm^{rs} and Assignes forever he the sayd James Littlefeild his heires Exec^{rs} and Adm^{rs} and Assignes I do hereby Declare to be truly and Rightly Possessed of each of every Part and Parcell of the abovementioned Premises, and shall be the sayd James Littlefeild his Heires Exec^{rs}, Adm^{rs} and Assignes, shall have, hold, and Injoy all and every Part and Parcell of the Premises granted and sold to them forever/ And I doe hereby Covenant and Promise to

Jon Buckland
to
Ja Littlefield

and with the sayd James Littlefeild that I am before the Ensealing hereof the true and Lawfull and Right Owner and Possessor of all the abovementioned Premises, and that I have full Power and myself to make lawfull Exchange and Seale of the Premises, and I do further Covenant and Promise thall all and every part of the Premises above granted are free and Clear from all former gifts, grants Bargains Legacyes, Dowries Joynters, Mortgages Judgments Executions, and all other Incumbrances whatsoever, and do Promise to Warrant and Defend the Title and Interest of the Premises from me my heires, Exec^{rs}, Adm^{rs} and Assignes, and from any person and Persons under me or by my Meanes or by proCurement/ In Testimony of all and Every of the Premises I have hereunto sett

Book VI, Fol. 25.

my hand and Seale this 14th day of Aprill Anno Domini 1687 and in the third Year of the Reign of our Soveraign Lord the King James the Second of England &c/ I Sarah Buckland the wife of John Buckland, do freely [25] Consent to the above Bill of Sale and sett to my hand and Seale/ Signed Sealed and Delivered in Presence of us

   William Hammond
   Jonathan Hammond   John ┼ Buckland his marke
                                       & Seale (seale)
                        Sarah ⌒ Buckland
                        her Marke & Seale. (seale)

   Wells in the Province of Main the 9th July 1687 John Buckland and Sarah Buckland his Wife personally appeared before me the Subscriber being one of his Majtie Councill for this his Territory and Dominion of New England/ And Acknowledged the above Instrument to which they have sett to their handes and Seales to be their Voluntary Act and Deed/
                                                        Edward Tynge.
   A true Copy of the Originall Instrument transcribed and Compared this 13th May 1688, Attests/
                                     Tho : Scottow Depty Registr

Rowl Young
   to
Robt Young

        To all Christian People to whom this Present Deed of Gift shall Come/ Know yee That I Rowland Young Senr of the Town of York in the Province of Main ffisherman, together by and with the Consent freewill and Agreement of Joanna my now wife for and in Consideration of the Naturall Love and Affection we do bear to our Son Robert Young, As allso for diverse other good Causes and Considerations us thereunto moving have given, granted Alienated,

Enfeofed and Confirmed and hereby do give grant Alienate Infeofe and Confirm unto him the said Robert Young our son and his heires forever Ten Acres of Land together as it is now bounded and layd out, which is a Part of y^t Lott or Tract of Land which was formerly my now wifes Fathers Robert Knights Land where he formerly lived and is now in the Tenure and Possesion of me the said Rowland Young Senr, my Assigne or Assigns lying and being in York in the Province of Main which Ten Acres of Land being part of the said Roberts Knights farm or Lott of Land is layd out or bounded by a Small Brook or fresh Water, which is near unto the house of Mary Sayward Widow which Brook is South, or thereaboutes from the sayd house, from the Said Brook Southeast thirty two Pole to a Small Alder Tree marked on four sides, from the Allder Tree South west fivety Poles to a white Oake marked on four sides, from the sayd white Oake Tree North West nearest thirty two Poles unto three Small Oakes growing and standing together all marked, and so to Run North east fivety Poles unto the sayd Brook abovementioned, which four Lines compleates the sayd Ten Acres of Land, hereby granted and Confirmed/ To have and to hold the said Ten Acres of Land together with the Appurtenances unto him the sayd Robert our Son and his heires forever only his wife Mary Young is to have ye free Use & benefitt of it during her Naturall life in as full large and Ample Manner to all Constructions Intents and Purposes as I the sayd Rowland Young and Joanna my wife may or can Estate the same freed and discharged from all other or former Gifts grants sales Mortgags Joynters whatsoever made had Committed or Done by me the said Rowland or any my ancestors, and I the sayd Rowland Young do Acknowledge that the sayd Lott or Tract of [26] Land is Really mine Owne and that I have full power to dispose of it by Vertue

Rowl Younge To Robt Younge

of my father in Law Robert Knights Right Gift and Grant to me as it was the sayd Robert Knights at any Time while he Lived and I the sayd Rowland Young and Joanna my now wife for us our Heires Exec rs, Adm rs and Assignes and for every and either of us do hereby Covenant Promise and Agree to and with the sayd Robert Young our Son and his Heires and to and with either of them that he the Sayd Robert Younge and his heires forever and Mary his wife during her Naturall life shall or may from the Date of these Presents henceforth from Time to Time and at all Times hereafter shall Quietly and peceably, have hold Manure and Injoy and Possesse the sayd Tract of Ten Acres of Land be it more or lesse as it is above bounded & we doe hereby bind us our Heires Executors & Adm rs agaynst us the said Rowland Young and Johanna my wife our heires, Exec rs, Adm rs and Assignes the sayd Land to Defend and agaynst all other Person or Persons whatsoever Claiming the sayd Ten Acres of Land or any Part or parcell thereof forever the Lord Proprietor of the Province of Main, Rents only excepted/ In wittnesse hereof we the sayd Rowland Younge and Joanna my wife have hereunto sett our hands and Seales this third Day of June in thirty second Year of the Reign of our Soveraign Lord Charles the Second, of England Scottland ffrance and Ireland King Defender of the fayth, Annoq Dom 1680, and further we grant unto our aforesayd son as an adittion to what is formerly expressed the full breath of that Land belonging to us all and every Part of it, so far as John Leades his Lott, and in Length the whole Quantity, so far as our Interest doth Extend as wittnesse our handes and Seales, allwayes Provided that our sayd son Robert Younge and his

Rowld Young to Robt Young:

Assignes do allow us something Considerable out of the s^d Lands if our Necessity shall Require it

Signed Sealed and Robert Younge his
  Delivered in the presence
  of Arthur Bragdon   mark R and (seale)
  Daniell Livingstone   Joana Young her

         mark F and.(Seale)

Rowland Young Senr and Joanna his Wife came before me this 7th day of September 1685 and owned this Instrument to be their Act and Deed

         Edw Rishworth Just p^s

A true Copy of the Originall Instrument transcribed and Compared this 13th May 1688 as Attests

         Tho: Scottow Dep^t Regis^t

Tho Danforth
to
Jer Moulton

To all to whom these Presents shall Come I Thomas Danforth of Cambridge in New England, Deputy Govern^r, of Boston in the Massachusetts Collony and President of the Province of Main in New England send greeting &c Know yee that I the sayd Thomas Danforth for & in Consideration of the Summ of twenty Poundes good and Lawfull Money of England to me in hand payd by Jeremiah Moulton of York in the Province of Main husbandman before the Enfeoffing and Delivery hereof/ The Receipt whereof I the sayd Thomas Danforth do hereby Acknowledge, & my self therewith to be fully Satisfyed/ Have for my self and Partnerers, given granted, bargained, sold delivered & Confirmed, and by these Presents do fully freely and absolutely, give, grant bargain sell deliver and [27] Confirm unto the sayd Jeremyah Moulton his heires Exec^rs, Adm^rs and Assignes a Certain Tract of

BOOK VI, FOL. 27.

Land lying in York in the Province of Main one the Poynt, commonly called Gorge Poynt, which Land formerly belonged to S^r fferdinando Gorges as Proprietor to the sayd Province, with all Cricks and Coves that do belong to the sayd Tract of Land with all and Singular the Woodes and Underwoodes and all Appurtenances whatsoever to the sayd Land belonging, or in any wise appertayning and all Priveledges thereto belonging with all other Vacant Land which legally is not yett layd out, or now belonging to any other Person/ To have & to hold the sayd Tract of Land lying as afores^d and premises, hereby bargained and sold unto the Sayd Jeremyah Moulton his heires, Exec^rs, Adm^rs, and Assigns as his and their Own proper good and Estate forever to his and their own proper use and behoof forevermore And I the sayd Thomas Danforth for my self Executors Adm^rs and Assignes and every of them together for and in the behalf of my Patrners do Covenant Promise and grant, to and with the sayd Jeremyah Moulton his heirs Exec^rs, Adminis^rs and Assignes by these Presents, that I the sayd Thomas Danforth on the day of the Date hereof, and att the Tyme of the Ensealing and Delivery hereof, have in my self full Power good Right and lawfull Authority to give grant bargain sell deliver and Confirm the sayd Tract of Land and Premises hereby granted and sold unto the sayd Jeremyah Molton his heires Exec^rs, Adm^rs and Assignes forevermore in manner and form aforesayd/ And allso that he the sayd Jeremiah Moulton, his heires Exec^rs Adm^rs and Assignes, or any of them shall and lawfully may from Time to Time, and at all Times hereafter peceably and Quietly, have hold use and Injoy the s^d T Tract and Poynt of Land and Premises hereby bargained and sold without any Manner of Lett Suite Trouble Eviction, Ejection, Molestation, Disturbance Challenge Clayme Deniall or Demand whatsoever of or by me the sayd Thomas Danforth my heires Exec^rs Adm^rs, and Assignes or any of them, or of

*Tho: Danforth
to
Jerm Moulton*

Book VI, Fol. 28.

or by the Govern^n and Company of the Massachusetts Collony or of or by any other Person or Persons w^{t}soever lawfully clayming, or to Clayme from by or under me, my Act or Title/ In Wittnesse hereof I have hereunto Putt my hand and Seale this 27th Day of December Anno Dom^i 1684
Sealed and Delivered in   Tho Danforth/ (Seale)

Tho: Danforth
to
Jer: Moulton

Presence of.
ffrancis Johnson/
Thaddeus Makerty.

John, Hayward Not^r Pub^c

This Instrument was Acknowledged by Thomas Danforth Esqr to be his Act and Deed this 27th of December 1684
         Before Sym Broadstreat Governour

A true Copy of the Originall Instrument transcribed and Compared this 20th May 1688 Attests
         Tho : Scottow : Dep^t Regis^{tr}

To all Christian People to whom these Presents shall Come/ Edward Gillman of Exeter in the Province of New Hampshire send greeting Now Know yee, that the abovementioned Edward [28] Gillman for diverse good Causes me thereunto moving more especially for in Consideration of five and Twenty Pound to me in hand payd by Joseph Hill of Kittery in the Province of Mayn, the Receipt whereof and of every part and Parcell thereof I Acknowledge and therewith fully Satisfyed Contented and payd, have given granted bargained Sold Aliened Infeofed made over and Confirmed/ And by these Presents doe for me my heires, Exec^{rs}, Adm^{rs}, and Assignes forever freely clearly and Absolutely, give grant bargain Sell Aliene Infeofe make Over and Confirm unto him the sayd Joseph Hill his heires Exec^{rs}, Administr^{rs} and Assignes forever a Certain Peice or

BOOK VI, FOL. 28.

Edw Gillman
to
Jos: Hill

parcell of Land Scituate lying and being in the Town of Kittery afores^d Joyning to the head or North East Side of Sam^{ll} Hill Land which he bought of Stephen Paul being in breadth Seventy eight Pole, and so to Run backward upon a Northeast and by East Line till forty Acres be compleated/ To have and to hold the above given and granted Premises with all the Priveledges and Appurtenances thereunto belonging or in any wise appertayning, to him the sayd Joseph Hill his heires Exec^{rs} Adm^{rs} or Assignes forever and y^t the s^d Hill shall and May from Time to Time and at all Times hereafter Improve and make use of the aforesayd Premises, without any· Molestation Lett Deniall or hinderance from or by me the sayd Gillman my Heires or Assignes And further I doe Ingage and Promise for me my heires and Assignes to and with the sayd Hill, agaynst all Persons whatsoever laying any Just Clayme thereunto forever to Warrant and Defend by these Presents/ In Wittnesse whereof I have sett my hand and seale this five and twentieth day of Aprill One thousand Six hundred eighty and Six/ 1686

The words for me my heires and Assignes were Interlined before the Sealing and Delivering

Signed Sealed & Delivered   Edward Gillman : (seale)
   in Presence of.   Edward Gillman came and Acknowl-
Chrystian Remich   edged ye above written Bill of Sale
Joseph Hammonds   to be his Act and Deed this 27th
                      of Aprill 1686, before me
                           Charles ffrost Just Peace.

Stephen Paule and Katherine his wife freely consented to the above written Instrument and gave up all their Right Title and Interest therein this 27th Aprill 1686 before Charles Frost Just Peace

                       Stephen Paule. (seale)
        Kattherine Paule /   marke (seale)

BOOK VI, FOL. 29.

A true Copy of the Originall Deed of Sale as afores^d transcribed and Compared this 20th May 1688 Attests/
Tho: Scottow: Depu^{ty} Regis^{tr}

Jon Buckland
to
Will Taller

To all Christian People to whom these Presents shall Come/ John Buckland send greeting Know ye that I John Buckland of Wells in the Province of Main in New England with the free Consent of Sarah my Wife, for severall good Causes and Considerations me there unto moving, and more especially for and in Consideration of nine Poundes to me in hand delivered and sufficiently Assured to be Payd by William Taller, which is to my satisfaction & wherewith I am fully Contented, have for me [29] my heires Exec^{rs} Adm^{rs} have bargained sold granted Infeofed and Confirmed, and by these Presents do sell Infeofe and Confirm unto William Taller of the aforesayd Town and Province, his heires Exec^{rs} Adm^{rs} and Assigns forever all my Marsh on the West Side of Kennebunck River beginning at the Middle ffalls where the Salt Water doth flow over & to Run up by the River Side till my Boundes be Ended, whither it be more or lesse with all the Appurtenances and Priveledges thereunto belonging with Commons and Commonages with all other Conveniencyes belonging freely and quietly to have and to hold without any Matter of Clayme or Deniall of me

Jon Buckland
to
Willm Taller

the sayd John Buckland or any Person or Persons either from by or under me my heires Exec^{rs} Adm^{rs}, and Assignes forever, he the sayd William Taller, his heires Exec^{rs}, Adm^{rs}, and Assignes I do hereby declare to be truly and Rightly Possessed of the Marsh abovesayd, and that he the sayd William Taller his heires Exec^{rs} Adm^{rs} and Assignes shall peceably and Quietly have hold & Injoy all the abovesayd Premise granted &

sold to them forever/ And I do hereby promise and Covenant to and with the sayd William Taller that the Premises granted and sold are free and Clear from all Gifts grants bargains leases Dowries Mortgages Judgem^{ts} and all other Incumbrances whatsoever and do Promise to Warrant and Defend the Title and Interest of the Premises, from me my heires, Exec^{rs}, Adm^{rs} and assignes, and from any Person or Persons under me or by my Meanes or Procurement/ In Testimony whereof I have sett my hand and seale this eighth day of July One thousand Six hundred eighty and five/

Signed Sealed and   John Buckland
Delivered in Presence
of Sam^{ll} Wheelright   *I* his Marke & (seale)

Sarah Buckland her Mark. /*f9*/ (seale)

John Buckland and Sarah his wife Came before me this 22th day of July 1685 and owned this Instrum^{t} abovewritten to be their free Act and Deed/

                       Edw: Rishworth Jus^{t} peace

A true Copy of the Originall Instrument transcribed and Compared as afores^{d} this 20th of May 1688 Attests/

                     Tho: Scottow: Dep^{t}, Regis^{t}

Ben Bernard
to
Jos Bernard

To all Christian People to whom these Presents shall Come/ Benjamen Bernard of Dover in the Province of New hampshire in New England yeoman and Sarah his Wife Sends Greeting Know yee that I the abovementioned Benjamen Bernard and Sarah my wife for diverse good Causes and Considerations us moving thereunto, more especially for and in Consideration of the Summ of fivety Poundes in Currant Money of New England in hand Received before the Signing and Sealing hereof of Joseph Bernard of Barwick in the Towneship of Kittery in new England wherewith we Acknowledge our Selves fully satisfyed Contented and Payd, and thereof and every part and parcell thereof do Acquitt and forever discharge the Sayd Joseph Bernard his heirs [30] and Assignes by these Presents/ Have absolutely given grrnted bargained sold Aliened Enfeofed and Confirmed, and by these Presents do absolutely give grant bargain Sell Alien Enfeofe and Confirm unto the abovenamed Joseph Bernard a Peice or Parcell of Land being by Measure fivety Acres scituate and being in the Township of Kittery, that Land which I Bought of Joseph Bernard formerly being bounded on the South with the Land of Richard Tozer, & on the West with the River that parts Dover and Kittery, and on the North with the Land of John Price & on the East with the Common Land. To have and to hold the abovementioned peice or parcell of Land with the housing and fencing on it to him the sayd Joseph Bernard and his heires and Assignes forever to his only proper Use benefitt and behoof forever, and the sayd Benjamen Bernard and Sarah his wife for themselves their heires and Assignes do Covenant promise and grant to & with the sayd Joseph Bernard his heires and Assignes, that they the sayd Benjamin Bernard and Sarah his Wife, have in themselves good right full Power and lawfull Authority the above given and granted Premises to sell and Dispose of & that the same and every Part and parcell thereof are free and Clear, and freely and Clearly Acquitted exonerated and discharged of and from all & all manner of former gifts grants Leases, Mortgages Intailes Wills Judgments, Executions power of Thirds and all other Incumbrances of what Nature and kind soever had made done, Acknowledged Committed or Suffred to be done or Committed, whereby the sayd Joseph Bernard his heires or Assignes shall or may any wayes be Molested in Evicted or Ejected out of the above granted Premises or

*Ben Berna·d
to
Jos Bernard*

Book VI, Fol. 31.

any Part or parcell thereof by any Person or Persons whatsoever, having Claiming or pretending to have or Clayme any Legall Right Title Interest claime or Demand of in or to the above granted Premises, and the said Benjamen Bernard and Sarah his wife do for themselves their heires, Exec^{rs}, Adm^{rs}, and Assignes Covenant Promise and Grant to and with the sayd Joseph Bernard his heires and Assignes the abovegranted Peice or parcell of Land with the housing fencing and priveledges thereto belonging to Warrant and forever Defend from all Persons excepting the Lord Proprietor by these Presents/ In Wittnesse whereof the sayd Benjamen Bernard and Sarah his Wife have hereunto sett their handes and seales this twenty fourth day of August in the Year of our Lord One thousand Six hundred eighty & seven and in the third year of the Reign of our Soveraign Lord James the Second by the Grace of God of England Scotland ffrance and Ireland King Defender of the fayth &c.

Ben Bernard
to
Jos Bernard

Signed Sealed and.   Benjamen Bernard (seale)
   Delivered in presence   mark of
   of us George Broughton   Sarah *CD* Bernard (seale)
     Peter Knap

Benjamen Bernard and Sarah Bernard his wife personally appeared before me the [31] Subscriber being One of his Majestyes Councill & Acknowledged the above Instrument to be their volontary Act and Deed this 1th November 1687
                                Edward Tynge.

A true Copy of the Originall Instrument transcribed and Compared this 20th May 1688 Attests/
                        Tho : Scottow : Dep^t Regis^t

This Indenture made the third Day of November Anno Domⁱ, One thousand six hundred Eighty seven, Annoq RR^s Angliæ &c^a Tertio/ Between John Allcock of Kittery

Book VI, Fol. 31.

Jon Allcock
to
Shubll Dumer

Elldest Son of Joseph Allcock, the eildest son and heir of John Allcock of York within the Province of Main in his Majestyes Territory and Dominion of New England Yeoman Deceased on the One Part, and Shubnell Dumer of Yorke aforesaid Clerk of the other Part/ Wittnesseth/ That the sayd John Allcock for and in Consideration of the Summ of Six Poundes Currant Money of New England to him in hand by the sayd Shubaell Dummer at the Ensealing and Delivery of these Presents well and truly Payd, the Receipt whereof the said John Allcock doth hereby Acknowledge, and thereof doth forever Acquitt, and Discharge the said Shubaell Dummer his heires Exec^{rs}, Adm^{rs} and Assignes firmly by these Presents/ Hath Given granted, Released and Quitt Claimed, And by these Presents Doth freely fully and absolutely give grant Release and Confirm unto the said Shubaell Dummer in his Actuall Possesion now benig/ A certain Tract or Parcell of Upland in Quantity Fivety eight Acres or thereaboutes Little more or lesse/ Lying scituate within the Towneship of York aforesaid near the Rivers Mouth being the one half or Moiety of a Neck of Land commonly Called and known by the Name of Farmer Allcocks Neck, who was the above mentioned John Allcock Deceased, and whereof he dyed seised this said Moiety thereof abutting Notherly upon the other Moiety now in the Possesion of George Snell, Easterly upon the Sea, Southerly upon the Land of Henry Millberry, or however otherwise abutting or Bounded/ And four Acres or theraboutes be it More or lesse of Salt Marsh lying on the Western branch of York River afores^d, commonly called and known by the Name of Farmer Allcock Marsh and whereof he dyed seized/ Allso all the Estate, Right Title and Inheritance, Use Property Interest, Claim

Jon Alcock
to
Shubll Dumer

Challenge, Pretention or Demand of the sayd John Allcock first above Named of in or unto the sayd Tract or Parcell of Up Land and

Marsh both which the sayd Shubaell Dummer severall Yeares since Purchased of John Twisden Administra[rs] to the Estate of Joseph Allcock his Aforesaid father Deceased/ To have and to hold the said Moiety or half Part of said Neck of Upland and Parcell of Salt Marsh, with all buildings and Improvements thereupon whatsoever, Rights Libertyes Commonages profitts priveledges and Appurtenances thereto belonging, unto the sayd Shubaell Dumer his heires and assignes/ To his and their own Proper Use benefitt and behoof forever/ And the said John Allcock for himself his heirs Exec[rs] and Adm[rs] doth by these Presents Covenant Promise Grant and Agree to and with the sayd Shubaell Dummer his heires and Assignes/ That he the sayd Shubaell Dummer his heires and Assignes Shall and May at all Times and Times forever hereafter lawfully peceably [32] and Quietly hold Use Possese and Injoy all the above granted and Released Premises, with the Rights Members and Priveledges and Appurtenances thereof w[th]out the Lest Lett Deniall Suite Troubell, Molestation Claime Challenge or Demand of him the said John Allcock his heires Exec[rs] or adm[rs] or of any other Person or persons whomsoever from by or under him them or either of them/ And doth hereby forever Quitt Claim unto the Same or any Part thereof/ And to all Action of Right Title Challenge or Demand thereunto/ In wittnesse Whereof the sayd John Allcock hath hereunto sett his hand and seale the day and Year first above written/

Signed Sealed and Deliverd   John Allcock (seale)
in presence of us.

Jon Allcock
to
Shubll Dumer

John Gidding,
George Gidding, Is[a] Addington/

Boston in New England November the 3[d], 1687 Then Appeared before me the within Named John Allcock and Acknowledged this Writing and Instrum[t] to be his Act and Deed/

                                Edw: Randolph.

Book VI, Fol. 32.

A true Copy of the Originall Deed or Instrum^t transcribed and Compared this 2^d of June Anno Dom^i 1688 Attests

      Tho : Scottow Dep^t Regis^tr

This Indenture made the ffive and Twentieth day of June in the ffowerth yeare of the Raigne of our Soûaigne Lord James the second by the grace of God of England Scotland ffrance and Ireland King Defender of the fayth &c And in the yeare of our Lord God One Thousand six hundred and Eighty Eight Betweene Richard White of the Towne of Kittery in the Provynce of Mayne on the one parte And Henry Dering of the Towne of Boston in New England Merchant on the other parte Witnesseth that the said Richard White for and in consideraçon of the sume of Thirty pounds to him in hand paid by the said Henry Dering att and before the sealing and delivery of these p^rnts the receipt whereof he doth hereby acknowledge and thereof and of every parte thereof doth accquitt release and discharge the said Henry Dering his Heires Exec^rs Adm^rs and Assignes forever by these p^rnts Hath given graunted bargayned and sold And by these p^rnts doth give graunt bagayne and sell unto the said Henry Dering his Heires Exec^rs Adm^rs And Assignes for ever All that Messuage Tenement or dwelling house scituate and being in Kittery aforesaid wherein the said Richard White doth now Inhabite and dwell And alsoe all that Ninety acres of Vpland which he the said Richard White lately purchassed of Ephraim Crockett beginning att the bridge att the head of Broad boate Harbour and Running from thence North West along by York Line One hundred and sixty Poles into the Woods and Ninety Poles in breadth South West being bounded on the South East with a smal piece of Salt

Rich: White
 to
Henry Dering

Book VI, Fol. 33.

Marsh which Thomas Crockett late of Kittery aforesaid deced did usually mow (leaving out the places where John Billing and James Wiggens built their houses And alsoe All the Marsh beginning att the Bridge and soe running in the breadth of ffifty acres of the abovesaid Vpland on the south East of it. Which Marsh is bounded with the said Vpland on one side And Broad-boate Harbour Crick on the other side And alsoe a small stripp of Marsh lyeing on the North East side of the Neck above the Bridge Together with all and singular proffitts comodities priviledges and advantages whatsoever to the same belonging or in any wise appertayning And all ways waters water courses Yards Backsides Easments Woods Vnderwoods Meadows Leasows pastures ffeedings comons proffitts and comodities whatsoever wth thappurtences unto the same or any parte thereof belonging or in any wise appertayning And the Revercon and Revercons Remainder and Remainders of [33] all and singular the said p'misses or any parte there of And true Coppyes of all such deedes Evidences and writeings which concerne the same or any parte thereof To have and to hold the said Messuage or Tenement Lands and p'misses and all and singular the p'misses aforesd wth thappurtences unto the sd Henry Dering his Heires Execrs Admrs and Assignes To the onely and proper use and behoofe of him the sd Henry Dering his Heires Execrs Admrs and Assignes for ever Provided allways and itt is fully agreed by and betweene the said parties to these p'sents that if the said Richard White his Heires Execrs Admrs or Assignes or any of them do and Shall well and truly pay or cause to be paid unto the sd Henry Dering his Heires Execrs Admrs or Assignes the severall sumes and att the severall tymes herein after mencōned & Expressed (That is to say) the full sume of Seaven

Rich White
to
Hen: Dering

pounds Ten shillings att or upon the last day of October next ensueing the date hereof and the like sume of seaven pounds Ten shillings att or upon the last day of Aprill then next following and the like sume att or upon the last day of October which Shall be in the yeare of our Lord God One Thousand Six hundred Eighty Nine, And the like sume of Seaven pounds Ten shillings att or upon the last day of Aprill then next following without fraud or Covin All which payments are to be paid in Marchant^ble^ staves or heading (as the money price shall then be in Piscataqua River att the severall tymes of payment as aforesaid) That Then this p^r^sent Indenture to be voyd frustrate and of none effect the sd p^r^sents or any thing herein contayned to the contrary in any wise notw^th^standing But if default be made in the said payments or any or either of them that then this Indenture to stand and remayne in full force effect and vertue And the said Richard White doth for him selfe his Heires Exec^rs^ and Administrators Covenant promise and agree to and with the said Henry Dering his Heires Exec^rs^ and Adm^rs^ by these p^r^sents in manner & forme following That is to say That he the said Richard White now att the tyme of the sealing and delivery of these p^r^sents is and doth stand lawfully and actually seized of and in the said Lands Tenements and p^r^misses of a good lawfull absolute and indefeazible Estate of inheritance in ffee simple and that he hath good right full power and lawfull authority to graunt and convay the sd p^r^mises unto the said Henry Dering and his Heires and Assignes for ever and that ffree and cleare and freely and clearly acquitted Exonerated and discharged of and from all and all maner of former and other guifts graunts bargaynes sales Leases Joyntures Dowers Mortgages Statutes Entayles or any other incumbrances whatsover shall be remayne and continue unto the said Henry Dering and his Heires forever

Richd White
to
Henry Dering

from and after the Nonpayment of the sumes aforesd or any or either of them And alsoe that it shall and may be lawfull to and for the said Henry Dering his Heires Exec^rs^ & Adm^rs^ or either of them imediately after the Nonpayment of either of the said sumes att the tymes a foresd to enter the said Messuage or Tenement Lands and p'misses and the same to enjoy as his and their owne proper use and behoofe and in some short tyme make sale of the said p'misses for the payment of the sumes aforesd and the overplus if any be to returne to the sd Richard White his Heires or Assignes allowing unto him the said Richard White his Heires Exec"' or Adm"' the space of Six Moneths to redeem the said p'misses And alsoe that he the sd Richard White his Heires Exec"' or Adm"' shall and will performe any further act or deede for the more sure settling of the said p'misses unto the said Henry Dering his Heires [34] Exec"' Adm"' or Assignes as aforesd as by the said Henry Dering his Heires Exec"' or Adm"' or by his or their Councell Learned in the Law att the proper cost and charges of the said Dering his Heires Exec"' or Adm"' shall be reasonably devised and required And alsoe for the further security of the said sume of Thirty pounds unto the said Henry Dering he the said Richard White doth by these p'nts give and graunt to the sd Henry Dering Two Redd Cows Topp Cutt and splitt in the neare eare which said Cows the said Henry Dering his Heires Exec"' or Adm"' are to have to their owne proper use and behoofe imediately after the Non payment of either of the sumes aforesd In Witnes whereof the said Richard White hath hereunto sett his hand and Seale the day and yeare first wthin written./

Rich. White
to
Henry Dering

Sealed and delivered
in the p'sence of
   Richard White
    his Marke

(sigillum)
(Ric White)

Francis Hooke ⎫ Provynce ⎫
William Hooke ⎬ of ⎬ ss:
Henry Barter ⎭ Mayne ⎭

       Memorand that this day being the 25th day of June 1688 Richard White personally

Book VI, Fol. 34.

appeard before me and owned this Instrum^t to be his Act and deede

Francis Hooke Jus : Quo

Memorandum that it was agreed betweene the abovesd Richard White and Henry Dering by his Attorney that the abovesd staves are to be paid and delivered att the dwelling house of Captn Hooke in Kittery att the price abovesd dated this 25th day of June 1688

Will : Hooke Attorney to y^e
sd Dering

Ric : White   his Marke

Richd White
to
Hen : Dering

Livery and seizin given and delivered by the abovesaid Richard White unto the abovenamed Henry Dering by his Attorney of the house and lands above mencõnd according to Law this 24th day of June 1688 in the p^{r}sence of

Francis Hooke

Jno Moore   Marke

Will Hilton   Marke

William Hooke

A true Coppy of the Originall Deede or Instrument transcribed and compared this ffifth day of July Anno Dni 1688
attests Tho : Scottow :
Dep^t Regis^{tr}

Book VI, Fol. 35.

Know all men by these pʳsents that I Henry Dering of the Towne of Boston in New England Merchant Doe Nominate impower and appoint William Hooke of Boston aforesaid my true and lawfull Attorney for me and in my name to demand recieve or to use any way or meanes to recover any sume or sumes of goods of Estate money or effects by account specialty promise assignmᵗ or any other way whatsoever due or payable to me the said Dering Giveing and by these pʳsents granting to my said Attorney full and ample power to proceed prosecute and conclude any of my concernments as aforesd att any Court or Courts Eastward of Boston aforesaid and accquittances or other discharges or receipts for me and in my name to deliver and recieve and to act and performe in the pʳmisses as fully and amply in every respect as if I my self were [35] personally pʳsent Ratifying and allowing and holding firme and staple whatsoever my sd Attorney shall lawfully doe or cause to be done in and about the aforesd pʳmisses In Witnes whereof I have hereunto sett my hand & seale this fowerteenth day of March Anno RRˢ Jacobi secdi nunc Angł &c quarto Annoq Dni 168¾

Henry Dering to William Hooke

Sealed and delivered   Henry Dering (seal)
in the pʳsence of
    Theodor Attkison
    Benjamin Faireweather

Boston 14ᵗʰ March 168¾

Henry Dering personally appeared before me one of the Councill in this his Majesties Territory and Dominion & acknowledged the above written Instrument to be his act and Deede

    Jnº Vsher

A true Coppy of the above written Instrument transcribed and compared wᵗʰ the originall this 6ᵗʰ day of July Anno Dni 1688 Attests

    Tho: Scottow: Depᵗ Regisᵗʳ

Book VI, Fol. 35.

Wittnes these p'sents that I Joseph Hodsden of the Towne of Yorke Doe for my selfe my Heyres Executors Adm^{rs} sell make over Enfeoffe unto Silvanus Davis his Heires Executors Adm^{rs} and Assignes for and in consideracon of ffifteene pounds paid to me in hand before the insealeing and delivery of these p'sents by the sayd Davis to say all that parcell of land and swamp thereunto belonging scituate att Nonsuch p in the Towne of ffalmouth being about one hundred and Twenty Acres more or lesse as p the Towne Records doe appeare with all mañer of priviledges and appurtenances thereunto belonging in and upon the said Land and swampe for him the sd Davis his Heyres Executors Administrators and Assignes to have and to hold forever all and singular all the fore dementioned p^{r}misses and I the said Joseph Hodsden Doe bind my selfe my Heires & Executors Administrators in the sume of fforty pounds of Currant money of New England unto the sd Davis or Assignes that I the said Hodsden and my wife Tabitha Shall signe and seale to a firm Bill of sale according to the true intent and meaneing of what is above written upon all demands as Witnes my hand & seale this second day of June in the third yeare of his Majesties Reigne Annoq Dni 1687/

Joseph Hodsden to Sylvanus Davis

Sealed Signed & delivered in p'sence of us
Joseph Hodsden (seal)
Henry Crosslee
his signe
Elizabeth Clearb

ffalmouth provynce of Mayne June the second day 1687 Joseph Hodsden did acknowledge this Instrum^t to be his act and deede as above specified before me

Edward Tyng one of the Councill

Book VI, Fol. 36.

A true Coppy of this Instrument or deed transcribed out of the Originall and therewith compared this 12th day of of July 1688
                Attests
                        Tho : Scottow Dep't Regis'r

Know all men by these p'sents that I Thomas Wells of the Towne of Almsbury in the County of Essex in his Majesties Territory and Dominion of New England in America Minister haveing formerly purchased severall quantities or parcells of Vpland and Meadow scituate lyeing and being in the Towne ship of Wells in the Provynce of Mayne in New England as may more particularly appeare by convayances or Bills of sale of the same under the hands & seales of Thomas Thaurley of Newberry Dat Jan'ry 8th 1667 and Nicholas Cole of Capeorpus Dated June 25th 1669 ffor and in consideracon of a valuable sume of good pay by Bill unto me [36] secured by Nicholas Cole Jun of the Towne of Wells in the Provynce of Mayne abovesaid Labourer and for divers other good and Lawfull motives me thereunto induceing Have Covenanted bargayned and sold And by these p'sents Doe fully Clearly and absolutely Give grant bargayne sell Alienate Enfeoffe confirme and make over unto said Nicholas Cole Jun all my right title and interest unto and in all and every of the contents of sd Deedes or Bills of sale and every quantity or parcell of upland or meadow in either or both of them contained expressed specified or Intended for sd Nicholas Cole Jun To have and to hold to use occupy possess and enjoy as a good sure and absolute ffee simple estate of inheritance to the Proper use behoofe and benefitt of himselfe his Heires Executors Administrators or Assignes for ever without Lett suite hindrance or interrupcon from

Tho: Wells to Nico Cole Jun

me the sd Wells or any of my Heires Executors and Administrators or any other person or persons in by from or under me or them or any of us And I the said Wells doe by these p^{r}sents both for my selfe my Heires Execut^{rs} and Adm^{rs} Covenant promise and engage to and with sd Nicholas Cole jun his Heires Executors Adm^{rs} or Assignes to Warrantize defend and maintaine the Sale of the demised p^{r}misses agst all Lawfull challenges claymes or demaundes that may be had made or Laide unto ye whole or any parte or parcell thereof by vertue of any gift grant bargayne sale Alienacon or convayance of the same made by me the said Wells or any other person or persons whatsoever for me or in my name or by my approbacon or procurement And Doe moreover by these p^{r}sents acknowledge to have given the demised p^{r}misses together with the above mentioned bills of sale into ye possession of sd Nicholas Cole Jun And in confirmacon of the p^{r}misses I have hereunto subscribed my hand and sett to my seale this Nineth day of August An: Dom: One Thousand six hundred Eighty and seaven And in the Third yeare of his Majesties Reigne/

Tho: Wells to Nico Cole Jun

Subscribed sealed and delivered/ Thomas Wells (a seal)
   in the p^{r}sence of us
      Henry Blasdall
      Nathan Littlefield

Tho: Wells to Nico Cole Jun

Thomas Wells personally appeareing acknowledged this Instrument to be his Act and Deed Sept: 9th 1687 before me
                      William Stoughton

A true Coppy of the Originall Deed of Sale as aforesd transcribed and compared this Last day of March 1689 Attests
              Tho: Scottow Dep^t Regis^{tr}

This Indenture made between William Burrage and Joshua Scottow both of Scarborough in the Provynce of Mayne testifieth that Whereas there was an agreem^t or sale made to William Burrage by said Scottow of a parcell of Marsh Land in said Scarborough according to a Deed Dated the Nineteenth day of October 1685 the bounds of the said Land not being clearly expressed nor under stood and noe seizin or possession given of the same, these are to declare that the said Deed or agreement though under hand and Seale, acknowledged and recorded is Delivered up cancelled and hereby declared to be Null and of noe force in Law and is in consideracon of an agreement made between the said Scottow and Burrage of the same date wth these p^{r}sents/ And the said William Burrage for himselfe Heires Executors and Administrators doth unto the said Joshua Scottow his Heires or Assignes relinquish all Claym [37] right or title whatsoever unto the said parcell of Marsh Land in the above Deed mentioned In Witnes of the p^{r}misses the said William Burrage hath hereunto set his hand and seale Blackpoint the 1th of Novemb^r 1687 and in the iiij^d yeare of the reigne of our soueraigne James the ij^d by the grace of God King of England Scotland &c

William Burregh (seale)

Signed Sealed and delivered
in p^{r}sence of
    mark
John ℘ Morton
John Howell

This deed or Instrument above was acknowledged by William Burregh before me the subscriber being one of his Maj^{ties} Councill for this his Dominion of New England the 30th July 1688

Edward Tyng

Book VI, Fol. 37.

A true Coppy of the Originall Instrument as aforesaid transcribed and compared this 8th of Aprill 1689
Attests T Scottow Dep^t Reg^r

At a Generall Court of Election held at Boston the 12th of May 1686 by the Governour & Company of the Massachusetts Bay in New England

Court Electio grant to Josh Scottow   In Answer to the Petition of Joshua Scottow/ The Court grants the Petition of five hundred Acres of Land as an Addition to the five hundred Acres formerly granted, & to be in the Same Place, and on the same Condition in full of all Demands

A true Copy Attests.

Edward Randolph Secret

A true Copy of the Originall Instrument aforesaid transcribed & Compared this 12th of Aprill 1689
Attests Tho Scottow Dep^t Regis^t

Articles of Agreement made & Concluded on between Anthony Brackett Junr of Casco Bay on the one Party and Abraham Drake Senr of Hampton in the County of Norfolk, both of New England/

Whereas the s^d Anthony Brackett Widdower is lately Joyned in Marriage, with Susanna Drake single woman, and the Elldest Daughter of the s^d Abraham Drake of Hampton/ Therefore Know yee That I the s^d Anthony Brackett have covenanted and Agreed, and by these presents do Covenant and Agree, in and with the s^d Abraham Drake as a ffeofee in Trust, for & in behalf of the s^d Susanna my present wife/ That I doe by these Presents, Instate the s^d Susanna by way of Joynter one half of all my Lands & Housing, which I had in Casco Bay, or Shall have, according to the true Estimatio & Value thereof/ To have & to hold the s^d Landes Meadowes, and Marshes, and all the Priveledges and Appurtenances thereof, with all Woodes Timber, and Waters and other Appurtenances belonging to one Moiety of my whole Estate there at Casco for her free Joynter during her Natturall life and to be and Remain to her and her Male Heires begotten of her Body by me the s^d Anthony Brackett her present Husband/ Made this Promise before Mariage, I doe Consent to it, with my hand and seale, and what the Lord Shall Add unto my Estate during our Naturall Lives together Made at Blackp^t, the 30th September 1679

Wittnesse, Thomas Scottow/   Anthony Brackett (seal)

This Instrument above written was Acknowledged by Anthony Brackett to be his Act & Deed before me the day & Year above Written

                       Josh Scottow Associate

A true Copy of the Originall Instrument transcribed and Compared this 14th Aprill 1689 Attests

                       Tho Scottow Dep^t Regis^r

[38] Thomas Jones aged Seventy yeares Testifieth that about forty yeares agoe he being Servant to Mr Alexander Shapleigh, was set to work to make a fence by the Marsh Side that belonged to said Shapleigh at Sturgeon Creek begining at ye Southeast Side of John Heards house by Sturgeon Creek and from thence to the little brooke by Nicholas ffrosts house. And the s^d ffrost desired of s^d Shapleigh a way to be left from the s^d Creek to his house which said Shapleigh granted it and left a way which hath bin used from time to time without deniall of the s^d Shapleigh or any of his Successors that ever said Jones knew of to this day.

Book VI, Fol. 38.

Taken upon oath this Second day of May 1679
Before me
John Wincoll Assotiate

A true Copie of the originall oath Transcribed and compared the 10th day of Novembr 1701 p Jos: Hamond Registr

John White aged. 70. yeares Testifieth that about two and forty years agoe Mr Alexander Shapleigh and Mr James Treworgie did agree wth the Neighbours dwelling at and about Sturgion Creek that there should be always a high way from Nicholas ffrosts house down to Sturgeon Creek and Soe along to the Ceaders And the sd high way hath bin held ever Since without Interuption.

Jno Whites Oath

Taken upon oath this 5th day of May 1679
Before me John Wincoll Assotiate

A true Copie of the originall Transcribed and compared the : 10 day of Novembr : 1701

p Jos: Hamond Registr

Barwick Novembr 14. 1702

Recd of my brother John Gowen the Sum of three pounds six shillings & eight pence being in full of that part of my father William Gowens Estate which he ye sd John Gowen was appointed to pay me before ye Decease of my Mother Elizabeth Gowen/

Wittness { Willm M Rogers (his mark) / Thomas Penny }

p Lemuel Gowen

A true Copie of ye originall Transcribed & compared Decembr 5th 1702/

p Jos Hamond Regr

BOOK VI, FOL. 38.

To all Christian People to whome these presents shall come Greeting/ Know yee that I Gabriel Tetherly of Kittery and Susanna my wife, in the County of York in New England Shipwright, for and in consideration of the Sum of thirty two pounds in Money and Merchandize to us in hand alredy paid by Samuel Penhallow of Portsm⁰ in yᵉ Province of New Hampshiere in New England Shopkeeper wᵗʰ which Sum we Acknowledge our Selues fully Satisfied & paid And doe hereby Acquit and Discharge yᵉ sᵈ Samˡˡ Penhallow his heires Executʳˢ and Adminʳˢ from every part & parcell thereof for ever, have giuen granted bargained and Sold, and by these presᵗˢ doe giue, grant, bargain, Sell, Alien, Enfeoffe confirm and make over unto yᵉ sᵈ Samˡˡ Penhallow his heires Executʳˢ Administratʳˢ and Assignes one certain Lott or parcell of land lying & being in Thomas Spinneys Creek or Cove comonly soe called, containing one hundred and twenty six pole or rods in Length from yᵉ east end of John ffernalds ten Acres Lott behind yᵉ great Cove upon An East line And forty pole or rod in breadth at yᵉ west end upon a North line, and thirty eight pole broad at yᵉ east end bounded on yᵉ South with yᵉ land of Richard Kings; on yᵉ North & West with the land of John ffernalls; and on yᵉ east with yᵉ Comons; which said Lott or tract of land is in full thirty Acres granted me by the town, Measured and laid out August Eighteenth. 1679. by Captain John Wincoll then Survʳ together with all manner of Priviledges and Appurtenances thereunto belonging or what else hereafter may be Appurtaining. To have and to hold to him yᵉ sᵈ Samˡˡ Penhallow his heires Executʳˢ Adminʳˢ & Assignes, all the abouesᵈ lott or tract of land butted & bounded as aforesᵈ with all manner of Priviledges in any kind Appurtaining ffor ever/ And I yᵉ sᵈ Gabriel & Susana Tetherly doe by these presents bind our Selues our heires Executʳˢ and Adminʳˢ to Warrant & Defend unto yᵉ sᵈ Samˡˡ Penhallow his heires Executʳˢ Adminʳˢ and Assignes all yᵉ abouesᵈ tract or lott of land, together with all yᵉ Priviledges thereunto belonging for ever from all & every mannʳ of psons whatsoever that shall prove or pretend to any manner of Claim title or Interest in any kind or nature whatsoever ffrom by or under us/ In Testimony to all and Singular yᵉ Premises, I yᵉ sᵈ Gabriel Tetherly and Susanna my wife have hereunto sete our hands & affixed our Seales this : 16ᵗʰ day of Aprill Anno Domini : 1695.

                                  Gabriel Tetherly (his seale)

Signed Sealed & Delivered   her
  in yᵉ presents of us   Susanna ST Tetherly (her seale)
  Jacob Remick   mark
  Beriah Higgins

Gabriel Tetherly Appeared this 18ᵗʰ of June 1695, and Acknowledged the above Instrumᵗ to be his Act & Deed, before me   Tho Packer Jusᵗ Pˢ

A true Copie of yᵉ origenall Deed Transcribed & compared. this. 26ᵗʰ day of Augˢᵗ 1699.

                                  Jos Hamond Registʳ

[39] These presents Witnesseth that I Samuel Penhallow wᵗʰin Mentioned for and in Consideration of yᵉ Sum of thirty two pounds Currant money of New England by me in hand received of John Dennet Junʳ of Porstmᵒ in yᵉ Province of New Hampshier, have bargained & sold unto yᵉ sᵈ John Dennet his heires Executʳˢ Adminʳˢ or Assignes all that land in Spinneys Creek, with yᵉ Priviledges belonging Mentiond in the within Deed And I yᵉ sᵈ Samˡˡ Penhallow for me my heires Executʳˢ and Administratʳˢ doe by these presents giue grant bargain sell Assigne and set over unto the sᵈ John Dennet his heires Executʳˢ Adminʳˢ and Assignes all my Right title and Interest in and unto this Deed and to all things therein contained in as large and Ample manner

Book VI, Fol. 39.

as I have ye same from the within Mentioned Gabriel and Susanna Tetherly/ In witness whereof I have hereunto set my hand and seal this 28th of Augst 1699.
Signed Sealed & Delivered   Sam^{ll} Penhallow (his seal)
  in the presence of.
  Cha : Story.
  Samuel Hill
  Mary King.
  Nicholas Gowen.

Samuel Penhallow and Mary his wife Appeared before me the Subsriber, he ye s^d Samuel Acknowledging this same to be his Act and Deed & she ye s^d Mary deliuering up her thirds in point of Dowery/ August 28th 1699/
                        Mary Penhallow (her seal)
                    Jos Hamond Jus^{te} Peace

A true Copie of ye origenall Deed or Assignm^t transcribed & compared this 2^d day of Septemb^r 1699.
                    p Jos Hamond Regist^r

To all Christian People to whome these presents shall come Greeting in our Lord God everlasting. Know yee that I Isaac Goodridge of Kittery in ye County of York in New England Yeoman, for Divers good causes and valluable considerations me hereunto moveing but more Especially for and in consideration of ffiftie pounds in Money to me in hand paid by my Aunt Mrs Margret Addams of the same place Spinster/ the receipt thereof I doe by these presents Acknowledge And my self therewith contented and paid and of every part thereof And freely Acquit ye s^d Margret Addams for the same, Have giuen granted Aliened bargained Sold Enfeoffeed and confirmed And by these presents doth fully clearly and Absolutely giue grant bargain sell Aliene Enfeoffee and confirme unto ye said Margrett Addams her heires and Assignes for ever all that house and Land lying in the Township of Kittery in the County of York aboues[d]. And that Tract of Land and house that I bought of Samuel King late of Kittery as Appears by a Deed of Sale under y[e] s[d] Kings hand bearing Date y[e] sixteenth day of June in y[e] year of our Lord one thousand six hundred and Ninety Six as by s[d] Deed on Record doth more at large Appear reference thereunto being had, together with all and singular its Rights, Memb[rs] Jursidictions and Appurtenances together with the buildings, orchards, yards Easments lands Meadows feedings, pastures, woods, under woods, timber, Quarries of Stone, Mines and Mineralls of what kind soever and all Heredittaments & Appurtenances to y[e] s[d] house and land belonging or in any wise Appertaining & y[e] Reversion & reversions remaind[r] & remaind[rs] of all and Singular y[e] above Mentioned Premises And all Estate Right title Interest Possession propertie claim and Demand whatsoever, of him y[o] s[d] Isaac Goodridge in or to y[e] Same, with all Deeds writings Euidences Trascripts Escripts and Monuments whatsoever, touching or concerning y[e] Premises or any part or parcell of them/ To haue and to hold all y[e] s[d] house & land and all and Singular other y[e] Premises hereby granted bargained & sold with their and every of their rights, Memb[rs], and Appurtenances whatsoever unto y[e] s[d] Margrett Addams her heires and Assignes to y[e] onely proper use and behoof of y[e] s[d] Margret Addams her heires & Assignes for ever/ And the s[d] Isaac Goodridge for himselfe and his heires the s[d] house & land and all and singular other y[e] Premises before granted bargained & sold with y[e] Appurtenances unto y[e] s[d] Margret Addams & her heires to y[e] onely proper use and behoofe of y[e] s[d] Margret Addams her heires & assignes for euer against him y[e] s[d] Isaac Goodridge his heires and Assignes for euer And all other psons Claiming from by or under him/ And shall & will Warrant & foreuer Defend by these presents And y[e] s[d] Isaac Goodridge doth for himselfe his heires

Execut[rs] and Administrat[rs] couenant promise grant and agree to and with y[e] s[d] Margret Addams her heires and Assigns and euery of them by these presents in manner and form following that is to say that y[e] s[d] Isaac Goodridge at y[e] time of y[e] Sealing of these presents is Siezed & in full possession of all and singular ye aboue Mentioned Premises And hath within himselfe full power & Lawfull Authority to sell & dispose of y[e] same And that y[e] Premises are free from all incumbrances whatsoeuer, as Sales gifts bargains joyntures and Dowers Judgm[ts] and Executions and all whatsoeuer And that is shall & may be Lawfull for y[e] s[d] Margret Addams her heirs and Assignes to take up ocupie & possess y[e] same for euer y[e] Peaceable and quiet possession thereof to Warrant and for euer Defend against all persons laying Lawfull Claim thereunto. In witness hereof I haue set unto my hand & Seal this fourth day of Aprill one thousand six hundred Ninety & Nine

Signed sealed sealed and deliuered in
   y[e] presents of us   Isaac Goodridge (his seale)
   John Addams
   An Couch
   W[m] Godsoe

Isaac Goodridge Appeared before me y[e] Subscrib[r] one of the Memb[rs] of his Maj[ties] Council of y[e] Prouince of y[e] Massachusets Bay and Justice of Peace within y[e] same And Acknowledged y[e] above Instrum[t] to be his Act & Deed this 11th Septemb[r] 1699   Jos Hamond

A true Copie of the origenall Deed Transcribed & compared this 11th Septemb[r] 1699
                         p Jos Hamond Regist[r]

[40] Know all men whome it may concern that I Job Alcock of York Resident doe Assigne and Deliuer ouer a

parcell of Land and all that belongs to it to Edward Cock his Yeares Execut^{rs} or Assignes the aboues^d Land to lay as followeth begining at Westermost Creek laying from Goodman Braggingtons to ye old Bound tree Joyning to Goodman Cards Land Soe Northeast till it comes to ye head of ye Creek/ The aboue said Job Alcock doth hereunto put his hand & seale this 6th of Augus : Anno Domini 1670

Tests   Job Alcock (his seale)

  John Dauis

  John Penwill

Cap^{tn} Job Alcock Appeared before me this sixth day of Septemb^r 1699. And Acknowledged this Instrument to be his Act & Deed as attests.

                         John Plaisted Justis Peace

A true Copie of ye origenall Transcribed and compared this 5th day of Octob^r 1699.

                         p Jos Hamond Regist^r

Know all men by these presents that I Edward Cock now Resident at New York for diuers good causes and Considerations me hereunto moveing haue Assigned ordained & made, And in my Stead and place by these presents put & constituted my Honoured Mother Agnes Kelly of s^d New York afores^d to be my true sufficient and Lawfull Atturney. Giuing and hereby Granting to my s^d Atturney, full power Authority & Speciall Comission for me and in my name and to my use and behoofe to ask demand sue for Levie require recover & receiue all and every Such Debts Wares Sum or Sums of Money lands housing Edifices of what kind or nature soever or in whose hands or Custodie soever any Such Debts Wares lands &c as to me ye Constituant doth belong, or that did belong formerly to my father Edward Cock late of York In ye County of York in New England Dece^d — or that shall hereafter at any time be due, owing paiable or Appertaining to me, of and all and every pson or psons within ye s^d County of York in ye Province of the Massachusets Bay by any way or means whatsoever And in Default of Deliuery or payment, or other Damage done me in any of my Lands or other Estate or thing belonging belonging to me or that did heretofore belong to my Deceased Father Edward Cock, by any pson or psons whatsoever/ All and every Such pson or psons to Attach Arest Sue Implead Imprison and cause to be condemned & from Prison again (when need shall be) to deliuer, Alsoe upon Judgm^t obtained their Estates or psons in Execution to take and hold untill Satisfaction giuen and thereupon from under Execution to release And on receits & recoveries Acquittances and other Lawfull Discharges to Seale and deliuer/ Alsoe to compound and agree with any pson or psons for any of s^d lands or Estate/ And appearance for me and in my behalfe to make And in any Court or Courts of Judicature before any Judges or Justices there to defend reply and make answer in all causes Matters & things which may concern me/ Atturney or Atturneys under her to substitute and at pleasure to revoke Generally to doe Execute and Accomplish all & whatsoev^r I my selfe might or could doe psonally/ hereby promising to ratifie alow & hold of Vallue for ever all that my Said Atturney or her Substitutes shall Lawfully doe in ye Premises by vertue of these presents. In witness whereof I haue hereunto put my hand and Seale, this fifth day of Septemb^r one thousand six hundred Ninety and Nine: 1699

Signed Sealed & deliuered   Edward Cox (his seal)
  in presents of us.
  John Key his mark
  Hannah Key her mark

Edward Cocks Appeared before me ye Subscriber one of ye memb^{rs} of his Maj^{tis} Council of ye Province of ye Massachusets Bay and Justice of Peace wth in the same And owned ye above Instrum^t to be his Act & Deed this 5th Septemb^r 1699/

Jos Hamond

A true Copie of ye aboue written Letter of Atturney Transcribed & compared this fifth day of Octob^r 1699

p Jos Hamond Regist^r

Be it known unto all men by these presents that I Samuel Wheelwright of ye towne of Wells in ye County of York and in ye Province of the Massachusets Bay in New England Gen^t Severall good causes & considerations Me thereunto Moveing and more Especially for and in consideration of a Valluable Sum of forty pounds to me alredy in hand paid by Jonathan Littlefield of ye afores^d Town and County haue giuen, granted, Infeeoffed and confirmed and by these presents doe Giue, grant Infeoff and confirm freely fully and Absolutely unto ye aboue s^d Jonathan Littlefield frome me my heires Execut^rs Administrat^rs and Assigns a certain tract or pcell of Upland Scituate and being in the Town of Wells and bounded as here followeth/ The upper or Northeast end of Said lands buts upon ye high way or Road which lies near ye now Dwelling house of ye abouesaid Jonathan Littlefield And on ye Northeast side bounded by ffrancis Littlefields land and on ye Southwest bounded as ye fence now stands And soe that breadth from ye aboue said high way or Road, down to ye Marsh on ye Southeast, which land is Nineteen Acres and three quarters of an Acre, with all ye Appurtenances Priviledges & conveniencies whatsoever thereunto belonging freely & quietly. To haue & to hold without any Matter of Challenge Claime or Demand of me ye said Samuel Wheelwright or any other pson or psons either from by or under me my heirs Execut^rs Administrat^rs

& Assigns forever he y⁰ sᵈ Jonathan Littlefied his heires Execut⁰ Administrat⁰ and Assigns I doe hereby Declare to be truly and Rightly Possessed of y⁰ abovesᵈ Premises & every part thereof And that he y⁰ sᵈ Jonathan Littlefield his heirs Execut⁰ Administrat⁰ and Assigns shall Peaceably & quietly haue hold and Enjoy y⁰ aboue land with all y⁰ Appurtenances granted [41] and sold to them for ever And I doe hereby Promise & covenant to and with y⁰ said Jonathan Littlefield that I am before y⁰ ensealing hereof true & Lawfull & right owner of the Premises granted & sold/ And that I have full and lawfull power to make lawfull Sale of y⁰ same And I doe further couenᵗ & Promise that all & every part of y⁰ Premises granted and sold are free and clear from all former gifts grants Leases Legacies, Judments Dowries Morgages Excutions and all other Encombrances whatsoever And I doe promise to Warrant and Defend y⁰ title & Interest of y⁰ aforesᵈ Land and every part of it from me my heires Execut⁰ and Administrat⁰ And from all other pson or psons whatsoever under me or any by my means or procuremᵗ In testimony whereof I haue hereunto Affixed my hand and Seale this fourth day of Octobʳ in y⁰ year of our Lᵈ Anno Dom : one thousand six hundred and Ninety Nine.   Samᵘ Wheelwright (his seale)

Signed Sealed & deliuered in   Hester Ƨ Wheelwright. (her seale)
the presents of us
Richard Cutt
Samuel ffernald
Jonaⁿ Hamond

The aboue named Samᵘ Wheelwright Esqʳ Appeared before me y⁰ Subscribʳ one of y⁰ Membⁿ of his Majᵗˢ Council of the Prouince of y⁰ Massachusets Bay and Justice of Peace wᵗʰin the same and owned y⁰ aboue written Instrumᵗ to be his Act & Deed/ And Mʳˢ Hester Wheelwright at y⁰ same time Appeared and gaue up all her Right of Dower in & to y⁰ Premises abouesᵈ/ And alsoe Mʳ John Wheelwright

and Mary Wheelwright his wife Appearing gave up and freely Surrendred all their Right, Title and Interest of, in and unto y⁰ aboue giuen and granted Premises, from them their heires Execut⁽ⁿ⁾ Administrat⁽ⁿ⁾ And Assignes, to him y⁰ aboue Mentioned Jonathan Littlefield his heires or Assigns for ever And thereto haue set their hands and Seales in y⁰ presents of y⁰ Witnesses to y⁰ aboue Deed/ This fifth day of Octob⁽ʳ⁾ 1699/   John Wheelwright (his seal)
       Jos Hamond   Mary Wheelwright (her seal)

    A true Copie of y⁰ origenall Deed of Sale with y⁰ Acnowledm⁽ᵗ⁾ thereof./ And John Wheelwrights & his wifes Surrendring their Interst thereto/ Entred and Compared this 5ᵗʰ of Octob⁽ʳ⁾ 1699

                     p Jos Hamond Regist⁽ʳ⁾

    Whereas I Jonathan Littlefield of y⁰ Town of Wells in y⁰ County of York in y⁰ Province of the Massathusets Bay in New England, haue bought of M⁽ʳ⁾ Sam⁽ˡˡ⁾ Wheelwright & of his Son, John Wheelwright of y⁰ afores⁽ᵈ⁾ Town and County, a certain tract of Upland as may Appear by a Bill of Sale under their hands bearing Date of y⁰ 4ᵗʰ Octob⁽ʳ⁾ 1699.

    Now know all men by these presents that I Jonathan Littlefield doe by these presents bind my selfe my heires Execut⁽ⁿ⁾ Administrat⁽ⁿ⁾ and Assignes in y⁰ Penall Sum of fiue pounds mony to y⁰ aboues⁽ᵈ⁾ M⁽ʳ⁾ Sam⁽ˡˡ⁾ Wheelwright And M⁽ʳ⁾ John Wheelwright And to their heires Execut⁽ⁿ⁾ Administrat⁽ⁿ⁾ and Assigns that I & my Success⁽ʳˢ⁾ shall and will Annually And always set up and Maintain a good sufficient fence where it now stands in y⁰ Deuiding line between M⁽ʳ⁾ Sam⁽ˡˡ⁾ Wheelwright and my selfe on y⁰ Southwest Side of that Land w⁽ᶜʰ⁾ I bought of s⁽ᵈ⁾ Wheelwright/ The aboues⁽ᵈ⁾ Sum of fiue pounds is to be forfeited and paid upon every breach or defect in s⁽ᵈ⁾ Jonathan Littlefield or his Successors in in this

obligation. Whereunto I have set my hand and seale this fourth day of Octob^r in ye year of our Ld Anno Dom. 1699. Signed Sealed and Deliuered   Jonathan Littlefield (his seal)
in presents of
Jonathan Hamond
Richard Cutt
Samuel ffernald

The aboue named Jonathan Littlefield Appearing before me owned the aboue Obligation to be his Act and Deed this, fifth day of Octob^r 1699 :

                      Jos Hamond Jus^{ta} Peace

A true Copie of ye origenall obligation Transcribed and Compared this 5th of Octob^r 1699.

                      Jos Hamond Regist^r

To all Christian People whome the these presents may concern Richard Toziar and Elizabeth his wife, of Barwick in the County of York in ye Province of the Massachusets Bay in New England Sendeth Greeting/ Know ye that the said Richard and Elizabeth, for and in consideration of a certain sum of Money to them in hand paid or otherwise at ye Sealeing of this Instrum^t Satisfactorily Secured by Lewis Bane of York in ye County and Province abouesaid haue giuen, granted, bargained, sold, Alienated, Enfeoffed and confirmed And doe by these presents Giue, Grant, Bargain, Sell, Alienate, Enfeoffe confirm and fully freely and Absolutely make over unto the said Lewis Bane, a certain parcell of Land Upland and Meadow Land containing, by Estimation, twenty fiue Acres be it more or less, Scituate Lying and being in ye Township or precincts of York being formerly in ye Possession of James Sharp, but of late in the Improvem^t of s^d Lewis/ The Road going to ye new Mill Creek passing thrô it and Soe Deviding it into two parts, ye one

part lying on yᵉ South Side of yᵉ way being about ten Acres, bounded on yᵉ North Side by yᵉ Road on yᵉ South Side by a Brook runing out of yᵉ spring comonly called yᵉ Spruce Swamp spring, Westwardly by Land of John Parker and Eastwardly by Land of John Preble & Philip Adams the other part abutting about twenty Rods on yᵉ North Side of yᵉ way being bounded Eastwardly by John Prebles Land And westwardly by Land formerly Isaac Everets And runing Northerly as far as the Lotts Adjoyning Together with all yᵉ Rights Benefits Imoluments and Aduantages on Appertaining [42] unto or any wayes at any time Redownding from yᵉ same or any part or parcell thereof. To have and to hold, and quietly and Peaceably to ocupie possess and Enjoy yᵉ sᵈ Land and Appurtenances, as a Sure Estate in ffee Simple to him the sᵈ Lewis his heires Executʳˢ Administratʳˢ & Assignes for ever/ Moreouer yᵉ said Richard and Elizabeth for themselues their heires Executʳˢ & Adminʳˢ, to & with the sᵈ Lewis his heires Executʳˢ Adminʳˢ and Assignes doe Indent covenant Engage and Promise, the Premises with all their Priuiledges & Appurtenances, from all former Grants Gifts Sales Rents Rates Dowryes Demands & Incumbrances as alsoe all future Claimes Suites or Interuptions to be had or Comenced by them their heires Executʳˢ Adminʳˢ or Assignes or any pson or psons whatsoever (upon grounds preceeding the Date of this Instrumᵗ) for ever to Warrantise & Defend by these presents. In witness whereof yᵉ sᵈ Richᵈ Toziar & Elizabeth his wife haue hereunto set their hands & Seales this third day of Novembʳ in yᵉ year of our Lord one thousand six hundred & Ninty Eight and in yᵉ tenth year of the Reign of William the third, King of Great Brittain &c.   Richard Toziar (his seal)
Signed Sealed & deliuered   Elizabeth Toziar (her seal)
   in presents of us.
   Elizabeth Wade
   James Emery
   John Wade

BOOK VI, FOL. 42.

York/ May y* 8th 1699/ Richard Toziar came and Acnowledged this aboue written Deed of Sale to be his Act and deed/ before me/ Abrā Preble, Justice of Peace

A true Copie of y* origenall Deed of Sale Transcribed & compared this 6th of Octobr 1699.

p Jos Hamond Registr

Hooper
to
Barter

Kittery in the County of York in New England March 5th 169¾ Know all men by these presents that I Thomas Hooper of York in the County of York Yeoman for Divers good causes and considerations me hereunto moving Especially for and in consideration of twenty six pounds in Money to me in hand paid by Henery Barter of Kittery in s^d County Marinǝ, the recipt thereof I doe Acknowledge and my selfe therewith contented and paid and every part thereof And doe hereby Acquit y* s^d Henry Barter for y* same for y* consideration aboves^d which is for y* Needy use and Nessessities of my ffamily for Sutinance of y* same/ Have giuen granted bargained and sold And doe by these presents bargain sell Alienate Enfeoff and confirm unto y* s^d Henry Barter his heires and Assignes for ever All that tract of Land containing twenty seven Acres three quarters of an Acre and twenty six pole of Land Scituated and Lying in y* Township of Kittery in Spruce Creek bounded by Nicholas Tucker with an Northeast Line and with y* Creek of water Southwar and by Cap^{tn} Thomas his line Eastward/ S^d Tract Lying in y* form of a Triangle And is that Tract of Land which was bequeathed unto s^d Hoopers wife Elizabeth, by Cap^{tn} ffrancis Champernown Esqr Dec^d And Since Deliuered unto s^d Hooper by Mrs Mary Champernoun Relict and Executrix to y* Dec^d aboues^d as doth more at large Appear by y* last Will & Testam^t of y* Dec^d, together with all y* Priviledges

Book VI, Fol. 42.

& Appurtenances thereunto belonging As Creeks Coves water Courses Runs Rivolets high ways & easments Timb^r Stone wood under woods Standing or Lying thereon To haue and to hold all and Singular the aboues^d Land and Appurtenances thereunto belonging, unto ye Sole benefit use and behoofe of him ye s^d Henry Barter his heirs and Assigns for euer, ffurthermore I ye s^d Thomas Hooper doe for my selfe my heires or Assigns Covenant to and with ye s^d Henry Barter his heires or Assignes that ye Premises are free from all incumbrances whatsoever as Gifts Sales Morgages Joyntures Dowries and Seruices And that it shall and may be Lawfull for ye s^d Henry Barter his heires or Assignes to take use Ocupie & Possess ye s^d tract of Land every part thereof to his own proper use benefit and behoofe for ever and that I ye s^d Hooper haue ffull power to sell and dispose of the Same and that I am ye true and proper owner thereof at ye time of ye Signing and Sealing hereof And that I am Lawfully Siezed of every part and pcell thereof, the peaceable Possession thereof to Warrant and Maintain unto ye s^d Henry Barter and his heires and Assignes for ever against all manner of psons Laying Claim thereunto in true Testimony hereof I haue hereunto set my hand and Seale this fifth day of March one thousand six hundred Ninety Seven Eight 169⅞ the signe of

Signed Sealed and Deliuered   Thomas ⚓ Hooper (his seal)
  in the presents of us.
John Woodman
Anna Bran
Wm Godsoe.

Thomas Hooper Appeared before me and owned this Instrument to be his Act and Deed. 26. March. 1698

        Wm Pepperrell Js pes

Elizabeth Hooper Apeared before me and freely Acknowledged that she gaue up her Right of Dowry unto ye s^d Henry Barter as is in this Instrum^t above Expressed According to true Meaning. Witness my hand and Seale this 26th day of March 1698

       Elizabeth ⌒ Hooper (her seal)
      Wm Pepperrell Js pes

A true Copie of ye origenall Deed of Sale Transcribed & Compared this tenth day of Octob^r 1699.

        p Jos Hamond Regest^r

[43] Know all men by these presents That I Thomas Hooper of ye County of York in New England, Yeoman Doe owe and stand firmly Indebted unto Henry Barter of the Town of Kittery in New England afores^d Marrifi in ye full & Just Sum of ffifty two pounds Currant Money of New England to be paid to ye s^d Henry Barter or to his Certain Atturney his Execut^{rs} Admin^{rs} or Assigns to ye which paym^t well and truly to be made I bind me my heires Execut^{rs} Admin^{rs} firmly by these presents/ Sealed with my Seal/ Dated this 5th day of March 169⅞ In ye year of our Lord God one thousand six hundred Ninety Seven eight

The condition of this Obligation is such that if ye aboue bounded Thomas Hooper his heires Execut^{rs} Administre^{rs} Doe and shall well and truly obserue pform Accomplish fully And keep all and Singular ye Covenants grant Articles Clauses & and agreem^{ts} which are and ought to be obserued pformed Accomplished fullfilled and kept Mentioned and Comprised in one Indenture or bargain & Sale bearing Equall Date with these presents/ Made between ye said Thomas Hoper on ye one part and ye aboue named Henry Barter on ye other part in all things According to ye true Intent & Meaning of ye same Indenture of bargain & Sale/ That then this

Hoopers obligation to Barter

Book VI, Fol. '43.

Obligation to be Voyd & of none Effect or Else to be and remaine in full force Effect and Vertue.

Signed Sealed and delivered
 in the presents of us.
 Wm Pepperrell.
 Andrew Pepperrell

The mark of
Thomas ⌒ Hooper (his seal)

   The 26th of March, 1698/
Then Thomas Hooper came and Acknowledged this Instrument to be his free Act and Deed
     Before me Wm Pepperrell Js Pes
A true Copie of ye origenall Obligation Transcribed and compared this tenth day of, October, 1699
     p Jos Hamond Regist^r

To all Cristian People to whome these presents shall come John Gowen alias Smith of the town of Kittery in ye County of York in ye Province of the Massachusets Bay in New England Marrifi Sends Greeting/ Know yee that I John Gowen alias Smith afores^d for diuers good causes me thereunto moveing, more Especially for and in consideration of the Sum of fiue and twenty pounds of Lawfull money of New England to me in hand paid and Secured to be paid before ye Ensealing and deliuery of these presents by Black Will, Negroe formerly belonging to Maj^r Nicholas Shapleigh of Kittery in s^d County Deceased the receipt whereof I Acknowledge And of euery part and parcell thereof And therewith fully satisfied contented and paid haue giuen granted bargained and sold And by these presents for me my heires Execut^{rs} Administrat^{rs} and Assigns for euer, doe ffreely clerely and absolutely giue grant bargain and sell unto him ye s^d Black Will his heirs Execut^{rs} Admin^{rs} and Assigns for euer/ A certain Piece or parcell of Land Scituate lying and being in the town of Kittery afores^d containing one hundred Acres being two grants of the town one grant of fiftie Acres to me the s^d John Gowen and ye other fiftie Acres being granted to my brother, William Gowen Deceased both grants bearing Date Aug^st ye 21st 1685. As at large Appears upon Kittery town book/ And laid out July: 14 : 1694 as also Appears on ye town book being butted and bounded as followeth/ Viz^t a hundred and fifty pole in length, East and west And a hundred pole in breadth North and South, bounded on ye west wth Maj^r ffrosts land and on ye South with ffrancis Blachford William Sanders and Some Comons And on ye East with Some Comons and high way in part, and a corner tree of Maj^r ffrosts out Lot and North with John Heards Ashen Swamp and Mrs Hamonds Swamp and Some Comons. To haue and to hold ye afores^d hundred Acres of Land with all ye timb^r, wood, trees standing lying thereon With all and Singular ye priuiledges and Appurtenances thereto belonging or in any wise Appurtaining to him ye s^d Black Will his heirs or Assigns for euer And to his and their own proper use benefit and behoof And that the s^d Black Will his heirs or Assigns shall and may from time to time and at all times hereafter use ocupie and improve the afores^d premisses without any Molestation let deniall or hinderance/ And I ye s^d John Gowen Alias Smith doe couenant and promise to and with ye s^d Black Will, the s^d land and premisses for euer to Warrant and Defend against all persons whatsoever Claiming any Right title or Interest thereunto from by or under me my heires or Assigns for euer. In witness whereof I haue hereunto Set my hand and Seale this fifth day of Decemb^r in ye year of our Lord one thousand Six hundred Ninety & Six And in the Eighth year of ye Reign of our Soveraign Ld William ye third King over England &c

Signed Sealed & deliuered   John Gowen, Alias Smith (his seal)
  in ye presents of us
John Newmarch
John Leighton
Jos Hamond Junr

York ss/ Kittery Nouemb{r} 10{th} 1699 The aboue named John Gowen Alias Smith personally Appearing Acknowledged y{e} aboue written Instrum{t} or Deed of Sale to be his Act & Deed

Before me Jos Hamond Jus{ts} Pea

A true Copie of the origenall Instrum{t} Transcribed and Compared this 10{th} of Novemb{r} 1699.

p Jos Hamond Register

York ss, Kittery June 28{th} 1701

Mercy Gowen wife of y{e} within named John Gowen psonally Appeaing before me Joseph Hamond Justice of Peace within y{e} County of York Acknowledged this Instrum{t}, and gave up all her right of Dower to y{e} Premisses therein mentioned.

Jos: Hamond

A true Copie of y{e} Originall Transcribed & compared June: 28{th}: 1701/

p Jos: Hamond Regist{r}

[44] Know all men by these presents that I Enoch Hutchins of Kittery in the County of York Yeoman for and in consideration of y{e} sum of ten pounds in Money to me in hand paid by M{r} James Johnson of the same place Millwright y{e} recipt y{r}of I doe Acknowledge and my self therewith Satisfied paid and contented And doe by these presents Acquit y{e} s{d} James Johnson for y{e} same. Have bargain and sold and doe by these presents bargain Sell and Set over and for euer confirm unto the said James Johnson his heires and Assignes for euer, a certain tract of Land lying in y{e} Township of Kittery, Near York Road And is part of that tract of Land that was laid out unto me y{e} said Enoch Hutchens in the year, 1694, June y{e} 9{th} by Cap{tn} John Wincoll And takes its begining at y{e} Easterend thereof, and on

Norther Side next York Road, and is in Length one hundred & seven pole East North East and West south west And in breadth thirty pole North : North west and South Southeast Containing twenty Acres of Land as it is now bounded and laid out by Wm Godsoe Surv^r of s^d Town, together with all & Singular the Priuildges and Appurtenances thereto beloinging, as Timber wood and und^r wood Quarry of Stone Mines and Mineralls of what kind soever that shall be found therein And precious Stones/ To haue

<small>Hutchins to Johnsons</small>
and to hold the s^d Tract of Land as it is bounded and Described unto ye s^d James Johnson his heires & Assigns for ever, against me ye said Enoch Hutchins my heires or any other psons under me or Authorized by me And furthermore I ye s^d Enoch Hutchins doe covenant to and with ye s^d James Johnson his heires and Assigns in behalfe of my selfe my heires Execut^rs and Administrat^rs that ye Premises are free from all Incumbrances whatsoever as Sales,Gifts Mortgages Joyntures Dowers Rents and Seruices And that I am ye true and Proper owner thereof and of euery part thereof And that I haue within my selfe full power & Lawfull Authority to Sell and Dispose of ye same And I am in full Possession and am Lawfully Seized of ye same and of euery part thereof at ye ensealing and Deliuery of these presents And that it shall and may be Lawfull for ye said James Johnson or any vnder him to take Use Ocupie and Possess the same without ye Let hinderance or Molestation of me ye s^d Enoch Hutchins or any other under me or Authorized by me/ The Peaceable and quiet Possession thereof to Warrant and Maintain against all psons laying Lawfull Claime thereto the Kings most Excellent Majestie only Excepted Witness my

hand and Seal this twenty Sixth day of Octob[r] one thousand Six hundred Ninety and Nine. 1699

Signed Sealed and deliuered   Enoch Hutchins (his scale)
  in presents of us the Subscrib[rs]
  Thomas Rice.
  Isaacke Goodridge
  W[m] Godsoe.

York ss/ Kittery Novemb[r] y[e] 3[d] 1699

The aboue named Enoch Hutchins psonally Appearing Acknoledged y[e] aboue Instrument or Deed of Sale to be his Act and Deed Before me

                      Jos Hamond Jus[ts] Peace

A true Copie of y[e] origenall Transcribed and Compared this 3[d] day of Novemb[r] 1699

                      p Jos Hamond Register

    To all Christian People to whome these presents shall come I James Emery of Kittery in y[e] Province of Maine in New England and Elizabeth my wife send Greeting Know ye that I y[e] s[d] James Emery and Elizabeth my wife for & in consideration of forty fiue shillings to us in hand paid & by us received haue giuen granted and Covenanted Enfeoffed bargained, sold, and made over, and by these pres[ts] doe giue, grant, Enfeoffe, bargaine, sell confirm and make over unto Charles ffrost of the aboues[d] Town and Province, a certaine Marsh or piece of Medow ground scituated Lying and being on y[e] North Side of Sturgeon Cricke Comonly known or called by the name of y[e] barren Marsh being bounded as followeth Viz[t] on y[e] West side wth a Creek which parts Reinold Jinkins his Marsh and this, and on y[e] South Side with Stirgeon Creek and on the East Side with an other certain Cricke which comes out of y[e] woods And on y[e] North bounded with y[e] Upland being about two Acres more or Less, all and all and singular yᵉ sᵈ Marsh/ To haue and to hold, from the day of yᵉ Date hereof, to yᵉ proper use and behoofe of yᵉ abouesᵈ Charles ffrost his heires Executʳˢ Administratʳˢ and Assignes for euer And I yᵉ sᵈ James Emery and Elizabeth my wife Doe couenant promise and agree to and with yᵉ sᵈ Charles ffrost to Warrantize yᵉ Sale of all and every part of yᵉ abouesᵈ Premises, that yᵉ sᵈ Charles ffrost shall, both he his heires Executʳˢ Administratʳˢ and Assignes from time to time and at all times for euer hereafter haue, hold, use, ocupie possess and enjoy all and singular yᵉ abouesᵈ Premises without any lett hinderance Molestation or Interuption of me yᵉ abouesᵈ James Emery or Elizabeth my wife our heires Executʳˢ or Assignes or any other pson or psons whatsoever Lawfully Claiming, in by from or under us or either of us our heires Executʳˢ or Assigns/ further for and in consideration of yᵉ Satisfaction aboue specified I sell and make ouer unto yᵉ said Charles ffrost yᵉ aboue Mentioned Marsh with all yᵉ priuiledges as Witness our hands this twentieth day of Decembʳ in yᵉ fourteenth yeare of Reign of oʳ Soueraign Lord Charles yᵉ Second, by yᵉ grace of God of England Scotland ffrance and Ireland King Defendʳ of yᵉ ffaith &c. Anoq̄ Domini : 1662

Emery to ffrost

Sealed Signed and Deliuered   James Emery (his seal)
  In presents of us.
    The mark of.   the ⌒ mark of
  Peter ⟲ Grant.   Elizabeth Emery (her seal)
  John ffrost

Peter Grant Appeared before me yᵉ Subscribʳ this 14ᵗʰ day of Nouembʳ 1699/ and made oath that he saw James Emery and Elizabeth his wife Signe Seale & Deliuer the aboue Instrumᵗ as their Act and Deed, And that he yᵉ sᵈ Peter Grant did Signe it as a Witness, And that he alsoe Saw

John ffrost Signe it as a Witness in the presents of y" s"
Emery and his wife/

Jos Hamond Jus" Peace

A true Copie of y" origenall Deed of Sale Transcribed and Compared this 14"" day of Nouemb" 1699.

p Jos Hamond Regist"

[45] Know all men by these presents that I Thomas More of York And Administrat" to the Estate of my father William More late of York Dec" doe for and in consideration of y" loue I beare unto my brother in Law Daniel Dill of York, but more particularly for and in consideration of a Portion which I am willing to giue unto my s" brother in Law who was husband unto my own Sister Dorithy More and other causes me thereunto Moving, haue granted & freely giuen unto y" s" Daniel Dill his heires Execut" Administrat" or Assignes, one tract of upland containing twenty Acres lying in y" Township of York, near to a place Called Scotland being butted and bounded as followeth, to say Joyning to a piece of Marsh which was formerly Maj" John Davis of y" one side and the high way on y" other side with a little gutter at y" head of y" said Land which was formerly in Possession of my father Moore Deceased being given to him by s" town of York it being twenty Acres more or less within s" bounds To have and to hold use ocupie Possess enjoy and improve unto y" s" Daniel Dill his heires and Assignes for ever with all y" priviledges whatsoever Containing therein to enjoy and improve Peaceably & quietly without any fet or Molestation by me my heires Execut" or Administrat", disclaiming for ever my Right or Propriety therein with Warranty from all other pson or psons whatsoever Claiming any Right

More to Dill

therein/ In witness whereof I haue hereunto Set my hand and Seale this Seventeenth day of March one thousand Six hundred and Ninety three 1693/4.

Signed Sealed & Deliuered   Thomas More (his Seale)
   in the presents of us
      the Mar of
  Timothy ⌕ Markue
      the mark of
  Lewis 〰 Williams

Thomas Moore came and Acknowledged this Instrument to be his Act and Deed to Daniel Dill this Seventeenth day of March, 1693/4 before me

                       ffrancis Hooke Just: Pea

A true Copie of y⁕ origenall Deed Transcribed and Compared this 20th Novemb^r 1699

                       p Jos Hamond Regist^r

            Barwick Novemb^r 19th 1702

Rec^d of my brother John Gowen ye Sum of four pounds Eighteen shillings & four pence which makes in full of Six pounds thirteen shillings & four pence that he ye s^d John Gowen was appointed to pay my wife Sarah Gowen for her part of our father Wm Gowens Estate before ye Decease of our Mother Elizabeth Gowen as p Distribution bearing Date Jan^{ry} 19 : 1696

                       William Smith

Witness { Daniel Emery
         { Lemuel Gowen

A true Copie of the originall Transcribed & compared Decemb^r 5 1702

Book VI, Fol. 45.

To all Christian People to whome this present writing shall come/ Know y*, That I Miles Thompson Sen*, of Barwick in the Province of Maine in New England for a Certain Sum ·in hand paid and by me Received, haue giuen granted Alienated and confirmed, And doe by these presents giue grant Alienate and confirm unto my Son Thomas Thompson of y* Town and County abouesaid, the whole of my Home Lot with y* Addition belonging to it Lying in y* Town and County abouesaid, containing by Estimation fourscore Acres more or less, bounded Northerly by the Land of Benony Hodsden, Southerly by the Land of James Heard, Easterly by the Town Comons Westerly by the Riuer Together with all y* Priviledges thereunto belonging, Likewise my housing barns orchard Cattle Swine sheep Husbandry Tackling, And all my working tooles, only I doe reserue my two old oxen to be at my Disposall, y* aboue mentioned to be to my Son Thomas Thompson his heires Execut* Administrat* and Assignes, Who shall from time to time and at all times Use ocupie Possess and Enjoy them quietly and peaceably for from by or under me or any any other pson or psons Laying any Legall Claime thereunto To haue and to hold them in ffee Simple for ever/ This is to be understood that I doe make ouer y* aboue named things on these conditions That my Son Thomas Thompson doe pay or cause to be paid Annually well and truly two fiueths of y* Product of y* grain Cyder wooll Cattell Swine shall be raised upon y* s^d Land, Alsoe that he shall not make Sale of any Cattle that shall be raised on the said Land without my consent Likewise that my aboues^d shall Provid us or either of us if we see cause conuenient habitable house room, procure y* grinding of our corn And Provide for us a Sufficiency of Suteable wood and draw it Home to us, the abouesaid conditions to be performed unto me y* said Miles Thompson dureing my

Miles Thompson
·to his Son Tho.

Naturall Life And if God by his Providence shall take me away by death before Ann Thompson my wife, then my Son Thomas Shall truly pay or cause to be paid the thirds of ye aboue Specified things and shall bring ye abouesaid product to my said wife in any convenient place nere Piscatqua Riuer And likewise keep her two Yews which said Yews shall be at her Disposall And likewise I doe reserue all my household Moveables to be for ye Use and Disposall of my abouesaid wife my Son Thomas fulfilling ye abouesaid Conditions I haue set to my hand and Seale to ye true performance of my aboues^d obligation. This Decemb^r ye third one thousand Six hundred Ninety and four.

Signed Sealed and Deliuered   Miles Thompson (his seale)
 In the presents of us.
 Edward Tompson   Ann   Thompson (her seal)
 Thomas Rhodes
 Samuel Small   her mark

Miles Thompson & Ann Thompson Acknowledged the above written Instrum^t to be their Act & Deed, this 3^d of Decemb^r 1694 Before me   Charles ffrost Just : Peace

A true Copie of ye origenall Transcribed and compared Decemb^r 1st 1699   p Jos Hamond Regist^r

[46] This Indenture made the Eleauenth day of January Anno Domini One thousand Six hundred Ninety Nine Annoq̨ R R^s Gulielmi Tetii Angliæ &c undecimo. Between John Plaisted of Portsm^o in the Province of New Hampshiere in New England Merchant of the one part, And Eliakim Hutchinson of Boston in ye County of Suffolk within his Maj^{tys} Province of the Massachusets Bay in New England afores^d Esqr on ye other part Witnesseth that the s^d John Plaisted for and in consideration of ye Sum of fiue hundred pounds currant money in New England to him in hand at

and before the Ensealing and deliuery of these presents well and truly paid by the s^d Eliakim Hutchinson the receipt whereof is hereby Acknowledged. Hath giuen granted bargained sold Aliened Enfeofed released and confirmed And by these presents doth freely fully and Absolutely giue, grant, bargain, Sell, Alien, Enfeoffe, release, convey & confirm unto ye s^d Eliakim Hutchinson his heires and Assigns for ever All that his Tracts parcells and quantity of Land containing Six hundred Acres be it more or less, Scituate Lying and being on both Sides ye little Riuer of Newgewanack Alias Neichewanak within ye Township of Kittery in ye County of York formerly cald the Province of Maine And Now part of ye Province of the Massachusets Bay aboves^d ffour hundred and fourteen Acres, parcel whereof was formerly Surveyed and Measured by Cap^{tn} John Wincoll, as Appears by a draught or plat of the Same by him made and Signed the 25th day of May 1682 relation being thereunto had for ye lines and boundaries thereof (Excepting onely out of the four hundred and fourteen Acres, thirty three acres and three quarters of an Acre of Land which were heretofore granted out of the same as follows Viz^t To John Emeson ten Acres thereof, To Daniel Gooding Senr Eleven Acres & three quarters y^{r}of and the other twelue acres for the Accomidation of ye Meeting house & Ministry in the upper part of ye town of Kittery afores^d) One hundred and thirty acres another parcel of which afores^d tract of Land consists of Upland Swamp & Meadow which lies at ye Southeast end of Bonibissie pond (soe called) containing two hundred and Eighty pole in length South east and by east down to ye riuer being bounded on ye Northwest with the high way by ye head of ye s^d Pond And on the Southwest with ye Land of Roger Plaisted Junr, Northesterly with ye present Commons and Southeasterly with the riuer. Sixty Acres another parcel of which afores^d Tract of Land being Meadow,

Plaisted to Hutchinson

Book VI, Fol. 46.

lies at a place cald by ye name of Totnock And three Acres an other parcel thereof lies at ye Northwest end of Bonibissie pond afores^d Adjoyning to a Meadow known by the name of Broughton's Meadow, Alsoe ten Acres an other parcel thereof being Marsh lies half a Mile or thereabouts below a Marsh known by ye name of ye long Marsh & is comonly cald Whites Marsh And an other parcel thereof (which was formerly Richard Nasons) is a Small piece of Land cald by the name of pipestaue point which begins at s^d point and runs down along ye riuer unto ye next fresh water crick being in breadth four Rod from ye bank head and runs upon a Straight line between ye point and ye Creek, holding its full breadth all along ye bounds afores^d Together with all and Singular other Tracts and parcels of Land whatsoever Granted by ye Town of Kittery afores^d unto ye s^d Eliakim Hutchinson or to his brother William Hutchinson And alsoe the ffalls in Newichewanick riuer afores^d comonly cald Assabumbedock ffalls with ye stream water, water courses Dams and banks (Reserving the priviledge of ye river and Stream for the Transportation of Timb^r Loggs and Boards &c as is Usual and has been formerly Accustomed Together alsoe with all and Singular the houses Edifices buildings Mills woods underwoods, trees, Timb^r, Swamps, Stones, Mines, Mineralls, Springs, Ponds, pooles, runs rivolets, fishing, fowling, hawking, hunting, Rights, Members, profits, priviledges comodities Hereditaments emoluments and Appurtenances whatsoever upon, belonging or in any wise appertaining unto ye s^d Tracts and Severall parcels of Land herein before granted or any any part thereof or accepted taken or known as part parcel or memb^r thereof or therewith now used ocupied or enjoyed (Excepting onely and reserving unto his Maj^{tie} his heires and Success^{rs} all pine trees standing growing or being upon ye s^d Land or any part thereof of four & twenty Inches Diameter fitting to make Masts for his Maj^{trs} Ships and one fifth part

of all Gold and Silver oare that from time to time and at all
times hereafter shall be there gotten had and obtained)
Alsoe all ye Estate right title Interest Inheritance use prop-
ety possession Claim and Demand whatsoever of him ye s^d
John Plaisted and his heires of in to or out of ye s^d Tracts
parcels and quantity of Land herein before bargaied and
sold and every part thereof and all and singular other y^e
Premisses and of, in, to and out of all other Lands and
Timb^r whatsoever at any time heretofore granted unto ye s^d
Eliakim Hutchinson and his s^d brother William Hutchinson
or either of them by ye town of Kittery afores^d or by Robert
Tufton Mason Esqr Grandson and heir of Cap^{tn} John Mason
of London Esqr Deceased And ye revertion and revertions
Remainder and remainders rents Issues and profits of y^e
said granted premises and every part and parcel thereof,
with all Deeds writings Escripts and Miniments touching
or concerning ye Same All which Tracts and parcels of
Lands and premisses mentioned to be in and by these presents herein before granted and sold unto ye s^d Eliakim
Hutchinson his heirs & Assignes were by Deed Indented
bearing Date ye day before ye day of ye Date hereof granted
bargained and sold for and under ye considerations and reservations therein mentioned by the said Eliakim Hutchinson
ye herein before named grantee unto ye s^d John Plaisted
ye herein before named granter and to his heires and Assigns
for ever. To have and to Hold the severall Tracts parcels
of Land and all and Singular ye premisses with ye rights
memb^{rs} and Appertenances herein and hereby granted bargained and Sold or meant mentioned or intended to be
granted bargained & sold and every part and parcel of
ye Same (Excepting and reserving always as is above excepted & reserved unto ye s^d Eliakim Hutchinson his heirs
and Assignes To his and their only proper Use benefit and
behoofe for ever, as in his first & former Estate before his
Sealing & Executing ye afores^d Deed Indented bearing Date

yᵉ day next before yᵉ day of yᵉ Date hereof And under and Subject nevertheless to yᵉ same paiments and Quit rents to be rendered Yeelded and paid unto the before named Robert Tufton Mason his heires or Assignes by yᵉ sᵈ Eliakim Hutchinson his heires or Assigns As by yᵉ sᵈ Deed or any covenant therein, yᵉ said John Plaisted his heirs or Assigns are liable unto. Provided alwayes and upon condition nevertheless And it is yᵉ true intent and meaning of these presᵗˢ and of yᵉ parties to yᵉ Same, Any thing before written to yᵉ contrary notwithstanding That if yᵉ sᵈ John Plaisted his heirs Executʳˢ Adminʳˢ or Assigns Shall & doe well and truly pay or cause to be payd unto yᵉ said Eliakim Hutchinson his heires Executors Adminʳˢ or Assignes the full and Just Sum of five hundred pounds in good Siluer pieces of eight of Sevill piller and Maxico at yᵉ rate of Six Shillings p piece, each piece of eight to weigh full Seventeen penny weight Troy, at on or before the twelfth day of January which will be in yᵉ yeear of our Lord God Seventeen hundred And in Default of paying the sᵈ whole Sum of five hundred pounds at or before yᵉ sᵈ twelfth day of January Anno Domini Seventeen hundred Shall and doe fully compleat yᵉ sᵈ paymᵗ of five hundred pounds principle money, within yᵉ Space of three years thence next and Imediately following & in the Interim Shall and doe well and truely pay or cause to be paid unto yᵉ sᵈ Eliakim Hutchinson his heires Executʳˢ Adminʳˢ or Assigns, Interest Annually after yᵉ rate of six pounds p Cent in like Currant Money as aforesᵈ for such part & soe much of [47] the sᵈ Sum of five hundred pounds as shall remaine behind and unpaid from and after yᵉ aforesᵈ twelfth day of January Anno: Seventeen hundred untill yᵉ sᵈ payment of five hundred pounds be fully compleated and ffinished Then yᵉ before written Deed of bargaine and Sale or Mortgage And every grant Clause and Article therein to Cease Determine be utterly voyd and of none Effect, but in Default of making yᵉ aforesᵈ paym^{ts} According to ye true intent and meaning of the Proviso or condition above written Then the s^d before written Deed and every Article therein to abide remain and continue in full force Strength and Vertue to all Intents constructions & purposes in ye Law whatsoever And the s^d John Plaisted for himself his heires Execut^{rs} & Admin^{rs} doth covenant grant and Agree to and with ye s^d Eliakim Hutchinson his heirs and Assigns by these presents in Manner ffollowing That is to Say that in case Default be made by ye s^d John Plaisted his heires Execut^{rs} or Admin^{rs} of performing ye condition or Proviso above mentioned And that the money therein Mentioned to be paid, be not well and truly paid According to ye tenour true intent and meaning therof, it shall and may be Lawfull to and for ye s^d Eliakim Hutchinson his heires or Assigns, forthwith and Imediately after such Default made to enter into and upon and possession to take of all and Singular the Lands and Premisses herein before granted or mentioned or intended to be granted And have hold Use ocupie possess and enjoy the Same & every part thereof, to him ye s^d Eliakim Hutchinson his heires and Assigns To his & their only proper Use benefit and behoofe for ever As in his first and former Estate before his conveying the same to ye s^d John Plaisted as is before expressed And under And under and Subjects to ye Quit rents and payment in ye afores^d Deed of coveyance of the Same Mentioned and Expressed/ And that ye s^d John Plaisted his heirs Execut^{rs} and Admin^{rs} from that time and thence forward will Warrant and Defend the s^d granted & bargained premisses and every part and parcell thereof unto ye s^d Eliakim Hutchinson his heirs and Assigns for ever against all and every pson and psons whomsoev^r hauing Claiming or pretending to have or Claim any Lawfull Estate right title or Interest in or to the s^d granted premisses or any part thereof by or under him the s^d John Plaisted In witness whereof the s^d parties to these presents Indentures

haue interchangeably Set their hands and Seales the day and first within written John Plaisted (his Seal)
Signed Sealed and Deliuered
  by John Plaisted within named
  In presents of us.
  Isaac Addington.
  Edw : Turfrey.

Boston Jan'y 11 : 1699

The above named John Plaisted personally appearing before me ye Subscrib^r one of ye Council and Justice of ye Peace within his Maj^{ty*} Province of ye Massachusets Bay in New England Acknowledged ye before written Instrum^t to be his Act and Deed.

                            Isaac Addington.

A true Copie of the origenall Transcribed and Compared this 15th day of ffebruary, 1699.

                        p Jos Hamond Regist^r

•

To all People unto whome these presents shall come, George Turfrey of Boston in New England Merch^t now resideing at Saco in the Province of Mayn in New England aforesaid Sendeth Greeting Whereas ffrancis ffoxcroft of Boston afores^d Merch^t and ye s^d George are Joynly concerned together in a Saw Mill now in building at Saco afores^d by the s^d Turfrey as alsoe in ye Joynt Use and Supply of the same for ye cutting of Timber boards plank and Slitwork &c. And whereas ye s^d ffrancis ffoxcroft is considerably more money out in disburse for ye building and purchasing of Nessessaries oxen Utensells and geers for the use & Service of ye carrying on ye s^d Mill, than ye s^d Turfrey is out on ye same on his part. Now know yee that I ye s^d George Turfrey for the Securing the payment of all Such Summe and Summs of Money with interest upon ye Same

BOOK VI, FOL. 47.

as y⁰ sᵈ ffrancis ffoxcroft alredy hath and shall hereafter Disburse lay out and expend in Nessessaries for y⁰ sᵈ Mill on my accompt more then for carrying on y⁰ sᵈ ffoxcrofts halfe part Have giuen granted bargained sold assigned set over and confirmed, and by these presents Doe ffully freely cleerly and absolutely giue grant bargain Sell Assign set over and confirm unto the sᵈ ffrancis ffoxcroft his Execut⁽ʳˢ⁾ Admin⁽ʳˢ⁾ and Assigns All that my Moyety or full halfe part Share Right title Interest property Claime and demand of in to and out of the aforesᵈ Saw Mill standing on Saco river with all y⁰ runing going Geers and Utensells and Appurtenances wᵗsoever now thereunto belonging and hereafter to y⁰ Same to be thereunto belonging Used Ocupied or Serving And alsoe all that my Moiety or halfe part share right and Interest of in and to all Such oxen as already are and shall

Turfrey
to
ffoxcroft

hereafter be purchased for y⁰ Use and Service of sᵈ Mill To have and to hold all y⁰ above granted and bargained premisses and every part and parcel thereof unto the said ffrancis ffoxcroft his Execut⁽ʳˢ⁾ Admin⁽ʳˢ⁾ and Assignes to his and their own Sole and proper Use benefit and behoof for ever And I the sᵈ George Turfrey at y⁰ time of y⁰ Ensealing hereof doe avouch my selfe to be the true sole and Lawfull owner of all the afore bargained premisses Having in my selfe full power good right and Lawfull Authority to grant Sell and dispose thereof in manner as aforesᵈ ffree and Clear and Cleerly Acquitted Exonerated and discharged of and from all and all manner of former and other gifts Grants bargains Sales titles troubles Charges and Incumbrances whatsoever And ffurther I doe hereby covenant pomise bind and Oblige my selfe my heires Execut⁽ʳˢ⁾ and Admin⁽ʳˢ⁾ to warrant and Defend all y⁰ aboue granted and bargained premisses with the Appurtenances unto y⁰ sᵈ ffrancis ffoxcroft his Execut⁽ʳˢ⁾ Admin⁽ʳˢ⁾ and Assignes for ever against the Lawfull Claimes and demands of all people whomesoever Provided alwayes And upon condition nevertheless being the true intent and meaning of these presents and parties to the same any thing herein contained to y* contrary thereof in any wise notwithstanding That if I the s^d George Turfrey or my heires Execut^{rs} or Admin^{rs} shall and doe well and truly pay or cause to be paid unto the s^d ffrancis ffoxcroft or to his certain Atturney Execut^{rs} Amin^{rs} or Assignes at Boston afores^d in Currant money of New England upon demand all Such Sum & Sums of Money with Lawfull Interest thereupon as upon Adjustments of Accompts shall Appear, the s^d ffoxcroft to haue expended and laid out on s^d Mills for Accompt of me s^d Turfrey on my afores^d part thereof Then this present writing and every grant and Article thereof to be voyd and of none Effect or else abide in full force and Vertue/ In witness whereof I have hereunto set my hand and Seal y* Eighth day of Augst Anno Domini 1699. In y* Eleventh year of y* Reign of our Soveraign Lord King William y* third over England &c.

Signed Sealed & deliuered in y* George Turfrey (his seal)
  presents of us
  John Pride
  Jonathan Judd/

[48] Suffolk ss./ Boston 21st August 1699/
John Pride and Jonathan Judd psonally Appearing before me ye Subscrib^r made oath that they were present and did See y* aboue named George Turfrey Signe Seal and deliuer this Instrum^t as his Act and Deed Jur̃ Cor:

                        Jeri: Dum̃er Jus: Pea:

Boston: 22^d ffeb^{ry} 1699/ the afore named George Turfrey then personally Appeared before me y* Subscrib^r one of his Maj^{tys} Councill and Justice of y* Peace within the Province of y* Massachusets Bay And Acknowledged this Instrument to be his Act and Deed/

                        Elisha Cooke

Book VI, Fol. 48.

A true Copie of the origenall Transcribed & Compared this 28th day of ffebruary : 1699.

p Jos Hamond Registr

To all Christian People to whome these presets Shall come Greeting Know ye that I William Breaden of Taunton in ye County of Bristoll in his Majtys Province of ye Massachusetts Bay in New England Marrinr Acknowledge that I have received of Nicholas Morey of ye abovesd Town and County one hundred pounds Currant money of New England before ye Signing and Sealing this Instrumt, In consideration of ye receit of sd hundred pounds money I sd William Breaden doe for my selfe my heires Executn Adminrs, Giue grant bargain Sell Alienate Enfeoffe and confirm unto sd Nicholas Morey his heirs all that Land and Meadow that my father in Law Joseph Cross of Wells in the Province of Mayn in New England Deceased gave me by his last Will and Testament bearing Date, March ye Second day in ye year, 168¾ may Appear, butted and bounded as by sd Will and ye Deeds sd Cross had of ye purches of sd Lands and Meadow the which is Scituate lying in sd town of Wells formerly in sd Province of Mayn aforesd being three hundred Acres more or less, I sd William Breaden doe for my selfe my heires Executn & Adminrs Acknowledge ye abouesd sum of one hundred pounds to be full Satisfaction And am therewith fully Satisfied & payd for every part and parcell thereof And doe hereby Exonerate Acquit release & discharge sd Morey his heires Executn Adminn and Assigns for every part and parcel thereof I sd William Breaden doe for my selfe my self my heirs Executn & Adminr Giue grant bargain Sell Alienate Enfeoff and confirm All my Right title and Interest that I ought to haue or haue in ye aboue bar-

Breaden
to
Moorey

gained premises in Possession or in reversion by vertue of ye aboves^d Will of s^d Cross Deceased, to s^d Nicholas Morey his heirs Execut^{rs} Admin^{rs} or Assigns with all ye Appurtenances and priviledges that thereto pertain and belong/ To have and to hold to Ocupie and Possess for ever to his & their proper Use/ further I s^d William Bready doe for my selfe my heirs Execut^{rs} Admin^{rs} Auouch s^d bargained Premises aboue Mentioned to be ffree & clere from all Incumbrances whatever by Morgage Gift or Deed of Gift or Dower or Joynter or womans thirds or Judgment Execution or troubles in the Law, to said Morey his heires Execut^{rs} Admin^{rs} or Assigns Alsoe I s^d William Breaden Covent^t for my selfe my heirs Execut^{rs} Admin^{rs} to and with s^d Mory his heires Execut^{rs} Administrat^{rs} and Assigns that I am ye rightfull owner of ye above bargained premises And that it is an Estate in ffee Simple, further I s^d Breaden bind my self my heires Execut^{rs} Admin^{rs} to s^d Morey his heirs Execut^{rs} Admin^{rs} and Assigns in ye Sum of two hundred pounds money to be truly paid to s^d Morey his heirs Execut^{rs} Admin^{rs} or Assigns if either s^d Breaden his heirs Execut^{rs} Admin^{rs} or Assigns or any by from or under him or them shall Molest disturb hinder Eject Evict s^d Mory his heirs Execut^{rs} Admin^{rs} or Assigns in all or any part of ye aboves^d bargained premisses And to doe and perform whatsoeuer Act or Acts may be needfull for ye more sure making of s^d bargained premisses whether by Acknowledgm^{ts} of this Instrument or any other thing that is needfull or rquisit In witness hereto I haue set my hand and Seal this twentieth day of ffebruary One thousand Six hundred Ninety and nine, in ye Eleuenth year of his Maj^{tys} Reign Willm the third King ouer England &c.

Signed Sealed and delivered   William Breaden (his seal)
  in the presents of us.
  Malachi Holloway
  William Carr
  Samuel Dauis

Book VI, Fol. 48.

Memorandum, that on ye tenth day of January one thousand Six hundred Ninety nine then in Bristoll William Breaden ye Signer & Sealer of this Instrument psonally Appeared and Acknowledged this Instrument to be his free volluntary Act & Deed.

Coram John Brown Justice

A true Copie of ye origenall Deed Transcribed and Compared this: 28th ffebruary 1699

p Jos Hamond Regist^r

To all Chistian People to whom these presents shall come Nicholas Morey of ye Town of Taunton in ye county of Bristoll in his Maj^{tys} Territory and Dominion of ye Massthusets Bay in New England Sendeth Greeting Know yee that I Nicholas Morey sundry good causes and considerations me thereunto mouing and more Especially for and in consideration of seventy pounds Currant money to me in hand paid and well assured to be p^d by Joseph Hill of Saco in ye County of York in his Maj^{tys} Province of ye Massachusets Bay in New England have bargained granted and sold a certain parcel or tract of Upland Meadow and Marsh ground Lying Scituate and being in ye Town of Wells which Land I lately purchased of William Breaden and by Will giuen to him by Joseph Cross of Wells Deceased which land is bounded on the West side by a small Creek or brook comonly called Crosses Creek and soe bounded by that brook till it comes up to ye high way and then up into the Maine Land upon ye same point as other Lands Adjoyning to it runs And on the East side bounded by a Lott of Land now belonging to William Parsons Alsoe all ye Marsh ye whole breadth of s^d Land to run down to ye great riuer caled Webhannt riuer Alsoe Six Acres of Marsh more lying near ye Neck of Land part of it

Moorey to Hill

Joyning to Jonathan Hamonds Marsh/ I haue giuen granted Aliened Enfeoffed released Assigned and confirmed and by these presents doe fully freely and Absolutely giue grant Alien Enfeoffe Assign release and confirm unto y'' aboves'' Joseph Hill his heires Execut'' & Assigns for euer all and Singular y'' before mentioned granted premisses buildings housing woods underwoods Comons and all other profits priviledges Rights comodities Heredittaments Emoluments and Appurtenances to y'' same belonging or in any [49] kind Appurtaining And alsoe all y'' Estat Right title Interest use possession Dower thirds Claims reversion remaind'' property and demand whatsoeuer of me y'' s'' Nicholas Morey my heires Execut'' and Assignes of in and to the same and every part thereof To have and to hold all y'' before mentioned Enfeoffed confirmed premisses with the Appurtenances unto y'' s'' Joseph Hill his heires and Assigns for ever to his and their own Sole and proper Use benefit and behoofe from henceforth and for euer, freely, peaceably and quietly without any manner reclaim Challenge or contradiction of me y'' s'' Nicholas Morey my heires Execut'' or Assigns or of any other person or persons whatsoever by their or any of their means title or procurement in any manner or wise & without any Account or recouing or answer therefore to them or any in their names to be giuen rendered or done in time to come soe that Neith'' I y'' s'' Nicholas Morey my heires Execut'' Admin'' or Assignes or any other person or persons whatsoever by them for them or in their names of any of them at any time or times hereafter may Ask Claime Challenge or demand in or to y'' premisses or any part thereof any right title Interest use possession or Dower, but from all and every Action of right title Claime Interest Use possession and demand thereof they and every of them to be utterly Excluded and for euer by these presents Debarred In witness whereunto I haue set my hand and Seal this four and twenty day of ffeb'''' in y'' year of our Lord Anno

Dom: one thousand Six hundred and Ninety Nine And in y⁰ 11ᵗʰ year of our Soueraign Lord Wᵐ the third of England &c King

Signed Sealed and deliuered   Nichˢ Moorey (his seale)
  in presents of.
  John Wheelwright
  Jonathan Hamond

Nicholas Moorey came personally before me this 24ᵗʰ day of ffebruary 1699. and did Acknowledge this aboue written Instrument to be his Act and Deed.
      p Samˡˡ Wheelwright Jus: Peac:

A true Copie of the origenall, Transcribed and compared this 28ᵗʰ ffebʳʸ 1699.
       p Jos Hamond Registʳ

To whome these presents shall come Greeting/ Know yee that I John Rennalls of Cape Porpus in yᵉ Province of Mayn Alias Kenebunck Riuer in New England ffisherman haue sold unto Nicholas Moorey of yᵉ aboue sᵈ Town & Province a parcell of Land Scituate lying and being on yᵉ East of Kenebunk Riuer abouesaid at a place called yᵉ long Creek or Mast Coue ouer against Gillums point that is twenty poles or Rods up stream from the Creeks mouth or entrance into sᵈ long Creek as the maine riuer runneth And three score poles down Stream as sᵈ riuʳ runneth from yᵉ mouth of yᵉ abouesᵈ Creek soe that the Maine riuer is to be the bounds of one side of sᵈ land, but sᵈ twenty poles up stream and three score poles down stream to be Measured on Streight lines, not as yᵉ riuer runeth in Crooks And sᵈ land is to extend Six score poles back into the woods on each side from sᵈ riuer on Northeast lines And a Streight line to be yᵉ bounds on yᵉ head of sᵈ Land in yᵉ woods from yᵉ Extent of yᵉ side lines, Soe that I sᵈ John Rennalls diuers

BOOK VI, FOL. 49.

good Causes me thereunto moving haue sold y⁰ aforementioned land six score poles one way and fourscore y⁰ other way, but more Especially for the Sum of ten pounds in money to me in hand paid before y⁰ ensealing hereof And a Cow and Calfe lawfully Assured to be paid to me May next after this Date wherewith I s^d Jno Rennalls doe Acknowledge

Renals
to
Moorey

my selfe to be fully Satisfied for y⁰ s^d land I haue sold to y⁰ aboues^d Nicholas Moorey as afores^d I s^d Rennalls doe for my selfe my heires Exec^{rs} Admin^{rs} & Assigns doe Alienate enfeoff and confirm y⁰ aboues^d land and long Creek with all the priviledges there belonging to s^d Nicholas Moorey his heires Execut^{rs} Admin^{rs} and Assigns. To haue and to hold to ocupie and possess it/ Alsoe I John Rennalls doe bind my Selfe my heires Execut^{rs} Admin^{rs} and Assigns by these pres^{ts} to pay s^d Nicholas Moorey twenty pounds in Sterling Money his heirs Execut^{rs} and Assigns if I doe not Acknowledge this Instrum^t before Lawfull Authority or giue s^d Moorey an other Deed of Sale for y⁰ premisses if s^d Moorey desire it According to Law. In witness hereunto I haue set my hand & Seal this second day of January 1687. In y⁰ Reign of James y⁰ Second

    his   his
Gilbert B Endicot   John F Rennalls (his seal)
   mark   mark

    his
Richard ᛃ Crose
   mark

March 3$^d_1$ 168$\frac{7}{8}$ Liuery & Siesen p turf and twig giuen of y⁰ within land to Nicholas Moorey by John Rennalls.

     his   his
Witness Richard O Crose   John F Renals
     mark   mark

   his
Nathan P Presbury
  mark

BOOK VI, FOL. 50.

Suffolk ss/

Boston Dec: 6. 1699

Gilbert Endicot psonally Appearing before me ye Subscrib^r one of his Maj^{ts} Justices of ye Peace for ye County of Suffolk made oath that he was present and saw John Renals Signe Seal and deliuer the with written Instrum^t as his Act and Deed and that he set his hand thereto as a witness Also that he saw Richard Crose Sign as a witness.

Jur^t Cor̃ me Jno Eyre

A true Copie of ye origenall Transcribed and compared this. 28th ffeb: 1699

p Jos Ham̃ond Regist^r

[50] To all Christian People to whome these presents Shall come Greeting/ Know yee that I James Pendleton of Westerly Alias ffeversham in ye Collony of Rhoad Island and Providence Plantations in America Yeaoman Acknowledge that I have receiued of of Nicholas Moorey of Taunton in ye County of Bristoll in his Maj^{ts} Province of the Massachusets Bay in New England Yeoman the Just Sum of one hundred pounds in currant money before Ensealing this Instrum^t, In consideration whereof I s^d James Pendleton doe for my selfe my heirs Execut^{rs} Admin^{rs} giue grant bargain Sell Alienate Enfeoffe and confirm unto s^d Nicholas Moorey his heirs Exec^{trs} Admin^{rs} or Assigns a certain tract of Land Scituate lying and being on the west side of Saco River in New England Containing by Estimation Six hundred Acres butted and bounded as by Maj^r William Phillips his Deed to my honoured father Brian Pendleton bearing Date the 4th day of May, 1664 may appear, And by said Maj^r Phillips his giuing s^d Brian Pendleton possession of s^d Six hundred Acres of land and therein Setting forth more distinctly the bounds thereof, on ye 24th day of April, <u>1673</u> May ap-

BOOK VI, FOL. 50.

pear/ All and Singular the aforenamed lands with all the Appurtenances libberties and priviledges in any way or manner thereto belonging Also as it is giuen to me s^d James Pendleton by my honoured father Brian Pendleton Dec^d by his last Will and Testam^t bearing Date Aug^st ye 9th 1677, may Appeer that is the Six hundred Acres of Land afores^d,

Pendleton to Moorey

the whole premisses abous^d I s^d James Pendleton doe for my selfe my heirs and Success^rs Giue grant bargain Sell Alienate Enfeoffe and confirm to s^d Nicholas Moorey his heirs Success^rs or Assigns To haue and to hold to ocupie and possess it to his and their proper use for euer. further I s^d James Pendleton doe hereby Acknowledge for my Selfe my heires and Success^rs the receipt of ye one hundred pounds aboues^d to be in full for all the aboue bargained premisses and am hereby fully Satisfied and paid for euery part thereof, hereby Exonerating releasing and Acquitting s^d Moorey his heirs & Success^rs for for euery part and particle of the aboue bargained premisses, Also I s^d Pendleton doe for my selfe my heirs and Success^rs to s^d Moorey his heirs and Assigns that I haue good Right and Lawfull Authority to sell ye aboue bargained premisses And that they are free and Cleare from all Incumbrances whatever whether by Mortgage gift or Dower or womans thirds or any other Sute or Sutes Judgm^t or Judgements of Court or Courts Execution or Executions or any troubles in ye Law making good ye title & sale aboues^d In witness hereto I haue set my hand and seal this 23^d day of January 1699 or 1700: In ye Eleventh year of his Maj^ties Reign William the third King ouer England &c.

Signed Sealed and deliuered   James Pendleton (his Seal)
    in the presents of us
    George Denison
    Joseph Pemberton
    Joseph Pendleton

Book VI, Fol. 50.

Cap^{tn} James Pendleton personally Appeared & Acknowledged the aboue written Deed before me the Subscrib^r Dated in Stonington January ye 23^d 1698/9

Samuel Mason Assistn^t

A true Copie of the origenall Transcribed and Compared ffeb^{ry} 28th 1699.

p Jos Hamond Regist^r

Saco ffebruary 23^d 1699/ Possession entred upon and taken of all ye Premisses contained in the within written Deed by the within written Nicholas Moorey p turf and twig in the presents of us whose names is underwritten as Attests   John Hill.
                                  Jos. Hill.

A true Copie   p Jos Hamond Regist^r

Whereas we John Batson of the town of Cape Porpois in the County of York And Samuel Hill of Charles town both in ye Province of ye Massachusets Bay in New England haue good title to seuerall tracts or parcells of land at Cape Porpois, together with a Riuer called Cape Porpois Riuer where we are now building a Saw Mill/ Now Know all men by these presents that we ye aboue mentioned John Batson & Samuel Hill for Diuers good causes and considerations us thereunto Inducing haue taken Joseph Storer of Wells in the County and Prouince aforesaid to be a partner with us in s^d Mill and doe by these presents giue grant make ouer Enfeoffe and confirm unto the afores^d Joseph Storer, one quarter part of s^d Mill now building with one quarter part of all other places in s^d Riuer that is capable or conuenient for ye building of an other Mill or Mills with two Acres of Land on the west side of s^d Riuer and two Acres on ye East side of s^d Riuer for the conuenient Landing and transporting of timber or boards, together with all other profits and Priuiledges of timb^r for ye use of ye s^d Mill or Mills to him ye said Joseph Storer his heires Execut^rs Admin^rs for euer/ the s^d Joseph Storer is to Carry on one third part of the timber work his labour Equall with s^d Batson and Hill untill ye Mill be raised And afterward to be at one quarter part of

Batson Hill & Storer

all other charges about ye said Mill or Mills that shall or may hereafter by us be built upon s^d Riuer And to haue one quarter part of ye profit of ye s^d Mill or Mills/ We doe hereby bind our selues each to other in the Sum of fifty pounds to be at proportionable charges in carrying on the work from time to time in either Mill or Mills that we shall build upon s^d Riuer/ it is further agreed upon by us the s^d Partners that if either of us be minded to Sell or Let his part, he shall make ye first tender to the other partners of the same/ to the real and true performance of all ye Articles aboues^d According to ye true Intent and meaning thereof without fraud or deceit we haue Set to our hands and Seales this 22nd day of January, 1698/700

Signed Sealed and deliuered	John Batson (his seal)
In presents of.	Sam^ll Hill (his seal)
Joseph Hill	Joseph Storer. (his seal)
Jonat^n Hamond	

John Batson & Sam^ll Hill and Joseph Storer came before me this 22^d day of January and Acknowledged this aboue Instrum^t to be their Act and Deed/

p Sam^ll Wheelwright Jus: peace

A true Copie of ye origenall Instrum^t Transcribed and compared this ffeb^ry 28th 1699.

p Jos Hamond Regist^r

[51] To all People to whome this present Deed of Sale shall come. Know yee that I Matthew Austine of York in ye County of York in ye Province of the Massachusets Bay in New England for and in consideration of ye Sum of Six pounds currant Money of New England to me in hand paid at & before the ensealing and deliuery thereof by Micum Maccantere of s^d York, the receipt whereof I doe hereby Acknowledge and my selfe therewith to be fully satisfied contented and paid And thereof and of and from euery part and parcell thereof for me ye s^d Matthew Austine my heirs Execut^n Admin^n and Assigns doe exonerat Acquit and fully discharge him ye s^d Micam Maccantier his heirs Ex^n Admin^n & Assigns for euer by these presents Haue giuen granted bargained sold Aliened Enfeoffed & and confirmed And by these presents Doe giue grant bargain Sell Alien enfeoff convey and confirm unto him ye s^d Micum Maccantier his heires & Assigns. that my piece of parcell of Upland lying and being at a point against Goose coue in in ye s^d town of York, which is to run twenty pole by the riuer side & so backward untill ten Acres be compleated as is specified in ye grant upon Record in York July ye first 1656 or how ever otherwise bounded or reputed to be bounded together with all ye profits priviledges and Appurtenances to ye same land belonging with all ye Right, Title, Interest, Claim and demand which I ye s^d Matthew Austine now haue or in time past haue had or which I my Exe^n or Admin^n in time to come may might should haue or in any wise ought to haue of, in, or to ye aboue granted premisses. To have and to hold for ever the s^d premisses to him and his heirs for euer and to their sole and proper use benefit and behoofe And I the s^d Matthew Austine for me my heirs Execut^n Admin^n &c, doe couenant promise and grant to and with him ye s^d Micum Maccantier his heirs & Assigns that at and before the ensealing & deliuery hereof I am ye true Right. & proper owner of the

Austine to Maccantier

aboue granted premisses and their Appurtenances And that
I haue in my selfe full power, good right and Lawfull Authority the same to grant & confirm unto him ẙ s^d Micum
Maccantier his heirs and Assigns as afores^d and that the
same and euery part thereof is free & clere. Acquitted &
discharged of & from all other gifts, grants, bargains, Sales,
leases, Mortgages, titles, troubles, Acts Alienations and Incumbrances whatsoever And that it shall and may be Lawfull to and for ẙ s^d Micum Maccantier his heirs and Assigns
ẙ afores^d premisses and euery part thereof from time to
time and at all times for ever hereafter to haue, hold, use,
improue, ocupie, possess, and enjoy Lawfully peaceably and
quietly without any Lawfull Let, deniall, hinderance, Molestation and disturbance of or by me or any other person
or persons from by or und^r me or my procurem^t, And that
ẙ sale hereof against my self my heirs Execut^rs Admin^rs &
Assigns and against all other persons whatsoever Lawfully
claiming or demanding ẙ same or any part y^rof I will for
ever saue harmless warrant & defend by these presents
And that I my heires Exec^rs Admin^rs shall and will make
perform & Execute such other further Lawfull & reasonable
Act or Acts thing or things as in Law or equity can be devised or required for ẙ better confirming and more sure
making of ẙ premisses unto ẙ s^d Micum Maccantier his
heirs or Assigns According to ẙ Laws in this Province/ In
witness whereof I haue hereunto set my hand and Seal the
tenth day of Decemb^r in ẙ year of our Lord one thousand
Six hundred Ninety & four Annoq : R : R R Guilielmi &
Mariæ Angliæ &c. Sexto/

Signed Sealed and deliuered   Matthew Austin (his seal)
    In presents of us.   her
    John Hancock   Mary M Austin (her seal)
    Edward Beal.   mark

    Matthew Austin & Mary Austin his wife made Acknowledgm^t of this bill of Sale unto ẙ s^d Micum Maccantier as their Act and Deed before me Sam^ll Donnell Esqr one of their Maj^ties Justices of ye Peace in York, this 11th day of Decemb^r 1694.   Samuel Donnell Justis peace

    The aboues^d ten Acres was laid out by Mr Sam^ll Donnell & Mr James Plaisted and is thus bounded, on ye south east with the land of Arthur Bragdon Senr, the next line Northwest runs 20 poles by ye Riuer side, then ye next line fourscore pole runs Northeast thrō Arthur Bragdon's land Junr, bounded at the top by a heap of stones/ nextly from that heap of stones runs ye line southeast to ye Land of Arthur Bragdon Senr/ As Witness our hands the Date aboue writt
                                         Samuel Donnell
                                         James Plaisted
A true Copie of the origenall Transcribed & compared Jan^ry 5th 1699   p Jos Hamond Regist^r

    To all people to whome these presents shall come, Samuel Johnson now resident in Kittery in ye County of York in ye Collony of ye Massachusets Bay in New England Sends Greeting, Now Know yee that I the aforementioned Samuel Johnson for diuers good causes me thereunto Moueing, more Especially for and in consideration of four pounds of Lawfull money of New England to me in hand paid at and before ye ensealing & deluery of these presents by Andrew Neal of Barwick in ye County afores^d the receipt whereof and of euery part and parcell thereof I Acknowledge And therewith fully Satisfied contented and paid Haue giuen

Johnson to Neal

granted bargained Sold Aliened Enfeoffed and confirmed And by these presents for me my heirs Execut^rs Admin^rs and Assigns doe freely clerely and Absolutely giue grant bargain Sell Alien Enfeoffe and confirm unto him ye s^d Andrew Neal his heirs

Execut[rs] Admin[rs] and Assigns for euer, a certain piece or parcell of Salt Marsh containing two Acres, Scituate lying and being in y[e] town of York in y[e] County afores[d] And on y[e] South side of y[e] Riuer of s[d] York Joyning upon M[r] Dummers land on y[e] one side and upon y[e] Widow Hatch on the other side which s[d] Marsh was formerly James Grants of York afores[d] Deceased and by him giuen to his wife Hannah Grant, as appears by his last Will & Testam[t], whom I y[e] s[d] Johnson afterward Married. To have and to hold the s[d] piece or parcel of Marsh with all y[e] priuiledges and Apurtenances thereto belonging or in any wise Appurtaining with all Right, Title, Interest, claim and Demand which I the s[d] Johnson now haue or in time past haue had or which I my heirs Execut[rs] Admin[rs] or Assigns in time to come may might should or in any wise ought to have of, in, or to the aboue granted premisses or any part thereof, to him y[e] s[d] Andrew Neal his heirs or Assigns for ever and to his and their proper use benefit & behoofe for euer more And I y[e] s[d] Samuel Johnson for me my heirs &c doe [52] covenant promise and grant to and with y[e] s[d] Andrew Neal his heirs and Assigns that at and before y[e] Ensealing and deliuery of these pres[ts] I am the true right and proper owner of y[e] aboue premisses and y[e] Appurtenances And that I haue in my selfe good Right full power & Lawfull Authority y[e] aboue giuen and granted premisses to Sell and dispose of And y[t] the same is free and clere and freely and clerely Acquitted Exonerated & and Discharged of and from all former gifts grants bargains sales Judgm[ts] Executions power of thirds and all other Incumbrances whatsoever And that the s[d] Andrew Neal may from time to time and at all times hereafter haue hold enjoy and peaceable possess use and Improue the same w[th]out any let deniall hinderance or Molestation from me my heirs or Assigns and further doe promise and engage for ever to warrant and defend y[e] said title against all manner of persons whatsoever Lawfully

Claiming any right title or Interest thereunto In witness whereof I haue hereunto set my hand and seal this thirtieth day of Decemb' in y* year of our Lord one thousand Six hundred Ninety and Six And in y* Eighth year of his Maj^{ts} Reign ouer England &c.

Signed Sealed and Deliuered   Samuel Johnson (his seal)
   In the presents of us.
   Peter Wittum.
   Daniel Robinson
   Joseph Hamond Junr
   York ss/ Kittery, Octob^r 15th 1699

The within named Samuel Johnson psonally Appearing before me y* Subscrib^r one of his Maj^{ts} Justice of y* Peace Acknowledged the within Instrum^t to be his Act & Deed.
                                                       Jos Hamond

A true Copie of y* origenall Transcribed and compared Octob^r 15th 1699   p Jos Hamond Regist^r

   The Depositions of James Johnson and Thomas Rice being of full age

these Deponents testifie and say that they being at Spruce Creek about fourteen or fifteen years agoe with Mr Thomas Wethers & Mr John Shapleigh we the Depon^{ts} heard Mr Wethers afores^d ask said Shapleigh how much land would Serue him for a landing place for his Mill to lay boards & loggs on upon y* eastern side of y* Creek, the s^d Shapleigh replyed that from y* head of y* little Coue or Creek that comes out of y* Eastern Creek Streigh ouer to Mr Johnsons land would be enough to Serue his turn, then Mr Wether called y* Depon^t, Thomas Rice, to take an ax and mark y* trees Streight ouer to Mr Johnsons land from y* head of y* little coue, which he did doe according to his desire/ then y* s^d said to Mr Shapleigh if that land within

Book VI, Fol. 52.

ye head of the little coue and Johnsons land be not enough I will giue the more, then the s^d Shapleigh replyed it is enough & he desired noe more/ the land Mentioned is about two Acres More or less, Joyning to ye Mill and soe from said Johnsons land by the Crick to the little point at ye mouth of ye Eastern Crick, And further Saith not.

Taken upon oath ye 22^d day of Jan^{ry} 1699 Before me

Jos : Hamond Jus^{ts} Peace

A true Copie of ye origenall Transcribed & compared, Jan^{ry} 22^d 1699

p Jos Hamond Regist^r

To all People to whome this present Deed of Sale shall come, I John Shapleigh of Kittery in ye County of York in ye Province of ye Massachusets Bay in New England Gentleman Send Greeting Know yee that for and in consideration of the sum of forty five pounds in Currant money in New England to me in hand well and truly paid at and before ye ensealing and deliuery of these presents by Nathaniel Keen of ye Same town County & Province afores^d Yeoman ye receipt whereof I doe hereby Acknowledge and my selfe therewith to be fully satisfied & paid and of and from every part and parcel thereof for me ye s^d John Shapleigh my heires Execut^{rs} Admin^{rs} and Assigns doe exonerate Acquit and fully discharge him ye said Nathaniel Keen his heires Execut^{rs} Admin^{rs} and Assigns by these presents for ever I ye s^d John Shapleigh have giuen, granted, bargained, Sold, Aliened, enfeoffed, and confirmed, And by these presents doe for my selfe my heires Execut^{rs} Admin^{rs} & Assigns fully freely and Absolutely giue grant bargain Sell Alien enfeoffe convey and confirm unto him ye s^d Nathaniel Keen his heires and Assigns, A certain tract of Land containing one hundred Acres Scituate Lying and being in y⁰ township of Kittery at a place comonly called by y⁰ name of y⁰ Western Creek, butted and bounded as followeth to say begining in y⁰ Southwest gutter at y⁰ bottom of y⁰ lower ffalls & from thence runing upon a North Northwest line one hundred and Sixteen poles, then to run upon a west South west line one hundred and thirty poles, then to run upon a South or North line one hundred and Eighteen poles, then to run on an East Northeast or west south west line sixty five poles, then North west or Southeast thirty eight poles and from thence runing upon West south west or an east North east line eighty four poles to run to y⁰ place where y⁰ bounds first began, containing one hundred Acres together with all y⁰ Appurtenances and Priviledges that now doth or ever hereafter shall Appertain as wood or Woods Timb^r or und^r groves standing or lying thereon And all Water Courses/ To have and to hold the s^d tract of Land with y⁰ Appurtenances and Priviledges thereunto belonging or in any wise Appurtaining with all y⁰ Right title Interest Claim & Demand which I y⁰ s^d John Shapleigh now haue and in times past haue had or which I my heires Execut^{rs} Admin^{rs} or Assigns may might should or in any wise ought to haue in time to come of in or to y⁰ above granted Premisses or any part thereof to him y⁰ Said Nathan^{ll} Kene his heirs and Assigns for ever And to y⁰ sole and proper Use benefit and behoofe of him his heires &c for evermore And I y⁰ said John Shapleigh for me my heires Execut^{rs} Admin^{rs} and Assigns doe covenant promise and grant to and with him y⁰ s^d Nathan^{ll} Kene his heires Execut^{rs} Admin^{rs} and Assignes that at and before y⁰ ensealing and Deliuery hereof I am y⁰ true right and prop^r owner of y⁰ above mentioned premisses And their Appurtenances And that I haue in my selfe full power and good right and Lawfull Authority y⁰ same to grant and confirm unto him y⁰ s^d Nathan^l Kene his heirs and Assigns and that y⁰ same &

Shapleigh to Keen

euery part thereof is free and clere Acquitted and discharged of & from all former and other gifts grants bargains sales leases Mortgages Dowers titles troubles Acts Alienations and incumbrances whatsoever And that it shall and may be Lawfull to and for ye s^d Nathaniel Kene his heires &c the afores^d premisses and euery part thereof from time to time and at all times forever hereafter to haue hold Use ocupie improve and possess Lawfully and Quietly as his own proper right of Inheritance in fee Simple without any lawfull let deniall Molestation or Interuption of or by me or any person or persons from by or under me or by my procurem^t, & that ye Sale thereof And every part thereof against my selfe my heires Execut^{rs} Admin^{rs} and Assigns and against all other persons whatsoever the Kings [53] Maj^{tie} onely excepted, Claiming and Lawfully Demanding the same or any part thereof I will for ever Saue harmless warrant and Defend by these presents. In witness whereof I ye s^d John Shapleigh haue hereunto set my hand & Seal after ye word Southwest was incerted interlined in ye thirteenth line, this third day of July Anno Dom̃: One thousand six hundred Ninety & Nine And in ye Eleventh year of ye Reign of our Soveraign Lord William ye third of England &c King

Signed Sealed & Deliuered   John Shapleigh (his Seal)

In the presents of us   Lydia Webber and Mary Beckham
John Pickerin Senr Appeared before me ye Subscrib^r
the mark of   and made oath that they saw
Lydia ⌐ Webber   John Shapleigh Signe & Seal
the mark of   this Instrum^t & Deliuer it as his
Mary M Beckham   Act & Deed this fourth of ffebruary 1699.

                           John Plaisted Jus. Peace

A true Copie of ye origenall Transcribed and compared this 5th March 1699

                     p Jos Ham̃ond Regist^r

BOOK VI, FOL. 53.

York ss/ Kittery March 6th 1699

The within named John Shapleigh psonally Appearing before me the Subscrib[r] one of y[e] Members of his Maj[us] Council of y[e] Province of y[e] Massachusets Bay and Justice of Peace within ye same. Acknowledged the within Instrum[t] or Deed of Sale to be his Act and Deed/

         Jos Hamond
A true Copie   p Jos Hamond Regist[r]

Abraham Lord
to
Abbot & Nason

Whereas Abraham Conly some time of Kittery in the Province of Maine in New England did by his last Will and Testament bearing Date y[e] first day of March 1674 giue and bequeath unto me Abraham Lord a certain Legacie of land and Marsh lying and being in Stirgeon Creek in s[d] Town & Province/ which said land and Marsh my father Nathan Lord sold unto Thomas Abbet and Jonathan Nason Deceased, as may at large Appear by my s[d] fathers Deed under his hand and Seal together with my mother Lords consent as doth alsoe Appear by a Deed under both their hands bearing date y[e] twenty eighth of June one thousand six hundred Seventy and eight, which s[d] Deed was giuen by my s[d] father and Mother unto s[d] Abbet and Nason without my consent or Approbation the which has caused a contest in Law between s[d] Abbet Nason and my self And for a finall Issue whereof, Be it known unto all manner of persons to whom this Instrument or writing shall come that I Abraham Lord y[e] Subscriber hereof, for y[e] consideration of that money paid by s[d] Abbet and Nason as Alsoe for y[e] consideration of forty pounds to me in hand paid and secured to be paid by s[d] Thomas Abbet and Sarah Nason y[e] Relict and Administratrix of s[d] Jonathan Nason the which s[d] Sum I y[e] s[d] Abraham Lord doe hereby acknowledge and my self to be fully Satisfied and contented, doe for a further Assurance of all that tract of Land being about forty Acres onely excepting what land my Grandfather Conly disposed of to one Peter Wittum being about three Acres out of s^d forty together with all ye great Marsh Adjoyning to s^d Land being ten Acres more or less And is bounded as in my s^d father and Mother Nathan and Martha Lords Deeds under their hands and Seals All which land and Marsh I ye s^d Abraham Lord doe hereby Acknowledge to haue bargained and by these presents doe bargain Sell Alienate and confirm unto ye s^d Tho: Abbet and Sarah Nason their heires Execut^{rs} Admin^{rs} and Assigns for ever To haue and to hold all ye before Mentioned land and Marsh with all ye Priuiledges and Appertenances whatsoever thereunto belonging or in any wise Appertaining unto them ye s^d Abbet and Nason their heirs Execut^{rs} Admin^{rs} and Assigns and that for euer without ye least let Interuption or Molestation of me ye s^d Abraham Lord my heirs Execut^{rs} & Administrat^{rs} or any pson or psons whatsoever Claiming any Just Right title or Interest to all or any part of ye before mentioned bargained and Sold Lands and Marsh together with all the timber trees woods and under woods standing lying and growing upon s^d land, by from or under me ye s^d Lord my heires Execut^{rs} & Administrat^{rs} or any any of them And that for ever. And further more I ye s^d Abraham Lord doe by these presents oblige my self my heirs Exec^{rs} and Admin^{rs} firmly by this presents that if at any time hereafter ye aboues^d Abbet and Nason shall find fault that this my Deed be not Sufficient & Legall for ye confirming of all ye Rights title Claim & Interest that euer I had or ought to haue to all and euery part of ye before Mentioned land & Marshes unto them ye s^d Abbet and Nason their heirs Execut^{rs} Admin^{rs} and Assigns and that for ever, I say then and in that case I doe hereby oblige my self &c to Sign and Seal any other writing or Deed as shall be Judged by learned men in y⁰ law to be Legall and Sufficient to confirm all my s⁴ wright that euer I had or ought to haue to all & euery part of y⁰ aboue bargained & sold premisses unto them y⁰ s⁴ Abbet & Nason their heirs &c for euer/ In confirmation whereof I haue hereto Set my hand and Seal this: 11ᵗʰ of May 1695

Signed Sealed and Deliuered   Abraham Lord (his seal)
   in presents of   mark
   John Pickerin   Tho: Butler   Susanna S Lord (her seal)
   Samuel Burnum   John Cooper   her
   Efram E Joy his mark.

County of   Abraham Lord and Susana his wife came
   York   before me this 20ᵗʰ of May 1697. And Acknowledged y⁰ within written Instrument to be their free Act & Deed.   Charles ffrost Just peace

A true Copie of y⁰ origenall transcribed & compared this. 20ᵗʰ ffebʳʸ 1699
                     p Jos Hamond Registʳ

[54] Know all men by these presents that I Thomas Abbet of Kittery in the County of York in y⁰ Province of Massachusets Bay for and in consideration of y⁰ Sum of ffifty pounds of Lawfull money of New England to me in hand paid by Joshua Downing and John Leighton of Kittery afores⁴, Have giuen granted and sold And by these presents doe for me my heirs Executʳˢ Adminʳˢ and Assigns fully and Absolutely giue grant bargain and Sell Assign and set ouer unto y⁰ s⁴ Joshua Downing and John Leighton All my Right title Interest Claim and Demand of, in and to all my part of y⁰ land & Marsh mentioned in y⁰ within writted Deed of Sale made by Abraham Lord unto Sarah Nason and my self with all y⁰ Priuiledges thereto belonging as in s⁴ Deed on y⁰ other side is expressed To haue and to

hold yᵉ sᵈ Land and Marsh with yᵉ Appurtenances, unto them yᵉ sᵈ Joshua Downing and John Leighton their heirs Executⁿ Adminⁿ or Assigns for ever more from me yᵉ sᵈ Thómas Abbet my heirs and Assigns In witness whereof I haue hereunto set my hand and Seal this fiue and twentieth day of March one thousand Six hundred Ninety and nine And in yᵉ Eleuenth Year of our Soueraign William yᵉ third King of England &c.

Abbet to
Downing &
Leighton

Signed Sealed and de- Thomas Abbet (his seal)
liuered In presents of us

Wᵐ Vaughan
John Abbet
Jos Hamond

County York ss/ Kittery ffebᵣ 29ᵗʰ 1699

The aboue named Thomas Abbett psonally Appearing before me yᵉ Subscribʳ one of his Maᵗˢ Council of the Province of yᵉ Massachusets Bay And Justice of Peace within yᵉ same, Acknowledged the aboue Instrumᵗ to be his Act and Deed   Jos Hamond

A true Copie of yᵉ origenall Assignment Transcribed and Compared the 29ᵗʰ day of ffebᵣ 1699.

p Jos Hamond Registʳ

To all People to whome this present Deed of Sale shall come/ I Thomas Abbet of Kittery in yᵉ County of York in yᵉ Prouince of yᵉ Massachuset Bay in New England Blacksmith Send Greeting Know yee that for and in consideration of the full sum of ffifie pounds in currant Money of New England to me in hand well and truely paid at and before yᵉ ensealing and Deliuery of these presᵗˢ by Joshua Downing and John Leighton of Kittery in yᵉ County and Province aforesᵈ Yeomen, the receipt whereof I doe hereby

Acknowledge and my self therewith to be fully Satisfied contented and paid And thereof and of and from euery part and pcell thereof for me y⁴ s⁴ Thomas Abbet my heirs Executrˢ Adminrˢ and Assigns doe Exonerate Acquit & fully discharge them y⁴ s⁴ Joshua Downing and John Leighton their heirs Executrˢ Adminrˢ and Assigns for euer, I y⁴ s⁴ Thomas Abbet haue giuen, granted, bargained, Sold, Aliened, Enfeoffed and confirmed And by these presents doe for me my heires Executrˢ Adminrˢ and Assigns fully freely and Absolutely giue, grant, bargain, Sell, Alien, Enfeoffe, conuey & confirm, unto them the s⁴ Joshua Downing and John Leighton their heires & Assigns all that my part, Portion, Right, Title and Interest, of in and unto a certain piece or parcell of land scituate lying and being near Stirgeon Creek in yᵉ township of Kittery aforesᵈ containing about forty Acres which land together with all my part of yᵉ great Marsh Adjoyning to s⁴ land, being by Estimation ten Acres more or less, wᶜʰ land and Marsh I bought in partnership & Equall proportion with Jonathan Nason late of Kittery Deceased, of Nathan Lord late of s⁴ Kittery Deceased as by Deed of Sale under y⁴ hand and seal of s⁴ Nathan Lord bearing Date the twenty eighth of June one thousand six hundred seuenty eight, referrence thereunto being had may more at large Appear, together with all y⁴ profits priuiledges and Appurtenances to y⁴ s⁴ land and Marsh belonging or in any wise Appurtaining To haue and to hold y⁴ part portion or one halfe part of all yᵉ s⁴ piece or parcells of land and Meadow or Marsh being butted and bounded as by y⁴ aforsᵈ recited Deed from Nathan Lord or how euer else bounded or reputed to be bounded, with all Right, Title, Interest Claim and Demand which I y⁴ said Thomas Abbet now haue or in time past haue had, or which I my heirs Executrˢ Adminrˢ or Assigns in time to come, may, might, should or in any wise ought to haue of, in or to y° aboue granted premisses or any part thereof to them y° s^d Joshua Downing and John Leighton their heires or Assigns for euer And to the sole and proper Use benefit and behoofe of them the s^d Joshua Downing and John Leighton their heires Execut^rs &c for euer more. And I y° s^d Thomas Abbet for me my heires Execut^rs Admin^rs & Assigns doe couenant promise and grant to and with y° s^d Joshua Downing and John Leighton their heirs and Assigns that at and before y° ensealing & deliuery thereof, I am the true Right and proper owner of y° aboue premisses and the Appurtenances/ And that I have in my selfe good right full power and lawfull Authority y° same to grant and confirm unto them y° said Joshua Downing and John Leighton their heirs and Assigns as afores^d And that y° same & euery part thereof is free and Clere Acquitted and Discharged of and from all other & former gifts, grants, bargains, sales, leases, Mortgages, titles, troubles, Acts, Alienations and Incumbrances whatsoever And that it shall and may be Lawfull to and for y° s^d Joshua Downing and John Leighton their heirs & Assigns the afores^d premisses and euery part thereof from time to time and at all times for euer hereafter to haue hold Use Improue ocupie Possess and enjoy Lawfully peaceably and quietly without any Lawfull let deniall hinderance Molestation or disturbance of or by me or any other person or persons from by or under me or by my procurem^t and that y° sale thereof and euery part thereof against my self my heires Execut^rs Admin^rs and Assignes and against all other persons whatsoever Lawfully Claiming the same or any part thereof I will for euer Saue harmless warrant and Defend by these presents And that I my heirs Exscut^rs & Administrat^rs shall and will make perform and Execute such other further lawfull and reasonable Act or Acts thing or things as in Law or Equity can be deuised or required for the better confirming

Abbot to Downing & Leighton

and more sure making of the premisses unto the s⁴ Joshua Downing and John Leighton their heires Execut^rs Admin^rs & Assigns According to y⁰ Laws of this Province/ In witness whereof I y⁰ s⁴ Thomas Abbet haue hereunto Set my hand & Seal y⁰ fiue & twentieth day of March in y⁰ Eleuenth year of y⁰ Reign of our Soveraign Lord William y⁰ third by the grace of God of England Scotland ffrance and Ireland, King Defend^r of the ffaith Anno Domini one thousand six hundred Ninety & nine : 1699

Signed Sealed & deliuered in presents of Us.
    Wm Vaughan
    John Abbot
    Jos Hamond

Thomas Abbot : (his seal)

York ss/ Kittery ffeb^ry 29 : 1699

The aboue named Thomas Abbet psonally before me the Subscrib^r one of y⁰ memb^rs of his Maj^ties Council of y⁰ Province of the Massachusets Bay, And Justice of Peace within y⁰ same, Acknowledged the aboue Instrum^t to be his Act & Deed   Jos Hamond

A true Copie of y⁰ origenall Transcribed & Compared this 29 : ffeb^ry 1699.

                       p Jos Hamond Regist^r

[55] To all people to whome these presents shall come I Sarah Nason Relict Widow and Administrat^r to y⁰ Estate of my husband Jonathan Nason late of Kittery in y⁰ County of York in y⁰ Province of the Massachusets Bay in New England Deceased send greeting/ Know yee that I Sarah Nason for and in Consideration of y⁰ Sum of ffifty pounds currant money of New England to me in hand well and truly paid at and before y⁰ ensealing and deliuery of these

presents by Joshua Downing and John Leighton of Kittery in y' County & Province aforesaid Yeomen, the receipt whereof I doe hereby Acknowledge and my selfe therew[th] to be fully Satisfied contented and paid And thereof and of and from euery part and parcell thereof for me y' s[d] Sarah Nason my heires Execut[rs] Admin[rs] and Assigns doe Acquit Exonerate and fully discharge them y' s[d] Joshua Downing & John Leighton their heires Execut[rs] Admin[rs] and Assigns for euer/ I y' s[d] Sarah Nason haue giuen granted bargained Sold Aliened Enfeoffeed and confirmed And by these presents doe for me my heirs Execut[rs] and Admin[rs] fully freely and Absolutely giue grant bargain Sell Alien Enfeoffe convey and confirm unto them y' s[d] Joshua Downing and John Leighton their heires And Assigns all that my part portion Right title and Interest of in and unto a certain piece or parcel of land lying and being Scituate near Stirgeon Creek in y' township of Kittery on y' South Side of s[d] Creek containg about forty Acres which land together with my Moiety or one halfe part of y' great Marsh Adjoyning to s[d] land being by Estimation ten Acres more or less

Sarah Nason to Downing & Leighton

which land and Marsh my s[d] husband Jonathan Nason bought in partnership and Equall proportion with Thomas Abbot of Kittery afores[d] of Nathan Lord late of s[d] Kittery Deceased as p Deed of Sale under hand and seal of s[d] Lord bearing Date June 28: 1678, referrence there unto being had may more at large Appear/ And Since confirmed to me by Abraham Lord (who Appeared to be y' Right owner thereof) as Appears by Deed under his hand and Seale bearing Date. 11. May 1695. together with all y' profits priuiledges and Appurtenances to y' s[d] land and Marsh belonging or in any wise Appurtaining To have and to hold y' s[d] part portion Moity or one halfe part of all y' s[d] pieces or parcels of Meadow or Marsh being butted and bounded as by y' afore recited Deed from Nathan Lord or how euer else bounded or or reputed to be bounded with all Right title Claim and demand which I yᵉ sᵈ Sarah now haue or in time past haue had or which I my heires Executⁿ or Adminⁿ in time to come may might should or in any wise ought to haue of in or to yᵉ aboue granted Premisses or any part thereof to them yᵉ sᵈ Joshua Downing and John Leighton their heires or Assigns for euer more And I yᵉ sᵈ Sarah Nason for me my heirs Executⁿ Administratⁿ and Assigns doe couenant promise and grant to and with them yᵉ sᵈ Joshua Downing and John Leighton their heirs and Assigns That at and before yᵉ ensealing and deliuery thereof I am yᵉ true Right and proper owner of yᵉ aboue premisses & the Appurtenances And that I haue in my selfe good Right full power and Lawfull Authority the same to grant and confirm unto them yᵉ sᵈ Joshua Downing & John Leighton their heirs and Assigns as aforesᵈ And that yᵉ Same and euery part thereof is free and clere Acquitted and discharged of and from all other and former gifts grants bargains Sales eases Mortgages titles troubles Acts Alienations and Incombrances whatsoeuer And that it shall and may be Lawfull to and for yᵉ sᵈ Joshua Downing & John Leighton their heirs and Assigns yᵉ aforesᵈ premisses and euery part thereof from time to time and at all times for euer here after To haue hold use ocupie possess and enjoy Lawfully peaceably and quietly without any Lawfull let deniall hinderance Molestation or disturbance of or by by me or any other person or psons from by or under me or by my procuremᵗ And that yᵉ Sale thereof and euery part thereof against my self my heires Executⁿ Adminⁿ and Assigns And against all other persons whatsoeuer Lawfully Claiming yᵉ Same or any part yʳof I will for euer Saue harmless warrant and defend by these presents & that I my heires Executⁿ and Adminⁿ shall and will make perform & execute Such other further

Lawfull Act or Acts thing or things as in Law or Equity can be deuised or required for y° better confirming and more Sure making of the premisses unto y° s^d Joshua Downing and John Leighton their heirs or Assigns According to y° Laws of this Prouince In witness whereof I haue hereunto Set my hand and Seal the Nine and twentieth day of ffebruary in the twelfth Year of y° Reign of our Soueraign Lord William the third ouer England &c. Anno Domini one thousand Six hundred Ninety nine. 1699 the

Signed Sealed and deliuered
   In presents of us   Sarah ⌇ Nason (her seal)
        her   mark of
  Amy ⌇ Neal
     mark
Jonathan Nason
Jos Hamond

County York ss/ Kittery ffeb^y 29th 1699

The aboue named Sarah Nason personally Appearing before me y° Subscrib^r one of y° Memb^rs of his Maj^tys Council of y° Prouince of the Massachusets Bay & Justice of Peace within y° Same Acknowledged the aboue Instrum^t to be her Act and Deed.   Jos Hamond

A true Copie of y° origenall Transcribed and Compared this 29th of ffebruary : 1699.   p Jos Hamond Regist^r

The Deposition of Ensign Thomas Abbot Senr and Sargeant Christopher Banfield testifying & say that some time in y° 1683. Cap^tn Wincoll Agent and partner for and in y° land at Stirgeon Crick Swamp did lay out unto Leonard Drown and giue him Possession of Sixty Acres of land more or less butting upon s^d Stirgeon Creek on these terms fol-

Abbot & Bampfields Oaths

lowing, that is to Say, the s^d Drown was to make improuement of s^d land for and in behalfe of ye Proprietors, s^d Wincoll declaring himself to be one, that ye s^d Drown was to enjoy s^d Sixty Acres of land for his pains if s^d Land did fall in s^d Wincolls part or Deuidend, if not, s^d Wincoll did engage that ye s^d Drown should haue s^d Land of ye Priet^rs upon good and reasonable terms And s^d Drown did take Possession and build and plant & improue and is at this day in Possession at this day by himselfe or Tenant and euer hath declared he would Stand and fall by ye Propriet^rs & ffurth^r saith not

Taken upon oath this twenty fifth of April one thousand seuen hundred/ Before me   Jno Plaisted Jus^ts Peace

Witness our hands { Thomas Abbott
{ Christo : Bampfield

A true Copie of ye origenall Transcribed & compared. this 21st May 1700.

Jos Hamond Regist^r

[56] At a Legall town Meeting held at Kittery May 24th 1699. Granted unto Daniel Green his heires or Assigns for ever thirty Acres of land if he can find it clere of former grants. Attests.   Jos Hamond Cler

Know all men by these presents that I Daniel Green of Kittery for and in consideration of Eight Shillings in Money to me in hand paid by Joseph Hill of ye Same town/ haue giuen granted Assigned and set over And by these presents doe fully & Absolutely giue grant Assign and Set over & confirm unto him ye s^d Joseph Hill his heires or Assigs for ever ye aboue mentioned

Green to Hill

grant of thirty Acres of Land/ In witness whereof I have hereunto Set my hand & Seal this 28th day of March 1700.
Signed Sealed & Deliuered
  In presents of us.   his
  Michael Whidden   Daniel ⌒ ╲Green (his seal)
  Jos Hamond.   mark

York ss/ Kittery March 28th 1700

The above named Daniel Green psonally Appearing before me yͤ Subscribr one of his Mats Justices of Peace within yͤ County of York Acknowledged yͤ aboue Instrumt to be his Act & Deed.   Jos Hamond

A true Copie of yͤ origenall Transcribed & Compared
March 28 : 1700   p Jos Hamond Cler

 At a Legall town meeting held at Kittery May 24th 1699./ granted unto John Morgrage his heires or Assigns for ever ten Acres of land if he can find it clere of former grants   Attests Jos Hamond Cler

Know all men by these presents that I yͤ above named John Morgrage doe Sell Assign and convey unto Robert
Morgrage to Cutt Cutt of Kittery his heires Executrs Administratrs and Assigns for ever All yͤ above mentioned grant of ten Acres of land/ To have and to hold from me yͤ Said John Morgrage my heires & Assigns for ever more. In witness whereof I haue hereunto Set my hand and Seal this Sixteenth day of July one thousand seven hundred   his
Signed Sealed & delivered   John ꟻMorgrage (his seal)
 in presents of us.   mark
 Mary Champernown
 Jos Hamond

BOOK VI, FOL. 56.

York ss/ The aboue named John Morgrage psonally Appearing before me y* Subscrib* one of his Ma** Justices w*h*in the County York Acknowledged y* above Instrum* to be his Act and Deed.

Jos Hamond

A true Copie of y* origenall Transcribed and compared July 16th 1700

p Jos Hamond Regist*

At a Legall town meeting held at Kittery May 16, 1694/ Granted to Walter Deniver ten Acres of land provided he improve it within one year after it be laid out by building or fencing & improving a considerable part thereof otherwise to return again to y* town And to be laid out Clere of former grants.

A true Copie taken out of Kittery town book

p Jos Hamond Cler

Know all men by these presents that I Walter Deniver above named for and in consideration of a Valluable sum of Money to me in hand paid at and before y* ensealing and delivery of these presents by Robert Cutt of Kittery, haue

Deniver to Cutt Sold Assigned and conveyed And doe for me my heires and Assigns for ever, Sell, Assign convey and confirm unto him y* s*d* Robert Cutt his heirs &c/ All y* aboue grant of ten Acres of land To haue and to hold to him y* s*d* Robert Cutt his heirs Execut*r*s & Assigns for ever from me y* s*d* Walter Deniver my heirs &c for ever/ In witness whereof I have hereunto Set my

BOOK VI, FOL. 56.

hand & Seal this Sixteenth day of July one thousand Seven hundred

Signed Sealed and deliuered   Walter ╳ Deniver (his Seal)
  In pres^{ts} of us.   mark
  Jos Hamond
  Richard Cutt
  York ss : Kittery July. 16. 1700

The above named Walter Deniver psonally Appearing before me ye Subscrib^r one of his Maj^s Justices in s^d County Acknowledged ye aboue Instrum^t to be his Act And Deed.
                                            Jos Hamond

A true Copie of ye origenall Transcribed & compared this 16th July : 1700   p Jos Hamond Cler

At a Legall town Meeting held at Kittery May 16. 1699. Granted unto Thomas Hooper twenty Acres of land provided he improue it within one year after it be laid out by building or fencing and improving a considerable part thereof otherwise to return again to ye town.

A true Copie as Appears of Record in Kittery town Book. Examined   p Jos Hamond Cler

Know all men by these presents that I Thomas Hooper of Kittery in ye County of York in ye Province of ye Massachusets Bay in New England for and in Consideration of ye Sum of twenty Shillings to me in hand paid by Robt Cutt of ye Same place Shipwright the receipt whereof I doe Acknowledg And myself therewith to be fully Satisfied and paid Have giuen granted and Sold And by these presents doe for me my heirs Execut^{rs} Admin^{rs} and Assigns for ever fully and absolutely giue, grant, bargain, sell, make over and confirm unto him ye s^d

Hooper to Cutt

Robert Cutt his heires and Assigns All my Right, Title and Interst of in and to ye above grant of twenty Acres of land To have and to hold, ye same without any Molestation let deniall or hinderance from me y^{e s^d} Hooper or any other pson or psons from by or under me or by my procurem^t In witness whereof I haue hereunto Set my hand and Seal this third day of May. 1700/

Signed Sealed and deliuered   Thomas ⌒ Hooper (his seal)
   in presents of us
   Hannah Hamond
   Jos Hamond

Thomas Hooper psonally Appearing before me the Subscrib^r one of his Ma^{ts} Justices of Peace within ye Province of ye Massachusetts Bay Acknowledged the aboue written Instrum^t to be his Act & Deed. At Kittery May 3^d 1700
                                                 Jos Hamond

A true copie of ye origenall Transcribed & compared this 3^d May 1700.
                                       p Jos Hamond Regist^r

[57] At a Legall town Meeting held at Kittery May 24th 1699. Granted unto John Thomson his heires or Assigns for ever thirty Acres of land if he can find it clere of former grants, A true copie as Attests.   Jos Hamond Cler

Know all men by these presents that I John Thompson of Kittery in the County of York in ye Province of ye Massachusets Bay have Sold Assigned and confirmed And by these presents doe for me my heirs Execut^{rs} and Admin^{rs} fully and Absolutely Sell Assign convey and confirm All my right title, Interest, Claim & Demand of in and to y^e

Book VI, Fol. 57.

Tomson to Cutt

aboue grant of thirty Acres of Land unto Robert Cutt of yᵉ Same place Shipwright his heires Executʳˢ Adminʳˢ or Assigns for ever, to be to his and their own proper use benefit & behoof for ever more, for which grant of land I doe Acknowledge to haue Recᵈ of yᵉ sᵈ Robᵗ Cutt full Satisfaction to my content In witness whereof I haue hereunto set my hand and Seal this thirteenth day of April, 1700

Signed Sealed and deliuered   John Tomson (his seal)
  In the presents of us.
  Hannah Storer
  Jos Hamond
  York ss/ Kittery April 13ᵗʰ 1700/

The aboue named John Tomson psonally Appearing Acknowledged yᵉ aboue written Sale to be his Act & Deed.
                    Before me Jos Hamond Jusᵗˢ Peace

A true Copie of yᵉ origenall Transcribed and Compared April : 13ᵗʰ 1700
                        Jos Hamond Registʳ

At a Legall town meeting held at Kittery May 24ᵗʰ 1699/ Granted unto Samuel ffernald his heirs and Assigns for ever, thirty Acres of land if it may be found clere of former grants.

  A true Copie taken out of Kittery town Book
                      p Jos Hamond Cler

ffernald to Cutt

Know all men by these presents that I Samˡˡ ffernald of Kittery in yᵉ County of York in the Province of yᵉ Massachusets Bay have Sold Assigned and conveyed And doe by these presents for me my heirs Executʳˢ & Assigns for ever; Sell Assign, convey and confirm unto Robᵗ Cutt of sᵈ Kittery his heirs and

Assigns (for a Valuable Sum of Money to me in hand paid by yᵉ sᵈ Cutt) All yᵉ above grant of thirty Acres of land. To have and to hold yᵉ sᵈ grant to him yᵉ sᵈ Robert Cutt his heirs &c as aforesᵈ In witness whereof I haue hereunto set my hand and Seal this Sixteenth day of July. one thousand Seven hundred.

Signed Sealed and Deliuered   Samuel Fernald (his seal)
  In presents of us.
Mary Champernown
Jos Hamond
York ss/ Kittery July 16 : 1700.

The aboue named Samᵘ ffernald psonally Appearing before me yᵉ Subscribʳ one of his Maᵗˢ Justices in sᵈ County Acknowledged yᵉ aboue Instrumᵗ to be his Act & Deed

             Jos Hamond

A true Copie of yᵉ origenall Transcribed & compared July : 16. 1700

         p Jos Hamond Registʳ

At a Legall town meeting held at Kittery May 24. 1699/ Granted unto Mʳ Richard Cutt thirty Acres of land to him his heirs and Assigns for ever if he can find it clere of former grants.

A true Copie taken out of Kittery town Book

         p Jos Hamond Clerͬ

Richd Cutt
to Robt Cutt

Know all men by these presents that I Richard Cutt aboue named for and in consideration of a Valuable Sum of money to me in hand paid at and before the ensealing and deliuery of these presents by my brother Robert Cutt of Kittery, doe grant bargain & sell to him his heirs Executʳˢ Adminˢ and Assigns for ever All yᵉ aboue grant of thirty Acres of Land. To haue & to hold to him y⁰ sᵈ Robᵗ Cutt his heirs and Assigns for ever from me yᵉ sᵈ Richard Cutt my heires &c for ever more In witness whereof I haue hereunto Set my hand and Seale this Sixteenth of July. 1700.

Signed Sealed and deliuered Richard Cutt (his seal)
 In presents of us.
   her
 Lydia ✗ Nelson
  mark
 Jos Hamond

York ss/ Kittery July: 16: 1700

The aboue named Richard Cutt psonally Appearing before me yᵉ Subscribᵣ one of his Maᵗˢ Justices in sᵈ County Acknowledged yᵉ aboue Instrumᵗ to be his Act and Deed
         Jos Hamond

A true Copie of yᵉ origenall Transcribed & compared this. 16. July. 1700.
       p Jos Hamond Regᵣ

At a Legall town Meeting held at Kittery May 24ᵗʰ 1699/ Granted unto Jacob Smith his heirs or Assigns for ever thirty Acres of Land, if he can find it clere of former grants/

A true Copie taken out of Kittery town Book.
       p Jos Hamond Cler

Know all men by these presents that I yᵉ above named Jacob Smith for and in consideration of a Valluable Sum of Money to me in hand paid at and before yᵉ Ensealing and

Smith to Cutt

deliuery of these presents by Robert Cutt of Kittery Have sold Assigned and conveyed And by these presents doe for me my heirs and

Assignes for ever, Sell Assigne, convey & confirm unto him y⁰ sᵈ Robert Cutt his heirs and Assigns All y⁰ above grant of thirty Acres of Land/ To haue and to hold, unto him y⁰ sᵈ Robert Cutt his heirs &c for ever-more from me y⁰ sᵈ Jacob Smith my heirs and Assigns for ever/ In witness whereof I have hereunto Set my hand and Seal, this thirtieth day of July one thousand Seven hundred: 1700.

Signed Sealed & deliuered   Jacob Smith (his seal)
   in presᵗˢ of us
   Jos Hamond Junʳ
         his
   George ⌒ Cresy
        mark

York ss/ July 30ᵗʰ 1700

The abou named Jacob Smith psonally Appearing before me Acknowledged y⁰ aboue Instrumᵗ to be his act & Deed
                          Jos Hamond Jusᵗˢ Pea.

A true Copie of y⁰ origenall Transcribed & compared this 30: July: 1700/
                          Jos Hamond Registʳ

Fletcher to Pope

[58] Know all men by these presents that I Pendleton ffletcher late of Winter harbʳ for and in consideration of y⁰ Sum of three pounds ten shillings alredy Satisfied me by Richard Pope now resident in Kittery, whereof & wherewith I doe Acknowledge myselfe to be fully Satisfied and contented for a neck of land comonly called y⁰ Middle neck which is on y⁰ Eastern Side of y⁰ little River comonly called Scadlocks River within y⁰ township of Winter harbour in y⁰ Province of Maine, butting on y⁰ one Side to the Salt Meadows, runing East to a cove called Whale cove And bounded on the other

Side with ye Sea, three or four Score Acres being more or less To have and to hold the s^d Neck of Land with all its Appurtenances and every part thereof unto ye said Richard Pope his heires Execut^{rs} Administrat^{rs} and Assigns for ever freely peaceably and quietly to possess ocupie and enjoy with all ye Prviledges thereunto belonging, as his own proper Estate for ever without any lett or deniall of me ye s^d Pendledon ffletcher my heires Execut^{rs} Admin^{rs} or any of us only ye s^d Richard Pope is, and his heirs Execut^{rs} Admin^{rs} or Assigns are hereby enjoyned when required thereunto, to give liberty to the owners of ye afores^d Marsh unto which ye s^d Neck is butted soe much timber of ye s^d neck as is nessessary to fence in ye s^d Marsh from time to time then I ye s^d Pendleton ffletcher for my self my heirs &c. doth covenant promise and grant to ye s^d Pope that all ye before mentioned Premisses at ye time of ye delivery hereof is free from all other Sales or bargains whatsoever, And that I the s^d ffletcher is y^e proper owner thereof with warrantys against all psons whatsoever and that for ever by these presents/ Unto all which I have hereunto Set my hand and Seale this eighth day of June Anno Dom, one thousand six hundred Ninety and one.

Signed Sealed and delivered   Pendleton ffletcher ($_{seal}^{his}$)
   in the presents of us.
      the mark of
Robert   Saturly
Mary Hooke.

Mr Pendleton Fletcher came and Acknowledged this Instrum^t to be his Act and Deed unto Richd Pope this eight day of June 1691. before me.

                       ffrancis Hooke Just Pea.

A true Copie of y^e originall Transcribed and compared this. 17 day of June 1700

                     p Jos Hamond Regist^r

Book VI, Fol. 58.

This Indenture made ye first day of Novemb^r Anno Domĩ one thousand Six hundred Ninety and three, Annoq R R^s et Reginæ Guliel et Mariæ Angliæ &c Quinto Between Elihue Gunnison of Kittery in their Ma^{ts} Province of ye Massachusets Bay in New England Shipwright of one part and William Pepperrel of Kittery afores^d Marrin^r on ye other part Whereas on ye seventeenth day of Septemb^r in ye second year of ye Reign of King James ye Second of England &c. Annoq Domĩ 1686. John Palmer Esqr one of ye then Council in ye afores^d Kings Plantation and Colony of New York and Comission^r for ye granting and confirming of Lands within the County of Cornwall in s^d Colony Pursuant unto ye Comission and Authority to him given by the R^t Honble Coll Thomas Dongan then Lieu^t and Govern^r of ye s^d Colony for and in behalfe of our Late Soveraign Lord ye s^d King James then Supream Lord, of ye Plantation and Colony afores^d by Pattent under ye hand of s^d Palmer and Seal of ye Colony of New York afores^d of ye last Menc̃oned Date duly Entred upon Record, Did give, grant, Ratifie and confirm unto the s^d Elihu Gunnison then Living in ye County of Cornwall afores^d all That Tract or parcell of Land within the bounds of James Town in the afores^d County containing five hundred Acres Lying and being at ye place or neck of Land called Bucklands Neck, begining at a certain place known by ye name of Corbitts Sound to ye Southwest of ye s^d Neck, from thence along ye upland by the River called by the name of Damaris Cotty River, Soe North : north east to ye narrow of s^d Neck known by ye name of Winagance or carrying place, from thence East south east over the said Winagans to ye cove in ye back River, from thence along ye upland by the s^d River South : south west to ye s^d Corbitts Sound and to ye Eastward of the same, from thence along s^d upland by s^d Corbits Sound to ye place where began, Alsoe fiftie Acres of Meadow part whereof to be laid

Gunnison to Pepperrell

out at that Meadow which is at ye Westward Side of Damaris Cotty and cove against bread and Chees Island, the rest to be laid out where most convenient/ To have and to hold the s^d five hundred Acres of upland fifty Acres of Meadow with all and Singular its Appurtenances unto ye s^d Elihu Gunnison his heirs and Assigns to the Sole and only proper use, benefit and behoofe of ye s^d Elihu Gunnison his heirs and Assigns for ever; Yeelding and paying therefore Yearly and every year unto our aforemenc͠oned late Soveraign Lord his heirs or Success^{rs} or to such Govern^r or other Officers as from time to time shall be by him or them Appointed to receive the Same on every twenty fifth day of March as a Quitt rent or Acknowledgm^t for the s^d Land four bushells and an halfe of Merchantable wheat or the Vallue thereof in money as in and by s^d Pattent is at large Exprest reference whereto being had more fully may Appear. Now this Indenture Witnesseth that ye s^d Elihu Gunnison for and in consideration of ye Sum of Ten pounds Currant Money of New England to him in hand well and truly paid before the ensealing & delivery of these presents by ye s^d William Pepperrell the receipt whereof to full content and Satisfaction he ye said Elihu Gunnison doth hereby Acknowledge & thereof and of every part thereof doth Acquit Exonerate and Discharge ye s^d William Pepperrel his heirs Execut^{rs} Admin^{rs} and Assigns and every of them for ever by these presents, hath given, granted, bargained and sold Aliened Enfeoffed conveyed & confirmed And by these presents Doth fully freely cleerly and Absolutely give grant bargain Sell Alien Enfeoffe convey and confirm unto ye s^d William Pepperrel his heirs & Assigns for ever One Full Moiety or halfe part of all afore mentioned Tract or parcel of Land Lying within ye bounds of James Town in ye County of Cornwall afores^d Containing in the whole five hundred Acres, As alsoe one Moiety or full halfe part of ye afores^d fifty Acres to be [59] laid out as afores^d Together with all and Singular the Timber trees woods under woods profits priviledges Rights comodities heredittaments Emolum^{ts} & Appur^{ces} whatsoever to ye s^d Moiety of Land and Meadow belonging or in any wise app^{r}taining And alsoe all ye Estate, Right, Title, Interest use property Possession reverçon remaind^r Claime and Demand whatsoever of him ye s^d Elihu Gunnison and his heirs of in and to ye same To have and to hold all ye above granted and bargained Premisses with their Appur^{ces} and every part thereof unto ye said William Pepperel his heirs and Assigns for ever to his and their only Sole & proper use benefit and behoofe from henceforth and for ever more/ Yielding and paying therefore unto our Soveraign Lord and Lady, the King & Queen their heires or Success^{rs} &c. The one Moiety of ye afores^d Añuall Quit Rent in manner as afores^d And ye s^d Elihu Gunnison for himselfe his heirs Execut^{rs} and Admin^{rs} doth hereby covenant promise grant and Agree, to & with ye s^d William Pepperrell his heirs and Assignes in manner Following That is to say That att and Imediately before the time of ye Ensealing and delivery of these presents, he the s^d Elihu Gunnison is the true Sole & Lawfull owner And stands Lawfully Siezed of and in all the afore bargained Premisses with th'Appurtenances in his own proper Right of a good perfect & Indefeasible Estate of Inheritance in Fee Simple, having in himselfe full power good Right and Lawfull Authority to grant sell convey and Assure the same in manner & form afores^d Free and Clere and Clerely Acquitted Exonerated and Discharged of and from all and all manner of former and other gifts grants bargains Sales leases releases Mortgages Joyntures Dowers Judgm^{ts} Executions Entails forfeitures And of and from all other titles troubles Charges and encumbrances whatsoev^r had made comitted done or Suffered to be done by the s^d Elihu Gunnison his heirs or Assigns at any time or times before the Ensealing hereof And Further that ye s^d Elihu Gunnison doth hereby Coven^t promise grant and agree bind and oblige himselfe his heirs Execut^{rs} & Admin^{rs} from time to time and at all times for ever hereafter to warrant & defend all ye above granted & bargained Premisses with th'appur^{ces} thereof unto ye said William Pepperrell his heires and Assigns for ever (in his and their peaceable possession and Seizen) against ye Lawfull Claimes of all and every pson and persons whomesoever, from by or und^r me or by my procurem^t/ In witness whereof ye s^d Elihu Gunnison and Elizabeth his wife/ In Testimony of the Relinqushm^t of all her Right of Dower and power of thirds to be had & Claimed in and to ye s^d Premisses, have hereunto Set their hands and Seales, the day and year first above written/ The words from by or und^r me or by my procurem^t were inserted before Signing Sealing and deliuery of these presents in ye fifty fifth line. Signed Sealed and deliuered   Elihu Gunnison (his seal)

in presents of us.
William ffernald
John Newmarch
John fford.
York ss/
Kittery June. 17th 1700.

The above named Elihu Gunnison psonally before me ye subscrib^r one of ye memb^{rs} of his Ma^{ts} Council of ye Province of ye Massachusets Bay and Justice of Peace within ye same/ Acknowledged the above Instrum^t to be his Act and Deed.

Jos Hamond

A true Copie of ye originall Transcribed and compared.
June 17 : 1700   p Jos Hamond Regist^r

Know all men by these presents that I Sarah Pope Widow, now resident in ye Town of Kittery for and in consideration of ye Sum of three pounds ten shillings alredy paid me by M{r} William Pepperrell of Kittery, whereof & wherewith I doe Acknowledge myselfe to be fully Satisfied and contented for a neck of land comonly called y{e} Middle neck which is on y{e} Western side of y{e} little River comonly called Scadlocks River within the township of Winter harb{r} in the County of York, butting on y{e} one Side to the Salt Meadows, runing East to the cove called Whale Cove and bounded on the other side with y{e} Sea three or four score Acres being more or less To have and to hold the s{d} neck of Land with all y{e} Appurtenances and priviledges as sold unto my late husband Richard Pope Dec{d} And now belongeth to me Relict and Administratrix to the Estate of y{e} said Richard Pope Deceas{d}, which neck of Land was purchased and bought by my late husband Pope, of M{r} Pendleton ffletcher as may appear by a Deed of Sale und{r} the s{d} Fletchers hand bearing date y{e} eighth day of June one thousand six hundred Ninety and one, which said neck of Land I doe by these presents Alienate enfeoffe sell and confirm unto the aboves{d} M{r} William Pepperrell his heires Execut{rs} Admin{rs} & Assigns for ever freely peaceably and quietly to enjoy without any lett or deniall of me the s{d} Sarah Pope my heires Execut{rs} or Admin{rs} or Assigns or any by or under me And alsoe I doe by these presents further engage that y{e} said M{r} Pepperrell his Execut{rs} and Assigns Shall at all times when required give Liberty to me and my heires &c and owners of y{e} Marsh unto which y{e} s{d} Neck is butted, to cut soe much timb{r} of y{e} s{d} Neck as is nessessary to fence s{d} Marsh from time to time on which consideration I y{e} s{d} Sarah Pope doth coven{t} for my selfe and heires &c, nevermore to Claim any Right or propriety to y{e} s{d} Neck/ And furthermore doe afirm that all y{e} aforementioned Premises at y{e} time of y{e} delivery hereof is free from all other Sales or Incumbrances whatsoever and that I y{e} s{d} Pope is y{e} proper owner thereof, with Warrantys against all persons whatsoever and that for

Pope to Pepperrel

ever by these presents. unto all which I haue hereunto Set my hand and Seale this first day of September Anno Dom̃. One thousand six hundred ninety and four.

The word score interlined before ye Signing hereof under ye eight line.

Signed Sealed and delivered   the mark of
   In ye presents of us.   Sarah Pope. (her seal)
Daniel Rindge
    The mark of
Patience P Creasie

Sarah Pope came. and Acknowledged this Instrum^t to be her Act and Deed this first day of Septemb^r 1694/ Before me

                       ffrancis Hooke Jus^t pea

A true Copie of the origenall Transcribed and Compared the : 17th of June. 1700/.

                       p Jos Ham̃ond Regist^r

[60] To all People to whome these presents shall come Know yee that I Elihu Gunnison of Kittery in ye County of of York Shipwright for and in consideration of ye sum of six pounds in money to me in hand paid by Samuel Prey of ye same place Marrin^r at and before ye Ensealing and deliuery of these presents wherewith I confess myselfe to be fully Satisfied contented and paid Have bargained and sold and by these presents doe fully clerely and Absolutely bargain and sell Alien Enfeoffe and confirm unto ye s^d Samuel Prey his heirs and Assigns for ever all that tract of Land whereon his now dwelling house standeth containing one cre and a halfe more or less fronting Crooked lane or branch of the Maine River of Piscataqua being twelve pole in breadth by s^d River and soe to Low-water mark ye same

breadth and to run back by the same breadth to the present high way or road that goes to y® point or to y® s^d Elihu Gunnisons house or ferry and is bounded on y® Northwest by the lands of Mr Hubert, by an Northeast line And Southwest with Crooked Lane, And y® above s^d highway on Northeast And Southeast with y® Lands of y® s^d Gunnison, together with all y® Appurtenances and Priviledges Easments profits comodities Hereditaments whatsoever thereunto belonging or in any wise Appurtaining To have and to hold the s^d tract of Land as it is bounded set forth and described And every part thereof unto y® only use benefit and behoofe of him y® s^d Samuel Prey his heirs and Assigns for ever And y® s^d Elihu Gunnison for himselfe his Execut^rs and Admin^rs & for every of them, doth covenant promise and grant to and with y® s^d Samuel Prey his heirs Execut^rs Admin^rs and Assigns by these presents that at y® time and before y® ensealing of these presents that he y® s^d Elihu Gunnison was Lawfully Siezed of y® above mentioned Lands and every part thereof And that I now have full and good Right and Lawfull Authority and true title to grant Alien bargain sell and confirm the before bargained Premisses unto y® s^d Samuel Prey his heires and Assignes in manner and form as above s^d And that y® Premisses are free from all Incumbrances whatsoever, As sales gifts Joyntures Dowers Mortgages Judgm^ts Executions and all whatsoever had made comitted suffered or done by y® s^d Elihu Gunnison or any other person under him And that from henceforth it shall and may be Lawfull for y® s^d Samuel Prey to take use ocupie possess and enjoy the s^d land to his own proper use benefit and behoofe for ever, the peaceable & quiet possession thereof to warrant and maintaine against all persons that shall lay a Lawfull Claime thereunto in Testimony hereof I have hereunto set

Gunnison to Prey

my hand & seale this twenty third day of August One thousand six hundred ninety & nine.

Signed Sealed and delivered   Elihu Gunnison (his seal)
    in presents of us
    George Ingersoll
    Wm Godsoe.

Mr Elihue Gunnison Appeared before me the Subscrib^r at Portsm° in New Hampshier this sixth day of Decemb^r 1699. And Acknowledged the above Instrum^t to be his Act and Deed.   Sam^{ll} Penhallow Jus^{te} p^{ce}

A true Copie of the originall Deed Transcribed & compared this third day of July 1700.

                      p Jos Hamond Regist^r

Know all men by these presents that I John Heard of Kittery in ye County of York in the Province of ye Massachusets Bay in New England Yeoman, for and in consideration of ye sum of one pound and sixteen shillings of Lawfull money of New England to me in hand paid at and before ye Ensealing and Delivery hereof by John Nemarch of ye same town County and Province afores^d/ the receipt whereof I doe hereby Acknowledge and myselfe therewith fully Satisfied have given granted bargained and sold and doe by these presents give grant bargain sell Alien and Enfeoffe unto ye aboves^d John Newmarch his heirs and Assigns a certain tract of land lying and being in ye township of Kittery containing fifty Acres as it was laid out and bounded to me ye s^d John Heard by the Survei^{rs} of ye town of Kittery William Godsoe and Nicholas Gowen on ye 26 of Augst 1699. the bounds of s^d land are as followeth Viz^t begining at ye North end of Maj^r Hooks farm lying near ye Road which goeth from Spruce to Stirgeon Creek And is in length one hundred and Eighty eight poles North and South And in breadth forty four poles east and west/ bounded on ye east by yᵉ sᵈ John Newmarchis land on yᵉ South by Majʳ Hookes land And on yᵉ west and North by the Comons Together with all yᵉ Appurtenances and Priviledges to sᵈ land or any part of it belonging or any ways Appertaining provided yᵉ sᵈ land be not laid out in any Persons propriety To have and to hold sᵈ land with all yᵉ Appurtenances thereof and euery of yᵉ above granted premisses unto yᵉ sᵈ John Newmarch his heires and Assigns for ever And to yᵉ sole proper use benefit and behoofe of him yᵉ sᵈ John Newmarch his heirs &c. for evermore/ And yᵉ sᵈ John Heard doth for himselfe his heirs &c covenant and promise to and with yᵉ sᵈ John Newmarch his heirs &c/ That it shall and may be Lawfull to and for yᵉ sᵈ John Newmarch his heirs Executʳˢ Adminʳˢ and Assigns for ever hereafter quietly and peaceably to have hold use ocupie possess and enjoy to his and their use and uses all yᵉ Demised premisses with every of yᵉ Appurtenances free and clere as a good and absolute Estate of Inheritance in ffee simple without any condition whatsoever soe as to alter and make Voyd yᵉ same provided as above that yᵉ sᵈ Land or any part of it be not laid out in any particutlar propriety And I yᵉ sᵈ John Heard for my selfe my heirs &c the sᵈ bargained and sold premisses unto yᵉ sᵈ John Newmarch his heires &c. against all manner of psons from by or under me And against all other psons will warrant and Defend by these presents for ever In witness whereof I yᵉ sᵈ John Heard have hereunto set my hand and seal this nineteenth day of April Anno Domini One thousand & Seven hundred.

marginal note: Heard to Newmarch

Signed Sealed & dd   John Heard. (his seal)

  in yᵉ presents of us
  Mercy Smith.
  Hannah Hamond
  York ss/ Kittery April 19ᵗʰ 1700

Book VI, Fol. 61.

The above named John Heard personally Appearing before me yᵉ Subscribʳ one of yᵉ membʳˢ of his Majᵗˢ Council of yᵉ Province of yᵉ Massachusets Bay and Justice of Peace within yᵉ same Acknowledged the above Instrument to be his Act & Deed.

Jos Hamond

A true Copie of yᵉ originall Transcribed and compared this: Nineteenth day of April: 1700.

p Jos Hamond Registʳ

Be it known unto all men by these presents that I Diggory Jefferyes of Kittery in New England have for and in consideration of yᵉ Sum of Sixty pounds sterling to me in hand secured by Mʳ Roger Dearing of Kittery Shipwright whereof and wherewith I doe Acknowledge my selfe to be fully Satisfied and contented for a parcel of land and housing being in yᵉ aforesᵈ Town of Kittery, have given granted bargained Sold Aliend enfeoffed and confirmed And doe by these presents give grant bargain and sell unto yᵉ sᵈ Mʳ Dearing his heires Executⁿ Adminⁿ or Assignes one dwelling house and other out housing thereunto belonging, with one hundred Acres of upland and Marsh Adjacent unto yᵉ sᵈ house forever [**61**] which sᵈ house and land did formerly belong to George Pamer and afterwards Possessed by Docter Henry Greenland and then Possessed by William Broad Decesed and afterwards by my selfe as may Appear more at large by Severall conveiances; which sᵈ housing and Land lyeth in yᵉ aforesᵈ town of Kittery in yᵉ Lower part thereof, butted and bounded as followeth that is to say, on yᵉ west side bounded by Majʳ Shapleighs Land begining at a place comonly called yᵉ Steping Stones which is near to a Small Neck of land which formerly John Pearce lived on and from thence on a North and beast line to a hemlock tree marked with a D and an I. And from thence by marked trees to a fresh brook And from thence Southwarly to run to y͏ͤ afores͏ͩ Steping Stones which brook is Adjacent unto a piece of land comonly called Lockwoods land To have and to hold the afores͏ͩ housen & land with all trees woods priviledges and Appurtenances thereunto belonging to y͏ͤ only use and behoofe of y͏ͤ s͏ͩ M͏ͬ Dearing his heires Execut͏ͬˢ Administrat͏ͬˢ or Assigns and to and with every of them by these presents/ And that all y͏ͤ aforementioned at y͏ͤ time of ensealing and delivery of these presents are and shall at all times hereafter be and remain and continue clearly Acquitted and discharged or otherwise saved and kept harmless from all former gifts and bargains whatsoever And from all other pson or psons whatsoever Claiming any Interest therein or any part thereof shall and will warrant and forever defend According to y͏ͤ true intent & meaning of these presents And to noe other intent use or purpose whatsoever/ Always provided that y͏ͤ s͏ͩ M͏ͬ Dering his heirs Execut͏ͬˢ Admin͏ˢ or Assignes doe not hind͏ͬ or Interupt me and my now wife Ann Jefferys in y͏ͤ quiet possession of y͏ͤ aboves͏ͩ housing and Land during our Naturall lives with all y͏ͤ priviledges thereunto belonging, then this Deed to stand good and firm against me and heirs &c for ever; to which I have hereunto set my hand and seal this first day of Septemb͏ͬ Anno Dom̃. 1694.

Signed Sealed and delivered   the mark of
   in presents of us   Diggory D Jeffry (his seal)
   Clement Jackson   the mark of
   Andrew Hallye   Ann. A Jeffry (her seal)

Diggory Jeffery and Ann his wife came & Acknowledged this Instrument to be their Act and Deed to M͏ͬ Roger Dering, this first day of Septemb͏ͬ 1694. Before me
                         ffrancis Hooke Just Peace

Book VI, Fol. 61.

A true Copie of ye originall Transcribed and Compared April 1st 1700

p Jos Hamond Regist^r

Stackpole
to
Wade

Know all men by these presents that I James Stagpoll of Dover in New Hampshier in New England husbandman for a Sum of money in hand paid or secured by Mr John Wade Minist^r of Barwick in the County of York in New England, doe by these presents sell and confirm a certain parcle of Land Scituate in s^d Barwick near the Meeting house which I bought of Epraim Joy Dec^d Containing three Acres and a quarter be it more or less being forty Rod in Length and thirteen Rod in breadth bounded on the southeast by the way going from the great work to the River Northeast by Mr John Plaisteds land Sometime called Parkers field Northwest by the Burying place in ye Land of Humphrey Spencer, heir to William Spencer Deceased; Southwest by land of s^d Spencer or the Countrey Road, with all the housing trees fences & Priviledges pertaining thereto/ And Assigne Ephraim Joys Deed from William Spencer of s^d Land, with the Indorsed Assignm^t thereon, to s^d Mr John Wade his heires and Assigns for ever. To have and to hold and quietly to possess and enjoy ye same or According to pleasure to dispose of it as an Estate in Fee Simple without Molestation or Interuption from my selfe my wife my heires Execut^{rs} Admin^{rs} or Assigns fully discharged from all former and other gifts, Sales, Mortgages, Rents, thirds or Legall Incumbrances for ever, In witness whereof I have hereto set my hand and seal this twenty second day of Novemb^r In ye year of our Lord one thousand six hundred & Ninety nine And the Eleventh year of ye Reign of William the third.

Signed Sealed and delivered James Stagpoll (his seale)
  In presets of.
  Thomas Goodin
  Samuel Savery
  Timothy Gerrish
    York ss, Kittery April 8th 1700

The above named James Stackpole psonally Appearing before me ye Subscrib^r one of ye memb^{rs} of his Ma^{ts} Council of the Province of ye Massachusets Bay And Justice of Peace within ye Same Acknowledged ye above Instrum^t to be his Act and Deed.

                                    Jos Hamond

A true Copie of ye original Deed Transcribed and compared this Eigth day of April 1700.

                        p Jos Hamond Regist^r

This Indenture made ye one and thirtieth day of Octob^r Anno Dom one thousand six hundred Ninety four, Annoq, R R^s et Reginæ Gulielmiæ et Mariæ Angliæ &c. Sexto, Between Ephraim Turner of Newport on Rhode Island in New England Brasiar of ye one part and Benjamin Gillam of Boston in the County of Suffolk in ye Province of the Massachusets Bay in New England Marrin^r Son of Zechariah Gillam Sometime of Boston Marrin^r Deceased of ye other part, Witnesseth, that ye s^d Ephraim Turner for and in consideration of Eight Shillings of Lawfull money of New England

Turner to Gillam   to him in hand paid by Benjamin Gillam afores^d And before ye Ensealing and Delivery of these pres^ts Hath Bargained and sold and by these presents doth Bargain and sell unto the s^d Benjamin Gillam his heirs Executⁱˢ Adminⁱˢ and Assigns All that piece or parcel of land Scituate lying and being upon Saco River in yᵉ County of Yorkshiere or Province of Mayn in New England which William Phillips and Bridget his wife Granted unto Zechariah Gillam afores⁴ and the s⁴ Ephraim Turner by one Deed under yᵉ hands and seales of s⁴ William Phillips and Bridget Phillips bearing Date yᵉ Eighth day of July one thousand Six hundred Seventy Six, as alsoe one eighth part of a Mine lying in yᵉ Countrey above s⁴ Saco River, And all yᵉ Timbʳ, trees, woods, underwoods profits comodities and Appurtenances whatsoever to yᵉ s⁴ tract of land Mine & land trees and Appurᶜᵉˢ whatsoever thereunto belonging or in any wise Appurtaining or therewᵗʰ or any part thereof Demised, letten used ocupied or enjoyed, or Accepted reputed taken or known as part parcel or membʳ thereof, & yᵉ reverc̃on reverc̃ons [**62**] Remaindʳ & remaindⁱˢ Rents Issues and profits of s⁴ Lands and premisses and every part and parcel thereof To have and to hold the s⁴ tract of land containing five hundred Acres, as alsoe yᵉ Mine, and, all and Singular yᵉ Premisses hereby granted and Sold or herein before menc̃oned meant or intended to be bargained and sold And every part and parcel thereof with their and every of their Appurtᶜᵉˢ unto yᵉ s⁴ Benjamin Gillam his Execut⁴ˢ Adminⁱˢ and Assigns from yᵉ day next before yᵉ day of yᵉ Date of these presᵗˢ unto yᵉ full end & term of one whole year from thence next ensuing and fully to be compleat and ended to yᵉ end and intent that yᵉ s⁴ Benjamin Gillam may be in yᵉ Actuall possession of yᵉ s⁴ lands Mine and Premisses And may hereby And by a Subsequent grant release or other conveyance hereafter to be made of the Premisses And by force of the Statute for Transferring Uses into Possession be enabled to Accept and take yᵉ reverc̃on and Inheritance of yᵉ s⁴ lands and Premisses to him yᵉ s⁴ Benjamin Gillam his heirs and Assigns, to and for yᵉ only proper use and behoofe of him s^d Benjamin Gillam his heirs and Assigns for ever, Yielding & paying for ye Premisses unto ye s^d Ephraim Turnor his heires or Assigns, the yearly Rent of a pepper corn only upon ye last day of ye s^d Term of one whole year if the same shall be then Lawfully Demanded. In witness whereof ye parties to these present Indentures interchangeably have set to their hands and Seales, the day and year first above written.

Ephraim (his seal) Turnor

Signed Sealed and delivered Boston in New England
in the presents of Novr pr^o 1694.
Arthur Mason Junr
Joseph Webb. Mr Ephraim Turnor psonally

Turnor to Gillam

Boston from March. pr^o 169¾ Entred and Recorded with ye Records of Deeds for the County of Suffolk Lib: 18th pa: 82/3 Attest^r Joseph Webb Reg^r

appearing before me ye Subscrib^r one of their Ma^ts Council in the Province of ye Massachusets Bay and Justice of Peace in ye same Acknowledged this Instrum^t to be his Act & Deed/.   Sam Sewall

A true Copie of ye origenall Transcribed and compared the 21st day of Septem: 1700/

p Jos Hamond Regist^r

This Indenture the twelfth day of Decemb^r Anno Domini 1698. in the tenth year of the Reign of our Soveraign Ld William the third by the grace of God of England Scotland ffrance and Ireland King Defend^r of ye ffaith &c Between Ephraim Turnor of Rhode Island in New England formerly of Boston in ye County of Suffolk within his Ma^ts Province Province of ye Massachusets Bay in New England Brazier of ye one part, And Benjamin Gillam of Poston afores^d Marrin^r of ye other part Witnesseth/ that ye s^d Ephraim Turnor for and in consideration of ye Sum of five Shillings Lawfull money of New England to him in hand paid by the s^d Benjamin Gillam at or before ye Ensealing and delivery of these presents, the receipt whereof the s^d Ephraim Turnor doth hereby Acknowledge hath bargained and sold And by these presents doth Bargain and sell unto the said Benjamin Gillam his Execut^{rs} Admin^{rs} and Assigns All that tract piece or parcel of Land Scituate lying and being near to Saco River in ye County of Yorkshier or ye Province of Mayn, containing by Estimation four hundred Acres or thereabouts, be the same more or less/ Butted and bounded Northeasterly by ye land formerly Zechariah Gillams & s^d Ephraim Turnors, but now ye land of ye s^d Benjamin Gillam, As will Appear by a Deed thereof made and Executed According to Law from ye s^d Ephraim Turnor to ye s^d Benjamin Gillam bearing date the first day of Novemb^r Anno Domini one thousand Six hundred Ninety and four Northwesterly by ye land of William Hutchinson formerly called Liscombs Lott Southeasterly or Southwesterly on ye Southeasterly or Southwesterly side of West brook by the land of Maj^r Bryan Pendleton and runing between ye bounds of ye s^d Hutchinson and Pendleton about four Miles from Saco River afores^d, As contained in a Deed, duly and Lawfully Executed under ye hands and Seales of William Phillips & Bridget his wife made to ye s^d Ephraim Turner which bears date ye eighth day of July one thousand Six hundred Seventy and Six/ And alsoe all wayes waters timber trees woods Rents profits Priviledges, Hereditaments Emoluements comodities and Appur^{ces} whatsoever to ye s^d Tract or parcel of land belonging or in any wise Appurtaining or therewith used ocupied or enjoyed Accepted reputed taken or known as part parcel or memb^r thereof And ye rvercon and rever͠cons, remaind'r and remaind'rs thereof/ And alsoe all y'e full & whole Estate Right, Title, Interst use possession property Claim Inheritance And Demand whatsoever of him y'e s'd Ephraim Turner of in or to y'e s'd Tract or parcel of Land and Premisses, with the Appurtenances, To have and to hold all and Singular y'e s'd Tract or parcel of land and Premisses, with the Appur'ces to y'e s'd Benjamin Gillam his Execut'rs Admin'rs and Assigns from y'e day before y'e Date hereof, and for and during the term of one whole year from thence next ensuing and fully to be compleat and ended Yielding and paying therefore the Rent of one Pepper corn at y'e feast of S't Michael y'e Arch Angell, if y'e same be Demanded/ To the intent that by vertue of these presents and of y'e statute for Transferring of uses into Possession the s'd Benjamin Gillam may be in y'e Actuall Possession of y'e Premisses and be enabled to Accept a Grant of y'e rever͠con and Inheritance thereof, to him his heirs and Assigns for ever/ In witness whereof y'e s'd Ephraim Turnor hath hereunto set his hand & Seal the day and year first above written.

Turnor to Gillam

     Ephraim (his seal) Turner

Signed Sealed & delivered
 In the presents of us
 John Gerrish
 John Vallentine

Suffolk ss/ Boston in New England 13th Decemb'r 1698

The within named Ephraim Turnor psonally Appearing before me y'e Subscrib'r one of his Ma'ts Justices of the Peace for the County afores'd Acknowledged this Instrum't to be his free Act and Deed   Jer Du͠mer.

 Boston Decemb'r 29th 1698

Recorded with y'e Records of Deedes for y'e County of Suffolk Lib XIX, pa : 37.

      p Ad'ton Davenport Regist'r

BOOK VI, FOL. 63.

A true Copie of the originall Transcribed and Compared the 21st Septemb^r 1700

p Jos Hamond Regist^r

[63] This Indenture made the first day of Novemb^r Anno Dom^i One thousand six hundred Ninety four Annoq R R^s et Reginæ Gulielmiæ et Mariæ Angliæ &c Sexto/ Between Ephraim Turnor of on Rhode Island in New England formerly of Boston in ye County of Suffolk in ye Province of the Massachusets Bay in New England Brazier of the one part And Benjamin Gillam of Boston afores^d Marin^r, Son of Zechariah Gillam Sometime of Boston afores^d Marin^r, Dec^d of the other part/ Whereas by one Deed or writing under ye hands and Seales of William Phillips of Saco in ye County of Yorkshiere or Province of Maine in New England afores^d & Bridget his wife bearing Date the eighth day of July Anno Domini one thousand Six hundred seventy & six Acknowledged and Recorded with ye Records of the County of York, did give grant Alien Enfeoffe and confirm unto Zechariah Gillam afores^d and to ye afores^d Ephraim Turnor a certain pcel or Tract of Land lying on Saco River on ye southwest side thereof, being about five hundred Acres, bounded on the Northeast side wth Saco River on the Northwest with Liscombs Lott, now ye land of William Hutchinson (with this Addition to the grant afores^d) Runing over West brook home to ye land of Maj^r Bryan Pendletons Southeasterly And from low water mark of Saco River afors^d, runing between ye afores^d boundaries of Hutchinsons and Pendletons including West brook up into the Country, untill the full and Just quantity of five hundred Acres be Measured To have and to hold the s^d tract or parcell of Land butted bounded and Measuring as afores^d, with all ye timb^r

Turnor
to
Gillam

trees woods und^r woods thereon, standing growing or belonging, Alsoe one eighth part of a Mine, lying & being up in the Countrey above Saco River in which Maj^r Thomas Clark, Mr Edw. Tyng Senr Mr John Hull and s^d William Phillips and others were partners, with one eighth part of all ye Lands woods trees and priviledges thereunto belonging or in any wise Appurtaining to them ye said Sons in Law Zechariah Gillam & Ephraim Turnor their heirs & Assigns for ever As by s^d Deed bearing Date as afores^d Relation being thereunto had may more plainly and at Large Appear/ Now this Indenture Witnesseth That ye s^d Ephraim Turnor As well for and in consideration of Eight pounds of good and Currant money of New England to him in hand well and truly paid by the s^d Benjamin Gillam at & before the Sealing and delivery of these presents, the receipt whereof he the s^d Ephraim Turn^r doth hereby Acknowledge And himselfe to be therewith fully paid & satisfied, and thereof and of every part and parcel thereof doth fully and Absoutely Acquit release and for ever discharge the s^d Benjamin Gillam his heires and Assigns for ever by these presents, And for other good causes and considerations him s^d Ephraim Turnor thereunto moving Hath granted bargained sold Aliened released and quit Claimed and confirmed, And by these presents Doth fully and Absolutely, grant, bargain, Sell Alien release quit Claim and for ever confirm unto ye s^d Benjamin Gillam in his Actuall Possession of ye s^d Lands herein mentioned with their Appurtenances, being by Vertue of one Indenture of Lease or bargaine and Sale to him thereof made for one year, by and from ye s^d Ephraim Turner bearing Date the day next before the day of ye Date of these pres^ts and by force of ye Statute for Transferring uses into Possession in that behalfe made and provided, And to ye heires of ye s^d Benjamin Gillam All that afores^d parcel or Tract of land Scituate Lying and being upon Saco Riv^r afores^d in y^e

BOOK VI, FOL. 63.

County of Yorkshier or Province of Maine And all and every the woods, timb^r, trees Standing and growing thereon And all and every part & parcel thereof with all ye profits liberties priviledges comodities Rights hereditam^{ts} and Appur^{ces} whatsoever to ye afóres^d Tract or parcel of land belonging or in any wise Appurtaining or therewith or any parcell thereof Demised Letten used ocupied & enjoyed or accepted reputed taken or known as part parcell or memb^{rs} thereof/ And the reverc͠on and reverc͠ons remaind^r and remaind^{rs} Rents Issues profits of ye s^d Lands and Premisses And alsoe ye s^d Eighth part of a Mine lying and being in ye Countrey above Saco River as is before mentioned with one eighth part of all the woods trees and priviledges thereunto belonging or in any wise Appurtaining And all the Estate Title Interest possession Rents reverc͠on property benefit Claim and Demand of him the s^d Ephraim Turner and his heires of in and to the s^d Lands & Premisses hereby granted And of in and to every part and parcel thereof To have & to hold the s^d Tract or parcel of Land butted bounded and measuring and containing as afores^d with ye liberties priviledges and premisses hereby granted bargained, sold released and quitclaimed and confirmed or hereby meant or mentioned to be granted bargained sold released quitclaimed and confirmed As alsoe s^d Eighth part of s^d Mine with all ye Premisses therewith granted unto the s^d Benjamin Gillam his heires and Assignes for ever to and for ye only poper use and behoofe of him s^d Benjamin Gillam his heires and Assignes for evermore And ye s^d Ephraim Turner for himselfe and his heires/ All ye above mentioned Tract of land Eighth part of the Mine afores^d with all the premisses and Appur^{ces} thereto belonging ag^t himself his heires unto ye s^d Benjamin Gillam his heires and Assigns shall and will Warrant and Defend And ye s^d Ephraim Turner doth covenant promise and grant to and with ye s^d Benjamin Gillam his heires and Assignes, in manner and form following That is to say that yᵉ sᵈ Ephraim Turnor is the true and Lawfull owner of yᵉ above granted Premisses by vertue of yᵉ afore resited Deed of William Phillips and Bridget his wife of a good and perfect Estate of Inheritance in ffee simple And hath in himselfe full Right and Lawfull power and Authority yᵉ Same to convey and Assure And that yᵉ sᵈ Benjamin Gillam shall and may peaceably and quietly have hold use Ocupie Possess and Enjoy all yᵉ before hereby granted and bargained Premisses and every part thereof, free and cleer & cleerly Acquitted and Discharged of and from All and all manner of former and other gifts grants bargains Sales Leases Joyntures Dowers Judgments Executions Entailes And of and from all other Titles, troubles, Charges and Incumbrances whatsoever had made done or comitted or Suffered to be done by him sᵈ Ephraim Turnor at any time before yᵉ ensealing and Delivery of these presents And further yᵉ sᵈ Ephraim Turnor doth Covenant and agree to and with yᵉ sᵈ Benjamin Gillam that he will at yᵉ proper Costs and Charges of sᵈ Benjamin Gillam his heires or Assignes make doe Acknowledge Execute and cause or procure to be made Acknowledged and Executed all and every Such Lawfull and reasonable Act or Acts Device and Devices conveyances and Assurances whatsoever for yᵉ better and more Absolute conveying Settling Assuring & confirming yᵉ sᵈ Tract of Land and All yᵉ before granted premisses and Appurtenances and every part thereof unto and upon yᵉ sᵈ Benjamin Gillam his heires and Assigns for ever as by his or their Council learned in yᵉ Law shall be reasonably Devised Advised or required And lastly it is covenanted granted declared & agreed by and between yᵉ parties to these presents and is the true Intent and meaning of these presents that all and every yᵉ fine and fines recovery and recoveryes conveyances and Assurances whatsoever Alredy made Levied Acknowledged and Executed of the Premisses hereby granted, and yᵉ force Effect and Execution of them & every of them shall be and enure And shall be Deemed Adjudged taken and Construed to be & enure and is hereby Declared to be and enure to and for ye only proper use and behoofe of the sd Benjamin Gillam and to his heires and Assigns for ever And for noe other use intent or purpose whatsoever/ In witness whereof ye sd Ephraim Turner hath hereunto set his hand and Seal, the day and year first aboue written.

Ephraim (his seal) Turner

Sealed and delvered in
  presets of us
  Arthur Mason Junr
  Joseph Webb.

                    Boston in New England Novembr prio 1694

	Mr Ephraim Turner psonally Apearing before me ye Subscribr
Boston/ March pro 169¾ Entred and recorded with ye Records for Deeds for ye County of Suffolk Lib: 18 : 83 : 4 : 5	one of ye Council of their Mats Province of the Massachusets Bay and a Justice of ye Peace in ye Same Acknowledged this Instrumt to be his Act and Deed
Attest p Joseph Webb Regr	Sam̅ Sewall

A true Copie of ye origenall Transcribed & compared Sepr 21st 1700

                    p Jos Ham̅ond Regr

[64] This Indenture made the thirteenth day of Decembr Anno Domini 1698 And in the tenth year of the Reign of our Soveraign Lord William the third by the grace of God of England Scotland ffrance and Ireland King Defendr of the ffaith &c/ Between Ephraim Turner of Rhode Island in New England, formerly of Boston in the County of Suffolk

within his Majesties Province of yᵉ Massachusets Bay in New England, Brazier of yᵉ one part. And Benjamin Gillam of Boston aforesᵈ Marinʳ of yᵉ other part Witnesseth. That yᵉ sᵈ Ephraim Turnor for and in Consideration of yᵉ Sum of nine pounds Curᵗ money of New England, to him in hand well and truely paid by the sᵈ Benjamin Gillam at and before yᵉ ensealing and delivery of these presents the receipt whereof he yᵉ sᵈ Ephraim Turner doth hereby Acknowledge to full content and satisfaction And thereof and of every part & parcell thereof doth fully and absolutely Acquit Exonerate and Discharge yᵉ sᵈ Benjamin Gillam his heirs and Assigns for ever by these presents hath given granted, bargained sold, Aliend, Enfeoffeed, Released, quit Claimed and Confirmed And by these presents doth fully freely cleerly and Absolutely give, grant, bargain, sell Alien Enfeoffe release quit Claim and confirm unto yᵉ sᵈ Benjamin Gillam, in his Actuall Possession of yᵉ Lands and Tenements hereafter mecōned now being by vertue of a bargain and sale for a year to him thereof made by the sᵈ Ephraim Turnor by Indenture bearing date the day next before yᵉ day of yᵉ Date into hereof and by force of yᵉ Statute for Transferring of uses Possession. All that Tract piece or parcell of Land Scituate lying and being near to Saco River in the County of York-

Turnor
to
Gillam

shier in yᵉ Province of yᵉ Maine containing by Estimation four hundred Acres or therabouts be the same more or less, butted and bounded Northeasterly by yᵉ Land formerly Zechariah Gillams, and sᵈ Ephraim Turners but now yᵉ land of yᵉ sᵈ Benjamin Gillam (as will Appear by a Deed to him thereof made and Executed According to Law from yᵉ sᵈ Eprhraim Turner bearing Date yᵉ first day of Novembʳ Anno Domini one thousand six hundred Ninety and four) Northwesterly by yᵉ Land of William Hutchinson formerly called Liscombs Lott Southeasterly or Southwesterly on yᵉ Southeasterly or Southwesterly side of West Brook by the land of Majʳ

Bryan Pendleton And runing betwen the bounds of y̌ Lands of y̌ s^d Hutchinson and Pendleton about four Miles from Saco River afores^d as contained in a Deed duly and Lawfully Executed under y̌ hands & seales of William Phillips and Bridget his wife made to y̌ s^d Ephraim Turnor, which bears date y̌ eighth day of July one thousand Six hundred seventy and six And alsoe all wayes waters, timber, trees Rents, woods, profits, priviledges, hereditam^ts, Emolum^ts, comodities and Appur^ces whatsoever to y̌ s^d Tract or parcell of land belonging or in any wise Appurtaining or therewith used ocupied and enjoyed, Accepted, reputed taken & known as part parcel or memb^r thereof, And y̌ reversion & revesions remaind^r & remaind^rs thereof And also all y̌ full and whole Estate Right Title Interest use possession prop^r ty Claim Inheritance and Demand whatsoever, of him y̌ s^d Ephraim Turnor of & to y̌ s^d tract or parcel of land and Premisses with y̌ Appurtenances And alsoe all Deeds minnements and writings concerning y̌ Premisses/ To have and to hold y̌ s^d Tract or parcel of Land and all and Singular other y̌ Premisses with their Appur^ces unto y̌ s^d Benjamin Gillam his heirs and Assigns for ever To his and their only proper use benefit and behoofe for evermore/ To be holden of y̌ Lords of y̌ ffee by the rents therefore due and of right Accustomed to be paid/ And y̌ s^d Ephraim Turnor for himselfe his heires and Assigns the afores^d tract of land and all other the Premisses with y̌ Appur^ces unto y̌ s^d Benjamin Gillam his heirs & Assigns against himself y̌ s^d Ephraim Turner his heirs and Assigns, and against all persons whatsoever Claiming by from or under him or any of them shall and will Warrant and for ever Defend by these presents And the s^d Ephraim Turnor for himself his heirs and Assigns doth by these presents Covenant, promis grant and agree, to and with y̌ s^d Benjamin Gillam his heirs and Assigns in manner & form following that is to say, that he y̌ s^d Ephraim Turner is y⁰ true sole and Lawfull owner of all y⁰ above granted and released Premisses, and rightfully and Lawfully siezed thereof in a good sure perfect and Indefeazible Estate of Inheritance in ffee Simple, and hath in himselfe full power good Right and Lawfull Authority to grant release convey and Assure y⁰ same as in manner afores[d], And that y⁰ s[d] Benjamin Gillam his heirs and Assignes shall and may peaceably and quietly have hold use ocupie possess and Enjoy all y⁰ before hereby granted Premisses with y⁰ Appur[ces] and every part and parcel thereof free & cleere and cleerly and absolutely Acquitted and discharged of and from all and all manner of former and other gifts grants bargains sales Leases releases Joyntures Dowers Judgm[ts] Executions and of and from all other Titles troubles Charges & Incumbrances whatsoever, had done comitted or suffered by him y⁰ s[d] Ephraim Turner at any time before y⁰ Ensealing and delivery of these presents, And further that y⁰ s[d] Ephraim Turner his heires and Assigns at any time or times hereafter, shall and will at y⁰ proper Costs and Charges of y⁰ s[d] Benjamin Gillam his heires or Assigns when thereunto requested and Demanded, make, doe, Acknowledge Execute and perform And cause and procure to be made done Executed suffered and performed all and every such further and other Lawfull & reasonable Act & Acts thing and things, and devices and Assurances or conveyances in y⁰ Law whatsoever for y⁰ further better and more absolute conveying settleing, and Assuring of the s[d] Tract piece or parcell of Land herein before granted with y⁰ Premiss and Apur[ces] unto and upon y⁰ s[d] Benjamin Gillam his heires and Assigns for ever, According to the true intent and meaning of these presents, as by his or their Council Learned in the Law shall be reasonably Devised Advised or required. In witness whereof the s^d Ephraim Turner hath hereunto set his hand and seal ye day and year first aboue written

Ephraim (his seal) Turnor

Signed Sealed and delivered
 In the presents of us.
 John Gerrish.
 John Vallentine
 Not^ry Pub^liq.
 Suffolk ss/ Boston in New England
13th Decemb^r 1698.

The within named Ephraim Turnor personally Appearing before me ye Subscrib^r, one of his Ma^ts Justices of ye Peace for ye County Afores^d acknowledged this Instrum^t to be his free Act and Deed.

Jer: Dumer

A true Copie of ye originall Transcribed and compared Septemb^r the 21st 1700.

p Jos Hamond Regist^r

To all People before this Deed of gift shall come Greeting Now know ye that I Peter Hinkson of Linn in the County of Essex in this his Ma^ts Province of the Massachusets Bay in New-England husbandman for and in consideration of the love and good will that I bear to my Son Peter Hinckson of ye town of York in the Province of Maine, with Divers other good causes and considerations mufing me thereunto, the consideration whereof is to me ye s^d Peter Hinckson full and Ample satisfaction/ Have given granted bargained Alienated Infeoffed and [65] confirmed and doe by these presents further give, grant, bargain, Alienate Infeoffe and confirm unto ye s^d Peter Hinckson, a certain parcell of land containing by Estimation twenty and three Acres more or less. And it is situate in ye township of

Black point or Scarbro in the Province of Mayn and it is bounded Northerly with yᵉ land of William Shelding, Westerly with yᵉ land of John Mackenny and Christopher Picket, Southerly with the land of Joshua Scottoway, Easterly with yᵉ land of William Batting, And Alsoe a parcel of Marsh containing by Estimation ten Acres more or less And it is situate in yᵉ township of Black point abouesaid and it is bounded on yᵉ west and on yᵉ North with yᵉ land of John Libby, Southerly by the Land of Richard More, Easterly with yᵉ pine Crick/ And alsoe an other parcell of Upland and Marsh containing by Estimation fifty & Six Acres more or less, cituate in yᵉ township of Black point abovesᵈ bounded North and East with nonesuch River/ West with a little Brook, & from thence Ranging with two Mark trees upon a strait line to Nonesuch bridg together with yᵉ housing, fencing, timber, wood, grass, herbig, stones, ways uses members Heredittaments profits and improfments thereof/ To have

Peter Hinckson to his son Peter

and to hold all and Singular yᵉ above granted Premisses with what ever else is thereunto belonging or in any ways Appurtaining to him yᵉ sᵈ Peter Hinckson, him his heirs Lawfully begotten of his body, but if he die without Issue, to be to Elizabeth his wife during her naturall life And then to return to his father Peter Hinckson abovesᵈ or to his heires And this to be to their one only proper use benefit and behoof from henceforth and for ever more/ And further I yᵉ said Peter Hinckson doe for my selfe my heires Execut.ʳˢ and Admin.ʳˢ promise Covenant and grant to and with yᵉ sᵈ Peter Hinckson my son, his heirs Execut.ʳˢ Admin.ʳˢ that I am at this day and untill yᵉ Signing and Sealing of this Instrument, the true and Rightfull owner of the above granted Premisses And therefore have good Right full power and Lawfull Authority to make sale there—conuanc—of and that yᵉ sᵈ Peter Hinckson his heirs Lawfully begotten of his body as is above mentioned shall or may at all times and from time to time for ever hereafter peaceably and quietly have hold ocupie possess & injoy the same a good true absolute sure Indefesable title of Inheritance in ffee simple without the Lawfull Suit let hinderance Molestation controdiction or expultion of me the s^d Peter Hinckson or any other person or persons from by or under me, hereby promising for my selfe my heirs and Assigns to warrant maintain and Defend the above granted Premisses and every part thereof to the s^d Peter Hinckson his heires or Assignes for ever/ from all former gifts grants bargains Sales Leases Joynt^{rs} Dowers Wills entails Mortgages bonds or forfitures or any and all manner of Such like trouble had made or done at any time and from any other person or persons Lawfully Claiming or having any Right title or Intrust therein or any part thereof In witness whereof I ye s^d Peter Hinckson have set to my hand and afixed my seal this Sixteenth day of Novemb^r Anno Dominij Sixteen hundred Ninety and nine/ And in ye Eleventh year of our Soveraign Lord ye King over England &c.

Signed Sealed and delivered
   In pres^{ts} of.   Peter ⊕ Hinckson (his seale)
   John Hathorn Junr his mark
   Eben^r Hathorn
   Leuing Pearse

Peter Hinckson above named Acknowledged the above written Instrum^t to be his Act and Deed, Salem Novemb^r ye 18 : 1699. Before me John Hathorn one of the Council and Justice of Peace.

A true Copie of ye originall Deed Transcribed & compared. Apr^{ll} 3^d 1700

                                    p Jos Hamond Regist^r

Know all men by these presents that I Samuel Spinney of Kittery in ye County of York in New England Yeoman with ye consent of Elizabeth my wife, for Divers good and valuable considerations me hereunto moving, but more Especially for & in consideration of ye Sum of thirty four pounds in money to me in hand paid by my beloved brother John Spinney of ye same place Yeoman, the receipt thereof I doe Acknowledge And my selfe well and truely contented and paid And doe by these presents Acquit ye s^d John Spinney for the same for ye consideration aboves^d I ye s^d Samuel Spinney Have given, granted, bargained and sold, And doe by these presents Give, grant bargain and sell Enfeoff and for ever confirm unto ye s^d John Spinney his heires and Assigns All that Tract of Land lying in ye township of Kittery in ye County aboves^d containing forty Acres of Land be it more or Less And is Scituate and lying between ye great Cove and Spruce Creek and is bounded on the west with ye land of the late John Green, And on the South side with ye land of Thomas Spinney Senr and Thomas Spinney Junr and on ye North side with Staples lands and others And is that tract of land that was granted unto me by the town of Kittery and laid out by Cap^{tn} John Wincoll as by ye Records doth more at large Appear, together with all the woods underwood timber and trees standing or lying thereon with all the Appurtenances and priviledges thereunto belonging or in any wise Appurtaining unto ye same To have and to hold all and Singular ye above bargained Premisses and every part thereof unto ye only and sole use benefit and behoofe of him ye said John Spinney his heires and Assigns for ever more And furthermore I the s^d Samuel Spinney doe covenant for my selfe my heires Execut^{rs} and Admin^{rs} with ye s^d John Spinney his heirs & Assigns that ye Premisses are free from all encombrances whatsoever, as Joyntures, Dowers, gifts, Sales Mortgages or quit Rents And that at the time of ye ensealing hereof I am ye true and proper owner of the same and have within my selfe full power and Lawfull Authority

S. Spinney
to
J Spinney

to dispose of y̆ᵉ same And that it shall and may be Lawfull for yᵉ sᵈ John Spinney at all times hereafter to take use ocupie and Possess yᵉ Same. without the let or hinderance of me yᵉ sᵈ Samuel Spinney or any other person under me/ the Peaceable and quiet Possession thereof to warrant and maintaine against all persons whatsoever laying Lawfull Claim thereunto In witness hereof I have hereunto set my hand and Seal this twenty fift day of Novembʳ one thousand Six hundred Ninety & Nine : 1699

Signed Sealed and delivered   Samuel Spinney (his seal)
  in presᵗˢ of
Thomas Spinney Senʳ
James Spinney
Wᵐ Godsoe

Know all men by these presents that I Elizabeth Spinney doe freely Surrender all my Right of Dowery to yᵉ within mentioned Land in this Instrument, witness my hand this 25ᵗʰ Novembʳ 1699   The Signe of
    Elizab (E) Spinney.

York ss/ Kittery Augˢᵗ 12ᵗʰ 1700

The within and aboue named Samuel Spinney and Elizabeth his wife personally Appearing before me the Subscribʳ one of his Maᵗⁱˢ Justices of Peace for yᵉ County of York Acknowledged this Instrumᵗ to be their Act & Deed.

        Jos Hamond

A true Copie of yᵉ origenall transcribed & compared Augˢᵗ 12ᵗʰ 1700.

        p Jos Hamond Regʳ

[66] To all People to whome these presents may come Greeting/ Know ye that I Christian Remich of Kittery in yᵉ County of York in New England planter for and in consideration of an Execution obtained at a Superior Court at

Boston against s^d Remich by Sam^ll Spinney of Kittery afores^d Have, given, granted bargained and Sold And by these presents doe give grant bargain and sell Alien Enfeoffe and confirm to him ye s^d Sam^ll Spinney his heires and Assigns for ever a certain Lot of land lying and being in Kittery afores^d containing fifteen Acres and an halfe more or Less, with a frame now standing thereon with all ye wood und^r wood Herbage &c/ bounded as followeth Viz^t on ye West with Land formerly in Possession of Richd Kearle, on ye South with Thom^s Spiney Senr/ on ye East with Sam^ll Spinney, on ye North with John Dennet Sen with the priviledges of an high way, if there be any high way reserved in John Dennets Deed, runing from thence to ye water side, To have & to hold ye Premisses with the Priviledges and Appurtenances to ye same Appertaining or in any wise belonging to him ye s^d Sam^ll Spinney his heirs and Assigns for ever/ And I ye s^d Christian Remich for me my heirs Execut^rs Admin^rs doe covenant promise and grant to and with the said Sam^ll Spinney his heires Execut^rs and Admin^rs and Assigns/ That I have good Right full power and, Lawfull Authority to grant bargain and sell the above granted Premisses And that it is free from all incumbrances of thirds Mortgages &c/ And doe further oblige my selfe to warrant & Defend ye same to him his heirs and Assigns And that he shall & may at all times And from time to time forever hereafter, hold ocupie Possess and enjoy ye Premisses in and by these presents bargained And Sold without ye Lawfull lett contradiction and deniall of me ye aboves^d Christian Remich or of my heirs Exec^rs Admin^rs or Assigns, them or any of them or of any other pson whatever, Claiming or having any right or Intrest therein by from or und^r me/ In Testimony whereof I ye aboves^d Christian Remick have hereto set my hand and seal the twelfth day of June in ye twelfth year of the Reign

Remich to Spinney

of our Soveraign Lord William the third over England Scotland ffrance and Ireland King Defend[r] &c Anno Dom : 1700

the words if there be any high way reserved in John Dennets Deed between y[e] 14 : & 15th lines were enterlined before Signing.

Signed Sealed and and   Christian Remich (his seal)
  Delivered In presents of y[e] Subscrib[rs]
  John Spinney
  Jacob Remich
  Tho[s] Phipps

           Province of New Hampshier.

Christian Remich personally Appeared before me y[e] Subscrib[r] this 22[d] June 1700/ And Acknowledged the above Instrum[t] to be his Act and Deed.

                         Sam[ll] Penhallow Jus[t] Pe[c]

A true Copie of y[e] origenall Transcribed and compared this 12th July. 1700

                     p Jos Hamond Regist[r]

Know all men by these presents that I Christian Remich of Kittery in y[e] County of York in New England planter am holden and firmly doe stand bounden to Sam[ll] Samuel Spinney of Kittery afores[d] Planter, in the Penall Sum of one hundred pounds currant money of New England, to be paid to him y[e] s[d] Samuel Spinney his certain Atturney, his heires Execut[rs] Admin[rs] or Assigns, to y[e] which paiment well and truly to be made I bind me my heires Execut[rs] Admin[rs] firmly by these presents.

Dated in Portsm[o], this twelfth day of June, Anno Dom : 1700

             The condition of this obligation is such that if the above bounden Christian Remich his heires Execut[rs] Admin[rs] & Assigns Shall neither directly nor indirectly by themselves nor by any others Arest implead, or comence any Lawfull Suit whatever in any Court or before any Jus-

Remich to Spinney

tice or Justices of the Peace against Sam^ll Spinney afores^d his heirs Execut^rs Admin^rs or Assigns for any matter or difference that has or might, have, arise between them ye s^d Christian Remich and Sam^ll Spinney upon any ocation whatever from ye begining of the world unto this day And more particularly Shall not Arrest implead imprison or in any way or by any means whatever Molest or trouble ye s^d Samuel Spinney about a certain Lot of Land lying in Kittery at ye head of Thos Spinney Senr his old twenty Acre Lot, which has now of late been in contest between them Neither for any Matter that has hapned for the time past nor for aney thing that may happen for ye future at any time referring to s^d Land/ That then this present Obligat^n to be Voyd and of noe Effect, or Else to remain in full force & vertue

Signed Sealed and Delivered   Christian Remich (his seal)
in the presents of Subscrib^rs
John Spinney
Jacob Remich
Thos Phipps

Province of New Hampshier

Christian Remich personally Appeared before me the Subscrib^r this 22^d June 1700. And Acknowledged ye above Instrum^t to be his Act and Deed.

Sam^ll Penhallow Jus^t Pea^c

A true Copie of ye origenall Transcribed and compared this 12th July 1700   p Jos Hamond Regist^r

[67] Know all men by these presents that I Thomas Abbot, Senr, of Kittery in ye County of York of ye Province of ye Massachusets in New England, for divers good causes and considerations me hereunto Moving have given granted Alienated & confirmed And doe by these presents give grant

Alienate and confirm unto my beloved son John Abbot of y⁰ Town and County above said, A certain parcel of Land,

Tho Abbot to his son John

lying and being in y⁰ town and County aboves⁴ containing about five and twenty Acres more or less bounded as followeth, on y⁰ west with y⁰ head of my home Lot and on the North by Peter Grants Land and on y⁰ Northeast with Richard Nasons land and on the South with Daniel Goodens and John Greens Additions Land And on y⁰ East with y⁰ top of y⁰ Rockie hill As appears by marked trees, which said parcel of land shall be to my Son John Abbot and his heirs as a quiet and peaceable Possession for ever with all y⁰ Priviledges and Appurtenances thereunto belonging with trees woods under wood waters water courses &c To have and to hold all and Singular the priviledges thereunto belonging, only I reserve to my selfe my fire wood if I see cause to take it off that land my life time, or fencing Stuff if I want it Dated in Berwick in Kittery in y⁰ year of our Lord one thousand seven hundred in y⁰ Eleventh year of y⁰ Reign of our Soveraign Lord William y⁰ third by the grace of God King of England &c.

Signed Sealed and delivered   Dated March y⁰ 27ᵗʰ 1700/
   in the presents of us   Thomas Abbot (his seal)
   Josiah Goodridge   her
   Job Emery.   Elizabeth E Abbot (her seal)
   Daniel Emery   mark

York ss/ Kittery Septemb ͬ 16 : 1700

Ensign Thomas Abbott personally Appearing before me y⁰ Subscrib ͬ one of y⁰ Memb ͬˢ of his Maᵗˢ Council of y⁰ Province of y⁰ Massachusets Bay and Justice of Peace within y⁰ same Acknowledged this Instrumᵗ to be his Act and Deed/
                                       Jos Hamond

A true Copie of originall Deed Transcribed and compared this 16ᵗʰ Septemb ͬ 1700.
                         p Jos Hamond Regist ͬ

Book VI, Fol. 67.

To all Christian People to whome these may come/ Know yee that I Daniel Gooding Senr, of ye town of Kittery in ye County of York in New England wth the consent of Sarah my wife, have bargained and sold unto Jonathan Stone of ye same town and County and Countrey and to his heires for ever, a certain parcel of Marsh it being and lying on ye North side of the pond comonly called and known by the name of Humphrey's pond it containing about five or six Acres be it more or less, with ye one halfe of all my land lying & Joyning to ye Marsh afores^d, the which halfe is to be at ye s^d Stones Election & Choyce which whole tract of land contains about one hundred Acres and runing on a North east by east line one hundred and Sixty Rods long & one hund & five rods broad, of which land I the s^d Gooding have sold ye one halfe thereof wth all ye Marsh afores^d unto the fores^d Jonathan Stone, And by these presents doe bargain sell and Ratifie and confirm the fores^d land and Marsh with all the Appurtenances and privileges thereunto belonging unto ye fores^d Stone and to his heirs for ever/ for and in consideration of ten pounds in currant Money of New England to me in hand paid And further I the fores^d Daniel Gooding doe firmly by these presents bind my selfe my heirs Execut^rs Admin^rs and Assigns unto the fores^d Jonathan Stone and to his heirs for ever to warrant ye aboues^d Premisses unto them and defend them from any person or persons that shall lay any Claim unto ye aboves^d Premisses, And for confirmation hereof I set to my hand and seal the seventeenth day of May in ye year of our Lord one thousand Six hundred Ninety and Eight/

Gooden to Stone

Signed Sealed & Delivered
  in ye presents of us.
  Witt. James Warren
  Peter Nowell

the mark of
Daniel ⟨D⟩ Gooding (his Seal)
the mark of
Sarah ⟨⟩ Gooding (her seal)

York ss/ Kittery Septemb^r 16th 1700

Book VI, Fol. 67.

The above named Daniel Gooden Sen[r] personally Appearing before me y[e] Subscrib[r] one of the memb[rs] of his Ma[ts] Council of y[e] Massachusets Bay and Justice of Peace within y[e] Same Acknowledged this Instrum[t] to be his Act & Deed

Jos Hamond.

A true Copie of the originall Deed Transcribed and compared this 16th Septemb[r] 1700.

p Jos Hamond Regist[r]

These presents witnesseth that I Daniel Gooding of Berwick in y[e] town of Kittery in y[e] County of York in New England, doe for Divers good causes and considerations thereunto me moving And Epecially in respects of that love I doe bear unto my Sons William Gooding & Moses Gooding, doe give grant and confirm unto my fores[d] sons William and Moses all the remaining part of a certain parcel of land which I had given me by fores[d] town with all other priviledges of timb[r] and other Appurtenances upon that land thereunto belonging to them their heirs and Assigns for ever To have and to hold all and Singular that part of land that is to say, begining at y[e] head of my Sons Daniel Goodings land which I gave him and bounds alredy set unto him And from thence taking y[e] whole breadth and runing to y[e] extent of the head bounds of all the lands that I have or ought to have there which lands, I with y[e] consent of my wife doe confirm unto them as aboves[d] As Witness my hand and seal this y[e] Nineteenth day of March And in y[e] year of our Lord God one thousand six hundred Ninety $\frac{six}{seven}$.

D: Gooden to his Son Will & Moses

Signed Sealed and in y[e] presents of.	Daniel ⌒ Gooding (his seal) Se[r] his mark	
Witt: James Warren Jun[r] Thomas Gooding.	Sarah S Gooding. (her seal) her mark	

Book VI, Fol. 68.

Daniel Gooding Sen⟨r⟩ & Sarah his wife Acknowledged y⟨e⟩ above written Instrument to be their free Act and Deed, this 20⟨th⟩ May, 1697. Before me

      Charles ffrost Jus⟨t⟩ Peace.

A true Copie of y⟨e⟩ originall Deed Transcribed and compared, Septemb⟨r⟩ 16⟨th⟩ 1700   p Jos Hamond Regist⟨r⟩

[68] Know all men by these presents that I y⟨e⟩ within named William Gooding doe Assign make over and confirm all my Right Title and Interest that I have or ought to have to this within written Deed of Gift, unto y⟨e⟩ within named Moses Gooding to him his heirs Execut⟨rs⟩ Admin⟨rs⟩ and Assigns for ever to have and to hold all and singular the Appurtenances and priviledges thereunto belonging for and in consideration of thirty pounds in current money of New England or Merchantabe pay at money price, of which money I y⟨e⟩ aboves⟨d⟩ William Gooding have thirteen pounds in hand paid and have taken bills for y⟨e⟩ remainder of y⟨e⟩ money, As Witness my hand and Seal this the Nineteenth day of March and in y⟨e⟩ year of our Lord God one thousand Six hundred ninety and six-seven/

W: Gooden
to
Moses: Gooden

Signed Sealed and delivered William Goodin (his seal)
 in the presents of us.
 James Warren Jun⟨r⟩
 Thomas Gooding.

Deliverance Gooding y⟨e⟩ wife of y⟨e⟩ aboves⟨d⟩ William Gooding gives her Right of Dowry to y⟨e⟩ aboves⟨d⟩ Premisses as Witness my hand and Seal.

     Deliverance 𝒪 Gooding (her seal)
       her mark.

County York

William Gooding and Deliverance his wife Acknowledged the above written Instrum⟨t⟩ to be their ffree Act and Deed this 20⟨th⟩ of May 1697. Before me

      Charles ffrost Jus⟨t⟩ Peace

Book VI, Fol. 68.

A true Copie of the originall Transcribed and compared this 16th Septembr 1700/

p Jos Hamond Registr

This Indenture made ye twenty second day of July in ye year of our Lord One thousand & Seven hundred/ between Martha Taylor Widow of John Taylor of Barwick, in Kittery in the County of York in ye Province of ye Massachusets in New England And Executrix to his last Will and Testament, on ye one pty and William Goodwin, of the same Town (her Son in Law) on ye other party Witnesseth, That ye sd Martha (According to her best Prudence for her own Maintainance and the good of her daughters) Hath given, granted and sold to the said William Goodwin And doth hereby Effectually to him make over and confirm The homestead, house, Barn, orchard and all Priviledges thereto Left to her for her Maintenance by her sd husband/ To have and to hold and Quietly to Possess and Enjoy the same as her proper Estate firmly Secured and to be Secured by her, her heirs, Executrs and Adminrs from any Just Claims thereto laid by any person whatsoever to himselfe his heires, Executrs Adminrs or Assigns for ever, Upon condition of his performance of the Terms following And ye sd William doth for himselfe his heirs Executrs & Adminrs covenant and agree with sd Martha that she shall enjoy during her naturall life, of ye Premisses, the one halfe of ye Garden as now in fence and three Apple trees which she shall first make Choyce of, And her liberty to dwell in the dwelling house if she think meet And that he or they shall Añually pay to her or According to her order ye Sum of Eight pounds, one quarter in money an other in Merchantable Indian corn, an other in Merchantable pork & beefe the other quarter in Cyder or Pro-

Martha Taylor & William Gooden

vision as sold for money, on or before Christmass day. And to afford her Attendance in any time of her sickness, and to carry it dutifully and Peaceably toward her at all times during her life, And to afford at his own Charge when dead a decent and Christian buriall, And more over to pay within five years after her Decease ye sum of ffifteen pounds in ye Merchantable Product of s^d Place According to her last Will and in case of his not fulfilling these Articles, that she or her Assigns shall have full power and liberty to reenter upon and Possess ye Premises in the same Tenure as before ye Signing this Instrum^t In witness whereof the above named parties have hereto set their hands and Seales the day & year abovesaid

Signed and delivered   Martha Taylor (her seal)
  in presents of us   her mark
  James Waren   William Goodwin (his seal)
  Thomas Goodin
  John Wade

York ss/ Kittery Septemb^r 16th 1700

The within named Martha Taylor & William Goodin psonally Appearing before me the Subscrib^r one of the Memb^{rs} of his Ma^{ts} Council of ye Province of the Massachusets Bay and Justice of Peace within the same Acknowledged this Instrum^t to be their Act and Deed/.

                                   Jos Hamond

A true Copie of the originall Transcribed and compared this 16th Septemb^r 1700.   p Jos Hamond Regist^r

To all Christian People to whome these presents shall come Greeting/ Know yee that I Nicholas Turbet and Elizabeth his wife of the town of Kittery in ye Province of the Massachusets Bay in New England for and in consideration of a Valluable sum partly in hand paid and ye rest secured to be paid by Daniel Goodin Junʳ of yᵉ same town and Province, Have given granted bargained sold Infeoffeed and confirmed And doe by these presents for themselves their heirs Executⁿ and Adminⁿ give grant bargain sell Infeofee and confirm unto yᵉ aforesᵈ Daniel Goodin Junʳ fifteen Acres of upland lying in yᵉ town of Kittery aforesᵈ being a part of a hundred Acres of land formerly granted by yᵉ town of Kittery unto Thomas Spencer, near Wilcocks pond And alsoe one fifth part of yᵉ halfe of that Marsh or Meadow land called yᵉ further Marsh lately belonging to yᵉ aforesᵈ Thomas Spencer Deceased and to his wife Patience after his Decease And Since yᵉ Decease of yᵉ sᵈ Patience Spencer falleth to yᵉ sᵈ Turbet and his sᵈ wife as part of their Portion with all our title to any other part of sᵈ Spencers land And now by the said Nicholas Turbet and Elizabeth his wife sold unto yᵉ foresᵈ Daniel Goodin Junʳ. To have and to hold all the above bargained Premisses with all yᵉ Appurtenances Priviledges and comodities whatsoever thereunto belonging or in any wise Appurtaining to him the sᵈ Daniel Goodin Junʳ his heirs Executⁿ Adminⁿ and Assigns for ever freely Acquitted Exonerated and discharged of and from all manner of former Gifts, grants, bargains, Sales, Mortgages, Leases, Dowries or other Incumbrance whatsoever. And doe hereby warrant and defend yᵉ same against all [69] manner of persons laying any Lawfull Claim or title thereunto or to any part or parcell of the Premisses by from or under yᵉ sᵈ Nicholas Turbet and Elizabeth his wife/ ffor confirmation of the Premisses yᵉ sᵈ Nicholas Turbet and Elizabeth his wife have hereunto set their hands and seales, this fourth day of January, one thousand six hundred Ninety three, Ninety

Turbet to Goodin

four in y[e] fifth year of their Majesties Reign/ of England Scotland France & Ireland Defend[n] of y[e] Faith &c.

Signed sealed and Delivered   Nicholas ⟋ Turbet (his seale)
   in pres[ts] of
   Thomas Goodin   his mark
   Humphrey Spencer
   William ⋈ Hearle   Elizabeth ⋈ Turbet (her seal.)
      his mark   her mark

I Richard Check eldest son to y[e] within named Elizabeth Turbet doe give my free consent unto y[e] within written Sale of Land and doe wholly relinquish all or any Right that I have in any of the land within Mentioned, unto the within named Daniel Goodin Jun[r] and to his heires and Assigns for ever As witness my hand and Seal this three and twentieth day of April 1694

Signed Sealed and delivered   Richard Cheeke (his seale)
   in pres[ts] of us
   Margaret ⊓ Stagpole
      her mark
   John Wincoll

York ss/ Kittery Septemb[r] 16th 1700

Nicholas Turbet and Elizabeth his wife personally Appearing before me y[e] Subscrib[r], one of y[e] Members of his Ma[ts] Council of y[e] province of y[e] Massachusets Bay and Justice of Peace within y[e] same Acknowledged this within Instrument to be their Act and Deed/

                                Jos : Hamond

A true Copie of y[e] originall Deed together with Richard Cheeks consent thereto on y[e] back side of s[d] Deed/ Transcribed and compared this 16th of Septemb[r] 1700

                      p Jos Hamond Regist[r]

Book VI, Fol. 69.

Know all men by that I John Wincoll of Strawberry Bank Marin^r for and in consideration of ye sum of fforty pounds in hand paid before ye Sealing & delivering hereof by William Hearle of the Parish of Unity and County of York/ Planter the receipt whereof I the s^d John Wincoll doe hereby Acknowledge And hereof doth Acquit ye s^d William Hearle his heirs Execut^{rs} Admin^{rs} or Assigns for ever, Have granted bargained and sold unto ye s^d William Hearle, All that Tract of Land it being by Estimation twenty four Acres or there abouts be it more or Less/ being bounded with the land of Richard Nasons on ye South Side and west/ And on ye North and west with part of Thomas Spencers Land, And on the East and North with ye land of Daniel Goodings Land And on ye East with part of Humphreys Land, And wth part of Thomas Spencers Land on ye South And is lying and being within ye Parish of Unity and County of York afores^d/ To have and to hold the said tract of Land with ye Appurtenances And privildges thereunto belonging unto him ye s^d William Hearle his heirs & Assigns for ever in as large and Ample manner as I ye s^d John Wincoll can or may grant or state ye same/ Warranting him ye s^d William Hearle his heirs Execut^{rs} Admin^{rs} and Assigns for ever against all mañer of persons whatsoever/ from by or und^r me ye s^d John Wincoll/ In witness whereof I ye s^d John Wincoll have set my hand and Seale this present fifth day of April in ye year of our Lord One thousand Six hundred and Ninety nine

Signed Sealed & delivered   John Wincoll. (his seal)
  in the presents of us.   Deborah Wincoll (her seal)
  James Warren
  James Emery
  Daniel Goodin

Wincoll to Hearle

Book VI, Fol. 69.

John Wincoll and Deborah Wincoll Acknowledged this within written Instrum^t to be their Volluntary Act and Deed, the fifth day of Aprill 1699. Before. Kinsley Hall.
of the Councill.

A true Copie of ye originall Deed Transcribed and compared this 16th day of Aprill. 1700.
p Jos : Hamond Regist^r

Be it known to all men by these presents that I Humphrey Spencer of Barwick in ye County of York in ye Province of ye Massachusets Bay in New England Vintner In consideration of two pounds and nine shillings to me in hand paid by Mr John Wade of ye s^d Parish Minist^r the receipt whereof I doe hereby Acknowledge and my selfe to be therewithall fully satisfied/ Have sold, and by Turfe and Twig delivered And by these presents doe sell and deliver unto ye s^d Mr John Wade a piece of Upland Scituated in s^d Barwick, bounded Eastwardly by s^d Wades Land bought of James Stagpole, Southwardly by ye way leading toward ye great works (soe called) And on ye westwardmost side by the Countrey Road, it being a Triangle, containing by Measure Eighty five Pearches, with all ye Priviledges and Appurtenances thereof/ To have and to hold the s^d bargained Premisses to ye s^d Mr John Wade his heires Execut^{rs} Admin^{rs} & Assignes to ye only proper use and behoofe of him s^d Wade his heirs Execut^{rs} Admin^{rs} and Assigns for ever And I ye s^d Humphrey Spencer doe oblige my selfe, heires Execut^{rs} and Admin^{rs} the Premises hereby sold, against all persons whasoever (Excepting Robt Tufton Mason his heirs Execut^{rs} Admin^{rs} and Assigns, pretending title thereto from s^d Robert) to Mr John Wade his heires Execut^{rs} Admin^{rs} & Assigns to Warrantise and for ever De-

Spencer to Wade

fend by these presents/ In witness whereof I have hereunto set my hand and Seal this sixteenth day of Septemb^r Anno Domini One thousand and seven hundred Annoq Regni Guli^{mi} 3^u J. P. Magni Britainæ &c Regis Decimo Secundo Signed Sealed and Delivered   Humphrey Spencer (his seal)

In presents of us.
Daniel Stone
Thomas Goodin
William Earle
his ⪷ mark
York ss/

Kittery Septemb^r 16th 1700/ the above named Humphrey Spencer psonally Appearing before me the Subscrib^r one of his Ma^{ts} Council of ye Province of ye Massachusets Bay and Justice of Peace within the same Acknowledged this Instrum^t to be his Act & Deed   Jos Hamond

A true Copie of ye originall Transcribed and Compared this 16th Septemb^r 1700/   p Jos Hamond Regist^r

[70] Be it known unto all men by these presents that Benoni Hodsden Barwick in the County of York in ye Province of ye Massachusets Bay in New England in consideration of that love and affection which he beareth toward his own Naturall Dutifull eldest son Joseph Hodsden And for Divers good Causes and considerations him thereunto Moveing Hath Given granted, bargained, sold Alienated, Enfeoffed & confirmed/ And doth by these presents fully, freely clerely and Absolutely, Give, grant, bargain, sell Alienate, Enfeoffe, confirm and make over unto his said Son Joseph Hodsden, his heirs Execut^{rs} Admin^{rs} and Assigns Two certain Tracts of Land Adjoyning one to ye other Scituated Lying and being in s^d Barwick in ye Town of Kittery. The lesser pcell being bounded as followeth Viz^t

Book Fol. VI, 70.

Northwardly by the way that goes from s^d Benonis house to Nathan Lords/ Westwardly by the Countrey Road as it was setled in the year one thousand six hundred & eight/ Southwardly by land of Thomas Thompson, And Eastwardly by land of Nathan Lord and partly by ye greater Tract of land by these presents Alienated, containing by Estimation twenty Acres be it more or Less/ the greater Tract, being bounded Westwardly by Land of Thomas Thompson and partly by the forenamed & described little parcel, Southwardly and Eastwardly by the Town Comons And Northwardly by land of Nathan Lord/ Containing by Estimation forty two Acres be it more or Less, part being Swamp & part upland with all ye s^d Benonis Right Title, Interest or Propriety in either of & both the s^d parcels of Land And every benefit Appurtaining to them or either of them. To have and to hold and quietly and Peaceably to Ocupie Possess and enjoy ye hereby granted Premisses whether Upland or Swamp Together with all trees, timber, bushes, shrubs, windfalls, old loggs, underwoods, herbs, plants, grass, springs, brooks, streams, gullys water, Courses, Rocks, Stones, Mines of Gold, Silver, Tyn, Copper, Mercury, Lead or Iron &c Mettalls & Mineralls, Lying being or growing upon, arising proceeding or Derived from ye Premisses or being in ye Aiery or Subterranious parts thereof/ As alsoe all ye profits priviledges fruits Imoluments comodities Advantages liberties benefits Accomodations And Prerogatives in any wise Appurtaining thereto or by any improvem^t redounding from the Same, to his proper use benefit and behoof as an Estate in Fee Simple, fully discharged from all Gifts Sales Mortgages Dowries Titles Claims or Incumbrances whatsoever, to ye s^d Joseph Hodsden his heirs & Assigns for ever. In witness w^{r}of the s^d Benoni Hodsden hath set to his hand & Seal this seventeenth day of November, In ye year of our Lord One thousand Six hundred & Ninety nine And in y^e

Benoni Hodsden to his son Joseph

Eleventh year of yᵉ Reign of William the third King of Great Brittain &c.

Signed Sealed and Delivered   Benony Hodsden (his seal)
  In yᵉ presents of us.
  Daniel Emery
  Philipe Hubord
  James Emery

York ss/ Kittery Septembʳ 16ᵗʰ 1700

Benoni Hodsden and Abigail his wife psonally Appearing before me yᵉ Subscribʳ one of yᵉ membⁿ of his Majesties Council of yᵉ Province of yᵉ Massachusets Bay And Justice of Peace within the same, the sᵈ Benoni Acknowledged this Instrumᵗ to be his Act and Deed And yᵉ sᵈ Abigail his wife freely gave up all her right of Dower of in and to the Premisses therein Mentioned/

Jos: Hamond

A true Copie of yᵉ originall Transcribed & compared Septembʳ 16: 1700.

p Jos Hamond Regʳ

Know all men by these presents that We Nicholas Gowen alias Smith & John Gowen alias Smith both of Barwick in Kittery in yᵉ County of York in yᵉ Province of yᵉ Massachusets Bay In New England, doe Joyntly and Unanimously Choose Mʳ John Wade of sᵈ Parrish Ministʳ & Mʳ John Plaisted of Portsmouth to Judge & Determine between us what may be an Equall Division of yᵉ homestead which was our father William Gowen Alias Smiths, And yᵉ Estate which was formerly Trustrum Harrisons, Adjoyning thereto, between us, And alsoe how far Each of us are concerned & obliged in reason, to Allow to our Mother her thirds, and to our brethren and Sisters their Portions hereby impowering yᵉ sᵈ persons to goe over, View and Measure yᵉ Lands, observe

Book VI, Fol. 70.

ye buildings and improvem^t thereon, & puse our papers and Demand Answers unto their questions to either of us, soe far as they may se the same Nessessary to regulate and Inform their Judgm^t of ye Case/ Yielding to them full power & and Authority after their Satisfactory enquiry & search, to bring in their award as a finall Division of these controversies and other Depending thereupon or in case they cannot agree in their Judgm^{ts}, to chuse an Umpire to Determine in their stead, Moreover we agree to Acquess in ye award of ye afores^d Arbitrat^{rs} or their Umpire as an unanswerable and full conclusion of ye s^d differences for ever And hereto we doe bind our selves each to other in ye Sum of one hundred pounds to be paid by that person that shall not Acquiess y^r Judgm^t, his heirs Attorney Assignes Execut^{rs} or Admin^{rs} Allways provided that ye s^d Arbitrat^{rs} or their Umpire impowered by them under their hands and seals shall give in their award in writing under their hand and seal as their Act and Judgm^t on or before ye tenth day of September Ensuing, In witness whereof, we have set to our hands & seals this tenth day of July in y^e year of our Lord One thousand Seven hundred

Nicolas Gowen, Alias Smith (his seal)
John Gowen Alias Smith (his seal)

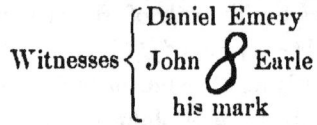

Witnesses { Daniel Emery
John 8 Earle
his mark }

York ss/ Novemb^r 6th 1700.

Daniel Emery and John Hearle personally Appearing before me the Subscrib^r, one of his Ma^{ts} Justices of Peace within y^e County of York/ made oath that they were pres^t and did see Nicholas Gowen and John Gowen Alias Smith, Signe Seal & Deliver this Instrum^t as their Act and Deed, and that they Signed thereto as Witnesses/

Jos: Hamond

Book VI, Fol. 71.

A true Copie of ye origenall Transcribed and Compared/ Novr 6th 1700

p Jos Hamond Regist^r

Whereas certain Differences have risen between Nicholas Gowen Alias Smith and John Gowen Alias Smith about ye Division of their father William Gowen Alias Smiths homestead, And the lands of Trustrum Harrison Added and Adjoyning thereto, as also concerning their Mothers thirds and ye other Childrens Portions &c. As more fully Appears in an Obligation under their hands and Seals Dated ye tenth day of July Anno Domini One thousand seven hundred/ Wherein they have fully referred the Devision of s^d Differences to ye Judgm^t of us the Subscrib^{rs}/ We therefore having Deliberately According to our best Light considered ye Case and Willing a ffinal Issue be made to their controversie doe Deliver our Award as followeth.

Imprimis/ We Award that Nicholas & John Gowen shall rest Satisfied with the Map [71] of s^d Lands signed by us as the foundation of ye Devision.

2 We Award that ye Deviding line shall begin in ye head line, one hundred & Eleven Rods from ye Southwardly end thereof, And from thence run straight to ye most Northerly corner of ye barn that was their fathers And thence straight to ye Gutter in Broughtons Swamp (soe called) Sixty eight Rods from ye Southwest Corner of the Land

3 We Award and Adjudge to Nicholas, All ye Land housing fences Orchards & Priviledges Included in ye Northward Devision, And in like manner to John All ye Lands housing fences Orchards and Priviledges Included in ye Southwardly Division of s^d Lands Excepting to Nicholas ye use of that Orchard Adjoyning to ye Garden for seven years/

4 We Award that John be at Equall Charge with Nicholas in Legal Defending of Trustrum Harrison unto Nicholas from all persons Molesting him by Vertue of a Title Derived from s^d Trustrum Harrison And if s^d Lands shall by Law, be taken from Nicholas by means of Such a Title, Then John shall Peaceably Deliver to Nicholas as much of his Land as an Addition to Nicholas his remaining Lands, as shall According to ye Judgm^t of two Indifferent men Mutually Chosen by them, make Nicholas his Portion of Land Equall wth Jn^{os}

5 We Award that Nicholas and John are Equally concerned to pay ye Children their Portions and to Allow their Mother her thirds, And if either of them have alredy paid or Allowed more than halfe ye Portion or thirds to their Mother and the Children or any of them, then ye other shall pay to him as much as he hath paid or Allowed above ye halfe,

6 If their Mother agree with them to receive an Annuall rent for her thirds then they shall Equally pay towards ye same. otherwise either of them shall be Liable to Allow ye other yearly ye vallue of halfe the thirds which she hath from ye others Division, which shall be recived by Improving lands or otherwise as they can best agree during their Moth^{rs} life

7 We Award that whatsoever Sum̄ hath been paid from Either to other for any particular Priviledge in ye last Division before this shall be repaid & no Covenant whatsoever shall oblige either of them to pay ye other any Sum which was to have been paid on ye afores^d Account.

8 We Award that Nicholas shall have liberty to ease himself of allowing any thing for thirds Excepting of the thirds of that land that was his fathers, by Acquitting his Seven years Right in ye orchard on ye South Side of ye Deviding line.

9 We Award that this our award shall not Extend to the

Siezing of any grayn hay grass husbandry Instrum^{ts} or ye like which may happen to be in ye Portion of each oth^r by means of this new line/ Nor shall it make a Right to either in any Estate not Accounted Dividable in ye line of ye last Division before this And time shall be allowed for ye removall of any such thing According to ye quallity thereof, as we or either of us formerly Advised with shall Direct

10 We Award that ye Charges of this Arbitration be paid by Nicholas & John in Equall proportion.

11 Finally We award that not only ye psons themselves but as well their Atturney heires Execut^{rs} Admin^{rs} and Assigns are priviledged or obliged by this our Arbitration as ye case may require/ And for confirmation of this our award we have set to our hands & seales this Seventh day of Septemb^r in ye year of our Lord One thousand and seven hundred, after ye Enterlining [men] in ye fourth Article & eight words belonging to ye Sixth Article in these presents

John Plaisted (his seal)
John Wade (his seal)

York ss/ Novemb^r 6th 1700/ Daniel Emery psonally Appeared before me ye subscrib^r one of his Ma^{ts} Justices of ye Peace in s^d County of York, and made oath that he was p^{r}sent & did se Mr John Wade deliver ye above award, in his own & Mr John Plaisteds name on ye 9th day of Septemb^r 1700.

Jos: Hamond

York ss/ Jan^{ry} 2^d 1700

Joseph Hamond Junr personally Appearing before me ye Subscrib^r, one of his Ma^{ts} Justices in s^d County of York made oath that he was pres^t and did Se Mr John Wade deliver ye above award in his own & Mr Jno Plaisteds name And y^t he & ye above named Daniel Emery were called & desired to bear Witness thereof.

Jos Hamond

Book VI, Fol. 71.

A true Copie of ye originall Transcribed & compared Novemb^r 6. 1700/ p Jos Hamond Regist^r/

To all People to whome these presents shall come/ Know ye that I Richard King of Kittery in ye County of York in ye Province of ye Massachusets Bay in New England Shipwright for and in consideration of ye Sum of twenty pounds of Lawfull money in New England to me in hand well and truly paid by John Dennet Junr of Portsmouth in ye Province New Hampshiere house Carpenter the receipt whereof I Acknowledge and my selfe therewith fully satisfied contented and paid, and of & from every part and parcell thereof doe for me my heires Execut^{rs} and Admin^{rs} freely Acquit Exonerate and Discharge him ye said John Dennet his heirs and Assigns for ever/ Have given, granted, bargained, sold, Aliened Enfeoffed and confirmed, And by these presents doe for me, my heirs, Execut^{rs}, Admin^{rs}, and Assigns freely clearly and Absolutely, give, grant, bargain, sell, Alien Enfeoffe convey and confirm unto him ye s^d John Dennet his heirs Execut^{rs} Administrat^{rs} and Assigns a certain piece or parcel of Land, containing twenty Acres which was granted to me by ye Town of Kittery ye 18th of August 1679. Seventeen Acres a halfe and twenty pole whereof was laid out to me July 16th 1694 as Appears on Kittery Town Book more at Large/ referrence thereunto being had, Lying and being Scituate in ye Township of Kittery afores^d at ye East end of John ffernalds Land bounded on ye North with John ffernalds land and Gabriel Tetherlyes Land And on ye East with Isaac Remich and on ye South with a high way of a pole Lying between Isaac Remichs land and s^d Kings land it being a hundred and forty one pole in length East and by north and twenty pole

Book VI, Fol. 71.

King
to
Dennet

in breadth, or how ever else bounded or reputed to be bounded/ Together with ye profits priviledges and Appurtenances to ye s^d land belonging or in any wise Appurtaining To have and to hold ye s^d piece or parcel of land with ye Appurtenances thereto belonging with all Right Title, Interest Claim and Demand, which I ye said Richard King now have or in time past have had or which I my heires Execut^{rs} Admin^{rs} or Assigns in time to come, may might should or in any wise ought to have of in or to ye above granted Premisses or any part thereof, to him the s^d John Dennet Junr his heires or Assigns for ever, And to ye sole and proper use benefit and behoof of ye s^d John Dennet his heirs &c for ever more And I the said Richard King for me my heires Execut^{rs} Admin^{rs} and Assigns doe covenant promise and grant to and with him ye s^d John Dennet his heirs and Assigns that at and before ye Ensealing and Delivery hereof I am ye true Right and proper owner of ye above Premisses and ye Appurtenances And y^t I have in my selfe, good Right full power and Lawfull Authority the same to grant and confirm unto him ye s^d Dennet his heirs and Assigns as aforesaid And y^t the same and every part thereof is free and clear Acquitted and Discharged of and from all former and other gifts grants bargains sales Leases Mortgages titles troubles Acts Alienations and Incumbrances whatsoever And that it shall and may be Lawfull to and for ye s^d John Dennet his heirs and Assigns ye afores^d Premisses and every part thereof from time to time and at all times for ever hereafter, To have hold use ocupie Possess and enjoy Lawfully peaceably and quietly without any Lawfull let deniall hinderance Molestation or disturbance of or by me or any other person or persons from by or under me or by my procurem^t And that ye sale thereof against my self my heirs Execut^{rs} Admin^{rs} and Assigns and against all other persons Lawfully Claiming ye same or any part thereof I will forever Save harmless

Warrant and Defend by these presents, And that I my heirs Execut^{rs} Admin^{rs} and Assigns Shall and will make perform & Execute such other and further Lawfull and reasonable Act or Acts thing or things as can be Devised Advised or required for ye better confirming and more sure making of the Premisses to him ye said John Dennet his heirs or [72] or Assigns according to the Laws of this Province In witness whereof I the s^d Richd King have hereunto set my hand and Seal this fourth day of Novemb^r In ye twelfth year of ye Reign of our Soveraign Lord William ye third, by ye grace of God, of England Scotland France & Ireland King Defend^r of ye ffaith &c In ye year of our Lord one thousand Seven hundred 1700.

Signed Sealed and Delivered
  In the presents of us
  Samuel Smaley
  Hannah Hamond
  Mary Storer.

Richard R King (his seal)
    his mark
Mary King. (her seal)

York ss/ Kittery Novemb^r ye 4th 1700

Richd King and Mary his wife personally Appearing before me the Subscrib^r one of ye Members of his Ma^{ts} Council of ye Province of ye Massachusets Bay, & Justice of Peace within ye same, The s^d Richd King Acknowledged this Instrum^t to be his Act and Deed, And ye s^d Mary King his wife ffreely gave up her Right of Dower, of, in & to ye above given and granted Premisses/

                              Jos: Hamond

A true Copie of the originall Deed Transcribed and compared this 4th Novemb^r 1700.   p Jos Hamond Regist^r

To all Christian People to whome this present Deed of Sale shall come Greeting Know yee that I Andrew Brown Planter, now of York, formerly of Black point, Alias Scarborough, in yᵉ Province of Mayn for Divers good causes & considerations me hereunto Moving but more in speciall for yᵉ consideration of seventy pounds Currant Money alredy received in hand from yᵉ hand of George Vaughan of Portsmº in the Province of New Hampshiere/ the receipt whereof I doe Acknowledge and yᵗ I am fully Satisfied therewith And doe for ever Acquit and Discharge yᵉ sᵈ Vaughan his heirs Executʳˢ Adminʳˢ and Assigns of and from every part and penny thereof Have given granted bargained sold Enfeoffed released delivered and confirmed And by these presents doe fully freely and Absolutely, give, grant bargain sell Enfeoffe release deliver and confirm unto yᵉ sᵈ Vaughan his heirs Executʳˢ Adminʳˢ & Assigns for ever to say one hundred Acres of Upland and fifty Acres of Salt Marsh Adjoyining to sᵈ upland Lying and being in yᵉ aforesᵈ Black point Alias Scarborough And is a Neck of land formerly in the Possession of one Henry Wats Decᵈ And yᵉ sᵈ Marsh lying on yᵉ South Side of sᵈ Neck of Land if so much can be found on yᵉ North Side of the River which is near Capᵗⁿ John Pickerins of Portsmº, Sold to him by my Predesessʳ yᵉ sᵈ Henry Watts And if there be not Sufficient to make up sᵈ fiftie Acres of Marsh on that Side yᵉ Mill River Then yᵉ remaindʳ to be mad up of as good Marsh as can be found on the Southwest side of yᵉ sᵈ Mill River as near as the sᵈ Vaughan shall think convenient to yᵉ sᵈ upland And whereas Henry Watts my Predesessʳ hath sold unto yᵉ sᵈ Pickerin the Priviledge of an high way to pass and repass from & to yᵉ sᵈ Mill over yᵉ Neck of Land and Marsh Adjoyning, I yᵉ sᵈ Brown do oblige my selfe and heirs to make good the sᵈ high way to yᵉ sᵈ Pickerin, As also to leave a Sufficient plot of Marsh for yᵉ digging of Turf for yᵉ securing and mending yᵉ Dam of sᵈ Mill that so yᵉ sᵈ Vaughan may not be cut short of his hundred and fiftie Acres of upland and Marsh which by these presents I do confirm to him And is bounded as fol-

Brown to Vaughan

loweth (Vid^z) The land to begin at ye end of s^d Neck which fronts Southward and so to run up towards ye falls Northward till one hundred Acres of land be compleated if so much can be found on ye Southerly Side of ye ffalls, ye land to run as ye Creek does which runs up to s^d falls And hath on ye East Side of s^d Creek another neck of Land Sold by my self to Mr William Cotten of s^d Portsm^o as likewise I doe sell grant and confirm by these presents unto ye s^d Vaughan ye one half of ye s^d ffalls & Stream both of fresh water and of ye Salt Creek which Joyns to his land, the other half being sold by self to ye s^d Cotten together with all trees and woods on ye s^d upland, Profits, priviledges & Advantages of ye s^d Streams both Salt and fresh/ To have and to hold all ye Premisses with all Priviledges to him ye s^d Vaughan his heirs & Assigns for ever, the title of which I will Warrant for him ye s^d Vaughan and his heirs for ever Against all Persons whatsoever/ To Performance of which I bind my self my heirs Exec^rs and Admin^rs to y^e s^d Vaughan his heirs & Assigns As Witness my hand and Seal this 22^d day of Novemb^r One thousand Six hundred Ninety & Nine : 1699

Sealed and Delivered   Andrew Brown ($^{his}_{seal}$)
  in presents of.
  Robt Elliot
  Nich^o Heskins

Then Andrew Brown personally Appeared before me the Subscrib^r one of his Ma^{ts} Justices of Peace and Council for y^e Province New Hampshier And Acknowledged the within written Instrum^t to be his Volluntary Act & Deed/

                         Robt Elliot of ye Council
New Castle Septemb^r 5th 1700

Then Andrew Brown gave quiet and Peaceable Possession of ye within Mentioned upland and Marsh to Mr William Cotten of Portsm^o for and in behalf of the s^d Vaughan within Mentioned by Turf and Twigge & in behalf of all the Premisses within Mentioned.

In presents of us

  Joseph Alexander

  Richard *R* Hunywell
         his mark

A true Copie of y° originall Transcribed and Compared this 14th day of Octob r 1700.

                    p Jos: Hamond Regist r

Be it known unto all whom this may concern that I John Sharp of Winter Habour which in y° yeer of our Lord. 1679. dwelt in y° town of Kittery And there was granted unto me y° s d John Sharp forty Acres of land within y° Bounds of Kittery/ I y° s d Sharp have sold unto John Morrell Sen r of y° same Town all my Righ and title in that land above mentioned to him y° said Morrell his Eares Admin rs or Assigns for ever/ I y° s d Sharp doe own my selfe fully satisfied, by a Mare already rec d whereunto I have hereunto set my hand and Seal. this 1. first day of ffebruary. 1685.

(margin: Sharp to Morrell)

Signed Sealed and Delivered The mark of ᴗ Sen r (his seal)
  in y° presents of us   John Sharp
      Witness

Edward Sargent

Phenis Hull

Cap tn Edward Sargent Appeared y° Eleventh day of Novemb r 1700. and Made oath that he did Se John Sharp Sign Seal & deliver this above written Instrum t as his Act and Deed, And that he being called did Sign as a witness & did Se Phenis Hull Sign as a witness at the same time/ Before me   Daniel Peirce, Justice of y° Peace

  A true Copie of y° originall

[73] To all People to whome these presents shall come Greeting/ Know yee that I Sarah Jordan Widdow, relict of Robert Jordan late of Spurwincke in the Township of Scarborough in ye Province of Mayn in New England Clark for and in consideration of a good and Valluable Sum to me in hand paid before ye Ensealing and Delivery of these presents by John Hincks of Portsm^o in the Province of New Hampshiere in New England afores^d Esqr whereof I the s^d Sarah Jordan doe Acknowledge ye receipt thereof And of every part and parcell thereof Doe Absolutely Acquit and discharge ye s^d Jno Hincks his heirs and Assigns & every of them for ever by these presents: Have given granted, bargained, sold, Aliened and confirmed, And by these presents doe fully clearly and Absolutely give, grant, bargain, sell, Alien & confirm to John Hincks Esqr afores^d his heires and Assigns for ever, one half part of a parcel of Land called Nonesuch to be Equally and Indifferently divided containing one thousand Acres more or less with half of all buildings houses out houses orchard, Gardens Upland woodland or Meadow land, formerly in ye Ocupation of my late husband Robert Jordan afores^d And now in ye Possession of me ye said Sarah Jordan.

Sarah Jordan to John Hincks

Excepting only out of the one thousand Acres afores^d a parcel of Upland of one hundred Acres and twenty Acres of Marsh land Sold to John Samson his heires and Assigns/ And Nine Acres of Marsh & land unto my son Robert Jordan To have and to hold the afores^d land being ye one half as afores^d with all conveniences and Appurtenances thereto belonging to ye s^d John Hincks Esqr his heirs and Assigns for ever And to their sole, proper, use, behoof & benefit And the s^d Sarah Jordan relict as afores^d/ for her self her heirs Execut^{rs} and Admin^{rs}, doth promise and grant to and with ye s^d John Hincks Esqr his heires, Execut^{rs}, Admin & Assigns, and to and with every of them y^t the s^d Sarah Jordan at ye time of the ensealing hereof doth stand & is Lawfully Siezed of the aforementioned Land and houses of a good & Lawfull Inheritance without any condition or Limitation of form^r bargains Sales Mortgages Leases or other Incumbrances whatsoever And that ye s^d John Hincks Esqr his heirs and Assigns shall and may from hensforth and for ever Peaceably and quietly Have hold ocupie Possess and Enjoy ye s^d bargained Land, houses, orchard, Garden, sold as above from ye s^d Sarah Jordan relict as afore^d, and from her late husband Robert Jordan as afores^d their heirs and all and every person or persons having or Claiming or which shall or may have or Claim or pretend to any right title Interest unto any part or parcel of ye s^d land by from or under my late husband Robert Jordan or me ye s^d Sarah Jordan relict as afores^d And that ye s^d Sarah Jordan shall and will be redy at any time or times hereafter upon reasonable request and at ye Charge and Cost of ye s^d John Hincks Esqr his heirs or Assigns to make and Acknowledge, or cause to be made and Acknowledged any Deed or Deeds Act or Acts thing or things Assurance or conveyance According to Law for ye further more better and perfecter Assurance and sure making the said Land by these presents Mentioned to be Sold to ye s^d John Hincks his heirs and Assigns for ever. In witness whereof I ye s^d Sarah Jordan have hereunto set my hand and Seal this tenth day of Novemb^r in ye second year of ye Reign of our Soveraign Ld James ye second by the grace of God King &c Annoq Domini, 1686

Signed Sealed and Delivered/   Sarah Jordan (her/seal)
  In the presents of us.   her ~~~ mark
  Jeremiah Jordan
  Deberoyh W Jordan
     her mark

The above Enterlining was done before ye Signing & Sealing & delivery of ye above Deed

Book VI, Fol. 73.

A true Copie of ye originall Deed of Sale from Mrs Sarah Jordan to Jno Hincks Esqr Transcribed & Compared March 3^d 1700.

p Jos. Hamond Reg^r

Province of New Hampsh^r   July 17th 1714/ Deberoh Jones who was formerly Deberoh Jordan ye wife of Jeremiah Jordan dec^d, psonally Appeared and made oath that she saw Sarah Jordan Sign Seal & Deliver this Instrum^t as her Act & Deed & that Jeremiah Jordan did at same Time Sign with her as a witness Before me/

Sam^ll Penhallow Justice peace

Recorded According to ye Original Oath July 19th 1714/

p Jos: Hamond Reg^r

James the Second by the grace of God of England Scotland ffrance and Ireland King Defend^r of ye ffaith &c. To all to whome these presents shall come, Greeting, Whereas our trusty and Loving Subject John Hincks Esqr one of the Memb^rs of our Council in the Teritory and Dominion of New England, hath by his Petition presented to Sr Edmund Andros K^t our Cap^tn Generall and Govern^r in Chief of our s^d Teritory and Dominion, Prayed our Grant & confirmation for a certain Tract or parcel of Vacant and unappropriated Land herein after perticularly set forth and Described, and whereon he Intendeth to make present Settlem^t and improvem^t, which request for his incouragem^t therein we being willing to grant. Know Yee, That of our especiall Grace we have given granted Ratified and confirmed And by these presents doe for us our heirs and Successors Give grant Ratifie and confirm unto the s^d John Hincks his heires and Assigns for ever/ All that certain Tract or parcell of Land Scituate

Sr Edmd Andros to John Hincks

Lying and being within y⁶ bounds of Scarborough in the Province of Maine And is part of a Neck of land there, comonly called and known by y⁶ name of Nonesuch Neck, begining at a certain stake placed by the side of Nonesuch River, and from thence Ranging North northwest two Degrees thirty Minits Northerly, one hundred Seventy Eight Chains to an Elme tree which standeth by Nonesuch River side And is marked on both sides with four Notches & from thence by the Riv' as it runs to a certain point in the River called Beaver-Knucke And from thence South and by East five Degrees thirty Minutes Southerly one hundred & Sixty two Chains to the said River where is a Stake placed And from thence by the River as it runs to y⁶ place where first begun, bounded on the West and East with Vacant land And on y⁶ North and South with Nonesuch River aforesaid/ Containing in all one thousand two hundred Eighty and five Acres as by the Survey and Draft thereof [74] may more fully Appear together with all and Singular the trees Timber woods, underwoods Moores Marshes Meadows Hereditaments and Appurtenances whatsoever to y⁶ said tract or parcel of Land within the bounds and Limits aforesaid belonging or in any wise Appurtaining (Excepting and always reserving out of this grant Ten Acres of Meadow now in y⁶ Tenure and Occupaĉon of Richard Hunywell of Scarborough aforesᵈ, To have and to hold all the before Mentioned tract or parcell of land and Premisses with their and every of their Appurtenances Except before excepted unto y⁶ sᵈ John Hincks his heires and Assigns to y⁶ sole and only proper use benefit & behoof of the said John Hincks his heirs and Assigns for ever Yielding rendring and Paying therefore Yearly and every year for ever on the feast of the Annunciacon of the Blessed Virgin Mary unto us our heirs and Successʳˢ or unto our Capᵗⁿ Generall and Governour In chiefe for y⁶ time being or to such other officer or Officers as by us our heirs and Suc-

cess^n shall be from time to time Impowered and Appointed to receive ye same The Annuall Rent of one bushell of Merchantable Winter wheat or five shillings in Currant money in New England in Liew and stead of all Rents Services Dues Duties and Demands whatsoever for the Premisses. In Testimony whereof we nave caused the great Seal of our s^d Territory and Dominion afores^d to be hereunto Affixed Witness Sr Edmund Andros Kn^t; our Cap^tn Generall and Govern^r in Chief of our said Territory and Dominion of New England at Boston the twenty Ninth day of ffebruary In the fourth year of our Reign And In ye year of our Lord God One thousand Six hundred Eighty and Seaven
Passed by order in Council. {seal} E. Andros
The day of the Date hereof
  p John West D Secry
A true Copie of the originall Transcribed & compared this 3^d of March : 1700/
      p Jos : Hamond Regist^r

This writing witnesseth that I William Hooke now Governour of Accamenticus in New England, and one of ye Patentees of that Plantation for and in consideration of a Marriage heretofore solemnized between Henry Simson of Accamenticus aforesaid And Jane ye Daughter and heir of Walter Norton Lieutenant Collonel/ Sometime a Pattentee of this Plantation, but now Deceased, as also for Divers other good causes and considerations me hereunto moving. Have Given Granted and confirmed And by these presents doe give grant and and confirm to the afores^d Henry Simson his heires and Assignes, one pcell of Land in Accamenticus aforesaid/ Bounded with ye land of Roger Gard lately set out by me ye s^d William Hook And Samuel Maverick one other of ye Pattentees on the North side ye River of Accamenticus on ye west side ye Bass creek And from thence Northeast Joyning with ye land of Arthur Bragdon on ye South side And the bounds of Accamenticus on ye east side Together wth the third part of a pcell of Meadow ground lying on ye North Side of a pcell of land lately granted to Roger Gard aforesaid neare ye head of ye River of Accamenticus/ To have and to hold ye aforesaid land with thapurtenances to ye said Henry Simson his heires and Assigns for ever, the said Henry Simson Yielding paying and performing to our Soveraign Lord the Kings Matie all Such Rents and reservations as in ye Pattent for this Plantation are Expressed In witness whereof I ye said William Hooke have hereunto set my hand & Seale the thirteenth day of March in ye fourteenth year of ye Reign of our Soveraign Lord King Charles. Anno Domi. 1638.

Wm Hook
Hen. Simson

Sealed and Delivered   William Hooke (his seal)

  In the presents of.   Memorand that these two lines were
  William Tompson   enterlined before ye Sealing and
  Roger Gard.   Delivery hereof.

A true Copie of the originall Transcribed and compared Decemb^r 23^d 1700.

                         p Jos Hamond Regist^r

Know all men whom these presents doe or shall concern that I Jane Simpson Alias Bond now living and dwelling in ye Town of York in ye Province of Mayn where I have lived and having been taken care and provided for about 14 or 15 years with Nessessary Cloathing and diet with my only and loving son Henry Simpson who hitherto hath taken a filial care of me And upon good Causes and considerations and so more Especially that he doe continue further care of me by providing Nessessary Cloathing food and Apparrell for

Book VI, Fol. 74.

Jane Simpson
to
Hen: Simson

me, during my Naturall life. Doe hereby give, grant, bargain, sell, Enfeoffe and confirm, as ye Sole and only heir of my father Captain Walter Norton Deceased, All my Lands Cattle, goods, Chattells and whatsoever other Interests belonged to my aforesaid father Capt Norton Deceased and afterward enjoyed by my former husband Henry Simpson Deceased by whome I had this my only Son Henry Simpson with whome I doe now dwell and reside/ Have upon ye above named considerations given granted bargained sold Enfeoffed and confirmed unto my s^d Son Henry Simpson, to his heires Execut^{rs} Admin^{rs} and Assignes for ever, of all my lands, goods and whatsoever Appurtains unto me as his proer Right, to dispose of and ord^r at his pleasure, with all ye Imunities priviledges Comonages thereto in any wise belong to my s^d Son Henery his heirs and Assigns for ever, And I doe further promise and Covenant with my s^d Son Henry Simpson that ye Lands Hereditam^{ts} or whatsoever else doe belong to me are free and Clear, from all bargains, sales leases Mortgages Judgm^{ts} Executions and all other entanglem^{ts} whatsoever And further I ye afores^d Jane Simpson doe further stand obliged, with my selfe heirs and Assigns to warrant and Defend ye Premisses herein Expressed and contained against all persons whatsoever as my own Just and proper Right Claiming and pretending any Just Claime from by or under me or by any means of my procurem^t In Testimony whereunto I have hereunto afixed my hand and Seal this 16th day of June 1688. one thousand six hundred eighty eight, In ye fourth year of ye Reign of Soveraign Lord James the Second of England Scotland France and Ireland King. Defend^r of the ffaith &c

Signed Sealed & Delivered in pres^{ts} of/
John Preble
John Parsons

Jane Simpson her mark ℐ (her seal)

Book VI, Fol. 75.

A true Copie of yᵉ originall Transcribed & compared this 23ʳᵈ Decembʳ 1700/   p Jos Hamond Registʳ

[75] To all Christian People whome these presents may concern/ Thomas Southerine and Elizabeth Southerine his wife in York in yᵉ County of York in yᵉ Province of the Massachusets Bay in New England Sendeth Greeting/ Know ye that yᵉ sᵈ Thomas Southerine and Elizabeth Southerine, for and in consideration of a certain Sum of Money to their hand paid or otherwise at yᵉ Sealing of this Instrumᵗ satisfactory secured by by Walter Burks of York, Soul Alinated Enfeoffed confirme fully freely and Absolutely make ouer unto yᵉ sᵈ Walter Burks a certain pcell of Marsh lying in yᵉ sᵈ West branch betwixt John Browns and John Parkers with all the writes and Benefits Emoluments and Advantages on Appertaining from yᵉ same or any part or parcel thereof. To have and to hold and quietly and Peaceably to Ocupie Possess and enjoy the said Land and Appurtinances as a Sure Estate to him yᵉ sᵈ Walter Burks his heires Execⁿ Adminⁿ or Assignes for ever/ Moreover yᵉ sᵈ Thomas and Elizabeth Southerine for themselves their heires Executⁿ and Adminⁿ to and with yᵉ sᵈ Walter Burks his heires Executⁿ Adminⁿ and Assignes doe Indent, covenant, engage and Promise the Premisse with all their Priviledges and Apurtenances from all former grants, gifts, Sales, rents Dowryes Demands and Incumbrances, As alsoe all future Claimes Suits or Interruptions to be had or Comenced by them their heires Executⁿ Adminⁿ or Assignes or any person or persons whatsoever upon grounds proceeding yᵉ Date of this Instrumᵗ, for ever to Warrantise and Defend by these presents In Witness whereof yᵉ sᵈ Thomas Southerine and Elizabeth Southerine his wife have hereunto Set their hands and seales, this

*Southerine
to
Waltr Burks*

seventeenth day of Septembʳ one thousand Seven hundred the one halfe of yᵉ Marsh properly belonging to the sᵈ Walter Burks.

                                    marke

Signed Sealed and De-   Thomas 🔾 Southerine (his seal)
  livered In the presents   Elizabeth Southerine (her seal)
of us.

Nath: Freeman.

Eliezar Johnson

Thomas Southerine & Elizabeth his wife Acknowledged this to be their Act and Deed the 17ᵗʰ of 7ber : 1700
                    Before me   Abra : Preble Justis Peace

A true Copie of the originall Transcribed and compared this 4ᵗʰ Octobʳ 1700   p Jos Hamond Registʳ

These may certifie whome it may concern that I Mary Write of York in yᵉ County of York, in yᵉ Province of the Massachusets Bay doe freely Acknowledge yᵗ I yᵉ sᵈ Mary Write my heirs Executʳˢ Adminʳˢ or Assignes doe truly and freely give grant unto my said Elizabeth Southerine her heires Executʳˢ Adminʳˢ or Assignes all my wright & title of the sᵈ within Mentioned Marsh Lying between John Browns and John Parker Lying now between yᵉ sᵈ Weste branch of York River formerly in yᵉ Possession of Nicholas Davis but now Actually in yᵉ Possession of Thomas Southerine and Elizabeth his wife/ Given under my hand and Seal this Seventh day of Septembʳ One thousand Seven hundred.

Mary Wright to Eliza: Southern

Signed Sealed and deliuered   Mary Wright (her seal)
  In the presents of us.

Nathˡˡ Freeman

Eliezar Johnson

A true Copie of yᵉ originall Transcribed and Compared this 4ᵗʰ Octobʳ 1700/
                                    p Jos Hamond Regʳ

Book VI, Fol. 75.

To all to whome these presents may come. I Thomas Wise of Ipswich in New England ffisher^m In the County of Essex Send Greeting and soforth : Know yee that I ye s^d Thomas Wise for and in consideration of Eleven pounds five shillings to me in hand paid by Daniel Black of York in ye County of York Wever before ye ensealing and delivery hereof, the receipt whereof I ye s^d Thomas Wise doe hereby Acknowledge and my self with these to be fully contented satisfied and paid, And have for my self my heires Execut^rs Admin^rs and Assignes Given, granted, bargained, sold, Delivered and confirmed and by these presents doe fully freely and Absolutely give, grant, bargain, sell, deliver and confirm unto the s^d Daniel Black his heires Execut^rs Admin^rs and Assignes a certain Tract of land lying and being within the town of York afores^d on a place comonly called or known by ye name of the burnt plain, containing Eleven Acres, being bounded in form and manner as followeth/ by Mr Edward Rishworths Lot on the West/ begining by y^e

Wise
to
Black

Swamp on ye South to a Red Oak Stump, and from thence North ninety one poles, and from thence East and by South twenty four poles, and from thence Sixty four poles, South/ And from thence Southwest twenty eight poles, And from thence West and by South five Rod to ye said red oak stump, With all and Singular ye woods under woods & timb^r, Timb^r trees priviledges or Appurtenances whatsoever thereunto belonging/ To have and to hold ye s^d Land and Premisses hereby bargained and sold unto the said Daniel Black his heires Execut^rs Admin^rs and Assigns as his and their own proper goods and Estate for ever, and to his and their own proper use, and behoof for evermore And I ye s^d Thomas Wise with my heires Executors Admin^rs and Assignes, doe Covenant promise and grant to and with ye said Daniel Black his heirs Admin^rs and Assignes by these presents that I the said Thomas Wise on ye day of the Date hereof and at ye time of the ensealing and Delivery hereof have in my self full power good Right and Lawfull Authority to give, grant, bargain, Sell deliver and confirm the s^d Land and Premisses hereby bargained and sold unto the said Daniel Black his heires Execut^{rs} Admin^{rs} and Assignes for evermore in manner and form afores^d And alsoe that ye s^d Daniel Black his heires Execut^{rs} Admin^{rs} and Assignes or any of them shall or Lawfully may from time to time or at all times hereafter peaceably and quietly have hold use and enjoy the s^d Land and Premisses hereby bargained for and Sold, without any manner of lett Suit trouble hinderance Molestation Disturbance Challenge Claims Denialls or Demands whatsoever of or by me the s^d Thomas Wise my heires Execut^{rs} Admin^{rs} and Assignes, or any of them or of or by any other person or persons whatsoever Lawfully Claiming or to Claime, from or by under me, my act or title/ In witness whereof I have hereunto put my hand and Seal this twenty fourth day of Septemb^r one thousand Six hundred Ninety Eight And in ye tenth year of his Ma^{ts} Reign over England.

Signed Sealed and Deliuered   Thomas Wise (his seal)
  in ye presents of these Witnesses
  Matthew Austine
  Abraham Preble Juſt

Ipswich Septemb^r 16 : 1700/ Then Thomas Wise personally Appeared & Acknowledged this Instrum^t to be his Act and Deed, & at ye same time his wife Eliz gave up her Right of Dower Before John Apploton : J Peace

A true Copie of ye originall Transcribed & compared, Octob^r 4th 1700.   p Jos : Hamond Regist^r

[76] To all Christian People to whome these presents shall come or may concern Know ye that I Emanuel Davies late of ye Town of Cape Porpoise in the Province of Maine,

now of New Town in ye County of Middlesex in ye Province of the Massachusets Bay in New England husbandman, for and in consideration of ye Sum of Eight pounds ten shillings Currant Lawfull Money of New England to me in hand well and truly paid by Samuel Hill of Charles Town in ye County of Middlesex afores^d and in ye Province afores^d Marin^r, the receipt whereof I doe hereby Acknowledge and my self therewith to be fully Satisfied contented and paid at & before the Signing Sealing and Delivery of these presents And thereof and of every part and parcel thereof doe Acquit Exonerate and Discharge him ye s^d Samuel Hill his heires Execut^{rs} Admin^{rs} and Assignes for ever Have given granted bargained and Sold Aliened Enfeoffeed & confirmed And by these presents doe fully freely clearly and absolutely give, grant, bargain, sell, Alien Enfeoffe convey and confirm, unto him ye s^d Samuel Hill his heires & Assignes for ever/ a Certain tract or parcell of land containing forty Acres more or less by Estimation, the same Scituate Lying and being within ye limits and bounds of the town of Cape Porpoise in ye Province of

<small>Davis to Hill</small> Mayn butting & bounded as followeth Viz^t Adjoyning to ye field of Richard Young begining at the foot of the little River falls which river is next unto ye Cape afores^d and from ye foot of ye falls afores^d runs along ye water side unto a pine tree by a great Rock near unto ye water side And from ye afores^d tree runing upon a Nor Norwest line into the woods untill it doe Abutt upon ye land of the afores^d Richard Youn upon that Side, or how ever ye same is other butted and bounded or reputed to be bounded the same being formerly sold by Henry Hatherly to s^d Richard Young as p Deed of Sale thereof bearing Date Jan^{ry} 1671 doth there fully Appear together with all our Right Title and Interest Claim and Demand whatsoever in and unto threescore Acres of upland Adjoyning to the aboves^d forty Acres given to Richard

Young by yᵉ town of Capeporpoise, together with thirteen Acres of Marsh, Seven Acres whereof lyeth at a place comonly called Princes Rock/ the other six Acres of sᵈ Marsh lying and being up towards Millers and yᵉ opening of the Pines the sᵈ thirteen Acres of Meadow being formerly given to William Randall by the town of Cape Porpoise together with all and Singular yᵉ trees woods under woods stones, Rights Members profits priviledges hereditamⁿ yᵉ sᵈ granted Premisses and every part and parcel thereof in upon and unto any ways belonging or in any wise Appurtaining whatsoever As also all yᵉ Estate right Title Dower Interest Use Propertie Claime and Demand whatsoever of me yᵉ sᵈ Emanuel Davis and Mary my wife our or either of our heires Executⁿ or Adminⁿ in and to yᵉ same/ To have and to hold yᵉ sᵈ forty Acres of land together with yᵉ sᵈ Sixty Acres thereunto Adjoyning, as also together with yᵉ sᵈ thirteen Acres of Meadow all and every of sᵈ parcells butted and bounded as aforesaid with all and Singular yᵉ Members profits priviledges and Appurtenances to the same and every of them And parcells of land and Meadow belonging unto the said Samuel Hill his heires and Assigns for ever. And to his and their own proper Use benefit and behoof for ever/ And I yᵉ sᵈ Emanuel Davis for my self my heirs Executⁿ & Adminⁿ Doe covenant promise and grant & agree to and with yᵉ sᵈ Samuel Hill his heirs Executⁿ Adminⁿ and Assignes that at yᵉ time of this bargain and Sale I am yᵉ true Sole & Lawfull owner of all and every yᵉ above bargained Premisses and stand Lawfully siezed of and in the same in a good and absolute Estate of Inheritance in Fee simple And have good Right in my self full power & Lawful Authority to sell and Dispose yᵉ Same as aforesᵈ to him yᵉ sᵈ Samuel Hill his heires and Assignes free and clear and clearly Acquitted Exonerated and Discharged of and from all former and other gifts, grants bargains, Sales, Leases, Mortgages, Wills, Entailes, Joyntures, Dowers, Judgmⁿ,

Extents forfitures, Executions, Rents, Titles, troubles or Incumbrances whatsoever and Demand or Demands whatsoever and by whomesoever together with sufficient Warranty the same and every part and parcell thereof to defend for ever hereafter together with y⁰ priviledges and Appurtinances thereof to him the s^d Samuel Hill his heires and Assigns against y⁰ Lawfull Claim and Demand of any person or persons whomsoever In witness whereof I y⁰ said Emanuel Davis and Mary my beloved wife In Acknowledgm^t of her full and free consent to this my Act and Deed & in token of her resignation and giving up of all her Right of Dower and thirds in all and every of the above bargained Premisses have hereunto set our hands & Seales this 27th day of ffebruary Anno Domini 169¾. Annoq R Ris & Reginæ Gulielmi & Mariæ Angliæ &c. Septimo.

Signed Sealed & Delivered the words [in a good & absolute
  In presents of us. Estate of Inheritance in ffee
  Sam^ll Phipps Simple] between y⁰ 29. & 30.
  William Hurry lines before signing ensealing
  Joseph Phipps Emanuel Davis (his seal)

Charlestown ffeb: 27th 169¾
Then rec^d y⁰ w^thin mentioned Mary Davis ⌀ her mark (her seal)
sum of eight pounds ten Charlestown ffeb: 27th 169¾
shillings of s^d Sam^ll Hill, Emanuel Davis & Mary his wife
being in full of y⁰ purchase consideration within
mentioned I say rec^d p me
  Emanuel Davis

psonally Appearing before me
One of their Ma^ts Justices of
y⁰ Peace for y⁰ County of
Middlesex, in y⁰ Province of
y⁰ Massachusets Bay And Acknowledged y⁰ above written
Instrum^t to be their Voluntary Act and Deed/
      Samuel Hayman

A true Copie of the originall Transcribed & compared this 22^d July 1700.
      p Jos Hamond Regist^r

Know all men by these presents that I Robert Elliot & Margery Elliot of Black point in ye Province of Maine Yeoman for and in consideration of the Naturall love and Affection we bear unto our Son in Law Emanuel Davis and unto his now wife Mary Davis Have of our free will Given granted Enfeoffed and confirmed And by these presents doe fully freely absolutely give grant Enfeoffe and confirm All

Elet to Davis

that our Right & Title to a parcell of Land Lying and being in ye Town of Cape Porpoise in this Province of Maine to ye vallue of forty Acres formerly Sold by Henry Hatherly to Richard Young as by Deed of Sale bearing Date the Second day of Jan^ry 1671. more fully will Appear, the Butts and [77] bounds Viz^t forty Acres being there specified together with all our Right and title whatsoever of threesore Acres of upland Adjoyning to ye above^sd forty Acres given to Richard Young by the Town of Cape Porpoise together with thirteen Acres of Marsh, Seven Acres whereof lyeth at a place comonly called Princes Rock, the other Six Acres of Marsh lyeth up towards Millers and ye opening of ye pines, the s^d thirteen Acres of Meadow being given to William Randall by ye town of Cape Porpoise/ To have and to hold ye s^d tracts of land to ye s^d Emanuel Davis and Mary Davis his now wife to him and his heires for ever all that our s^d Right and title to ye s^d Land, to wit of ye s^d forty Acres with the s^d Sixty Acres thereunto Adjoyning together with ye afores^d thirteen Acres of Meadow as on ye other side expressed To have hold use ocupie and enjoy all ye aboves^d tracts of land, with all ye profits priviledges and Imunities thereunto belonging And I the Robert Elliot and Margery my now wife doe hereby Acquit & release all our Right and Title to s^d land as above expressed binding us o^r heires Execut^rs Admin^rs to ye s^d Emanuel Davis and Mary his now wife and their heires for ever that shall quietly and Peaceably Use Ocupie and enjoy all ye s^d tracts of Land without any lett Molestation

Book VI, Fol. 77.

or trouble from by or under us our heires Execut^{rs} Admin^{rs} and Assignes/ In Witness of ye Premisses we have hereunto affixed o^r hands and Seales this 13th June. 1687. And in ye third Year of ye Reign of our Soveraign James ye Second King of Great Brittain &c

Signed Sealed and Delivered
  In presents of us.
  Thomas Scottow
  Henry ✦ Elkins
            marks
  John ✦ Marshall

Robert R Ellet (his seal)
Margery M Ellet (her seal)
      marks
the words y^e Second day of Jan^{ry} enterlined before Signing & Sealing

Portsm^o Jan^{ry} y^e 6th 169$\frac{3}{4}$. Robert Ellett Appeared before me and Acknowledged that he Signed this Instrum^t & afixed his Seal to y^e same & y^t his wife Signed & Sealed at y^e same time/ Attests

                      Tho : Packer Jus p^s

A true Copie of y^e origenall Transcribed & compared this 22^d July 1700

                      p Jos Hamond Reg^r

Johnson to Junkins

To all People to whome this pres^t Deed of Sale shall come Sam^{ll} Johnson of Kittery in ye County of York in ye Province of ye Massachusetts Bay in New England and Abigail his wife send Greeting Know yee that we ye s^d Sam^{ll} and Abigail Johnson for and in consideration of ye Sum of Seven pounds sterling to us in hand well and truly paid at & before ye ensealing and Delivery of these presents by Alexander Junkins of York in s^d County and Province The receipt whereof we doe hereby Acknowledge and our selves therewith to be fully Satisfied contented and paid and thereof, and of and from every part & parcell y^r of doe for us our heires Execut^rs Admin^rs and Assigns freely & clearly Acquit Exonerate and Discharge him ye s^d Junkins his heires and Assigns for ever. Haue given granted bargained sold Aliened Enfeoffed and confirmed/ And by these presents doe for us our heires Execut^rs Admin^rs and Assignes, freely clearly and Absolutely give grant bargain Sell Alien Enfeoffe convey and confirm unto him ye s^d Alexand^r Junkins his heirs and Assigns a certain piece or parcell of Upland containing ten Acres Lying and being Scituate in ye township of York in the County and Province afores^d, on ye Eastward Side of ye brook butting upon Mr Jeremiah Moltons land And Siding upon Constant Rainkings land or however Else bounded or reputed to be bounded, which s^d ten Acres of land was given by James Grant late of s^d York Deceased unto his then wife (whome afterward ye s^d Samuel Johnson Married) as may & doth appear by s^d Grants last will & Testament referrence whereunto being had doth more at large Appear To have & to hold ye said ten Acres of land with all and singular ye priviledges and Appurtenances thereunto belonging or in any wise Appurtaining, with all ye right title Interest Claim & demand which we ye s^d Sam^ll Johnson and Abigail Johnson now have or in time past have had or which we our heirs Exec^rs Admin^rs or Assigns may might should or in any wise ought to have in time to come of in or to ye above granted Premisses or any part thereof

Johnson to Junkins   to him ye s^d Alexander Junkins his heires or Assigns for ever And to ye sole and proper use benefit and behoofe of him the s^d Alexander Junkins his heires &c forevermore And we ye s^d Sam^ll Johnson and Abigail Johnson for us our heirs Execut^rs Admin^rs & Assigns doe covenant promise and grant to and with ye s^d Alexand^r Junkins his heirs &c/ that at & before ye Ensealing & Delvery hereof we are ye true right & proper owners of ye aboves^d Premisses with the Appurtenances

And that we have in o'selues good right full power and Lawfull Authority y° same to grant & confirm unto him y° s⁴ Alexand' Junkins his heirs and Assigns as afores⁴ And that the same and every part thereof is free and clear Acquitted and Discharged of & from all former and other gifts grants bargains Sales Alienations & Incumbrances whatsoever, had made comitted done or Suffered to be done by us y° s⁴ Sam¹¹ and Abigail Johnson our heirs &c at any time before y° Ensealing of these presents And that it shall and may be Lawfull to and for y° s⁴ Alexand Junkins his heirs & Assigns from time to time and at all times forever hereafter quietly and peaceably to have hold use Possess and enjoy the afores⁴ Premisses without any manner of Let hinderance or disturbance and that y° sale thereof against our selves our heirs Execut'ⁿ Admin'ⁿ or Assigns and against all other persons whatsoever Lawfully claiming y° same or any part thereof we will forever save harmless warrant and defend by these presents In witness whereof we y° s⁴ Samuel Johnson & Abigail Johnson have hereunto Set our hands and seales, this twenty eighth day of October in y° year of our Lord one thousand Seven hundred/ And in y° twelfth year of y° Reign of our Soveraign L⁴ William y° third by y° Grace of God of England Scotland ffrance & Ireland King Defend' of y° ffaith &c

Signed Sealed & Delivered in   Samuel Johnson (his seal)
   y° presᵗˢ of us   her
   William Barkwell   Abigail 🆃 Johnson (her seal)
   Hannah Hamond   mark
      her
   Hannah C. Key
       mark

York ss. Kittery Octob' 28 1700

Sam¹¹ Johnson & Abigail his wife psonally appearing before me y° Subscrib' one of her Majᵗˢ Justices of the peace

Book VI, Fol. 78.

for s^d County of York Acknowledged this Instrument to be their Act and deed.   Jos Hamond

A true Copie of ye Originall Transcribed & compared Octob^r 28th 1700

          p Jos Hamond Reg^r

[78] To all Christian People to whome these shall come Greeting Know ye that we John Shapleigh of Kittery in ye County of York Gentleman And William Godsoe of ye same place in consideration of one hundred pounds in money to us in hand paid by Mr James Johnson of ye same place Milwright the receipt whereof we doe hereby Acknowledge and ourselves therewith contented and paid And Acquit ye s^d James Johnson for ye same Have bargained and sold And doe by these presents bargain and sell set over & for ev^r confirm unto ye s^d James Johnson his heirs and Assigns for ever Sixty two Acres of Land Lying in ye Township of Kittery at ye head of Spruce Creek together with all ye timb^r and wood standing or Lying thereon with all ye Priviledges and Appurtenances thereunto belonging or in any wise Appurtaining thereunto & takes its begining at Cap^{tn} ffernalds ffarm And is in length one hundred & sixty pole west & be south and East & be North And in breadth sixty pole south & by East & North and be west and Joyns to ye Salt Marsh, containing Sixty Acres of land the other two Acres lying on the South Side of ye afores^d tract of Sixty Acres And begins at a Bridge going over a Brook or run of water And runs & runs North and B west to ye bounds of ye s^d Sixty Acres, thirty two pole And from s^d brook by Kittery Road twenty four pole North Northeast And from that Extent North and be west thirteen pole to ye bounds of s^d Sixty Acres aboves^d To have and to hold all ye aboves^d tract of

Marginal note: Shapleigh & Godsoe to Johnson

land containing Sixty two Acres of land unto ye said James Johnson his heires Execut^{rs} Admin^{rs} or Assigns for ever unto his and their own proper use benefit and behoof for evermore/ And furthermore we the s^d John Shapleigh and William Godsoe Doe for our selves our heires Execut^{rs} And Admin^{rs} covenant to and with ye s^d James Johnson his heires Execut^{rs} or Admin^{rs} and Assigns that the Premisses are free from all Incumbrances whatsoever as Joyntures Dowries Sales or Gifts Mortgages or any ye like Incumbrances And that we are the true and proper owners thereof And have full power to sell and Dispose of ye same The peaceable & quiet Possession thereof to warrant & maintain against all persons laying a lawfull Claim thereunto Excepting and reserving out of the Premisses, liberty for my brother and Sister Curtis and their heires to set a fence on ye upland Joyning to the Marsh to secure ye s^d Salt Marsh by the Edge thereof, doing as little damage as may be/ In testimony hereof we have hereunto set our hands & seals this twenty fifth day of June one thousand Seven hundred 1700,

Witnes   John Shapleigh (his seal)
   John Pickerin   William Godsoe. (his seal)
   Joseph Curtis
       the mark of
   Samuel 𝓘𝓒 Johnson

York ss/ Septemb^r 25th 1700

Lt John Shapleigh personally Appearing before me the Subscrib^r one of his Ma^{ts} Justices of Peace in ye County of York Acknowledged this Instrumen to be his Act and Deed.

                                     Jos Hamond

Kittery June 25th 1700/ Memorand that Peaceable and Quiet Possession was given of ye with mentioned land contained in this Instrum^t in presents of us who are ye Subscrib^{rs} by ye with named John Shapleigh & William Godsoe. Attests
   John Pickering
   Joseph Curtis

Book VI, Fol. 78.

York ss Octob{r} 12{th} 1700

The within named William Godsoe personally Appearing before me y{e} Subscrib{r} one of his Ma{ts} Justices in y{e} County of York Acknowledged this Instrum{t} to be his Act and Deed.

Jos Hamond

A true Copie of y{e} originall Transcribed and compared this 12{th} Octob{r} 1700   p Jos Hamond Regist{r}

This Indenture made y{e} twenty six day of June Anno Domini 1685. and in y{e} first Year of the Reign of our Soveraign Lord James y{e} Second by y{e} grace of God of England Scotland France and Ireland Defend{r} of the faith &c, Between Thomas Danforth Esq{r} President of his Ma{ts} Province of Maine in New England on y{e} one party & ffrancis Champernown Gen{t} of Kittery upon Piscataqua River on y{e} other party Witnesseth, that whereas y{e} above named Thomas Danforth, [by y{e} Govern{r} and Company of y{e} Mattachusets Collony in New England, the now L{d} Propriet{r} of y{e} above named Province of Maine, at a Generall Assembly held at Boston on the Eleventh day of May. 1681] is fully Authorised and Impowered to make Legall confirmation unto y{e} Inhabitants of y{e} aboves{d} Province of Maine of all y{e} land and Propriety to them Justly Appurtaining or belonging within y{e} Limits and bounds of s{d} Province, Now Know all men by these presents that I y{e} s{d} Thomas Danforth Pursuant to y{e} trust in him reposed and power to him given as aboves{d} by and on y{e} behalf of y{e} Govern{r} and Company of y{e} Mattachusets Collony afores{d} Have given granted and confirmed And by these pres{ts} doth fully clearly and absolutely give grant and confirm unto y{e} above named ffrancis Champernown those two tracts of land whereof he is now Seized Scituate lying and being w{th}in the limits and bounds of the above named Province And are bounded as followeth the one of y⁰ sᵈ tracts or parcells being the neck of land whereon yᵉ sᵈ ffrancis Champernown doth now dwell, and is Scituate on yᵉ East Side of yᵉ Rivers mouth of Piscataqua River and So along yᵉ Sea Side Eastward to yᵉ Mouth of yᵉ River called brave boat Harbour and thorow or along sᵈ River in yᵉ Entrance thereof into the river of Piscataqua aforesᵈ, and from thence again Southward along yᵉ River of Piscataqua as aforesᵈ to yᵉ Sea, the whole containing by Estimation four hundred Acres of land or otherwise be the same more or less And yᵉ other tract or parcell is Marsh land Scituate lying and being on yᵉ Northeast side of the afore named Brave boat Harbour as yᵉ Same was alotted & laid out by Richard Vines Esqʳ Steward Generall unto Sʳ Fardinando Gorges who was some time Lᵈ Proprietʳ of yᵉ above named Province containing by Estimation five hundred Acres be yᵉ Same more or less To have and to hold yᵉ abovesᵈ tracts or parcels of land by these presᵗˢ granted and Confirmed be yᵉ same more or less, With all the Soyls, ground, woods and underwoods Havens, Ports, Rivʳˢ waters, Lakes fishing, Mines and Mineralls, as well Royall Mines of Gold and Silver and other precious Stones, Quarries and all & Singular other comodities, Jurisdictions, Royalties, Priviledges, Franchises, Preheminances whatsoever which yᵉ sᵈ tracts or parcels of land & Premises or wᶜʰ any part or parcel thereof, Saving Excepting and reserving only out of this present grant yᵉ fifth part of all yᵉ Oare of Gold or Silver found or to be found in or upon the Premisses or any part or parcell thereof due unto his Maᵗⁱᵉ his heires & Successʳˢ and now or at any time reserved or to be reserved, unto yᵉ sᵈ ffrancis Champernown his heires and Assignes, to yᵉ only proper use and behoof of him yᵉ sᵈ ffrancis Champernown his heires and Assigns for ever, He yᵉ above named ffrancis Champernown his heires and Assigns for ever hereafter Yielding and paying in consideration thereof to yᵉ Governʳ and Company of

Danforth to Champrnown

y̆ᵉ Massachusets Collony or to yᵉ President of sᵈ Province by them Authorized and Impowered for yᵉ time being or to other their Agent or Lawfull Assign or Assignes, twenty Shillings in Currant money Yearly and every Year for ever hereafter And in case of Neglect to make full payment of sᵈ twenty Shillings as above Annually it shall then be Lawfull for yᵉ President of sᵈ Province for yᵉ time being or for other yᵉ Agents or Assigns of yᵉ Governʳ & Company of yᵉ Massachusets Collony to Levy and make Distress upon yᵉ Estate of any of yᵉ Inhabitants of [79] said Land for yᵉ time being as Well for sᵈ Annual Rent as alsoe for all Costs & Charges Accruing and arising upon the same and yᵉ Estate so Levied or Distreined to bear, Drive or carry away, with so much as it shall Cost to convey yᵉ same to any place as shall by Such Agent President or Treasurʳ of yᵉ Province be appointed within the said Province/ In Witness hereof yᵉ parties have hereunto Interchangeably set their hands and Seales the day and year above mentioned.

Signed Sealed and Delivered   Thomas Danforth Presidᵗ (his seal)

In the presents of.
John Wincoll
John Penwill

Thomas Danforth Esqʳ came before me this 29ᵗʰ of June 1685. and owned yᵉ above sᵈ Instrument to be his Act and Deed.

John Davis Depty Presidᵗ

A true Copie of the originall Transcribed and Compared Augˢᵗ 2ᵈ 1700

p Jos Hamond Registʳ

To all Christian People to whome these presents shall come/ I Joshua Atwater of Boston in New England Mercer, Send Greeting Know ye that yᵉ said Joshua Atwater for

Book VI, Fol. 79.

divers good causes and consideraçons him thereunto moving More Especially for and in consideration of threescore thousand feet of good and Merchantable pine boards to him yᵉ sᵈ Joshua Atwater by Humphrey Scammon of Saco in yᵉ Province of Maine in New England in hand paid or Secured to be paid, with the which paiment the said Joshua Atwater is fully Satisfied contented and paid Have granted bargained and Sold Aliened Enfeoffeed and confirmed And by these presents doe give, grant bargain Sell Alien Enfeoffe and confirm unto the sᵈ Humphrey Scammon his heires and Assignes for ever, All that his Saw Mill on Dunston ffalls in Scarborow, together with yᵉ fall and priviledge of timbʳ four Miles about the Mill, Alsoe fiftie Acres of upland Adjoyning to yᵉ falls on yᵉ Northeast, and a parcell of Meadow below yᵉ Mill as far down as Robert Nicholls his Marsh as yᵉ same was confirmed unto Benjamin Blackman by a town grant of whom yᵉ said Joshua Atwater Purchased yᵉ same Together with all and Singular yᵉ Appurtenances and priviledges thereunto belonging or in any wise Appurtaining And all his Right Title and Interest of in & to the same and every part and parcell thereof To have and to hold the sᵈ Mill ffalls and priviledge of timber fiftie Acres of upland and parcell of Meadow be it more or less as abovesᵈ with yᵉ Liberties priviledges and Appurtenances thereunto belonging or in any wise Appurtaining unto him yᵉ sᵈ Humphrey Scammon his heires and Assigns and to his and their only proper use benefit and behoofe for ever And yᵉ sᵈ Joshua Atwater for himself his heires & Assignes covenanteth promiseth and granteth to and with yᵉ sᵈ Humphrey Scammon his heires and Assignes that he hath full power and Lawfull Authority the same to sell and dispose of And that yᵉ same and every part of the above granted Premises with their liberties priviledges and Appurtenances now be, and from time to time shall be remaine and continue to be yᵉ proper right and Inheritance

*Atwater
to
Scammon*

of him the s^d Humphrey Scammon his heires and and Assignes without ye least Suite let trouble Molestacon contradiction deniall Eviction or ejection of him the s^d Joshua Atwater his heires or Assigns or by or from any other person whatsoever having, Claiming or pretending to have or Claime a right title or Interest thereunto or to any part or parcell thereof And that ye same and every part thereof with their Liberties priviledges and Appurtenances thereunto belonging is free and clear and freely and clearly Acquitted Exonerated and discharged of and from all and all manner of other gifts grants Leases Mortgages Joyntures wills entailes Judgments Executions Dowers & all other Incumbrances whatsoever, had made done Acknowledged comitted or Suffered to be done, Suffered and Committed by him ye s^d Joshua Atwater his heirs or Assignes or by or from any other person or persons whatsoever claiming any right or title thereto under him his heires or Assignes. In witness whereof the s^d Joshua Atwater hath hereunto put hand and seal this twentieth day of July, in ye year of our Lord God One thousand Six hundred and Eighty Seaven And in ye third yeare of ye Reign of our Soveraign Lord James the Second by the grace of God King of England Scotland ffrance and Ireland &c./

       Joshua Atwater (his seal)

 Memorand The Eight twentieth day of July Sixteen hundred eighty seaven Livery and Seisin with Turf and twig, of all ye within Mentioned premisses was delivered by the within Mentioned Joshua Atwater In ye presents of us

 T Sheppard
 Benj Blackey
 William Milborne

 A true Copie of the origenall Deed of Sale Transcribed and compared this 2^d of Jan^{ry} 1700.

       p Jos Hamond Regist^r

BOOK VI, FOL. 80.

To all Christian People to whome this present Deed of Sale shall come, John Tenny of Kittery within ye County of York in ye Province of ye Massachusets Bay in New England ffisherman and Margrett his wife Send Greeting/ Know ye that ye s^d John Tenny and Margrett his wife for and in consideration of the Sum̄ of twenty five pounds Currant money of New England to them in hand paid before ye ensealing and Delivery of these presents by Humphrey Scammon of the same Town County and Province afores^d Yeoman, the receipt whereof they doe hereby Acknowledge And themselves therewith to be fully satisfied contented and paid/ And thereof and every part thereof doe Acquit [80] Exenerate and Discharge the s^d Humphrey Scammon his heires Execut^{rs} and Administrat^{rs} for ever by these presents, Have given, granted, bargained, sold, Aliened Enfeoffed and confirmed And by these presents doe fully freely Clearly & absolutely give grant bargain Sell Aliene enfeoffe convey and confirm unto him ye said Humphrey Scammon his heires and Assignes for ever All that their tract of Land and Marsh or piece or parcell of land & Marsh Scituate lying and being in the township of Saco on ye North Side of Saco River, containing by Estimation about four hundred Acres be it more or less butted and bounded on ye one side by Saco River near ye Mouth of s^d River then by ye Sea Side to ye Mouth of Goose fare river, And from ye mouth of s^d Goose fair river to a pine tree on ye North Side of Goose fare River by the uper Wading place, then to ye root of a pine tree near Goose fare old path then to ye mouth of ye great Gutt com̄only called by the name of Shaws gutt where ye first bounds begin, which land & Marsh was formerly Henry Waddocks as by Deed of Sale from John Richards Thomas Lake & Joshua Scottow may Appear bearing Date ye first day of Novemb^r one thousand six hundred fifty & seven and is ye s^d John Tennys by Vertue of a Deed from

Tinny to Scamon

Jane Waddock Administratrix to yᵉ Estate of Henry Waddock Deceased Together with all yᵉ profits priviledges comodities and Appurtenances whatsoever to yᵉ sᵈ parcell or tract of Land belonging or in any wise Appurtaining To have & to hold the sᵈ tract or parcell of land and Marsh, butted and bounded as aforesᵈ, with all other the above granted Premisses and every part and parcell thereof unto the said Humphrey Scammon his heirs and Assignes for ever to yᵉ only proper use benefit and behoof of him yᵉ sᵈ Humphrey Scammon his heires & Assigns for evermore/ And yᵉ sᵈ John Tenny and Margret his wife for themselves their heires Executʳˢ and Adminʳˢ Doe hereby Covenant promise & grant to and with yᵉ sᵈ Humphrey Scammon his heires and assigns in following manner and form, that is to say, that at yᵉ time of yᵉ ensealing of these pʳˢᵗˢ they the said John Tenny and Margret his wife are the true Sole & Lawfull owners of all yᵉ afore bargained Premisses And that they have in themselves full power good right and Lawfull Authority to grant Sell convey & Assure the same unto yᵉ sᵈ Humphrey Scammon his heires and Assignes in aforesᵈ manner and form And that yᵉ sᵈ Humphrey Scammon his heires and Assignes shall and may by force and Vertue of these presents, from time to time and at all times forever hereafter Lawfully peaceably & quietly have hold use ocupie possess and enjoy yᵉ above granted Premises with their Appurtenances free and Clear and Cleerly Acquitted and Discharged of and from all and all manner of former and other gifts, grants, bargains Sales Leases Mortgages Joyntures Dowers Judgments entailes forfitures & all other troubles and incumbrances whatsoever And yᵉ abovesᵈ Premisses with their Appurtenances and every part and parcell thereof unto him the sᵈ Humphrey Scammon his heires and Assignes Against yᵉ sᵈ John Tenny and Margret his wife, their heires Executʳˢ and Adminʳˢ And against all other persons whatsoever Any ways Lawfully

Tinny to Scamon

Book VI, Fol. 80.

Claiming or Demanding ye same or any part thereof shall and will Warrant and Defend for ever by these presents. In witness whereof the s^d John Tinney and Margret his wife have hereunto set their hands and Seales the fourth day of June Anno Domini One thousand and Seven hundred Annoq̨ Regni Regis Gulielmi tertii Angliæ &c xii
Signed Sealed & Delivered

 In the presents of. The words Marsh twice in ye thir-
 John Newmarch   teenth line and river in ye seven-
 Joan Dearing.   teenth line & Marsh in ye twenty
   his   sixth line were incerted before
 John   Donnell Signing and Sealing.
   mark   John Tinny (his seal)
           her
       Margrett   Tinny (her seal)
The 23^d of Novemb^r 1700. mark

then John Tenny & Margret his wife Appeared and did Acknowledge this Instrum^t to be their free Act and Deed/ Before me   Wm Pepperrell Js Pes

A true Copie of ye originall Transcribed and Compared the second day of Jan^{ry} 1700. p Jos Hamond Regist^r

---

To all Christian People before whome these presents shall come/ William Sanders of Kittery in ye Province of Maine sendeth Greeting, Now Know ye that I ye afore mentioned William Sander for divers good causes me thereunto moving/ More Especially for and in consideration of fourteen pounds of lawfull money of New England to me in hand paid by John Gelding of ye town and Province afores^d/ the receipt whereof and of every part and pcell thereof I acknowledge and therewith fully satisfied contented and paid/ Have given granted bargained and sold and by these

BOOK VI, FOL. 81.

Sanders
to
Gelding

presents doe for me my heires Execut^{rs} Admin^{rs} and Assignes forever freely clearly and absolutely give grant bargain and sell unto him ye s^d John Gelding his heires Execut^{rs} Admin^{rs} and Assignes for ever All that piece or parcell of Land which was granted to me by the town of Kittery in ye year one thousand six hundred Eighty and two, Scituate lying and being in ye town of Kittery near Surgeon Creek brook, Containing thirty Acres, Eighty poles in length East and West And Sixty poles in breadth North and South/ bounded on ye west with ffrancis Blachfords land in part And bounded on the South in part with Maj^r ffrosts and ye North and East and part of the South bounded with present comons as Appears by ye return of the Surveying of s^d land bearing Date Septemb^r ye first one thousand six hundred Eighty and three/ To have and to hold ye above given and granted Premisses with all ye Priviledges and Appurtenances thereto belonging or in any ways Appurtaining/ Together with a dwelling house [81] Erected upon ye s^d land And ye s^d Gelding shall and may from time to time and at all times hereafter Improve and make use of ye aforesaid Premisses to his own proper benefit and behoof, without any Molestation let or hinderance from me ye s^d Sanders or any other person or psons Claiming any right title or Interest thereunto from by or under me In Witnesse whereof I have hereunto set my hand and Seal this fifteenth day of April in the year of our Lord one thousand six hundred Ninety and one.

Signed Sealed and Delivered   William Sanders (his seal)
  in the presents of.   his mark CV
  Jos Hamond
  Mercy Hamond   Sarah S Sanders
Province of New Hampshier   her mark

Sarah Brawn, formerly the wife of William Sanders personally Appeared before me the Subcrib^r this 29th day of Octob^r 1700 & Acknowledged the above Instrum^t to be her

Act and Deed And that she fully Acquits and surrenders her thirds of Dowryship/

       Sam[ll] Penhallow Jus[ts] Pea

A true Copie of the originall Deed Transcribed & compared this tenth day of Decemb[r] 1700,

       p Jos: Hamond Regist[r]

To all Christian People to whome this present Deed of Sale shall come/ I Elizabeth Witherick y[e] wife of Robert Witherick of Summer town in y[e] Countrey of Carolina Send Greeting/ Know yee that I Elizabeth Witherick by vertue of a letter of Atturny from my s[d] husband Robert Witherick for and in consideration of y[e] Sum of two hundred pounds of Currant money in New England to me in hand paid before y[e] ensealing and delivery of these presents by Richard Cutt of Kittery in the County of York in y[e] Province of y[e] Massachusets Bay in New England Yeoman the receipt whereof I do hereby Acknowledge and my self therewith to be fully Satisfied and paid And thereof and of every part thereof do Acquit Exonerate & discharge the s[d] Richard his heires Execut[rs] and Admin[rs] for every by these presents Have given granted bargained sold Aliened Enfeoffed and confirmed And by these p[r]sents doe for my self my heires &c fully freely and Absolutely give grant, bargain, sell, Aliene Enfeoffe and confirm unto him y[e] s[d] Richard Cutt his heires and Assigns for ever y[e] Moiety or one half part of all that parcell of Land and Marsh Scituate lying and being in Kittery in New England afores[d] Comonly called or known by y[e] name of Champernowns Island Together with all y[e] comodities priviledges and Appurtenances belonging or in any wise Appurtaining to said land and Marsh To have & to hold he s[d] land and Marsh with all y[e] Appurtenances thereunto be-

(margin: Witherick to Cutt)

BOOK VI, FOL. 81.

longing unto ye s^d Richard Cutt his heires Execut^{rs} Admin^{rs} and Assigns for ever to ye only proper use benefit and behoof of him ye s^d Richard Cutt his heires &c forever more And I ye s^d Elizabeth Witherick doe for my self my heires Excut^{rs} & Admiñ^{rs} hereby covenant and promise to and with ye s^d Richard Cutt his heires Execut^{rs} Admin^{rs} and Assignes in manner and form following, that is to say that at ye time of ye ensealing and Delivery of these presents I ye s^d Elizabeth Witherick am ye true owner and Lawfull owner of the above bargained Premisses And that I have in my self full power good right and lawfull Authority to grant sell convey and Assure ye same unto ye s^d Richard Cutt his heires &c in manner and forme afores^d And that ye s^d Richard Cutt his heires Execut^{rs} Admin^{rs} or Assigns shall and may by force and Vertue of these p^rsents from time to time & at all times for ever hereafter Lawfully peaceably and quietly Have hold use ocupie and enjoy ye above granted Premisses with their Appurtenances/ And every part and parcell thereof free and clear & clearly Acquitted and discharged of and from all and all manner of former and other gifts grants bargains sales Leases Mortgages Joyntures Dowers titles troubles Acts Alienations and Incumbrances whatsoever had made comitted done or Suffered to be done by me ye s^d Elizabeth my heires Execut^{rs} Admin^{rs} or Assignes At any time or times before ye ensealing hereof And ye aboves^d Premisses with their Appurtenances and every part thereof to him ye s^d Richard Cut his heires Execut^{rs} Admin^{rs} and Assignes Against my selfe my heires Execut^{rs} & Admin^{rs} and each and every of them And against all other person or persons whatsoever any ways Lawfully Claiming or Demanding the same or any part thereof from by or under me shall and will warrant & Defend for ever by these p^rsents In Witness whereof I ye s^d Elizabeth Witherick have hereunto set my hand and Seal (after ye enterlining of ye words by or under me against ye twenty fourth line) this twentieth day of Au-

Book VI, Fol. 82.

gust in yᵉ year of our Lord one thousand & seven hundred And in yᵉ twelfth year of of his Maᵗⁱᵉ Reign William yᵉ third ouer England &c. King.

Signed Sealed and delivered   Elizabeth Whetherick (her seal)
  in the presents of us
  John Newmarch
  Jos Hamond Junʳ
  Aaron Scriven

York ss/ Kittery Augˢᵗ 20ᵗʰ 1700

Mʳˢ Elizabeth Whetherick psonally Appearing before me yᵉ Subscribʳ one of the membʳˢ of his Maᵗⁱᵉ Council of yᵉ Province of the Massachusets Bay And Justice of Peace within yᵉ same Acknowledged this Instrument to be her Act and Deed/

                                    Jos : Hamond

A true Copie of the originall Deed Transcribed and compared this 20ᵗʰ Augˢᵗ 1700.   Jos Hamond Registʳ

To all to whome these pʳsents shall come I Mary Champernown of Kittery in yᵉ County of York in yᵉ Province of the Massachusets Bay in New England. Widdow send Greeting

Champernown to Cutt   Know ye that for and in consideration of yᵉ Sum of two hundred pounds in Currant mony of New England to me in hand well and truly paid at and before yᵉ Ensealing and delivery of these pʳsents. by my son Richard Cutt of yᵉ same town County and Province aforesᵈ Yeoman/ the receipt whereof I doe hereby Acknowledge & my self therewith to be fully satisfied contented and paid and of and from every [82] part and parcell thereof for me yᵉ sᵈ Mary Champernown my heires Executʳˢ Adminʳˢ and Assignes doe Acquit and fully discharge him yᵉ sᵈ Richard Cutt his heires Executʳˢ Adminʳˢ and Assignes for ever by these pʳsents I have given granted bargained sold

Book VI, Fol. 82.

Aliened Enfeoffed and confirmed/ And by these p'sents doe for my self my heires Execut'rs Admin'rs and Assignes fully freely and Absolutely give, grant, bargain, sell, Aliene Enfeoffe and confirm unto him y'e s'd Richard Cutt his heires and Assigns for ever, the Moiety or half part of all that tract or parcell of land and Marsh scituate lying and being in Kittery in New England afores'd Comonly called or known by y'e name of Champ'rnoons Island, which Island is bounded with M'r Nath'll ffryers on y'e West and brode bote harbour on East together with all y'e housing that is now on y'e s'd Island and all other priviledges profits and Appurtinances belonging to y'e one half part of s'd Island, To have and to hold y'e above mentioned land and Marsh and housing with y'e Appurtenances thereunto belonging with all y'e right title Interst Claime and Demand which I y'e s'd Mary Champernown now have or in time past have had or which I my heires Excut'rs Admin'rs or Assignes may might should or in any wise ought to have in time to come of in or to y'e above granted Premsses or any part thereof to him y'e s'd Richard Cutt his heires & Assignes for ever And to y'e sole and proper Use benefit and behoof of him y'e said Richard Cutt his heires &c for evermore And I y'e s'd Mary Champernoon do for my self my heirs Execut'rs Admin'rs and Assignes Covenant & promise to and with the s'd Richard Cutt his heires &c. that at and before y'e Ensealing & delivery hereof I am y'e true right and Lawfull owner of the aboves'd Premisses And that I have in my self full power good right and Lawfull Authority to grant and confirm y'e same unto him y'e s'd Richard Cutt his heirs and Assigns as afores'd And that y'e same and every part thereof is free and Clear of and from all other former gifts grants, bargains, Sales, Alienations and Incumbrances whatsoever had, made, comitted Done or suffered to be done by me y'e s'd Mary Champernoon my heires &c at any time or times before the ensealing hereof And that it shall be Lawfull to and for y'e s'd Richard

Cutt his heirs and Assigns yͤ afores⁴ Premisses from time to time and at all times for ever hereafter quietly and peaceably have hold use and enjoy without any manner of lett trouble or disturbance whatsoever of or by me my heires &c or any of them or of or by any other person or persons whatsoever Lawfully Claiming yͤ Same or any part thereof from by or under me And yͤ Sale hereof against myself my heires &c And And against all other persons Claiming yͤ same or any part thereof from by or und͟r me I will for ever warrant and Defend by these presents In witness whereof I haue hereunto set my hand & Seal this twentieth day of Aug͟ˢᵗ in yͤ year of o͟ʳ Lord one thousand Seven hundred And in yͤ xɪɪ year of his Maᵗⁱ Reign William yͤ 3ᵈ over England &c King. Signed Sealed and Delivered   Mary Champernown (her seal)

in yͤ p͟ʳsents of
Jos Haṁond Jun͟ʳ
John Newmrch.
Aaron Scriven

York ss/ Kittery Aug͟ˢᵗ 20ᵗʰ 1700

M͟ʳˢ Mary Champernown personally Appearing before me yͤ Subscrib͟ʳ one of yͤ Memb͟ʳˢ of his Maᵗⁱ Council of the Province of yͤ Massachusets Bay and Justice of Peace within yͤ same Acknowledged this Instrument to be her Act and Deed.

Jos Haṁond

A true Copie of yͤ originall Transcribed and compared Aug͟ˢᵗ 20ᵗʰ 1700

p Jos Haṁond Regist͟ʳ

Gentlmen/ To the Select men of the Town of York.

Having had discourse with Sundry of your Inhabitants relating to yͤ Straight and nessessity of your town for want of a corn Mill having had Sundry thoughts thereabout doe make you this offer (which I Judge all things considered is rashonall) which if you Judge Expedient, please to present to y° Inhabitants in gener¹¹ town Meeting as fol: Viz^t/ first I say this, if your town will give and confirm unto me and my heirs for ever y° whole sole right and priviledge of the Mill Creeks where Mr Henry Saword built his Mills as alsoe all y° towns Right and Intrust in those Lands and Medo and timber formerly granted by y° town to Web, Clark, Rushford and Ellinggam and all priviledges to them belonging with the Arreredges of rent, I say then and on that condition I will be obleged, both me and my heires to erect a good Sufficient Corn Mill and for ever maintain y° Same at my own proper cost for grinding y° towns corn for y° usuall Toll allowed through y° Countrey/ this I offer thoue I know I cannot have half y° advantage those persons formerly had for what timber was near and convenient is all gone besides I must forthwith lay out above 150$^£$ and have nothing for many years for all the toll of your towns corn will not pay a mans wages this seven years for tending y° Mill however if this be taken up with and a Voate past by your Inhabitants for Impowering y° Select men or some other Meet psons to enter into Articles with me on those conditions, shall on Notice from such Attend their Moshon I further Add that in y° mean time while I can Erect a Mill in your town I will always keep one of my Mills ready to grind your corn as you come/ Not else at present but await your resolve hereabout.

Soe remain Gentlemen, Yours to Serve John Pickerin.

Dated this 20th of ffeb^r 169$\frac{3}{4}$

Gentlemen I also ad and desire you to take care that if I should want timber for building y° Mill that I may have it on any mans land where I can find it most convenient as also 2 days work of each man in Town as I shall have occation about y° Mill and Dam, with libertie to build s^d Mill or Mills where I pleas in York.

BOOK VI, FOL. 83.

A true Copie of y⁰ originall Transcribed and compared Jan⁷⁷ 9th 1700.

p Jos Hamond Regist.ʳ

1 Voted at a Legall Town Meeting in York y⁰ 18th of March 169⅞ Compliance with the within proposals.

2 That Mr Samuel Donnell, Lᵗ Abraham Preble Senʳ Arthur Bragdon Senʳ and Joseph Wier, them or y⁰ Majʳ part of them are hereby fully Impowered in y⁰ behalf of sᵈ Town to enter into covenant with John Pickerin, Senʳ, of Portsm⁰ in behalf of our Town for y⁰ Erecting and Maintaining of a Corn Mill for grinding y⁰ towns Corn for y⁰ usuall toll taken throw y⁰ Countrey And to confirm unto him y⁰ sᵈ Pickerin and his heires &c for ever, all those lands, timbʳ, trees, stream and streams of waters both salt and fresh in those Creekes where Mill or Mills have been formerly built by Ellingam & Gail or Sayword, with all priviledges of rent & all priviledges and Advantages to y⁰ sᵈ Creeks or Stream, or Streams of water belonging wᵗʰ priviledges of timber as granted by sᵈ town to those Mills or Mill and any other thing or things for sᵈ Pickerins incouragemᵗ, to Act doe & pform in our behalf/ And whatsoever Covenᵗ or agreemᵗ shall be made by & between sᵈ Pickerin and y⁰ persons before named or y⁰ Majʳ part of them shall be held good vallid & made good in all respects as fully as if y⁰ whole had done y⁰ same.   James Plaisted town Clerk

A true Copie of y⁰ originall, and was written on y⁰ back side of y⁰ aboue letter, Transcribed and Compared Jan⁷⁷ 9th 1700.   p Jos Hamond Regist.ʳ

[83] Pursuant to a Voat Past at a Publick town meeting in York y⁰ 18th of March 169⅞ relating to agreement with John Pickerin for Erecting a Corn Mill for y⁰ benefit of the

town in grinding their corn, In which Voate we Samuel Donnell, Abraham Preble, Arthur Bragenton & Joseph Wier or ye Major part of us being fully Impowered to enter into Covenant with s^d Pickerin relating to ye foregoing Premises for building of a Mill as more at large Appeare by s^d Voate and s^d Pickerins letter and Proposalls on Record/ which agreem^t being made by us our s^d town is to perform.

Now know all persons to whom this Instrum^t of writing shall come or concern that we Samuel Donnell, Abraham Preble & Arthur Bragenton by Vertue of ye aboue power from our s^d town have fully and absolutely agreed with s^d Pickerin & Mr James Plaisted whom s^d Pickerin desires to be his partner in ye concerns And doe hereby fully and Absolutely in ye behalf of our town agree with s^d Pickerin and s^d Plaisted at s^d Pickerins request in manner following Viz^t

first on ye conditions hereinafter specified we ye Subscribers hereof by Vertue of the power above mentioned from our town doe by these presents fully & absolutely give grant and confirm unto ye s^d Pickerin and Plaisted at s^d Pickerins request the full sole and whole Rights & Priviledges of that whole stream or streams of water both fresh and salt runing throo the Creek where Ellingam, Gail & Saword former built Mills together with all ye benefit & Priviledges of s^d Creeks for building Mill or Mills As also all those lands timber & Medos granted on on conditions, to ye s^d Gal Ellingam & Saword, Web Clark & Rushford with all ye timber, trees, woods and underwoods standing growing or lying on s^d Lands together with all ye Arerages of Rent and all ye whole right & Interest that ever s^d town had, has, or of right ought to have to all or any part of ye before mentioned Creeks Stream or Streams of water, lands Medos trees rights & all Rents unto him ye s^d Pickerin and Plaisted at s^d Pickerins request their heires Execut^{rs} Admin^{rs} and Assigns for ever And to and for noe other use intent or purpose whatsoever.

2ly The s^d Pickerin and Plaisted for ye consideration of ye holding & enjoying of all and every part of ye above bargained and Mentioned particulars, doe by this present Covenant, and engage to and with ye s^d Samuel Donnell Abraham Preble & Arthur Bragenton in behalf of their Town of York that they ye s^d Pickerin and Plaisted will Erect and build at their own proper Cost and Charge a good Sufficient Corn Mill, and so keep and maintain the same for grinding ye whole Inhabitants of ye tows corn for ye Usuall Toll taken throw the Countrey/ And that they will keep and maintain ye same for those ends forever. And in Case it should so fall out that such Mill so built should happen to be burnt or otherway destroyed, that then in that case said Pickerin and Plaisted or their heires Execut^rs & Admin^rs and Assigns shall forthwith with all convenient Speed possible, to be shore within one year at furthest build and Erect such other Mill or Mills and so maintain ye same as may be sufficient for grinding ye s^t towns corn & that for ever, the first Mill to be built by ye last of July next at ye furthest

3ly We ye s^d Donnell Preble and Bragenton doe also further Ingage in behalf of our afores^d Town that we and all our Inhabitants are and be obleged and Ingaged to grind all their corn for their particular use for ever and to grind with no other so long as s^d Pickerin Plaisted & their heires &c shall perform ye before mentioned Ingagem^t of keeping and maintaining a Mill or Mills for those ends.

4ly and lastly for ye true performance of all and every particular of all the Premisses aboue Mentioned, we ye s^d Donnell, Preble and Bragenton for and in behalf of our town, And Pickerin and Plaisted for themselves doe bind themselves Joyntly and Severally, that is to say s^d Donnell, Preble and Bragenton doe Ingage ye s^d town, and s^d Pickerin and Plaisted for themselves Each to ye other in ye full Sum of five hundred pounds for ye true performance on both parties to be made good by the non performer of any thing in y[e] above Articles, to y[e] perform[r] As Witness our hands and Seales this : 19th day of Decemb[r] 1697. one thousand six hundred Ninety Seven.

Signed & Sealed Samuel Donnell (his seal)
  in presents of Abra : Preble (his seal)
James Gooch Arthur Bragdon (his seal)
Matthew Austine John Pickerin (his seal)
John Hancock James Plaisted (his seal)

The word Assignes in the Second Article were soe enterlined by consent of all parties

The persons above mentioned in these Articles is to be understood Pickerin of Portsm[o] in the Province of New Hampshier And Plaisted, Donnell, Preble & Bragenton all of York in y[e] Province of Maine, not being Specified before agreed thus to be entred here And y[e] names Web, Clark & Rushfort in y[e] first Article Alsoe y[e] timb[r] trees with liberty to build y[e] aboves[d] Mill or Mills any where in York

January y[e] 8th 1700. Cap[tn] Abraham Preble/ M[r] Sam[ll] Donnell/ Arthur Bragenton Sen[r]/ And John Pickerin Sen[r] Appeared before me y[e] Subscrib[r] one of his Ma[ts] Justices of Peace for y[e] County of York And Acknowledged y[e] within Instrum[t] of writing or Articles to be their Act and Deed the day and year first above written./

                          Will Pepperrell Js Pes

A true Copie of y[e] origenall Transcribed and compared Jan[ry] 9th 1700. p Jos Hamond Regist[r]

To all Christian People to whome this present writing shall come/ Know yee that I James Emery, Sen[r], of Barwick Alias Newachwonock of y[e] pvince of Maine in New England with y[e] concent of Elizabeth my wife for Di– good

Book VI, Fol. 84.

Emery
to
Waymouth

causes me thereunto Moving but Especially for and in consideration of fourteen pounds in Merchantable pay with which I Acknowledg my selfe Satisfied Have given granted and confirmed And doe by these presents Absolutely [84] and clearly giue grant make over and confirm unto Edward Waymouth of the same town and Province, All that lot of land Lying at ye head of a Creek commonly called by ye name of Mast creeke near ye River of Piscataqua & bounded by ye land of Mr Thomas Broughton on ye South containing, of Meadow and Upland by Estimation thirty Acres be it more or less as it hath bin & now is bounded by ye town above named, with all ye profits and Appertinances thereunto belonging To have and to hold ye aboves^d thirty Acres of land respectively to proper use and behoof of ye aboves^d Edward Waymouth his heires Execut^{rs} Admin^{rs} & Assigns for ever And I ye aboves^d James Emery doe covenant promise and agree for my self my heires Execut^{rs} Admin^{rs} and Assigns to and with ye aboves^d Edward Waym^o his heires Execut^{rs} Admin^{rs} and Assignes to warrant ye sale of ye aboves^d Premises And to free ye s^d thirty Acres of land from all former gifts Deeds Sales or Engagements whatsever/ Ld Propriet^r Excepted/ And that ye s^d Edward Waymouth his heires Execut^{rs} Admin^{rs} and Assignes from henceforth and for ever shall from time to time and at all times have hold use ocupie possess and enjoy all and every part of ye s^d Premisses without any lett suite hinderance or Molestation of me ye s^d James Emery and Elizabeth my wife our heirs Execut^{rs} Admin^{rs} and Assignes or any other person or persons lawfully Claiming, in by from or under us or any or either of us or any or either of our heires Execut^{rs} Admin^{rs} or Assignes/ In witness whereof I ye s^d James Emery and Elizabeth my wife have hereunto set our hands and Seales this twenty sixth day of May one thousand six hundred and Eighty Six.

Signed Sealed & Delivered   James Emery   (his seal)
  In ye presents of us   The Elizabeth
  John Emerson.   mark of ~~ Emery (her seal)
  Daniel Emery

Province of Maine in New England James Emery Senr personally Appearing before me William Stoughton Esqr one of his Ma^ts Council for his Teritory of New England Acknowledged this Instrum^t to be his Act and Deed Octob^r 12 : 1686

                          William Stoughton

A true Copie of ye originall Transcribed and compared Septemb^r 30th 1700.

                          p Jos : Hamond Reg^r

Morrell to ffernald

Know all men by these presents that I John Morrell Senr, of Kittery in the County of York Bricklayer, for ye consideration of sixty pounds in mony to me in hand paid by John ffernald Sen, of ye same place Yeoman the receipt thereof I doe Acknowledge And my self therewith contented and paid And doe by these presents Acquit ye s^d John ffernald for ye same in consideration of ye above said Sum I ye s^d John Morrell Have given granted bargained and sold And doe by these p^rsents Absolutely fully and freely give grant bargain & sell unto ye s^d John ffernald his heires and Assignes for ever Sixty Acres of land lying In ye township of Kittery between ye great Cove and ye head of Spruce Creek near Cap^tn ffernalds farm And is bounded on ye Northwest with Thomas Spinney and on ye Southwest with Jacob Remich and on Southeast with ye hill and swamp comonly called by ye name of Crockets and on ye Northeast with or near Captain ffernalds farm so

Book VI, Fol. 84.

Accounted together with all the timb{r} wood and underwood thereon with all y{e} Appurtenances and priviledges thereunto belonging To have and to hold all y{e} s{d} tract of land as it is hereby bargained and discribed to y{e} only use benefit and behoofe of him y{e} s{d} John ffernald his heires and Assignes for evermore And furthermore y{e} s{d} John Morrell doth covenant to & with the s{d} John ffernald that y{e} s{d} lands are free from all Incumbrances w'soev{r} as sales gifts Mortgages Joyntures or Dowries And that he y{e} s{d} John Morrell was y{e} true and proper owner thereof At y{e} time of y{e} ensealing hereof & that he had full power and Lawfull Authority to dispose of y{e} Same, y{e} Peaceable and quiet Possession thereof to warrant & maintaine against all persons laying a Lawfull Claim thereunto, the Kings Ma{tie} and his Success{rs} only Excepted/ Witness my hand and Seal this twenty second day of Decemb{r} one thousand Seven Seven hundred 1700

Signed Sealed & Delivered   John Morrell (his seal)
  In y{e} p'sents of us.   her
       his   Sarah ǁ Morrell (her seal)
  James ⌇ ffernald   mark
     mark
Thomas ffernald
Jos Hamond.

York ss/ Kittery Decemb{r} 28{th} 1700

John Morrell and Sarah his wife personally Appearing before me y{e} Subscrib{r} one of the Memb{rs} of his Ma{ts} Councill of y{e} Province of y{e} Massachusets Bay And Justice of Peace within y{e} same y{e} s{d} John Morrell Acknowledged this Instrum{t} to be his Act & Deed And the s{d} Sarah Morrell freely gave up all her right of Dower of in & to y{e} Premisses/

                        Jos Hamond

A true Copie of y{e} originall Transcribed and compared Decemb{r} 28{th} 1700

                p Jos Hamond Regist{r}

BOOK VI, FOL. 85.

At a Legall town Meeting held at Kittery May 16 1694/ Granted to Moses Goodwin twenty Acres of land provided he improve it within one year after it be laid out by building or fencing & improving a considerable part thereof otherwise to return again to y² town.

A true Copie taken out of Kittery town Book.

p Jos Hamond Cler

Know all men that Moses Goodwin, and Abigail his wife, of Barwick in y² County of York in New England doe Assigne and make over All their Right title and Interest in y² above written town grant of twenty Acres of land And all their Right in any lands on the Account thereof, to Abraham Lord of Barwick his heires & Assignes for ever. [85] To have and to hold the same for ever In Witness whereof y² s^d Moses & Abigail Goodwin have set to their hands and Seales this sixth day of Novemb^r Anno Domini one thousand Seven hundred

Goodin to Lord

Signed Sealed and Delivered   Moses   his 𝒪   Goodwin (his seal)
   In presents of.   mark
   John Plaisted
   John Hill.   her
   Ichabod Plaisted   Abigail X Goodwin (her seal)
York ss Kittery Novemb^r 6th 1700   mark

Moses Goodwin and Abigail his wife psonally Appearing before me y² Subscrib^r one of his Ma^ts Justices of Peace in y² County of York Acknowledged this Instrument to be their Act and Deed.

Jos Hamond

A true Copie of y² originall Transcribed and compared Novemb^r 6th 1700.   p Jos Hamond Regist^r

Know all men by these presents that I John Shapligh of Kittery in yᵉ County of York Gent¹¹ for Divers good Causes and Considerations me hereunto Moving but more Especially for and in consideration of sixteen pounds and ten shillings in Money to me in hand paid by Walter Deniver of yᵉ same place Shipwright at & before yᵉ Ensealing and delivery of these presents, wherewith I confess my self to be fully Satisfied contented and paid Have bargained and sold And by these presents doe fully clearly and Absolutely bargain and sell unto yᵉ sᵈ Walter Deniver his heires or Assignes for ever in plain and open Market after yᵉ manner of New England, thirteen Acres and almost a quarter of Land Lying in yᵉ town of Kittery between Crooked lane and Spruce Creek And takes its begining at yᵉ Cross way that goes to yᵉ point & Strawberry bank, toward yᵉ Northeast end of yᵉ late Mʳ Thomas Wethers his home lot And is part of sᵈ lot And runs from the said Cross way South Joyning to yᵉ high way that goes to yᵉ point forty pole and from that Extent Southwest & by west by Mʳ Cutts line forty pole and from thence Northwest forty pole near to yᵉ high way to Strawberry bank or Woodmans fferry & from thence by sᵈ high way to yᵉ first station on a straight line containing thirteen Acres and a quarter of an Acre Almost. Together with all yᵉ wood & underwood & Advantages thereto belonging To have and to hold all yᵉ sᵈ tract of land & yᵉ Appurtenances thereof unto yᵉ only use benefit and behoofe of him yᵉ sᵈ Walter Deniver his heires or Assignes for ever And I yᵉ sᵈ John Shapleigh doe for my self and my heires Covenant to & with the sᵈ Walter Deniver and his heires that yᵉ Premisses are free from all manner of Incumbrances whatsoever, as Sales gifts Mortgages and Joyntures And that I am yᵉ true and proper owner thereof at and before yᵉ ensealing of these presents And that I have wᵗʰin my self full power and Lawfull Authority to dispose of yᵉ same/ the peaceable and quiet

Shapleigh to Deniver

Possession thereof to Warrant and Defend against all persons laying a lawfull Claime thereunto/ In witness hereof I have set to my hand & seal this twenty sixth day of Decemb^r Vulgarly called Saint Stephens day, one thousand Seven hundred 1700

Signed Sealed & delivered   John Shapleigh (his seale)
   in presents of us
   Richard Bryar
   Daniel Jones
   Wm Godsoe

To all People to whome this present Deed of Sale shall come I Job Alcock of New Hampshier in New England Shipwright Send Greeting. Know yee that for and in consideration of twenty five pounds of Currant Money in New England to me in hand well and truly paid at and before ye ensealing & Delivery of these presents by Samuel Pray of Kittery in the County of York in ye Province of the Massachusets Bay in New England Marrin^r the receipt whereof I doe hereby Acknowledge And my self to be fully & intirely satisfied & paid And thereof And of and from every part thereof for me ye s^d Job Alcock my heires Execut^{rs} Admin^{rs} and Assignes Doe Exonerate Acquit and fully Discharge him ye said Samuel Pray his heires Execut^{rs} Admin^{rs} & Assignes by these presents for ever, I ye s^d Job Alcock have given, granted, bargained, sold, Aliened, Enfeoffed & confirmed And by these presents doe for my self my heires Execut^{rs} Admin^{rs} and Assignes fully freely and Absolutely give, grant, bargain, sell, Alien, Enfeoffe convey and confirm unto ye s^d Samuel Pray his heires and Assignes a certain tract or parcel of Land Scituate Lying and being in ye township of York containing fiftie Acres which tract of Land was granted to ye s^d Alcock by ye town of York on y̆ first day of May Anno Domini 1685/ And laid out to him by y̆ Select men of s^d town on y̆ 18th day of May Anno Domini 1686. As by ye Records of s^d town referrence thereunto being had doth & may plainly Appear, being Butted and Bounded as followeth/ That is to say begining at a Elm tree marked four square standing in a little run of water on y̆ Northwest Side of Daniel Livingstones Land then Northeast and by North one hundred & twelve poles to a Elm tree marked on four sides/ then North west & by west Sixty one poles to a white oak tree marked on four

Alcock
to
Pray

sides, Then Southwest & by South Sixty four poles to a white oak tree marked on three sides, on y̆ Southeastward of Alexand^r Maxfields Marsh, Then Northwest twenty six poles to a Asp tree marked on four sides Then Southwest and by South forty eight poles to a stake marked on four sides, Then Southeast & by East to the tree where y̆ bounds first began Together with all y̆ profits and priviledges to y̆ s^d land belonging or in any ways Appurtaining To have and to hold y̆ s^d tract or parcel of Land with ye Appurtenances thereunto belonging with all ye right title Claim and demand which I ye s^d Job Alcock now have or in time past have had or which I my heires Execut^{rs} Admin^{rs} or Assignes may might should or in any wise ought to have in time to come, of in or to ye above granted Premisses or any part thereof to him the s^d Sam^{ll} Pray his heires & Assignes for ever And to ye sole and proper use benefit & behoof of him ye s^d Sam^{ll} Pray his heires &c for evermore And I ye s^d Job Alcock for my self my heires Execut^{rs} and Admin^{rs} doe covenant promise and grant to & with the s^d Sam^{ll} Pray his heires and Assignes that at & before ye Ensealing & delivery hereof I am ye true right and proper owner of ye above mentioned Premisses and their Appurtenances And that I have in my self full power good right & Lawfull Authority ye same to grant and confirm unto him ye s^d Sam^{ll} Pray his heires & Assignes as afores^d And that ye same and every part thereof is free and Clear & clearly Acquitted and Discharged of and from all former and other gifts grant bargains sales Leases Mortgages Dowries titles troubles Alienations and Incumbrances whatsoever And that it shall and may be Lawfull to and for ye s^d Sam^{ll} Pray his heires & Assignes the afores^d Premisses and every part thereof from time to time and at all times for ever hereafter to have hold use ocupie improve Possess & enjoy Lawfully peaceably and quietly without any lawfull let denial hinderance Molestation or disturbance of or by me or any person or persons from by or under me or by my procurement And that ye Sale thereof against my self my heires Execut^{rs} and Administrators and against all other persons [86] whatsoever Claiming and Lawfully Demanding ye same or any part thereof from by or under me I will for ever Save harmless Warrant and Defend by these p^{r}sents. In Testimony whereof I ye s^d Job Alcock have hereunto Set my hand and Seal this first day of January in ye year of our Lord one thousand Seven hundred Annoq Regni Regis Gulielmi tertii Dei Gratiæ Angliæ &c Duodecimo

Signed Sealed and Delivered   Job: Alcock (his seale)

In the presents of us.

Sam^{ll} Penhallow

Hen: Penny.

Job Alcock personally Appeared before me the Subscrib^r at Portsm^o (This first day of January one thousand and Seven hundred) one of his Ma^{ts} Justices of Peace for ye Province of New Hampsh^r and Acknowledged the above Instrum^t to be his Act and Deed.

Sam^{ll} Penhallow

A true Copie of the originall Transcribed and compared Jan^{ry} 4th 1700

p Jos Hamond Regist^r

BOOK VI, FOL. 86.

To all People to whome this present Deed of sale shall come/ Richard Cutt of Kittery within ye County of York in ye Province of the Massachusets Bay in New England, Yeoman, & Joanna his wife Send Greeting Know yee that ye s^d Richard Cutt and Joanna his wife for and in consideration of ye Sum̄ of two hundred and fifty pounds Currant money of New England to them in hand paid before ye Ensealing and delivery of these presents by Tobias ffernald of ye same Town County and Province afores^d Shipwright, the receipt whereof they doe hereby Acknowledge and themselves therewith to be fully satisfied contented and paid And thereof and every part thereof acquit Exonerate & discharge ye s^d Tobias ffernald his heirs Execut^{rs} Administrators and Assignes for ever by these presents Have given granted bargained sold Aliened Enfeoffed and confirmed/ And by these presents doe fully freely clearly and absolutely give grant bargain sell Alien Enfeoffe and confirm unto him the s^d Tobias Fernald his heires Execut^{rs} Admin^{rs} or Assignes for ever all that Tract and parcell of Land on which they now dwell, Scituate Lying and being in ye Township of Kittery afores^d containing by Estimation Eighty five Acres be ye same more or less/ being Butted and bounded as followeth, that is to say, begining at ye Middle of ye Cove at Low water mark against Mr William Scrivens Warf and Land and soe to run back up ye s^d Cove to a stake fixed on ye Edge of ye bank by Mr Robert Cutts Land to a white ash tree And then one hundred thirty four poles North by s^d Cutts Land and from this s^d center ye s^d Cutts doth Allow ye s^d Fernald a Cart Road of two Rods broad down to Broad Cove And from ye above mentioned North line by Mr Cutts to run one hundred and six pole upon a Southwest & by west line by ye land of John Amerediths and Mr Withers Deceased Then Sixty three poles South to a Beach tree then down to ye Middle of ye Cove to low water Mark by the land that was

Cutt to ffernald

Book VI, Fol. 86.

Mr William Deaments Deceased then to run along by that branch of yᵉ River comonly called by yᵉ name of Crooked lane till it come to yᵉ first statian in yᵉ aforesᵈ Cove Together with one dwelling house and Barn standing thereupon and all other profits priviledges Rights comodities hereditamᵗˢ and Appurtenances whatsoever to yᵉ sᵈ tract of land belonging or in any wise appurtaining To have and to hold the sᵈ tract or parcel of land, butted bounded and containing as aforesᵈ with all yᵉ above bargained premisses and every part and parcel thereof unto yᵉ sᵈ Tobias Fernald his heires Executʳˢ Adminʳˢ or Assignes for evermore And the sᵈ Richᵈ Cutt and Joanna his wife for themselves their heires Executors and Adminʳˢ doe hereby Covenant promise and grant to and with yᵉ sᵈ Tobias Fernald his heires Executʳˢ Adminʳˢ or Assignes in yᵉ following manner and form That is to say, that at yᵉ time of yᵉ ensealing and delivery of these pʳsents, they the said Richard Cutt and Joanna his wife are yᵉ true sole and Lawfull owners of all yᵉ afore bargained premisses And that they have in themselves full power good Right and Lawfull Authority to grant sell convey and Assure to him the sᵈ Tobias Fernald yᵉ Same, and to his heires Executʳˢ Adminʳˢ and Assignes in aforesᵈ manner and form And that yᵉ sᵈ Tobias Fernald his heires & Assignes shall and may by force and vertue of these pʳsents from time to time and at all times for ever hereafter Lawfully peaceably and quietly have hold use ocupie possess and enjoy yᵉ above granted Premisses with their Appurtenances and every part and parcel thereof free and clear and freely and clearly Acquitted & discharged of and from all and all manner of former and other gifts grants bargains sales Leases Mortgages Joyntures Dowries Judgments Executions Wills Entailes forfitures And of and from all other titles troubles charges and Incumbrances whatsoever had made committed done or Sufferred to be done by them the sᵈ Richard Cutt & Joanna

Cutt
to
ffernald

his wife or either of them their or either of their heires or Assignes at any time or times before the ensealing hereof And y⁰ above s^d Premisses with all their Appurtenances and every part and parcel thereof unto him the s^d Tobias Fernald his heirs and Assignes the s^d Richard Cutt and Joanna his wife their heires Execut^rs and Admin^rs & each & every of them against all & every other person whatsoever any wayes Lawfully Claiming or Demanding y⁰ same or any part thereof by from or under them or any of them Shall and will warrant and defend for ever by these presents In witness whereof the s^d Richd Cutt & Joanna his wife have hereunto set their hands and Seales y⁰ twenty second day of August Anno Dom one thousand & Seven hundred.

Signed Sealed & delivered   Richard Cutt (his seal)
  in y⁰ p^rsents of us   Joanna Cutt (her seal)
William ffernald Senr
Solomon Cotten
William Bryar.

York ss/ Kittery Feb^ry 18th 1700

the above named Richd Cutt & Joanna his wife personally Appearing before me y⁰ Subscrib^r one of the memb^rs of his Ma^ts Council of y⁰ Province of y⁰ Massachusets Bay and Justice of Peace within y⁰ same Acknowledged this Instrument to be their Act and Deed.

                            Jos: Hamond

A true Copie of y⁰ originall Transcribed & compared Feb^ry 18⁰ 1700   p Jos Hamond Regist^r

[87] Know all men by these presents that I Adrian ffry of Kittery in y⁰ County of York and Province of y⁰ Massachusets Bay in New England planter, for many good Causes and considerations me moving hereunto Especially for the Naturall love and affection I bear unto my loving son

William ffry as also for y⁰ comfortable provision for my self and my wife Sarah during our Naturall lives have granted Demised and to ffarm letten unto my fores^d loving son William ffry, a certain tract of land lying in Kittery afores^d Joyning to Creeks mouth on y⁰ south side of s^d Creek containing about Nine Acres^y be it more or less with y⁰ Oorchard upon it And twenty Seven Acres more of land lying on and near horsidown hill bounded on y⁰ East with Maj^r ffrosts land and Comons and on y⁰ South with John Morrells land and Comons, and on y⁰ North with a high way, To have and to hold all and Singular y⁰ above Demised and granted Premisses with all y⁰ Appurtenances thereunto belonging unto him y⁰ s^d William ffry his heires and Assignes during y⁰ whole Terme of y⁰ Naturall lives of y⁰ afores^d Adryan ffry and Sarah his wife, his s^d father and Mother, upon y⁰ rent hereafter expressed And after y⁰ s^d Adrian and Sarah his wife To have and to hold all and Singular y⁰ above granted Premisses with all thappurtenances &c/ to him y⁰ s^d William ffry and his heires for ever in ffee simple without rent or other Incumbrances whatsoever and y⁰ s^d Williams rent for y⁰ fores^d lands during y⁰ lives of his s^d father and Mother shall Maintain good fences and make good improvem^t

Adrian ffry
to
his son Wm

of y⁰ s^d lands and shall pay unto his s^d father the one halfe of whatsoever grain shall grow upon y⁰ land at Sturgeon Creek mouth, together wth the one half of the Cyder and Perry that y⁰ Orchard shall yeeld/ And allow unto his said father y⁰ use of one Acre of land yearly during y⁰ lives of both father & Mother of that land that lies next y⁰ great river, and in case y⁰ Mother shall out live the father he is to pay the same rent, to her/ And for y⁰ land at horsidown hill afores^d the s^d William shall allow his s^d father and Mother or longest liver of them the free use of the now dwelling house And a quarter of an Acre of land for a garden with libertie to cutt and carry off such firewood or building timber as they shall have occation for their own use and when their abillities shall fail and need be, s^d William shall help his s^d father and Mother or either of them in cutting & carying s^d timber or firewood and to pay his s^d father or either of them during their lives yearly one third part of whatsoever grain ye s^d land shall Yield he well fencing and improving s^d land/ And s^d William shall receive two Cowes from his s^d father and winter them from year to year untill s^d Cowes with their increase of calves shall amount to ye number of Six and then his father or mother and he shall divide the increase between them in halves, in ye mean time his s^d father and Mother or either of them, to have all ye milk of ye s^d two Cowes And after ye first devision made the said William shall carefully keep four neat Cattle for his s^d father or Mother dureing their lives as above s^d with Sufficient winter meat Always allowing his s^d father or mother to take ye Milk of two Cows if there be so many, And when ye four neat Cattle afores^d shall amount in their Increase unto ye number of Six, then s^d increase to be devided in halves as afores^d and so to continue from year to year so long as said father or Mother shall live And further if s^d father or Mother shall procure any sheep, he s^d William shall take and keep them winter and summer for ye one half of ye increase of the lambs and wooll And the s^d William is never to keep above ye number of ten for his s^d father or Mother both of Stock & increase and if any difference or controversie shall arise between the parties to these presents it shall be determined by Indifferent men Mutually chosen by both partys And for confirmation of the Premisses both parties to these presents have Interchangeably set to their hands and Seales to these presents and an other of the same tenour/ Octob^r 12th Anno. Dom̃. 1692.

the word William in the Margent entred before Signing & Sealing hereof

Signed Sealed & delivered Adrian ffry
  in the presents of us his **A** mark (his seal)
Robert Allen
John Wincoll Sarah ffry
  her **SF** mark (her seal)

Robert Allen appeared before me and made oath that he saw Adryn ffry Sign and Seal ye abovesaid. Instrum^t to which he set his hand as a witness, and Cap^{tn} Wincoll set his hand to as a witness at ye same time/

Septemb^r 16th 1695.

                    Charles ffrost Just^e peace

A true Copie of ye originall Transcribed & Compared. March 12th 1700

                    p Jos Hamond Regist^r

This Writing witnesseth that I Nicholas Shapleigh of Kittery in New England Merch^t with the consent of my wife Alice Shapleigh for and in consideration of the Sum of two hundred and fiftie pounds Sterling to me in hand paid, the receipt whereof I doe hereby Acknowledge and therewith to be fully Satisfied, have and do for my selfe my heires Execut^{rs} and Administrat^{rs}, bargain sell Alien Enfeoff convey and make over unto Humphrey Chadborne of Kittery in New England afores^d all that parcell of Marsh lying and being Scituate at or in Sturgeon Creek within the precincts of Kittery afores^d and is on ye Northermost side of the said Creek being bounded by the upland on ye Northwest and by the afore mentioned Sturgeon Creek on ye Southeast side, by ye known bounds that are betwixt Nicholas ffrost and me Nicholas Shapleigh on ye Northeast side, And on ye South-

Shapleigh to Chadborn

west side by ye known bounds that are betwixt John Heard of Sturgeon Creek afores^d and me Nicholas Shapleigh, As alsoe all my right title and Interest of and in a tract of land which was granted unto me the s^d Nicholas Shapleigh by the Inhabitants of the town of Kittery afores^d lying and being Adjoyning to ye afores^d Marsh and is bounded by ye land of ye afores^d Nicholas ffrost on ye one side And by the land of the afores^d John Heard on ye other side And soe runs away Northwest from ye s^d Marsh All which land and Marsh with all and Singular ye premisses thereunto belonging together with all the woods, under woods timber and timber trees, And all other priviledges and Immunities whatsoever, he ye s^d Humphrey Chadborn is to Have & to hold unto him ye s^d Humphrey his heires and Assignes forever, free & cleare Acquitted and Discharged of and from all former and other bargains Sales Mortgages Joyntures Dowers titles troubles Alienations, prevaricacones & Incumbrances whatsoever, had made or done by me ye s^d Nicholas Shapleigh or by any other person or persons whatsoever from by or under me. And I ye s^d Nicholas Shapleigh doe for my self my heires Execut^{rs} & Administrat^{rs} Covenant promise & agree to and with ye s^d Humphrey Chadborn his heires and Assignes to warrant & make good [88] the title and sale of all and singular ye afore Demised Premisses and every part and parcell thereof unto him ye afores^d Humphrey Chadborn his heires and Assignes from time to time and at all times from henceforth hereafter And that he ye s^d Humphrey his heires Execut^{rs} & Administrat^{rs} shall and may peaceably and quietly ocupie possess and Enjoy all ye afore Demised Premisses and every part and parcell thereof without the Lawfull let trouble hinderance Molestacon or Disturbance of me ye s^d Nicholas Shapleigh or of any other person or persons whatsoever Lawfull claiming Interest or right in or unto ye afore Demised Premisses or any part thereof from by or under me And lastly that I the s^d Nicholas Shapleigh shall and will at any time hereafter upon ye reasonable request of him ye s^d Humphrey his heires Execut^rs Administrat^rs and Assignes give and make unto him or them or any or either of them any oth^r further or better assurance of in or unto ye afore Demised premisses or any part thereof as shall be According to Law adjudged to be necessary requisite and Expedient. In witness whereof I ye s^d Nicholas Shapleigh and my wife Alice Shapleigh have hereunto set our hands and Seales this Eleventh day of April in ye year of our Lord one thousand Six hundred Sixty and three Anno Dom. 1663

Signed Sealed & Delivered   Nicho: Shapleigh (and seal)
   in presents of us.   Alice Shapleigh (and seale)
   ffrancis Champernowne
   Thomas Kemble

This Instrument of writing was Acknowledged by Nicholas Shapleigh and Alice his wife to be their Act and Deed this 20th 5mo 67. before us

           ffran: Champernowne Jus^t
           Edward Johnson Justice

A true Copie of the originall Deed of Sale Transcribed and Compared this 8th April 1701

           p Jos Hamond Regist^r

County of York

These may certifie whome it may concern that I John Shapleigh of Kittery doe release and for ever set free one Negroe man comonly called Black Will which was formerly Maj^r Nicholas Shapleighs and now in my Possession I doe by these presents release and for ever set free from me my

Shaplegh
to
Black Will

heires Execut[rs] Administrat[rs] and from all persons whatsoever laying any Lawfull Claime to or right to him Witness my hand Kittery 13th ffeb[ry] 1700/.

John Shapleigh

York ss/ Kittery March 21st 1700/.

The above named John Shapleigh psonally Appearing before me y[e] Subscriber one of his Ma[ts] Justices of y[e] Peace in s[d] County of York Acknowledged this Instrument of Release, to Black Will therein named, to be his Act and Deed/

Jos: Hamond

A true Copie of y[e] above release with y[e] Acknowledgem[t] thereof Transcribed and compared this 2[d] April 1701

p Jos Hamond Regist[r]

Know all men by these presents that I John Bracy of York in New England Taylor for and in consideration of a certain Sum to me in hand paid by M[r] Jeremiah Molton of said town have bargained and sold And doe by these presents bargain sell Alien Enfeoffe confirm and make over all my right title and Interest lying and being in York afores[d] consisting in lands Meadows housing of any kind, whether by gift, grant, purchase or otherwise unto y[e] said Jeremiah Molton his heires Execut[rs] Administrat[rs] and Assignes To have and to hold for ever/ And I y[e] s[d] John Bracy doe hereby Oblige my self my heires Execut[rs] and Administrat[rs] to Warrant and Defend all my s[d] Right title and Interest from by by and under me/ Given under my hand & seal in York Apr[ll] 8th 1696.

Bracy
to
Molton

Signed Sealed and delivered
In the presents of us.
John Pickerin
Sam[ll] Penhallow

his
John ℗ Bracy (and seale)
mark

BOOK VI, FOL. 88.

John Bracy came & Appeared before me this Eighth day of Aprill 1696, and Acknowledged this above written Instrum^t to be his own Act and Deed/
Job: Alcock Jus. pes

A true Copie of ye originall Instrum^t Transcribed & compared this 2^d April 1701
p Jos: Hamond Regist^r

To all People unto whome these presents shall come/ Mehetable Warren Widow Elisha Hutchinson Esqr and Elizabeth his wife all of Boston within ye County of Suffolke in New England being Co-heires of Major Thomas Clark late of the same Boston Merchant Deced, Send Greeting Know yee that we the s^d Mehetable Warren Elisha Hutchinson and Elizabeth Hutchinson for and in consideration of ye Sum of three hund pounds Currant Money in New England, one hundred pounds, part thereof to us in hand paid the receipt whereof we doe hereby Acknowledge/ And the other two hundred pounds at and before the ensealing and Delivery of these presents secured in the Law to be paid by Joseph Hammond Esqr, David Libbey, Matthew Libbey Daniel ffogg and Stephen Tobey, the s^d Hammond and Tobey being of Kittery in ye Province of ye Massachusets Bay, And ye s^d Libbeys & ffogg of Portsmouth in ye Province of New Hampshier in New England. Have given, granted, bargained, sold, released, Enfeofed and confirmed And by these presents Doe freely fully and absolutely Give, grant, bargain sell release Assigne Enfeoffe & convey and confirm unto ye s^d Joseph Hammond David Libbey Matthew Libbey Daniel ffogg and Stephen Tobey their heires and Assignes for ever All that our certain tract of Land Scituate and Lying at a certain place comonly called and known by

Warren and Hutchinson to Hamond & company

the name of the long reach in Piscataqua River within ye township of Kittery afores^d (the s^d tract of land being called and known by the name of Mr Knowles his Purchase or by what other name or names the s^d land is now called and knon According as ye same was laid out and Platted by John Evans in presents of ye Select men of Kittery on ye twentieth day of June [89] Anno 1682 and Allowed of by the Generall Court held at Boston on ye seventh day of May Anno 1684, the s^d Land Measuring by the s^d Platt thereof returned into ye said Court two hundred and forty rod in breadth between Watts ffort and ffranks ffort runing towards York five hundred and Eighty rods Northeast and by East And contains eight hundred and Seventy Acres in ye whole, Excepting and reserving out of this Sale Thirty Acres or thereabouts lying within ye Limits and boundaries aboves^d now in ye Possession of Joshua Downing, Together with all and singular ye trees timber, Woods, underwoods, waters, water Courses Swamps, Meadows, Meadow grounds rights, members, profits, priviledges, comodities, Advantages, hereditaments, emoluments and Appurtenances whatsoever upon, belonging or in any wise Appurtaining to the s^d Granted tract of land or any part or parcell thereof and the revertion and revercons, remaind and remainders, rents Issues and profits thereof And all the Estate right, Title, Interest, Inheritance, use, property, possession Claim and Demand whatever, of us ye s^d Mehetable Warren, Elisha Hutchinson and Elizabeth Hutchinson and of each and every of us and of our and each and every of our heires of in & to the same/ To have and to hold the s^d tract of Land and every part and parcel thereof (Excepting as is before Excepted) and all and singular ye premisses and Appurtenances herein before granted bargained and sold, unto ye s^d Joseph Hamond David Libbey Matthew Libbey Daniel ffogg and Stephen Tobey their heires & Assignes To their only proper use benefit and behoof for ever/ And we the s^d Mehetable Warren Elisha Hutchinson and Elizabeth Hutchinson for our selves our heires Execut^{rs} and Admin^{rs} Do hereby Covenant grant and agree to and with the said Joseph Hamond David Libbey, Matthew Libbey Daniel ffogg and Stephen Tobey their heirs and Assigns in manner following (that is to say) That we the said Mehetable Warren, Elisha Hutchinson and Elizabeth Hutchinson at and untill the ensealing and Delivery of these presents are ye true and Lawfull owners of the s^d Tract of Land and premisses herein before granted (Excepting as afores^d) And stand Lawfully Seized thereof in our, or some of our own proper right as a good perfect and Absolute Estate of Inheritance in ffee Simple, without any man^r of condition revercon or Limitation of use or uses whatsoever so as to alter Change defeat or make voyd ye same And have full power good right and Lawfull Authority to grant sell and assure ye s^d Land and premisses in manner as afores^d And that ye same are free and clear and clearly Acquitted and Discharged of and from all former and other gifts grants bargains sales Leases releases Mortgages Wills entailes Judgments Executions titles troubles Charges & Incumbrances whatsoever And further that we ye s^d Mehetable Warren, Elisha Hutchinson & Elizabeth Hutchinson our heires Execut^{rs} and Administrat^{rs} shall and will Warrant & defend the s^d tract of Land and Premisses herein before bargained and sold (Excepting as before Excepted) unto ye s^d Joseph Hamond David Libbey Matthew Libbey Daniel ffogg and Stephen Tobey their heires and Assignes for ever against ye Lawfull Claims and Demands of all and every person and persons whomsoever/ for ye making good of which Warranty bargain and Sale above mentioned we have also delivered unto ye s^d Grantees an obligation under our hands and Seales bearing even date with these presents of ye Penalty of five hundred pounds/ In Witness whereof we have hereunto set our hands and seales ye Eighteenth day of Decemb^r Anno Domini one thousand six hundred Ninety nine Annoq R R⁸ Gulielmi 3ᵗⁱⁱ Angliæ &c undecimo

Signed Sealed and Delivered in yᵉ presents of
Benjᵃ Alford/ William Manly

Elisha (and/seal) Hutchinson, Elizabeth (and/seal) Hutchinson, Mehetable (and/seal) Warren

Suffolke ss/ Boston 18ᵗʰ Decembʳ 1699.

The within named Mehetable Warren/ Elisha Hutchinson Esqʳ and Elizabeth his wife personally Appearing before me the Subscribʳ one of his Maᵗʸˢ Justices of the Peace within the County of Suffolke Acknowledged the within written Deed or Instrument to be their Act and Deed.

John ffoster.

A true Copie of yᵉ originall Deed of Sale from Mʳˢ Mehetable Warren Elisha Hutchinson Esqʳ and Elizabeth his wife, to Joseph Hamond and Company as on yᵉ foregoing Pages, the above Acknowledgmᵗ being written on yᵉ back side of yᵉ sᵈ Deed/ Transcribed and Compared the 30ᵗʰ Decembʳ 1699.   p Jos Hamond Registʳ

Whereas we Joseph Hamond, Stephen Tobey, David Libby, Matthew Libby and Daniel ffogg of Kittery in yᵉ County of York have bought & purchased of Mʳˢ Mehetable Warren Elisha Hutchinson Esqʳ and Elizabeth his wife a certain parcel of Land within yᵉ township of Kittery Lying and being scituate between Wats ffort and ffranks ffort (so called) fronting Piscataqua river being an hundred and forty poles in breadth and running back into yᵉ woods toward York river as at large Appears by a Deed of Sale from sᵈ Mehetable Warren and Company referrence thereunto being had Now for yᵉ Division of sᵈ Land According to true intent and meaning we the above named doe Mutually agree as follows (that is to say) that the said Hamond is to have his part on y" Northwest Side of s^d tract of Land And Daniel ffogg next to s^d Hamond, and Matthew Libby next to s^d Fogg, & David Libby next to s^d Matthew Libby and Stephen Tobey next to s^d David Libby being ye Lowermost or Southeast side of s^d tract or parcel of Land And we doe further Mutually agree and consent that ye s^d Joseph Hamond shall have and hold to him and his heirs & Assignes for ever one third part of ye whole tract of Land afore mentioned, he having already paid ye one third of one hundred pounds at ye Signing and Sealing of the Deed of Sale and stands Engaged to pay one third part of ye remaining two hundred pounds which is yet to pay And in consideration of some Lands in ye Possession of Joshua Downing &c which hinders the said Hamonds from butting upon ye Main river as ye rest doe, we the above named doe therefore Mutually agree and consent that the s^d Joseph Hamond his heires and Assignes for ever shall have hold and quietly Possess and enjoy Eighty & eight poles of s^d Land in breadth and to run ye whole Length of the s^d tract of Land And ye other four, namely Stephen Tobey David Libby Matthew Libby & Daniel ffogg are to have thirty eight poles apiece to them their heires and Assignes for ever/ for ye true performance of which Agrement We bind and Oblige us our heires Execut^{rs} [90] Administrat^{rs} and Assignes for ever firmly by these presents In witness whereof we have hereunto Set our hands and Seales this twenty first day of March Anno Dom. 1700/1,

Hamond & Company

Book VI, Fol. 90.

Signed Sealed and delivered	Jos Hamond	(and seal)
In the presents of us.	Stephen Tobey	(and seal)
Jacob Remich	his	
Jos: Hamond Jun{r}	David ⤴ Libby	(and seal)
Mary Storer.	mark	
	his	
	Matthew ⅍ Libby	(and seal)
	mark	
York ss/	Daniel ffogg	(and seal)

  Kittery March 21st 1700

 Maj^r Joseph Hamond/ Stephen Tobey David Libby Matthew Libby and Daniel Fog. personally Appearing before me ye Subscrib^r one of his Ma^{ts} Justices of ye Peace within the County of York Acknowledged this Instrum^t to be their Act and Deed.

          Wm Pepperrell

 A true Copie of ye originall agreement Transcribed & compared this 21st March: 1700/1.

       p me Jos: Hamond Regist^r

 Know all men by these presents that I Daniel Black of York in ye Province of Maine Weaver/ In consideration of twenty five pounds eighteen shilling which I am Indebted to Mr James Gooch of Boston in ye Province of ye Massachusets Bay in New England Merchant, doe give grant bargain sell Alienate make over Enfeoffee and confirm from me my heires Execut^{rs} Administrat^{rs} and Assignes to Mr James Gooch afores^d his heires Execut^{rs} Administrat^{rs} and Assignes my now dwelling house and Barn, together with that three Acres of land on which s^d house and barn doth stand be it

Black to Gooch

more or less, bounded as followeth Viz^t by ye high way and the land of Job Young on two sides, and on the other two sides by ye Meeting house Creek and a gully runing from y® high way into s⁴ Creek, only half an Acre Excepted belonging to y® house of John Pennel; as also the fencing on s⁴ land with all priviledges and Appurtenances thereto belonging. To have and to hold without any Molestation by my self or any other by from or under me for ever/. The condition of this Deed is such that if s⁴ Black doe well & truly pay or cause to be paid to Mr Gooch afores⁴ y® full and Just Sum of twenty five pounds & eighteen shillings above mentioned on or before y® first day of Novemb^r which will be in y® year one thousand seven hundred and five Currant Money of New England or that wch shall be Equivalent, Then y® above written Deed to be Voyd, or else to be in full force.

Signed Sealed & delivered   Daniel Black (and seal)
 in presents of.
Samuel Moody
Joseph Smith

Septemb^r 5th 1700/ Daniel Black came and Acknowledged this above written Instrum^t to be his Act & Deed before me/   Abra: Preble Justis peace

A true Copie of y® originall Transcribed and compared. Octob^r 26th 1700.   p Jos: Hamond Regist^r

To all Christian People to whome these presents shall come Greeting in our Lord God everlasting/ Know yee that we Nathaniel Rayns and John Woodman Administrat^{rs} to the Estate of John Deament late of Kittery in y® County of York for divers good Causes and considerations us hereunto moving, but more Especially for and in consideration of ffiftie five pounds in Currant money to us in hand paid by Mr Nicholas Walden of Portsmouth in y® Province of New Hampshier Taylor the receipt thereof we doe Acknowledge and our selves therewith contented and paid & doe by these presents Acquit and Discharge ye s^d Walden for ye same for ye consideration afores^d And by Vertue of power given unto us ye s^d Administrat^rs aboves^d by the Justices of his Ma^ts Superiour Court of ye s^d Province of Massachusets Bay as will Appear on Record referrence thereunto being had Have hereby given granted bargained and sold, and doe by these presents give grant bargain sell Alien and for ever confirm unto ye s^d Nicholas Walden his heires and Assignes for ever All that house and land that was ye late John Deaments lying in ye Town of Kittery at a place comonly called Crooked lane, on ye Northeast side of Berrys Island, containing by Estimation forty Acres of land be it more or Less, bounded by ye River of Piscataqua Thomas Withers and others, together with all ye out housing Orchards and gardens & fencing thereunto belonging or in any wise Appurtaining with all ye timber wood and underwoods Quarries of Stone Mines & Mineralls of what kind soever/ To have and to hold all and Singular ye aboves^d house & land with all ye Appurtenances and priviledges thereto beloinging unto ye sole and only use of him ye s^d Nicholas Walden his heires

Rayns and Woodman to Walden

and Assignes for ever, And furthermore we ye s^d Administrat^rs doe for our selves our heires Execut^rs and Administrat^rs Covenant to and with ye s^d Nicholas Walden his heires & Assigns that ye Premisses are free from all encumbrance whatsoever by us made or Sufferred to be done by any others as gifts, grant, Mortgages Joyntures of Dowers And that we as we are Administrat^rs to s^d Estate are ye true & proper owners thereof And have within our selves full power & Lawfull Authority to dispose of ye same and every part thereof And that it may be Lawfull for the s^d Walden at any time and at all times hereafter to take use Ocupie and Possess ye Same to his own only use and behoof for ever or any other person Lawfully Authorized by him and that without the let or hinderance or obstruction of us or either of us yᵉ above Administratʳˢ or any under us, the Peaceable and quiet possession thereof for ever to warrant and Maintain against all persons whatsoever, Lawfully laying Claim thereunto, the Kings most Excellent Majestie only Excepted Witness our hands and Seales this thirteenth day of April one thousand Six hundred Ninety and Nine. 1699

Signed Sealed and Delivered Nathaniel Raynes (and Seale)
  To presents of us. John Woodman. (and Seale)
Dodevah Curtis
Jonathan Mendum
  the sign of
John ✕ Braun.
Wᵐ Godsoe.

The 3ᵈ of March, 1701/
  then Mʳ Nathaniel Raynes & Mʳ John Woodman Volluntary Appeared and Acknowledged this above written to be their free Act and Deed to Mʳ Nicholas Walden delivered yᵉ day and year above written Acknowledged before me
                    Wᵐ Pepperrell/ Js pes

A true Copie of yᵉ originall Transcribed & compared May 8ᵗʰ 1701
                  p Jos: Hamond Registʳ

[91] To all people to whome this present Deed of sale shall come I John Downing of Dover in yᵉ Province New Hampshier in New England husbandman send greeting Know yee that for and in consideration of yᵉ Sum of one hundred & fiftie pounds of good and Lawfull Money to me in hand paid at and before yᵉ ensealing and delivery of these presents by Joseph Hill of Kittery in yᵉ County of York in yᵉ Province of yᵉ Massachusets Bay in New England aforesᵈ Turner/ the receipt whereof I doe hereby Acknowledge and

Book VI, Fol. 91.

my self therewith to be fully Satisfied contented and paid and thereof, and of and from every part and parcel y[r] of doe for me y[e] s[d] John Downing my heires Execut[rs] Administrat[rs] and Assignes Exonerate Acquit and fully Discharge him y[e] s[d] Joseph Hill his heires Execut[rs] Administrat[rs] and Assignes by these presents forever. I the s[d] John Downing Have given granted bargained sold Aliened Enfeoffed and confirmed And by these presents doe for me my heires Execut[rs] Admin[rs] and Assignes fully freely and Absolutely give grant bargain sell Alien Enfeoffee convey and confirm unto him y[e] s[d] Joseph Hill his heires and Assignes All that my certain house and land lying & being scituate in y[e] township of Kittery afores[d] Abutting on Piscataqua river in a place comonly called y[e] long reach on y[e] Southwest, Peter Staples land on y[e] Northwest, y[e] s[d] Hills land and Lissons on y[e] Northeast, and y[e] land formerly Charles Nelsons on the Southeast in part, or however Else bounded or reputed to be bounded by a Deed of Sale given me by Richard Hilton bearing Date y[e] Sixteenth of May 1699 reference thereunto being had (Excepting and Reserving only three Acres mentioned in y[e] afores[d] Deed and does there at large Appear) together with a certain piece or parcel of fresh Marsh or Swamp y[e] bounds whereof alsoe fully & largely Appear in y[e] afores[d] Deed it being about a Mile & half from y[e] s[d] house Lott containing ten Acres be it more or less, together alsoe with a grant of forty Acres given me by y[e] Town of Kittery May 24th 1699. as Appears on Record/ Seventeen Acres and a half being alredy laid out at y[e] Northeast side of Simons Marsh by y[e] Mast way at y[e] head of John Greens lott, the bounds whereof doe more fully Appear by y[e] return of y[e] laying out thereof bearing Date July y[e] 24th 1699. together with all and singular y[e] Edifices, barns, stables, out houses, orchards, Gardens and what ever else being within y[e] boundaries afores[d], with all profits priviledges and

Downing to Hill

Appurtenances to yᵉ sᵈ lands belonging or in any wise Appurtaining To have and to hold, the sᵈ house lands Marsh with all yᵉ timber trees standing or lying on sᵈ land barns stables out houses Orchards Gardens &c. with yᵉ Appurtenances thereto belonging, with all right, title, Interest, Claime and Demand which I yᵉ said John Downing now have or in time past have had, or which I my heires Executrˢ or Assignes in time to come, may, might, or in any wise ought to have of in or unto yᵉ above granted Premisses or any part thereof, to him yᵉ sᵈ Joseph Hill his heires or Assignes for ever And to yᵉ sole and proper use benefit and behoof of him the sᵈ Joseph Hill his heires &c for evermore And I yᵉ sᵈ John Downing for me my heires Executrˢ and Assignes doe Covenant promise and grant to and with him the sᵈ Joseph Hill his heires and Assignes that at and untill yᵉ Ensealing & delivery thereof I am yᵉ true right and proper owner of the aboue Premisses & yᵉ Appurtenˢ And that I have in my Self good right full power and Lawfull Authority the same to grant and confirm unto him the said Joseph his heires or Assignes as aforesaid And that yᵉ same and every part thereof is free and Clear Acquitted and Discharged of and from all former and other gifts, grants, bargains, sales, Leases, Mortgages troubles Acts Alienations and Incumbrances whatsoever And that it shall and may be Lawfull to and for yᵉ sᵈ Joseph Hill his heires or Assignes yᵉ aforesᵈ Premisses & every part and parcel thereof from time to time and at all times for ever hereafter To have hold use improve Ocupie possess and enjoy Lawfully peaceably & quietly without any Lawfull lett hinderance Molestation or disturbance of or by me or any other person or persons from by or under me or by my procurement And that yᵉ sale thereof against my self my heires or Assignes and against all other persons whatsoever Lawfully Claiming yᵉ same or any part thereof (Except there happen a Chief Lᵈ Proprietʳ) I will forever save harmless warrant & Defend

BOOK VI, FOL. 91.

by these presents In witness whereof I ye s^d John Downing have hereunto set my hand & seal the twenty third day of January in ye Eleventh year of ye Reign of our Soveraign Ld William ye third by ye grace of God of England Scotland ffrance & Ireland King Defend^r of ye faith &c. And in ye year of our Lord one thousand six hundred Ninety and nine: 1699.

Signed Sealed and Delivered   John Downing. (and seal)
   In the presents of us.   her
   Jos: Hamond Junr   Susanna X Downing (and scale)
   Samuel Spinney   mark
   Mary Whipple
         her
   Hannah *p* Key
        mark

Kittery March 11th 1700/

The above named John Downing personally Appearing before me ye Subscrib^r one of his Majesties Justices of the Peace within the County of York Acknowledged the above written Deed or Instrument to be his Act & Deed And Susanna ye wife of ye s^d Downing Appearing at the same time, gave up all her right of Dower of, in or to the above granted Premisses & thereto affixed her hand & seal

                                        Jos: Hamond

A true Copie of the originall Instrum^t Transcribed & Compared March 11th 1700.   p Jos: Hamond Regist^r

Whereas we Joseph Hamond, Stephen Tobey, David Libby, Matthew Libby and Daniel ffogg of the Town of Kittery in ye County of York in ye Province of ye Massachusets Bay in New England Doe stand bound and firmly Obliged Joyntly and Severally unto Edward Hutchinson of Boston in New England afores^d Merchant, for ye paym^t of two hundred pounds Cur[t] money in New England at two Equall paym[ts] as may and doth Appear by a bond given under our hands and Seales bearing Date in y[e] year 1699.

<u>Hamond</u>
<u>&</u>
<u>Company</u>

reference thereunto being had which sum of Money is for and in consideration of a certaine parcel of land which we y[e] above named Joseph Hamond & company bought and purchased of M[rs] Mehetable Warren Elisha Hutchinson Esq[r] and Elizabeth his wife as p their Deed of Sale bearing Date Decemb[r] 18th 1699. And there being no distiction made in s[d] Obligation what each person is to pay we doe therefore by these presents Mutually consent and agree that y[e] above named Joseph Hamond (for and in consideration of his having Eighty and Eight poles in breadth of s[d] land as may appear [92] by agreem[t] Made between us y[e] s[d] Joseph Hamond and Company bearing even Date with these presents) shall and hereby is obliged to pay one third part of y[e] said two hundred pounds and y[e] other to pay y[e] other two thirds Equally And we doe further agree consent and engage each to other that if it should so happen y[t] one or more of us y[e] above named shall make Default an d not pay his or their due proportion by these presents agreed upon, that he or they making such default shall forfeit his or their proportion of land herein Mentioned to to y[e] person or persons observant and paying y[e] same. In confirmation whereof we have hereunto set our hands and Seals this twenty first day of March. 1700

Signed Sealed and Delivered	Jos : Hamond	(and seal)
In presents of us.	Stephen Tobey.	(and seal)
Jacob Remich	his	
Jos Hamond Jun[r]	David ⌒∫ Libby	(and seal)
Mary Storer	mark	
	his	
	Matthew 𝓜 Libby	(and seal)
	mark	
	Daniel ffog.	(and seal)

Book VI, Fol. 92.

York ss/ Kittery March 21ˢᵗ 1700.

Majʳ Joseph Hamond, Stephen Tobey, David Libby Matthew Libby and Daniel ffogg, personally Appearing before me yᵉ subscribʳ one of his Maᵗˢ Justices of yᵉ Peace within yᵉ County of York Acknowledged this Instrumᵗ to be their Act and Deed/

Wᵐ Pepperrell

A true Copie of the originall Transcribed and Compared March 21ˢᵗ 1700

p Jos Hamond Registʳ

Be it known unto all men by these presents whome it may concern that I Nathaniel ffuller Weaver living in yᵉ town of Ipswich in yᵉ County of Essex in New England, for Divers good and Valluable Causes and considerations me thereunto moving And Especially for and in consideration of money to me in hand paid and received before yᵉ Sealing and delivery of these presents And for which I doe Acknowledge myselfe to be fully Satisfied And therefore have given, granted bargain sell pass away and make over unto Mʳ Peter Tappin of Newberry in yᵉ County abovesᵈ in New England two hundred Acres of land that was Mʳ Harlakinden Simons and belongeth to yᵉ first Division Lying and being at Cockshall yᵉ which sᵈ land was purchased of yᵉ sᵈ Simons by the abovesᵈ ffuller as may appear by yᵉ originall List where yᵉ rest of the purchasers are entred and recorded, the sᵈ tract of land lying at yᵉ head line of the township of Wells in yᵉ County of York Joyning to Saco River at the Northwest and on Mousom river Southeast yᵉ sᵈ land to have and to hold quietly to possess and enjoy with all singular yᵉ priviledges and Appurtenances thereunto belonging unto the sᵈ Tappen his heires Executrˢ Administratrˢ or Assignes for ever as his and

ffuller to Tappen

their own proper wright and Inheritance withou let hinderance or Molestation from me my heires Execut^{rs} Administrat^{rs} or Assignes or any other person or persons whatsoever laying any Lawfull Claim or title thereunto for ever; And for true performance of the same I bind my my self my heires Execut^{rs} and Administrat^{rs} or Assignes unto ye aboves^d Tappen his heires Execut^{rs} Administrat^{rs} or Assignes. And In witness hereunto I have set my hand and seal this Eleventh day of June in ye year of our Lord one thousand six hundred Ninety and four/ In ye County of York was enterlined before signing & sealing.

Signed Sealed & Delivered   Nathaniel ffuller (and seal)
  In presents of us.
  John Stewart
  James Taylor
  John Hareis

Nathaniel ffuller personally Appeared and Acknowledged the above written Instrum^t to be his Act and Deed July the 28th 1694.

                     Thos Wade Justice of peace

A true Copie of ye originall Transcribed and compared May 8th 1701

                     p Jos: Hamond Regist^r

To all People to whome these presents shall come I Samuel Ingolls, Senr, of Ipswich in ye County of Essex in ye Province of ye Massachusets Bay in New England America send Greeting. Know yee that I ye s^d Samuel Ingolls Senr for divers good causes and considerations me thereunto Moving but Especially for and in consideration of a Valluable Sum̄ in hand paid unto me by Mr William Titcomb of Newberry in ye County and Province afores^d to my full Satifaction and content And I doe Accordingly for my self my heires Execut^{rs} and Administrat^{rs} Acquit Exonerate and Discharge ye s^d Mr William Titcomb his heires Execut^{rs} and Admin^{rs} by these presents Have given, granted, bargained, sold, Enfeoffed and confirmed And doe by these presents fully freely clearly and Absolutely give, grant, bargain sell Enfeoffe and confirm unto ye s^d Mr William Titcomb one hundred Acres of land being part of a tract of land which I ye s^d Samuel Ingolls Senr with Severall others Joynt purchasers, purchased of Mr Harlakenden Symonds of Ipswich in ye County aforesaid which s^d tract of land is Six Miles in

Ingolls
to
Titcomb

Length and four Miles in breadth known by the name of Coxhall in ye County of Yorkshier in ye Province of Maine as it is bounded as followeth Viz^t at ye southeast end p^{t}ly by ye line of the township of Wells And p^{t}ly by ye line of ye township of Cape Porpois, and on ye Northeast side partly bounded by ye line of ye land formerly Maj^r William Phillips his land And p^{t}ly upon the comon land. And on the Northwest End the land is bounded on ye Comon land and bounded on ye southwest side with ye land of ye s^d Symonds as by a Deed of Sale under ye hand and seal of ye s^d Mr Harlakenden Symonds bearing Date June 12th Anno Dom 1688 And by him Acknowledged June 22, 1688 before John Usher Esqr and Entred with ye Records of ye County of York Octob^r 12 1693 in fol: 48. more at large may Appear Andd ye s^d Samuel Ingolls Senr for my self my heires Execut^{rs} and Administrat^{rs} doe covenant and promise to and with ye s^d Mr William Titcomb his heires Execut^{rs} and Administrat^{rs} and Assignes that ye s^d one hundred Acres of land and every part and parcel thereof is free and Clear and freely and clearly Exonerated discharged and Acquitted of and from all former gifts grants bargains sales Alienations charges Mortgages Dower, Joyntures, Extents, Judgm^{ts} Executions and all other encumbrance whatsoever And I ye s^d Samuel

Ingolls Sen{r}, for my self my heires Execut{rs} & Admin{rs} doe and shall from time to time and at all times Warrantize and Maintain the s{d} bargained Premisses with all and singular the Appurtenances and priviledges and comodities [93] to y{e} s{d} hundred Acres of land herein Mentioned belong as namely trees wood und{r} wood standing or lying on y{e} s{d} land, with all y{e} Meadows Swamps waters, water courses Mines or Mineralls in or upon y{e} s{d} land whatsoever or wheresoever it be against all manner of Persons whatsoever Claiming or pretending to have any Just & lawfull Right & title or Interest to y{e} s{d} bargained Premisses or any part or parcle thereof To have and to hold y{e} s{d} bargained Premisses and every part and parcel thereof to him the s{d} M{r} William Titcomb his heires Execut{rs} Admin{rs} and Assignes for ever/ In witness and confirmation of all y{e} above written I y{e} s{d} Samuel Ingolls Sen{r} have hereunto set my hand and seal this fifteenth day of June. Anno Dom. Sixteen hundred Ninety and four, Annoq Regni Regis et Regine Gulielmi et Mariæ Nunc Angliæ &c Sexto   Samuel Ingolls (his seal)
Signed Sealed and delivered
  by M{r} Samuel Ingolls Sen{r}
  to M{r} William Titcom in presents
  of us
  Thomas Hart
  Robert Lord Jun{r}
  Jacob Tappin

L{t} Sam{ll} Ingolls made his Appearance July y{e} 16{th} 1694 and did Acknowlege this Instrum{t} to be his Act and Deed Before me

    Samuel Appleton Justice of y{e} Peace

A true Copie of the originall Transcribed and and compared this Eighth day of May : 1701.

     p Jos Hamond Regist{r}

Book VI, Fol. 93.

To all Christian People to whome this present writing shall come Greeting/ Know yee that I John Harris of Ipswich, Locksmith, in the County of Essex New England for and in consideration of the Sum of about ten pounds in currant Money received before ye confirmation hereof in full satisfaction And for Divers other good and Lawfull causes me thereunto Moving, Have given, granted, bargained sold Enfeoffed & confirmed and by these presents Do fully clearly and asbolutely give, grant, bargain, sell, Enfeoffe and confirm unto Jacob Tappin yeoman of Newbury in ye County of Essex New England and to his heires and Assignes for ever two hundred Acres of land be it more or less being part of that tract of land that was Mr Harlakenden Simonses Six Miles in Length and four Miles in Breadth known by

Harris
to
Tappan

ye name Cocks-Hall in ye County of Yorkshiere in ye Province of Mayn And is bounded as followeth Viz at the Southeast end partly upon ye line of the township of Wells and partly upon the line of ye township of Cape Porpoise And on ye Northeast Side, partly bounded by ye line of ye land formerly Maj^r William Phillips his and partly upon ye comonland, And on ye Northwest end the s^d land is bounded on ye Common land & bounded on the Southwest side with ye land of Mr Harlakinden Symonds, And I the said John Harris for my self my hires Execut^{rs} Admin^{rs} and Assignes Doe coven^t and promise to and with the aboves^d Jacob Toppan his heirs Execut^{rs} Admin^{rs} & Assignes that ye s^d bargained Premisses and every part thereof is free and clear & freely and clearly Exonerated Discharged and Acquitted from all former gifts & grants Sales Alienations Changes Mortgages Dowrys Joynters and all other encumbrances whatsoever And I ye s^d Harris for my self my heires Execut^{rs} Administrat^{rs} and Assignes, doe and shall from time to time and at all times Warrantize and maintain the bargained Premisses with all and Singular the Appurtenances and Priviledges and Comodities, as namely the trees wood under wood standing or lying upon s^d land, with all Meadows Swamps waters & water Courses Mines and Mineralls in or upon ye s^d land whatsoever or wheresoever it shall be, against all manner of persons whatsoever from by or under me pretending to have any Just or Lawfull right or title unto ye s^d bargained Premisses or any part or parcell thereof. To have and to hold ye s^d two hundred Acres of land and every part thereof to him ye s^d Jacob Toppan his heires Execut^{rs} Admin^{rs} and Assignes for ever In witness and confirmation of all ye above written I ye s^d John Harris have hereunto set my hand and Seal Dated this thirty first of March in ye year of our Lord God one thousand Six hundred Ninety Six. And in ye eight year of ye Reign of our Soveraign Lord King William.

Signed Sealed and delivered   John Harris (his seal)

in ye pres^{ts} of us witnesses.

Caleb Moody Senr

Philip ffouler.

Cutting Noyce

John Harriss appeared ye first day of April 1696. in ye eight year of his Ma^{ts} Reign and Acknowledged ye above written Instrument to be his Act and Deed before me.

                   Daniel Pierce Justice of ye Peace.

A true Copie of ye originall Transcribed & compared this 8th day of May : 1701.

                   p Jos : Hamond Regist^r

Know all men by these presents that I John Shapleigh of Kittery in the County of York Gent^l for Divers good causes and considerations me thereunto moving but more Especially for and in consideration of Sixteen pounds and ten shillings in Money to me in hand paid by Walter Deniver of the same place Shipwright at & before ye Ensealing and Delivery of these presents wherewith I confess my self to be fully satisfied contented and paid Have bargained and sold and by these presents doe fully clearly and Absolutely bargain & sell unto the s⁴ Walter Deniver his heires or Assignes for ever in plain and open Market after y° manner of New England Thirteen Acres and almost a quarter of land lying in y° town of Kittery between Crooked lane and Spruce Creek and takes its begining at y° Cross way that goes to y° point and Strawberry Bank toward the Northeast end of the late Mr Thomas Withers his home Lott, And is part of s⁴ Lott And runs from y° s⁴ Cross way south, Joyning to the high way that goes to y° point, forty poles, And from that Extent southwest and be west by Mr Cutts line forty pole and from thence Northwest forty pole near to y° high way to Strawberry bank or Woodmans fferry, And from thence by s⁴ high way to y° first station on a streight line, containing thirteen Acres & a quarter of an Acre almost/ together with all y° wood and underwood & Advantages thereto belonging. To have and to hold all y° s⁴ tract of land & y° Appurtenances thereof unto y° only use benefit and behoof of him y° s⁴ Walter Deniver his heires or Assignes for ever And I y° s⁴ John Shapleigh doe for my self and my heires Covenant to and with y° s⁴ Walter Deniver and his heires that y° Premisses are free from all manner of incumbrances whatsoever, as sales gifts Mortgages & Joyntures, and that I am y° true and proper owner thereof at and before y° ensealing of these presents And that I have within my selfe full power & Lawfull Authority to despose of y° same the peaceable and quiet Possession thereof to Warrant and Defend against all persons laying a Lawfull Claim thereunto [94] In Witness hereof I have set to my hand and seal, this twenty

Shapleigh to Deniver

Book VI, Fol. 94.

sixth of Decemb^r vulgarly called Saint Stephens day, one thousand seven hundred, 1700.

Signed Sealed and Delivered   John Shapleigh (his seal)
  In presents of us.
  Richard Briar
  Daniel Jones
  Wm Godsoe.

To all People to whome this p'sent Deed of Sale shall come Nathaniel ffryar of New Castle in ye Province of New Hampshier in New England Esqr sendeth Greeting. Know Yee that I ye s^d Nathaniel ffryar for and in consideration of one thousand pounds Currant money of New England to me in hand well and truly paid at and before ye Ensealing and Delivery of these presents by Robert Elliot of New Castle afores^d Esqr. the receipt whereof to full content and satisfaction I doe hereby Acknowledge And thereof, and of every part and parcell thereof Doe acquit Exonerate and Discharge ye s^d Robert Elliot his heires Execut^{rs} Administrat^{rs} and Assignes and every of them for ever by these presents Have given granted bargained sold Aliened enfeoffed conveyed and confirmed And by these presents doe fully freely clearly and absolutely give, grant, bargain, sell, Alien, Enfeoffe, convey and confirm unto ye s^d Robert Elliot his heires and Assignes for ever All that my Island Scituate Lying and being on ye Eastern side and at ye Mouth of Piscataqua river in ye Province of Maine.

ffryer to Elliot

Comonly called or known by ye name of Champernoons Island, which I ye s^d ffryar formerly purchased of Cap^{tn} ffrancis Champernoone of Piscataqua river afores^d Gent/ containing one thousand Acres be ye same more or less (Excepting Eighty Acres of land Lying upon s^d Island which I ye s^d ffryar have given to my Son in Law John Hincks, Together with all and singular the housing Edifices buildings and fences standing thereon/ And all the land as well upland as Marsh or Meadow salt or fresh all ye wood, underwood timber and timber trees Mines Mineralls ways easments waters water Courses profits Priviledges Rights Liberties Immunities hereditaments Emmoluments and Appur^ces whatsoever upon and to ye s^d Island belonging or in any Appurtaining or therewith now used Ocupied or enjoyed Accepted reputed taken or known as part parcell or member thereof and ye revercon or revercons remainder and remainders Rents Issues and income thereof And alsoe all my Estate right title Interest Inheritance use Possession prop^rty Claime and Demand whatsoever of in and to ye s^d granted and bargained Premisses and every part thereof With all Deeds writings and Evidences relating thereto To have and to hold ye afores^d Island with all other th'above granted and bargained Premisses with th'appurtenances and every part and parcel thereof (Except as before excepted) unto ye s^d Robert Elliot his heires and Assignes for ever to his and their own sole and proper use benefit and behoofe from henceforth and for evermore Absolutely without any manner of condition redemption or revocation in in any wise And I ye said Nathaniel ffryar for me my heires Execut^rs and Admin^rs Doe hereby Covenant promise grant and agree to and with ye s^d Robert Elliot his heires and Assignes in manner and form following, That is to say, that I ye s^d Nathaniel ffryar at ye time of thensealing hereof and untill ye Delivery of these presents, am true sole and Lawfull owner of all ye afore bargained Premisses and stand Lawfully Siezed thereof in my own proper right of a good sure and Indefeasable Estate of Inheritance in ffee simple Having in my self full power good right & Lawfull Authority to grant, sell, convey and Assure ye Same unto ye s^d Robert Elliot his heires and Assignes for ever, in manner and form afores^d And according to ye true Intent and meaning of these presents And that ye s^d Robert Eliot his heires and Assignes shall and may by force and Vertue of these p^rsents from henceforth and for ever Lawfully peaceably and quietly have, hold use ocupie Possess and enjoy the above granted and bargained Premisses with th'appurtenances (Except as above Excepted) free & cleere and clearly Acquitted Exonerated and Discharged of and from all and all manner of former and other gifts grants bargains Sales Leases releases Mortgages Joyntures Dowers Judgmets Executions Entailes fines forfeitures Siezures amerciaments And of and from all other titles troubles charges and Incumbrances whatsoever/ And further that I ye s^d Nathaniel ffryar for my self my heires Execut^rs and Admin^rs and every of them doe hereby covenant and grant to warrant and Defend all the above granted and bargained Premisses with the Appurtenances and every part and parcell thereof (Excepting only as above excepted) unto ye s^d Robert Elliot his heires and Assignes for ever gainst ye Lawfull Claim and Demands of all and every person & persons whomsoever And at any time or times hereafter to give and pass such further and ample assurance and confirmation of ye Premisses unto the s^d Robert Elliot his heires and Assignes (at his and their own proper costs) as in Law or Equity can or may be reasonably Devised Advised or required. In witness whereof I ye s^d Nathaniel ffryar have hereunto set my hand and seal the twentieth day of August Anno Domī one thousand seven hundred In ye twelfth year of ye Reign of our Soveraign Ld King William ye third over England &c.

     Nath: ffryer (his seal) Senr

Signed Sealed and/.
 delivered in ye p^rsents of us
 Nicho Heskins,
 Edward Kennard

BOOK VI, FOL. 95.

New Hampshier ss

Nich : Heskins & Edw : Kennard both appearing before me ye Subscrib^r made oath that they saw Nathaniel ffryer Sign Seal & deliver ye within Instrum^t as his Act and Deed & they each Signed as Witnesses.

New Castle ye 21 Dec : 1700. Theodore Atkinson J Peace

A true Copie of ye originall Transcribed & compared May 26 : 1701 p Jos : Hamond Register

[95] Know all men by these presents that I Harlakinden Symonds of Ipswich in ye County of Essex in New England in the Massachusets Collony Gen^t/ for & in consideration of a Mare and alsoe a considerable Sum of money to me in hand paid before ye Sealing of these presents/ Have bargained & Sold and doe by these presents bargain sell Alien and confirm/ me my heires Execut^{rs} Administrat^{rs} and Assignes unto Robert Greenough of ye towne of Salem in ye same County & Collony of New England afores^d a considerable parcell of Land of one hundred Acres Upland and Meadow Viz^t a due & Just proportion of both where s^d Greenough shall Chuse out of a tract of land belonging to s^d Symonds Lying and being scituate above ye township of Wells and Cape Porpoise with all ye profits priviledges and

Symonds
to
Greenough

Appurtenances thereto in any wise belonging unto me s^d Grenough my heires Execut^{rs} Admin^{rs} and Assignes, To have and to hold Ocupie and peaceably and quietly to possess and enjoy for ever/ without any let hinderance Incumbrance or Molestation from by or under me s^d Symonds my heires Execut^{rs} Administrat^{rs} or Assignes for ever In witness of all and Singular ye Premisses I have hereunto set my hand & seale this fourth day of ffebruary in the year of our Lord one thousand Six hundred Eighty and four.

Signed Sealed and Delivered   Harlakinden Symonds (and/seal)
  In presents of.
  Daniel Epes Junr
  John Emerson

Mr Harlakinden Symonds Aknowledged the above written Instrum^t to be his Act and Deed, And Mrs Elizabeth Symonds his wife freely resigned up her right or title of Dowry therein/ Salem May 15th 1685.

                    Before me   John Hathorn Assistant

A true Copie of ye originall Transcribed and compared 31st 1701

                          p Jos: Hamond Cler

Wooden to Curtes

To all People to whome these p^{r}sents shall come I John Wooden now resident in Salem in ye County of Middlesex in ye Province of ye Massachusets Bay in New England husbandman send greeting Know yee that I ye s^d John Wooden for and in consideration of ye Sum of twelve pounds Curr^t money of New England to me in hand paid at and before the ensealing and delivery of these p^{r}sents by Benjamin Curtis of Kittery in ye County of York in s^d Province, house Carpenter the receipt whereof I doe hereby Acknowledge and my self therewith to be fully satisfied contented and paid And thereof and of and from every part thereof I doe acquit Exonerate and Discharge ye s^d Benjamin Curtis his heires Execut^{rs} Admin^{rs} and Assignes for ever by these p^{r}sents Have given granted bargained sold Aliened Enfeoffed & confirmed And by these p^{r}sents doe fully clearly and absolutely Give grant bargain sell Alien Enfeoffe convey and confirm unto him ye s^d Benjamin Curtis his heires Execut^{rs} Admin^{rs} & Assigns

for ever a certain piece or parcell of Land lying and being
Scituate in ye township of Wells in ye County of York containing Eighty Acres being butted and bounded as follows,
that is to say, begining at ye little River, so called, and on
the North Side thereof being thirty six poles in breadth
Joyning upon ye river and soe runing back from s^d river
upon a North Northeast line till Eighty Acres be completed
And bounded on ye East with ye land formerly Thomas
Coles, or how ever Else bounded or reputed to be bounded
which land was granted to me ye said Woodden by ye town
of Wells as may Appear on Record in s^d town book reference thereunto being had/ together with a town grant of
ten Acres of Meadow in any part of Wells where it may be
found cleare of former grants or proprieties/ with all profits
priviledges and comodities whatsoever to s^d piece or parcell
of land belonging or in any wise Appurtaining To have and
to hold ye s^d piece or parcell of land butted & bounded as
afores^d together with s^d grant of ten Acres of Meadow with
all ye priviledges as afores^d to him the s^d Benjamin Curtis
his heires Execut^{rs} Admin^{rs} or Assignes for evermore And I
ye s^d John Woodden for my self my heires Execut^{rs} Admin^{rs}
and Assignes doe hereby Covenant promise and grant to
and with ye s^d Benjamin Curtis his heires Execut^{rs} Admin^{rs}
and Assignes that at and before ye ensealing and delivery
hereof I am the true sole and proper owner of ye above bargained premisses And that I have in my self good right full
power and Lawfull Authority ye same to sell & convey unto
him ye s^d Benjamin Curtis his heires &c as afores^d And that
ye s^d Benjamin Curtis his heires or Assignes shall and may
from time to time and at all times for ever hereafter Lawfully peaceably and quietly have hold use ocupie possess &
enjoy ye above s^d Premisses with their Appurtenances and
every part thereof, free and clear Acquitted and Discharged
of and from all former and other gifts grants bargains Sales
leases Mortgages Joyntures Dowers Executions power of

thirds And of and from all other Incumbrances whatsoever by me made, done of suffered to be done at any time before y° enseyling hereof And that I y° s^d John Woodden against my self my heires Executors Admin^rs and Assignes and against all other persons whatsoever Lawfully Claiming y° same or any part thereof I will for ever Save harmless Warrant and Defend by these p'sents In witness w^r of I y° said John Woodden have hereunto set my hand and seal the third day of April Anno Domini one thousand seven hundred and one. 1701.

Signed Sealed and Delivered   John Wooden (and seale)
   In the presents of us.
              her
Hannah (9 Key
           mark
   Jos: Hamond

York ss/ Kittery April 3^d 1701

John Wooden personally Appearing before me the Subscrib^r one of his Ma^ts Justices of Peace in the County of York Acknowledged this Instrum^t to be his Act and Deed/
                              Jos: Hamond

A true Copie of y° originall Transcribed and compared this third day of April, 1701.
                        Jos: Hamond Regist^r

This Indenture made March y° 14th 1690. Witnesseth that I Jane Withers of the town of Kittery in y° Province of Maine in New England Widow and Relict of Mr Thomas Withers Deceased for divers good causes and considerations me hereunto moving, but Especially for the love I bear unto my daughter Elizabeth Berry of the same place, have given

Mrs Withers   and granted and confirmed unto my Daughter
   to   Elizabeth Berry all my right title and Interest
Elizabth Berry   in my land from Edmund Hamans' Reaching

home to Peter Lewis', aboth sides the Easting Creek, the title and Interest thereof to my s⁴ daughter Elizabeth I give by y⁰ desire of my husband which is Deceased by his order and my [96] desire I give all y⁰ Marshes lying between M⁷ ffernalds house and Edmund Hamans' aboth sides of y⁰ Creek for ever/ And my s⁴ Daughter promiss⁰ to let it out for my use as long as I shall live And my land at Egle point I will give to my s⁴ Daughter Elizabeth all my right title and Interest from and in that place Eagle point Joyning home to my house Lott improved land and pasture ground, woodland and woods in whose possession Soever it may be I give to my daughter Elizabeth to her and her heires Execut^{rs} Admin^{rs} or Assignes for ever Sealed and delivered in y⁰ presents of us whose names are underwritten.

   John Blanne   The W mark
   John Woodman   of Jane Withers. (and seale)

Mrs Jane Withers came and Acknowledged this Instrum^t to be her Act & Deed this 31 March 1691.   Before me
                               ffrancis Hooke Jus^{ts} Pec.

A true' Copie of y⁰ originall Transcribed & compared, June, 13th 1701.   p Jos : Hamond Regist^r

Maid y⁰ 1st are to say   Anno 1691. Ap^{ll} y⁰ first :

Memorandum that I Jane Withers widow and relict of my Deceased husband Thomas Withers, Declare hereby to future Satisfaction of all or any person or persons that may either Claim or be concerned in or about y⁰ land or Meadows mentioned or contained upon y⁰ other side of this paper Deed of gift, That whereas I Jane tooke into my consideration in y⁰ time of my widowhood for fear with all, of Neglecting alsoe to fulfill y⁰ desire of my husband Withers afores⁴ not knowing my own resolution of mind concerning Marriage or what other Changes might follow I had found by much experience of my said Daughter Elizabeth Berry I Acknowledge my selfe satisfied gratified and p^d w^tever Vallue the meadow was and is now worth/ And doe therefore Acquit & discharge the afores^d my daughter Elizabeth Berry from any further demand of Arreares or benefits from her my s^d Daughter Elizabeth but that she and her ofspring might improve possess and enjoy ye same for ever/ either during her own life or any oth^r heires Execut^rs or Assignes for ever or put it of to Sale as Nessessitie may compell or constraine. As I freely confirm under my hand and Seale In p^rsents of

  Jno Davise.   the mark of Mrs Jane
  & Joseph Berry
Kittery ss/ June 13th 1701.   Withers   (and seale)

Mrs Jane Godsoe, formerly Withers, personally Appearing before me ye Subscrib^r one of his Ma^ts Justices of the Peace within ye County of York Acknowledged this above written to be her Act and Deed, done in the time of her Widowhood.   Jos : Hamond

A true Copie of ye originall Transcribed and compared June 13th 1701   p Jos : Hamond Regist^r

---

To all Christian People to whome these presents shall come, Stephen Tobey of Kittery in ye County of York in ye Province of ye Massachusets Bay in New England sends greeting, Know yee that I Stephen Tobey afores^d for divers good causes me thereunto moving, more Especially for and in consideration of ye Sum of five and twenty pounds good and Lawfull money in New England to me in hand well and truly paid and secured in ye Law to be paid at and before ye ensealing and Delivery of these presents by Jacob Smith of the afores^d town County and Province Have given granted bargained Sold Aliened Enfeoffed and confirmed And by

these presents doe for me my heires Execut[rs] Admin[rs] and
Assignes fully freely and absolutely give grant bargain sell
Alien Enfeoffe convey and confirm unto him y[e] s[d] Jacob
Smith his heires Execut[rs] Admin[rs] and Assignes for ever, all
my Right title and Interest of in and to y[e] one half part of a
certain parcell of Land within the township of Kittery which
I bought in partnership with Joseph Hamond David Libby
Matthew Libby and Daniel ffogg./ of M[rs] Mehetable Warren Elisha Hutchinson and Elizabeth his wife as p Deed of
Sale under their hands and Seales Bearing Date Decemb[r]
18th 1699. my proportion thereof being Eight and thirty
poles in breadth as Appeares by a Mutuall agreement made
between me y[e] s[d] Steph Tobey & s[d] Hamond and Company
under our hands and Seals bearing Date March 21st 1700. ref-

Tobey to Smith

erence thereunto being had which s[d] half part
hereby sold unto y[e] s[d] Jacob Smith is bounded
as followeth, that is to say beginning at a
marked tree on y[e] Northeast Side of y[e] rode that goes from
y[e] corner of Thomas Hunscombs orchard fence toward Kittery Northwestward, and from that tree, which is on y[e]
Southeast Side of s[d] land, to run Northwest and by North
y[e] whole breadth of my Land which is thirty eight rods and
run back that whole breadth upon a Northeast & by east
line between y[e] lands of David Libby on y[e] Northwest and
Thomas Hunscomb on y[e] southeast to y[e] Extent and head
bounds of s[d] Hunscombs land And from thence the s[d] Smith
is to take y[e] Northwest half part of y[e] s[d] thirty eight poles
and to run back upon y[e] s[d] Northeast & by east point the
full breadth of Nineteen poles Joyning with s[d] David Libby
on y[e] Northwest to y[e] utmost extent of my s[d] Land And if
it doe happen that y[e] s[d] Smiths part according to y[e] afores[d]
bounds (when Justly Measured) be more than s[d] Tobeys
part, he is to pay y[e] s[d] Tobey proportionably to y[e] price he
is to give for y[e] halfe part according to y[e] number of Acres/
And if it happen to be less than y[e] one halfe then y[e] s[d]

Tobey is to make ye like abatement/ To have and to hold the s^d piece or parcel of Land with ye Appurtenances thereto belonging with all right, title, Interest, Claime and Demand which I ye s^d Stephen Tobey now have or in time past have had, or which I my heires Execut^{rs} Admin^{rs} or Assignes in time to come may, might, should or in any wise ought to have of in or to ye above granted Premisses or any part thereof to him the [**97**] the s^d Jacob Smith his heires or Assignes forever And to ye sole and proper use benefit and behoof of him ye s^d Jacob Smith his heires Execut^{rs} &c forevermore/ And I the s^d Stephen Tobey for me my heires Execut^{rs} Administrat^{rs} and Assignes doe Covenant Promise and grant to & with him the s^d Jacob Smith his heires and Assignes that at and before ye ensealing and delivery of these presents I am ye true right and proper owner of the above Premisses and the Appurtenances And that I have in my self good right full power and Lawfull Authority the same to grant and confirm unto him ye s^d Jacob Smith his heires & Assigns afores^d And that ye same and every part thereof is free and cleare Acquitted and discharged of and from all other and former gifts grants bargains sales Leases Mortgages titles troubles Acts Alienations and Incumbrances whatsoever by me done or suffered to be done and that it shall and may be Lawfull to and for him ye s^d Jacob Smith his heires or Assignes the afores^d premisses and every part thereof from time to time and at all times forever hereafter To have hold use improve Ocupie Possess & enjoy Lawfully peaceably and quietly without any Lawfull Let deniall hinderance Molestation or disturbance of or by me or any other person or persons from by or under me or by my procurement And that ye Sale thereof against my self my heires Execut^{rs} Admin^{rs} and Assignes Lawfully Claiming ye same, or any part thereof, I will for ever save harmless Warrant and Defend by these presents And that I my heires Execut^{rs} and Admin^{rs} shall and will make perform and Execute such other further Lawfull and reasonable Act or Acts thing or things as in Law or Equity can be Advised Devised or required for ye better confirming and more sure making of ye Premisses unto him ye s^d Jacob Smith his heires or Assigns According to ye Laws of this Province/ In witness whereof I ye s^d Stephen Tobey have hereunto set my hand and seal the sixteenth day of May in the thirteenth year of ye Reign of our Soveraign Lord William the third King over England &c. Anno Domini One thousand Seven hundred and one, 1701.

Signed Sealed & delivered   Stephen Tobey (and seal)
   in the presents of us
   John Rogers.
   Jos: Hamond

York ss/ Kittery, May 16th 1701

The above named Stephen Tobey personally Appearing before me the Subscrib^r one of his Ma^{ts} Justices of the Peace within the County of York Acknowledged this Instrum^t to be his Act and Deed.

                                   Jos: Hamond

York ss/ Decemb^r 8th 1701

Hannah Tobey ye wife of ye above named Stephen Tobey psonally Appearing before me ye Subscrib^r one of his Ma^{ts} Justices of ye Peace within s^d County did give and surrend^r all her right of Dower of in and to ye above premisses and did affix her hand and seal thereto.

                                   Jos: Hamond

A true Copie of ye originall Transcribed & compared Decemb^r ye eighth: 1701   p Jos: Hamond Regist^r

To all Christian People that these presents shall come to Greeting in our Lord Know yee that I Peter Staple of Kittery in ye County of York for and in consideration of

Love good will & affection which I have and doe bear towards my welbeloved son John Staple of Kittery in the County of York Carpenter have given and granted and by these presents doe freely clerely and absolutely give and grant to y[e] s[d] John Staple and his heires for ever a certain tract or parcel of Land containing thirty Acres scituate and lying in y[e] town of Kittery in the County of York Joyning to and bounded with Joshua Remich his Land on y[e] Northwest and with y[e] land that formerly was James Spinneys on y[e] Northeast & with William Tetherly Land on y[e] same side And on y[e] Southeast with Samuel Spinney & William Racklifs land To have and to hold all y[e] s[d] Land with all y[e] priviledges thereunto belonging unto y[e] s[d] John Staple and his heires from henceforth as his & their proper Land for ever absolutely without any manner of condition as I y[e] s[d] Peter Staple have Absolutely and of my own Accord put in further testimony In witness whereof I have hereunto set my hand and seal y[e] Eighten day of June And y[e] thirteenth Year of y[e] Reign of our Soveraign Lord William the third, King of England And in y[e] Year of our Lord one thousand Seven hundred and one.

Peter Staple to his son Jno

Signed Sealed and Delivered   Peter *P* Staple (his Seale)
    In the presents of.   his mark
    Jacob Remich
    Peter Stapell
    Mary Stapel

York ss/ Kittery June 24 : 1701

The above named Peter Staple psonally Appearing before me y[e] Subscrib[r] one of his Ma[ts] Justices of y[e] Peace in y[e] County of York Acknowledged this Instrum[t] to be his Act and Deed.

                           Jos: Hamond

A true Copie of y[e] originall Transcribed and compared this 24th day of June 1701.

                         p Jos Hamond Regist[r]

BOOK VI, FOL. 97.

Know all men by these presents that James Warren Senʳ of Barwick in Kittery in yᵉ County of York in yᵉ Province of yᵉ Massachusets Bay in New England In consideration of yᵉ Naturall affection that he beareth toward his son Gilbert Warren of yᵉ same Town, and the conditions hereafter in this Instrument Mentioned/ Hath given sold and fully confirmed unto his sᵈ son Gilbert, And doth by these presents give sell and absolutely confirm to him a certain parcel of Land containing forty Acres Scituate in York near the Bridge comonly called York Bridge on yᵉ Eastward side of that branch of York River (bounded as is Expressed in a return of its being Laid out Signed by Abraham Preble Survʳ and Lewis Bane Select man both for York Signed by them March Seventeenth day one thousand Six hundred and Ninety eight or nine) Together with all the Priviledges and Appurtenances belonging thereto To him yᵉ sᵈ Gilbert and

*James Warren
to
his son Gilbert*

his heires for ever To have and to hold the Premisses and Appurtenances to yᵉ only proper use and benefit of sᵈ Gilbert and his heires for ever/ And sᵈ James doth engage the premisses and Appurtenances from all persons laying any Claime thereto, to sᵈ Gilbert and his heires for ever to Warrantise and Defend by these presents, to which he alsoe binds his heirs Executʳˢ and Administratʳˢ/ Be it known moreover that yᵉ sᵈ Gilbert doth Covenant promise and engage as a Condition of this conveyance above referred to, to pay yearly as long as his father or mother shall live yᵉ Sum̄ of thirty Shillings in Currant money to his father or Mother or their order/ And in case sᵈ Gilbert or his heires During sᵈ James his life or his present wifes, shall refuse to make sᵈ paymᵗ/ Sᵈ James shall have power to reenter on thirty Acres of yᵉ Premisses Lying together most unimproved And have as good a title as before yᵉ Sealing of these presents In witness whereof the sᵈ James & Gilbert have set to their hands and Seales

BOOK VI, FOL. 98.

this twenty fifth day of March in y⁰ year of our Lord One thousand Seven hundred and one

Signed Sealed and DD   James ┼┼┼ Warren (his seale)
  in y⁰ presents of us   his
         his   mark
    James 𝒜 Stackpole   Gilbert G Warren (his seal)
      mark   mark
John Wade

York ss: Kittery June 16ᵗʰ 1701

The within named James Warren & Gilbert Warren personally Appearing before me y⁰ Subscriber one of his Maᵗˢ Justices of y⁰ Peace for the County aforesᵈ Acknowledged this Instrumᵗ to be their Act & Deed

                                          Jos: Hamond

A true Copie of y⁰ originall Transcribed & compared this: 16. of June. 1701.   p Jos: Hamond Registʳ

[98] At a Legall town Meeting held at Kittery May 16ᵗʰ 1694./ Granted unto Joseph Weeks provided it be in no former grant/ A true Copie.

                              p Jos: Hamond Cleȓ

Know all men by these presents that I Joseph Weekes above named Do sell Assigne and make over all my right title and Interest of in and to the above grant of Land to Mʳ Elihue Gunnison of Kittery his heires &c.

Weekes   for ever. from me y⁰ sᵈ Weekes my heires &c/
to
Gunnison   Witness my hand and Seale. Decembʳ 24ᵗʰ 1700.

Signed Sealed and Delivered   Joseph Weekes (and seal)
  In presents of.
        her
  Hannah 𝒟 Key
        mark
Jos. Hamond

BOOK VI, FOL. 98.

York ss. December 24th 1700

Joseph Weekes personally Appearing before me y⁰ Subscrib' one of Ma'⁸ Justices of Peace in y⁰ County of York Acknowledged this Instrum' to be his Act and Deed/

Jos Hamond

A true Copie of y⁰ originall Transcribed and compared Decemb' 24th 1700/.

p Jos: Hamond Regist'

At a Legall town Meeting held at Kittery May 24th 1699. Granted unto Nicholas Weekes his heires &c. thirty Acres of Land if he can find it clear of former grants. Attests

Jos Hamond Cler

Know all men by these presents that I y⁰ above named Nicholas Weekes Do Sell Assigne and make over all my right title and Interest of, in and to y⁰ above grant of Land to M' Elihue Gunnison of Kittery his heires and Assignes for ever from me y⁰ s⁴ Weekes my heires &c for evermore Witness my hand and Seal Decemb' 24th 1700/

Weekes
to
Gunnison

Nicholas Weekes (his seal)

Signed Sealed and Delivered
 In prents of.
   her
 Hannah ◯ Key
   mark
 Jos: Hamond

York ss. Decemb' 24th 2700

Nicholas Weekes personally Appearing before me y⁰ Subscrib' one of his Ma'⁸ Justices of Peace in y⁰ County of York Acknowledged this Instrum' to be his Act and Deed.

Jos Hamond.

A true Copie of y⁰ originall Transcribed and compared Decemb' 24th 1700. p Jos Hamond Regist'

Know all men by these presents that I Thomas Spinney of Kittery in ye County of York Yeomⁿ Have given granted bargained Exchanged and Sold unto my Son Samuel Spinney all that tract of Land lying near ye great Cove containing eight Acres or thereabout more or less Lying at ye head or East end of the Land I formerly gave him where his house now stands referrence thereunto being had And is in breadth at west end twenty four pole and at east end thirty two pole in breadth And in Length fiftie two pole And is bounded on ye South with my own Land And on all other parts with his own Land, and runs back from ye head of his house Lott on an East line as it had been formerly laid out by Cap^{tn} Wincoll together with all ye wood and under wood and timber thereon To have and to hold ye s^d tract of land to him ye s^d Samuel Spinney his heires or Assigns for evermore to his and their own proper use benefit and behoofe and furthermore I ye s^d Thomas Spinney doe covenant for my selfe & my heires with ye s^d Samuel Spinney and his heires that ye Premisses are free from all incumbrances by me made and that I am ye true and proper owner thereof at ye time of ye sealing these presents, the peaceable Possession thereof to Warrant & maintaine against all persons Laying a Lawfull Claime thereunto In witness hereof I have set to my hand and seal this twenty third day of Decemb^r One thousand Seven hundred : 1700.

[margin: Tho: Spinney to his son Sam^{ll}]

Signed Sealed and Delivered   Tho: Spinney. (his seal)

   In the presents of us

   John Spinney

   the sign **HF** of

   Hannah ffernald

   Wm Godsoe.

York ss/ Kittery July 8th 1701.

The above name Thomas Spinney personally Appearing before me ye Subscrib^r one of his Ma^{ts} Justices of Peace for

BOOK VI, FOL. 98.

ye County of York Acknowledged this Instrumt to be his Act and Deed.

Jos Hamond.

A true Copie of ye originall Transcribed and compared July 8th 1701.

p Jos Hamond Registr

Know all men by these presents that I Samuel Spinney of Kittery in the County of York Have given, granted, bargained, Exchanged and sold unto my Honoured fathr Mr Thomas Spinney of ye same place all that Tract of Land lying at ye head of his old Lott behind Alcock and by ye side of Samuel ffernalds containing seven or eight Acres of Land be it more or less, being in Length by Came or Adams North and South forty four pole from an oak where Samuel ffernalds name and my father have bin formerly Sett, And from that corner tree by Samll ffernalds line twenty four poles and on ye North side twenty eight pole,

Samll Spiney to his father Tho: Spiney Together with all ye wood and under wood and Timbr thereon, To have and to hold all ye sd tract of Land unto ye only use benefit and behoof of him ye sd Thomas Spinney his heires or Assignes for evermore. And furthermore I ye sd Samll Spinney doe covenant for my self and my heires with ye sd Thomas Spinney and his heires that ye Premisses are free from all incumbrances whatsoever by me made and that I am ye true and proper owner thereof at ye time of ye ensealing hereof the peaceable and quiet Possession thereof to warrant and maintaine against all persons laying a Lawfull Claim thereunto/ In witness hereof I have set to my hand and Seal this twenty fourth day of Decemb{r} one thousand Seven hundred: 1700.

Signed Sealed & delivered   Samuel Spinney (and seal)
   In presents of.
   John Spinney
   the Sign H F of
   Hannah ffernald

York ss, Kittery July 8th 1701.

The above named Samuel Spinney personally Appearing before me y* Subscrib{r} one of his Ma{ts} Justices of Peace for the County of York Acknowledged this Instrument to be his Act and Deed.

                                                Jos: Hamond

A true Copie of the originall Transcribed and compared July 8th 1701.   p Jos Hamond: Regist{r}

[99] Kittery in y* County of York/ Know all men by these presents that We Hannah ffernald Relict and Executrix of the last Will and Testament of Sam{ll} ffernald late of Kittery Deceased/ And Nathaniel ffernald Heir of y* s{d} Sam{ll} ffernald afores{d} for y* consideration and in Exchange for a tract of Land bought and Exchanged with our father and Grand father M{r} Thomas Spinney of the Town and County aboves{d} containing fifteen Acres and a half of Land lying in Kittery afores{d} above the great Cove at y* head of Alcocks Lott and Joyning to our own Land, being in Length Ninety four pole and in breadth twenty six pole and a halfe as it is bounded and laid out for y* consideration and in Exchange for y* aboves{d} Land we y* s{d} Hannah ffernald and Nathaniel ffernald aboves{d} Doe by these presents give, grant, barguine and sell unto y* s{d} Thomas Spinney his heires or Assigns for ever All that tract of Land lying and being at

BOOK VI, FOL. 99.

ye entrance of ye Pulpit reach at ye point and is bounded by the river of Piscataqua and ye great Cove and the Lands of ye s^d Thomas Spinney, containing Seven Acres and a half more or less, and is ye home Lott of ye s^d Sam^{ll} ffernald Deceased, together with ye appurtenances thereto belonging or in any ways Appurtaining To have and to hold all the s^d tract of land be it more or less unto ye only and sole use of him ye s^d Thomas Spinney his heires or Assignes for ever/ And further more we ye s^d Hannah ffernald and Nathaniel ffernald above s^d Doe for our selves and our heires covent^t to and with ye s^d Thomas Spinney and his heires, that ye Premisses are free from all Incumbrances whatsoever And that we are the true and proper owners thereof, and have within our selves full power and Lawfull Authority to sell and Dispose of the same, the peaceable and quiet Possession thereof to Warrant and Defend/ In witness hereof we have set to our hands and seales this twenty fifth day of June One thousand Seven hundred & one 1701

Hannah & Nath: ffernald to Tho. Spiney

Sign^d and Seal^d and Delivered
  In presents of us.
Samuel Spinney
  The Sign of
Mary   Spinney
Wm Godsoe

The Signe of
Hannah H ffernald (and seal)
Nathaniel ffernald (his seal)

York ss/ Kittery July 8th 1701

The above named Hannah ffernald and Nathaniel ffernald personally Appearing before me ye Subscriber one of his Ma^{ts} Justices of Peace for ye County of York Acknowledged this Instrument to be his Act & Deed

                                Jos: Hamond

A true Copie of ye originall Transcribed and Compared July 8th 1701.

                        p Jos: Hamond Regist^r

Book VI, Fol. 99.

York ss/ Novemb^r 6th 1702/

The within named Nathaniel Fernald p'sonally appearing before me ye Subscrib^r one of her Ma^{ts} Justices of the peace within s^d County Acknowledged ye Instrum^t within written to be his Act and Deed, thô made in the time of his non age yet now resigns up all his right, title & Interest of in & to ye Premisses within named, unto his Uncle John Spinney Execut^r to ye within named Thomas Spinney Dec^d.

Jos: Hamond

A true Copie of Nathaniel ffernalds Acknowledgm^t being on ye back side of ye originall Instrum^t/ Transcribed and compared, Novemb^r 6. 1702.

p Jos: Hamond Reg^r

Know all men by these presents that I Thomas Spinney of Kittery in ye County of York Yeoman. for ye consideration and Exchange of a tract of land bought and Exchanged with my daughter Hannah ffernald Relict and Executrix of Samuel ffernald late of Kittery Deceased, And Nathaniel ffernald son and heir of the s^d Samuel ffernald aboves^d, And doe by these presents for ye consideration of their home Lott Joyning to my now dwelling house bounded by the River of Piscataqua and ye great Cove and my own land containing seven Acres and a half be it more or less for ye consideration of ye Exchange, and in Lieu y^rof I ye s^d Thomas Spinney have given, granted bargained and sold unto the said Hannah ffernald and Nathaniel ffernald aboves^d, ffifteen Acres & a half of Land Lying at ye head of Alcocks Lott, And is in length Ninety four pole and in breadth twenty six pole and a halfe, bounded by their own land Southward and westward, And my own Northward, and Margaret Adams land Eastward, together with all the priviledges and Appurtenances thereunto belonging unto ye s^d

Tho Spinney to Hannah. & Nath^{ll} ffernald

Hannah ffernald dureing her naturall life & after her Decease unto ye s^d Nathaniel ffernald his heires or Assignes for ever as ye above s^d Seven Acres and a half had bin given to him ye s^d Nathan^{ll} by his s^d father refferrence thereunto being had/ To have and to hold ye said tract of Land and every part thereof with all ye Appurtenances thereunto belonging unto ye only and sole use of her ye s^d Hannah ffernald and ye said Nathaniel ffernald his heires and Assignes for ever, And furthermore I ye s^d Thomas Spinney Doe for my self and my heires Covenant to & with ye s^d Hannah ffernald and Nathaniel ffernald and their heires that ye Premisses are free from all incumbrances whatsoever And that I have within my self full power to dispose of the same/ the Peaceable and quiet Possession thereof to Warrant and Maintaine In witness whereof I have set to my hand and Seal this twenty fifth day of June One thousand seven hundred and one. 1701 The words [and a half] interlined.

Witness us   Tho: Spinney (his seal)
 Samuel Spinney
  the mark of
 Mary   Spinney
 Wm Godsoe.

York ss Kittery July 8th 1701

The above named Hannah ffernald and Nathaniel ffernald personally Appearing before me ye Subscrib^r one of his Ma^{ts} Justices of Peace for s^d County, Acknowledged this Instrum^t to be their Act and Deed.

             Jos: Hamond

A true Copie of ye Originall Transcribed and compared July 8th 1701

          p Jos Hamond Regist^r

Know all men by these presents that I Thomas Spinney, Senr, of Kittery in ye County of York in New England Yeoman for Divers good and Valluable considerations me hereunto moving, but more Especially for and in consideration of ye Sum of Six pounds in money to me in hand paid by Thomas Woster of Portsm^o in New Hampshier Yeoman receit whereof I doe acknowledge & my self well and truly contented and paid, and doe by these presents Acquit ye s^d Thomas Worster for the same for ye consideration aboves^d I ye s^d Thomas Spinney Have given granted bargained and sold, And by these presets give grant bargain and sell Enfeoffe and for ever confirm unto the s^d Thomas Worster his heires and Assignes All that tract of Land lying in ye township of Kittery in the County [100] aboves^d containing five Acres of Land and is scituate and lying between ye great Cove & Spruce Creek and is bounded on ye west with ye Land of John Tomson, and on ye south side with Land of Peter Dixon And on ye east with ye s^d Worster his own Land, And on ye North with ye Land of John Spinney And is part of fifteen Acres of Land that was granted unto me by town of Kittery and laid out by Captⁿ John Wincoll as by ye Records doth more at large Appear, together with all ye woods under woods Timber and trees standing or Lying thereon, with all ye Appurtenances and priviledges thereunto belonging or in any ways Appurtaining unto ye Same. To have and to hold all and Singular ye above bargained Premisses and every part thereof unto ye only and sole benefit and behoof of him ye s^d Thomas Worster his heires and Assignes for evermore/ I the s^d Thomas Spinney doe covenant for my self my heires Execut^{rs} and Administrat^{rs} with the said Thomas Worster his heires and Assignes that the Premisses are free from all Incumbrances whatsoever As Joyntures Dowries gifts sales Mortgages And that at the time of the Ensealing hereof I am the true and proper owner of the same and have within my self full power and Lawfull

Authority to dispose of ye same And that it shall and may be Lawfull for ye s^d Thomas Worster at all times hereafter to take use ocupie and Possess the same without ye lett or hinderance of me the s^d Thomas Spinney or any other person under me, the Peaceable and quiet Possession thereof to warrant and maintain against all persons whatsoever laying Lawfull Claim thereunto/ In witness hereof I have hereunto set my hand and Seal this sixth day of July one thousand seven hundred and one: 1701.

Signed Sealed and Delivered   Tho: Spinney (and a seln)

  In the presents of.

  James Spinney.

  Hannah *HF* ffernald

  John Spinney.

York ss/ Kittery July 8th 1701

The above named Thomas Spinney personally Appearing before me ye Subscrib^r one of his Ma^{ts} Justices of Peace in s^d County Acknowledged this Intrument to be his Act and Deed.

                               Jos. Hamond

A tru Copie of the originall Transcribed and compared July. 8th 1701   p Jos: Hamond Regist^r

---

Nicholas Walden to John Woodman

Know all men by these presents that I Nicholas Waldron of Portsmouth in the Province of New Hampshier Taylor in consideration of Seventy pounds in money to me in hand paid by Mr John Woodman of Kittery in the County of York fferry man the receipt thereof I doe confess and my self therewith contented and paid have given granted bargained and sold And doe by these presents give grant bargain and sell unto the s^d John Woodman his heires or Assignes for ever a certain house & Land Lying in the Township of Kittery in y^e

County of York at a place known by y⁎ name of Crooked Lane on y⁎ Northeast Side of Piscataqua River over against Witherses Island and is that house and Land that was the late John Diaments of Kittery and in y⁎ Ocupation of the s⁴ Woodman And is that house and Land that I y⁎ s⁴ Waldron purchased of Mʳ Nathaniel Raynes and John Woodman aboves⁴ as Appeares by an Instrument under their hands as they were Administratⁿ to y⁎ Estate of the s⁴ John Diament bearing Date April 13ᵗʰ 1699. together with all y⁎ lands housing and out housing orchard and Gardens fields and pastures thereunto belonging or in any ways Appurtaining as they were conveyed unto me by the aboves⁴ recited Instrument by the s⁴ Administratⁿ to all intents constructions and purposes To have & to hold all y⁎ above mentioned house and Lands and Appurtenances thereunto belonging unto y⁎ only use benefit and behoof of him y⁎ s⁴ John Woodman his heires Executⁿ Administratⁿ or Assignes for evermore And I the s⁴ Nicholas Waldron doe for myself my heires Executⁿ Administratⁿ Covenant to and with the said John Woodman his his heirs Executⁿ Adminⁿ or Assignes that y⁎ Premisses are free from all incumbrances whatsoever by me made And that I have full power and Lawfull Authority to dispose of y⁎ same And that I am y⁎ true and proper owner thereof at and before y⁎ Ensealing of these presents the Peaceable and quiet Possession thereof to Warant and Maintain against all persons Laying a Lawfull Claim thereunto the Kings most Excellent Majᵗⁱᵉ only excepted, In witness hereof I have set to my hand & Seal this Second day of January one thousand Seven hundred: $\frac{1700}{1701}$.

Memorand̃ the word owner enterlined between line y⁎ twenty fourth and twenty fifth before Signing

Signed Sealed and Delivered   Nicolas Walden (and seal)
  in presents of us.
  John Shepard Senʳ
  John Shepard Junʳ
  Wᵐ Godsoe

BOOK VI, FOL. 101.

Nicholas Walden came before me Rich[d] Waldron one of his Ma[ts] Council and Justice of Peace for y[e] Province of New Hampshier and Acknowledged y[e] above Instrum[t] to be his Act and Deed.
Portsm[o] in New Hampsh[r] 17[th] June 1701   Rich[d] Waldron.

A true Copie of y[e] originall Transcribed and compared July 24[th] 1701   p Jos Hamond Regist[r]

Let all men know by these p[r]sents that we John Heard of Kittery in the County of East York Husbandman, And Shuah Heard late wife of James Heard Dece[d]/ of y[e] same town and County afores[d] Widow/ are hereby held and firmly bound unto John Neal of y[e] same town and County Husbandman in y[e] full & whole sum of two hundred pounds Lawfull money and Currant in New England to be paid unto y[e] s[d] John Neal or to his certain Atturney his heires Execut[rs] Admin[rs] or Assignes or to one of them at one intire paym[t] unto which paym[t] well and truly to be made and done we doe bind our selves and either of us Joyntly and Severally for y[e] whole and in y[e] whole our heires Execut[rs] & Administrators firmly by these presents Sealed with our Seales And Dated y[e] first day of Novemb[r] in y[e] twenty eight year of y[e] Reign of our Soveraign L[d] Charles y[e] Second, by the grace of God of England Scotland ffrance and Ireland King Defender of the ffaith Anno Dom 1676.

John & Shuah Heard to John Neal

The Condition of this present Obligation is such that whereas James [101] Heard of the town of Kittery and County aboves[d] Deceased, the son of thabove bounden John Heard And late husband of thabove bounden Shuah Heard for severall years since and for a true and Valluable consideration for himself his his heires Execut[rs] Admin[rs] and Assignes did clerely really and Absolutely bargain and sell unto thabove named John Neal his heires Execut[rs] Admin[rs] and Assignes the halfendeal of a certain Lot or tract of Land granted unto the s[d] James Heard and one Thomas Etherinton, Deceased, by the town of Kittery afores[d] and since laid out and bounded to them and since the sale thereof unto y[e] said Neale Divided between y[e] s[d] John Neale and y[e] Administrat[r] or Administrat[rs] of y[e] s[d] Thomas Etherintons Estate to both to both their contents and agreement/ Which lott or tract of Land as it was granted and as it is laid out Lyeth and is bounded on y[e] North or thereabouts by a lott or tract of Land some times heretofore granted unto one W[m] Ellingham And Southerly by lands granted unto one M[rs] Katherine Treworgie And Westerly by y[e] river of Piscataqua/ And Easterly by y[e] Commons which s[d] Moietie or halfendeale of y[e] s[d] Lott the s[d] Neale now Possesseth & enjoyeth; Now for as much as the s[d] James Heard Deceased, did not by his Deed under his hand according to Law confirm the said Land unto y[e] s[d] Neale as he ought to doe, being prevented by death/ Thabove boundens John Heard and Shuah Heard doe hereby confess and Acknowledge that y[e] s[d] halfendeal of y[e] s[d] Lott of Land with thappurtenances and priviledges thereunto belonging or in any wise Appurtaining or ought to Appurtain or belong to it were by y[e] s[d] James Heard clearly really and Absolutely sold and delivered unto y[e] s[d] John Neale And Seizen & Possession taken by him Accordingly and thafores[d] valluable consideration or price greed on to be paid for y[e] s[d] Land and every part and parcle thereof fully duly and truly satisfied & paid long since by y[e] s[d] John Neale unto y[e] s[d] James Heard And thereof and every part & pcell thereof thabove boundens John and Shuah Heard doe for themselves their heires Execut[rs] Admin[rs] and Assignes Acquit y[e] s[d] John Neale his heires Execut[rs] Admin[rs] & Assignes for ever/ Now if thabove boundens John Heard and Shuah Heard or either of them they their heires Execut[rs] Admin[rs] and Assignes and

Book VI, Fol. 101.

every of them doe from time to time and at all times hereafter pmit and suffer yͤ sᵈ John Neale his heires Executʳˢ Administratʳˢ or Assignes and every and either of them quietly and peaceably to have hold ocupie possess and enjoy that foresᵈ halfendeal or tract of Land as it is now Divided with yͤ Appurtenances and priviledges thereunto belonging or in any wise are or ought to be Appurtaining thereunto without their or either of their Lawfull let suit trouble deniall disturbance or Molestation, putting out of them yͤ sᵈ John and Shuah Heard or either of them or either of their heires Executʳˢ Adminʳˢ or Assignes Lawfully Claiming the sᵈ halfendeal or tract of Land or any part or parcel thereof And further if thabove boundens John and Shuah their heires Executʳˢ Adminʳˢ and Assignes or any or either of yᵐ upon request made to them or either of them by the above named John Neale his heires Executʳˢ Adminʳˢ or Assignes doe: doe any further Act or Acts thing or things in yͤ Law as shall be Judged meet and Nessessary to be done for yͤ better confirming and clear conveying and Settleing of yͤ sᵈ halfendeale or tract of Land unto yͤ sᵈ Neale his heires Executʳˢ Adminʳˢ or Assignes that then this pʳsent obligation shall be voyd and of none effect or Else to be and remaine in full power force & vertue

Sealed Signed & delivered
  in yͤ presents of us   The mark of John 〔mark〕 Heard (his seal)
  Andrew Searle
  the mark of   the mark of
  William W ffurbish   Shuah 〔mark〕 Heard (her seal)

John Heard & Shuah Heard Acknowledged yͤ above Obligation to be their free Act and Deed with their hands and Seales to it this 12ᵗʰ day of Janʳʸ 1676: Before me
                       John Wincoll Assotiate

A true Copie of the originall Transcribed and compared: May 12ᵗʰ 1701
                    p Jos Hamond Registʳ

Book VI, Fol. 101.

Know all men by these presents that I John Neale, Senr, of Barwick of ye Province of the Massachusets in New England for Divers causes and considerations me hereunto moving, but Especially for ye love I doe bear unto my Naturall Son Andrew Neale of ye town & Province aboves^d Have given granted Alienated and confirmed And by these presents Doe give grant Alienate and confirm unto my aboves^d son Andrew Neale his heires Execut^{rs} Administrat^{rs} and Assignes the one half of that Lott or tract of Land which I now live upon and that my now dwelling house standeth on/ Viz^t the North Side of ye land next ye Widow fforgusons from ye rivers side up to ye old fence near a bridge called Forgusons bridge as it is this day bounded and marked out with stakes and called by the name of the old field be it half

<small>John Neal
to
Andrew Neal</small> more or less And residue of that Land from that fence by fforgusons bridge to be Equally Divided into two parts, the s^d Andrew to have that part which lyeth Northerly next to ye s^d Widow fforgusons And ye other half of ye Lott I doe reserve to my self which Lot of Land in ye whole containeth by Estimation fivety Acres from the waters side to ye head of the Lott with the Addition be it more or less The half of the s^d Lott to be to my Son Andrew his heirs Execut^{rs} Administrat^{rs} or Assignes/ To have and to hold the same for ever so that my Son Andrew shall from time to time and at All times Use Ocupie Possess and enjoy the s^d Land together with all the Priviledges thereunto belonging quietly and Peaceably free from all Molestation from me ye abovesaid John Neale my heires Execut^{rs} Administrat^{rs} and Assignes or any other person or persons whatsoever laying any Legall Claim thereunto To the true performance of y^e above written I

Book VI, Fol. 102.

have set to my hand and Seale this Decemb^r the fourth: 1694. Annoq, Sexto Gulielmo Nostri Regis Tertij Angliæ &c
Signed Sealed and Delivered
   In the presents of us.   John ┼ Neale ($_{mark}^{his}$)
   Daniel Goodin   his mark
   Nathan /\ Lord his   Joan ⊃ Neale ($_{seale}^{her}$)
        mark   her mark
   Edward Tompson
John Neal and Joan Neale Acknowledged the above written Instrument to be their Act & Deed this 26th of Decemb^r 1694/ Before me.
                          Charles Frost Jus^t peace
   A true Copie of the originall Transcribed and compared this : 12th May 1701.   p Jos : Hamond Regist^r

   Know all men by these presents That whereas I John Neal Senr of Barwick of the Province of ye Massachusets in N. England Have given and confirmed unto my son Andrew Neal the one half of my Land Lying and being in ye town & Province aboves^d by a Deed of Gift made over to my said son bearing Date Decemb^r ye 4. Anno Domini : 1694 Soe

John Neal
to
Andrew Neale

Likewise know Yee that I John Neale Senr abovesaid doe by these presents grant Alienate and confirm unto my above named Son Andrew Neale the other halfe of my whole Living, Lands, Tenements, All grants of Lands, Rights titles, Moveables, Goods Chattells &c/ belonging to my s^d Living to be to him his heires Execut^{rs} Admin^{rs} and Assignes To have and to hold ye same for ever so that my son Andrew shall from time to time and at all times Use Ocupie Possess [102] and enjoy ye aboves^d things, Living Lands &c, wth all their Appurtenances quietly and freely from all Molestation from me ye aboves^d John Neale my heires Executors Administrat^{rs} and

Assignes or any other person or persons Laying any Legall Claim thereunto. This is to be understood that I doe make over this last half of my Living to my Son Andrew only upon these conditions that he shall Maintain or cause to be comfortably maintained me ye abovesaid John Neale his father and Joan Neale my wife During our Naturall lives in any sutable and convenient place near or wth my Son Andrew And likewise that my Son Andrew doe well and truly pay or cause to be paid the full and Just Sum̄ of ten pounds in Valuation either to my self or to my wife Joan Neale/ which s^d Sum̄ shall be at our disposall to whome we shall se meet Be it also further known that my son Andrew shall have no libertie to sell or convey away this said halfe of my Living untill he shall fulfill or cause ye aboves^d Obligation to be fulfilled/ these conditions being performed I have set to my hand and Seale for y^e confirmation of y^e above written This Decemb^r y^e fiveth Anno Domini 1694. Annoq̄ Sexto Gulielmi Regis Nostri tertij Angliæ &c/

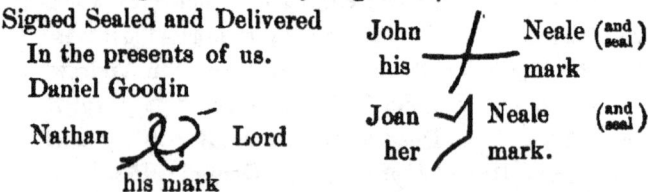

Signed Sealed and Delivered   John   Neale (and seal)
In the presents of us.   his   mark
Daniel Goodin

Nathan   Lord   Joan   Neale   (and seal)
his mark   her   mark.

Edward Tompson

John Neale and Joan Neale Acknowledged the above Instrum^t to be their Act and Deed this 26th of Decemb^r 1694 Before me

                         Charles Frost Jus^t Peace

A true Copie of ye originall Transcribed and Compared this 12° May. 1701   p Jos : Ham̄ond Regist^r

This Indenture made ye tenth day of January Anno Domini One thousand six hundred Ninety nine/ Annoq̄ R R^s

Book VI, Fol. 102.

Guliemi Tertii Angliæ &c Between Eliakim Hutchinson of Boston in the County of Suffolk within his Ma*tis* Province of y*e* Massachusets Bay in New England Esq*r* and Sarah his wife of y*e* one part And John Plaisted of Portsmouth in y*e* Province of New Hampshier in New England afores*d* Merchant on y*e* other part Witnesseth that the s*d* Eliakim Hutchinson and Sarah his s*d* wife as well for and in consideration of the sum of five hundred pounds currant money in New England to them y*e* said Eliakim Hutchinson and Sarah his wife by y*e* s*d* John Plaisted at and before y*e* ensealing and Delivery of these p*r*sents well and truly paid to y*e* full content and satisfaction of y*e* s*d* Eliakim Hutchinson and Sarah his wife as for and under y*e* yearly Rent payments and reservations hereinafter mentioned and expressed to be Yielded rendred and paid by y*e* s*d* John Plaisted his heires or Assignes Have given, granted, bargained, Sold Aliened, Enfeoffed, released and confirmed And by these pres*ts* Doe freely fully and absolutely give, grant, bargain, sell, Alien Enfeoff, release, convey & confirm unto y*e* s*d* John Plaisted his heires and Assignes for ever All that their Tract parcels and quantity of Land containing Six hundred Acres be it more or less, scituate Lying and being on both sides y*e* little river of Newgewanack Al*s* Newichewanick within the Township of Kittery in the County of York formerly cald y*e* Province of Maine And now part of y*e* Province of the Massachusets Bay aboves*d*, four hundred and fourteen Acres parcel whereof was formerly Surveyed and Measured by Cap*tn* John Wincoll as Appears by a Draught or platt of the same by him made and signed y*e* 25*th* day of May Anno: 1681. relation being thereunto had for y*e* lines and boundaries thereof (Excepting only out of y*e* s*d* four hundred and fourteen Acres thirty three Acres and three quarters of an Acre of Land which were heretofore granted out of the same as follows. Viz*t* to John Emerson ten Acres thereof To

Eliakim Hutchinson to Jno Plaisted

Book VI, Fol. 102.

Daniel Gooding Sen[r] Eleven Acres and three quarters thereof and y[e] other twelve Acres for y[e] Accomodation of the Meeting house and Ministry in y[e] upper part of y[e] Town of Kittery afores[d] One hundred and thirty Acres an other parcel of which afores[d] Tract of Land consists of Upland Swamp and Meadow which lies at y[e] southeast end of Bonny Bissie Pond (so called) Containing two hundred and Eighty pole in Length Southeast and by East down to y[e] river being bounded on y[e] Northwest with y[e] high way by y[e] head of the s[d] Pond and on y[e] Southwest with y[e] Land of Roger Plaisted Jun[r]; Northeasterly with y[e] present Comons and Southeasterly with the river/ Sixty Acres another parcel of which afores[d] Tract of Land being Meadow Lies at a place cald by y[e] name of Totnock. And three Acres an other parcel thereof lies at y[e] Northwest end of Bonny Bissy Pond afores[d] Adjoyning to a Meadow known by y[e] name of Broughtons Meadow, Alsoe ten Acres an other parcel thereof being Marsh Lies half a Mile or thereabouts below a Marsh known by y[e] name of y[e] Long Marsh and is comonly cald White's Marsh And an other parcel thereof (which was formerly Richard Nasons) is a small piece of Land cald by y[e] name of Pipe staff point which begins at s[d] point and runs down along y[e] river unto y[e] next fresh water Creek being in breadth four rod from y[e] bank head and runs upon a Straight Line between y[e] point and the Creek holding its full breadth all along y[e] bounds afores[d] Together with all and Singular other Tracts and parcels of Land whatsoever granted by y[e] Town of Kittery afores[d] unto y[e] s[d] Eliakim Hutchinson or to his Brother William Hutchinson whose right he hath purchased And also y[e] ffalls in Newichewannack riv[r] afores[d] comonly cald Asabumbedock ffalls, with y[e] stream, waters water courses Dams and banks reserving y[e] Priviledge of y[e] river and stream for y[e] Transportation of Timber Loggs and Boards &c. as is usual and has been formerly accustomed/ Together also with all and Singular y[e] houses, Edifices, buildings, Mills, woods, underwoods, trees, timber, swamps, stones, Mines, Mineralls, Springs, Ponds, Pooles, runs Rivolets, fishing, fouling, hauking, hunting, Rights, Members, profits priviledges comodities, her editam^{ts} emoluments and Appurtenances whatsoever upon, belonging or in any wise Appurtaining unto ye s^d Tracts and severall parcels of Land herein before granted or any part y^{r}of (which are now in ye present Tenure and Possession of ye s^d John Plaisted) or accepted taken or known as part parcel or member thereof, or therewith now used Ocupied or enjoyed Excepting only and reserving unto his Matie his heires and Successors all pine trees standing growing or being upon ye s^d Land or any part thereof, of four and twenty Inches Diameter fitting to make Masts for his Ma^{ts} Ships, And one fifth part of all Gold & Silver Oare that from time to time and at all times hereafter shall be there gotten had and obtained/ Also all ye Estate, right, title, Interest, Inheritance, use, Property, Possession, Dower, Claim and Demand whatsoever of them ye s^d Eliakim Hutchinson and Sarah his s^d wife and of each of them, And likewise of ye before named William [103] Hutchinson and of their and every of their heires of, in, to or out of ye s^d Tracts parcels and quantity of Land herein before bargained and sold and every part thereof and all and singular other ye Premisses; And of, in, to and out of all other Lands and Timber whatsoever granted unto ye s^d Eliakim Hutchinson and William Hutchinson or either of them at any time heretofore by ye Town of Kittery afores^d or by Robert Tufton Mason Esqr and ye revertion and revercõns remainder and remainders rents, Issues and profits of the s^d granted premisses and every part and parcel thereof; with all Deeds writings Escripts and miniments touching or concerning ye same/ To have and to hold the severall Tracts, parcels of Land, and all and singular ye premisses with ye members and Appur^{ces} herein before granted bargained and sold, or meant, mentioned, or intended to be granted bargained and sold and every part and parcel of y same (Excepting and reserving always as is above Excepted and reserved) Unto y'' s'^d'' John Plaisted his heires and Assignes To his and their only proper use benefit and behoofe for ever And the s'^d'' Eliakim Hutchinson and Sarah his wife for themselves their heires Execut'^rs'' and Administrat'^rs'' and each and every of them Do covenant grant and agree to and with y'^e'' s'^d'' John Plaisted his heires and Assignes by these presents in manner following That is to say that for for and notwithstanding any act matter or thing at any time heretofore had made comitted done or suffered to be done by them the s'^d'' Eliakim Hutchinson & Sarah his wife or either of them or by y'^e'' before named William Hutchinson or any other person or persons whatsoever in their any or either of their names, or by their, any or eiher of their meanes title assent consent privity or procurement, the s'^d'' John Plaisted his heires and Assignes shall and may from time to time and at all times forever hereafter Lawfully peaceably and quietly have hold use Ocupie possess and enjoy all & Singular the before herein granted Tracts and parcels of Land & premisses And have receive & take to his and their only proper use and behoofe the rents Issues and profits thereof, & that y'^e'' s'^d'' granted premisses now are and at all times hereafter shall be and remain unto y'^e'' s'^d'' John Plaisted his heires and Assignes free and clear and clearly Acquitted and discharged of and from all former and other gifts, grants, bargains, sales, Mortgages, releases Joyntures, Dowers, Judgments, Excutions, titles, troubles, Charges, and Incumbrances whatsoever, had, made, comitted, done or suffered by the s'^d'' Eliakim Hutchinson and Sarah his wife and William Hutchinson afores'^d'' or by any or ether them or by any or either of their meanes or procurement And that they y'^e'' s'^d'' Eliakim Hutchinson and Sarah his wife their heires Execut'^rs'' and Admin'^rs'' shall and will warrant and Defend all and singular the s'^d'' granted and bargained premisses unto yᵉ sᵈ John Plaisted his heires and Assignes for ever against all and every person and persons whomsoever, having claiming or pretending to have or claime any right title Estate or Interest therein from by or under them the sᵈ Eliakim Hutchinson and Sarah his wife or yᵉ sᵈ William Hutchinson or any or either of them And also that they yᵉ sᵈ Eliakim Hutchinson and Sarah his wife & their heires at any time hereafter at yᵉ request, cost and Charges of yᵉ sᵈ John Plaisted his heires or Assignes shall and will make Seal and Execute Such further Instruments writings Acts and things for yᵉ confirmation and more sure making of yᵉ sᵈ granted and bargained premisses unto yᵉ sᵈ John Plaisted his heires and Assignes as by his or their Council learned in the Law shall be Lawfully or reasonably Devised Advised or required so as the same containe no other or larger Warranty than what is above written And the sᵈ John Plaisted for himself his heires Executʳˢ and Adminˢ doth covenant grant and agree to and with yᵉ sᵈ Eliakim Hutchinson his heires and Assignes by these presents That he yᵉ sᵈ John Plaisted his heires Executʳˢ or Adminˢ shall and will well and truly pay or cause to be paid unto Robert Tufton Mason aforesᵈ (who was grand son and heir of Capᵗⁿ John Mason of London Esqʳ Deceased) or to yᵉ Lawfull heires or Assignes of sᵈ Robert Tufton Mason (if thereunto required or Demanded) upon the five and twentieth day of Decembʳ yearly and in every year successively for ever hereafter the full and Just Sum̄ or quitt rent of forty shillings currant money in New England p annum, for part and parcell of yᵉ Land above bargained and sold which yᵉ sᵈ Eliakim Hutchinson formerly purchased of sᵈ Robert Tufton Mason, And shall and will likewise pay unto yᵉ sᵈ Robert Tufton Mason his Lawfull heires or Assignes on yᵉ sᵈ five & twentieth day of Decembʳ yearly and every year for ever hereafter (if demanded) for yᵉ grants and priviledge of yᵉ Saw Mill part part of yᵉ premisses herein before granted, the full and Just quantity of three thousand foot of Boards for every hundred thousand thousand foot which from time to time hereafter shall be there sawn and also all other payments and Quitrents reserved by and payable unto the s^d Robert Tufton Mason his heires or Assignes according to ye Tenure true intent and meaning of a Covenant grant and agreement on ye part and behalfe of ye s^d Eliakim Hutchinson in a certain Indenture bearing Date ye 16th day of Decemb^r 1687. made and mentioned to be made between ye s^d Robert Tufton Mason on ye one part and ye s^d Eliakim Hutchinson on ye other part in and by which Indenture ye s^d Robert Tufton Mason hath bargained and sold unto ye s^d Eliakim Hutchinson his heires and Assignes certain Tracts or parcels of Land which are part of ye premisses herein before granted to ye s^d John Plaisted And ye s^d Indenture is at ye time of ye Executing of these pres^{ts} delivered unto him s^d Plaisted. And further ye s^d John Plaisted for himself his heires Execut^{rs} and Admin^{rs} doth covenant and grant to and with the s^d Eliakim Hutchinson his heires and assignes that he ye s^d John Plaisted his heires Execut^{rs} or Adm^{rs} shall and will well and truly pay or cause to be paid unto ye s^d Robert Tufton Mason his heires or assignes (if Demanded) all Such Sum and Sums of Money and Such quantity of Boards as have alredy grown due to ye s^d Robert Tufton Mason or his heires for rent or quitrent of any of the premisses as afores^d and the Arrearages thereof according to ye s^d Covenant of ye s^d Eliakim Hutchinson in ye afore recited Indenture Since the Date thereof, And shall and will at all times hereafter well and sufficiently defend keep harmless and indempnify ye s^d Eliakim Hutchinson his heires Exec^{rs} & Adm^{rs} of and from ye same and all Actions and Suites to be therefore brought or prosecuted against him or them by ye s^d Robert Tufton Mason his heires or assignes And ye payments above mentioned to be made by and on ye part of the s^d John Plaisted to be in full of all rents Acknowledgm^{ts} dutys and Services for the above granted premisses and every part and parcell thereof to any person or persons whatsoever excepting only what is above reserved unto his Ma^{ty} his heirs and Success^{rs} In witness whereof the s^d parties to these present Indentures have interchangeably set their hands and Seales the day and year first above written.

   E^m (.$^{md.}_{seal}$) Hutchinson Sarah ($^{and}_{seal}$) Hutchinson

Signed Sealed and Delivered
 by Eliakim Hutchinson and
 Sarah his wife : in p^{r}sents of us
 Is^a Addington
 Edwd Turfrey

Boston Jan^{ry} 11th 1699

The within named Eliakim Hutchinson and Sarah his wife personally Appearing before me the Subscrib^r one of y^e Council and Justice of the Peace within his Ma^{tys} Province of the Massachusets Bay in New England Acknowledged the within written Instrum^t to be their volluntary Act and Deed/

           Is^a Addington

A true Copie of ye originall Transcribed and compared May. 4th 1701   p Jos Hamond Register

[104] This Indenture made the sixth day of ffebruary Anno Domini One thousand six hundred ninety and nine Annoq, R R^s Gulielmi Tertii Angliæ &c Undecimo. Between John Plaisted of Portsmouth in ye Province of New Hampshiere in New England Merchant and Mary his wife of ye one part And John Hill of ye same place Gen^t on ye other part Witnesseth y^t ye s^d John Plaisted and Mary his wife for And in consideration of ye Sum of one hundred and sixty six pounds 13^s 4^d currant money of New England to them ye s^d John Plaisted and Mary his wife by the said John Hill

at and before yᵉ ensealing and Delivery of these presents well and truly paid, to yᵉ full content and satisfaction of yᵉ sᵈ John Plaisted and Mary his wife as for and under yᵉ yearly rents payments & reservations hereafter mentioned and Expressed, to be Yielded rendred and paid by the sᵈ John Hill his heires or Assignes. Have given granted bargained sold Aliened Enfeoffed released & confirmed And by these presents doe freely fully and absolutely give grant bargain sell Alien Enfeoffe release convey and confirm unto yᵉ sᵈ John Hill his heires and Assignes for ever one full third part yᵉ whole in three parts equally to be Divided of all that their Tract parcel and quantity of Land containing six hundred Acres, be it more or less Scituate Lying and being on both sides yᵉ little river of Newgewanack Alⁱ Newichewanick within yᵉ Township of Kittery in yᵉ County of York, formerly called yᵉ Province of Maine And now part of the Province of the Massachusets Bay abovesᵈ, four hundred And fourteen Acres parcel whereof was formerly Surveied & Measured by Capᵗⁿ John Wincoll as Appears by a Draught or platt of yᵉ same by him made and signed yᵉ 25ᵗʰ day of May Anno 1681. relation being thereunto had for yᵉ lines and boundaries thereof Excepting only out of yᵉ sᵈ four hundred and fourteen Acres thirty three Acres and three quarters of an Acre of Land wᶜʰ were heretofore granted out of the same as follows Vizᵗ to John Emerson ten Acres thereof ; to Daniel Gooding Senʳ Eleven Acres and three quarters thereof And yᵉ other twelve Acres for yᵉ Accomodation of yᵉ Meeting house & Ministry in yᵉ upper part of the Town of Kittery aforesᵈ/ One hundred thirty Acres another parcel of which aforesaid tract of Land consists in Upland Swamp and Meadow which lies at yᵉ southeast end of Bonny Bissie pond (so called) containing two hundred and Eighty in Length Southeast and by east down to yᵉ river being bounded on the Northwest with yᵉ high way by the head of yᵉ sᵈ Pond

Jno Plaisted
to
Jno Hill

And on yᵉ Southwest with the Land of Roger Plaisted Junʳ Northeasterly with yᵉ present Comons and Southeasterly with yᵉ river Sixty Acres an other parcel of which aforesᵈ Tract of Land, being Meadow, lies at a place cald by yᵉ name of Totnock. And three Acres an other parcel thereof lies at yᵉ Northwest end of Bonny Bissie Pond aforesᵈ Adjoyning to a Meadow known by yᵉ name of Broughton's Meadow Also ten Acres an other parcel thereof being Marsh lies half a Mile or thereabouts below a Marsh known by yᵉ name of the long Marsh and is comonly cald Whites Marsh, and an other parcel thereof which was formerly Richard Nasons) is a small piece of Land, cald by yᵉ name of pipe staff point which begins at sᵈ point and runs down along the river into yᵉ next fresh water Creek, being in breadth four rod from the bank head And runs upon a streight line between yᵉ point & and the Creek holding its full breadth all Along the bounds aforesᵈ Together with all and singular other tracts and parcells of Land whatsoever granted by the town of Kittery aforesᵈ unto Eliakim Hutchinson of Boston in the County of Suffolk within his Maᵗⁱᵉˢ Province of the Massachusets Bay in New England Esqʳ or to his brother William Hutchinson (whose right he hath purchased and also the ffalls in Newichewannack River aforesaid comonly called Assabumbedock ffulls with the stream Waters, watercourses, Dams and banks) reserving the priviledge of the river and stream for yᵉ Transportation of timber Loggs & boards &c. as Usuall and hath been formerly accustomed Together also with all and Singular yᵉ houses, Edifices, buildings, Mills, woods, underwoods, trees, timbʳ, swamps stones, Mines, Mineralls, Springs, Ponds, Pooles, runs, rivolets, ffishing, fowling, hawking, hunting, Rights, members, profits, priviledges, comodities, Hereditamᵗˢ, Imoluments and Appurtenances whatsoever upon, belonging or in any wise Appurtaining unto the sᵈ tracts and severall parcels of Land herein before grunted or

Book VI, Fol. 104.

any part thereof (which are now in ye present Possession of the s^d John Plaisted or accepted taken or known as part parcel or member thereof, or therewith now Used Ocupied or enjoyed) excepting only and reserving to his Ma^{ty} his heires and Successors All pine trees standing growing or being upon the said Land or any part thereof, of four and twenty Inches Diameter fitting to make Masts for his Maties Ships, And one fifth part of all Gold and Silver Oare that from time to time and at all times hereafter shall be there gotten had & obtained Also all the Estate Right title Interest Inheritance use property possession Dower Claim and Demand whatsoever of them ye s^d John Plaisted and Mary his wife and of each of them and likewise of the before named Eliakim Hutchinson and William Hutchinson and of their and every of their heires of, in to or out of the s^d tracts parcels and quantity of Land herein before bargained and sold and every part and parcel thereof and all and singular other other ye premisses And of, in, to and out of all other Lands and timber whatsoever granted unto ye s^d Eliakim Hutchinson & William Hutchinson or either of them at any time heretofore by ye town of Kittery afores^d or by Robert Tufton Mason Esqr And ye reverc̄on and reverc̄ons remaind^r and remaind^{rs} Rents Issues and profits of ye s^d granted premisses and every part and parcel thereof To have and to hold the severall Tracts, p^rcels of Land, and all and Singular the premisses with ye Members and Appurtenances herein before granted bargained and sold or meant mentioned or intended to be granted bargained or sold, and every part and parcel of the same (Excepting and reserving alwayes as is above excepted and reserved) unto ye s^d John Hill his heires & Assignes to his and their only proper use benefit and behoofe for ever And the said John Plaisted and Mary his wife for themselves their heires Exec^{rs} and Admin^{rs} And each and every of them Do coven^t grant and agree to and with yᵉ sᵈ John Hill his heires and. Assignes by these presents in manner following (That is to say, that for and Notwithstanding any Act matter or thing at any time heretofore had made, comitted, done or suffered to be done by them yᵉ sᵈ John Plaisted & Mary his wife or either of them or by the before named Eliakim Hutchinson or William Hutchinson or any other person or persons whatsoever in their any or either of their names or by their any or either of their means title assent consent, privity or procuremᵗ the sᵈ John Hill his heires & assignes shall and may from time to time and at All times for ever hereafter Lawfully, peaceably And [105] quietly have hold use Occupie possess and enjoy All and Singular yᵉ before herein granted Tracts and parcels of Lands and pʳmisses, and have receive and take to his and their only proper use and behoofe, the rents Issues and profits yʳof And that yᵉ sᵈ granted premisses now are and at all times hereafter shall be and remaine unto the said John Hill his heires and assignes free and clear And clearly Acquitted and Discharged of and from all former and other gifts grants bargains sales Mortgages Releases Joyntures Dowers Judgmᵗˢ Executions Titles troubles, charges and incumbrances whatsoever had, made, comitted, done or sufered by yᵉ said John Plaisted and Mary his wife, or by yᵉ sᵈ Eliakim Hutchinson or William Huchinson aforesᵈ or by any or either of them, or by any or either of their meanes or procuremᵗ. And that they yᵉ sᵈ John Plaisted and Mary his wife their heires Execʳˢ and Admʳˢ shall and will Warrant and Defend all & singulʳ the sᵈ granted and bargained premisses unto yᵉ said John Hill his heires and Assignes for ever agᵗ all and every person & persons whomsoever, having claiming or pretending to have or Claim any right title or Interest therein from by or under them yᵉ sᵈ John Plaisted and Mary his wife or yᵉ sᵈ Eliakim Hutchinson and William Hutchinson or any or either of them And alsoe that they yᵉ sᵈ John Plaisted and Mary his wife and their heires at any time hereafter at yᵉ request Cost and Charges of yᵉ sᵈ John Hill his heires or assigns shall and will make seal and Execute such further Intrumᵗˢ writings Acts and things for yᵉ confirmation and more sure making of yᵉ said granted and bargained pʳmisses unto yᵉ said John Hill his heires and Assignes as by his or their Council Learned in yᵉ Law shall be Lawfully or reasonably devised advised or required soe as the same, contain no other or larger Warrantry than what is above written And the said John Hill for himself his heires Execʳˢ & Admʳˢ doth Covenᵗ grant and agree to and with yᵉ sᵈ John Plaisted his heires and assignes by these presents That he yᵉ sᵈ John Hill his heires Execʳˢ or Adminʳˢ shall and will well and. truly pay or cause to be paid unto Robert Tufton Mason aforesᵈ (who was grand Son and heire of Capᵗⁿ John Mason of London Esqʳ Decᵈ, or to yᵉ Lawfull heires or assignes of sᵈ Robert Tufton Mason/ if thereunto required or Demanded/ upon yᵉ five and twentieth Day of Decembʳ yearly and in every Year successively for ever hereafter the full and Just Sum̅ or quit rent of thirteen shillings four pence currᵗ money of New England p annum for part and parcel of yᵉ Land above bargained and Sold which yᵉ sᵈ Eliakim Hutchinson formerly purchased of the sᵈ Robert Tufton Mason/ And shall and will likewise pay unto the said Robert Tufton Mason his Lawfull heirs and Assignes on yᵉ sᵈ five and twentieth day of Decembʳ yearly and every year for ever hereafter/ if Demanded/ for yᵉ grants and priviledges of yᵉ Saw Mill part of yᵉ premisses herein before granted the full third part of three thousand foot of boards for every hundred thousand foot which from time to time hereafter shall be there Sawn/ And also all other paymᵗˢ and quit rents reserved by, and payable unto the said Robert Tufton Mason his heires or assignes according to the Tenor true intent and meaning of a Coven^t grant and agreem^t on ye part and behalf of ye said Eliakim Hutchinson in a certain Indenture bearing Date the 16 Decemb^r 1687. made and menc̃oned to be made between ye said Robert Tufton Mason of the one part and ye said Eliakim Hutchinson on the other part, in and by which Indenture ye said Robert Tufton Mason hath bargained and sold unto ye s^d Eliakim Hutchinson his heires and assignes, certaine Tracts and parcells of Land which are part of the Premisses herein before granted to ye s^d John Hill. And ye said Indenture is at the time of ye executing of these p^rsents in ye hands or Custody of ye s^d Plaisted And further ye said John Hill for himself his heires Exec^rs and Adm^rs doth Covenant and grant to and with ye said John Plaisted his heires and assignes that he ye s^d John Hill his heires exec^rs and Adm^rs shall and will well and truly pay or cause to be paid unto ye said Robert Tufton his heires or assignes, if Demanded, all such sum̃ and sum̃s of Money and quantity of boards as have already grown due to the said Robert Tufton Mason or his heires for rent or quitrent of any of ye premisses as aforesaid and ye Arrearages thereof according to ye s^d Covenant of ye s^d Eliakim Hutchinson in ye afore recited Indenture since ye Date thereof & shall and will at all times hereafter well and Sufficiently Defend keep harmless and Indempnify the s^d John Plaisted his heires Execut^rs and Adm^rs of and from ye same And all Actions and Suits to be therefor brought or prosecuted ag^t him or them by the said Robert Tufton Mason his heires or Assignes and ye paym^ts above Mentioned to be made by and on ye part of ye said John Hill to be in full of all rents Acknowledgments duties and Services for ye above granted p^rmisses and every part & parcell thereof to any person or persons whatsoever Excepting only what is above reserved to his Ma^ty his heires and Successors In Witnesse ye s^d parties to these present Indentures interchangeably have set their hands and Seales the day and year first above written/.

John (and a Seal) Hill

Sealed and Delivered
  In the presents of.
  Sam^{ll} Penhallow
  Cha: Story.

6th February: 1699

John Hill within Mentioned came this day before me and acknowledged ye subscribing and setting his hand and seale to the Indenture as his Act and Deed for ye use of ye within named John Plaisted.

Sam^{ll} Penhallow Jus^t Pe^c

A true Copie of ye originall Transcribed and compared this twelfth day of May 1701.

p Jos: Hamond Regist^r

John Plaisted & John Hill

This Indenture made ye seventh day of ffebruary Anno Domini 1699. And in ye eleventh year of ye Reign of our Soveraign Lord William ye third, by ye grace of God of England Scotland France and Ireland King Defend^r of ye ffaith &c/ Between John Hill of Portsm^o in ye Province of New Hampshiere in New England Gentleman of the one part, and John Plaisted of ye same place Merchant, on ye other part/ Whereas the s^d John Hill by one bond or obligation bearing Date with these presents stands firmly bound unto [106] ye said John Plaisted in the Sum or penalty of three hundred thirty and three p^{ds} six shillings and eight pence Currant Money of New England, for ye true payment of one hundred Sixty and Six pounds thirteen shillings and four pence like Lawfull Money of New England without Interest at or before ye tenth day of January next ensuing the Date of these p^{r}sents as in and by y̆ᵉ sᵈ recited bond or obligation, relation being thereunto had it doth and may may more fully and at large Appear. Now this Indenture Witnesseth that yᵉ sᵈ John Hill for yᵉ further and better Security and Securing the payment of yᵉ sᵈ sum of one hundred sixty & six pounds 13ˢ and 4ᵈ at yᵉ said day and time, in the condicõn of yᵉ sᵈ recited bond or Obligation mentioned and Expressed and for and in consideration of five shillings of Currᵗ money of New England to him in hand, before yᵉ ensealing and delivery of these pʳsents well and truly paid by yᵉ sᵈ John Plaisted the receipt whereof yᵉ sᵈ John Hill doth hereby Acknowledge And also for Divers other good causes and considerations him thereunto Moving Hath Demised granted bargained and sold, and by these pʳsents doth Demise, grant, bargain and sell, unto yᵉ said John Plaisted his Execⁿ Admⁿ and Assignes One full third pᵗ the whole in three parts Equally to be Divided, of All that Tract, parcel and quantity of Land containing six hundred Acres be it more or less, Scituate Lying and being on both Sides yᵉ little River of Newgewanack, Alias Newichewanick within the Township of Kittery in yᵉ County of York formerly called the Province of Maine and now part of the Province of the Massachusets Bay, four hundred & fourteen Acres parcell whereof was formerly Surveyed and Measured by Capᵗⁿ John Wincoll, as appears by a Draught or platt of the same by him made and Signed yᵉ 25ᵗʰ day of May Anno. 1681 : relation being thereunto had for the lines and boundages thereof Excepting only out of yᵉ four hundred and fourteen Acres, thirty three Acres and three quarters of an Acre of Land which were heretofore granted out of the same as followeth Vizᵗ to John Emerson ten Acres thereof to Daniel Gooding Senʳ Eleven Acres and three quarters thereof And yᵉ other twelve Acres for yᵉ Accomodacõn of the Meeting house and Ministry in the upper part of y̆ Town of Kittery afores⁴, One hundred and thirty Acres an other parcell of which afores⁴ Tract of Land; consists in Upland Swamp and Meadow, which lies at y̆ Southeast end of Bony Bissy pond (so called) containing two hundred and Eighty poles in Length South east, and by east, down to y̆ River, being bounded on y̆ Northwest with the high way by the head of y̆ s⁴ pond, And on the Southwest, with y̆ land of Roger Plaisted Junr Northeasterly with the p^rsent Comons, And Southeasterly with the River. Sixty Acres an other parcell of which afores⁴ Tract of Land being Meadow, lies at a place called Totnock. And three Acres an other parcel thereof lies at y̆ Northwest end of Bony Bissy pond afores⁴ Adjoyning to a Meadow known by the name of Broughtons Meadow, Also ten Acres an other parcel thereof being Marsh, lies half a Mile or thereabouts, below a Marsh known by the name of long Marsh, And is comonly called Whites Marsh And an other parcel thereof which was formerly Richard Nasons; is a Small piece of Land, called by the name of Pipestaff point which begins at s⁴ point & runs down along y̆ river unto y̆ next freshwater Creek, being in breadth four Rod from the Bank head And runs upon a Streight line between y̆ point and the Creek, holding its full breadth all along the bounds aforesaid together alsoe with all and Singular other Tracts and parcels of Land whatsoever granted by y̆ Town of Kittery afores⁴ unto Eliakim Hutchinson of Boston in the County of Suffolk within his Ma^ts Province of the Massachusets Bay afores⁴ Esqr or to his brother William Hutchinson whose right he hath purchased, And alsoe y̆ ffalls of Newichewanick River afores⁴ comonly called Asabumbedock ffalls with the stream water water Courses Dams and Banks, Reserving the priviledge of the River and stream for the Transportation of Timber, Loggs, Boards &c as is Usuall and hath been formerly Accustomed. Together with all and Singular y̆ house Edifices buildings

Book VI, Fol. 106.

Mills, woods under woods trees timber swamps stones Mines Mineralls Springs Ponds Pooles ruñs Rivolets fishing fowling hawking hunting Rights Members profits priviledges Comodities Hereditam^{ts} Emolum^{ts} and Appurtenances whatsoev^r to the said granted and bargained Premisses belonging or in any wise Appurtaining (Excepting only and reserving to his Majesty his heires and Successors all pine trees standing growing or being upon ye s^d granted p^{r}misses or any part thereof, of four and twenty Inches Diameter fitting to make Masts for his Ma^{tis} Ships And one fifth part of all Gold and Silver Ore, that from time to time and at all times hereafter shall be there gotten had and Obtained, And ye Reverc̃on and reverc̃ons Remainder and remainders of all and Singular ye s^d p^{r}misses And all the Estate, Right, title Interest property and Demand whatsoever, of him the said John Hill his heires Exec^{rs} and Adm^{rs} of in and to ye above granted & bargained p^{r}misses And of in and unto every or any part or parcell thereof To have and to hold all the said full third part of all the afores^d tract and parcel of Land, And all and Singular other the p^{r}misses above by these p^{r}sents Demised granted bargained and sold, or mentioned or intended so to be with their and every of their Appurtenances and every part and parcel thereof, unto the said John Plaisted his heires Exec^{rs} Adm^{rs} & assignes from ye day of the date of these p^{r}sents unto ye full end and term of one thousand years from thence next ensuing fully to be compleated and ended Yielding and paying therefor yearly during the said Term unto ye s^d John Hill his heires or assignes the rent of one peper corn at ye feast of the Nativity of our Lord Com̃only Christmas day in every day if Lawfully Demanded Provided Always and nevertheless and upon condition, and it is the true intent and meaning of these p^{r}sents And of the s^d parties thereunto That if ye said John Hill his heires Exec^{rs} or Adm^{rs} or any of them Doe in discharge of ye s^d recited bond or obligac̃on and according to the Tenour and true meaning of the condicon thereof well and truly pay or cause to be paid unto y² s^d John Plaisted his Exec^rs Adm^rs or Assignes the said Sum of one hundred Sixty and Six pounds 13^s 4^d of Currant money of New England at or before the tenth day of January next ensuing ye date of these p^rsents/ without Interest/ or within three years after ye said bond or Obligation shall become due, he ye s^d John Hill his Exec^rs Admin^rs or Assignes paying interest unto ye said John Plaisted his Exec^rs Adm^rs or Assignes, for ye three yeares last mentioned, or for such part of the s^d Sum of one hundred Sixty Six pounds 13^s 4^d as shall remain unpaid that then and from thenceforth this present Demise and every Clause Coven^t grant matters and things herein [107] contained shall cease Determine and be utterly voyd ffrustrate and of none effect to all intents and purposes whatsoever as if ye same had never been made any thing in these presents contained to ye contrary hereof in any wise notwithstanding And the s^d John Hill doth for himself his heires Exec^rs and Adm^rs Coven^t and agree to and with ye said John Plaisted his heires Exec^rs Adm^rs or assignes in manner and forme foll/ That is to say/ That he ye s^d John Hill hath in himselfe full power good right title, and Lawfull & Absolute Authority in the Law to Demise grant bargain and sell the above mencõned p^rmisses unto the s^d John Plaisted his Execut^rs Adm^rs or Assignes for and During all ye s^d Term of one thousand years in manner and form afores^d And That it shall and may be Lawfull to & for ye said John Plaisted his Exec^rs Adm^rs or assignes imediately after Default shall be made in the paym^t or payments of the s^d sum of one hundred sixty six pounds 13^s 4^d or any part thereof as is nominated or specified in the provisoe afore mencõned, into and upon all and singular ye afore Demised and bargained p^rmisses with ye App^rs to enter, and the same from thenceforth peaceably and quietly To have hold Ocupie possess and enjoy, And to have take and receive, the rents, Issues and profits thereof to his and their own proper use and uses for and During all the then residue and remaind^r of the said Term of one thousand years hereby granted, without any Let, Suit, trouble, Molestacõn, interupcõn or Disturbance of him ye said John Hill his heires or assignes or any of them, or of any other person or persons whatsoever Claiming by from or under him, them or any of them And freed and Discharged, of and from all manner of former or other gifts grants bargains Sales, Leases, Intailes, Joyntures, Dower and titles of Dower Mortgages Judgm^ts, Execucõns, Extents, debts, Acts, titles, troubles, Claims demands and Incumbrances whatsoever In witness whereof the parties aboves^d to these presents Interchangeably have set their hands and Seales the day and year first before Mencõned.

John (his seal) Hill

Sealed and Delivered
  In the presents of.
  Sam^ll Penhallow
  Cha: Story.

7th of ffebruary. 1699

John Hill within Mencõned came this day before me, and Acknowledged the Subscribing and setting of his hand and Seale to ye Indent^e as his Act and Deed for ye use of the w^thin named John Plaisted/

Sam^ll Penhallow. Jus^ce Pec

A true Copie of the originall Transcribed and compared this 12th May: 1701   p Jos: Hamõnd Regist^r

---

Wm Ashly
   to
Jonath: Littlefield

Know all men by these presents that I William Ashleigh of the Town of Wells in the Province of Mayn in New: England Yeoman with the full and free consent of Elizabeth my wife, severall good causes and considerations me thereunto moving, and more

Especially for and in consideration of forty pounds Starling of Lawfull money of New England to me in hand alredy paid by Jonathan Littlefield of the aforesaid Town and Province, Have given, granted, Enfeoffed and confirmed/ And by these presents doe give, grant, Enfeoffe and confirm, fully and Absolutely unto ye aboves^d Jonathan Littlefield, from me my heires Exec^{rs} Adm^{rs} and Assignes My sole right title & Interest of one hundred and forty Acres of upland as it is bounded by ffrancis Littlefields Land on ye North side, and a Lott of Land belonging to John Trott on ye south side And butting upon the high way next to Mr Wheelwrights land, with a dwelling house and Barn upon ye s^d Land, the land runing up into the Country from the high way as before bounded, being seven and twenty poles in breadth till one hundred and forty Acres be compleated, Together with all Cornfields fences gardens pastures Comons comonages woods and under woods with all and singular the Appurtenances and priviledges any wise Appurtaining or belonging alsoe a parcel of Marsh at ye Neck of land, bounded by Jonathan Hamond on the Northeast and ye sea-wall on ye Southeast, and soe by ffrancis Littlefields Marsh on ye other sides/ Alsoe a parcel of Marsh which I bought of ffrancis Littlefield called the Six Acres all which land and Marsh as Scituate and being in the Town of Wells/ All the premisses above named I the said William Ashleigh have granted and confirmed unto ye aboves^d Jonathan Littlefield his heires Exec^{rs} and Adm^{rs} for ever freely and quietly to Have and to hold. without any matter of Challenge Claime or Demand of me the said Wm Ashleigh or any person or persons either from by or under me my heires Exe^{rs} Adm^{rs} and assigns for ever. he ye s^d Jonathan Littlefield & his heires Exec^{rs} Adm^{rs} and assignes I doe hereby declare to be ye truly and Right possess^r of each and every part and parcell of ye Premisses above granted, And that he ye s^d Jonathan Littlefield his heires Exec^{rs} Adm^{rs} and assignes shall peaceably and quietly have hold and enjoy all and every part and parcell of the p'misses given & granted to them for ever And I doe here promise and Coven^t to and with ye s^d Jonathan Littlefield that all ye Estate given and granted and every part and parcel of it are free and cleare from all rights grants bargains leases Dowers Judgm^ts Morgages Executions and all other Incumbrances whatsoever And that I am at this present before ye ensealing hereof the true and Right owner of the p'misses given and granted And doe promise to Warrant & defend the title and Interest of the p'misses from me my heires Exec^rs or from any person or persons either from by or under me by my means or procurem^t In Testimony whereunto We Wm Ashleigh & Elizabeth Ashleigh have set our hands and Seales this sixth day of October in the Year of our L^d one thousand Six hundred and Eighty four And in the thirty ninth yeare of ye Reign of our Soveraign Ld Charles Secund^e by the grace of God of England Scotland ffrance & Ireland King Defend^r of the ffaith &c.

Signed Sealed and Delivered   William   Ashleigh (his seal)
   In the p'sents of us   his mark
   Jonathan Hamond
   Thomas Web.   Elizabeth Ashleigh (her seal)
                                    her mark

William Ashleigh and Elizabeth Ashleigh came and Acknowledged this Instrument to be their Act and Deed.

Before me.   Sam^ll Wheelwright Jus Peace

A true Copie of the Originall Transcribed and Compared July 2^d 1702

                    p Jos : Hamond Regist^r

[108] To all Christian People whome whome these presents may concern/ Dodeuer Curtis and Elizabeth his wife

BOOK VI, FOL. 108.

(of Kittery in ye County of York in ye Province of the Massachusets Bay in New England) send Greeting Know Ye that the s^d Dodevah & Elizabeth, And in consideration of a certain Sum of money to them in hand paid or otherwise at the signing of this Instrum^t satisfactorily secured by Lewis Bane and Job Curtis of York in ye County and Province afores^d (Have given, granted, bargained, sold Alienated Enfeoffed and confirmed, And fully ffreely and absolutely make over unto ye s^d Lewis Bane and Job Curtis, a certain parcell of upland and Meadow containing fifty Acres more or less, it being the one quarter part of two hundred Acres of land and Meadow given by the town of York unto Richard Banks, Thomas Curtis, Samuel Twisden and Abra^m Preble in York, and known by the name of Situate plaine and Sittuate Marsh, and is bounded in York book is specified, the which was never as yet Divided/ Therefore ye s^d

Dodevah Curtes
to
Lewis Bean
and
Job Curtes

Dodever & Elizabeth doe for themselves their heires Exec^{rs} Admin^{rs} and Assignes doe by these presents fully confirm the afores^d quarter part of the afores^d 200 Acres of Land and Meadow Adjoyning unto ye s^d Lewis Bane and Job Curtis, unto them their heires Exec^{rs} Adm^{rs} and Assignes for evermore. Adjoyning together with all the rights benefits Emolum^{ts} and Advantages on Appertaining unto it or any part of it or at any time redowing from ye same. To have and to hold, and quietly and peaceably to Ocupie Possess and enjoy the said land and Appurtenances as a Sure Estate in ffee simple as aboves^d, Moreover the s^d Dodevah and Elizabeth for themselves their heires Exec^{rs} Adm^{rs} and Assignes, to and with the s^d Lewis and Job their heires Exec^{rs} Admin^{rs} and Assignes Doe Indent, Coven^t engage & promise the Premisses with all their priviledges and Appurtenances from all form^r grants, gitts Sales or Interuptions to be had or Comenced by them their heires Exec^{rs} Adm^{rs} or

Assignes or any other person or persons wthsoever upon grounds preceeding the Date of this Instrum^t, for ever to Warrant and Defend by these presents. In Witness whereof ye s^d Dodfer Curtis and Elizabeth his wife have hereunto Set their hands and Seales this fifth day of Octob^r in ye year of our Lord one thousand Seven hundred/ And in the twelfth year of the Reign of William ye third, King of Great Brittain &c.

Signed Sealed and Delivered   Dodevah Curtis (his seal)
   In presents of.   (a seal)
   John Shapleigh
   Joseph Curtis.

                        County York/

Kittery July ye 10th 1701/ the above named Dodevah personally Appearing before me the Subscriber one of his Ma^{ts} Justices for ye County afores^d Acknowledged the above Instrum^t to be his Act and Deed

                                        Samuel Donnel

A true Copie of the originall/ Transcribed and Compared/
                       p Jos : Hamond Regist^r

Be it known unto all men by these presents that I Philip Cooper of Boston in the County of Suffolk in the Province of the Massachusets Bay in New England Seaman, Eldest Son of Philip Cooper Late of York in New England Husbandman Dec^d Have Assigned ordayned and made and in my stead and place by these presents put and Constituted my good friend Sarah Wright of Boston afores^d Spinster to be my true sufficient and Lawfull Atturney giving and hereby Granting unto my s^d Attorney full power Authority & Special Comission for me and in my name and to my use & behoofe to aske Demand Sue for Levie require recover receive and take out of ye hands Custody and possession of all and

Philip Cooper
to
Sarah Wright

every person and persons whomsoever it doth shall or may concern, All and singular such debt and debts sum and sums of money, Lands, Tenem^{ts} hereditam^{ts} Effects of things and other Estate whatsoever which is are or hereafter shall be due, owing belonging or Appurtaining unto me by any manner of ways or means whatsoever and upon recovery or receipt thereof to give due Acquittances and discharges/ And if need be to Appear and ye person of me Constituant to represent before any Judges, Justices or Ministers of ye Law in any Court or Courts of Judicature, And there in my behalf to answer defend and reply to all Actions matters and things relating to ye premisses or otherwise howsoever and to Sue Arrest Attack cite, plaint prosecute Implead imprison and condemne And out of prison again when need shall be to deliver, As alsoe to contest in Law in most Ample manner untill Definitive Sentance And I doe hereby Authorise and Impower my s^d Attorney to grant, bargain, sell and make sale of all or any my lands Tenem^{ts} & hereditaments with ye Appurtenances thereof, Scituate and Lying in York or Else where in New England afores^d for my best Advantage to any person or persons minded to buy the same, And in due form to Execute Legall conveyance or conveyances thereof to ye person or persons soe buying the same, And as my Agent to Act, manage and Negotiate all my matters affaires and concerns of every sort and kind to full Effect. Attorneys one or more under her my s^d Attorney to make and Substitute, and at pleasure again to revoake/ And Generally, in, touching and concerning the premisses and ye Dependances thereof, to doe, say, Execute, compound, Determine and finish all and whatsoever I the Constituat might or could doe personally present, Ratifying, allowing and holding firm and vallid, All and whatsoever my s^d Attorney shall Lawfully doe or cause to be done in and about ye premisses by vertue of these presents And I doe hereby revoak and make voyd all former power trust and Authority by me granted unto my brother Joseph Cooper of York afores^d, Husbandman, by Letter of Attorney or otherwise for or about ye contents of the premisses or for any other matter or thing whatsoever/ In witness whereof I have hereunto set my hand seale the seventh day of Novemb^r Anno Domī one thousand six hundred Ninety and nine In the Eleventh year of the Reigne of our Soveraign Lord King William the third over England &c

Signed Sealed & delivered
  in presents of us.   The ∮ mark of
Thomas Harper   Philip Cooper (his seal)
Eliezer Moody Scr.

       Suffolk ss Boston Novemb^r 7th 1699

The above named Philip Cooper personally Appearing before me the subscrib^r one of his Ma^{ts} Justices of Peace for ye County afores^d Acknowledged this Instrum^t to be his Act and Deed.

                                        Samuel Sewall

A true Copie of ye originall Letter of Attorney Transcribed and compared this 4th July : 1701.

                            p Jos : Hām̄ond Regist^r

[109] To all Christian People to whome this Deed of Sale shall come or concern Know yee that I Sarah Wright of Boston in the County of Suffolk in New England spinster having by vertue of a Letter of Attorney to me given by Philip Cooper of Boston afores^d Seaman, Eldest Son of Philip Cooper late of York in New England husbandman Deceased, bearing date seventh day of Novemb^r one thousand six hundred ninety nine, relation thereto being had will at Large Appear, Impowering me ye said Sarah to Sell or otherwise dispose of and make sale any or all those

Lands Tenem^{ts} &c in York or Else where/ Now know all persons to whom this present deed shall come that I the said Sarah Wright by Vertue of the afores^d power for divers good and Lawfull causes and considerations me hereto moving, but more in Speciall for the consideration of Eleven pounds fifteen shillings Currant Money to me in hand paid by Lewis Bane and Andrew Brown now of York aboves^d the receipt whereof I doe hereby Acknowledge and my self fully satisfied contented and paid And thereof and of every part parcel & penny thereof doe by this presents for ever Acquit and Discharge them ye s^d Bane and Brown their heires Exec^{rs} Adm^{rs} and Assignes and every of them, have and by this pres^t Deed by vertue of the power to me as aboves^d, bargain, sell, Alien, Enfeoff, release deliver and confirm unto them ye s^d Andrew Brown & Lewis Bane their heirs Exec^{rs} Adm^{rs} and Assignes for ever, to say a certain parcel or piece of Land Lying and being in York afores^d, being Eleven Acres and three quarters or thereabout, butted and bounded as followeth, with all the timb^r, trees, wood or underwoods standing, growing, lying and being on said Land with all ye priviledges thereto belonging or in any way Appertaining And is that same piece or parcel of Land that belonged unto the aboves^d Cooper Deceased, bounded by the Country Road through York Town & Nichewanick, or the Northerly end of s^d bargained and sold Land, on the Easterly side by a way that leads down toward York River on the westerly side by the Land of   Saward and the Land now in the possession of the s^d Andrew Brown/ To have & to hold all the s^d Lands According to ye bounds, with all the timb^r, trees, woods & underwoods standing, growing and being on said Land with all ye priviledges thereto belonging or in any wise Appertaining, Unto them ye s^d Brown and Bane their heires Exec^{rs} Adm^{rs} and assignes for ever in ffee Simple without the least trouble; interuption or Molestation of me

Sarah Wright
to
Lewis Bean
and
Andrew Brown

Book VI, Fol. 109.

ye s^d Sarah Wright or ye above s^d Philip Cooper his or their heires Execut^{rs} Adm^{rs} or any other pson or persons what ever Claiming any Right to all or any part of ye s^d bargained and sold Lands and priviledges and that for ever/ And that my selfe & s^d Cooper our heires Execut^r and Adm^{rs} will for ever warrant and Defend ye title thereof free and Clearly Acquitted secured and kept harmless of and from All and manner of former and other bargains, sales Judgm^{ts}, Executions rights of Doweris and all manner of incumbrances heretofore had made comitted suffered done by my selfe, the s^d Cooper our heires Execut^{rs} & Adm^{rs} for ev^r And further more that I will at any day or time hereafter if need require or ye s^d Cooper our heires &c. make and give unto the s^d Bane & Brown any such other Deed or writing as learned men in the Law shall Judge needfull for ye sure confirming of all ye s^d bargained Lands & priviledges unto the s^d Brown and Bane their heires Execut^{rs} Adm^{rs} or Assignes for ever for confirmation of the same I have hereunto set my hand and seal this 6th day of January : 1699.
Signed Sealed & delivered   Sarah Wright (her seal)
  in pres^{ts} of us
  Joseph Banks
  Daniel Black
  Eliezer Johnson
  Sarah Wright aboves^d came and Acknowledged ye above written Deed of Sale to be her Act and Deed, this 29th of of Jan^{ry} 1699. before me
       Abra : Preble Justis of peace
A true Copie of ye originall Transcribed & compared this
4 July 1701   p Jos. Hamond Regist^r

To all Christian People whome these presents may concern/ Arthur Bragden Junr and Sarah his wife, of York in

BOOK VI, FOL. 109.

the County of York in ye Province of the Massachusets Bay in New England Send Greeting, Know Yee that the s^d Arthur and Sarah for and in consideration of a certain sum of money to them in hand paid or otherwise at ye signing of this Instrum^t Satisfactorily secured by Lewis Bean & Job Curtis of ye Town, County, Province & Country aforesaid have given, granted, bargained, sold Alienated, Enfeoffed & confirmed And doe by these presents give, grant, bargain, sell, Alienate, Enfeoff and confirm fully freely and Absolutely make over unto ye s^d Lewis Bane and Job Curtis a certain parcel of Land, Upland Swamp & Meadow-Land, containing fiftie Acres being formerly granted to Samuel Twisden by ye town of York, Alsoe Richd Banks Thomas Curtis and Abraham Preble being Adjoynt partners with s^d Twisden the whole grant of ye four Lots being two hundred Acres, Lying and being within the township of York and known by ye name of Situate plains & Situate Marsh And is bounded as in York town booke is specified Page 34. and is not as yet divided, the which fifty Acres is one fourth part of ye whole grant of two hundred Acres, Together with all

<small>Arthur Bragdon
to
Lewis Bean
and
Job Curtes</small> ye rights benefits Emolum^{ts} & Advantages Appertaining unto it or redowning any ways or at any time from the same, both Land timber wood underwood Marsh or Meadow-ground, stream or streams of water there runing through the land or any part thereof, To have and to hold And quietly and peaceably to Ocupie and enjoy the s^d Land & Appurtenances as a sure Estate in ffee simple to them ye said Lewis and Job, their heires Exec^{rs} Adm^{rs} and Assignes for ever, moreov^r the said Arthur and Sarah for themselues their heires Exec^{rs} Adm^{rs} and to and with ye s^d Lewis and Job their heires Exec^{rs} Adm^{rs} and Assignes doe indent Covenant engage and promise, the p^{r}misses with all their priviledges and Appurtenances from all former grants, gifts Sales rents, rats, Dowries, Demands and Incumbrances,

as alsoe from all former Claimes Suites or Interuptions to be had or comenced by them their heires Exec^rs Adm^rs or assignes any person or persons whatsoever upon any grounds preceding ye date of this Instrum^t for ever to Warrantize & defend by these presents, In witness whereof the said Arthur Bragdon & Sarah his wife have hereunto set their hands and Seales, this twenty Eight day of Novemb^r in the year of our Lord one thousand seven hundred, And in the thirteenth year of ye Reign of William the third King of Great Brittain &c. It is alsoe agreed before the Signing of the above Instrum^t that ye aboves^d Lewis Bane and Job Curtis shall pay ye rent of the aboves^d stream if any shall hereafter arise, to this town of York or any Lawfull Propriet^r for s^d quarter part.

Signed Sealed and Delivered   Arthur Bragdon Jn^r (and a seal)
  In presents of.   Sarah Bragdon · (and a seal) ·
Joseph Banks
Abra^m Preble Jn^r

Arthur Bragdon Junr and Sarah his wife Acknowledged the above written Deed of Sale to be their Act and deed this 5th day of June: 1701. Before me
                      Abra: Preble Justis of Peace

A true Copie of the originall Transcribed and Compared: July: 4th 1701.
                  p Jos: Hamond Regist^r

[110] To all Christian People whome these presents may concern/ Henry Wright and Sarah his wife of Boston in the County of Suffolk in New England Sendeth Greeting, Know Yee that the said Henry and Sarah (for and in consideration of a certain sum of Money to them at ye Sealing of this Instrum^t Satisfactorily Secured by Andrew Brown of York in the Province of ye Massachusets Bay in New

England) Have given, granted, bargained Sold, Alienated, Enfeoffed & confirmed And doe by these p'sents, give, grant bargain, sell, Alienate, Enfeoffe and fully freely and Absolutely make over and confirm unto ye s^d Andrew Brown a Certain parcel of Land containing by Estimation Seventeen Acres and an halfe be it more or less, Scituate Lying and being in the township or Precincts of York, which land was formerly Edward Starts of York Deceased, Lying on the Northeast side of York river between ye Widow ffrethys Land & Homes^d Land Adjoyning to each abutting on afores^d River, twenty four Poles or Pearch in breadth And runing back ye same breadth from the river N: east an hundred and Seventeen Poles or Perch bounded at ye Northeast end by a small white Oake marked on four Sides at ye East corner, and on ye North corner by a small pine marked on four Sides, Together with all the rights, benefits, Emolum^{ts} and Advantages Appertaining to or any wayes at any time redowning from ye same or any part or parcell thereof, To have and to hold, and quietly and peaceably to Ocupie Possess and enjoy ye s^d Land and Appurtenances as a sure Estate in Fee Simple to him the s^d Brown his heires Exec^{rs} Adm^{rs} and Assignes for ever, Moreover the s^d Wright and his wife for themselves their heires Exec^{rs} and Adm^{rs} to and with the s^d Brown his heires Exec^{rs} Adm^{rs} and Assignes doe Indent Covenant egage and promise, the premisses with all their priviledges & Appurtenances from all former grants, gifts, sales, rents, rates Dowrys Demands and incumbrances as alsoe from all future Claimes, suites or Interuptions to be had or Comenced by them their heires Executors Adm^{rs} or Assignes or any person or persons whatsoever, upon grounds preceding the Date of this Instrum^t for ever to Warrantize and Defend by these presents. In witness whereof the s^d Henry Wright and Sarah his wife have hereunto set their hand and Seal, this tenth day of August in

Hen: Wright to Andrew Brown

the year of our Lord one thousand six hundred Ninety nine And in y[e] Eleventh year of the Reign of William the third King of Great Brittain &c.

Signed Sealed & delivered   Henry Wright (and a seal)
  In the presents of us   Sarah Wright
  Joseph Ware
  William Hooke
  Samuel Bragdon

Henry Wright came and Acknowledged this above written to be his Act and deed this: 10th day of Aug[st] 1699 Before me,

                  Abra: Preble Jus[te] of pea

A true Copie of the originall Transcribed & compared this 27th of Septemb[r] 1701.

               p Jos: Hamond Regist[r]

To all Christian People to whome this present Deed of Sale shall come/ John Partridge of Portsmouth in the Province New Hampshiere, Vintner, and Mary his wife sends greeting Know Yee that we y[e] s[d] John Partridge and Mary Partridge, for and in consideration of a Valuable Sum of money and other goods to us in hand well and truly paid at and before y[e] Ensealing and Delivery of these presents by Daniel Simpson of York in y[e] County of York in New England Cordwainer, the receipt whereof we doe hereby Acknowledge and therewith fully satisfied contented and paid, and thereof, and of and from every part and parcel thereof doe freely Acquit Exonerate and discharge him the said Daniel Simpson his heires and Assignes for ever by these presents Have given granted, bargained, Sold, Aliened Enfeoffed and confirmed And by these doe for us our heires Exec[rs] and Assignes for ever, freely clearly & absolutely give, grant, bargain, sell, Alien Enfeoffe Convey and confirm unto him the s^d Daniel Simpson his heires and Assignes All that our Right title & Interest of in and unto a certain house and Land Lying & being Scituate in ye Township of York afores^d bounded as followeth (that is to say) fronting on the Maine river on the south and a high way on the East next unto the Land that was formerly Mr Edward Rishworths and on the West Adjoyning to John Penwills, and on ye North the bounds yet unknown, Together with all other Lands Meadows Mowing ground pasturage Comonage &c, which I ye s^d John Partridge bought of Arthur Hughs and Sarah his wife as at large Appears by Deed of Sale under their hands and seales, bearing Date the twentieth day of January 169¾ reference thereunto being had, Together with ye profits, Priviledges & Appurtenances to ye s^d lands belonging or in any wise Appertaining. To have and to hold the s^d lands &c with the Appurtenances, wth all right, title, Interest, Claime and demand which we ye s^d John and Mary Partridge now have or ought to have of, in or unto ye above granted Premisses or any part thereof to him ye s^d Daniel Simpson his heires or Assignes for ever And to ye only proper usebenefit & behoofe of him ye s^d Daniel Simpson his heires &c for evermore, And we the said John Partridge and Mary Partridge for us our heires Exec^rs Adm^rs and Assignes doe Coven^t grant and agree to and with him ye s^d Daniel Simpson his heires and Assignes that at and before thensealing and delivery hereof, we are the true right and proper owners of the above Premisses and thappurtenances And that we have in our selves full power good right and Lawfull Authority the same to grant and confirm unto him ye s^d Daniel Simpson his heires and Assignes as afores^d and that it shall and may be Lawfull to and for ye s^d Daniel Simpson his heires and Assignes the afores^d Premisses and every part thereof from time to time and at all times for ever hereafter to have hold use Ocupie Possess and enjoy without any Lawfull let

Jno Partridge to Danll Simson

deniall, hinderance Molestation or disturbance of or by us or any other person or persons from by or under us or by our procurement and that ye sale thereof against our selves our heires Excut^{rs} Adm^{rs} and Assignes and against all other persons Lawfully Claiming ye same or any part thereof from by or under us our heires or [111] Assignes We will for ever save harmless Warrant and Defend by these p^{r}sents And that we our heires Execut^{rs} Adm^{rs} and Assignes shall & will make perform and Execute such other and further Lawfull and reasonable Act or Acts, thing or things as can be devised Advised or required for ye better confirming and more sure making of the Premisses to him the said Daniel Simpson his heires or Assignes (At his or their proper Cost According to ye Laws of this Province) In witness whereof we ye said John and Mary Partridge have hereunto set our hands and seales this Eight and twentieth day of June in the thirteenth year of the Reign of our Soveraign Ld William the third, and in the year of our Lord God One thousand seven hundred and one. 1701.

Signed Sealed and delivered   John Partridge (and seal)
   In the presents of us   Mary Partridge (and seal)
   Mercy Gowen
   John Rogers
   Jos: Hamond

         Kittery ss/ June ye twenty eigth 1701

The afore named John Partridge and Mary his wife, personally Appearing before me ye Subscrib^r one of his Ma^{ts} Justices of ye Peace within ye County of York Acknowledged this Instrum^t to be their Act & deed.

                                 Jos: Hamond

A true Copie of ye originall Transcribed and compared July 4th 17

                  p Jos: Hamond Regist^r

Book VI, Fol. 111.

Province of Massachusets

Nicho Moorey to Jos: Bayly

To all Christian People to whome these present Deed shall come. Nicholas Morey of Taunton In the County of Bristoll in his Ma^ts Province of the Massachusets Bay in New England Carpenter, Send Greeting Know yee that I ye s^d Nicholas Moorey, for and in consideration of the Sum of one hundred and five pounds in Currant Silver money to me in hand paid and Lawfully assured to be paid before the ensealing these present Deed by Joseph Bayly of Newbury in the County of Essex in the Province afores^d Yeoman, the receipt whereof I ye s^d Nicholas Moorey doe for my selfe my heires Execut^rs and Adm^rs acknowledge our selves to be fully contented satisfied and paid for every part and parcel of the Premisses herein contained hereby Exonerate, Acquit, release and discharge ye said Joseph Bayley his heires and success^rs for ye same for ever by these presents, Hath given, granted, bargained, sold, Alienated Enfeoffed and confirmed, one hundred and fifty Acres of Land and Meadow or salt marsh, scituate lying and being in the Township of Cape Porpoise, formerly in the Province of Maine now in the County of York in the Province of the Massachusets Bay afores^d the which land and Meadow I y^e said Moorey bought of Samuel Snow of Boston as by his Deed to me bearing date y^e 2th day of ffebruary 168$\frac{5}{6}$/ may Appear, butted and bounded as by the Antient boundaries of s^d ffarm is set forth by Ditches, salt water, Coves, lines, stakes &c All and singular the above bargained premisses with all the Appurtenances liberties and priviledges, as wood, timber, trees, brush, stones &c. that in any manner pertain to ye above bargained premisses, I s^d Nicholas Moorey doe for my selfe my heires and Success^rs Give, grant, bargain, sell, Alienate, Enfeoffe and confirm to the afores^d Joseph Bayley his heires Execut^rs & Admin^rs and Assignes for ever. To have and to hold to his and their proper use, and behoof for ever/ I s^d Nicholas Moorey doe for my selfe my heires & successors avouch that I have good Right and Lawfull Authority to dispose of y° above bargained p'misses, And that they are free and cleare from all manner of Incumbrances whatever whether Morgage, gift, or gift of Dower, womans thirds, Deed of Sale, Judgm' or Judgments of Court Execution or Executions or any manner of suit or suits trouble or trouble in the Law done or contracted, by me s⁴ Moorey or Assignes, or my procurem' or any other person laying any Lawfull Claim thereunto, Always holding firm stable all and singular the above bargained Premisses with all the Appurtenances thereto pertaining to be s⁴ Joseph Bayleys his heires and Successors for ever without let hinderance Ejection Eviction or controle/ In witnesse hereto I have set my hand and seal this twenty second day of Novemb' One thousand Seven hundred, In the twelfth year of his Ma" Reign, William the third King over England &c:

Signed Sealed & delivered   Nich' Moory (and seal)

  In presents of us.
  Edward
  John Kent
  Edward Sargent

It is to be understood that y° aboves⁴ Joseph Bayley as he is in Possession of y° fores⁴ Premisses, in part I give him the full possession of the whole as above written And as by other Deeds may Appear having relation to y° same.

Essex ss Newbury.

Nicholas Moory Appeared y° twenty second day of Novemb' 1701. And Acknowledged the above written Instrum' to be his Act & deed Before me
      Daniel Pierce Justice of the Peace.

A true Copie of the originall Transcribed and Compared the 4ᵗʰ July 1701.   p Jos: Hamond Regist'

BOOK VI, FOL. 112.

Be it known unto all whom it may concern that Jonathan Bass, son of the late Peter Bass, of York in the Province of Maine have received of Samuel Johnson of the same town and Province successor of G parker the full sum of five pounds According to y⁰ order of a Generall Assembly held in York the 25th of June 1684 as may Appear, I say received in full satisfaction According to y⁰ above mentioned order of y⁰ Generall held at y⁰ time aforesᵈ, wherefore, I Jonathan Bass son of the late Peter Bass doe According to order of the Generall Assembly held at York as abovesaid doe reverse, make voyd and of none Effect all former Instruments And [112] Obligations by the fore mentioned George Parker whose successor I Samuel Jobnson before named am, And doe hereby resigne all my former right & title in and unto the premises above mentioned, unto the abovesaid Samuel Johnson successor to George Parker for ever, Witness his hand and seale this 26th day of June, 1702.

Jonth Bass
to
Samll Johnson

Signed Sealed and delivered   The marke   of.
In the presents of.   Jonathan J Bass (and seal)
  John Carthero
  Eliezer Johnson
  Samuel Mattocks

Jonathan Bass personally appearing before me one of his Maᵗˢ Council and Justice of Peace for y⁰ Province of y⁰ Massachusets Bay in New England, did Acknowledge the above written Instrument to be his Volentary Act and deed, y⁰ 26th June 1701

John Philips

A true Copie of this Instrumᵗ Transcribed & compared the 4th of July: 1701.   p Jos: Hamond Registʳ

Book VI, Fol. 112.

To all People unto whome this present Deed of sale shall come, Samuel Sewall of Boston in the County of Suffolk within ye Province of ye Massachusets Bay in New England Esqr and Hannah his wife ye only daughter of John Hull late of Boston afores^d Esqr Dec^d send Greeting Know Yee that ye said Samuel Sewall and Hannah his wife for and in consideration of the summe of one hundred & twenty pounds Currant money in New England secured in the Law to be paid the s^d Samuel Sewall by & from Icabod Plaisted of Salmon falls within the Township of Kittery in ye County of York in the Province of Maine in New England afores^d Merch^t wherewith they Acknowledge themselves to be fully satisfied & and contented, As alsoe for divers other good causes and consideracõns them hereunto moving, they ye s^d Samuel Sewall and Hannah his wife Have given, granted, bargained, sold, aliened, released conveyed and confirmed, & by these presents for themselves and their heires Doe fully freely clearly and absolutely give grant bargain sell alien release convey & confirm unto ye said Icabod Plaisted his heires Exec^{rs} Adm^{rs} and assignes for ever All the Estate right title Interest Inheritance use Possession revercõn remainder property Claim and Demand whatsoever which the said Samuel Sewall and Hannah his said wife or either of them/ ever had now have or hath or that they or either of them their or ether of their heires or assignes or any of them at any time or times hereafter shall have may might should or in any wise ought to have or Claim of in to or out of the afores^d Salmon falls and grant of Timb^r upon & belonging to the Town and within the precincts of the Township of Kittery in the County of York and Province of Mayne afores^d either in respect or in right of their father ye said John Hull Dec^d or by any other manner of ways or means whatsoever/ To have and to hold all ye above granted bargained and released premisses with thapurtenances and every part and

*Samll Sewall
to
Ichabod Plaisted*

parcel thereof unto ye said Icabod Plaisted his heires Execut^rs Adm^rs and assignes to his and their own sole and proper use benefit and behoofe from henceforth and for ever, And the said Samuel Sewall and Hannah his wife for themselves their heires Execut^rs and Administra^rs doe hereby Covenant promise and grant to and with ye said Icabod Plaisted his heires Exec^rs Adm^rs and assignes in manner and form following That is to say that at and untill the time of thensealing and delivery of these presents they the said Samuel Sewall and Hannah his wife are true sole and Lawfull owners of all ye afore bargained Premisses And stand Lawfully seized thereof in their or one of their own proper right Having in themselves full power good right and Lawfull Authority to grant sell convey and assure the same in manner and form afores^d free and clear, and clearly Acquitted Exonerated and Discharged of and from all and all manner of former and other gifts, grants bargains sales Leases releases Mortgages titles troubles Charges and Incumbrances whatsoever had made comitted done or suffered to be done by ye said Samuel Sewall and Hannah his s^d wife or either of them at any time or times before thensealing hereof. And further ye s^d Samuel Sewall and Hannah his s^d wife for themselves their heires Excut^rs and Admin^rs and every of them doe hereby Covenant and grant to warrant and Defend all the above granted and released premisses with thappurtenances unto the said Icabod Plaisted his heires Execut^rs Adm^rs and assignes for ever against all and every person and persons whomsoever any Lawfully Claiming or Demanding any Estate right title or Interest therein by from or und^r them or either or any of them their or either or any of their heires or assignes In witnesse whereof the said Samuel Sewall and Hannah his s^d wife have hereunto set their hands

Book VI, Fol. 113.

and Seales the first day of May Anno Dom: 1701 Annoq, RR° Gulielmi 3 ii Angliæ Decimo Tertio

Signed Sealed and Delivered   Sam Sewall. (and seal)
    in presents of us.   Hannah Sewall (and seal)
    Eliezer Moody Scr./

Suffolk ss, Boston Septemb^r 20th 1701

Samuel Sewall Esqr and Hannah his wife the Subscribers to the within written Instrum^t Acknowledged the s^d Instrum^t to be their Act And deed/

            Before   Peter Sargeant Ju : Pec :

A true Copie of the originall Transcribed and compared the 1st of Octob^r 1701.   p Jos Hamond Regist^r

---

Be it known to all men by these pres^{ts} that I Harlakinden Symonds of Ipswich in ye County of Essex Gen^t for a valluable consideration to me in hand paid have given and granted and by these p^{r}sents confirmed unto my brother William Symonds of ye same town & County Gent : four hundred Acres of ground Meadow and pasture Lying in Coxhall (with Meadow to it as part of ye four hundred Acres proportionably as the tract of Land will Yield which

Harlakdn Symonds   ye s^d Harlakinden purchased of John Bush and
to   Peter Turbutt) this land lyeth in ye County of
Wm Symonds   Yorkshiere neare Maj^r Philips his land above

Cape Porpus township. To have and to hold ye s^d four hundred Acres of [113] ground with all and singular the Appurtenances to him the said William Symonds his heires and Assignes for ever And I the s^d Harlakinden Symonds doe covenant promise & grant to and with ye said William Symonds, that he the said William Symonds & his heires shall enjoy ye p^{r}misses without any Lawfull lett or Interuption from by or under me my heires or Assignes In witness whereof I ye said Harlakinden Symonds have hereunto set

BOOK VI, FOL. 113.

my hand & seale the 4th day of October Anno Dom 1670 Subscribed Sealed & delivered   Harlakinden Symonds (and seale)
In the presents of us.
Priscilla Symonds
John Greaver.
This was Acknowledged by the said Harlakinden to be his Act and Deed upon the 4th day of Octob^r 1670
        Before me   Samuel Symonds/ Assistant
A true Copie of the originall Transcribed and Compared the 16th Octob^r 1701   . p Jos : Hamond Regist^r.

To all Christian People to whome this present Deed of sale shall come Rachel Rew by vertue of a letter of Attorney dated the 22^d day of August: 1701 from her husband Thomas Rew of Boston in the County of Suffolk in ye Province of the Massachusets Bay New England Marriner, Mary Broughton and Sarah Johnson for her selfe and sister Rebekah Broughton by vertue of a Letter of Attorney from ye s^d Rebekah bearing Date ye 13 day of May 1700 all of them of Boston afores^d being the daughters and coheires of George Broughton late of Kittery in the County of York within ye Province of Maine Gent. Deceased of the one part, and John Rogers of Boston afores^d Gent of the other part Witnesseth that ye s^d Rachel, Thomas Rew, Mary Broughton and Sarah Johnson for her selfe and sister Rebekah Broughton for and in consideration of the sum of thirty five pounds currant money of Boston afores^d to them

Brougtons
    to
Rogers

at or before the ensealing and Delivery of these presents well and truly in hand paid by the s^d John Rogers, whereof and wherewith ye s^d Rachel Thomas Rew, Mary Broughton and Sarah Johnson for her selfe and sister Rebekah Broughton doth Acknowledge themselves to be fully satisfied contented & paid and thereof, and from every part thereof doe Acquit and discharge yᵉ sᵈ John Rogers his heires and Assignes for ever by these presents, Have given granted bargained sold Aliened conveied and confirmed and by these presents doe fully freely and Absolutely give grant bargain sell Alien covey & confirm unto him the sᵈ John Rogers his heires Executʳˢ Adminʳˢ and assignes, all our full Rite Title in the Salmon falls, at yᵉ East part of New England which lyeth on both sides of Newichawanack great river As all the land with all the wayes Easements woods trees Mines Mineralls Mills Iron work buildings fences rivers, water Courses, and Appurtenances to yᵉ sᵈ lands and all & every of them belonging or in any wise Appurtaining Whereof the sᵈ George Broughton died seized of or did of Rite belong or Appurtain to him at the time of his Deccase by virtue of Severall Deeds of Sale and town grants hereafter Mentioned referrence thereto being had may fully and plainly appear/ Vizᵗ two grants of the Town of Kittery Recorded yᵉ 13 of April 1671 for 120 Acres and Deed of Sale from Nicholas ffrost & Mary his wife Bearing Date 23ᵈ of March the 23 167$\frac{2}{3}$ for Sixty Acres of Land, one Deed of Sale from Roger Plaisted and Olive his wife bearing Date yᵉ 18 day of April 1671. for three Acres and one Deed of Sale from John Wincoll undʳ his hand and seale bearing Date yᵉ 24 day of July 1686./ To have & to hold the afore bargained Premisses with their Appurtenances to him the sᵈ John Rogers his heires Execʳˢ Adminʳˢ or Assignes and to his and their only proper use and behoof for ever freely peaceably and quietly without any matter of Challenge Claime or demand of us the sᵈ Rachel Thomas Rew Mary Broughton Sarah Johnson and Rebekah Broughton or any person or persons whatsoever for us or in our names by our cause or procurement And the sᵈ Rachel Thomas Rew Mary Broughton Sarah Johnson and Rebekah Broughton doth for themselves their heires Execʳˢ and Adminʳˢ Covenant promise grant to and with ye s^d John Rogers his heires and Assignes that ye premisses before bargained & and their Appurtenances are at and before ye ensealing hereof free and clear Acquitted and Discharged of and from all and all manner of former and other gifts grants bargains sales titles troubles Acts Alienations or incumbrances whatsoever And that we have in ourselves full power good rite and Lawfull authority the premises & every of them to grant bargain sell Alien convey and confirm unto him the s^d John Rogers his heires and Assignes as afores^d And he the s^d John Rogers his heires as afores^d shall and may for time to time and at all times for ever hereafter Have hold use improve Ocupie possess and enjoy the same and every of them with their Appurtenances free and Clear, without any Lawfull let hinderance forever hereafter Have hold use improve Ocupie possess and enjoy the same and every of them with their Appurtenances free and clear without any Lawfull Lett hinderance Molestation or disturbance had made or done or suffered to be done by us the s^d Rachel Thomas Rew Mary Broughton Sarah Johnson & Rebekah Broughton or from any person from by or under us And that we the s^d Rachel Thomas Rew Mary Broughton Sarah Johnson and Rebekah Broughton shall and will Warrant and Defend the sale of the s^d Premisses unto him the s^d John Rogers his heires and assignes against our selves & every other person Lawfully Claiming any rite thereto or Interest therein for ever by these presents And we the s^d Rachel Thomas Rew Mary Broughton Sarah Johnson and Rebekah Broughton our heires Exec^{rs} or Admin^{rs} shall and will doe any other further thing or things that may be for the better securing, secureing and more sure making the said premisses unto him ye s^d John Rogers his heires and assignes in manner as afores^d/ In witness wherof we the s^d Rachel for my self & husband Thomas Rew, Mary Broughton and Sarah Johnson for my self & sister Rebekah Broughton have hereunto set our hands and seales.

Book VI, Fol. 114.

Dated in Boston the sixt day of October Anno Dom. one thousand seven hundred & one, In yᵉ thirteenth year of the Reign of our Soveraign Lᵈ William King of great Brittain ffrance and Ireland &c/

Sarah Johnson (her seal)
the mark of Rachel Rew for (seal)
her husband Thomas 𝈦 Rew
the mark of Rchel ∫ Rew (her seal)
the mark of Mary ✕ Broughton (her seal)
the mark of Sarah Johnson for her sister
Rebeka ⅄ Broughton (seal)

Signed Sealed and Delivered
 in the presents of us
 Rich Ellis.
 Hannah Wright
Boston 7ᵗʰ Octobʳ 1701

Suff ss/ Sarah Johnson for her self & as Attorney to her husband Thomas Rew and Mary Broughton personally appeared before me the Subscribʳ one of his Maᵗˢ Justices of Peace for sᵈ County of Suffolk and acknowledged this Instrumᵗ to be their voluntary Act & Deed

Penn Townsend

A true Copie of yᵉ originall Transcribed and compared
Octobʳ 25 : 1701   p Jos Hamond Registʳ

[114] At a Legall Town Meeting held at Kittery May 16ᵗʰ 1694/ Granted unto Alexandʳ Dennet twenty Acres of Land to be laid out Clear of former grants provided he improve it within one year after it is laid out, by fencing or building and improving a considerable part thereof otherwise to return again to yᵉ Town

A true Copie as Appears of Record in Kittery town book.
Examined p Jos : Hamond Clerͬ

Book VI, Fol. 114.

Now know all men by these presents that I yᵉ above named Alexander Dennett have for a valuable consideration to me in hand paid by John Gelding of Portsmᵒ in the Province of New Hampshire/ Sold Assigned and made over and by these pʳsents for me my heires Execʳˢ and assignes freely and absolutely sell assigne make over and confirme unto yᵉ sᵈ John Gelding his heires or Assignes, all my right Title & Interest of in and to yᵉ above grant of twenty Acres of Land To have and to hold to him his heires and Assignes for ever. In witness whereof I have hereunto set my hand seale this fourteenth day of June: 1701.

Dennett to Gelding

Signed Sealed and Delivered   Alexander Dennet (his seal)
In the presents of us.

Mehetable W Dennet
(her mark)

Jos: Hamond

York ss/ Kittery July 14ᵗʰ 1701

The above named Alexander Dennet personally appearing before me the Subscribʳ one of his Maᵗˢ Justices of the Peace within yᵉ County of York Acknowledged this Instrument to be his Act & Deed

Jos: Hamond.

A true Copie of the originall Transcribed and compared yᵉ 7ᵗʰ Novembʳ 1701   p Jos: Hamond Registʳ

At a Legall town Meeting held at Kittery May 24ᵗʰ 1699/ Granted unto Robert Allen his heires or assignes for ever, thirty Acres of Land if he can find it clear of former grants
  A true Copie as Attests.
                              Jos Hamond Clerʳ

Book VI, Fol. 114.

Now know all men by these presents that I Robert Allen of Kittery in the County of York in the Province of the Massachusets Bay Have sold assigned & made over unto Mr John Newmarch of ye same place, all the above mentioned grant of thirty Acres of land To have and to hold ye aboves^d land with all ye priviledges and Appurtenances thereunto belonging to him ye said Newmarch his heires Excut^{rs} Admin^{rs} and assignes for evermore In Witness whereof I have hereunto set my hand and seale this Sixth day of Septemb^r one thousand seven hundred 1700/

Allen to Newmarch

Signed Sealed and delivered
  In the presets of us.
  Jos: Hamond
  Jos: Hamond Junr

Robert X Allen (his seal)
     mark

York ss/ Kittery Septemb^r 6 : 1700

The above named Robert Allen personally Appearing before me the Subscrib^r one of his Ma^{ts} Justices of Peace in s^d County of York Acknowledged this Instrum^t to be his Act & Deed   Jos: Hamond

A true Copie of the originall Transcribed and Compared Novemb^r 7th 1701   p Jos: Hamond

Know all men by these presents that I Aaron Pharies of Kittery in the County of York in the Province of the Massachusets Bay in New England fisherman for and in consideration of a valuable sum of Money to me in hand paid by John Newmarch of the same place the receipt whereof I doe hereby Acknowledge Have bargained sold and Delivered and by these presents doe bargain sell and deliver unto the said John Newmarch a certain grant of twenty Acres of Land that was granted to me by the town of Kittery May yᵉ twenty fourth in the year of our Lord one thousand six hundred Ninety & Nine as in yᵉ Records for sᵈ town may Appear together with all yᵉ Appurtenances and privildges thereunto belonging, To have and to hold the said grant & land therein granted with all yᵉ priviledges thereunto belonging unto yᵉ said John Newmarch his heires and Assignes as his and their owne proper right of Inheritance in ffee Simple for ever and to yᵉ only proper use and behoof of him yᵉ sᵈ John Newmarch his heires and assignes for evermore. And I yᵉ sᵈ Aaron Phares for my self my heires Executʳˢ & Adminʳˢ the sᵈ bargained premisses unto yᵉ sᵈ John Newmarch his heires Executʳˢ Adminʳˢ and Assignes shall and will warrant and for ever Defend against all and all manner of persons from by or under me by these presents. In witness whereof I have hereunto set my hand and seal this twenty second day of November Anno Domini one thousand and seven hundred And in yᵉ twelfth year of yᵉ Reign of our Soveraign Lord William the third King over England &c.

Pharies to Newmarch

Signed Sealed & delivered   Aaron Phares   (his seal)
   In yᵉ presents of us.   his **A** mark
   Henry Barter
       her
   Sarah **S** Barter
       mark

York ss/ January yᵉ 27ᵗʰ 17¾

Aaron Phares personally Appearing Acknowledged this Instrumᵗ to be his free act and Deed before me

                           Wᵐ Pepperrell Js pes

A true Copie of the originall Transcribed and compared this 7ᵗʰ of Novembʳ 1701.

                    p Jos : Hamond Registʳ

Know all men by these presents that I Benjamin Gooch of Wells in the County of York in ye Province of the Massachusets Bay in New England Planter send Greeting, Know yee that I ye s^d Benjamin Gooch for and in consideration of the Sum̄ of fourteen pounds good and Lawfull money of New England to me in hand paid and well Insured to be paid at ye ensealing hereof by John Wheelwright of s^d Wells Yeoman, the receipt whereof I doe hereby acknowledge, Have granted bargained sold Aliened enfeoffed & confirmed and by these presents doe freely fully and Absolutely give grant bargain sell Alien enfeoff and confirm unto ye aboves^d John Wheelwright his heires and Assignes all these severall pieces or parcels of Marsh ground scituate in Wells aboves^d containing by Estimation Eight Acres be it more or less and is part of that Marsh ground com̄only called or known by ye name of the little River Marsh being butted and bound as followeth (that is to say) all those three points of Salt and fresh Marsh lying upon and Joyning unto ye little river aboves^d begining at ye uper end of the Marsh formerly John Wellses and now in the Possession of Thomas Wells & Nathaniel Clark/ And soe to [**115**] run up the whole breadth of the s^d Marsh untill it butts upon an other piece of s^d Wellses Marsh as alsoe an other parcel of fresh Marsh begining at ye uper end of that piece of of s^d Wellses wher the points of Marsh butts upon, and so to run up to the head of a certain Cove on ye Northern side and up by ye s^d River the whole breadth of s^d Marsh which lyeth chiefly in two points by ye river and so to the upland untill an Elbow of the river comes pritty near to a birchen point of upland as it is now bounded and a stake set up in ye Marsh by s^d river with all ways waters water courses easments liberties feedings priviledges and Appurtenances thereunto belonging To have and to hold the above granted severall parcels of Marsh ground, with the rites liberties priviledges and Appurtenances whatsoever thereunto belong-

Gooch to Wheelwright

ing unto him ye s^d John Wheelwright his heires Execut^rs Admin^rs and Assignes to his and their only proper use benefit & behoof forever And I ye s^d Benjamin Gooch for myself my heires Execut^rs Administrat^rs and assignes doe covenant promise and agree by these presents that at ye time of this bargain and sale and untill ye Signing and Sealing hereof I am ye true sole and Lawfull owner of the above bargained premisses and of every part and parcell thereof and have in my self full power good right and Lawfull Authority to grant convey and asure the same unto ye s^d John Wheelwright his heires Exec^rs Admin^rs and assignes as a good perfect and absolute Estate of Inheritance in ffee simple, free and clear and clearly Acquitted Exonerated & discharged of and from all former and other gifts grants barguins sales leases Morgages entailes Joyntures and of and from all other titles and Incumbrances whatsoever and that ye s^d John Wheelwright his heires and Assignes shall and may by vertue of these presents forever hereafter Lawfully peaceably and quietly Have hold use Possess and enjoy the above bargained premisses and every part and parcel thereof without the least let deniall Suit trouble Molestation eviction or ejection of me the s^d Benjamin Gooch my heires Excut^rs Administrat^rs or assignes or of any other person or persons from by or under me or by my means act or consent procurem^t or default/ In witness whereof I the s^d Benjamin Gooch have hereunto put my hand and seal this twenty eighth day of Novemb^r one thousand seven hundred/ And in the twelfth year of the Reign of our Soveraign King William over England Scotland ffrance & Ireland &c

Signed Sealed and delivered   Benjamin Gooch (and a seal)
  In the presents of us.
  James Wakefield
     her
  Rebeckah + Wakefield
     mark

BOOK VI, FOL. 115.

York ss/ Wells Octob[r] 7th 1701

The above named Benjamin Gooch personally Appearing before me the Subscrib[r] one of his Ma[ts] Justices of y[e] Peace within y[e] County of York Acknowledged y[e] above Instrum[t] to be his Act and Deed

Abra: Preble.

A true Copie of the originall Transcribed and compared Octob[r] 7th 1701   p Jos: Hamond Regist[r]

To all Christian People to whome this present Deed of sale shall come, Know yee, that I James Treworgie Tanner, in the town of Portsm[o] in the Province of New Hampshiere,

Treworgie to Greely

for and in consideration of a certain sum of money to me in hand truly paid p Thomas Greely of y[e] Town & Province afores[d] Tanner, where with I doe Acknowledge my self to be fully satisfied Have bargained and sold And doe by these presents bargain sell Alien & Enfeoffe and set over unto the s[d] Thomas Greeley his heires Execut[rs] Admin[rs] and Assignes for ever a certain tract or parcell of Land containing fiftie Acres being and Joying to Edward Waymouths land near to Mast Cove in the town of Kittery as appears p a Copie of the town Record bearing Date the 23[d] of Novemb[r] 1685, together with a dwelling house and all Appurtenances belonging to y[e] afores[d] tract of Land, together with Eleven Acres as Addition to y[e] house Lott being a hundred and two poles in length East North East from y[e] ledge of rocks and a hundred poles in breadth south, southeast, bounded on the North with the land of Israel Hodsden and on the east with the comons at the third hill and on the south with the Comons as p y[e] severall marked trees which mensuration or grant is entred into the third book of Records for the Province of Mayn Page: 113. the 26. day of June 1682. p

Edward Rishworth Recorder together with all other Appurtenances belonging to the afores^d tract of Land, as woods trees water or water Courses, as alsoe all fence or fences Erected and Improved p my Predecess^r John Bready or my selfe All which land Limitted and mentioned as afores^d I doe Acknowledge my self to be truly and Justly Satisfied and fully contented and paid for the same To have and to hold, all the forementioned bargained Premisses with the Appurtenances thereunto belonging unto the s^d Thomas Greely his heires Execut^{rs} Admin^{rs} or Assignes for ever And I the said James Treworthy doe hereby Ingage to Warrant and defend the above bargained Premisses from any person or persons whatsoev^r that shall lay any Claime or title thereunto from by or under me my heires Execut^{rs} & Admin^{rs}/ And doe more particularly from all Claimes or pretences the heires of my predecess^r John Bready May by any manner of meanes or whatsoever pretend thereunto vnto the s^d Thomas Greely his heires Execut^{rs} Admin^{rs} and Assignes for ever And I doe hereby avouch my selfe to be invested with a full power to grant this Deed of Sale to all intents & purposes that the Law requires In witness whereof I have hereunto set my hand and Seal the Eighteen day of Novemb^r in the year of our Lord one thousand Seven hundred and one years And in the thirteenth year of the Reign of our Soveraign Lord William the third King of England Scotland ffrance and Ireland.   Signum

Signed Sealed and delivered   James ⦙ Treworthy (his Seale)
  In presents of us.
  John Macgoune   Ejus
  Daniel Jackson
  William Stacie
  Peter ⊢ Brook
    his mark

BOOK VI, FOL. 116.

York ss, Kittery Novemb[r] 21, 1701.

The above named James Treworgie personally Appearing before me the Subscrib[r] one of his Ma[ts] Justices of the Peace within y[e] County of York Acknowledged this Instrument to be his Act and Deed/.

Jos : Hamond

A true Copie of the originall Transcribed and compared the 21st Novemb[r] 1701. p Jos. Hamond Regist[r]

[116] Know all men by these presents that I John Littlefield and Patience Littlefield my wife, of Wells in the County of York in the Province of the Massachusets Bay in New England Divers good causes & considerations me thereunto moving and more Especially for and in consideration of that Naturall love and affection that I bear unto my Son Josiah Littlefield doe by these presents give and grant unto my Loving Son Josiah Littlefield of the aboves[d] Town and County his heires Execut[rs] Administrat[rs] and Assignes for ever a certain tract or parcel of Salt Marsh and thatch lands lying and being in the town of Wells on the Southeast Side of ogunquit river bounded as followeth, begining over against Daniel Littlefields Marsh where the Creek comes home to y[e] beach and so to run along between y[e] Creek and the Seawall along y[e] beach westward so far as the Sandy point be it.more or less All which Marsh or thatch land I doe from my self my heires Execut[rs] Administrat[rs] and Assignes give and grant unto my Loving Son Josiah Littlefield his heires Execut[rs] Administrat[rs] and Assignes, To have and to hold and peaceably to enjoy for ever all y[e] above s[d] tract of Marsh and thatch land I doe by these presents warrant and Defend the same from all persons whatsoever from by or under me or by my means or procurem[t] In witness whereof I have hereunto Set my hand and Seale this eighth day of

Captn Jno Littlefield to his son Josiah

August one thousand Six hundred Ninety and Six And in y⁰ eighth year of his Ma⁽ᵗˢ⁾ Reign.

Signed Sealed and delivered   John Littlefield.   (his Seal)
  In the presents of.
  John Wheelwright   Patience *p* Littlefield (her Seale)
  James X Emerson   mark

Cap^{tn} John Littlefield and Patience Littlefield came and personally Appeared before me this 8th day of August 1696/ And Acknowledged this Above Instrum^t or Deed of gift to be their Act and deed/ before me.

       Samuel Wheelwright Jus^{ts} Peace

A true Copie of the originall Transcribed and Compared from Octob^r 14th 1701   p Jos: Hamond Regist^r

---

To all People to whome this present writing shall come Samuel Hatch of Wells Sends Greeting/ Now Know ye that the aboves^d Samuel Hatch of Wells abovesaid in the County of York Province of the Massachusets Bay in New England Planter with Mary his wife for divers good and lawfull causes and considerations him thereunto Moving

Hatch to Littlefield   more Especially for and in consideration of ye Sum of Eighteen pounds in currant money of New England secured to be paid from Josiah Littlefield of Wells aforesaid partly by promise and partly by a bill of Eleven pounds bearing Date with these presents Hath given and granted and doth by these p^rsents fully clearly and Absolutely give grant bargain sell Alienate enfeoffe confirm and set over unto Josiah Littlefield aforesaid of Wells in ye County of York Province of ye Massachusets Bay in New England Millwright A certain piece or parcell of land lying and being in the township of Wells aboves^d containing about one hundred Acres be it more or less bound as followeth Northeasterly upon my own land, Southeasterly upon Ogunquit river, Southwesterly upon

Book VI, Fol. 116.

land in the possession of Josiah Littlefield afores^d and Northwesterly upon ye Town Comons being forty poles or rods in breadth, the one half of ye Land I purchased of Mr Bolls To have & to hold the aboves^d piece or parcell of land bounded or Estimated as afores^d with all ye priviledges rights or Appurtenances thereunto belonging or any ways Appertaining to ye proper use and behoofe of him ye aboves^d Josiah Littlefield his heires Execut^{rs} Administrat^{rs} or Assignes as a free Estate unto them in ffee simple for ever And ye aboves^d Samuel Hatch doth for himself his heires Exec^{rs} Admin^{rs} covenant and promise to and with ye aboves^d Josiah Littlefield his heires Execut^{rs} Admin^{rs} or Assignes that he is ye true and rightfull owner of ye above granted land at the time of the ensealing hereof, and that he hath full power good right & Lawfull Authority to Sell and dispose of the same/ Moreover he doth by these presents afirm and promise that it and every part thereof is free and clear, And fully clearly, and absolutely Acquitted and discharged of and from all other & former gifts, grants, bargains sales Dowries Alienations enfeoffments Joyntures rights Intrusions Mortgages or Incumbrances whatsoever by or from him or under him And that he will warrant and Defend the same from any person or persons whatsoever in by from or under him or by his cause or procurem^t or any other persons whatsoever laying any Legall Claim thereunto Lord proprie t^r Excepted/ In witnesse to and in confirmation of the premisses aboves^d the above named Samuel Hatch hath hereto set his hand and seal this twenty sixth day of April in the year of our Lord one thousand seven hundred and one.

Annoq, Regni Regis Guilielmi Tertii Anliæ Scotiæ Franciæ & Hibeniæ Rex ffid. Defens^r XIII.

Sam^{ll} Emery   Samuel Hatch (his seal)
James Gooch
May 28th 1701

BOOK VI, FOL. 117.

Then Samuel Hatch made personall Appearance and Acknowledged this above written Instrum^t to be his own voluntary Act & deed.

Before me. John Wheelwright Jus^{tis} Pea

A true Copie of the originall Transcribed and compared Octob^r 14th 1701. p Jos : Ham̅ond Regist^r

To all Christian People to whome these p^{r}sents Shall come Greeting Know Yee that I Nicholas Moorey of Taunton in ye County of Bristoll in his Ma^{ts} Province of the Massachusets Bay in New England Acknowledge that I have received of Lieu^t Joseph Storer Samuel Hill and John Batson all of ye County of York in ye Province afores^d Joseph Storer and Sam^{ll} Hill of the town of Wells and John Batson of Cape Porpoise the Just Sum̅ of thirty three pounds Currant money & Lawfully Assured to be paid before ye Ensealing this Instrument [117] In consideration of ye said sum̅ of thirty three pounds I ye s^d Nicholas Moorey doe for my self my heires Execut^{rs} & Admin^{rs} give, grant, bargain, sell Alienate Enfeoff and Confirm unto the aboves^d Joseph Storer Sam^{ll} Hill & John Batson their heires Exec^{rs} Adm^{rs} or Assignes Each of them an Equall share of two tracts of Land Scituate Lying and being in s^d town of Cape Porpoise, the one that I said Moorey bought of John Renols of Sixty Acres as p his Deed to me bearing date Jan^{ry} 2^d 1687. butted and bounded as set forth in s^d Deed, The other tract of an hundred Acres of land granted to s^d Moorey from ye town of Cape Porpoise afores^d Scituate Lying and being on Kenebunk River in Capeporpoise Township butted and bounded as s^d town grant setteth forth/ All and Singular the above bargained Premisses with all ye Appurtenances liberties and priviledges in any

Moorey to Storer, Hill & Batson

manner thereto pertaining I s^d Nicholas Moorey acknowledge my selfe my heires & Successors to be fully satisfied and contented and paid for all and every part thereof, giving granting bargaining selling Alienating Enfeoffeing and confirming s^d tracts of Land afores^d to s^d Joseph Storer Sam^{ll} Hill & Jno Batson To have and to hold, to them & their heires Exec^{rs} Admin^{rs} and Assignes for ever I s^d Nicholas Moorey doe for my selfe my heires and Successors avouch that I am the rightfull owner of the above bargained Premisses. And have in my Self full power to make sale of ye Same And alsoe that they are free & clear from all Incumbrances whether by Mortgage gift Dower or womans thirds Judgm^t or Judgments of Court Execution or Executions or any troubles in ye Law whatever Warranting to Defend the Title of all and Singular ye above bargained Premisses against all Just Claims of any person whatever to said Joseph Storer Sam^{ll} Hill and John Batson their heires Execut^{rs} Adm^{rs} and Assignes for ever/ In witness hereto I have set my hand and seale This : 2 : day of Octob^r 1701. in the thirteenth year of his Ma^{ts} Reign William the third, King over England &c/

Signed, Sealed and delivered   Nicholas Moorey (his seal)
   In the presents of us.
   William Sayer
   Sarah Sayer
County of York/

Nicholas Moorey personally appeared before me the Subscrib^r ye 2^d day of Octob^r 1701. one of his Ma^{ts} Justices of the Peace and acknowledged this above written Deed or Instrument with his hand & seal to be his Act & deed

                                   John Wheelwright

A true Copie of the originall Transcribed and compared Octob^r 7th 1701

                         p Jos : Hamond Regist^r

Book VI, Fol. 117.

Know all men by this present writing that I James Bredeen of this Town of Kittery doe sell Assigne and set over unto Peter Lewis of Kittery, thirty Acres of Land which he had for a town grant y⁰ 24 of May 1699. And to his heirs Execut™ Admin™ and Assignes for ever To have and to hold from me the said James Bredeen my heires and Assignes for evermore In which I have paid him for in money as in Witness whereof I have hereunto set my hand and seal this seventh day of Novemb' one thousand seven hundred.

Bredeen to Lewis

Signed Sealed and Delivered   James Bredeen (his seal)
In the p'sents of us.   his mark

The mark of Elizabeth Bodge

Andrew Lewis.

The 7th of Novemb' 1701

then James Bredeen Acknowledged this Instrum' to be his free Act and deed/ Before me.

W™ Pepperrell Js pes.

A true Copie of the originall Transcribed and Compared this 27th Novemb' 1701

p Jos Hamond Regist'

March the 14th 1700/ Then I received three pounds six shillings and eight pence of my brother John Gowen, which was his part to pay me according to the distribution of my father William Gowen Al' Smiths Estate Approved of by M' Samuel Wheelwright Judge of Probate bearing date Jan'⁷ y⁰ 19th 169¾. I say received by me.

Attests   James Gowen Al' Smith

William Smith
William Rogers
   his i mark

Book VI, Fol. 118.

A true Copie of yᵉ originall Transcribed and compared, Decembʳ 10ᵗʰ 1701.

Receipts from
James Gowen
&
Sarah Smith
to
John: Gowen

p Jos : Hamond Registʳ

March the 16ᵗʰ 1700/ Then I Sarah Smith Recᵈ of my brother John Gowen Alˢ Smith thirty five shillings in part of what he was to pay me when I should arive at yᵉ age of Eighteen Years, it being part of my Portion, as Appears on Record by the destribution of my fathers Estate, bearing date January yᵉ 19 : 169⁴⁄₉. I say Received by me

Attests

Sarah Smith
her mark

Eizabeth Gowen Alˢ Smith/
her mark
Mary Hamond/

A true Copie of the originall Transcribed and Compared : Decembʳ 10 : 1701.   p Jos : Hamond Registʳ

[118] To all Christian People to whome these pʳsents shall come Richᵈ Monson of Portsmᵒ in the Province of New Hampshiere in New England sends Greeting Know Yee that I Richᵈ aforesᵈ for Divers good Causes me thereunto moving more Especially for yᵉ Naturall love I have and doe bear unto my beloved son John Monson, as alsoe for and in consideration of a certain sum of money to me in hand well and truly paid at and before yᵉ ensealing and Delivery of these pʳsents by my sᵈ son John Monson of Kittery in yᵉ County of York in in yᵉ Province of the Massachusets Bay in New England aforesᵈ Have given granted bargained sold Aliened Enfeoffed and confirmed And by these pʳsents doe for me my heires Executʳˢ Adminʳˢ and Assignes freely clearly and Absolutely give grant bargain sell Alien Enfeoffe

convey and confirm unto him y® s^d John Monson & his wife
their heires Execut^rs Adm^rs and assignes for ever/ All that
my house and land in y® Township of Kittery afores^d lying
and being scituate on y® South of Spruce Crick wch land I
bought of Thomas Rice of s^d Kittery containing thirty and
two Acres of land wth som Marsh being bounded as followeth
Viz^t begining at a place called Ox point, And from the s^d
Ox point from a marked hemlock tree one hundred and
Sixty rods on a North Northwest line And on the South
side by the s^d Creek thirty two rods to a marked tree and
from thence one hundred and Sixty rods on a North Northwest line/ which contain thirty and two Acres
(or how ever else bounded or reputed to be
bounded) as does and may Appear by a Deed of
Sale under y® hands and seales of Thomas Rice afores^d and
Mary his wife, bearing Date y® twenty eighth day of June:
1680: refference thereunto being had To have and to hold
y® s^d house and piece or parcel of land and Marsh with the
Appurtenances thereto belonging, with all right title Interest Claim and demand which I y® s^d Richd Monson now have
or in time past have had or which I my heires Execut^rs
Adm^rs or Assignes in time to come, may might or in any
wise ought to have of in or to y® above granted Premisses
or any part thereof to him the said John Monson and Lydia
his wife their heires or Assignes for ever And to the sole
and proper use benefit and behoofe of him y® s^d John Monson & Lydia his wife their heires Execut^rs &c for evermore
And I the s^d Richd Monson for me my heires Exec^rs Adm^rs
and Assignes doe covenant promise and grant to and with
him y® s^d John Monson his heires and Assignes that at and
before y® ensealing and delivery of these presents I am y®
right true and proper owner of y® above p^rmisses and thappurtenances And that I have in my self good right full
power & Lawfull Authority y® same to grant and confirm
unto him y® s^d John Monson and Lydia his wife their

Richd Monson to Jno Monson

BOOK VI, FOL. 118.

heires & assignes as afores[d] And that y[e] same and every part thereof is free and clear Acquitted and Discharged of and from all former and other gifts, grants, bargains, sales, leases Mortgages titles troubles Alenations and Incumbrances whatsoever by me done or suffered to be done And that it shall and may be Lawfull to and for y[e] s[d] John Monson and Lydia his wife their heires or Assignes the afores[d] Premisses and every part thereof from time to time and at all times for ever hereafter. To have, hold, use, ocupie improve possess and enjoy Lawfully peaceably and quietly without any Lawfull let deniall hinderance Molestation or disturbance of or by me or by any other person or persons from by or under me or by my procurem[t] And that y[e] sale thereof against my self my heires Execut[rs] Adm[rs] and Assignes I will for ever Save harmless warrant and Defend by these p[r]sents And that I my heires Execut[rs] & Adm[rs] shall and will make perform and Execute such other further Lawfull and reasonable Act or Acts thing or things as in as in Law or Equity can be Advised Devised or required for y[e] better confirming and more sure making of the premisses unto him y[e] s[d] John Monson and Lydia his wife their heires or Assignes According to y[e] Laws of this Province, In witness whereof I y[e] s[d] Rich[d] Monson have hereunto set my hand and seal y[e] fifteenth day of Decemb[r] in y[e] thirteenth year of y[e] Reign of our Soveraign Lord William the third by y[e] grace of God of England Scotland ffrance & Ireland King Defender of the ffaith &c Anno Domini one thousand seven hundred & one : 1701

Signed Sealed and delivered in the presents of us.
    Samuel Spinney
    Samuel Monson
    Jos Hamond
York ss/ Decemb[r] 15th 1701

Richard R Monson (his seal)
    his mark

Book VI, Fol. 118.

The above named Richard Monson personally Appearing Acknowledged this Instrument to be his Act and Deed/
Before me   Jos : Haṁond J : Peace
A true Copie of the originall Transcribed and Compared this fifteenth day of Decemb^r 1701/
                              p Jos : Haṁond Regist^r

To all People to whome these p^{r}sents shall come Jacob Smith of Kittery in the County of York in the Province of the Massachusets Bay in New England and Priscilla his wife sends Greeting, Know Yee that we ye s^d Jacob Smith and Priscilla Smith for and in consideration of ye suṁ of fiftie four pounds good and Lawfull money in New England/ twenty one pounds part thereof to us in hand paid the receipt whereof we doe Acknowledge and the other thirty three pounds at and before thensealing and Delivery of these p^{r}sents Secured in ye Law to be paid by John Cotten of Portsmouth in ye Province of New Hampshier Have given granted bargained sold Aliened Enfeoffed and confirmed, and by these presents doe for us our heires Execut^{rs} Adm^n and Assignes fully freely and Absolutely give grant bargain sell Alien Enfeoffe convey and confirm unto him the s^d John Cotten his heires Execut^{rs} Adm^n and assignes forever, All that our piece or parcell of Land which I ye s^d Jacob Smith bought of Stephen Tobey of Kittery afores^d scituate lying and being in ye township of Kittery afores^d, being bounded as followeth, That is to say begining at a marked tree on the Northeast Side of the Country road that goes from the corner of Thomas Hunscombs Orchard fence toward Kittery Northwestward, and from that tree (which is on the Southeast Side of s^d Land) to run Northwest and by North the whole breadth of ye s^d Stephen Tobeys land which is thirty eight

Smith
to
Cotten

poles, And to run back that whole breadth upon a Northeast and by east line between yᵉ lands of David Libbey on yᵉ Northwest and the Land of Thomas Hunscomb on the Southeast to the Extent and head bounds of the sᵈ Hunscombs land And from thence the sᵈ Cotten is to have the Northwest half part of the sᵈ thirty eight poles and to run back upon yᵉ sᵈ Northeast and by east point yᵉ full breadth of Nineteen poles Joyning with sᵈ David Libbey on yᵉ Northwest and Stephen Tobey on the Southeast to yᵉ utmost Extent of their Lands, the sᵈ piece or parcell of Land being part of a certain Tract of Land which yᵉ sᵈ Stephen Tobey bought of Mʳˢ Mehetable Warren, Elisha Hanchinson & Elizabeth his wife, in partnership with Joseph Hamond David Libbey Mathew Libbey and Daniel ffogg as Appears by Deed of sale bearing Date Decembʳ 18ᵗʰ 1699 [119] And Recorded in the Sixth Book of Records for ye County of York Page the 88ᵗʰ & 89ᵗʰ and by yᵉ sᵈ Tobey sold unto yᵉ sᵈ Jacob Smith as appears by Deed of sale under sᵈ Tobeys hand and seal bearing Date yᵉ 16ᵗʰ of May 1701 referrence thereunto being had/ To have and to hold the sᵈ piece or parcel of Land with the Appurtenances thereto belonging or in any wise Appurtaining with all Right title Interest Claim and Demand which we yᵉ sᵈ Jacob Smith and Priscilla Smith now have or in time past have had, or which we our heires Execut⁽ⁿ⁾ Adm⁽ⁿ⁾ or assignes in time to come may might or in any wise ought to have of in or to yᵉ above granted Premisses or any part thereof to him the sᵈ John Cotten his heires or assignes for ever And to the sole and proper use benefit and behoofe of him yᵉ sᵈ John Cotten his heires Execut⁽ⁿ⁾ &c for evermore And we yᵉ sᵈ Jacob Smith and Priscilla Smith for us our heires Execut⁽ⁿ⁾ Administrat⁽ⁿ⁾ and assignes Doe covenant promise and grant to and with the sᵈ John Cotten his heires and assignes that at and before the Ensealing and Delivery of these pʳsents we are the true right and proper owners of the above Premisses & yᵉ

Book VI, Fol. 119.

Appurtenances as houses, out houses, Barn frame or frames of Barn or houses standing or being upon s^d Land And that we have in our selves good right full power & Lawfull authority to grant & sell and assure the s^d Land and Premisses in manner as afores^d and that ye same and every part thereof is free and clear Acquitted and Discharged of and from all former and other gifts grants bargaines sales Mortgages Leases titles troubles Acts Alienations and Incumbrances whatsoever by us done or suffered to be done And that it shall and may be Lawfull to and for ye s^d John Cotten his heires or assignes the afores^d Premisses and every part thereof from time to time and at all times forever hereafter to have hold use improve ocupie Possess and enjoy Lawfully peaceably and quietly without any Lawfull lett deniall hinderance Molestation or disturbance of or by us or any other person or persons from by or under us or by our procurem^t, And that ye sale thereof against our selves our heires Execut^{rs} Adm^{rs} and assignes Lawfully Claiming the same or any part thereof we will for ever save harmless warrant & Defend by these p^{r}sents And that we our heires Execut^{rs} and Adm^{rs} shall and will make perform and Execute Such other further Lawfull and resonable Act or Acts thing or things as in Law or Equity can be Devised Advised or required for ye better confirming and more sure making of the Premisses unto him the s^d John Cotten his heires or assignes according to ye Laws of this Province In witness whereof we ye s^d Jacob Smith and Priscilla Smith have hereunto set our hands and Seales the twelfth day of January in the year of our Lord one thousand seven hundred and one: 1701

Signed Sealed and Delivered   Jacob Smith   (his seal)
   In the p^{r}sents of us.   her
   Jos: Hamond Junr Priscilla ✗ Smith (her seal)
      her   mark
   Hannah ✗ Key
      mark

Book VI, Fol. 119.

York ss Kittery Jan⁊ 12th 1701.

The above named Jacob Smith and Priscilla his wife personally Appearing before me the Subscribr, one of his Mats Justices of ye Peace wthin the County of York Acknowledged this Instrumt to be his Act and Deed/

Jos: Hamond

A true Copie of the originall Transcribed and compared Jan⁊ 12th 1701 p Jos: Hamond Registr

To all Chistian People whome these presents may concern, that Thomas Moore and Hannah Moore his wife of York in ye County of York in ye Province of Maine in New England sendeth Greeting Know Yee that ye sd Thomas Moore and Hannah Moore for and in consideration of a certain sum of money to them in hand paid or otherwise at ye Sealing of this Instrumt satisfactory secured by John Morrell of Kittery in ye Province of Maine in ye County of York Plaisterrer sould Alienated Enfeoffyd and confirmed and doe by these prsents give and grant bargaine sell Alienated Enfeoffyd confirm fully ffreely and absolutely make over unto ye sd John Morrell a certain parcell of Land Lying near Mr Hulls Creek and soe forty rods or pole by the wood side southwest, westerly, and soe into ye upland Northwest till the sd forty Acres be Accomplished, with all ye rites and benefits Imolumts and Advantages on Appurtaining unto or any wise at any time redounding from ye same or any part or parcell thereof To have and to hold and quietly and peaceably to ocupie Possess and enjoy the sd Lands and Appurtenances as a sure Estate to him the said John Morrell his heires Execrs Admrn & assignes for ever Moreover the sd Thomas Moore and Hannah Moore for themselves their heires Executrn Adminrn to and with ye sd John Morrell his heires Execrs

*Moore
to
Morrell*

Admin[rs] and assignes doe Indent Cov[tt] Engage and promise the Premisses with all their Priviledges and Appurtenances from all former grants gifts sales, Rents rates Dowryes Demands and Incumbrances to be had or comenced by them their heires Exec[trs] or assignes or any person or persons whatsoever upon grounds preceeding y[e] Date of this Instrum[t] for ever to Warrantise and Defend by these p[r]sents In witness whereof the s[d] Thomas Moore and Hannah Moore his wife have hereunto set their hands and seales this twenty eighth day of Novemb[r] One thousand Seven hundred and one And in the thirteenth year of the Reign of our Soveraign Lord King William the third of Great Brittain &c.

Signed Sealed and Delivered   Thomas Moore (his seal)
  In the p[r]sents of us.   Hannah Moore (her seal)
Alie Donnell
Nath ffreeman

Thomas More and his wife Hannah Moore came this 28[th] day of Novemb[r] 1701 And acknowledged this Deed Sale to be their Act and Deed.

Before me/   Samuel Donnell Justis Peace

A true Copie of the originall Transcribed and compared Jan[ry] 2[d] 1701.   p Jos: Hamond Regist[r]

[120] York ss/ William the third by the grace of God of England Scotland ffrance and Ireland King Defend[r] of the ffaith &c/ — To the Sheriff of our s[d] County of York under Sheriff or Deputy Greeting/ — Whereas William Vaughan of Portsm[o] in the Province New Hampshier Esq[r] recovered Judgm[t] against the Estate of Henry Bodge of Kittery before our Justices of our Inferio[r] Court of Common Pleas holden for or w[th]in our County afores[d] on the first Tuesday of April 1701. for the sum of thirteen pounds

one shilling & 1ᵈ Debt or Damage And two pounds seven shillings & 2ᵈ costs of Suit as to us appears of Record whereof Execution remains to be done. We comand you therefore that of the goods Chattells or Lands of the sᵈ Henry Bodge Deceased, within yᵉ Precinct you cause to be paid and satisfied unto yᵉ sᵈ William Vaughan at yᵉ vallue thereof in money the aforesᵈ Sums being fifteen pounds eight Shillings & three pence in the whole with two shillings more for this writ And thereof alsoe to satisfie yʳself for yʳ own fees And hereof faile not and make return of this Writ with your doings therein unto our sᵈ Inferiour Court of Pleas to be holden at Wells upon the first Tuesday of July next Witness Joseph Hamond Esqʳ at Kittery the 19ᵗʰ day of April, 1701. In the thirteenth year of our Reign Annoq, Doñi 1701   Jos: Hamond Clerᵐ

Curtes to Vaughan

This may certifie whome it may concern that by vertue of the within Execution I made enquiry after the goods moneys and Estate of Henry Bodge within named to satisfie sᵈ Execution but could find none save two parcells of Land of sᵈ Bodges, the one eight Acres and the other twenty Acres bounded as followeth Vizᵗ sᵈ eight Acres lying on the North side of Spruce Creek, butting on the Creek at the westerly end and on the other three sides by David Hutchings, Rowland Williams & yᵉ parsonage land and is the land whereon Bodge lived in his life time, the other parcel being twenty Acres lies up in the woods, bounded by a run of water and Edmund Hamans & a twenty Acre Lot of my own as more at large doth appear by yᵉ town of Kittery Records relation thereto being had/ On these two parcels of Land I Levied the within Execution in June 1701. for satisfaction of the Judgment within mentioned & the Cost and my Charges And Appointed time and put sᵈ Lands on Sale but no person appeared to buy/ I tendered yᵉ sᵈ lands to sᵈ Vaughan for his satisfaction and my own ffees who Accepted thereof in full satisfaction of s^d Judgm^t, Cost, fees &c have accordingly delivered possession thereof unto s^d Vaughan as his proper right and Interest in ffee simple to him his heires Execut^{rs} Administrat^{rs} and assigns for ever, According to Law and no other ways. This done by me ye Subscrib^r June 1701 the whole sum̄ for ffees, Charges Judgm^t and Costs is sixteen pounds fourteen shillings and nine pence/.

Jos. Curtis Sheriff.

A true Copie of the originall Execution & ye return on the back side thereof Transcribed and compared Jan^{ry} 31st 1701/   p Jos : Ham̄ond Regist^r

---

Simpson to Partridge

Whereas Lt Roger Plaisted late of Kittery in the County of York Died Intestate and Roger Plaisted Junr Eldest son to ye s^d Lt Roger Plaisted being alsoe Deceased and leaving severall Children to whom of right and by the Laws of this Province a double share or Portion of ye s^d Lt Roger Plaisteds Estate doth belong Now Know all men by these p^{r}sents that Daniel Simpson of York in the County of York in ye Province of the Massachusets Bay in New England and ffrances his wife, (the s^d ffrances being one of ye Children of ye s^d Roger Plaisted Junr) for Divers good causes us ye s^d Daniel and ffrances thereunto moving, more Especially for and in consideration of a certain sum̄ of money to us in hand paid, and for other considerations to our full satisfaction and content, by John Partridge of Portsm^o in ye Province of New Hampshier in New England afores^d, the receipt whereof we doe hereby Acknowledge And thereof and of and from every part & parcel thereof doe for us our heires Execut^{rs} and Assignes freely Acquit Exonerate and fully discharge him ye s^d John Partridge his heires and assignes for ev^r by

BOOK VI, FOL. 120.

these p'sents have given granted bargained sold assigned made over and confirmed And by these presents doe for us our heires and assigns freely Clearly and Absolutely, give grant bargain sell Assigne make over and confirm unto him ye s^d John Partridge his heires and assignes All that our Right title part Portion Proportion Interest Claim and demand whatsoever which we ye s^d Daniel Simpson and ffrances Simpson have or ought to have of in or to ye Estate of our s^d Grandfather Lt Roger Plaisted or what shall or may at any time hereafter appear to be our right of or to s^d Estate in whose hands Custody or Possession soever it shall be found To have and to hold our s^d Right title Interest &c/ as afores^d to him ye s^d John Partridge his heires or assignes without any manner of let denial hinderance or disturbance from or by us ye said Daniel and ffrances Simpson or either of us our heires Execut^{rs} or assignes or any or either of them And we the s^d Daniel and ffrances our heires or assignes shall and will make perform and Execute such other and further Lawfull and reasonable Act or Acts, thing or things as can be devised advised or required for the better confirming and more sure making of the Premisses to him ye s^d John Partridge his heires or assignes According to y^e true Intent & meaning of these p^{r}sents In witness whereof we y^e s^d Daniel Simpson have hereunto set our hands and seales this second day of July in y^e year of our Lord One thousand seven hundred and one : 1701.

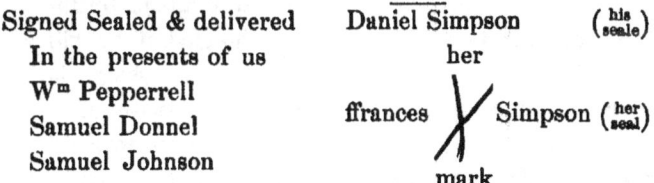

Signed Sealed & delivered   Daniel Simpson   (his seale)
  In the presents of us   her
  Wm Pepperrell
  Samuel Donnel   ffrances X Simpson (her seal)
  Samuel Johnson
                              mark

York ss/ The above named Daniel Simpson and ffrances his wife personally appearing before me ye Subscriber one of his Ma^{ts} Justices of ye Peace within the County of York

Book VI, Fol. 121.

Acknowledged this Instrum^t to be their Act and Deed this second July 1701
　　　　　　　　　　　　　　　　　　　Jos Hamond

A true Copie of ye originall Transcribed and compared from the second of July : 1701

　　　　　　　　　　p Jos : Hamond Regist^r

[121] To all Christian People whome these presents may concern John Clark of the Town of ffoxhall in the County of Suffolk within the Kingdome of England sendeth Greeting Know Yee that whereas Mr Roules an Indian Sagamore of Newechewannick sold unto Thomas Spencer of the same place And s^d Spencer to Mr Thomas Broughton Merchant a certain ffarm or parcel of Land Adjoyning to Quamphegan river and ffalls, as also half ye falls, which conveyances were authorised and confirmed by ye town of Kittery in ye year of our Lord 1651 The Land being bounded on ye Southeast side by ye brook next below the falls And by Humphrey Chadborns ffarm, on ye Northeast end by land of John Crafford The maine river and Salmonfall-brook bounding the remainder, it being ye Land comonly of late known by ye name of Docter Cooks Land at Quomphegan, on wch land, and suited to which ffalls the s^d Broughton Erected at his own Cost a Saw Mill And whereas ye s^d Broughton sold one sixth part of his s^d Land ffalls and Mill to George Cole of Dorchester in the County of Dorset in old England by Instrum^t bearing date Decemb^r 20th 1653. who gave it by will to his son John Cole, by whose death (in his nonage) it descended to his brother George Cole of ye Parish of St Andrew Holbourn in Middlesex Merchant And from s^d George to his wife ye mother of s^d Clark, And from her to s^d Clark : Therefore ye s^d John Clark now residing in New England for & in consideration of twenty pounds of Money Currant in New England to him in hand paid or to his sat-

<small>Clark to Abbott</small>

isfaction secured by Thomas Abbot, sen^r, of Barwick or Newechewanick in the County of York in ye Province of the Massachusets Bay in New England Hath given granted bargained Sold Alienated Enfeoffed confirmed And doth by these presents give grant bargain sell alienate Enfeoff confirm And ye delivery of by Turf and twig Acknowledge, to ye s^d Thomas Abbot his heires and assignes for ever The s^d Sixth part of s^d Lands and falls & Mills and Sixth part of all ye profits priviledges and Appurtenances thereof or any ways redounding therefrom or belonging thereto as timber, trees, under wood, brooks springs water Courses, or any remainder of s^d Mill as runing Geers Iron-work rubbish Dam̄ or Appurtenances thereto, stones, Mines or Mineralls or any thing whatsoever in any sort belonging to ye Premisses, To have and to hold a full and Clear sixth part of s^d ffarm and ffalls and Mill of Thomas Broughtons as above Mentioned Together with a Clear Sixth part of all Appurtenances thereto/ to ye said Thomas Abbot his heires Execut^{rs} Administrat^{rs} and Assignes from the ensealing and Delivery of these p^{r}sents for ever, to ye only proper use behoofe and benefit of the s^d Abbot his heires Execut^{rs} Adm^{rs} and Assignes as a free and Clear Estate for ever/ Moreover the s^d John Clark for himselfe his heires Execut^{rs} Administrat^{rs} to and with the s^d Thomas Abbot his heires Execut^{rs} Adm^{rs} and Assignes doth Coven^t grant promise and Engage the granted premisses against all persons whatsoever or any person whatsoever Laying Claime to the p^{r}misses or any part thereof or to any sum̄ or sum̄s of money due from ye same by vertue of any gift grant sale Dower thirds Mortgages, bill, bond Judgm^t Execution or other Legall fform or conveyance whatsoever to ye s^d Thomas Abbot his heires Execut^{rs} Adm^{rs} and assignes for ever to Warrant and Defend by these p^{r}sents/ In witness and for a full confirmation whereof the s^d John Clark hath hereunto set his hand and seale this third day of

Book VI, Fol. 121.

Septemb* In y* year of our Lord One thousand Seven hundred and one And in the thirteenth year of y* Reign of William the third King of Great Brittain &c

Signed Sealed and delivered   John Clark. (his seal)
 in the p*sents of us.
 Peter Wittum
 John Wade

York ss/ Septemb* 17th 1701

The above named John Clark personally appearing before me y* Subscrib* one of his Ma** Justices of y* Peace within y* County afores* Acknowledged this Instrum* to be his Act and deed/

             Jos : Hamond

A true Copie of y* originall Transcribed and compared from Septemb* 17th 1701   p Jos Hamond Regist*

To All Christian People to whome these p*sents shall come/ Know Ye that I Thomas Spinney, Sen*, of Kittery in the Province of Maine in New England Yeoman with the free consent of Margery my wife for many good causes and considerations us moving thereunto Especially for that naturall love and afection we bear unto our Loving Son James Spinney of the town and Province afores* Have freely given granted Enfeoffed Aliened and confirmed And doe by these p*sents for our selves and our heires for ever Absolutely and freely give grant Alienate Infeoffe and confirm unto the afores* James Spinney a certain Tract of Land Scituate and Lying in the lower part of the town of Kittery between y* great River and Spruce Crick in y* woods containing twenty Acres as it is bounded on the South with y* Land of John Morrell and on y* North with his own land

Tho: Spinney Senr and is bounded East and west with the rest of
 to   my Land And it is y* land on which his house
his son: James   standeth and a part of my town grant there

and now by me and my wife freely given as afores^d To have and to hold all ye above given Premisses with all and singular ye Appurtenances comodities and priviledges thereto belonging or in any wise Appertaining to him ye s^d James Spinney his his heires and assignes to his and their proper use and behoofe for ever For confirmation of the Premisses I the s^d Thomas Spinney Senr and Margery my wife have hereunto set our hands and seales this seven and twentieth day of Septemb^r Anno Dom one thousand six hundred eightie and nine And in the first year of the Reign of our Soveraign Lord and Lady William and Mary by ye grace of God of England ffrance and Ireland King & Queen Defenders of the ffaith &c.

Signed Sealed and delivered   Thomas Spinney   (his seal)
  In the presents of us.   Margery 𝍖 Spinney (her seale)
  John Spinney   her mark
  John Wincoll.

Province of Maine

Thomas Spinney Senr and Margery his wife did Acknowledge the within written Deed of Gift to be their free Act & deed this eight and twentieth day of Septemb^r 1689.
Before me   John Wincoll Jus^{ce} of Peace

A true Copie of ye originall Deed with ye Acknowledgm^t on ye back side thereof transcribed and compared ye twenty second day of Septemb^r 1701.

                        p Jos: Hamond Regist^r

Know all men by these p^rsents that I Thomas Spinney of Kittery in ye County of York in New England Cordwainer with ye consent of Christian my wife for Divers good & valluable considerations me hereunto moving but more Especially for and in consideration of the Sum of twenty pounds in mony to me in hand paid by Thomas Worsester of Portsmouth in New Hampshier Yeoman, recipt thereof I doe Acknowledge and my self well and truly contented and paid And doe by these p'sents Acquit y'e s'd Thomas Worsester for y'e same, for y'e consideration aboves'd I y'e s'd Thomas Spinney have given granted bargained and sold And doe by these p'sents give grant bargain and sell Enfeoffe and for ever confirm unto y'e s'd Thomas Worsester his his heires and assignes twenty Acres of land Lying in y'e township of Kittery in y'e County aboves'd and is Scituate and lying between y'e great Cove and Spruce Creek and is bounded on y'e west with the land of my father Thomas Spinney and on y'e North with y'e land of John Spinney and on y'e south with y'e land of Joshua Remich and on the East with my own Land And is that tract of land that was given me by my father Thomas Spinney as by a Deed under his hand doth more at large Appear together with all y'e woods under woods Timber and trees standing or lying thereon w'th all the Appurtenances and priviledges thereunto belonging or in any wise Appertaining to y'e same To have and to hold all and singular y'e above bargained Premisses and every part thereof unto y'e only and sole use benefit and behoofe of him y'e said Thomas [122] Worsester his heires and assignes for evermore/ I y'e said Thomas Spinney doe covenant for my self my heires Execut'rs and Administrat'rs with y'e s'd Thomas Worsester his heires and assignes that y'e p'rmisses are free from all Incumbrances whatsoever as Joyntures Dowries gifts Sales Mortgages or quit rents And that at the time of y'e ensealing hereof I am y'e true and proper owner of the same And have within my self full power and Lawfull Authoritie to dispose of the same And that it Shall and may be Lawfull for the s'd Thomas Worsester at all times hereafter to take use ocupie and possess y'e same, without the let or hinderance of me y'e s'd Thomas Spinney or any other person under me the peaceable and quiet possession thereof to warrant

Spinney to Worsester

and maintain against all persons whatsoever Laying Lawfull Claim thereunto: In witness hereof I have hereunto set my hand and Seale this twenty fift day of Decemb{r} One thousand Seven hundred; 1700
Signed Sealed and delivered
  in p{r}sents of   The Sign of (and a seale)
  William Wooster   Thomas Spinney
  John Spinney
  James Stoodleygh

York ss/ Kittery Septemb{r} 22{d} 1701

The above named Thomas Spinney personally Appearing before me y{e} subscrib{r} one of his Ma{ts} Justices of Peace in y{e} County of York Acknowledged this Instrum{t} to be his act and Deed/   Jos. Hamond

A true Copie of the originall Transcribed and Compared from Septemb{r} the 22{d} 1701.

           p Jos. Hamond Regist{r}

Know all men by these presents that I Christian Spinney doe freely surrender all my right of Dowery to y{e} within mentioned Land in this Instrum{t} Witness my hand this 25{th} of Decemb{r} 1701.

           The Signe of
           Christian Spinney

A true Copie of the Originall Surrender being on the back side of y{e} Deed of which y{e} above is a copie. Transcribed and compared from Septemb{r} 22{d} 1701

           p Jos. Hamond Regist{r}

To All Christian People to whome this present Deed shall come and concern Know Ye that I Humphrey Spencer now Resident at Nichewanak in the Province of Maine/

Son and heir to Humphrey Spencer Deceased, the son of Thomas Spencer of the same place Deceased also/ for Divers good and Lawfull Causes and considerations me hereunto moving, but more in speciall for the consideration of forty pounds currant money to me in hand paid by Thomas Gooding of y\ :sup:`e` same place aboves\ :sup:`d` the receipt whereof I doe hereby Acknowledge and my selfe fully Satisfied contented and paid and thereof of every part parcell and penny thereof doe by this p\ :sup:`r`\ sent Deed of sale for ever acquit Exonerate and discharge him y\ :sup:`e` s\ :sup:`d` Gooding his heires Exec\ :sup:`rs` Administrat\ :sup:`rs` and assignes freely fully and absolutely: Have given granted bargained Sold Enfeoffed released Delivered and confirmed And by this Deed of Sale doe freely firmly and absolutely, grant bargain Sell Alien Enfeoffe release deliver and confirm unto him y\ :sup:`e` s\ :sup:`d` Thomas Gooding his heires Execut\ :sup:`rs` Adm\ :sup:`rs` and assignes for ever to say a certain tract or parcel of Land lying and being at s\ :sup:`d` Nichewanick afores\ :sup:`d` be Estimation about thirty Acres more or less according to y\ :sup:`e` bounds hereinafter exprest, which s\ :sup:`d` land is part of a tract of Land formerly granted unto my Honoured Grand father Thomas Spencer above mentioned And by him given unto my afores\ :sup:`d` Dec\ :sup:`d` father Humphrey Spencer and to his heir which I am: s\ :sup:`d` tract of Land was granted as afores\ :sup:`d` by y\ :sup:`e` town of Kittery, the now sold part thereof is bounded as followeth begining at a piece of Land given by my Dec\ :sup:`d` Grandfather Thomas Spencer unto Daniel Gooding being part of y\ :sup:`e` afores\ :sup:`d` grant butting on s\ :sup:`d` Goodings Land along to a parcell of Marsh called and known by the name of Parkers Marsh and Joynes to y\ :sup:`e` brook or run of water that runs out of s\ :sup:`d` Marsh and so round by y\ :sup:`e` land formerly in y\ :sup:`e` possession of M\ :sup:`r` Richard Leader now in the possession of M\ :sup:`r` John Plaisted and Cap\ :sup:`tn` Hill and partly bounded by y\ :sup:`e` remaining part of my own Lands: so all round to y\ :sup:`e` place where it first begun with all the profits priviledges and

Marginal note: Spencer to Goodwin

Book VI, Fol. 122.

Advantages with all the Timber, trees, woods and under woods standing, growing, lying and being on s^d Land or any part thereof with all passages ways paths and conveniences to and from the s^d Land and all priviledges thereto belonging or in any wise Appertaining To have and to hold all and every part of ye s^d Land timber trees woods & under woods standing growing lying and being on s^d land and every part thereof with all the privileges and Advantages passages paths way & ways to and from s^d Land unto him ye s^d Gooding his heires Execut^{rs} Admin^{rs} and assignes for ever without the let trouble Interuption Molestation or hinderance of me the s^d Humphrey Spencer my heires Execut^{rs} or Admin^{rs} or any person or persons whatsoever that shall lay any Lawfull Claime unto all or any part of ye s^d bargained Land and Premisses and that for ever And that I the s^d Humphrey Spencer am at ye ensealing and delivery hereof the true and Lawfull owner of ye s^d bargained Land and have full power in my self & good and Lawfull right the same to dispose of as a sure right of Inheritance and will warrant Defend and make good ye title of s^d Land unto him ye s^d Gooding his heires Execut^{rs} Admin^{rs} and assignes for ever in ffee simple And that I and my heires Execut^{rs} and Administrat^{rs} will Save and keep harmless him the s^d Gooding his heires Execut^{rs} Adm^{rs} and assignes for ever from all and all manner of former and other bargains gifts sales Mortgages grants Judgments Executions right of Dowries and all other Incumbrances whatsoever heretofore made comitted suffered or done or that may or shall hereafter be made comitted suffered or done by me my heires Execut^{rs} Administrat^{rs} or an person or person whatsoever And that is and shall be Lawfull for the s^d Gooding his heires Execut^{rs} Admin^{rs} or assignes to enter into ye s^d bargained Lands timber and priviledges the same to have hold and peaceably enjoy as his and their own proper right and Interest in ffee simple from the day of the Date hereof and for ever with yᵉ Appurtenances thereof (Excepting only as above Excepted) unto yᵉ sᵈ Samˡˡ Checkley his heires & Assignes for ever against yᵉ Lawfull claimes and demands of all people whomsoever from by or under the sᵈ Joshua Scottow his heires or assignes And for yᵉ better Execution of these pʳsents the sᵈ Joshua Scottow hath and hereby doth constitute Authorise and Appoint and in his stead and place John Wheelwright of Wells in yᵉ Province of Maine aforesᵈ to be his true sufficient and Lawfull Atturney for him and in his name and stead to enter into and upon the sᵈ granted premisses or any part thereof Generally or in yᵉ name of the whole And Possession and Seizen in his name and stead Generally or in the name of the [132] whole to have and to take and after yᵉ same possession and seizin soe taken, Livery of Seizen and possession thereof for him and in his name and stead Generally or in the name of the whole to give or deliver to yᵉ sᵈ Samuel Checkley his heires or Assignes or certain Attorney in that behalf according to the true meaning hereof Ratifying allowing and confirming all and whatsoever my sᵈ Atturney shall Lawfully doe or cause to be done in and about the Premisses by vertue of these pʳsents, In witness whereof the sᵈ Joshua Scottow and Lidiah his wife, in Testimony of the relinquishment of her right of Dower and power of thirds in yᵉ Premisses, have hereunto set their hands and Seales the day & year first above written

Signed Sealed and Delivered   Josh : Scottow (his seal)
   in pʳsents of us   Liday Scottow (her seal)
John Ballentine
Thomas Cushing
Eliezer Moody Scr :

July 30ᵗʰ 1692. Capᵗⁿ Joshua Scottow and Lidia his wife personally Appearing before us, of their Maᵗˢ Council and Justices of the Peace for the Province of the Massa-

Book VI, Fol. 132.

chusets Bay in New England And Acknowledged this Instrument to be their voluntary Act and Deed.

Sam. Sewall
John Walley

A true Copie of the originall, Transcribed and compared April 13th 1702.   p Jos Hamond Regist^r

This Indenture made ye twenty third day of October Anno Domⁱ one thousand six hundred ninety and four Annoq, R R^s et Reginæ Gulielmi et Mariæ Anliæ &c. between Thomas Scottow of Boston in the County of Suffolke within their Ma^{ts} Province of of the Massachusets Bay in New England Marrin^r of ye one part And Sam^{ll} Checkley of Boston afores^d Merchant on the other part Witnesseth That ye s^d Thomas Scottow ffor and in consideration of ye sum of forty pounds Curr^t money of New England to him in hand well and truly paid before thensealing and delivery of these presents by ye s^d Samuel Checkley the receipt whereof to full content and satisfaction he doth hereby Acknowledge and thereof and of every part thereof doth Acquit Exonerate and Discharge ye s^d Sam^{ll} Checkley his heires Execut^{rs} Administrat^{rs} and Assignes and each and every of them by these p^rsents Hath given granted bargained sold Aliened Enfeoffed released conveyed and confirmed And by these p^rsents Doth fully freely clerely and Absolutely give grant bargain sell Alien enfeoffe release convey & confirm unto ye s^d Sam^{ll} Checkley his heir es and Assignes for ever One that his Farm containing one hundred and forty Acres of Land be the same more or less, scituate lying and being in the township of Scarborough in the Province of Main in New England afores^d That is to say one hundred Acres thereof being upland lies near to a brook comonly called or known by the name of

*Tho Scottow
to
Checkley*

Moores brook And soe to run Easterly along by y⁰ plantation formerly in y⁰ possession of Nathan Bedford since called Hubbards house the other remaining forty Acres thereof being Meadow and lies on a River comonly called or known by the name of Pigscutt River in the afores⁴ Township bounded with y⁰ Meadow of Andrew Brown Senʳ Westerly. And the Meadow of William Burrage near the mouth of sᵈ River formerly in the possession of George Taylor Northerly. Together with y⁰ afores⁴ house and all timber trees woods and under woods standing on y⁰ pʳmisses, ways Easments waters water Courses fishings fowlings profits priviledges rights comodities heredittaments Emolumᵗˢ and Appurᶜᵉˢ whatsoever to y⁰ sᵈ granted pʳmisses or to any part thereof belonging or in any wise Appertaining or therewith now used ocupied or enjoyed Accepted reputed taken or known as part parcel or member thereof And alsoe all y⁰ estate right title Interest use possession reverc͠on remaindʳ inheritance Claim property and demand whatsoever of him the sᵈ Thomas Scottow and his heires of in and to y⁰ same and every part thereof with all Deeds writings and evidences relating to or concerning y⁰ sᵈ granted pʳmisses To have and to hold all the before menc͠oned granted pʳmisses with their & every of their Appurtenances and every part thereof unto the sᵈ Samˡ Checkley his heires and assignes for ever to his and their own Sole and proper use benefit and behoofe from henceforth and for evermore Provided always and it is nevertheless conditioned concluded and agreed upon by and between the sᵈ parties to these pʳsence any thing within written to y⁰ contrary thereof in any wise notwithstanding That if y⁰ within Named Thomas Scottow his heires Executʳˢ Admʳˢ or assignes shall and doe well and truly pay or cause to be paid unto y⁰ above named Samˡˡ Checkley or to his heires Executʳˢ Admʳˢ certain Attorney or assignes in Boston afores⁴ y⁰ full and Just Summe of forty pounds currant money of New England at any time or times within or

Book VI, Fol. 132.

by yᵉ Expiration of three yeares from & next ensuing the day of yᵉ Date of these pʳsence without fraud coven or further delay That then this pʳsent Indenture Sale and grant and every Clause and Article thereof to Cease determine be Null voyd and of none Effect or else to abide and remaine in full force strength and vert with full Effect in Law And the sᵈ Thomas Scottow for himself his heires Executʳˢ and Admʳˢ and every of them doth hereby Covenant promise grant and agree to and with yᵉ sᵈ Samˡˡ Checkley his heires and Assignes in manner following, That is to say, that at yᵉ time of this pʳsent grant bargain and sale and unto then-sealing and Executing of these pʳsents he yᵉ sᵈ Thomas Scottow is the true sole and Lawfull owner of the afore bargained pʳmisses And stands Lawfully Seized thereof in his own proper right of a good sure and Indefeasible Estate of Inheritance in Fee Simple without any manner of condiĉon reverĉon or Limitation of Use or Uses whatsoever soe as to alter change defeat or make voyd yᵉ same And hath in himself full power good right & Lawfull authority to grant sell convey and confirm yᵉ same unto the sᵈ Samˡˡ Checkley his heires and Assignes in manner and form aforesaid And that from and after default made on yᵉ foremenĉoned payments the said Samˡˡ Checkley his heires and Assignes shall and may by force and vertue of these presence Lawfully peaceably and quietly enter into and upon, have hold use ocupie possess and enjoy the above granted pʳmisses with thappurtenances thereof Free and clear and clearly Acquitted exonerated and Discharged of and from all and all manner of former and other gifts grants bargains Sales Leases releases Mortgages Joyntures Dowers Judgmᵗˢ Executions entailes fines forfitures Seisures And of and from all other titles troubles Charges & incumbrances whatsoever And further doth hereby covenᵗ promise grant and agree bind & Oblige himſ his heires Execut ͬˢ and Adm ͬˢ from henceforth and for ever hereafter to warrant and Defend all yᵉ within granted and bargained p'misses with thappurtenances and every part thereof unto y̓e s̓d Sam̓ll Checkley his heires & assignes against y̓e Lawfull Claims and Demands of all & every person & psons whomsoever & whatsoever In Witness whereof y̓e s̓d Thomas Scottow hath hereunto set his hand and Seale y̓e day & year first above written

Signed Sealed and delivered   Thomas Scottow (his seal)
  in p'sents of us   and seal
  Tho: Cushing.
  Joseph Billing

The above named Thomas Scottow personally appearing before me y̓e Subscrib̓r one of y̓e Council of their Ma̓ts Province of y̓e Massachusets Bay & Justice of y̓e peace within y̓e same Acknowledged y̓e above written Instrum̓t to be his Act and Deed/   Is̓a Addington
Boston Octob̓r 29th 1694

A true Copie of y̓e originall Transcribe & compared. Ap̓ll 13th 1702:   p Jos: Hamond Register

[133] To all Christian People to whome these presents shall come. Peter Staple of Kittery in the County of York in the Province of the Massachusets Bay in New England and Elizabeth his wife send greeting/ Know Yee, that we y̓e s̓d Peter Staple and Elizabeth Staple for divers good causes us thereunto moving, more Especially for the love and Parentall affection which we bear unto our beloved son John Staple of y̓e same Town County and Province Have given granted Aliened and confirmed And by these p'sence doe for us our heires Exec̓rs Administrat̓rs and Assignes freely clearly and absolutely give grant Alien convey and confirm unto him y̓e s̓d John Staple his heires Execut̓rs Adm̓rs & assigns for ever one certain piece or parcel of Land

BOOK VI, FOL. 133.

containing thirty Acres Scituate Lying and being in the township of Kittery in y[e] County and Province afores[d], bounded on the Northwest with Josha Remichs Land, on y[e] Northeast y[e] Land formerly James Spinneys And with William Tetherlys land on the same side and on the Southeast with Sam[ll] Spinneys and William Rackliffs Land, or how ever else bounded or reputed to be bounded To have and to hold all y[e] aforementioned land with all and Singular the priviledges and Appurtenances thereunto belonging or in any wise Appertaining unto him y[e] s[d] John Staple his heires

Peter Staple to his son John Staple & assignes for ever, free and clear Acquitted and discharged of and from all former and other gifts grants bargains Sales Mortgages Alienations and incumbrances whatsoever And that he y[e] s[d] John Staple his heires or assignes shall and may from time to time and at all times for ever hereafter have hold use ocupie possess and enjoy y[e] above given and granted premisses with their Appurtenances without any Molestation let deniall or hinderance of or by us y[e] s[d] Peter and Elizabeth Staple our heires or assignes and that y[e] Sale thereof against our selves our heires Execut[rs] Adm[rs] and assignes & against all other persons whatsoever Lawfully Claiming the same or any part thereof we will for ever Save harmless warrant and Defend by these p[r]sence. In witness whereof, we the said Peter Staple and Elizabeth Staple have hereunto set our hands and Seales the fifteenth day of April in the fourteenth year of y[e] Reign of our Soveraign Lord William the third by the grace of God of England Scotland ffrance & Ireland King Defend[r] of the ffaith &c Annoq Domi on thousand seven hundred and two : 1702./

the words, containing thirty Acres between y[e] 5 and 6 lines And the word thereof between y[e] 14 & 15 lines were enterlined before the ensealing and Delivery of these presents.

Signed Sealed and delivered   Peter Staple. (his Seal)
   In the p'sence of us.   Elizabeth Staple (her seal)
       her
Hannah O Key
     mark
Jos : Hamond.

York ss/ Kittery April 15th 1702.

The above named Peter Staple and Elizabeth his wife personally Appearing before me the Subscrib^r one of his Maties Justices of the Peace within the County of York Acknowledged this Instrument to be their Act and Deed.

                                       Jos. Hamond

A true Copie of the originall Transcribed & Compared :
April 15th 1702   p Jos : Hamond Regist^r

A Mutuall agreement made between Josep Hill and Peter Staple Junr both of Kittery in ye County of York in the Province of the Massachusets Bay in New England relating to ye Dividing line between their Lands in the Long reach, vizt the Land formerly belonging to John Simmons now in the Possession of Joseph s^d Hill and ye Land formerly belonging to Peter Staple Senr & now in the Possession of ye s^d Peter Staple Junr As follows That is to say the s^d Hill and Staple doe mutually agree and consent that the dividing Line shall begin a Long Rock set down into the ground in the middle of a Gully at ye Lower end of ye Lane next ye River Piscatqua and from that Rock to run Northeast and by east (Nearest) unto a Rock set down into the ground in the middle of ye Lane between s^d Staples now dwelling house and the Meeting house And from thence to run back upon ye same point to an other rock set down into the ground upon the hill in the Lane between s^d Staples Land and s^d Hill land which he bought of Samuel Miller And so backward upon ye same point so far as their Lands Joyn/ And this to be a finall Issue of all Differences between them referring to s^d Lands And to continue and remain as a perpetuall bounds between the s^d Hill and Staple, of the above mentioned Lands to them their heirs and Assignes for ever. In witness & confirmation whereof the s^d Joseph Hill and Peter Staple have hereunto set their hands and Seales the second day of May in y^e fourteenth year of the Reign of our Soveraign Ld William the third Anno_q Domi. 1702.

Jos: Hill & Peter Staple

Signed Sealed and delivered   Joseph Hill (his seal)
  In the presence of us.   Peter Staple (his seal)

      her
Hannah 🜊 Key
     mark
Jos: Hamond

York ss/ Kittery May 2^d 1702

The above named Joseph Hill and Peter Staple personally Appearing before me the Subscrib^r one of his Ma^{ts} Justices of the Peace within ye County of York Acknowledged this Instrum^t to be their Act and Deed/

                                Jos. Hamond

A true Copie of the originall Transcribed and compared this 2^d day of May 1702.   p Jos Hamond Regist^r

---

This receit made ye 24th day of Octob^r/ Received of Charlles Nelsone 18 eighteen kentells of Refuse fish and five kentells of Merchantable fish and five barrells of Mackrell/ I say received by me

Gilbert Lug to Charles Nelson

                                Geelbut Lugh

BOOK VI, FOL. 134.

A true Copie of the originall Transcribed and compared May 2ᵈ 1702.   p Jos: Hamond Regʳ

Recᵈ of Charles Nelson twenty and one pound which is in full satisfaction for the part of Gilbert Luggs house and Land which he had with Waymouth Lissen/ I say Receᵈ
            p me Gilbert Luggs his ⁀◯ mark
Witness/ Peter Twisden

A true Copie of the originall Transcribed and compared May 2ᵈ: 1702   p Jos: Hamond Registʳ

[134] Know all men by these pʳsence that I Thomas Spinney of Kittery in the County of York Cordwainer for and in consideration of twenty pounds in money to me in hand paid by James ffernald of the same place Yeoman, the receipt thereof I doe Acknowledge and my self therewith contented and paid and Acquit him for the same Have given granted bargained and sold And doe by these pʳsence give grant bargain and sell unto the said James ffernald his heires or Assignes for ever a certain tract of Land containing Eleven Acres and a half lying in the township of Kittery in the County abovesᵈ And is part of my Land Joyning to my dwelling house and takes its begining at a little Ash tree that is a marked tree between my Cousin John ffernalds Land and mine And from that marked tree Northwest be North twelve pole to a stake and heap of stones and from thence west south west Seventy three pole to Thomas Wosters line And thence by Thomas Worcesters line to Jacob Remichs land thirty eight pole, And thence by Jacob Remichs line East Northeast thirty two pole to John ffernalds land And by John Fernald line North, Northwest sixteen odle to my own land And thence East to yᵉ aforesᵈ Ash tree

· Book VI, Fol. 134.

Tho: Spiney
to
James ffernald

our first Station To have and to hold all the above^d tract of land as it is bounded and described to ye only and sole use benefit & behoof of him ye s^d James ffernald his heires Execut^{rs} Adm^{rs} or Assignes for evermore/ And furthermore I the s^d Thomas Spinney doe for my Self and my heires Covenant to and with ye s^d James ffernald & his heirs that the Premisses are free from all Incumbrances whatsoever And that I am ye true and proper owner thereof at and before ye ensealing hereof And that it shall and may be Lawfull for the s^d James ffernald and his heires or Assignes for ever to take use ocupie and possess the Premisses with the Appurtenances and all the priviledges there unto belonging for evermore, from me the s^d Thomas Spinney and my heires for ever, the peaceable and quiet possession thereof to Warrant and for ever Defend against all persons Laying a Lawfull Claime thereunto Witness my hand and Seal this tenth day April one thousand seven hundred and two. 1702.

Signed Sealed and delivered Thomas Spinney (his seal)
 the sign of
 John ⟅ Shepard Senr
  the sign of
 Elizabeth ✗ Roberts
Wm Godsoe.
Apr^{ll} 10th 1702

Know all men by these presents that I Christian Spinney doe by these prsence render all my Right of Dowry in the above^d Land to James ffernald In witness whereof I have set my hand and seal.
      Christian Spinney (her seal)

York ss/ Kittery April 10th 1702.

The above named Thomas Spinney and Christian Spinney his wife personally Appearing before me ye Subscrib^r one of his Ma^{tts} Justices of the Peace within the County of York Acknowledged this Instrum^t to be their Act and Deed.

Jos. Hamond

A true Copie of the originall transcribed and Compared April 10th 1702   p Jos : Hamond Regist^r

Robt Wadleigh
to
Jno Wadleigh

To all Christian People unto whome these p^{r}sents shall come Greeting/ Now know ye that I Robert Wadleigh Senr of the town of Excester in his Majesties Province of New Hampshier in New England Yeoman ; for and in considera- tion of that Naturall affection which I bear unto my son John Wadleigh of the town of Salisbury in the County of Essex in his Ma^{tts} Province of the Massachusets Bay in New England Millwright And for divers other good and Lawfull motions me thereunto Inducing doe by these p^{r}sents firmly fully Clearly and absolutely give grant Alienate Enfeoffe confirm and make over unto ye s^d John Wadleigh All my right title and Interest unto and in the whole and every part and parcell of the Commonage or Commonages land or lands grant or grants, Indian rights or Indian Purchas priviledge or priviledges whether lying in Comon or impropriate within ye Townships of Wells and Kittery or Else where in any and every township place or places within ye Precincts of the County of York or ye Province of Mayn Eastward of Piscataqua River by any way or means unto me now Lawfully Appurtaining not already by or for me Legally disposed off and conveyed unto any other person or persons before ye Date and delivery of this Instrum^t for ye s^d John Wadleigh To have and to hold ye Premisses together with all and Singular of ye Priviledges and Appurtenances there- unto belonging as well as all and every of ye profits benefits produce & comodities thence any ways Lawfully to be deduced and Derived to ye sole & proper use behoofe and benefit of ye s^d John Wadleigh his heires Execut^{rs} Administrat^{rs} or assignes as a good sure and Absolute ffee simple Estate of Inheritance for ever without any let suit hinderance Molestation or interuption from me ye s^d Robert Wadleigh Senr or any of my heires Execut^{rs} or Adm^{rs} or any other person or persons, in, by, from for or under me or them or any of them at any time hereafter And in confirmation of the Premisses I have hereunto subscribed my hand and seal this twenty eighth day of Octob^r in the thirteenth year of ye Reign of our Soveraign Lord Will iii p ye grace of God of England Scotland ffrance and Ireland King Defend^r of ye ffaith &c Annoq Domini one thous^d seven hundred and one.

Enterlined under ye Eleventh line before Signed or delivered, Indian Rights or Indian Purchases.

Signed Sealed and delivered   Robt Wadleigh (his seal)
  In ye presence of us.
  Henry Wadleigh
  Jonathan Wadleigh
  Israel Young

Province of New Hampshier/

Cap^{tn} Robert Wadleigh Acknowledged ye above Instrum^t to be his Act and Deed Octob^r 28th 1701
  Before me   Peter Coffin Justis Peace
  A true Copie of ye originall Transcribed and compared May 13th 1702   p Jos: Hamond Register

---

[**135**] To all Christian People to whom this p^rsent come Know yee that I Daniel Dill, Senr, of York in the Province of the Massachusets Bay in New England send Greeting That out of my intire love and affection that I bear to my beloved son John Dill of ye same town and Province above s^d doe freely and absolutely Give grant Alien and confirm

unto my son John Dill his heires Execut[rs] Adm[rs] or assignes all my Estate now in my Possession as houses barns land Cattle horse kind hog sheep to be for my son John Dill his heires Execut[rs] Adm[rs] or assignes proper use behoof and benefit, the one half of the Increase and produce of my aboves[d] house and Land and the produce and increase of all Indian corn and English Graine which is produced from of the aboves[d] place And also half y[e] Increase of one Cow and heifer and the half the increase of one Sow and five Sheep and one Mare of one year old & y[e] vantage all y[e] aboves[d] Premisses I doe give grant Alien and confirm unto my aboves[d] Son John Dill his heires Execut[rs] Adm[rs] and assignes for ever And also the aboves[d] Stock of cows horse kind hog sheep shall be at y[e] end of every three year Equally divided the one half of y[e] Stock and half y[e] Indian corn and English Graine which produced from of the aboves[d] place shall be for my own proper use behoof & benefit during my Naturall life and y[e] other halfe of y[e] aboves[d] increase to be for my son John Dill proper use and disposall It is further agreed with my aboves[d] Son that I will have the whole comand of my now dwelling house to be free Egress and regress without y[e] least Molestation or hinderance from my Son during my Naturall life Alsoe I doe Give grant Alien and confirm unto my above son John Dill his heires Execut[rs] or assignes after my Decease All my now dwelling house barnes Lands with all my part of the stock as aboves[d] to be for my son John Dill on benefit use and disposall as free gift to my son John Dill for ever with all y[e] priviledges and Appurtenances thereunto belonging, I doe hereby bind my self my heires Execut[rs] and Adm[rs] to make good this my free gift against all person laying any lawfull Claim from by or under me I doe by this present I also order my son John Dill to pay as portions out of my Estate after my Decease to my Son Daniel Dill on Shilling and to my Son William Dill five Shillings and my

Daniel Dill to his Son Jno

son Joseph to shillings and to my Daughter Elizabeth forty Shillings money it is further agreed that my aboves^d son shall take dilligent care of the aboves^d stock in producing for them so that they be not lost through his neglect And my s^d son shall if please God I should be visited with sickness shall take care to povide for me as a dutifull ought to doe for his parents And in Testimony hereof we have hereunto set our hand and seal this fifteenth day of May one thousand Seven hundred and one in ye 13 year of Maj^{ts} Reign.

It is to be understood that ye aboves^d Daniel Dill Senr is to have halfe ye Increase of the orchard and ye whole use of ye garden which is upon ye abovesaid place.

Signed Sealed and Delivered   of Daniel Dill (his seal)
   In presence of us.
   John Pickerin Junr the mark ▽ and seal
   Arthur Bragdon Junr Dill

           mark
         the ◯ and seal
       of John Dill   (his seal)

Daniel Dill Senr and John Dill aboves^d came this 20th day of May: 1701. And Acknowledged ye above written to be their Act and Deed before me

               Abra: Preble Justis a peace

A true Copie of ye originall Transcribed and compared
May 22^d 1702   p Jos: Hamond Regist^r

To all Christian People Know Yee that we Harlakeden Symonds and Elizabeth Symonds his wife of the Town of Ipswich, in ye County of Essex within their Ma^{ts} Province of ye Massachusets Bay in New England for and in consideration of a Valluable Sum of courrant pay to us in hand paid before ye Sealing and Delivery of these p^{r}sents by John

Emerson, Junr, of Glocester in the same County of Essex within their Ma^{ts} Province of the Massachusets Bay in New England afores^d preacher of the Gopell And of which and every part & parcell thereof we doe Acknowledge our selves fully satisfied and paid have bargained and sold And doe by these p^{r}sence bargain sell Alien set over and confirm unto ye said John Emerson his heires Execut^{rs} Adm^{rs} and assignes for ever a certain tract or parcel of Land Meadow and pasture containing six hundred Acres being part of that tract of Land which I Harlakenden Symonds afores^d bought of John Sanders John Bush and Peter Turbut, and which was confirmed to me by ffluellen ye only son of Sosowen ye Sagamore Deceased which land lies and is Scituated in a place called Coxhall in ye Province of the Massachusets Bay formerly ye Province of Mayn in New England and next the two thousand Acres which I ye s^d Harlakenden Symonds sold to Thomas Baker and Timothy Dorman of Topsfield in the County and Province above named on the Northerly Side of it/ the Length of which six hundred Acres afores^d is Six Miles and ye breadth threescore or sixty poles or rods/ To have and to hold/ quietly and peaceably to possess & enjoy All the said six hundred Acre with all and Singular ye Rights profits Priviledges and Appurtenances thereunto in any wise belonging to ye sole & proper use benefit and behooff of him ye s^d John Emerson his heires Execut^{rs} Adm^{rs} and assignes for ever without any manner of incumbrance hinderance or Molestation whatsoever And we the said Harlakenden Symonds & Elizabeth Symonds aboves^d doe covenant and promise for ourselves our heires Execut^{rs} Adm^{rs} and assignes to and with s^d Emerson his heires Excut^{rs} Adm^{rs} and assignes by these p^{r}sents that we are lawfully seized on the Premisses and have full power in our own right to bargain grant sell &c/ And that it shall and may be Lawfull to and for him ye said Emerson his heires Exec-

*Symonds
to
Emerson*

ut" Adm" and assignes to hold ocupie possess and enjoy all y° s^d six hundred Acres of Land with all rights and priviledges as afores^d free and clear, freely & clearly discharged and Acquitted of and from all other and former bargains sales gifts grants titles Joyntures Dowers titles of Dowers Mortgages Judgm^ts Executions troubles Molestations or incumbrances whatsoever, had made, done or suffered to be done by us, s^d Harlakenden Symonds or Elizabeth Symonds our heires Execut" Adm" or assignes for ever And shall and will warrant y° right and title of all and singular y° premisses to him y° said Emerson his heires Execut" Adm" and assignes for ever against all manner of person or persons laying legall Claime thereto/ In witness of all and singular y° premisses we y° s^d Harlakenden Symonds and Elizabeth Symonds have hereunto set our hands and seales this twenty sixth day of October sixteen hundred Ninety three. Annoq Regni Regis et Regine Gulielmi & Mariæ Angliæ quinto.

Signed Sealed and Delivered   Harlakenden Symonds (his seal)
  In the presence of us.   Elizabeth Symonds   (her seal)
Nathaniel Burnum
William Woster.
Susannah Brown
    her ✚ mark

At a Generall Sessions of y° Peace holden at Ipswich March 25 : 1701 Nathaniel Burnum made oath that he was p^rsent & saw Mr Harlakenden Symonds sign seal & deliver this Instrum^t as his act & deed and he himself together wth William Woster & Susannah Brown, then Signed as Witnesses thereunto/ Sworn Attests

                        Steph : Sewall Cle

At an Inferi^r Court of Pleas holden at Newbury Septemb^r y° 30th 1701. Susannah Brown one of the Evidences to this Deed made oath that she was p^rsent & did see Harlakenden

Book VI, Fol. 136.

Symonds and Elizabeth his wife sign seal and deliver this Instrum^t & that Nathaniel Brown and William Woster with her signed as witnesses Attests

Seph : Sewall Cler

A true Copie of the originall Transcribed and Compared : May : 25th 1702   p Jos : Hamond Regist^r

[136] Know all men by these p^{r}sence that I John Croad of Salem in the County of Essex in the Province of the Massachusets Bay in New England Merchant Al^s Inholder for and in consideration of the sum of twenty pounds in money to me in hand well and truly paid by Samuel Ruck of Salem in ye County and Province afores^d Shipwright the receipt whereof I doe hereby Acknowledge and my self therewith fully satisfied contented and paid Have bargained sold Aliened assigned Enfeoffed set over and confirmed And doe by these p^{r}sence bargain sell Alien assigne Enfeoff set over and confirm unto ye s^d Samuel Ruck his heires and assignes All that my ffarm at Casco bay which I bought of Nathaniel Wallis of Beverly at a place known by the name of broad cove containing three hundred and nine Acres more or less alsoe Six Acres of land more or less lying in Salem afores^d at ye entrance on upon ye Southfield, bounded on the North with land of William Stacie on ye East with land of William Curtice, on ye South with land of Benj^a Allen or ye partition fence between ye Southfield propriet^{rs} and me, on ye South partly with ye Mill pond and partly with land belonging to ye owners of the Mill, To have and to hold the s^d two parcells of land unto him ye s^d Samuel Ruck his heires & assignes for ever And that ye same and every part thereof is free and clear from all and all manner of Incumbrance or incumbrances whatsoever And that it shall and may be lawfull to and for ye s^d Sam^{ll} Ruck his heires Execut^{rs} Adm^{rs} or

Croade
to
Ruck

assignes quietly & peaceably to use ocupie possess & enjoy yᵉ same from time to time and at all times for ever hereafter and every part therof without any manner of Reclaim Challenge or Demand from me yᵉ sᵈ John Croad my heires Executⁿ or Admⁿ from henceforth and for ever hereafter And I yᵉ sᵈ John Croad for my self my heires Execⁿ and Admⁿ yᵉ bargained Premisses and every part parcel thereof shall and will warrant Acquit and Defend him yᵉ sᵈ Samˡˡ Rnck his heires Executors Admⁿ or assignes in yᵉ quiet and peaceable possession thereof and of every part thereof from time to time and at all times for ever hereafter against all & all manner of persons or person laying legall Claim thereunto from by or under me my heires Executⁿ or Admⁿ and all other persons whatsoever. In Testimony whereof I yᵉ sᵈ John Croad have hereunto set my hand and seal this 13ᵗʰ day of Novembʳ Anno Domini 1701.

Signed Sealed and Delivered   John Croade (his seal)
    In the presence of.   Deborah Croad (her seal)
    Ed : Hillard
    William Cash

Essex ss/ John Croad personally Appeared before me yᵉ Subscribʳ one of his Maᵗⁱ Justices for sᵈ County and Acknowledged yᵉ above written Instrumᵗ to be his Act and Deed And Debrah his wife alsoe appeared and Relinquished her right of Dowry to yᵉ Estate above mentioned in this Instrumᵗ/

                                   Jonathan Corwin

Salem Novembʳ the 13 : 1701.

    A true Copie of yᵉ originall Transcribed & compared May 25ᵗʰ 1702   p Jos : Hamond Registʳ

    To all Christian people to whome these presence shall come/ James Plaisted of York in the County of York in yᵉ

BOOK VI, FOL. 136.

Province of ye Massachusets Bay in New England sends Greeting, Know Yee that I James Plaisted afores^d for and in consideration of the sum of twenty pound good and Lawfull money of New England to me well and truly paid at and before ye Ensealing and Delivery hereof by my Brother Ichabod Plaisted of Kittery in ye County and Province afores^d, the receipt whereof I doe hereby Acknowledge and therewith fully satisfied contented and paid and of and from every part & parcell thereof I doe Acquit Exonerate and Discharge him ye s^d Ichabod Plaisted his heires Execut^{rs} Adm^{rs} and assignes for ever/ I ye s^d James Plaisted have given granted bargained Sold Aliened Enfeoffed and confirmed and by these presence for me my heires Execut^{rs} and Adm^{rs} doe freely clearly and Absolutely give grant bargain sell Alien enfeoffe convey and confirm unto him ye s^d Ichabod Plaisted his heires And assignes for ever one certain piece or parcell of Land wthin the Township of Kittery afores^d Lying and being Scituate at Salmonfalls, bounded by ye Salmonfalls River Westerly, by ye lands formerly William Lords Northerly by ye high way Easterly And by ye land of late Cap^{tn} George Broughton Southerly which land is known by ye name of the ffort field containing about ten Acres be ye same more or less To have and to hold ye s^d

James Plaisted to Ichabod Plaisted

piece or parcel of land wth all its priviledges and Appurtenances thereunto belonging or in any wise Appertaining, to him ye said Ichabod Plaisted his heires Execut^{rs} and assignes for ever/ without any Molestation lett Deniall or hinderance of or by me the said James Plaisted my heires or assignes And that ye sale thereof against my self heires Execut^{rs} or assignes and against all other persons whatsoever Lawfully Claiming any right title or Interest thereunto from by or under me or by my procurem^t I will for ever Save harmless warrant and Defend by these presence/ In witness whereof I ye s^d James Plaisted have hereunto set my hand and Seale this Nineteenth day of May in yᵉ fourteenth year of yᵉ Reign of our Soveraign Lᵈ William yᵉ third by yᵉ grace of God King of England &c. And in yᵉ year of our Lord one thousand seven hundred and two : 1702./

Signed Sealed and Delivered   James Plaisted (his seal)
In yᵉ presence of us.
      her
Hannah Q Key
    mark
Jos : Hamond

York ss/ Kittery May 19ᵗʰ 1702.

The above named James Plaisted personally Appearing before me yᵉ Subscribʳ one of his Maᵗⁱˢ Justices of yᵉ Peace in sᵈ County Acknowledged this Instrumᵗ to be his Act and Deed.

                              Jos : Hamond

A true Copie of yᵉ originall Transcribed and compared this : 19ᵗʰ May 1702.   p Jos : Hamond Registʳ

[137] York Decembʳ the 27ᵗʰ 1702./ By request have renewed yᵉ bounds of a certain tract or parcell of upland lying on the southwest side of York River begining by said river at yᵉ Southeast Side of sᵈ lotts next unto yᵉ land of Samuel Bragdon Junʳ At a little run of water And so by sᵈ Bragdons lot of Land Southwest to Kittery bounds to a beech tree markt on four Sides which is from sᵈ River a little above a Mile And by said bounds to a black burch by Thomas Adams land mark on four sides standing in Kittery and York bounds and from thence by sᵈ Adamsᵉ bounds Northeast to the river again to a black burch markt four sides And so by the river to yᵉ place first began which is in breadth thirty five pole, in quantity seventy two Acres requested to be bounded by Abraᵐ Parker for Mⁿ Mary

Hooke And is Accordingly done by the consent of y͏ᵉ aboves͏ᵈ Bragdon and Adams whose land Joyn on both Sides and with their Assistance/ Witness my hand

       Abra͏ᵐ Preble, one of y͏ᵉ select
              men of York

A true Copie of the originall Transcribed and compared this 1͏ˢᵗ day of June : 1702/

       p Jos : Hamond Regist͏ʳ

This Indenture made y͏ᵉ fifteenth day of Novemb͏ʳ in the year of our Lord God one thousand six hundred eighty nine, Between John Thurston of the Town of Kittery in the Province of Mayn in New England Black smith and Hannah his wife on the one part And William Pepperrell of the town and Province afores͏ᵈ Marin͏ʳ on y͏ᵉ other part Witnesseth that y͏ᵉ s͏ᵈ John Thurston & Hannah his wife for and in consideration of y͏ᵉ sum of three pounds currant money of New England to them in hand paid by y͏ᵉ s͏ᵈ William Pepperrell at & before thensealing and delivery of these p͏ʳsence y͏ᵉ receipt whereof they doe hereby Acknowledge and thereof doe Acquit and discharge y͏ᵉ s͏ᵈ William Pepperrell his heires Execut͏ʳˢ & Adm͏ʳˢ for ever by these

Thurston to Pepperrell

p͏ʳsents and for other good causes and considerations them thereunto moveing Have granted bargained sold Aliened Enfeoffed and confirmed And by these p͏ʳsence doe grant bargain sell Alien Enfeoffe & confirm unto y͏ᵉ said William Pepperrell his Heires, and assignes for ever All that Tract or parcell of Land Lying in y͏ᵉ s͏ᵈ Town of Kittery, bounded Eastwardly by the land of M͏ʳ William Pepperell afores͏ᵈ, Westwardly by y͏ᵉ land of Cap͏ᵗⁿ ffrancis Hooke or land of M͏ʳ Benjamin Woodbridge, Southwardly by Piscataqua river towards its entring into y͏ᵉ sea And Northwardly by a back crick comonly called Crockets Crick being about forty four rod in length from Piscataqua river to yᵉ aforesᵈ Crick And ten rod wide as it hath been already laid out, and lately given and confirmed to them the sᵈ John Thirston & Hannah his wife by yᵉ sᵈ Mʳ Benjamin Woodbridge as by a Deed bearing Date yᵉ eighth day of this instant Novembʳ may more at large appear together with yᵉ revercõn and revercõns of the sᵈ Tract of land and the remaindʳ and remaindʳˢ thereof, And all profits, priviledges and Advantages whatsoever to yᵉ same belonging and all yᵉ Estate right title and Interest of yᵉ said John Thurston and Hannah his wife or either of them of in or to the same And alsoe all such Deeds and writings which concern the same or any part thereof, To have and to hold yᵉ sᵈ tract or parcell of land wᵗʰ the appurteñces unto yᵉ said William Pepperrell his heires and assigns for ever to and for yᵉ only and proper use and behoof of him yᵉ said William Pepperrell his heires and assignes for ever And the said John Thurston doth for himself and yᵉ sᵈ Hannah his wife and their heires covenant promise and grant to and with yᵉ said William Pepperrell his heires and assignes that they yᵉ said John Thurston and Hannah his wife doe stand lawfully seized of yᵉ aforesᵈ parcell of land of a good perfect and absolute Inheritance in Fee Simple and that they have full power and good right to grant and convey yᵉ said land to yᵉ sᵈ William Pepperrell his heires and assignes for ever And alsoe that he yᵉ sᵈ William Pepperrell his heires and assignes shall & lawfully may from time to time and at all times hereafter peaceably and quietly possess and enjoy yᵉ sᵈ land with thappurteñces without the lawfull Lett, Suit, trouble rejection or eviction or disturbance of them yᵉ sᵈ John Thurston and Hannah his wife or either of them or their or either of their heires or of any other person or persons whatsoever And alsoe that yᵉ sᵈ hereby sold premisses with thappurteñces now are and be and soe at all times hereafter shall be remain and continue unto the said William Pepperrell and his heires freely and clearly Acquitted exonerated & discharged from all former or other gifts grants bargains Sales Dowers Judgments Executions extents And of and from all Titles troubles charges & incumbrances whatsoever had made or done by them ye said John Thurston and Hannah his wife or either of them or any other person or persons whatsoever. And alsoe that ye s^d John Thurston and Hannah his wife and their heires or either of them shall and will at any time for and dureing ye space of seven years next ensuing, at ye reasonable request and at ye Charges in ye Law of ye s^d William Pepperrell his heires or assignes, make perform & execute or cause to be made perform^d and executed all such further Lawfull and reasonable Acts and Assurances for the better assurance of ye s^d land unto the said William Pepperrell and his heires and assignes for ever as he or they shall reasonably require, all which s^d Acts shall be and enure and shall be Adjudged and taken to be and enure to the only and proper use & behoofe of ye said William Pepperrell his heires and assignes for ever and to & for none other use intent or purpose whatsoever In witness whereof the said parties to these p^{r}sence have hereunto Set their hands and Seales the day and year first above written.

   John (his seal) Thurstun   Hannah (her seal) Thurstun
Sealled and Delivered and livery and seizin given and delivered according to law in the p^{r}sence of.

   The mark W of
Nicholas Weekes
Willm Hooke
John Bray.

   A true Copie of ye originall Transcribed and compared June 18th 1702/   p Jos: Hammond Regist^r

BOOK VI, FOL. 138.

[138] To all Christian People to whome this present Deed of sale shall come & concern Know ye that I John Pickerin of Portsm^o in ye Province of New Hampshier many good causes and considerations me hereunto moving but more in speciall for the consideration of Ninety pounds currant pay and money and ten hides of upper leather to me in hand paid and secured by William Pepperrell Esqr of Kittery in the Province of Mayn ye receipt whereof I doe hereby Acknowledge and my self fully satisfied contented and paid have bargained sold enfeoffed released delivered & confirmed And doe by this present bargain sell release deliver and confirm unto him ye said Pepperrell his heires Execut^{rs} Adm^{rs} and assignes for ever to say ye one half part of a Single Saw Mill together with ye full half of ye Stream of water whereon said Mill now standeth which is in the Town of York And on that place and fall where formerly Saw Mills hath been built And is called and known by ye name of the fall Mill brook and is that very Mill in partnership between Samuel Webber, Mathew Austine (both of York) and my self togetheth with all the Iron work (to say all my part) thereto belonging as also half the priviledge for cutting Timber on ye bounds in York to say ye one half of such Liberty as belongs to my selfe for cutting timber in s^d Comons and noe other ways To have and to hold the s^d half part of s^d Saw Mill with all things thereto belonging with the half part of s^d stream of water half part of priviledge in ye Comons for cutting timber, reserving liberty to my selfe my heires Execut^{rs} & Administ^{rs} as herinafter exprest, All ye rest to be to ye whole sole use benefit & behoof of him ye s^d Pepperell his heires Execut^{rs} Adm^{rs} and Assignes from ye day of ye date hereof and for ever, reserving to my self if ocation shall require full power & Liberty to build a corn Mill or Mills on s^d Stream And that neither ye s^d Pepperell nor his his heires Execut^{rs} Adm^{rs} nor no other by his or their means

Pickerin to Pepperrell

Book VI, Fol. 138.

or procurem^t shall ever hinder or Molest ye doing ye same nor hinder ye run of ye water for those ends of grinding the townes corn And I ye s^d Pickerin doe by this p^{r}sent warrant and will for ever Defend ye title thereof unto to ye s^d Pepperrell his heires Execut^{rs} Administrat^{rs} or assignes against all persons laying lawfull Claime to any part of the above bargained and sold half part of s^d Mill Dam or Dams flume or flumes and priviledge in ye Comons as afore mentioned together with halfe of all ye Iron work thereto belonging every thing as afore mentioned to be to ye only sole use benefit and behoof of him ye s^d Pepperrell his heires Execut^{rs} &c. for ever, for confirmation hereof I have hereunto set my hand and seal this eight day of August 1702 and in ye thirteenth year of the Reign of our Soveraign L^d the King.
Signed Sealed and Delivered   John Pickerin (and a seal)
  In presence of.
  Edward Beal
  Andrew Pepperrell
    Province of
    New Hamps^r

Captn John Pickerrin came before me the Subscrib^r and Acknowledged the above Deed to be his free Act and Deed, And Mary his wife alsoe acknowledged the Surrend^r of her right of Dower in ye above bargained & sold p^{r}mises.

John Plisted Just Peace
Before Jan^{ry} 27th 170½

A true Copie of ye originall Transcribed & compared July 18th 1702   p Jos : Hamond Regist^r.

Know all men by these p^{r}sence that I John Brawn of Kittery in ye County of York in ye Province of the Massachusets Bay and Anna my wife Divers good causes us thereunto moving and more Especially for and in consideration of a Valluable sum of money already in hand received doe by these p'sence give grant bargain sell Alienate Enfeoffe and confirm unto Mr William Pepperrell of ye aboves^d town and County a certain tract or parcell of Land lying and being in ye afores^d town of Kittery containing about half an Acre be it more or less, bounded as followeth/ on ye south side upon ye high way near the aboves^d Mr Pepperrells now dwelling house And on ye other three sides Joyning to ye land of Mr William Pepperrell afores^d All which lands with all the priviledges conveniencies and Appurtenances thereunto belonging to the s^d John Brawn and Anna my wife from our selves our heires Execut^{rs} Adm^{rs} and assignes for ever doe sell Alienate and confirm unto the aboves^d Mr William Pepperrell his heires Execut^{rs} Adm^{rs} and assignes for ever, To have and to hold all the lands aboves^d with all ye priviledges and Appurtenances thereunto belonging or any ways Appurtaining And further I ye s^d John Brawn and Anna my wife doe by these p'sence warrant and Defend ye title of ye same from any person or persons whatsoever laying Claime thereunto from by or under us or by our procurement & that I have full power of my self to Alienate ye same, and that I am ye true owner of all ye land aboves^d before ye Signing and Sealing of this Instrum^t whereof we have set to our hands and Seales this twenty seventh day of October, one thousand six hundred Ninety and five.

Brawn
to
Pepperrell

Signed Sealed and delivered
In the presence of us
Joseph Curtes
Richard Endle

John X Brawn (and a seal)
his mark

Anna + Brawn (and a seal)
her mark

John Brawn and Anna Brawn his wife Appeared before me this 27th day of Octob^r 1695 and Acknowledged this above Instrum^t to be their Act and Deed/

Sam^{ll} Wheelwright Jus Peace

Book VI, Fol. 139.

A true Copie of the originall Transcribed and compared June 18th 1702   p Jos. Hamond Registr

At a Legall town Meeting held at Kittery May 24th 1699/ Granted unto Hezekiah Elwell his heires &c/ thirty Acres of Land if he can find it clear of former grants.
    Attests   Jos Hamond Cler.

These p'rsents Witness that I Hezekiah Elwell doe sign over this within written grant to Mr William Pepperrell & to his heires for ever As witness my hand and Seal this 20th day of Aprill 1700
    Witness John ffenich.   the mak of
    Andrew Pepperrell.   Hezekias A Allowell (his seal)
June 17th 1700.
    The above named Hezekiah Elwell Acknowledged ye Assignmt to be his Act and Deed/ Before me/
                       Jos: Hamond J: Peace
A true Copie of ye originall grant & Assignmt Transcribed & compared June: 18 1702/
               p Jos: Hamond Registr

[139] At a Legall Town Meeting held at Kittery May 24th 1699/ Granted unto William Roberts forty Acres of Land to him and his heires & assignes for ever if he can find it Clear of former grants/
    Attests   Jos. Hamond Cler

Know all men by these p'rsence that I William Roberts above named for a valuable sum of money to me in hand paid by William Pepperrell Esqr doe Assigne & make over

BOOK VI, FOL. 139.

unto y⁰ s^d William Pepperrell of Kittery in y⁰ County of York in y⁰ Province of the Massachusets Bay, his heirs &c, for ever, all my right title & Interest of and in y⁰ above mentioned grant of forty Acres of Land Witness my hand and Seal this Eighteenth day of June 1702.

Signed Sealed & Delivered   his
 in presence of us.   William $\cancel{W}$ Roberts (his seal)
 Joshua Downing   mark
 Jos. Hamond Junr

York ss/ Kittery June 18th 1702.

 The within named William Roberts personelly Appearing before me y⁰ Subscrib^r one of her Ma^ts Justices of the Peace in y⁰ County of York Acknowledged this Instrum^t to to be his Act & Deed   Jos : Hamond

 A true Copie of y⁰ originall Transcribed and compared.
June 28th 1702   Jos Hamond Regist^r

 At a legall Town Meeting held at Kittery May 24th 1699. Granted unto Hugh Crocket his heires or assignes for ever, thirty Acres of land if he can find it Clear of former grants/
 Attests   Jos : Hamond Cler

 Know all men by these p^rsence that I Hugh Crocket, for a valluable sum of money sell assign & set over unto William Pepperrell Esqr, of Kittery in the County of York All my Right and Interest of and in the within named grant of thirty Acres of land to him his heires &c for ever. Witness my hand and Seal the Eighteenth day of June 1702.

       Hugh $\cancel{H}$ Crocket (his seal)
June 18th 1702/

Hugh Croket Acknowledged this to be his Act and Deed before me   Jos : Hamond J Peace

 A true Copie of y⁰ originall Transcribed & compared
June : 18 : 1702   p Jos : Hamond Regist^r

Book VI, Fol. 139.

At a Legall Town Meeting held at Kittery May 24th 1699/ Granted unto Joseph Crocket Junr his heires or Assignes for ever, thirty Acres of land if he can find it clear of former grants/   Attests   Jos: Hamond Cler̃ Kittery the 27 June 1701

    Know all men by these p^{r}sence that I Joseph Crocket of Kittery do sell all my right and title of ye s^d grant within Mentioned unto William Pepperrell his heires & Assignes for ever, as Witness my hand and seal   mark of
                       Joseph   Crocket Junr (seal)

    A true Copie of ye originall Transcribed & Compared June: 18: 1702   p Jos: Hamond Reg^r

---

Cleve to Bartlet

    These p^{r}sence Witnesseth that I George Cleve of Casco in New England Gen^t Have given, granted bargained and sold And by these p^{r}sence doe give grant sell and confirm unto Nicholas Bartlet late of Cape Porpois one hundred Acres of land lying together in Casco Bay, near unto ye house of me ye s^d George Cleeve to begin at ye Southwest Side of the cornfield now Imployed for Tillage and corn by me ye s^d George Cleeve, the bounds to begin at ye small water Lake which runneth into ye cove near ye s^d corn field and is to run Northwesterly into ye woods eight score pole And from ye cove southwesterly by the water side toward ye house of Michael Mitton one hundred poles, together with so much Marsh ground as is to be Appointed to any other Tenant for every hundred Acres To have and to hold all ye s^d Lands and Marsh ground together with all the Timb^r woods underwood upon ye premisses unto him ye s^d Nicholas Bartlet his heires and assignes untill ye end and Term of Nineteen hundred years be fully ended, for and in consideracõn of ye sum̃ of five pounds to me in hand paid before ye sealing and Delivery hereof,

And for y`<sup>e</sup>` yearly rent of two shillings a year to be paid yearly and every yeare unto him the s`<sup>d</sup>` George Cleeve his heires or assignes During all y`<sup>e</sup>` s`<sup>d</sup>` Term, and two days work of one man every year for all Services and Demands. In witness whereof I the said George Cleeve have hereunto set my hand and Seal this twenty six day of Decemb`<sup>r</sup>` in y`<sup>e</sup>` year of our Lord one thousand six hund fifty and one.

Sealed Signed & delivered   George (his seal) Cleeve
  in presence of us.
  Robert Howard Not: Publ:
  Benjamin Thwing
  Hope Alline

This writing on y`<sup>e</sup>` other side was Acknowledged by M`<sup>r</sup>` George Cleeve to be his Act and Deed y`<sup>e</sup>` 8`<sup>th</sup>` day of June 1661. before   J`<sup>no</sup>` Endecott Gov`<sup>r</sup>`

Entred and Recorded in y`<sup>e</sup>` 256 Page of y`<sup>e</sup>` third book of Records of the Notary Publike of the Massachusets Collony in New England the 11`<sup>th</sup>` of June. 1661./

       p Robert Howard Not: Publ./ Coloniæ Prædict

A true Copie of y`<sup>e</sup>` originall Transcribed and Compared
July 3`<sup>d</sup>` 1702   p Jos Hamond Regest`<sup>r</sup>`

Know all men by these p`<sup>r</sup>`sence that I Nicholas Bartlot, of Salem in y`<sup>e</sup>` County of Essex fisherman, who formerly lived at Cape Porpois, for and in consideration of the Sum of fifty shillings to me in hand paid by John Higginson Jun`<sup>r</sup>` of Salem afores`<sup>d</sup>` Merch`<sup>t</sup>` and Divers other causes moving me thereunto Have given granted bargained and Sold/ And doe by these p`<sup>r</sup>`sence fully and freely, give grant bargain Sell and confirm unto y`<sup>e</sup>` said John Higginson his heires Execut`<sup>rs</sup>` Adm`<sup>rs</sup>` & assignes for and During y`<sup>e</sup>` space & Term of eighteen hundred and fiftie one years, a certain tract or parcel of land Cituate in Casco Bay in y`<sup>e</sup>` Province of Mayn, near unto ye place where Mr George Cleeves did formerly dwell Containing one hundred Acres being [**140**] bounded as followeth to begin at the Southwest side of ye cornfield improved by ye said George Cleeves in the year 1651. ye bounds to begin at the Small water Lake which runeth into ye Cove near ye said corn field and is to run Northwesterly into the woods eight score pole And from ye cove Southwesterly by ye water side side toward the house or dwelling place of Michael Mitton one hundred poles which s^d land is part of ye land whereon ye Town of   was of late built in Casco Bay together with so much Marsh ground as is to be appointed to any other for every hundred Acres or wheresoever or howsoever it be otherwise laid butted and bounded together with all my right, title Interest Estate and Claime of in & to ye same and every part thereof To have and to hold the s^d tract or parcell of land containing one hundred Acres, butted and bounded as afores^d or

Bartlet
to
Higginson

howsoever laid, butted and bounded together with a proportion of Marsh ground as is to be Appointed to every hundred Acres Unto him ye s^d John Higginson his heires Executors Adm^{rs} and assignes for and dureing Space of Eighteen hundred & fiftie one yeares yet to come together with all my Right, title, Interst, Estate, Claime priviledges and Appurtenances to ye same any ways belonging, The which s^d tract of land and Marsh ground I purchased of ye said George Cleeves as by his Deed of Sale Acknowledged and recorded bearing Date ye 26 Decemb^r 1651 will at large Appear, And the s^d Nicholas Bartlet doth for himself heires Execut^{rs} Adm^{rs} and Assignes firmly covenant and agree to and with the said John Higginson his heires Execut^{rs} Adm^{rs} and assignes that at the time of the Signing this present Instrum^t of Sale, he s^d Nich^o Bartlet is the true and Lawfull owner of ye afore recited bargained Premisses & has in himself full power and lawfull Authority to sell and assure the same And that y^e

bargained premisses are free and cleare And freely & clearly Acquitted of and from all other gifts grants bargains Sales and Incumbrances whatsoever And that he will warrant and Defend yᵉ sᵈ John Higginson his heires Execut admʳˢ and assignes in yᵉ quiet and peaceable possession & enjoyment of the same and every part thereof against all manner of persons laying Legall Claime thereunto or any part thereof as witness his hand and Seal this third day of February $\frac{1699}{1700}$. And in the eleventh year of his Maᵗˢ Reign/ The word owner being enterlined before Signing.

Signed Sealed and Delivered   mark of
  in the presence of   Nicholas /B Bartlet (and seal)
  Steph: Sewall
  Barth: Brown

Essex ss/ Nicholas Bartlett personally appeared before me yᵉ subscribʳ hereof one of his Maᵗˢ Justices of yᵉ Peace for sᵈ County and acknowledged yᵉ above written Instrumᵗ to be his Act and Deed with his hand & Seal thereunto Affixed

Salem 3ᵗʰ February: $\frac{1699}{1700}$/   Benjᵃ Brown

Nich Bartlet to Jnᵒ Higginson Esqʳ recᵈ on file Apˡˡ 19: 1700

Essex ss: The within Deed is Recorded wᵗʰ yᵉ Records of sᵈ County in Lib. 14: ffol: 16:

                       p Steph: Sewall Regʳ

A true Copie of the originall Transcribed and Compared
July 3ᵈ 1702   p Jos Hamond Registʳ

Recᵈ of John Higginson Junʳ fifty shillings in money and goods in full satisfaction for the land conveied in yᵉ within bill of Sale.   Recᵈ p me the /B mark of
  Salem 3ᵈ ffeb. $\frac{1699}{1700}$/   Nicholas Bartlet

BOOK VI, FOL. 140.

Know all men by these p^rsence that I William Cock Senr now resident in Salem in the County of Essex in their Ma^ts Province of y^e Massachusets Bay in New England formerly an Inhabitant at Saggadehock in y^e Province of Main planter, for and in consideration of the Sum of fifty four pounds to me in hand paid by John Higginson Junr of Salem Merch^t the receipt whereof I doe Acknowledge and my self therewith fully satisfied and paid/ Have granted bargained and Sold And doe by these presence grant bargain sell Aliene Enfeoffe assigne set over and confirm unto ye s^d John Higginson his heires Execut^rs Adm^rs and assignes A certain tract of land Cituate and Lying at or near ye mouth of Sagadehock River on ye west side of said River in ye Province of Maine containing by Estimation about thirteen hundred Acres of Upland Meadow and Salt Marsh be it more or less And being that tract of land which I ye s^d William Cock bought of Thomas Atkins of Sagadehock afores^d Planter and which I lived upon many years And is bounded as followeth that is to Say, begining at ye head of long cove Marsh down ye Cove Easterly to ye point and soe round up ye River Northerly till you come to a Creek runing in from ye Main River westerly all along upon ye s^d Cove and River (which s^d Creek is ye bounds between ye land of Simon Newcomb & this tract of land hereby sold unto ye s^d Higginson)

Cock to Higginson

And so up to ye head of said Creek and from thence about half a Mile into the Main land westwardly unto a great Swamp And from thence Southwardly to ye head of ye Creek which goeth down to ye head of long Cove And thence down to ye head of long cove Marsh where we began the which s^d Creek is ye bound between ye land formerly in ye possession of Robt Edwards, and this tract of land hereby sold unto ye said Higginson and one Small Island lying in ye s^d River against ye s^d land commonly called Toms Island containing about five Acres more or less together wth the liberty of range for cattle and swine for feed upon ye land of ye s^d Thomas Atkins adjoyning thereunto And all Mines Mineralls wood trees waters water courses, flats, Rights, titles priviledges profits and Appurtenances whatsoever unto the said bargained premisses are any ways belonging and all the Estate right title Interest Use propriety, Possession Claime and Demand whatsoever of me ye s^d William Cock my heires Execut^rs Adm^rs or assignes of in and to ye same/ To have and to hold ye s^d tract of land and Island be they more or less as they are hereby bounded or as they ought or have been formerly bounded together with all ye rights titles priviledges Estate and Appurtenances thereunto any ways belonging unto him the said John Higginson his heires Execut^rs Adm^rs and assignes to his and their only proper use benefit and behoof for ever And I ye s^d William Cock doe by these presence covenant and promise for my Self heires Execut^rs Adm^rs and assignes to & with the s^d John Higginson his heires Execut^rs Adm^rs and assignes, that he the said William Cock is ye true and lawfull owner of all ye bargained premisses & hath full power and Lawfull authority to grant bargain Sell and assure unto the said John Higginson his heires Execut^rs Adm^rs and assignes as aforesaid all and singular ye afores^d ye afores^d Tract of land and Island with all ye rights titles priviledges and Appurtenances whatsoever And that ye said bargained premisses and every part thereof are free and clear & freely & clearly acquitted and Discharged of and from all former and other gifts grants Sales titles Dowers title of Dower Mortgages Judgm^ts Executions troubles, [141] Molestations and Incumbrances whatsoever And ye s^d William Cock doth hereby Olige himself heires Execut^rs Adm^rs and assignes to warrant and Defend the said John Higginson his heires Execut^rs Adm^rs and assignes in ye peaceable and quiet possession of all and Singuler ye bargained premisses for ever, against all manner of persons laying Legall Claime thereunto or any part

BOOK VI, FOL. 141.

thereof And Mary Cock the wife of ye s^d William Cock doth freely surrender up her right of Dowre of, in and to ye same as Witness their hands & Seales this twenty sixt day of July, one thousand Six hundred Ninety and three And in the fift year of their Ma^{ts} Reign/

Signed Sealed and delivered   William Cock (and a seal)
  In presence of us.   (a seal)
  John Robinson Senr
  John Marston Junr

William Cock Senr personally Appeared and Acknowledged this Instrum^t to be his Act and Deed this 27th July: 1693   Before me   Benj^a Brown Justs peace

William Cock to Cap^{tn} Higginson/ Rec^d ye 29th Augst 93

Essex ss/ Registed with the Records of Lands for said County at Salem. in Lib: 9th folio. 142/

                                      p Steph. Sewall Reg^r

A true Copie of the originall Transcribed & compared July 3^d 1702   p Jos Hamond Reg^r

The Testimony of John Cock aged about thirty four yeares, and Thomas Cock aged about thirty one years/ Testifieth and Saith, that they having been long inhabitants at Sagadehock in the Province of Maine doe certainly know that William Cock now of Salem did formerly live upon a certain Tract of land at Sagadehock in the Province of Maine for many yeares before ye Indian warr, which drove him off from it about ye year 1677/ in his own right, which land he bought of one Thomas Adkins who lived there as by ye Deed from said Adkins to ye s^d Cock (wch we have often seen may Appear) And in or about ye year 1686 our father John Cock, with us and ye rest of his family went and lived upon ye s^d William Cocks land afores^d in s^d William Cocks right

John Cocks Testimony

Book VI, Fol. 141.

untill ye Indian warr broke out again about ye year 1689. And we doe Testifie that ye bounds of the s^d tract of land was always accompted to be from ye head of long cove Marsh down to ye point being about a Mile And from thence up ye River to a Creek which is ye bound betwixt ye land of Simon Newcomb and this land of Wm Cocks which he has now sold unto John Higginson Junr of Salem And from ye mouth of s^d Creek up into ye woods we know not whither/ And that ye s^d Will Cock and our father in s^d Will Cock his right hath peaceably and quietly enjoyed ye afore mentioned parcell of land without any Claime from any person till diven of by the Indians/ John Cock and Thomas Cock both personally appeared before me the subscrib^r one of his Ma^{ts} Council & Justice of ye peace and Coram in ye County of Essex & made oath to ye truth of ye above written Evidence; ye words Wm Cock being twice enterlined at Salem: 14th Augst 1695/   Wm Browne

    A true Copie of ye originall Transcribed & compared July 3^d 1702/   p Jos: Hamond Reg^r

    John and Thomas Cocks Evidence relating to land at Sagadahock/

    Essex ss/ Augst 17th 95/ The within written Evidences are recorded with the Records of said County in Lib: 11th Folio 7mo   p Steph: Sewall Reg^r

    A true Copie of the originall Transcribed & compared: July 3^d 1702   p Jos: Hamond Reg^r

    Laurence Denis of Beverly of full age/ Testifieth and Saith that he formerly lived at Kenbeck river in New town and upon his certain knowledge Saith that William Cock now of Salem formerly lived upon a certain tract of Land at Sagadehock at ye mouth of Kenebeck river in ye Province of Maine for many years before ye Indian Warr, which drove him off from it about y* year : 1677. in his own right which s^d land said Cock bought of one Thomas Adkins who formerly lived in these parts, And that about y* year 1686. John Cock, brother in law to y* said William Cock with his family went and lived upon the s^d William Cocks land at Sagadehock untill y* Indian Warr broke out again about y* year 1689. And that y* said tract of land runeth up the river Joyning upon the land of Simon Newcome/

Laurence Denis his Testimony

Laurence Denis

Sworn Salem July y* 4th 1699./
Before

Essex ss Nov^r/ 3^d 99

John Hathorn Jus^t pe
Benj^a Browne Quorum

The within Evidence is registred wth y* records of s^d County in Lib : 13. folio : 177 : Exam̃ :

p Steph Sewall : Reg^r

A true Copie of the originall Transcribed & compared July 3^d 1702.   p Jos : Ham̃ond Reg^r

To all Christian people to whome these p^rsence shall come Know ye that ffrancis Littlefield Senr of Wells Yeoman in y* Province of Maine and in the County of York in New England in America sendeth Greeting, Know ye that I y* s^d ffrancis Littlefield Senr out of that Naturall Love & affection that I bear to my son James Littlefield of Wells as aboves^d And for divers and Sundry other considerations me thereunto moveing Have given, granted bargained and sold And doe by these p^rsence doe Absolutely and Clerely give, grant bargain sell Aliene assigne and set over and confirm unto my said son James Littlefield his heires Execut^{rs} Adm^{rs} and assignes All That house and land I lately bought of William ffrost lying and

ffr : Littlefield to Jas Littlefield

being in Wells, being bounded on the Westermost Side of that River called Webhannet River Joyning to s^d ffrancis Littlefield Junr Land and Mills containing in breadth thirty four poles and half from a Marked red oak tree at or near unto the bridge next unto my said Lot on the westermost side thereof and so thwart ye land unto the bounds of that Land formerly which was Edmund Littlefields late Deceased going down towards the sea southeasterly to ye fence a Small distance below the highway and soe to run back into ye woods until ye Lott of the Towns grant be fully Extended and Accomplished reserving only a high way for the Town and Country after ye Decease of my self and Rebeckah my now wife I doe further give unto my said Soñ James and to his heires Exec^{rs} and assigns as an Addition to ye Lands above given as is expressed in this bill of Sale soe much [142] Land out of this ffarm which I now live upon begining where my fence now stands above as to make it Equall for quantity of land with this s^d ffarme I now live upon and now in my possession And I give my said son James to make use of said Land for pasture or wood when he pleases but not to Aliente it in any wise untill I and my wife be dead And doe further give my s^d son James Littlefield his heires Exec^{rs} and assignes one hundred Acres of Upland upon Merryland plain bounded wth ye land of Thomas Littlefield to the North and soe extends fifty poles in breadth Southward and to carry same breadth east and west untill it be Accomplished with two Acres of Marsh Lying near Mr Sam^{ll} Wheelwrights Neck of Land Southerly And five Acres of Marsh more or less ten poles of Upland thereunto belonging lying at Merriland on each side the River/ with my Neck of Upland butting towards ye lower end of his Lott & the Salt Marsh that belongs to s^d Neck; being bounded with a fresh water creek that runs into ye Salt River/ And twenty pounds in comõn pay at or before I and my wifes Decease and all my Island soe called lying upon ye seawall with four Acres Salt Marsh Meadow butting to s^d Island with two Acres Salt Meadow Abraham Tilton bought formerly of Goodman Hamond on ye east side by a Creek/ And two hundred Acres upland and ten Acres of frash Meadow Lying at Merriland which I bought of Thomas Averil bounded with a little Pitch pine tree marked close by the Meadow side and a Maple tree in ye River at ye lower end of ffrancis Littlefield Junr Meadow and to run eighteen score pole down ye river on both sides/ Ye upland begins at ye afores^d Markt pine tree at the upper end of ye Meadow And to run Eight score poles by the Meadow westerly as bounded by ye marke trees untill it be compleated With all my right Title and Interest that I have or ought to have at the time of the Sealing of these presence in all the above s^d housing Arrable fences upland & Meadow with all woods underwoods Mines Mineralls Comonage profits priviledges and Appurtenances thereunto belonging To have and to hold all and singuler ye above granted and bargained Premisses with every part and parcel thereof with all the profits priviledges & appurtences to every part and parcel thereunto belonging With all my right title and Interest therein, unto the s^d James Littlefield my son and to his heires Exec^n Adm^n and assignes to his and their own proper use benefit and behoof for ever And I ye s^d ffrancis Littlefield doe by these presence coven^t and promise for my self my heires Execut^n Adm^n to and with the said James Littlefield my son his heires Execut^n Adm^n and assignes that at and imediately before ye ensealing of these p^{r}sence was ye true and Lawfull owner of all and Singuler ye afore bargained Premisses And that I have good right and Lawfull Authority in my own name to give grant bargain sell & convey the same as afores^d And that ye s^d James Littlefield my son his heires Exec^n and assignes shall and may by vertue and force of these presence from time to time and at all times for ever hereafter Lawfully peaceably & quietly have hold use ocupie possess and enjoy yᵉ above granted Premisses with their Appurtenances free and clear and freely and clearly Acquitted and Discharged of and from all manner of Gifts, grants bargains Sales Leases Mortgages Joyntures Dowers Judgmᵗˢ Executions forfitures troubles and encumbrances whatsoever had made done or suffered to be done by me yᵉ sᵈ ffrancis Littlefield or my heires Executʳˢ or assignes at any time or times before yᵉ sealing and delivery of these pʳsents And I yᵉ sᵈ ffrancis Littlefield my heires Executʳˢ shall and will from time to time and at all times for ever hereafter warrant and Defend yᵉ above granted Premisses with their Appurtenances and every part and every part and parcell thereof unto yᵉ sᵈ James Littlefield my son his heires Execʳˢ Admʳˢ and assignes for ever against all and every person or persons Laying Claime thereto or any part thereof by from or under me In witness whereof I have hereunto set my hand and seal the twentieth day of March one thousand six hundred eighty and two : three : Annoq̨ Regni Regis Caroli Secundi xxxi. Before Signing and Sealing hereof I give unto my Son James Littlefield his heires Executʳˢ and assignes one small Island that lyeth in the Middle of yᵉ river at yᵉ Lower end of my Marsh being called by yᵉ name of thatch Island to him and his heires for ever/ Littlefield in the third row was Interlined before Signing and Sealing and Delivery hereof/

Signed Sealed and Delivered   ffr : Littlefield (and a Seal)
  I presence of
  Rob : Lurton.
  George Pearson.
  ffrancis Littlefield Senʳ Acknowledged this above Instrumᵗ to be his Act and Deed/ this 3ᵈ day of May 1683/ before me
                    Samˡˡ Wheelwright Jusᵗˢ Peace
  A true Copie of the originall Transcribed and compared :
Sepʳ 18ᵗʰ 1702   p Jos : Hamond Regʳ

To all Christian People to whome this p^rsent Deed of Sale shall come I Thomas Moore of York in the County of York in the Province of the Massachusets Bay in New England send Greeting Know Yee that for and in consideration of the sum of Eight pounds good and Lawfull money of New England to me in hand well and truly paid at and before ye Ensealing and Delivery of these presence by Daniel Black of York in ye County afores^d and in the Province afores^d Weaver, the receipt whereof I doe hereby Acknowledge and my selfe therewith to be fully satisfied contented and paid and thereof and of & from every part and parcell thereof for me ye s^d Thomas Moore my heires Execut^rs Adm^rs and assignes doe Exonerate Acquit and Discharge him the said Daniel Black his heires Execut^rs Adm^rs and assignes for ever I ye s^d Thomas Moore have given, granted, bargained, sold, Alienated Enfeoffed and confirmed And by these presence doe for me my heires Execut^rs Administrators and assignes a certaine piece or parcell of Marsh lying and being Scituate in ye Township of York in ye Province afores^d by Estimation two Acres more or less being and lying up the s^d west branch of York river it being ye one half of the Marsh and Creek that is betwixt Elizabeth Adams and ye aboves^d More lying between ye Cove comonly called Mr Dumers cove and ye River, with all other ye priviledges and Appurtenances thereunto belonging or in any wise Appurtaining To have & to hold the s^d Marsh together with all and Singular ye rites titles priviledges Interest claimes and demands which I ye s^d Thomas Moore my heires Execut^rs or assignes now have or in time past have had, or in time to come may should or in any wise ought to have in and to ye above granted Premisses or any part thereof moreover I the said Thomas Moore doe covenant promise and grant that at and before [143] the ensealing and Delivery of these p^rsence I am ye true right and proper owner of the above granted p^rmisses and their Appurtenances, And that I have in my self good

Moore to Black

right full power and lawfull authority ye same to grant and confirm unto ye s^d Daniel Black as aboves^d and that ye same and every part thereof is free and clear Acquitted and Discharged of & from all former and other gifts grants bargaines sales leases Mortgages Dowers titles troubles and incumbrances whatsoever And that it shall and may be lawfull to and for ye s^d Daniel Black his heires Execut^{rs} Adm^{rs} and assignes the above granted Premisses and every part thereof from time to time and at all times forever hereafter to have and to hold use improve ocupie possess and enjoy Lawfully peaceably quietly without any lawfull let hinderance Molestation or disturbance Eviction or Ejection of or by me or any other persons by from or under me or my procurement And that ye sales thereof and every part thereof I will maintain against me my heires Execut^{rs} administrat^{rs} and assignes and against all other persons whatsoever Lawfully claiming or Demanding ye same or any part thereof And will farther more make perform & execute such other lawfull and resonable Act, or Acts, thing or things as in law or Equity can be devised or required for ye better confirming and more sure making over of these presence unto ye s^d Daniel Black his heires, Execut^{rs} adm^{rs} & assignes according to ye Laws of this Province In witness whereof I the s^d Thomas More, Hannah my wife have hereunto put our hands and Seales this Sixteenth day of March One thousand seven hundred one two and in the fourteenth year of the Reign of our Soverine Lord King William the third of Great Brittain &c.

The words that is betwixt Elizabeth Adams and the aboves^d More was enterlined between the 8 & 9 line as before Signed.

Signed Sealed & delivered   Thomas More (his seal)
  in the presence of us.   Hannah More (her seal)
  Samuel Addams
  Ales ffreeman
  Nath: ffreeman.

Book VI, Fol. 143.

Thomas More and Hannah his wife came and Acknowledg^d this Instrum^t to be their Act and Deed this sixteenth day of March 170¾ Before me

       Abra : Preble Justes of peace

A true Copie of the originall Transcribed and Compared.
July 6th 1702   p Jos : Hamond Reg^r

Know all men by these p^{r}sence that I Mary Webber of Charles Town in ye County. of Middlesex in the Province of Massachusets Bay in New England, late of Kenebeck in the Province of Main in New England afores^d Widdow for and in consideration of ye naturall love good will and affection I have and bear to my well beloved son Joseph Webber of Yarm^o in the County of Barnstable in the Province afores^d by these p^{r}sence as aforesaid Have given granted Aliened Enfeoffed assigned Set over conveyed and confirmed And further by these p^{r}sence doe fully freely clearly and absolutely give, grant, Alien enfeoffe assign set over convey and confirm unto him my said son Joseph Webber of the County and Province afores^d his heires and assignes for ever one full and whole seventh part of all that tract or parcel of Land and Meadow to me formerly given & confirmed by Deed of Gift by my loving brother John Parker late of s^d Kenebeck in the Province of Maine Decea^d, and that under his hand and Seale Legally Executed by which referrence thereto being had may more fully Appear, the whole of which s^d parcell of land and Meadow, as yet undivided is scituate lying and being within ye afores^d Province of Maine on ye Western Side of Kenebeck River butting and bounded as followeth Viz^t by the s^d Keneb eck River more or less four Miles more or less and soe round the point up Winnegance River And from ye s^d Winegans River over to ye Maine River, bounded by the

Mary Webber
to
Jos: Webber

land of William Baker which he formerly purchased of me
ye s^d Mary Webber together with one full seventh part of
all ye trees Timber woods brush, grass herbage under wood
brush stones waters and water Courses therein and thereon
and all uses profits priviledges and Appurtenances thereunto whatsoever belonging or in any wise Appertaining To
have and to hold the s^d full and whole seventh part of y^e
land Medow and Premisses and of every part and parcel
thereof with their Appurtenances whatsoever And one full
Seventh part of all my Estate, right, title, Interest use
property possession Claim and Demand in ye before given
and granted Premisses, unto him my s^d Soñ Joseph Webber
his heires and Assignes, to his and their own profit & sole
use benefit and behoofe for ever And I the s^d Mary Webber
for me my heires Execut^{rs} & Adm^{rs} Doe covenant promise
and grant to and with my said son Joseph Webber his heires
and assignes that at ye time of the ensealing & delivery
hereof, I am the true sole and Lawfull owner of all and
singuler ye above given granted and confirmed Premisses
with their Appu^{ces} And have in my self good right full
power and lawfull Authority to give grant convey and
Assure ye same in manner as afores^d being thereof Lawfully
and rightfully Sole Seized in a good perfect and absolute
Indefeasable Estate of Inheritance in ffee simple And that
he my s^d Son Joseph Webber his heires and assignes shall
and may from time to time and at all times for ever hereafter
Lawfully peaceably and quietly have hold Ocupie possess
and enjoy the above given granted and confirmed premisses
and every part and parcel thereof with their Appurtenances
without the let deniall ejection Interuption hinderance
Molestation or Expultion of me the s^d Mary Webber my
heires Execut^{rs} or adm^{rs} them or any of them or of any
other person or persons whatsoever Lawfully having or
Claiming any right title or Interest therein or any part or
parcel thereof by from or under me my heires execut^{rs} or

Adm⁰ by any other Lawfull ways or meanes whatsoever/ In witness whereof I the said Mary Webber have hereunto set my hand and seal, This 16th day of July, 1700 R Ris Gulielmi 3ᵗⁱⁱ Angliæ Duodecimo/. Memorand agreed by the parties hereto hereto before signing & sealing that this Deed of gifts shall not hinder yᵉ sale of the whole tract of land. Signed Sealed & delivered   Mary Webber (her seal)
  in the p'sence of us
  Samˡˡ Phipps
  Sarah Kettle her mark

Charlestown July 16th 1700/ Mary Webber personally Appeared before me the Subscribʳ one of his Maᵗˢ Justices of the Peace for yᵉ County of Middlesex in the Province of the Massachusets Bay and Acknowledged yᵉ above written to be her voluntary Act and Deed/.

                                 Samuel Hayman

A true Copie of yᵉ originall Transcribed and compared July 6th 1702.   p Jos: Hamond Regʳ

To all People to whome these p'sence shall come Joseph Webber of Yarmouth in the County of Barnstable in yᵉ Province of the Massachusets Bay in New England sendeth greeting &c Know yee, that yᵉ sᵈ Joseph Webber for and in consideration of yᵉ sum of twenty & six pound in currᵗ money of New England to him in hand at or before yᵉ en-

Webber   sealing & delivery of these p'sence by Thomas
to   Sturges of the Town and County aforesᵈ Yeo-
Sturges   man, well and truly paid the receipt whereof

he yᵉ sᵈ Joseph Webber doth hereby Acknowledge himself therewith fully satisfied and paid And thereof and of every part & parcell thereof [144] doth clearly Acquit exonerate and Discharge the sᵈ Thomas Sturges his heires Executʳˢ and Adm^{rs} and every of them by these p^{r}sence Hath given granted Aliened bargained sold enfeoffed and confirmed And by these p^{r}sence Doth fully clearly and absolutely give grant bargain sell Alien Enfeoffe and confirm unto ye said Thomas Sturges his heires and assignes for ever All his right and Interest in a certain tract or parcel of land and Meadow which he had by gift of his mother Mary Webber now of Charlestown in ye County of Middlesex in the Province afores^d Widow, which Intrest & right is one whole seventh part of all that tract of Land and Meadow as now it lies undivided which is scituaté Lying and being within ye Province of Maine on the wester side of Kenebeck river butted and bounded as followeth Viz^t by the said Kenebeck River four Miles more or less and soe round the point up Winegans river and from ye s^d Winegans river over to ye Maine river bounded by the land of William Baker which he formerly purchased of ye said Mary Webber together with one full seventh part of ye trees timber woods under woods grass herbage Rocks stones waters swamps water Courses, profits priviledges and Appurtenances whatsoever is belonging or in any wise Appertaining, together alsoe wth three parcels more of land which is scituate lying and being with ye Township of ffamouth in Casco Bay in ye Province of Maine afores^d one parcel whereof contains Sixty Acres more or less lying at ye head of long Creek-river towards ye Saw Mill, the land of John Skillins lying on ye Northwest side of it And ye afores^d Mary Webbers land on ye Southeast side of it, And one two Acre lot butting upon Queens street lying betwixt ye lott of the s^d Mary Webber on the one side & ffrancis Jeffries on ye other side And one piece more containing Six Acres more or less lying betwixt the land of Samuel York on ye one side and Richard Pierce on the other side Alsoe all his right & Intrest in one Neck of land called Parkers Neck lying in Saco within ye Province of Maine afores^d with all and singular ye rights members Jurisdictions lands Meadows feedings pastures woods underwoods swamps waters, ways Easm^{ts} profits comodities heredities and Appurtenancés whatsoever to ye s^d Premisses or to any of them is belonging or in any wise Appertaining And ye revertion & revertions, remaind^r and remaind^{rs} of all and singular ye before mentioned Premisses And also all the Estate right title Interest possession property Claim and Demand whatsoever of him ye s^d Joseph Webber, in or to ye same or in and to any part or parcel of them All Deeds writings Evidences Records, Court Rolles Escripts and Monuments whatsoever touching or concerning ye Premisses or any part or parcell of them To have & to hold all the s^d severall parcells of land above hereby granted bargained & sold and all and singular other ye p^rmisses hereby granted bargained and sold, with their & every of their rights members and Appurtenances whatsoever unto the s^d Thomas Sturges his heires and assignes, to ye only proper use benefit and behoof of the said Thomas Sturges his heires and assignes for ever And ye s^d Joseph Webber for himself his heires Execut^{rs} and Adm^{rs} Doth coven^t, promise, grant and agree to and with ye s^d Thomas Sturges his heires and assignes that at ye time of the ensealing and Delivery these p^rsence he is the true sole and Lawfull owner of all and Singular ye hereby granted and confirmed p^rmisses with their and every of their Appurtenances And that he hath in himselfe good right full power and Lawfull Authority to give grant convey and confirm the same in manner and form afores^d, he being thereof Lawfully, rightfully sole Seized in all the p^rmisses in a good perfect and Absolute Indefeasable Estate of Inheritance in ffee simple And that he ye said Thomas Sturges his heires and assignes and every of them shall or may by force and vertue of these p^rsence from time to time time and at all times for ever here after Lawfully peaceably and quietly have hold use ocupie possess and enjoy all ye above herein granted and confirmed p^rmisses and every part and parcel therof with their and every of their rights members and Appurtenances And have receive and take ye Rents Issues and profits thereof to his and their own proper use benefit and behoofe for ever without any lawfull lett, suit trouble denial Interuption Eviction or disturbance of him the s^d Joseph Webber his heires Execut^{rs} or assignes or of any other person or persons whatsoever lawfully Claiming by from or under him, them or any of them or by his or their meanes Act consent title Interest privitie or procurem^t In witness whereof he y^e s^d Joseph Webber hath hereunto set his hand and seal the eleventh day of Septemb^r Annoq̇ Dō one thousand seven hundred/

Signed Sealed and Delivered Joseph Webber ($^{his}_{seal}$)
 in the presence of.
 Lydia Thacher
 the mark ⟨mark⟩ of
 Paul Wittup.

with y^e words (in y^e Province of Main afores^d) over y^e 14 line, and y^e words Thomas Sturges his heires/ over y^e dash in y^e 32^d line, before ensealing hereof.

Barnstable ss/ at Yarmouth y^e 11th day of Septemb^r 1700. Then personally Appeared before me ye subscrib^r one of his Ma^{ts} Justices of peace for ye County afores^d Joseph Webber & acknowledged this Instrum^t to be his Act and Deed.

         John Thacher.

A true Copie of ye originall Transcribed & compared
July : 6th 1702   p Jos : Hamond Regist^r

Whereas there was granted by the select men of Kittery ye first of January 1676./ unto John and Jonathan Nason, a certain tract or parcell of Land being by Estimation about an hundred Acres, let it be more or less which s^d grant is on ye lower side of a cove known and called by the name of Mast cove in s^d Town being in breadth containing ye two next points to s^d cove and on the south side to run till it meet with Abraham Conley bounds And on ye North side above Waymouths Improved land to ye brook of water that runs into Mast cove. These p^{r}sence Witnessth that I John Nason above named have formerly, and by this presents writing doe freely firmly and absolutely for my self my heires Execut^{rs} and Adm^{rs} for ever quit all and all manner of Claim and Challenge of right to any part or parcell of the

John Nason
to
Jon^a Nason

above recited grant, unto my Loving Cousin Jonathan Nason, but that all and every of my whole part of s^d grant of Land be and remaine to be him ye s^d Jonathan Nasons my s^d Cousin and his heires & assignes for ever wthout ye least Molestation of me ye s^d John Nason my heires Exec^{rs} Adm^{rs} or assignes or any person or persons whatsoever Claiming any Right or Intrust thereunto from by or under me, them or any of us for ever/ In confirmation hereof I have hereunto set my hand and Seale this second day of July : 1702.   his

Signed Sealed & delivered
   in presence
   Joseph Littlefield
   Nathan Lord.

John ⌇ Nason (his seal)
mark

York ss/ July 2^d 1702

The above named John Nason personally Appeared before me, one of her Ma^{ts} Justices of ye Peace and Acknowledged this Instrum^t to be his Act and Deed.

                              Ichabod Plaisted

A true Copie of the originall Transcribed & compared : Septemb^r 25th 1702   p Jos Hamond Reg^r

[145] To all to whome these p'sence shall come I John Winford of York in New England Husbandman in y'e Province of Maine afores'd send Greeting & so forth/ Know Yee that I the said John Winford, for and in consideration of one stere delivered unto me by John Preble of York in the afores'd Province Husbandman before y'e ensealing and Delivery hereof the receipt whereof I y'e s'd John Winford doe hereby Acknowledge my self therewith to be fully satisfied contented and paid Have for my self my heires Execut'rs Adm'rs & Assigns given granted bargained sold delivered and confirmed And by these p'rsence doe fully freely and Absolutely give grant bargain sell deliver and confirm unto y'e s'd John Preble his heires Execut'rs Adm'rs and assignes a certain tract of Land lying and being in York afores'd containing five Acres more or less being bounded in manner & form following Viz't with y'e land of the John Preble on three sides and by y'e land of the s'd John Winford on y'e south being fifty pole in breadth with all and singular the woods und'r woods timb'r timb'r trees priviledges or Appurtenances whatsoever thereunto belonging or in any wise Appertaining To have and to hold the said land and p'rmisses hereby bargained and sold unto the s'd John Preble his heires Exec'rs Adm'rs and assignes as his and their own proper goods and Estate for ever and to his and their owne proper use and behoofe for evermore And I the s'd John Winford with my heires Execut'rs Adm'rs and assignes doe covent promise and grant to and with y'e s'd John Preble his heires Execut'rs Adm'rs and assignes by these p'rsence that I y'e s'd John Winford on the day of y'e Date hereof and at y'e time of y'e ensealing and Delivery hereof I have in my self full power good right and Lawfull authority to give grant bargain sell deliver and confirm the s'd land and p'rmisses hereby bargained and sold unto the s'd John Preble his heires Execut'rs Adm'rs and assignes for evermore in manner and form afores'd And also

Wentworth
to
Preble

Book VI, Fol. 145.

that he y⁰ s⁴ John Preble his heires Execᵘʳˢ admʳˢ and assignes or any of them shall or lawfully may from time to time & and at all times hereafter peaceably and quietly have hold use and enjoy y⁰ s⁴ land and Premisses hereby bargained and sold, without any manner of let suit trouble Eviction Ejection Molestation Challenge Claime deniall or demand whatsoever of or by me y⁰ s⁴ John Winford my heires Executʳˢ Admʳˢ & assigns or any of them or of or by any other person or persons whatsoever Lawfully Claiming or to Claim from by or under me my Act or title In witness whereof I have hereunto put my hand and seal the tenth of ffebruary 16⅜⅞

This being done by the consent of my wife Mathar Winford.

Signed Sealed and Delivered in pʳsence of us.
John Penwill

       his
Benjamin X York
    mark

John   his   Winford (his seal)
   mark

John Winford came the tenth of ffebʳʸ 16⅜⅞ And owned the aboves⁴ Instrument to be his Act and Deed Before me
                          John Davis Deptu Presidᵗ

A true Copie of the originall Transcribed and compared:
July 6ᵗʰ 1702   p Jos: Hamond Regʳ

Gooch
to
Bean

To all Christian People to whome this pʳsent Deed of Sale May come or concern Mʳ James Gooch of Boston in yᵉ County of Suffolk in yᵉ Province of the Massachusets Bay in New England send Greeting, Know yee that the s⁴ James for and in consideration of a certain Sum of money to him in hand paid or otherwise satisfactorily secured to be paid by Lewis Bane of York in yᵉ County of York in yᵉ Province & Country aboveˢᵈ Have given, granted Bargained sold allenated Infiefed and confirmed And doe by these pʳsence give grant bargain sell Allenate Infiffe and confirm and fully freely and absolutely make over and confirm unto the sᵈ Lewis Bane a piece or parcel of Land lying and being within yᵉ Township or presenᵗⁱˢ of York abovesᵈ and is in quantity thirty Acres be it more or lest Cituate upon yᵉ North east side of the high way that leads toward yᵉ Corn Mill with yᵉ house Lott of the abovesᵈ Lewis Bane on yᵉ North west side of it And on yᵉ South east bounded by the Land of the sᵈ Bane that he bought formerly of Richard Toziar And is in breadth by above said high way between sᵈ Banes two Lotts fifteen or sixteen poles be it more or lesse and runeth back northeastward as far as the Adjoyning Lotts, as more fully doth Appear upon York Town Book, which land was formerly in yᵉ possession of Jnᵒ Winthford and sold by him yᵉ sᵈ Winthford to Gilbord Endicot and by power of A turney to abovesᵈ Gooch from sᵈ Indecut Now he the sᵈ Gooch hath sold as abovesᵈ together with all Rights benefits Emoloments and Advantages both of Land Swame Meadow ground Timber timbʳ trees wood underwood standing lying or belonging to yᵉ same, on Appertaining or any wise at any time redowning from yᵉ same or any part thereof To have and to hold and quietly and peaceably to possess ocupie and injoy the same as a sure Estate in ffee simple to him the sᵈ Lewis Bane his heires Executʳˢ Admʳˢ and assignes for ever Moreover the sᵈ Mʳ James Gooch doth for himself and for the abovesᵈ Gilbord Indecutt and his heires Executʳˢ Admʳˢ and assignes to and with yᵉ sᵈ Lewis Bane his heires Executʳˢ Administratʳˢ and assignes doe covenᵗ Ingage and promise, the pʳmisses with all their priviledges and Appurtenances from all former grants gifts sales or interuptions as alsoe from all incumbrances whatsoever to be had or commenced by them yᵉ sᵈ Gooch and Gilbord their heires Execut⁰ Admⁿ or assignes or any person or persons whatsoever upon grounds proceeding yᵉ Date of this Instrumᵗ, for ever to warrant and Defend by these pʳsence/ As alsoe from all future Claimes, In witness whereof yᵉ abovesᵈ Mʳ James Gooch hath hereunto set his hand and seal this twenty third day of May one thousand seven hundred and two, in yᵉ fourteenth year of yᵉ Reign of our soveraign Lord William the third, King of Great Brittain &c.

Signed Sealed and Delivered   James Gooch (his seal)
   in presence of.
   Nath ffreeman
   Abraᵐ Preble Junʳ

Mʳ James Gooch came this twenty third day of May: 1702/ And Acknowledged this to be his Act and Deed.
                       Before me in York Samuel Donnell
                                  Jusᵗˢ peace

A true Copie of the originall Transcribed and compared
July: 6ᵗʰ 1702   p Jos Hamond Regʳ

Articles of agreemᵗ made between John Wells Thomas Wells Nathaniel Clark & Patience Clark his wife/ And Thomas Wells in yᵉ right of Sarah Lybbey all of them Children to John Wells late of Wells Deceased concerning the Division of yᵉ Estate that did belong to their father Deceased Intestate

Wells: John
Tho: Nathll   Imprimis/ It is agreed that Thomas Wells
Sarah &c   have in behalf of himself and of our Sister Sarah Lybbey thirty two poles or Rods in breadth of that parcel of land which adjoines to Joseph Sayer his land [146] or that is now in Joseph Sayers possession which is to run in length upon a Northwest and Southeast line According as yᵉ Lotts doe run And he is to begin next to Joseph Sayers and to run yᵉ the thirty one poles or Rods

upon a Northeast line which is ye breadth Also two third parts of that Marsh which belonged to our father aboves^d Deceased which lies upon the Eastwardmost branch of little River.

Item It is agreed that our Sister Patience Clark shall have fifteen pole of the aboves^d land which was our fathers to begin next to Thomas Wells and soe in breadth fifteen poles or rods upon a Northeast line and the length thereof upon a Northwest and Southeast line the whole length of the Lott/ likewise ye other third part of ye Meadow aboves^d lying upon ye Esterly branch of little River.

Item It is agreed that John Wells shall have ye remainder of ye Lott of Land Lying Northwest of Nathaniel or Patience Clark belonging to our late Deceased father/ likewise that John Wells shall have all the old Lott which our father lived upon lying between land of Benjamin Curtes Northeasterly and land land now in Possession of Mr John Wheelwright southwesterly together with all the Marsh thereunto belonging. And whereas there is a convenient falls in the aboves^d land that is Divided between us John Wells Thomas Wells Nathaniel & Patience Clark it is agreed that John Wells shall have five eighth parts of the priviledge at his disposall, and Thomas Wells shall have two eighths and Patience Clark one eight part of ye aboves^d priviledge And that each shall have free liberty of improving of their priviledge in ye ffalls aboves^d for building of a Saw Mill or Mills. Likewise that each of ye parties above named they and their heires and Success^{rs} shall have the priviledge of cutting or laying timb^r for ye use of the Mill likewise for transportation of timber or boards to or from the s^d Mill (when built) to any convenient landing place And this priviledge is to be both in that Lott that is Divided between them and in ye old Lott alsoe that falls to John Wells his share In witness to ye aboves^d agreem^t we the above named John Wells Thomas Wells Nathaniel Clark and Patience Clark have hereto put our hands and seales this third day of Aprill in yᵉ year of our Lord one thousand seven hundred and two And in the fourteenth year of his Maᵗˢ Reign. The words Nathaniel Clark and his wife in yᵉ uper line And Nathaniel in the second line of yᵉ lower Article now enterlined before Signing & sealing hereof

    John Wells, Thomas Wells and Nathaniel Clark

Signed Sealed and Delivered   John Wells   (and seal)
   In the presence of.   Thomas Wells (and seal)
   Thomas Wells   Nathaniel Clark (and seal)
   John Wheelwrigh

York ss/

John Wells, Thomas Wells and Nathaniel Clark personally Apeared before me yᵉ Subscribʳ one of his Maᵗˢ Justices of the Peace of this County and Acknowledged this above written Instrumᵗ in writing to be their free Act and Deed/ this third day of April one thousand seven hundred & two   John Wheelwright

  A true Copie of yᵉ originall Transcribed and compared July 6. 1702.   p Jos: Hamond Regʳ

    This Indenture made the ninth day of October one thousand seven hundred & two in yᵉ first year of yᵉ Reign of our Soveraign Lady Anne by the Grace of God over England Scotland ffrance and Ireland Queen Defendʳ of the ffaith &c between Joane Blagdon, Richard Tucker and Grace his wife all three of the Isles of Shoales in New England of the one part/ And Silvanus Tripe of the same Islands of yᵉ other part Witnesseth, that yᵉ said Joane Blagdon Richard Tucker and Grace his wife, as well for and in consideration of the sum of twenty pounds Currant money of New England to them or either of them in hand paid at or before thensealing and Delivery of these p'sence, the receipt whereof they doe hereby Acknowledge and thereof and of every part and penny thereof doe Acquit, release and discharge y⁰ sᵈ Sylvanus Tripe his heires Execᵗʳˢ Admʳˢ forever by these pʳsence, Also for Divers other good causes and considerations them thereunto Especially moving Have Demised, given, granted, bargained, sold, Aliened, Enfeoffed and confirmed and by these pʳsence doe give, grant bargain, sell, Alien, Enfeoffe, release and confirm unto y⁰ sᵈ Sylvanus Tripe his heires and assignes for ever All that tract or parcell of Land containing ten Acres Scituate lying and being in Crooked Lane in the Town of Kittery in y⁰ County of York in New England, being bounded as followeth Vizᵗ twenty pole or Rod by y⁰ waters side in breadth and soe to run back untill y⁰ sum of ten Acres be full and compleatly ended And on the Northwest side is bounded by the Land that was Thomas Wells, and on y⁰ Easterside by the Land of Robert Cutts his Land, which Tract of Land was purchased by Joane Blagdon formerly Widow Relict of William Deament Deceased, of Joshua Downing and Patience his wife as by a Dee under their hands bearing date the 21ᵗʰ day of June 1679 — may more at Large Appear, together with all wood under wood trees Timbʳ waters water Courses Easments profits priviledges, advantages and Appurtenances to y⁰ same or any part thereof belonging or in any wise Appertaining And free Ingress Egress & regress into & out of any part of the Demised pʳmisses And y⁰ revertion & revertions remainder and remaindʳˢ thereof and every part thereof And all y⁰ Estate right title and Interest of them y⁰ sᵈ Joane Blagdon Richard Tucker & Grace his wife or either of them of or into y⁰ same, together with true Copies if required/ of all such Deeds Evidences and writings which concern y⁰ same or any part thereof, To have and to hold, all and Singular the above bargained and sold pʳmisses with the Appurtenances unto y⁰ sᵈ Silvanus Tripe his heires

Blagdon & Tucker to Tripe

and assignes for ever to and for y*e* only and proper use and behoofe of him y*e* said Silvanus Tripe his heires and assignes And they y*e* s*d* Joane Blackdon, Richard Tucker and and Grace his wife doe for themselves or either of them, their or ether of their heires Exec*rs* or Adm*rs* coven*t* promise and grant to and with y*e* s*d* Silvanus Tripe his heires and assignes in manner and form following that is to say that they y*e* s*d* Joane Blagdon Richard Tucker and Grace his wife now at the time of the Sealing and delivery of these p'sence are seized of and in y*e* s*d* p'misses of a good and Lawfull & Indefeazeable right of Inheritance in ffee Simple And that they have full power [147] good right and Lawfull Authority to grant sell and convey y*e* s*d* Lands with y*e* Appurtenances unto y*e* said Silvanus Tripe his heires and assignes for ever And that freely and clearly Acquitted Exonerated and Discharged of and from all and all manner former and other gifts grants bagains Sales Leases Joyntures Dowers Judgments Executions Extents and all manner of Incumbrances whatsoever y*e* same shall be remaine and continue unto y*e* s*d* Silvanus Tripe his heires and assignes for ever; And alsoe they y*e* s*d* Joan Blackdon, Richard Tucker & Grace his wife, they their heires Execut*rs* Adm*rs* All and Singular y*e* aboves*d* p'misses shall and will warrant and for ever Defend unto y*e* s*d* Silvanus Tripe his heires and assignes for ever from any person or persons whatsoever Claiming any right title or Interest to y*e* same or any part thereof/ In witness whereof y*e* parties aboves*d* have hereunto put their put their hands and seales y*e* day and year first above written.

Signed Sealed and Delivered
and Livery & Seizen and Possession given in p'sence of us
John Geare
   the mark of
Sarah S Geare
Francis Tucker

the mark of
Joane X Blackdon (and seal)
Rich*d* Tucker (and seal)
the mark of
Grace 6 Tucker (and seal)

BOOK VI, FOL. 147.

Kittery County of York

the 10th Octob^r 1702/ then Mrs Joane Blagdon & Richard Tucker & Grace Tucker his wife personally appeared before me ye Subscrib^r and Acknowledged this above written to be their free Act and Deed

Wm Pepperrell Js pis

A true Copie of the originall Transcribed and compared Octob^r 13th 1702. p Jos : Hammond Reg^r

Know all men by these p'sents that I Daniel Goodwin Senr of Barwick in the County of York in the Province of the Massachusets Bay in New England in consideration of twenty pounds and thirteen shillings to me in hand paid by my Son Daniel Goodwin of ye same Town the receipt whereof I doe hereby Acknowledge and my self to be therewith fully satisfied Have Sold, and by these presence doe firmly sell and convey unto my s^d Son Daniel a parcell of Marish and Swamp Land Scituate in s^d Barwick in ye Marishes Comonly called Sluts Coner Marish contained now within fence being bounded Northwardly by my own Land or Marish Westwardly and Southwardly by my Son Thomas his Land And Eastwardly by Land of my son James his Widow and partly by Thomas Goodwins land It containing by Estimation Six Acres be ye same more or Less (the Northward line passing from a small white oak marked at ye west end by a pitch pine Marked, to a red oak Marked in ye East end of s^d line) Together with all ye Appurtenances thereto as wood, grass hay springs or ye like, or other benefits thereto belonging To have and to hold the hereby bargained p'misses to my s^d Son Daniel his heires Execut^{rs} Adm^{rs} & assignes and to their own proper Use and behoofe for ever And I ye s^d Daniel Goodwin Senr Doe Oblige my self my heires Execut^{rs} & Adm^{rs} the p^r misses

Danll Gooden to his son Danll

hereby sold against all persons whatsoever (Excepting all persons deriving a title from Robert Tufton Mason) To my s^d son Daniel his heires Execut^{rs} Adm^{rs} and assignes to Warrant & for ever Defend by these p^{r}sence In witness whereof I have hereto put my hand and seale this twenty first day of August in ye year of our Lord One thousand Seven hundred and one And in ye thirteenth year of King William the third his Reign over Great Brittain &c.

Signed Sealed and Delivered Daniel Goodwin his mark Senr (and a seal)
   In presence of Us.
   Jno Plaisted
   John Wade

The Land by these presence conveied was Delivered by Turf and twigg by Daniel Gooden Senr to Daniel Gooden Junr this first day of June one thousand Seven hundred and two in the presence of us.

                      Thomas Gooden } Witness
                      Daniel Goodin }

York ss

The above named Daniel Goodwin Senr personally Appearing before me the Subscrib^r one of his Ma^{ts} Justices of ye Peace within s^d County Acknowledged this Instrum^t to be his Act and Deed

                                      Jos: Hamond
A true Copie of ye originall Transcribed and Compared

To all Christian People to whome these p^{r}sence shall come Thomas Spinney of Kittery in the County of York in ye Province of ye Massachusets Bay in New England Cordwain^r and Christian his wife send Greeting, Know Yee that we ye s^d Thomas & Christian Spinney for and in consideration of the Sum of Nine pounds money to us well and truly paid at and before ye Ensealing and Delivery of these p^{r}sence by John Staple of yᵉ same Kittery Carpenter the receipt whereof we doe hereby Acknowledge & our selues therewith fully Satisfied contented and paid And thereof and of and from every part and parcel thereof we doe by these

Spinney to Staple

pʳsence Acquit & for ever discharge him yᵉ sᵈ John Staple his heires and Assignes We the sᵈ Thomas and Christian Spinney Have given granted bargained and sold And by these pʳsence doe for us our heires Executʳˢ Admʳˢ and assignes fully clearly and absolutely give grant bargain sell and confirm unto him yᵉ sᵈ John Staple his heires Executʳˢ Admʳˢ and assignes for ever one certain piece of parcell of Land containing twelve Acres And is part of that twenty Acres which I yᵉ sᵈ Thomas Spinney bought of my brother James Spinney near yᵉ Mast way in the Town of Kittery bounded as followeth Vizᵗ begining at the head of yᵉ sᵈ John Staples land (formerly Abraham Remichs) and on yᵉ head of John Spinneys land and is forty eight poles in [148] breadth, thirty five poles whereof lying upon yᵉ head of sᵈ Staples & thirteen poles upon yᵉ head of John Spinneys land Joyning to each and soe to run back upon an East line forty poles yᵉ same breadth/ To have and to hold the said piece or parcell of Land together with all and singular its Appurtenances, with all right title Interest Claime and Demand which we yᵉ sᵈ Thomas and Christian Spinney now have or in time past have had or or which we our heires or assignes in time to come, may might or in any wise ought to have of in or to yᵉ pʳmisses and that yᵉ same is free and clear Acquitted and Discharged of and from all other and former Gifts, grants bargains Sales Mortgages titles troubles and Incumbrances whatsoever had made done comitted or suffered to be done or comitted by us or either of us/ And we the said Thomas and Christian Spinney doe for us our heires and assignes covenant promise and grant to and with yᵉ sᵈ John Staple his heires and assignes that we the sᵈ Thomas and Christian

Book VI, Fol. 148.

Spinney are yᵉ true right and proper owners of the pʳmisses and every part thereof at & untill yᵉ ensealing and Delivery of these pʳsence And have in our selves good right full power and Lawfull Authority yᵉ same to sell and convey unto him yᵉ said Staple his heires and assignes, And that the sᵈ John Staple his heires Executʳˢ or assignes shall and may from time and at all times for ever hereafter have hold ocupie possess & enjoy the same and every part thereof without any Molestation let deniall or hinderance of or by us yᵉ sᵈ Thomas and Christian Spinney our heires or assignes and that yᵉ title thereof against our selves, heires Executʳˢ and assignes, and against all other peresons whatsoever Lawfully Claiming yᵉ same or any pᵗ thereof we will for ever save harmless warrant and Defend by these presence In witness whereof we have hereunto set our hands and Seales the eighth day of June in the first year of the Reign of our Soveraign Lady Anne by the grace of God of England Scotland ffrance & Ireland Queen Defendʳ of the ffaith &c. And in the year of our Lord One thousand Seven hundred and two. 1702.

Signed Sealed and Delivered   Thomas Spinney (and seal)
in the pʳsence of us.   Christian Spinney (and seal)

       her   her   mark
Hannah ∠ Key
       mark

Jos: Hamond

York ss/ June 8ᵗʰ 1702.

     The within named Thomas Spinney and Christian Spinney his wife personally Appearing before me the Subscribʳ one of her Maᵗˢ Justices of the peace within yᵉ County of York Acknowledged this Instrument to be their Act and Deed/   Jos: Hamond

     A true Copie of the originall Transcribed and Compared June the eighth, 1702.   p Jos Hamond Regʳ

Book VI, Fol. 148.

Be it Know unto all men by these p^rsence that I Peter ffolsham of Exeter in the Province of New Hampshier in New Engl^d Planter send Greeting/ Know Yee that I ye s^d Peter ffolsham for a valuable consideration to me in hand paid or Sufficient Security therefore by William Sawyer of Wells in the Province of Maine in ye s^d New England Planter doe therewth acknowledge my self fully satisfied contented and paid And thereof and of every part and parcell thereof doe Exonerate Acquit and Discharge ye said William Sawyer his heires Execut^{rs} Adm^{rs} and assignes for ever by these p^rsence Have given granted bargained sold Aliened Enfeoffed and confirmed And by these p^rsence doe give grant bargain sell Alien enfeoffe and confirm unto ye s^d William Sawyer his heires Execut^{rs} and Adm^{rs} for ever a certain parcell of Meadow and Upland Scituate Lying and being in Wells afores^d Excepting five Acres and a half heretofore alienated/ the s^d Meadow & upland being formerly purchased by me ye s^d Peter ffolsham of Robert Wadleigh Senr & John Wadleigh That is to Say one sixth part of the Farm or Estate of John Wadleigh formerly of ye afores^d Wells Dec^d And one third part of the Estate of the afores^d John Wadleigh, by account & Estimation one halfe of the Farm and Estate of the s^d Wadleigh : The other half being now in the Tenure and occupaĉon of ye afores^d William Sawyer, and adjoining to ye land of Thos Mills Dec^d To have and to hold the aforesaid Meadow and upland with all and singular ye woods trees timb^r under wood & all other ye Appurtenances thereunto belonging, unto ye s^d William Sawyer his heires Execut^{rs} adm^{rs} and assignes for ever Alsoe I ye s^d Peter ffolsham doe covenant promise and engage to and with ye s^d William Sawyer his heirs Execut^{rs} and Adm^{rs} and either of them, that I ye s^d Peter ffolsham am ye true proper and undoubted owner of the s^d bargained p^rmisses And that the s^d bar-

Folsham to Sayer

gained p^rmisses were free and clear and freely and clearly Exonerated acquitted and Discharged of and from all and all manner of former bargains sales gifts grants titles Mortgages suits Dowries and all other Incumbrances whatsoever from ye begining of the world untill ye sale and delivery hereof And also I ye s^d Peter ffolsham doe alienate assigne and make over from me my heires Execut^rs and Adm^rs unto ye s^d William Sawyer his heires Execut^rs and adm^rs for ever, and to his and their proper use & Interest for ever two third parts of the priviledge of a brook & falls that runs through part of ye above p^rmised land; and ye land formerly Thomas Mills Dec^d And further I ye s^d Peter ffolsham doe for my self my heirs Execut^rs and adm^rs Coven^t promise and engage to and with the s^d William Sawyer his heires Execut^rs and Adm^rs All & Singular the p^rmisses with ye Appurtenances thereunto belonging to warrant acquit and Defend for ever against any person whatsoever Claiming any Legall right Title or Interest of or into y^e same or any part or parcell thereof And in Testimony hereof I y^e s^d Peter ffolsham with Susañah my wife have hereunto set our hands and Seales this 27th of June Anno Domini 1689. Annoq̃ RR^s Willielmi tertij j^o

Seald & Deliverd
  in the p^rsence of
Edw: Smith
Samuel Leuitt

Peter $\mathcal{G}$ ffolsham (and seal)
    his mark

Susanna ✚ ffolsham (and seal)
    her mark

Peter ffoulshame owned this written Instrument to be his Act and Deed this sixteenth day of January Anno Dom: 1691. before me   Robt Pike Assis^t

  A true Copie of the originall Transcribed & compared Octob^r 8th 1702   p Jos Hamõnd Reg^r

[149] Know all men by these p'sence that I Thomas Thompson of Kittery in y° County of York Yeoman for the consideration of five pounds in money to me in hand paid by my brother Thomas Roads of the same place Joyner, the receipt thereof I doe confess and my self therewith contented and paid. Have given, granted bargained and sold And doe by these p'sence give grant bargain and sell unto y° s^d Thomas Roads his heires or assignes for ever All my right title and Interest in fifteen Acres and a quarter of Land being part of a grant unto me by the town of Kittery May 16 : 1694 : as by Record of s^d Town may more at Large Appear refferrence thereunto being had. To have and to hold, all y° s^d fifieen Acres & a quarter of Land unto y° only use benefit and behoof of him the s^d Thomas Road his heires and assignes for ever against me y° s^d Thomas Thompson and my heires for ever and furthermore I y° s^d Thomas Thompson doe for my self and my heires, Covenant to and with y° s^d Thomas Roads and his heires that the p'misses are free from all incumbrances by me made And that I am y° true & proper owner thereof at y° time of y° ensealing hereof, the peaceable & quiet possession thereof to warrant and maintain against all persons Laying a Lawfull Claim thereto from by or under me/ In witness hereof I have hereunto set to my hand and seal this 5th Decemb^r 1702

Thompson to Roads

Signed and Sealed in the p'sence   Thom. Thompson (and a seal)
of us y° Subscribers.
Samuel Shory
 the sign of
Jacob E Roads
Wm Godsoe

York ss. Decemb^r 24th 1702.

The within named Thomas Thompson personally appearing before me y° Subscrib^r one of her Ma^{ts} Justices of the

BOOK VI, FOL. 149.

Peace within s⁴ County Acknowledged the within written Instrum⁴ to be his Act & Deed

Jos : Hamond

A true Copie of the originall Transcribed and compared Decemb⁴ 24ᵗʰ 1702   p Jos Hamond Reg⁴

Whereas severall controversies hath happened between Dodavah Curtis of Kittery in the County of York and Mad^m Bridget Graffort of Portsmouth in ye Province of New Hampshiere lately Deceased about a certain Island which lies in the river of Piscataqua on ye E^tside of Strawbery Bank comonly called by ye name of Witherses Iland, which Island was formerly given by Mr Thomas Withers unto his two daughters, Mary & Eliz: Withers as by an Instrument made July 27, 1701. Now be it known to all men by these p'sence that I Dodevah Curtis who married s⁴ Eliz^th And we Samuel Keais and Samuel Penhallow Execut^rs and Legatees of the Estate of s⁴ Mad^m Bridget Graffort Relict and Sole Executrix of Mr Thomas Graffort Deceased, she alsoe ye s⁴ Bridget Graffort being formerly ye Relict and Sole Executrix of Thomas Daniel Esqr of Portsm^o who had ye one half of s⁴ Island sold him by one Thomas Rice who married s⁴ Mary Withers Be it further known by these p'sence for ye prevention of any further controversie that shall or may arise, that we the s⁴ Dodavah Curtis Samuel Keais & Sam^ll Penhallow for us our heires Execut^rs Adm^rs and assignes doe freely and willingly Divide Acquiess with and rest contented with the Division now laid out the s⁴ Curtis to have ye upermost end of s⁴ Island, ending at ye southermost end of the house as the bounds are now set, with all Priviledges thereunto belonging And ye said Keais and Penhallow to have the Lowermost end of ye s⁴ Island with all the Priviledges and Appurte-

Curtes:
Keais
Penhallow

nances thereunto belonging, runing from a great stump that lies on a bank fronting to ye great river and soe to run on a strait course to a forked oak tree, which lies between five or six from ye south end of s^d Curtis Dwelling house And soe runing Cross the s^d Island as it is now staked out by Richard Bryar & Joseph Weeks And further it is mutually agreed upon that ye great Cove which lies fronting to Strawbery bank shall be Equall in point of all manner of priviledges unto ye s^d Dodevah Curtis Sam^{ll} Penhallow & Sam^{ll} Keais their heires & assignes wharfing only excepted/ In Testimony to all and singular the Premisses Wee the s^d Dodavah Curtis, Sam^{ll} Penhallow and Sam^{ll} Keais Doe hereunto set our hands and fix our Seales this day of April in the yeare of our Lord one thousand seven hundred two.

Signed Sealed and Delivered Dodavah Curtis (and a seale)
   in the p^rsence of us. Samuel Keais (and a seal)
   Richard Bryar Sam^{ll} Penhallow (and a seal)
   Joseph Weekes.

A true Copie of the originall Transcribed and Compared the 28th Novemb^r 1702.

                            p Jos: Hamond Reg^r

  At a Legall town meeting held at Kittery May 24th 1699./ Granted unto Nicholas Morrell his heires and assignes for ever twenty five Acres of land if he can find it clear of former grants. Attests.

                            Jos: Hamond Cler

  Know all men by these p^rsence that I Nicholas Morrell of Kittery Have given granted and sold unto my brother John Morrell his heires & assignes for ever all my right title and Interest of in & unto five Acres of ye above mentioned grant

Nicholas Morrell
to
John Morrell

of twenty five Acres/ To have and to hold yᵉ sᵈ five Acres of land with thappurtenances thereunto belonging peaceably to enjoy yᵉ same without any let Molestation or hinderance from me yᵉ sᵈ Nicholas Morrell My heires or assignes for ever more In witness whereof I have hereunto set my hand and seale the eighteenth of Decembʳ Anno Dom : 1702.

Signed Sealed and delivered   Nicholas Morrell (his seal)
  in the pʳsence of.
  Jos : Hamond

York ss/ Decembʳ 18ᵗʰ 1702.

The above named Nicholas Morrell personally Appearing before me yᵉ subscribʳ one of her Maᵗˢ Justices of the peace wᵗʰin sᵈ County Acknowledged this Instrumᵗ to be his Act and Deed/   Jos : Hamond

A true Copie of the originall Transcribed and Compared : Decembʳ 18 1702   p Jos : Hamond Regʳ

[150] To all People to whome these presence shall come, Moses Voden of Kittery in the County of York in the Province of the Massachusets Bay in New England sends Greeting Know Yee that for and in consideraĉon of the sum̄ of six pounds ten shillings to me in hand well and truly paid at and before the Ensealing and Deli very hereof by Samuel Johnson of the same Kittery the receipt whereof I doe hereby Acknowledge and myself therewith to be fully satisfied contented and paid And thereof, and of and from every part and parcell thereof, I doe by these presence Acquit and discharge him yᵉ sᵈ Samuel Johnson his heires and Assignes for ever/ Have given granted bargained sold Aliened enfeoffed and confirmed, And doe for my heires Executʳˢ Admʳˢ and assignes freely clerely and absolutely, Give, grant, bargain, sell, Alien, enfeoffe convey & confirm

unto him y'e s'd Sam'll Johnson his heires Execut'rs Adm'rs and assignes All that thirty Acres of land granted to me by the town of Kittery the twenty fourth day of May 1699. And bounded and laid out by y'e towns survey'r March y'e 25th 1788 — as appears on Record in Kittery town book reference thereunto being had — Lying and being scituate on the North side of Sturgeon Creek in y'e township of Kittery afores'd the bounds and Metes thereof fully appearing in s'd town book/ by y'e return of the laying out thereof under y'e hands of the Surv'rs bearing date as afores'd To have and to hold y'e above s'd grant of land with all its priviledges and Appurtenances thereunto belonging or in any wise appertaining To him y'e s'd Sam'll Johnson his heires Execut'rs adm'rs and assignes for ever and to his and their only proper use

Voden to Johnson

benefit & behoof/ And that he y'e s'd Johnson his heires or assignes may from time to time and at all times for ever hereafter Have hold ocupie possess and enjoy the said p'rmisses and every part thereof without any manner of Lett hinderance Molestation or disturbance of or by me y'e s'd Moses Voden my heires or assignes or of or by any other person or persons whatsoever Claiming any right title or Interest thereunto from by or under me my heires or assignes as aforesaid And that y'e sale thereof and of every part and parcell thereof against my self my heires and assignes or any other person Lawfully Claiming the same from or by me my heires or assignes I will for ever save harmless warrant and Defend by these presence. In witness whereof I have hereunto set my hand and seal this twenty seventh day of Octob'r 1702

Signed Sealed and delivered   his
  In the presence of us.   Moses ◯ Voden (and seal)
        his   mark
  Matthew ⋂ Williams
         mark
  Jos : Hamond
York ss/ Octob'r 27 : 1702

Book VI, Fol. 150.

The within named Moses Voden personally Appearing before me Joseph Hamond one of her Ma^{ts} Justices of the peace within said County Acknowledged this Instrum^t to be his Act and Deed/ And Ruth his wife appearing at ye same time freely gave up all her right of Dower of in and to ye within named p'misses   Jos. Hamond

A true Copie of the originall Transcribed and compared, Octob^r 27th 1702   p Jos. Hamond Reg^r

Know all men by these presence that I Elizabeth Hole of Kittery in the County of York Gentlewoman/ Attorney unto my husband John Hole late of Kittery aforesaid, now Resident on ye Island of Barbadoes Merch^t for the consideration of ten pounds in money to my s^d husband in hand paid, and unto me ye said Elizabeth Hole Attorney aboves^d/ by John Gaskin Deceased and Joana his wife Relict of s^d Gaskin the receipt thereof I ye s^d Elizabeth Hole in the behalf of my said husband and my self I doe confess, and our selves therewith contented & fully paid And doe acquit ye s^d Gaskin and his heires for ever for the same for ye consideration aboves^d I the s^d Elizabeth Hole Have given granted bargained and sold And doe by these presence bargain and sell unto ye said Joana Gaskin and ye heires of the s^d John Gaskin Ten Acres of Land Lying at ye Northeast end of my s^d husband John Holes home plantation in the town and County aboves^d and is forty pole square And is that tract of land that my s^d husband sold and delivered possession of unto ye s^d John Gaskin Deceased, together with all ye timber and wood thereon with the appurtenances and priviledges thereunto belonging unto ye s^d Joana Gaskin and the heires of the s^d John Gaskin and their assignes for evermore against the s^d John Hole or his heires To have and to hold all ye s^d ten Acres of land above mentioned and every part thereof unto ye sole & only use benefit and behoofe of her ye s^d

Hole to Gaskin

Joanna Gaskin and yᵉ heires of the said John Gaskin and their assignes for ever/ against him yᵉ sᵈ John Hole or me the said Elizabeth Hole as I am a Lawfull attorney to my sᵈ husband abovesᵈ, moreovʳ I yᵉ sᵈ Elizabeth Hole as I am Attorney abovesᵈ Do for my self and yᵉ said John Hole and his heires Covenant with yᵉ sᵈ Joanna Gaskins and her heires that yᵉ premisses are free from all incumbrances And that yᵉ sᵈ John Hole is the true and proper owner thereof at and before yᵉ ensealing hereof, the peaceable and quiet possession thereof to warrant and for ever Defend against all persons Laying claim thereunto from by or under him yᵉ said John Hole or me yᵉ sᵈ Elizabeth Hole Attorney as abovesᵈ In witness whereof I have hereunto set my hand and seale this second day of May one thousand six hundred Ninety.

Witness   Elizabeth Hole (and a seale)

    the sign of
John ᴗ Shepard Senʳ
Wᵐ Godsoe.

York ss/ May 15ᵗʰ 1702.

The above named Elizabeth Hole personally appearing before me yᵉ Subscribʳ one of his Maᵗˢ Justices of the Peace within yᵉ County of York Acknowledged this Instrument to be her Act and Deed/

                                     Jos. Hamond

A true Copie of the originall Transcribed and compared
May 15ᵗʰ 1702.   p Jos: Hamond Regʳ

I Richard Vines Steward Genˡˡ unto Sʳ ffadinando Gorges Kᵗ Lᵈ proprietʳ of the Province of Mayn doe give and Grant unto Henry Simpson his heires and assignes for ever ten Acres of Marsh land upon yᵉ south side of the river of Accomenticus Lying opposit against yᵉ ffarm of Wᵐ Hook Gover: Yeelding and paying for yᵉ Premisses two shillings yearly

BOOK VI, FOL. 151.

upon ye 29 day of Septemb^r unto ye s^d ffardinando Gorges his heires and assignes/ In witness whereof I ye afores^d Richd Vines in ye behalf of ye s^d S^r ffardinando Gorges, have hereunto set my hand this 28th day of May 1640.
Witness; Will Hooke/   Rich: Vines

 Possession & Seizen of ye Land within menconed was delivered to ye wthin named Henry Simpson by Thomas Gorges Esqr the 29 day of June 1640 — In ye p^{r}sence of Wm Hooke Govern^r And Richd Cornish

 A true Copie of the originall Transcribed & compared:
July: 6: 1702   p Jos: Hamond Reg^r

[151] To all people to whome these p^{r}sence shall come David Libbey of Kittery in the County of York in the Province of the Massachusets Bay in New England Sends Greeting Know Yee that I ye s^d David Libbey for and in consideration of the sum of fifteen pounds currant money money of New England to me in hand well and truly paid at & before thensealing and delivery of these p^{r}sence by John Cotten of Portsm^o in ye Province New Hampsh^r the receipt whereof I doe hereby Acknowledge to full content and satisfaccon, & of & from every part and parcell thereof Doe hereby Acquit Exonerate and discharge him ye s^d John Cotten his heirs Execut^{rs} and Adm^{rs} for ever, I ye said David Libbey Have given, granted, bargained, sold Aliened Enfeoffed and confirmed/ And by these p^{r}sence Do freely clearly and absolutely Give, grant bargain, sell Alien enfeoffe, convey and confirm unto him ye s^d John Cotten his heires Execut^{rs} Adm^{rs} and assignes, a certain piece or parcell of Land lying and being scituate in the town of Kittery afores^d bounded as follows, that is to say by the high way that Leads from Thomas Hunscombs to Joshua Downings on the southwest, the breadth to begin at ye western corner of

Book VI, Fol. 151.

ye Land which s^d Cotten bought of Jacob Smith And from thence to run Northwest and by North twelve poles, And

David Libbey
to
Jno Cotten

from s^d line at s^d High way to run back into the woods upon a Northeast and by East line the whole breadth of twelve poles to ye utmost extent and head bounds of my land, containing thirty Acres be ye same more or less and is part of that land which I purchased in partnership of Mrs Mehetable Warren & company as p Deed of Sale on Record with ye Records of ye County of York appears at Large Together with all and singular the Priviledges & appurtenances thereto belonging or in any wise appertaining To have and to hold the said piece or parcell of land with all right, title, Interest, Claim and Demand which I ye s^d David Libbey now have or ought to have of in or to ye above bargained p'misses or any part thereof And that ye same is free and clear Acquitted and Discharged of & from all other or former gifts, grants, bargains Sales, Mortgages Leases and Incumbrances whatsoever, had made done comitted or suffered to be done or comitted by me the s^d David Libbey my heires or assignes And I ye s^d David Libbey doe covenant promise and grant to and with him ye said John Cotten that at and untill thensealing & delivery hereof I am the true right and proper owner of the above bargained p'misses and every part thereof And have in my self good right full power and Lawfull authority the same to sell and convey unto him ye s^d John Cotten his heires and assignes And that he ye said John Cotten his heires and assignes shall and may from time to time and at all times for ever hereafter, have hold use Ocupy possess and enjoy ye same and every part thereof without any Molestacon, Lett, Deniall hinderance or disturbance of or by me ye s^d David Libbey my heires or assignes And that the sale thereof against my self, heires Execut^{rs} or assignes and against all other persons Lawfully claiming the same or any part thereof, I will for ever save harmless warrant &

defend by these prsence In witness whereof I ye said David Libbey have hereunto set my hand and seale, the fourth day of January in the year of our Lord one thousand seven hundred and two. 1702.

Signed Sealed and Delivered David ~ Libbey (his seale)
In the presence of us. his mark
Jos: Hamond Junr
Stephen Tobey.

York ss/ Janry 4th 1702.

The above named David Libbey personally appearing before me the Subscribr one of her Mau Justices of the Peace within sd County Acknowledged this Instrumt to be his Act and Deed and Eleanor his wife appearing at ye same time resigned up all her right of Dower of in and to the above granted prmisses.

Jos: Hamond

A true Copie of the originall Transcribed and Compared: Janry 4th 1702. p Jos: Hamond Regr

Whereas I James Plaisted of York in the Province of Mayn have and am concerned with John Pickerin Senr in building that Saw and corn Mill now Erected in York (near the place Mr Henry Saywords Mills formerly Stood) The full quarter part of both sd Mills belonging to my self with all other priviledges as granted by the town of York unto ye sd Pickerin or my self, both of lands timber Marsh and all priviledges wtsoever/ Now know All persons to whome this present release & conveyance shall come or concern that I ye sd James Plaisted for divers good causes and considerations me hereto moveing, but more in Speciall for ye consideration of threescore pounds money and as money to me in hand paid and secured to be paid by the abovesd Pickerin, as alsoe for the ballance of all accounts between s^d Pickerin and my self from the begining of our dealing to ye date hereof concering ye s^d Mills, which we have ballenced on both sides, the which s^d mony & ballence as afores^d I doe hereby Acknowledge and my self fully satisfied and contented therewith, Have therefore bargained sold released delivered & confirmed and doe by this p^{r}sence for my self my heires Execut^{rs} and adm^{rs} bargain sell release deliver and confirm unto ye s^d Pickerin his heires Execut^{rs} Adm^{rs} & assignes for ever, to say all ye full quarter part of s^d Mills land timber Marsh and all priviledges thereto belonging or in any ways Appertaining and that I will warr^t and defend ye s^d quarter part as afore specified unto him the s^d Pickerin his heirs &c for ever In confirmation hereof I have hereunto set my hand and Seal 24th day of May : 1700.

<small>James Plaisted to Jno Pickerin</small>

Signed Sealed and delivered   James Plaisted (his seal)

In p^{r}sence of
Abra^m Preble Junr
Samuel Webber

County of York/ James Plaisted appeared before me and Acknowledged this Instrum^t to be his free Act and Deed./ June ye 17th 1700

Abra^m Preble Justice Peace

A true Copie of ye originall Transcribed and Compared July 7th 1702   Jos : Hamond Reg^r

To all Christian People to whome this p^{r}sent Deed shall come or concern that I John Pickerin Senr of Portsmouth in ye Province of New Hampshier, now resident in York in the Province of Mayn Sendeth Greeting in ye name of our Lord God everlasting, Know Yee that I ye said Pickerin with the consent of Mary my now wife for ye naturall and Parentary love we bear unto our well beloved son John

Pickerin, and to his wife and Children now resident in York
afores^d Have fully freely and absolutely And
Doe by this p^rsente Deed of Gift fully freely
and absolutely give, grant, Enfeoffe, release,
deliver and confirm unto him our s^d son and to his wife and
Children for ever, in form and manner following, to say, all
that my corn and Saw Mill now in our s^d sons Possession in
York, together with the point of land thereto adjoyning soe
far as the Gulley or place called formerly Galloping hill together with the full half of the Neck of land begining at ye head
of ye cove or Creek that runs up between s^d point of land and
the Creek & runs from the [152] place where it begins round
as said Creek and the river runeth down to Rowland Youngs
land according to ye town grant, to say, my said son to have
that halfe next his Mills with all the profits priviledges and
advantages both of land and water belonging to s^d Mills and
land or in any way Appertaining To have and to hold ye s^d
Corn and Saw Mills Neck or point of land, together with y^e
full half of the other neck of land with all ye priviledges
and Appurtenances thereto belonging or in any ways appertaining, unto him my said son and his heires for ever, as
followeth Viz^t to his now son John Pickerin, and if it happen that he die, then to the next Male of his body and to
his and their heires for evermore, such heir as afores^d allowing and paying unto his brother and sister, or brothers and
sisters such sum̄ or sum̄s as shall be by my s^d son ordered
or willed/ if no son, then to ye daughters in Equall proportion at my s^d sons discretion, but ye Mills and land to run
in the heir Maill as long as long as any remaineth, after
them to ye Mails as afores^d but this I doe always keep and
reserve full power and liberty to my self, to cutt of all or
any part of the entailm^ts afores^d notwithstanding this Deed,
if soe then ye whole shall be to my said sons disposall as he
shall se good, only this, and so it is to be understood, that
if my said sons wife happen to outlive him then she shall

*John Pickerin
to
his son John*

have hold and enjoy the full half thereof dureing her Widdowhood, but if she se cause to Marry she shall have dureing her life but one quarter part of the income of s^d Estate, the whole Estate to be improved and ye income thereof to be imployed for bringing up ye Children to learning and at ye age of twenty one Years ye Males and Eighteen ye females each of their parts both of principle and income to come into their hands if it should please God to take their father out of this life, otherways at his discretion, but Imediately after his Decease to come into their or either of their hands as before exprest, and after their mothers Decease all to come to them, All the above given Mills Lands and Priviledges I doe promise to warrant and Defend ye title thereof unto my s^d son and his wife and his heires as afore mentioned for ever against all and all manner of persons whatsoever laying any Lawfull Claime to all or any part of the herebefore given and granted p^{r}misses for ever, In consideration hereof both my self and wife have hereunto set our hands and seales this 26. day of Septemb^r 1700. — In the twelfth year of his Ma^{ta} Reign

Signed Sealed and delivered   John Pickerin (his seal)
  In presence of   Mary Pickerin (her seal)
  Joseph Moulton
  William Brasey
    the mark of
  Richard **R** Croker

County of York/ Augst 27th 1701.

John Pickerin and Mary his wife appeared before me the Subscriber and Acknowledged ye above Deed of Gift to be their free Act and Deed ye day aboves^d

                       Abra: Preble Justes Peace

A true Copie of the originall Transcribed and compared:
July 7th 1702   p Jos: Hamond Reg^r

Book VI, Fol. 152.

York, June 5th 1700/ Laid out to Mr James March, twenty two Acres & an half of land which was formerly granted to him by ye town Lying agaist Balld head, near to John Spencers land, on ye North: E. side of it, bounded as followeth, begining at a pitch pine tree standing by ye sea, & runing N: W. Sixty pole to a red oak marked on four sides, And then N: East to a Walnut tree marked on four sides and from thence to the sea side upon a S: E Course, laid out and bounded accord to grant as abovesd By us
         Abrā Preble Surveyr
     Daniel Black } Selectmen
     James Plaisted }

The within written return of Land Entred into York town Book Page: 147 — June ye 10th 1701. p me
         Abrā. Preble Town Clē.

A true Copie of the originall return wth ye entry on ye back side thereof Transcribed and compared. this 7th July: 1702 —   p Jos: Hamond Regr

To all people to whome this p'sent writing shall come James March in ye County of York in theare Mats Teritories and Dominion in New England, Saddler Sendeth Greeting. Know Yee that the sd James March for and in consideration of forty five shillings in money in hand paid by Mr John Pickerin Junr of York aforesd, the receipt whereof he doth Acknowledge and himself therewith fully satisfied and contented, have given, granted, bargained and sold, And doe by these p'sents fully clearly and absolutely, give grant bargain and sell unto ye sd John Pickerin his heires Executrs Admrs and assignes, one piece, parcel or tract of Land lying being & scituate in York at Balld head aforesd Containing twenty two Acres of Land more or less, bounded as follow-

Book VI, Fol. 152.

James March
to
John Pickerin

eth, begining at a pitch pine tree standing by the sea side and runing N : W. sixty pole to a red oak marked on four sides, and then N : E. to a Walnut tree marked on four sides, and from thence to ye sea side upon a S. E. Course To have and to hold to him the s^d John Pickerin, his heires Execut^{rs} Adm^{rs} and assignes All ye above piece or parcel of land bounded or containing as aboves^d with all the priviledges an appurtenances there unto belonging or any ways appertaining as a free and clear Estate In ffee simple for ever And ye s^d James March for himself his heires Execut^{rs} and Adm^{rs} doth covent^t and promise to and with the s^d John Pickerin his heires execut^{rs} Adm^{rs} and assignes that at the time of the ensealing and delivery hereof he is the proper owner of the above granted premisses, and that he hath good right full power and Lawfull Authority to Sell and dispose of the same as aboves^d And that the Same and every part and parcell thereof is free and clear from any Incumbrance whatsoever, & that he will Defend the same according to ye town grant from all persons whatsoever/ In witness the aboves^d James March with Mary his wife have hereunto their hands and seales this. 12. day of August and in the year of our Lord one thousand seven hundred and one And in the thirteen year of his Ma^{ts} Reigne

Signed Sealed and Delivered   James March (his seal)
In presence of us, Witnesses   her
Abra^m Preble Junr Mary W March (her seal)
Daniel Black   mark

James March personally appeared before me this 14th day of August 1701. and acknowledged this Instrument to be his Act and Deed.

               Before me Samuell Donnell Justis peace

A true Copie of the originall Transcribed and Compared :
July 7th 1702   p Jos : Hamond Reg^r

Book VI, Fol. 153.

[153] To all People to whome this p^rsent Deed of Sale shall come I Richard Bryar of Kittery in the County of York in the Province of the Massachusets Bay in New England Carpenter Send Greeting Know Yee that for and in consideration of ye sum of thirty pounds in Currant money of New England to me in hand well and truly paid at and before the Ensealing and Delivery of these p^rsents by John ffrink of ye same Town County & Province afors^d Yeoman the receipt whereof I doe hereby Acknowledge and my self therew^th to be fully satisfied contented and paid And thereof and of and from every part and parcell thereof for me ye s^d Richard Bryar my heires Execut^rs Adm^rs and assignes doe Exonerate Acquit and fully discharge him ye s^d John ffrink his heires Execut^rs Adm^rs and assignes by these p^rsents for ever I ye s^d Richard Bryar Have given granted bargained sold Aliened enfeoffed and confirmed and doe by these p^rsence for my self my heires Execut^rs Adm^rs & assigns fully freely and absolutely Give grant bargain sell Alien enfeoffe covey and confirm unto him ye s^d John ffrink his heires and assignes a certain percell of Land containing fiftie Acres scituate lying and being in the Township of Kittery which

Richd Bryar
to
John ffrink

land was given to Mary my wife by Will, by Cap^tn Francis Champernown Esqr and laid out by Mr William Godsoe surv^r and by him butted and bounded as followeth, to say begining at ye Northeast end of Nicholas Tuckers house lott in Spruce Creek and to run from thence in breadth fiftie four poles Northwest and Southeast And in length one hundred and forty eight poles Northeast and Southwest, bound by Mr Gunnisons land on the Northwest and Nicholas Tuckers land on the Southwest and on all ye sides with ye land of Cap^tn ffrancis·Champernown; Together with all the timber and wood standing or lying upon y^e. said land, and all other profits, priviledges and Appurtenances to ye s^d fiftie Acres belonging or in any wise appurtaining To have and to hold the s^d Tract of land

Book VI, Fol. 153.

with the appurtenances thereunto belonging, with all yᵉ Right, Title, Interest Claime & Demand which I yᵉ sᵈ Richard Bryar now have and in time past have had or which I my heires Executʳˢ Admʳˢ or assignes may might should or in any ways ought to have in time to come of in or to yᵉ above granted premisses or any part thereof to him the sᵈ John Frink his heires and assignes for ever And to yᵉ sole and proper use benefit and behoof of him the sᵈ Frink his heires &c. for evermore And I the sᵈ Richard Briar for me my heires &c Doe Covenᵗ promise and grant to and with him yᵉ sᵈ John Frink his heires &c that at and before yᵉ ensealing and Delivery hereof I am the true right and proper owner of the above menĉoned premisses and their Appurtenances And that I have in my self full power good Right and Lawfull authority the same to grant and confirm unto him yᵉ sᵈ John ffrink his heires or assignes And that yᵉ same and every part thereof is free and Clear of and from all former and other gifts grants bargains sales leases Mortgages Dowries Titles troubles Alienations and incumbrances whatsoever And that it shall and may be lawfull to and for yᵉ sᵈ John Frink his heires and assignes yᵉ aforesᵈ premisses and every part thereof from time to time and at all times for ever hereafter To have hold use ocupie improve possess and enjoy quietly and Lawfully without any Lawfull deniall hinderance Molestation or interuption of or by me or any person or persons from by or under me or by my procuremᵗ And that yᵉ sale thereof and every part thereof against my self my heires Execʳˢ Admʳˢ and assignes And against all other persons whatsoever Claiming or Lawfully Demanding yᵉ same or any pᵗ thereof I will forever save harmless Warrant & defend by these pʳsence/ In witness whereof I yᵉ sᵈ Richᵈ Briar and Mary my wife have hereunto set our hands and seales this thirteenth day of Octobʳ Anno Doɱ one thousand six hundred ninety & nine & in the Eleventh year of his Ma^ts Reign William the third over England Scotland &c King.

Signed Sealed and Delivered   Richard Briar (seal)
  In ye presence of us.   Mary Briar (seal)

the mark ⌐ of Hezekiah Elwell
William Briar

the mark of Y Sarah Esmond

York ss Feb^ry 4th 1702

The above named Richd Bryar personally appearing before me ye subscriber one of her Maties Justices of the Peace in s^d County Acknowledgd this Instrum^t to be his Act & Deed

And at the Same time Mary his wife Appeared and gave up all her Right of Dower therein.

                           Jos: Hammond

A true Copie of the originall Transcribed and compared Feb^ry 4th 1702/   p Jos: Hammond Reg^r

Know all men by these p^rsence that I Elihue Gunnison of Kittery in the County of York Shipwright for and in consideration of ye sum of forty seven pounds in money to me in hand paid by George ffrink of ye same place Yeoman, the receipt thereof I doe confess and my self therewith contented and paid and doe Acquit ye s^d George ffrink and his heires for ye same by these p^rsence for ever for ye consideration abovesaid I the s^d Elihue Gunnison aboves^d Have given granted bargained & sold and doe by these p^rsence Give grant bargain Alien sell and forever set over unto ye s^d George ffrink his heirs or assignes for ever a certain house and land containing thirty five Acres by Estimation be it more or less lying in the Township of Kittery near unto my now dwelling house/ Together with all the Appurtenances and priviledges thereunto belonging as wood underwood

Book VI, Fol. 154.

Elihu Gunnison
to
Geo: ffrink

timber and trees thereon of what quallity soever and is bound as followeth Viz^t on ye South east side of John Ingarsons Senr and John Ingarson Junr land I formerly sold them and runs from ye Kings high way thirteen pole and half wide or square from John Ingarson Junr his land by a North east line on both sides and is to run by ye s^d two Northeast lines as far as my land Extend from the s^d high way Northeastwards into the woods by ye same breadth of thirteen pole and half/ And alsoe to run downward from ye s^d highway to Spruce Creek by the lands of John Ingarson Senr & John Ingarson Junr the whole breadth from sd Ingarsons land to a Maple Stump standing on ye North side of the barrs that goe through to ye water side which Barrs are on ye South eastward of s^d Ingarsons land and so to run down from ye s^d high way and Maple stump to an ash stake pitcht by the Creek side and from that stake to John Ingarson Senr lane or landing which may be about Eleven pole in breadth more or less as it is now bounded and marked out the whole breadth & length from the said highway on ye one end, & Spruce Creek on ye other end And ye Ingarsons lands on the other side and my lands on ye southwest side And so on a straight line from ye afores^d Maple stump to the stake at the Creek side/ To have and to hold, all ye abovesaid house and land as [154] they are now bounded and discribed unto ye only and sole use benefit & behoof of him ye said George ffrink his heires or assignes for evermore And I ye said Elihue Gunnison doe for my self and my heires covenant to and with ye said ffrink and his heires and assignes that ye s^d premisses are free from all Incumbrances by me made And that I am the true and proper owner thereof And have within my self full power to make sale of the same the peaceable and quiet Possession thereof to warrant and for ever defend against all persons laying a Lawfull Claim thereunto/ In witness whereof I doe hereunto set my hand and seal this twenty

BOOK VI, FOL. 154.

Ninth day of May one thousand seven hundred and two: 1702.

Signed Sealed and Delivered   Elihue Gunnison (his seal)
   In presence of.
     the sign of
  Rachel *n C* Credifer
     the sign of
  Benjamin *B* Hamond
Wm Godsoe.

York ss Feb^{ry} 4th 1702

   The above named Elihue Gunnison personally Appearing before me the Subscrib^r one of her Ma^{ts} Justices of the Peace in s^d County Acknowledg^d this Instrum^t to be his Act and Deed And at ye same time   his wife Appeared and resigned up all her right of Dower of in and to ye above granted p^{r}misses   Jos : Ham̄ond

   A true Copie of the originall Transcribed and compared Feb^{ry} 4th 1702.   p Jos. Ham̄ond Reg^r

   Know all men by these p^{r}sence that I Elihue Gunnison of Kittery in the County of York in New England Shipwright for divers good causes and considerations me hereunto moveing, but more Especially for and in consideration of a Valluable sum̄ of Money to me in hand paid by Richard Endle of the same place Yeoman The receipt thereof I

Elihu Gunnison
*   to*
Richard Endle

doe acknowledge and my selfe therewith contented and paid Have bargained and sold And doe by these p^{r}sence bargain and sell set over & for ever confirm unto ye s^d Richard Endle his heires or assignes for ever all that Tract of Land lying in Spruce Creek containing sixty Acres of land And is part of that three hundred Acres of land that was granted unto my father Hugh Gunnison at Bryans point And is that tract of land whereon ye said Endle now dwelleth and long possest by his father Richard Endle Senr Dec^d And takes its begining at the North side of my Mill on ye North Side of my land And to ruñ in breadth southeast toward John Ingarson land Nineteen pole, and from that Exent of Nineteen pole in breadth to ruñ Northeast back into the woods as farr as my land Extends in length that way And alsoe that tract of land that lies on the South side of s^d Endles house bounded by the Creek and Ingarsons lane and the old high way as the s^d tract of land is now fenced And alsoe free liberty of thirty foot square of land where he s^d Endles father and Mother were buried for a burying place for ye s^d Endle and his family for ever ye same not to be plowed. Together with all ye Appurtenances and priviledges thereunto belonging unto ye above Mentioned tract of land on the Northeastward of s^d Endles house, with all ye wood and under wood and timb^r thereon Excepting and reserving unto me ye s^d Elihue Gunnison and my heires for ever out of the above mentioned p^rmisses ye Mill priviledge and water Course and liberty of landing doing ye s^d Endle as little Damage as may be/ To have and to hold all the above mentioned lands and p^rmisses unto the only use benefit & behoof of him ye s^d Richard Endle his heires or assignes for ever Except ye Mill priviledge above Excepted and the priviled granted to my brother Ingarson of three pole square by ye Creek as by a Deed to him bearing Date 1697. doth more at large appear And further I the s^d Elihue Gunnison doe coven^t for myself and my heires with the s^d Richard Endle & his heires that the p^rmisses are free from all Incumbrances by me made and that I am ye true and proper owner thereof And have full power to sell and Dispose of ye same, Peaceable and quiet possession thereof to warrant and Defend against all persons laying a Lawfull Claime thereunto from by or under me In Witness whereof I have hereunto set my hand and

Book VI, Fol. 154.

seal this seventeenth day of Decemb[r] one thousand seven hundred and one/

Witness   Elihue Gunnison (his seal)

  the Signe of

  John Ingarson Sen[r]

Samuel Skilin.

W[m] Godsoe Sen[r]

The 23[d] March 1701. M[r] Elihue Gunnison Appeared and Acknowledged this Instrum[t] to be his free Act and Deed/

  Before me   W[m] Pepperrell Js peace

  A true Copie of the originall Transcribed & compared the 8[th] March : 170⅔.   p Jos Hamond Reg[r]

**Bampfield
to
Richd Rogers**

Know all men by these p[r]sence that I Christopher Bamfield of Kittery in y[e] County of York with the consent and allowance of Grace my wife for and in consideration of y[e] sum of ten pounds to me in hand paid by Richard Rogers of Kittery in y[e] County of York at and before y[e] sealing hereof have bargained and sold and by these p[r]sence doe bargain and sell fully clerely and absolutely unto y[e] s[d] Richard Rogers ten Acres of land lying in the town of Kittery being bounded on the North side with s[d] Rogers his home lott and on y[e] south side with Peter Staple his land And Joying to y[e] river side and so runing back on a Northeast and by east line to y[e] head thereof To have and to hold the same ten Acres of land with all the priviledges and Appurtenances thereunto belonging to y[e] s[d] Richard Rogers his heires Execut[rs] Adm[rs] or assignes to his and their own proper use and uses for ever, and I y[e] said Christopher Bamfield my heires Execut[rs] and Adm[rs] against all persons whatsoever shall and will for ev[r] acquit & Defend by these p^rsence/ In witness hereof I the s^d Christop^r Bamfield and Grace Bamfield have hereunto afixed our hands and [155] seales this seventh day of April in ye year one thousand six hundred Ninety seven

Signed Sealed and Delivered   Christopher Bamfield (his seal)
   In presence of   Grace ⁁ Bamfield her mark (a seal)
Dependance Littlefield
Jacob Remich.
Thomas Hunscom

Know all men by these p^rsence that we the above named Christopher Bamfield and Grace Bamfield do hereby give grant and confirm unto John Rogers ye only son and heire of the above named Richard Rogers All and whatsoever addition or additions of land Adjoyning or appertaining to ye above mentioned ten acres of land which doth or ought to belong to us, with all Right title Interest Claim and Demand which we ye s^d Christopher Bampfield and Grace Bampfield now have or in time past have had, or which we our heires Execut^rs Adm^rs or assignes in time to come, may, might or in any wise ought to have of in or to ye premisses afores^d which was the true intent and meaning of, and ought to have been inserted in this Deed above written, made to his father Richd Rogers Dec^d To have and To hold the aforementioned premisses with all its priviledges and Appurtenances to him the s^d John Rogers heires Execut^rs Adm^rs and assignes for ever without any Molestation or hinderance of or by us our heires Execut^rs Adm^rs or assignes In Witness whereof we ye s^d Christopher and Grace Bampfield have hereunto set

Bampfield to Jno Rogers

Book VI, Fol. 155.

our hands and seales this twenty sixth day of May Anno Dom 1702

Signed Sealed and Delivered   Christopher Bampfield (his seal)
In presence of us.

Grace (her mark) Bampfield (her seal)

York ss May 27th 1702/

The above named Christopher Bampfield and Grace Bampfield personally appearing before me the subscriber one of his Maj⁺ⁱᵉˢ Justices of the Peace within the County of York, acknowledged the above Instrum* or Deed made to Richard Rogers Dec⁴ Together with the Additionall Instrum* to John Rogers as y⁰ Intent and meaning of the first, to be their Act and Deed.   Jos Hamond

A true Copie of y⁰ originall Deed to Rich⁴ Rogers and the Additionall Instrum* to John Rogers Transcribed and Compared. May 26 : 1702/

p Jos : Hamond Reg*

To all People to whome these p'sence shall come Daniel Fogg of Kittery in the County of York in y⁰ Province of y⁰ Massachusets Bay in New England sends greeting Know yee that I y⁰ s⁴ Daniel ffogg for and in consideration of the sum of twenty pounds currant money of New England to me in hand well and truly paid at and before thensealing and Delivery of these p'sence by James Staple of the same Kittery Taylor the receipt whereof I doe hereby acknowledg to full content and satisfaction And off and from every part and parcell thereof do hereby Acquit Exonerate and Discharge him y⁰ s⁴ James Staple his heires Execut" and Adm" for ever I y⁰ s⁴ Daniel Fogg Have given granted bargained sold Enfeoffed and and confirmed And by these p'rsence doe freely clearly and Absolutely Give sell grant bargain sell Alien enfeoffe convey and confirm unto him y'e s'd James Staple his heires execut'rs adm'rs and assignes a certain piece or parcell of Land lying and being scituate in y'e Town of Kittery afores'd begining on the Northeast side of the high way that leads from Thomas Hunscombs to Joshua Downings, bounded by y'e land of Matthew Libbey on y'e southeast and runing by the s'd highway sixteen poles Northwestward, and so to goe back into the woods upon a Northeast and by east Course that whole breadth to y'e utmost extent of my land containing about forty Acres be the same more or less And in part of that land which I purchased in partnership of Mrs Mehetable Warren and company as by their Deed of sale on Record appears at large Together with all and singular y'e Appurtenances and priviledges thereto belonging or in any wise appertaining To have and to hold the s'd piece or parcell of land with all right title Interest Claim and

Fogg
to
James Staple

Demand which I y'e said Daniel Fogg now have or in time past have had or which I my heires Execut'rs adm'rs or assignes in time to come, may might should or in any wise ought to have, of, in or to y'e above bargained p'rmisses or any part thereof And that the same is free and clear acquitted and Discharged of and from all other or former gifts grants bargains sales Mortgages and incumbrances whatsoever had, made, done, comitted or suffered to be done or comitted by me the s'd Daniel Fogg my heires or assignes And I y'e s'd Daniel Fogg doe coven't promise and grant to and with him y'e s'd James Staple that at and untill thensealing and delivery hereof, I am the true right and proper owner of the p'rmisses and every part thereof And have in my self good right full power and Lawfull authority y'e same to sell and convey unto him the said James Staple his heires & assigns And that he y'e said James Staple his heires or assignes shall and may from time to time and all times for ever hereafter have hold use ocupie possess and enjoy the same and every part thereof without any Molestaĉon let Deniall hinderance or disturbance of or by me the said Daniel Fogg my heires or assignes And that y⁰ sale thereof against my self my heires Executrˢ or assignes and against all other persons Lawfully Claiming y⁰ same or any part thereof from by or under me my heires or assignes I will for ever save harmless warrant and Defend by these presence In witness whereof I have hereunto Set my hand & seal the eighth day of December One thousand seven hundred & two. 1702

Signed Sealed and delivered   Daniel Fogg (ʰⁱˢ ˢᵉᵃˡ)
  In prence of us.
    witnesses { John Staple
                 { Jos : Hamond

York ss/ Decemb' 8 : 1702.

The wᵗʰin named Daniel Fogg personally appearing before me yᵉ subscriber one of her Majᵗˢ Justices of the Peace wᵗʰin sᵈ County Acknowledged this Instrumᵗ to be his Act and Deed :   Jos Hamond

York ss, March 16 : 1702/

    the wife of yᵉ above and wᵗʰin named Daniel ffogg personally appearing before me yᵉ subscriber one of her Maᵗˢ Justices of yᵉ peace within sᵈ County freely and volluntarily surrendred and gave up all her right of Dower of in & to yᵉ premisses wᵗʰin mentioned unto yᵉ within named James Staple his heires & assigns   Jos : Hamond

A true copie of yᵉ originall Transcribed & compared March : 16. 1702/   p Jos : Hamond Regʳ

[156] To all People to whome these pʳsence shall come I Matthew Libbey of Kittery in yᵉ County of York in yᵉ Province of the Massachusets Bay in New England send

Book VI, Fol. 156.

Greeting. Know Yee that for and in consideraĉon of the sum of ten pounds curr^t mony of New England to me in hand well and truly paid at and before thensealing and delivery of these p^{r}sence by James Staple of the same Kittery Tailor the receipt whereof I the s^d Matthew Libbey doe hereby acknowledge and my self therewith fully satisfied contented and paid And of and from every piece and parcell thereof Doe acquit and Discharge him the s^d James Staple his heires and assignes for ever, I the s^d Matthew Libbey Have given granted bargained sold aliened enfeoffed and confirmed And by these p^{r}sence Do freely clearly and absolutely Give, grant bargain sell alien enfeoffe convey and confirm unto him the s^d James Staple his heires Execut^{rs} Adm^{rs} and assignes, a certain piece or parcell scituate Lying and being in the town of Kittery afores^d begining at ye high way that leads from Thomas Hunscombs to Joshua Downings on the Northeast side of s^d highway bounded by the land of Daniel ffogg on ye Northwest and runing southeastward eight pole by s^d high way and so to goe back into the woods upon a Northeast and by east line the whole length of my land being by computation twenty Acres be the same

Libbey
to
Jas Staple

more or less And is part of that land which I purchased in partnership of Mrs Mehetable Warren and Company as by their Deed of Sale on Record at large appears Together with all and singular the appurtenances and priviledges thereto belonging or in any wise appertaining To have and to hold the s^d piece or parcell of land with all right title Interest claim and Demand which I ye said Matthew Libbey now have, or in time past have had, or which I my heires Execut^{rs} or adm^{rs} in time to come may, might should or in any wise ought to have of, in or to the s^d piece or parcell of land And that the same is free & clere Acquitted and Discharged of and from all former and other Gifts grants bargains sales Mortgages and incumbrances whatsoever had made done comitted or suffered to be done or comitted by me yᵉ sᵈ Matthew Libbey my heires or assignes And I the sᵈ Matthew Libbey Do covenᵗ promise and grant to and with him the sᵈ Staple that at and untill thensealing and Delivery hereof I am the true right and proper owner of the pʳmisses and every part thereof, and have in my self good right full power and Lawfull authority the same to sell and convey unto him the sᵈ James Staple his heires and assignes And that yᵉ sᵈ James Staple his heires Executʳˢ admʳˢ or assignes shall and may from time to time and at all times for ever hereafter Have hold ocupie possess and enjoy the same and every part thereof without any Molestacõn let denial hinderance or disturbance of or by me the sᵈ Matthew Libbey my heires or assignes And that yᵉ sale thereof against my self my heires Executʳˢ or assignes And against all other persons Lawfully Claiming yᵉ same or any part thereof from by or under me my heires Executʳˢ or assignes I will for ever save harmless Warrant & Defend by these pʳsence In witness whereof I have hereunto set my hand and seal the eighth day of Decembʳ one thousand seven hundred and two : 1702./

Signed Sealed and Delivered   his
  in pʳsence of us   Matthew 𝓜 Libbey (his seal)
witnesses { John Staple   mark
     { Jos : Hamond

York ss/ Kittery Decembʳ 8ᵗʰ 1702.

   The within named Matthew Libbey personally Appearing before me yᵉ Subscriber one of her Maᵗˢ. Justices of the Peace wᵗʰin sᵈ County Acknowledged this Instrumᵗ to be his Act and Deed

            Jos : Hamond

York ss Kittery Janʳʸ 15ᵗʰ 1702.

   The wife of the above and within named Matthew Libby personally Appearing before me yᵉ Subscribʳ one of her Maᵗˢ Justices of yᵉ peace within sᵈ County freely and voluntarily surrendred up all her right of Dower of in and unto yᵉ within pʳmisses unto yᵉ within named James Staple his heires and Assignes/ Jos : Haṁond

A true Copie of the orignall Transcribed & compared: from : Janʳʸ 15ᵗʰ 1702 p Jos Haṁond Regʳ

To all Christian People to whome this pʳsent Deed of Sale shall come Know Yee that I John Plaisted of Portsmᵒ in the Province of New Hampshier many good & Lawfull causes and considerations me hereunto moveing but more in speciall for the consideration of one hundred pounds of money to me in hand paid & secured to be paid by Benoni Hodsden in the Province of Mayn the receipt whereof I doe hereby Acknowledge and my self fully satisfied therewith Doe for my self my heires Executʳˢ and Administratʳˢ for ever acquit and Discharge him yᵉ sᵈ Hodsden his heires Executʳˢ & Admʳˢ from every part and penny thereof Have given granted bargained and sold, and Doe by this presents Grant bargain sell enfeoffe release deliver and confirm unto him the sᵈ Hodsden his heires Executʳˢ Admʳˢ & assignes a certain parcel of Lands, timber trees and woods thereon

Plaisted to Hodsden

lying and being in the aforesaid Town of Kittery, near a place called birch point on the North side sᵈ Hodsdens house and was part thereof granted by the town of Kittery unto Capᵗⁿ John Wincoll in the year one thousand six hundred fiftie and two Decembʳ yᵉ 16 & run out and renewed yᵉ bounds the twenty fourth of Aprill 1654 — as may more full Appear by sᵈ grant, which Lot of tract of Land was by the sᵈ Wincoll sold unto my honoured father Roger Plaisted the 13ᵗʰ of July 1660 as p Deed undʳ sᵈ Wincolls hand and seal and by my self purchased of my Sister Elizabeth Plaisted as p Deed under her hand and seal bearing date yᵉ sixth of July : 1693 as also sixty rods of land ajoyning to sᵈ Lott granted to my father by the town of Kittery Decembʳ yᵉ 13ᵗʰ 1669. To have and to hold the sᵈ two parcells of land, together with all the Timbʳ trees woods and underwood with all the priviledges thereto belonging according to the sᵈ town grant and bounds being about eighty Acres more or less unto him the sᵈ Hodsden his heires Executⁿ Admⁿ and assignes for ever, without the least trouble Molestation or Interuption of me yᵉ sᵈ John Plaisted my heires Execut ⁿ Admⁿ or assignes or any other person or persons whatsoever laying any Lawfull Claime to all or any part thereof from by or under me, them or any of them but that it is and shall be Lawfull for him the sᵈ Hodsden his heires Executⁿ or assignes the sᵈ parcells of lands timbʳ trees woods and underwoods To have hold and peaceably the same to enjoy as their own proper right in Fee Simple/ for confirmation hereof I have hereto set my hand and Seal this 2ᵈ day of Decembʳ one thousand six hundred Ninety eight. It is to be understood that the land sold by my self unto James Emery is not to be medled with but is reserved out of the above bargained land, to be to the sole use of the sᵈ Emery and his heires for ever without the least Interuption from the sᵈ Hodsden or his heires &c for ever.

Signed Sealed and Delivered   John Plaisted (his seal)
  In presence of
  John Pickerin Senʳ
  Job Alcock.

Province of New Hampshʳ Dec: 2ᵈ 1696

  Mʳ John Plaisted appeared before me Job Alcock one of his Maᵗˢ Justices of peace for sᵈ Province Acknowledged the above Deed to be his Act and Deed/

                             Job Alcock Jus: pea

  A true Copie of the originall/ Transcribed and Compared March 22ᵈ 1702.   ·   p Jos: Ham̃ond Regʳ

BOOK VI, FOL. 157.

[157] Know all men by these p'sence that I James Spinney of Portsm° in the Province of New Hampshier Yeoman for Divers good and valluable consideration me hereunto moveing but more Especially for and in consideration of the sum of ten pounds in Money to me in hand paid by my brother John Spinney of the Town of Kittery in the County of York Yeoman The receipt thereof I do acknowledge and my self well and truly contented and paid And doe by these presence acquit the s^d John Spinney for the same, for ye consideration abovesaid I ye s^d James Spiney Have given granted bargained and sold And doe by these p'sence give grant bargain and sell enfeoffe and for ever confirm unto ye said John Spinney his heires and assignes All that Tract of land Lying in the Township of Kittery in ye County aboves^d containing one Acre of Land be it more or less and is scituate and lying by the Main River of Piscataqua And is bounded on the North and East with ye land of the said John Spinney And on the west with the land of Thomas Fernald And is that land which was given me by my late

Jas Spinney
to
Jno Spinney

Hon^d father Thomas Spinney as by a Deed under his hand doth appear, bearing Date ye twenty second day of March one thousand six hundred ninety & four Together with all ye appurtenances and priviledges thereunto belonging or appertaining To have and to hold ye afores^d tract of Land and every part thereof unto the only and sole use benefit and behoof of him the said John Spinney his heires and assignes for evermore And furthermore I the s^d James Spinney doe covenant for my self my heires Execut^{rs} & Administrat^{rs} with the s^d John Spinney his heires and assignes, that ye p'misses are free from all Incumbrances whatsoever as Joyntures Dowrys gifts sales or Mortgages and that at the time of the ensealing hereof I am the true and proper owner of the same And have within my selfe full power & Lawfull Authority to dispose of the same And that it shall and may be Lawfull for the s^d John Spinney at all times hereafter to take use ocupie and possess the same without ye lett or hinderance of me the said James Spinney or any other person under me, The peaceable & quiet possession thereof to warrant and maintain against all persons whatsoever laying Lawfull Claim thereunto, In witness hereof I have hereunto set my hand and seal this nineteen day of Decemb^r one thousand seven hundred and two, And in the first year of her Ma^{ts} Reign Anne by ye grace of God Queen of England Scotland ffrance and Ireland Defend^r of the Faith &c/

Signed Sealed and Delivered } 1702/ James Spinney (his seal)
  In presence of us.
Thomas ffernald
the sign ✝ of
Mary ffernald
The Sign ℘ of
Lydia Harmon

York ss/ Jan^{ry} 27th 1702.

The above named James Spinney personally appearing before me ye subscrib^r one of her Ma^{ts} Justices of the Peace in s^d County Acknowledged this Instrum^t to be his Act and Deed

         Jos : Hamond

A true Copie of the originall Deed Transcribed and Compared, Jan^{ry} 27th 1702   p Jos : Hamond Reg^r

Know all men by these p'sence that I William Hilton of Exeter in ye Province of New Hampshier in New England Gentleman many good considerations Intentions and causes me thereto moveing — Have given granted and sold unto ffrancis Mercer of Portsm^o in the Province of New Hampshier afores^d Carpenter three Acres of Land or ground lying and being in the Town of Kittery in ye Province of Main in New England And next Adjoyning on ye one side to ye land, ground or plantation of one Charles Nelson & being eight rods or perches in breadth bound on the one end wth the River of Piscataqua and on the other side with ye land or plantation formerly appertaining unto one John Simons out of which the s^d three Acres have been given like as by these p'sence with ye consent of Rebecca my wife I doe hereby Demise give grant sell and enfeoffe unto ye afores^d Mercer his heires Execut^{rs} Adm^{rs} and assignes the above mentioned three Acres of Land with all the profits pleasures Appurtenances benefits and conveniences whatsoever therein or thereunto belonging or   and I doe by the advise and free consent of my afores^d wife bind me my heires Execut^{rs} adm^{rs} & assignes to save warrant and Defend unto ye s^d ffrancis Mercer his heires Executors adm^{rs} and assignes the

<small>Hilton to Mercer</small>   above Demised premisses from Generation to generation for ever from all manner of person persons whatsoever who can may or shall Claim any Interest right Challenge or Claim whatsoever in or unto the s^d Demised three Acres of ground by vertue of any Deed, gift grant right Interest Challenge or Claim whatsoever precedent the Date hereof In witness of the true meaning and for the true performance of all and every of what above mentioned the above William Hilton and Rebecca his wife have hereunto put their hands and affixed their Seales this second day of August in the year of our Lord God One thousand six hundred eighty and one

Signed Sealed and Delivered · William ⊤ Hilton (his/Ss)
   In the presence of us   his mark
   John Jackson   and seal
        mark   Rebecca R Hilton (her/seal)
   William W Hilton Junr her mark
       his
   Sam^{ll} Hilton
   Joseph Alexander ·

Book VI, Fol. 158.

The above named William Hilton came and Acknowledged the above written Instrum^t to be his proper Act and Deed the 28th May 1685/ Before me

R : Chamberlain Jus : P

Entred and Recorded according to y^e originall the 28th May 1685

R. Chamberlain Sec^r

Province New Hampsh^r
Portsm^o March 15th 170$\frac{2}{3}$

The within Deed is a true Copie this day taken out of y^e Records 3^d Book ffol : 279./ Compared

p Sam^{ll} Penhallow Record^r

A true Copie of y^e Copie of y^e originall Transcribed and Compared/   p Jos : Hamond Reg^r

[158] Know all men by these p^{r}sents that I John Hilton of Exet^r in the Province of New Hampshier in New England Yeoman Do hereby Acknowledge and confess myself to be owing and stand Justly Indebted unto ffrancis Mercer of Portsm^o in the Province of New Hampshier afores^d Carpent^r in the Just and full sum of one hundred pounds sterling Currant good money to be paid unto s^d Mercer his heires Execut^{rs} Adm^{rs} assignes or Lawfull Attorney at his or their will and pleasure for the true performance whereof I the s^d John John Hilton Do hereby bind me my heires Execut^{rs} adm^{rs} and assignes firmly by these p^{r}sents. As Witness my hand & seal ye 27th day of Octob^r Anñ Dom. 1686.

The Condition of the above obligation is such that if the above bounden Hilton his heires Execut^{rs} adm^{rs} and assignes Do well & truly confirm observe keep ratifie and make good at all times and time hereafter All and every the whole condition and true meaning of the sale of three Acres of Land formerly sold by

Hilton
to
Mercer

Book VI, Fol. 158.

the father of the s^d Hilton as at large Appeareth by a Deed under his hand & seal bearing Date the second day of August Anno Dom̃i. 1681. That then and in that Case the above Obligation to be voyd and of non Effect otherwise to stand remain and continue in full force & vertue in Law being p^rsent John Pickerin Senr   & seal

   Joseph Alexander   John H Hilton (his seal)
       mark   his mark

   Walter Crap
        his

Cap^tn John Pickerin appeared before me this 23^d of March one thousand seven hundred and two three, and made oath that he saw ye aboves^d John Hilton Signe Seal and Deliver ye above Instrum^t as his Act and Deed And that Joseph Alexander did sign as an Evidence at the same/
                         John Plaisted Jus^ts of Peace

A true Copie of the originall Transcribed and compared the 24th March 1702.   p Jos Ham̃ond Reg^r

---

Raynes to Woodman

This Indenture made this eight day of March in the first year of ye Reign of of our Soveraign Lady Anne by the grace of God of England Scotland ffrance and Ireland Queen Defend^r of ye Faith &. Anno Domini 170⅔ between Francis Raynes, Senr of the Town of York in the Province of the Massachusets Bay in New England Gentleman on the one part And John Woodman of Kittery fferryman of ye s^d County one the other part witnesseth that ye said ffrancis Rayns for and in consideraçon of a valluable sum̃ to him in hand already paid by the said John Woodman the receit whereof he doth by these presence Acknowledge And himself therewith to be fully satisfied hath granted bargained and sold,

And by these presence doth grant bargain and sell unto the said John Woodman his heires Execut^n Adm^n and assignes for ever a certain parcel of land upon the Eastward side of Broad boat harbour begining at a small point of upland pointing East into ye Marsh upon which point is the low^r bounds which is a forked tree marked And soe runneth North northwest up the Creek one hundred and Ninety poles And so backward untill three hundred Acres be fully compleated, provided it doth not intrench upon Mr Godfreys land with all the priviledges and Appurtenances thereunto belonging with all Evidences writing or Minuments of or concerning said premisses To have and to hold the s^d parcel of Land unto ye s^d John Woodman his heires & assignes for ever hereby Warranting ye said premisses from from any person from by or under him the s^d ffrancis Raynes or any person or persons else whatsoev^r unto the only use and behoof of him ye s^d John Woodman his heires Exec^{rs} adm^{rs} and assignes In witness whereof he ye s^d ffrancis Raynes hath hereunto set his hand and seal the day and year above written: Anno Dom^i: 170¾

Signed Sealed and Possession   the mark of
   given of ye above p^{r}mises   ffrancis ✚ Raynes sen^r (his seal)
   In the p^{r}sence of us
   Natha: Raynes Senr
   George Crusy
   Nath: ffreeman

York ss/ April ye 16th 1703.

   Cap^{tn} ffrancis Raynes personally appeared before me and Acknowledged this above written Deed to John Woodman to be his act and Deed/

                        Willm Pepperrell Js pes

York ss/ Apr^l ye 17th 1703.

   by request of aboves^d Woodman this aboves^d Instrum^t was Transcribed in York Town book

                 p me Abr^m Preble Town Cler

Book VI, Fol. 159.

A true Copie of yᵉ originall Transcribed and Compared Aprˡ 20ᵗʰ 1703. p Jos: Hamond Regʳ

To all Xtian People to whome this pʳsent writing shall come ffrancis Champernown of Kittery in yᵉ County of York Esqʳ sendeth Greeting Know Yee that I yᵉ said ffrancis Champernown for and in consideration of yᵉ sum of one hundred and fourscore pounds of Lawfull pay of New England, in hand before thensealing and delivery of these pʳsence well and truly paid by Walter Barfoot of Dover in yᵉ County of Portsmᵒ Chirurgeon the receipt whereof the sᵈ ffrancis Champernown doth hereby Acknowledge and him-

Champrnown
to
Barfoot

self to be fully satisfied and paid And thereof and of every part pcel and penny thereof doth Acquit Exonerate and Discharge the sᵈ Walter Barfoot his heires Executʳˢ and assigns and every of them for ever by these pʳsence. Hath granted bargained and sold Aliened Enfeoffeed conveyed, released assured, delivered and confirmed And by these pʳsence doth graint bargain and sell Alien Enfeoffe convey release assure deliver and confirm unto yᵉ sᵈ Walter Barfoot his heires & assignes All that tract piece or parcel of Upland and swamp Scituate lying and being in Kittery aforesᵈ at a place there called and known by yᵉ name of Spruce Creek or by what other name or names yᵉ same is called or known And containing two hundred and sixteen Acres being parcell of a Town grant of three hundred Acres given unto yᵉ sᵈ ffrancis Champernown by the Town of Kittery aforesᵈ as by yᵉ Records of the sᵈ town of Kittery will Appear which sᵈ quantity of two hundred [**159**] and Sixty Acres yᵉ sᵈ Francis Champernown doth hereby promise to lay out by Meetes and bounds or cause to be laid out unto the sᵈ Walter Barfoot his Executʳˢ Admʳˢ or assⁿˢ within one month next after yᵉ Date

hereof, Together with all paths, passages trees woods underwoods commons Easments profits comodities Advantages Emolum^{ts} hereditam^{ts} & Appurtenances whatsoever to ye s^d tract piece or parcel of Land belonging or in any wise Appertaining and also all ye right title claim interest use possession reverc̃on remaind^r and demand of him the s^d ffrancis Champernown of in and to ye s^d p^{r}misses And of in and unto every or any part or parcel thereof and at ye signing of the bargained p^{r}misses ye s^d Champernown had full power right title claim and Interest of and in ye s^d tract piece or parcell of land, And further ye s^d Champernown doth hereby promise and engage himself his heires Execut^{rs} Adm^{rs} and assignes to save Defend and keep harmless ye s^d Walter Barfoot his heires Execut^{rs} Adm^{rs} or assignes from any person or persons whatsoever Lawfully laying any Claim right title or Interest thereunto, To have and to hold the s^d tract piece or parcel of upland and swamp and every part and parcel thereof And all ways paths passages trees woods and under woods comons Easme^s profits comodities & advantages Emolum^{ts} Hereditam^{ts} and Appurtenances whatsoever unto ye s^d Walter Barfoot his heires and ass for ever And to ye sole and only proper use and behoof of the s^d Walter Barfoot his heires and ass for ever and to no other intent or meaning whatsoev^r In witness whereof I have hereunto set my hand seal this twenty first day of January in the one and twentieth year of ye Reign of our Soveraign Lord Charles ye Second of England Scotland ffrance and Ireland King Defend^r of the ffaith &c. And in ye year of our Lord God one thousand six hundred Sixty and Nine. 1669.
Signed Sealed and Delivered   Fran Champernown (and a seal)

In the presence of us.
Hen: Greenland
    the mark of
James   Skid
Tho: Watkins.

BOOK VI, FOL. 159.

James Skid appeared before John Hincks one of his Maj^{tys} Council for his Teritory & Dominion of New England, made oath that he set his hand as a Witness unto ye above Deed this 20th Augst 1688

            John Hinckes

Recorded in the Secretaries office for his Ma^{ts} Teritory and Dominion of New England at Boston ye fifth day of Apr^l 1689./

            John West D Sec̃ry

A true Copie of the originåll Transcribed and compared April 15th 1703   p Jos : Ham̃ond Reg^r

---

Barfoot to Lee

To all Xtian People to whome this p^rsent writing shall come Walter Barfoot Esqr in ye Province of New Hampshier in New England sendeth Greeting, Know Yee, that I ye s^d Walter Barfoot Esqr out of that Naturall love & affection that I bear to my Loving kinsman John Lee Marrin^r now of Portsmouth in this Province of New Hampshier, but formerly of Chadwell near London in old England, And for that great love and affection shown toward me in coming from his relations to se me, Hath given granted Aliened Enfeoffed convaed assured and delivered unto my said kinsman John Lee his heires Execut^{rs} Adm^{rs} or assignes all that tract piece or parcel of upland and swamp scituate lying and being in Kittery in his Ma^{ts} Province or County of York all which land I bought and purchased of ffrancis Champernown for one hundred and fourscore pounds as by Deed under ye hand and seal of ffrancis Champernown Esqr Dated ye twentie first day of January one thousand six hundred sixty and nine, more at large doth Appear, All which upland and swamp lyeth at a place there called and known by ye name of Spruce Creek or by what oth^r name or names ye same is called or known and containing two hundred & sixteen Acres which s^d quantity of two hundred and sixteen Acres ye s^d Walter Barfoot Esqr doth hereby give and lay out by Meetes and bounds or cause to be laid out unto John Lee my s^d kinsman his heires Execut^{rs} Adm^{rs} or assigns within one moneth next after ye Date hereof Together with all paths passages trees woods under woods Comons Easm^{ts} profits comodities advantages Emoluments hereditam^{ts} & appurtenances whatsoever, to s^d Tract piece or parcel of land belonging or in any wise appertaining And also all ye Right title Claimes Interest use possession revercon Remaind^r and demands of him the s^d Walter Barfoot Esqr of in and to ye s^d Premisses And of in & unto every or any part or parcel thereof And at ye time of the Gift & grant thereof ye s^d Walter Barfoot Esqr had full power Rite title Claime and Interest to and in ye s^d Tract piece or parcel of land to give and dispose off as aboves^d And further ye s^d Barfoot Esqr doth hereby promise and engage himself his heires Execut^{rs} Adm^{rs} and assignes to save defend and keep harmless the said John Lee my s^d kinsman his heires Execut^{rs} adm^{rs} or assignes from any person or persons whatsoever Lawfully laying any Claim Right title or Interest thereunto To have and to hold the s^d tract piece or parcel of upland & swamp & every part and parcel thereof And all ways paths passages trees woods & underwoods comons easments profits comoditys advantages Emoluments Hereditam^{ts} and Appurtenances whatsoever unto ye s^d John Lee my s^d kinsman his heires and assignes for ever And to ye sole and only proper use and behoof of ye s^d John Lee my said kinsman his heires and assiges for ever and to no other Intent or meaning whatsoever In witness whereof I have hereunto set my hand and seal this one and twentieth day of Novemb^r one thousand six hundred eighty and seven And in ye third year of the Reign of our Soveraign Lord James ye second of England Scotland & Defend^r of the ffaith 1687

Book VI, Fol. 160.

Memorand that in yᵉ sixt row it is mentioned yᵉ County of York, but now it is called his Maᵗⁱᵉ Province of Mayn/ Signed Sealed and Delivered   Walter Barfoot (his seal)

In p'sence of us.
Robᵗ Tufton
Tho Wiggin

Mʳ Thomas Wiggin & Mʳ Robert Tufton made oath that the saw Capᵗⁿ Walter Barfoot Signe seal & deliver yᵉ above Ded for yᵉ use above   Before

John Hinckes of yᵉ Council

A true Copie of yᵉ originall Transcribed and compared Aprˡ 15ᵗʰ 1703   p Jos : Hamond Regʳ

[160] At a Legall Town Meeting held at Kittery May 24ᵗʰ 1699/ Granted unto Moses Goodwin thirty Acres of land to him his heires and assignes for ever to be laid out Clear of former grants   Attests. Jos. Hamond Cleř

March 23ᵈ 170⅔/ I have sold yᵉ above grant of thirty Acres of land unto Gabriel Hambleton and Acknowledge myself fully satisfied/ Witness my hand.

his mark
Moses ✕ Goodin

At a Legall Town Meeting held at Kittery May 24ᵗʰ 1699/ Granted unto Job Emery his heirs and assignes for ever twenty Acres of land to be laid out clear of former grants.   Attests. Jos : Hamond Cleř

Book VI, Fol. 160.

March 23ᵈ 170¾. I have sold the above grant of twenty Acres of land unto Gabriel Hambleton and Acknowledge my self fully satisfied. Witness my hand.

Witness { John Gowen.   Job. Emery.
         { Samuel Small

York ss. Barwick/ Moses Goodwin and Job Emery personally appeared before me Ichabod Plaisted one of her Maᵗˢ Justices of yᵉ peace and Acknowledged yᵉ within written assignmᵗˢ to be their free Act and Deed this twenty sixt of March one thousand seven hundred and three: 1703

                         Ichabod Plaisted

A true Copie of yᵉ above grants assignmᵗˢ And Acknowledgmᵗˢ of Moses Goodwin and Job Emery to Gabriel Hambleton, Transcribed and with yᵉ originall compared this 26ᵗʰ April 1703.

                         p Jos: Hammond Regʳ

Know all men by these pʳsence that I James Emery senʳ, of Barwick in the County of york in yᵉ Province of the Massachusets in New England, for Divers good causes and considerations me hereunto moving, but Espcially for yᵉ love I doe bear unto my naturall son James Emery of the Town and Province abovesᵈ Have given granted Alienated and confirmed And doe by these pʳsence Give grant Alienate and confirm unto my said son James Emery a certain parcel of Land lying and being in the Town and County abovesᵈ containing by Estimation twenty Acres be it more or less bounded Northerly on the land of Daniel Goodin Senʳ begining at yᵉ foot of the land at a small Red oak tree And so runing on a south line to yᵉ land of Jnᵒ Plaisted/ Bounded Southerly on the land of John Plaisted runing on yᵉ south side till you come to a

Jas Emery to his son James

small brook called Stony brook, so to run as y⁰ said brook runeth, till you come to yᵉ sᵈ land of Daniel Goodin senʳ on yᵉ North All which parcel of land Together with all yᵉ Appurtenances thereunto belonging or that may or shall hereafter belong to or to be to my said son James Emery his heires, To have and to hold the sᵈ land for ever as a quiet and peaceable possession free from all Molestation from me yᵉ abovesᵈ James Emery senʳ my heires Executʳˢ or any other person or persons laying any Legall Claim thereunto, for from by or under me, likewise I do give to my said son James Emery half an Acre of ground as freely as yᵉ abovesᵈ tract of land, which sᵈ half Acre shall be where his now dwelling house standeth so that he shall have a free outlet from his house to yᵉ street, likewise I do reserve three quarters of a rod of land in breadth along by the side of Daniel Goodins land for to be a free way to be to yᵉ use of me and my heires for ever/ for yᵉ confirmation of the above written I have set to my hand and seal this January yᵉ second One thousand six hundred Ninety and four/ Annoq̃ Sexto Gulielmi Regis Nostri Tertij Angliæ. &c.

Signed Sealed and Delivered James Emery (his seal)
   In the presence of us.
      Jabez *Ja* Garland
         his mark
      Paul Averell
      Edward Tompson

James Emery Senʳ personally Appeared before me John Plaisted this 28ᵗʰ of Octobʳ 1702. and Acknowledged yᵉ above Instrumᵗ to be his Act and Deed./

                         John Plaisted Justis Peace

   A true Copie of the originall Transcribed and compared
March 1ˢᵗ 1702   p Jos: Hañiond Regʳ

Book VI, Fol. 160.

To all people to whome these p`r`sence shall come Know Yee that I Benoni Hodsden of Kittery in the County of York in y`e` Province of the Massachusets Bay in New England for and in consideration of the sum of seventy pounds Curr`t` money of New England to me in hand well and truly paid by Philip Hubbord of Kittery afores`d` in y`e` County and Province aforesaid the receipt whereof I doe hereby acknowledge and my self therewith to be fully satisfied contented and paid And of and from every part and parcel thereof Do for me my heires Exec`rs` Adm`rs` and assignee Acquit and Discharge him y`e` s`d` Philip Hubbord his heires and assignes for ever by these presence Have given granted bargained sold Aliened enfeoffed and confirmed, And by these p`r`sence do freely clearly and Absolutely, give grant bargain sell Alien enfeoffe convey and confirm unto him y`e` s`d` Philip Hubbord his heires Execut`rs` adm`rs` and assignes, a certain piece or parcel of land Lying and being scituate in Barwick in y`e` Township of Kittery afores`d` bounded as fol-

Hodsden
to
Hubbord

loweth Viz`t` begining at y`e` Lower corner of an old Ditch at a stake standing there and by the Road that leads down y`e` Town till it comes to y`e` high way that leads to y`e` Comons which way goes from y`e` landing place near my house And to go that way till it comes to a white oak marked on four sides Joyning to Nathan Lords land and from y`e` s`d` oak to a pine tree standing on the side of Birchen point brook (marked) And from s`d` tree to a white oak marked with y`e` letters H. N. and from s`d` tree westward by old bounds till it comes to a stake, which stake is the southwest corner bounds of James Emerys house Lot And from s`d` stake by y`e` s`d` Hubbords land till it comes to y`e` above mentioned Road at the Ditch, Containing about forty Acres of Land be y`e` same more or less together with all y`e` priviledges and appurtenances thereunto belonging or in any wise Appertaining To have and to hold the s`d` piece or parcel of land with all right title Interst

Claim and Demand which I y⁰ sᵈ Benoni Hodsden now have or in time past have, or which I my heires Execⁿ Admⁿ or assignes in time to come, may might should or in any wise ought to have of in or to yᵉ above granted premisses or any part thereof, To him yᵉ said Philip Hubbord his heires and assignes for ever And to y⁰ only proper use benefit and behoof of him y⁰ sᵈ Philip Hubbord his heires &c for evermore And I y⁰ sᵈ Benoni Hodsden for me my heires Execuᵗⁿ Admⁿ and assignes doe covenᵗ promise and grant to and with him yᵉ sᵈ Philip Hubbord his [161] heires Execuᵗⁿ & assignes that at and untill thensealing and delivery hereof I am yᵉ true right and proper owner of yᵉ above granted pʳmisses and thappurtenances And that I have in my self good Right full power and Lawfull Authority yᵉ same to grant and confirm unto him yᵉ sᵈ Philip Hubbord his heires and assignes as aforesᵈ And that yᵉ same and every part thereof is free and Clear Acquitted and Discharged of and from all former and other gifts grants bargains sales Mortgages leases titles troubles Acts Alienacōns and incumbrances whatsoever And that it shall and may be Lawfull to and for him yᵉ sᵈ Hubbord his heires and assignes yᵉ aforesᵈ Premisses and every part thereof from time to time and at all times for ever hereafter To have hold use ocupie possess & enjoy Lawfully peaceably and quietly without any Lawfull Lett deniall hinderance Molestation or disturbance of or by me y⁰ sᵈ Hodsden or any other person from by or undʳ me or by my procuremᵗ And that yᵉ sale thereof against my self my heires Execᵗⁿ and assignes I will for ever save harmless warrant and Defend by these presence In witness whereof I y⁰ sᵈ Benoni Hodsden have hereunto set my hand & seal this twenty fifth day of Aprˡ in yᵉ second year of yᵉ Reign of our Soveraign Lady Anne, by the grace of God of England Scotland ffrance and Ireland Queen Defendʳ of the Faith &c : 1703

Book VI, Fol. 161.

It is agreed before ye ensealing hereof that Joseph Hodsden has liberty for him his heires and assigns for ever for water water not Damnifying s^d Hubbord

Signed Sealed and Delivered   Benony Hodsden (seal)

In the presence of us

Witnesses {
   Daniel Stone
   Nathan (his mark) Lord
   Jos: Hamond
}

York ss/ Apr^l 25th 1703.

The within named Benoni Hodsden personally appearing before me y^e Subscrib^r one of her Maj^{tys} Justices of the Peace for s^d County Acknowledged this Instrum^t to be his Act and Deed, And at the same time Abigail y^e wife of s^d Hodsden Appeared and resigned up all her Right of Dowe_r of in or to y^e Premisses within Mentioned.

                                    Jos: Hamond

A true Copie of y^e originall Transcribed and compared, Apr^l 25th 1703   p Jos: Hamond Reg^r

---

Lord to Hodsden

Know all men by these presence that I Nathan Lord of Kittery in y^e County of York in the Province of the Massachusets Bay in New England Yeoman, for and in consideration and Exchange of a certain piece or parcel of Land bought and exchanged with Benoni Hodsden of Kittery in ye County and Province afores^d And do by these presence for the consideration of a certain parcel of land lying and being scituate in the Township of Kittery bounded on ye south with my own house Lot, on ye East with the Land I bought of Sivenus Knock And on the North with James Emery & by severall marked trees and other bounds as at large appears by an Instrum^t under s^d Hodsdens hand and seal bearing even Date with these presence referrence thereunto being had, containing twelve Acres be it more or less for ye consideration of wch Exchange and in Lieu thereof, I the s^d Nathan Lord have given granted bargained and sold And by these presence do for me my heires and assignes freely clearly & absolutely give grant bargain sell convey and confirm unto him ye s^d Benoni Hodsden a certain Lot of land Lying and being sciuate in ye Township of Kittery afores^d bounded on the Northwest wih Birch point brook and ye Hodsdens land on the Southeast or however Else bounded or reputed to be bounded, containing about seven Acres of land be ye same more or less And is that lot of Land whereon John Morrell formerly dwelt Together with all buildings fences orchards gardens thereon. To have and to hold the s^d lot of land with all and singular the priviledges and Appurtenances thereunto belonging or in any wise appertaining to him ye s^d Benoni Hodsden his heires Execut^{rs} Adm^{rs} and assignes and to his & their only proper use benefit and behoof for ever/ And I the s^d Nathan Lord doe coven^t promise and grant to and with him ye s^d Benoni Hodsden his heires & assignes that ye Premisses are free from any Incumbrance whatsoever And that I have in myself good Right full power and Lawfull Authority the same to sell and convey unto him ye s^d Hodsden his heires and assignes And that he the s^d Benoni Hodsden his heires and assignes shall and may from time to time and at all times for ever hereafter have hold use ocupie possess & enjoy the same and every part thereof Lawfully peaceably and quietly without any Lawfull Let deniall hinderance or disturbance of or by me ye s^d Lord my heires or assignes And that ye sale thereof against myself my heires and assignes and against any other person or persons Lawfully Claiming the same or any part thereof from by or under me my heires or assignes I will for ever save harmless

Book VI, Fol. 161.

warrant and Defend by these presence. In witness whereof, I have hereunto set my hand and seal this twenty fifth day of Apr^l in ye second year of the Reign of our Soveraign Lady Anne by the grace of God of England Scotland france and Ireland Queen Defend^r of ye Faith &c and in ye year of our Lord one thousand seven hundred and three : 1703.

Signed Sealed and delivered
 In the presence of us   Nathan his mark Lord (his seal)
 Daniel Stone
 Philip Hubord
 Jos : Hammond

York ss/ Apr^l 25th 1703.

The above named Nathan Lord and Martha his wife personally appearing before me ye subscrib^r one of her Ma^{ts} Justices of ye Peace in s^d County, ye s^d Nathan Acknowledged this Instrum^t to be his Act and Deed/ And ye s^d Martha freely resigned up all her right of Dower of in & to the above granted Premisses.

            Jos : Hammond

A true Copie of ye originall Transcribed and compared April : 25th 1703   p Jos : Hammond Reg^r

Know all men by these p^{r}sence that I Benoni Hodsden of Kittery in the County of York in the Province of the Massachusets Bay in New England Yeoman for the consideration and Exchange of a certain piece or parcel of Land bought and Exchanged with Nathan Lord of Kittery in ye County and Province afores^d And doe by these presence for ye consideration of a certain Lot of Land lying & being scituate in the Township of Kittery Adjoyning to my own Land and birch point brook And is that Lot of Land which was formerly John Morrells containing seven Acres be ye same more or less for

Hodsden to Lord

the consideration of which exchange and in Lieu thereof I ye s^d Benoni Hodsden Have given granted bargained and sold And by these presence doe for me my heires and assignes Give grant bargain sell and confirm unto him ye s^d Nathan Lord a [162] certain piece or parcel of land in s^d Town of Kittery bounded on ye south side with the s^d Lords house Lot/ on ye East with ye Land s^d Lord bought of Silvanus Knock and on the North with James Emery till it comes to a white oak marked with ye Letters H. N And from s^d oak across s^d Land till it comes to a pine tree which tree stands by ye side of birchpoint brook And is ye s^d Lords Northwest corner bounds of his house Lot, the corner mark being a red oak tree And so along by a white oak marked near upon a line till it comes to a white oak marked with ye Letters N. H. containing twelve Acres be it more or Less, Together with all ye priviledges and Appurtenances thereunto belonging To have and to hold the s^d piece or parcel of Land to him ye s^d Nathan Lord his heirs Execut^{rs} Adm^{rs} and Assignes And to his and their own proper use benefit and behoof for ever And I ye s^d Benoni Hodsden doe covenant promise and grant to & with him ye s^d Nathan Lord his heires and assignes that ye premisses are free from all incumbrances whatsoever And that I have in my self good Right full power and Lawfull Authority the same to sell and convey unto him ye s^d Lord his heirs and ass And that he ye s^d Nathan Lord his heires & ass shall and may from time to time and at all times for ever hereafter Have hold use ocupie possess & and enjoy the same Lawfully peaceably and quietly without any Lawfull Let denial hinderance Molestacon or disturbance of or by me my heires or assignes or any other person or persons Lawfully Claiming ye same or any part thereof from by or und^r me my heires or assignes, And that ye sale thereof against my selfe my heires or assignes I will for ever save harmless warrant and Defend by these presence In witness whereof I have hereunto set

BOOK VI, FOL. 162.

my hand and seal this twenty fifth day of April In the second year of the Reign of our Soveraign Lady Anne by the grace of God of England Scotland France and Ireland Queen Defender of the Faith &c/ And in the year of our Lord one thousand seven hundred & three 1703

Signed Sealed and delivered   Benony Hodsden (his seal)

   In the presence of us.
   Daniel Stone
   Philipe Hubord
   Jos Hamond.

York ss/ Apr¹ 25ᵗʰ 1703 :

The above named Benoni Hodsden and Abigail his wife personally Appearing before me yᵉ subscribʳ one of her Maᵗˢ Justices of yᵉ peace in sᵈ County. the said Benoni Acknowledged this Instrumᵗ to be his Act and Deed/ And the sᵈ Abigail his wife freely resigned up all her Right of Dower of in & to yᵉ above granted pʳmisses.

                                               Jos : Hamond

A true Copie of the originall Transcribed and compared Aprˡ 25ᵗʰ 1703   p Jos : Hamond Regʳ

Paul to Hill and Company

Know all men by these pʳsence that we Katharine Paul of Kittery in yᵉ County of York wife of Stephen Paul late of Kittery Shipwright Deceased, and surviveing heires of Mʳ Antipas Maverick late of Kittery Deceased, And John Paul Daniel Paul & Moses Paul and John Thomson and Samˡ ffernald sons in Law to sᵈ Katharine Paul, and all of them surviveing heires of the abovesᵈ Stephen Paul Deceased, Have for the consideration of thirty four pounds in money to us in hand paid before the signing and sealing hereof by Samˡ Hill and Joseph Hill and William ffry Yeomen & And Mʳ Joshua Downing of the same place, the receipt thereof we doe acknowledge and our selves therewith contented and paid and do acquit yᵉ sᵈ Samˡˡ Hill Joseph Hill William ffry and Joshua Downing for yᵉ same by these presence for yᵉ consideration abovesᵈ we yᵉ sᵈ Katherine Paul John Paul Daniel Paul Moses Paul John Thomson Samuel ffernald, Have given granted Aliend bargained & sold and doe by these pʳsence ffreely and Absolutely give grant bargain and sell unto yᵉ said Samˡˡ Hill Joseph Hill William ffry Joshua Downing All that our share Division or part of Land unsold lying between yᵉ Maine River of Piscataqua & Sturgeon Creek in the Township of Kittery as it was granted unto our Predesessʳ Mʳ Antipas Maverick February 17ᵗʰ 1653. as by an Instrumᵗ more at Large Appears together with all yᵉ timber wood or under woods thereon, Quarries of stone Mines Mineralls Creek waters Rivelets Coves and Landing, high ways Easments Appurtenances and priviledges whatsover thereunto belonging or in any wise appertaining unto them yᵉ sᵈ Samˡˡ Hill Joseph Hill William ffry and Joshua Downing and their heires for evermore To have and to hold, all the abovesᵈ tract of land and every part and membʳ thereof unto yᵉ sole and only use of them yᵉ sᵈ Samuel Joseph Hill William ffry and Joshua Downing their heires or assignes for ever more, And further more we yᵉ sᵈ Katharine Paul John Paul & Daniel Paul Moses Paul John Thomson Samˡˡ ffernald do for our selves and our heires covenant to and with the sᵈ Samˡˡ Hill Joseph Hill William Fry and Joshua Downing and their heires for ever that yᵉ premisses are free from all incumbrances by us made or or suffered to be done by others by our order, as Joyntures Dowers Sales gifts Mortgages and all what ever And that it shall and may be Lawfull for yᵉ sᵈ Samˡˡ Hill Joseph Hill William ffry Joshua Downing and their heires to take use possess ocupie and Improve yᵉ same and every part thereof without let or Molestation of us or any of us yᵉ sᵈ Katharine Paul John Paul Daniel Paul Moses Paul John Thomson Samuel ffer-

nald or our heires for ever hereafter, the quiet and peaceable possession thereof to Warrant and for ever Defend against all persons laying a Lawfull Claim thereunto from by or under us y⁰ sᵈ Katherine Paul John Paul Daniel Paul Moses Paul John Thomson Samˡˡ ffernald or our heires for ever more In Testimony hereof we have hereunto our hands set this twenty fourth of ffebruary one thousand seven hundred and two 170½   Moses Paul   (his seal)   the sign of
        John Tomson   (his seal) Katherine K Paul (her seal)
        Samˡ ffernald   (his seal) John Paul   (his seal)
        the sign of
        Abigail a Paul (her seal) Daniel Paul   (his seal)

Signed Sealed and delivered
   In presence of us
      the sign of
   Richard R King.
   Mary King.
   Wᵐ Godsoe.

Provin New Hampshier, March the 3ᵈ 170½

   Mʳˢ Katherin Paul and John Paul personally appeared before me yᵉ Subscribʳ of of his Maᵗⁱᵉ Justices of the peace and Acknowledged this Instrumᵗ to be their Act & Deed
                         John Woodman Justis of Peace

   A true Copie of the originall Transcribed and Compared Aprˡ 24ᵗʰ 1703   p Jos: Hammond Registʳ

   Know all men by these pʳsence that I Maverick Gilman of Exeter in the Province of New Hampshier in New England Cordwainʳ for Divers good & lawfull causes me hereunto Moveing but more Epecially for and in consideration of yᵉ sum of Eighty seven pounds in good and Lawtull moneys of New England to me in hand paid by Samuel Hill & Joseph Hill and William ffry Yeomen And Mʳ Joshua Downing, all of [163] The

Gillman to Hill and Company

BOOK VI, FOL. 163.

Province of Maine and Town of Kittery ye receipt thereof I doe confess & my self therewith contented and paid Have given granted bargained and sold, And do by these p^rsence freely and absolutely Give grant bargain and sell unto ye s^d Samuel Hill Joseph Hill W^m ffry and Joshua Downing All that tract of Land of mine as I am sole heir unto my Deceased father Mr Edward Gillman of Exeter above said Lying in ye Township of Kittery in the County of York between ye Main River of Piscataqua and Sturgeon Creek with a dwelling house thereon Together with all ye timb^r wood and woods standing or Lying thereon with all Mines and Mineralls Quarries of stone with all ye Appurtenances and priviledges thereunto belonging as Creeks Coves Landings waters high ways & easm^ts and all whatsoever thereunto belonging unto ye sole use of them ye s^d Sam^ll Hill Joseph Hill W^m ffry Joshua Downing their heires or assignes for ever And that tract of Land that was granted unto my Grandfather Mr Atipas Maverick by the Town of Kittery Feb^ry the 17th 1653. To have and to hold all ye above mentioned & described lands and and house or housing thereon and priviledges thereunto belonging unto ye only & sole use benefit and behoofe of them ye s^d Sam^ll Hill Joseph Hill William ffry & Joshua Downing their heires or assignes for ever hereafter against me ye said Maverick Gillman or my heires Execut^rs or administrators for ever/ And further I ye s^d Maverick Gillman doe for my self and my heires Execut^rs and Adm^rs Coven^t to and with ye s^d Sam^ll Hill Joseph Hill William ffry Joshua Downing and their heires Execut^rs Adm^rs or assignes for ever, that ye prémisses are free from all Incumbrances whatsoever by me made or suffered to be done of others And that I am the true and proper owner thereof And have full power & Lawfull Authority to sell and dispose of the same, the peaceable and quiet possession thereof to Warrant and for ever Defend against all persons laying a Lawfull Claime thereunto from by or under me, In witness hereof I have set to my hand and seal this fourth day of April one thousand seven hundred and two : 1702.

        Marvarrick Gillman (his seal)

Signed and Sealed in presence of
 me William Gillman
 Hannah ffoollet
 W^{llm} Godsoe

Marvarick Gillman personally appeared before me the Subscrib^r one of his Ma^{ts} Justices of Peace at Portsm° for ye Province of New Hampshier this 4th day of April 1702/ And Acknowledged the above Instrum^t to be his Act and Deed.

        Sam^{ll} Penhallow.

A true Copie of the originall Transcribed and compared Apr^l 24th 1703   p Jos : Hamond Reg^r

---

Tucker to Pepperrell

Know all men by these p^rsence that I Nicholas Tucker of Kittery in the County of York Yeoman, Have bargained and sold And doe by these p^rsence bargain and sell in plain and open Market after ye manner of New England, for the consideration of thirty four pounds in Money to me in hand paid by the worshipfull William Pepperrell Esqr the recipt thereof I doe confess and my self therewth contened and paid for the consideration aboves^d I ye said Nicholas Tucker have & doe by these p^rsence bargain and sell and for ever set over unto the s^d William Pepperrell Esqr and his heires for ever All that my dwelling house and lands thereunto belonging lying in the Township of Kittery, in Spruce Creek, with seven head of Neat Cattle and four sheep together with all my out housing and Barns Appurtenances & priviledges thereunto belonging, as timb^r wood or under woods thereon To have and to hold all the s^d house and land and Cattle herein Mentioned unto

the only and sole use of him y⁰ s^d William Pepperrell and his heires for ever And furthermore I y⁰ s^d Nicholas Tucker doe for my self & my heires Covenant to and with y⁰ s^d William Pepperrell and his heires that the p^rmisses are are free from all incumbrances whatsoever And that I have within my self full power to sell and dispose of the same, And that I am the true and proper owner thereof at y⁰ time of the signing and sealing hereof the peaceable possession thereof to warrant and Defend against all persons Laying a Claim thereunto, Always provided and to be understood that if the s^d Nicholas Tucker or his heires shall well and truely pay or cause to be paid unto y⁰ s^d William Pepperrell or his heires y⁰ full and Just Sum of thirty four pounds in money at or before the end and term of four years after the Date hereof. Then this Bill of sale is hereby declared to be voyd and of none Effect, otherwise to abide and remaine in full force power and vertue/ Witness my hand and seal this Eight day of Decemb^r one thousand seven hundred and one
Signed and Sealed in y⁰   Nicholas Tucker (his seal)
   p^rsence of us.
Richard Crucy
John Crowder.
York ss. March 1st 170¾

The within named Nicholas Tucker personally Appearing before me y⁰ subscrib^r one of her Ma^tys Justices of y⁰ Peace within s^d County Acknowledged this within written Instrum^t to be his Act and Deed/   Jos: Hamond.

A true Copie of the originall Transcribed and Compared March 1st 170¾   p Jos: Hamond Reg^r

8 March 170¼ Received in full of y⁰ within mentioned
                            p Wm Pepperrell

A true Copie of y⁰ originall as it is entred on the back side of Nicho^s Tuckers Mortgage to Mr Wm Pepperrell Transcribed & compared March 30 1708/
                        p Jos: Hamond Regist^r

This Indenture Made the twentyeth day of May in the fourteenth year of ye Reign of our soveraign Ld William the third, by the grace of God of England Scotland France and Ireland King Defend^r of ye ffaith &c. Between Jonathan Mendum of Kittery in ye Province of Maine in New England shipwright of the one part & Joseph Weekes of Kittery afores^d Yeoman Witnesseth That ye s^d Jonathan Mendum for and in consideraċon of the suṁ of fourteen pounds Currant money of New England to him secured to be paid by ye s^d Weekes before ye ensealeing and Delivery of these p^{r}sence And for divers other good causes & consideraċons him thereunto Moveing and Induceing hath Granted bargained sold & released and by these p^{r}sence doth grant bargain sell and release unto ye s^d Joseph Weekes (In his Actuall possession now being) And to his heires and assignes for ever All the Estate Right title Interest Use possession reverċon remaind^r property Claim and Demand whatsoever which he ye s^d Jonathan Mendum have or had, or which he his heires Execut^n Adm^n or assignes or any of them at any time or times hereafter shall have or may might should or ought to have or claime of in & to All that tract or parcell of Land Scituate lying and being in the town of Kittery afores^d being about twenty five Acres more or less and is part of that land bequeathed formerly to one Robert Mendum Dec^d brother to ye s^d Jonathan Mendum, by ye last Will and Testam^t of his Grand father Robert Mendum bearing Date the first day of May one thousand six hundred and Eighty two And is part of that land which was granted and lotted out unto him ye s^d Robert Mendum Grand father as afores^d by the town of Kittery December ye sixteenth day one thousand six hundred fifty and two Lying on the East side of spruce Creek begining at Turky point, and from thence along by the water side to a great pine, and from thence Northeast unto an Ashen Swamp formerly granted unto him ye s^d Rob-

Mendum to Weekes

ert Mendum as by s^d Town grant referrence being thereunto had may more fully appear and of in and unto every part and parcell thereof And of in and to ye reverĉon and reverĉons whatsoever of all and singular ye premisses herein before Mentioned to be granted bargained sold and Released, and of every part and parcel thereof with the appurtenances, And of in and unto all and singular woods, under woods & trees growing and being of in or upon the premisses, or any part or parcell thereof To have & to hold the said tract or parcel of land before mentioned/ be it twenty five acres more or less, woods under woods and trees growing upon the same, And all & singular other the p^rmisses herein before mentioned to be granted bargained sold & released And every part and parcell thereof with the Appurtenances, Together with the said Estate Right title Interest Vse possession Reverĉon Remainder property, Claim and Demand whatsoever of him ye said Jonathan Mendum and his heires of in and to ye same p^rmisses, And of in and to every part and parcel thereof with the App^rs unto the said Joseph Weekes and to the heires and assignes of the s^d Joseph Weekes, to ye only proper use and behoof of the s^d Joseph Weeks his heires and assignes for ever And the said Jonathan Mendum doth hereby Covenant for himself his heires Execut^rs and Adm^rs to and with the said Joseph Weeks his Exec^rs Adm^rs and assignes and to and with every of them by these p^rsence that neither he the said Jonathan Mendum nor his heires Exec^rs nor Adm^rs nor any of them nor any other person or persons for them or any of them or in ye name or names of them or any of them shall or will at any time or times hereaft^r ask Claim Challenge or Demand to have any manner of Estate Right title Interst or Demand of in or to the afore mentioned tract or parcel of land/ be it twenty five Acres more or less/ And all and Singular other the before granted bargained Sold and Released p^rmisses or any part or parcell thereof with the

Appurtenances, but that they and every of them shall be thereof and off and from every part and parcell thereof, from henceforth utterly Barred and Excluded for ever by these p'sence. And ffurther the said Jonathan Mendum for him self and his heires the said Tract or parcell of land/ be it twenty five Acres more or less/ And all and Singular other y'e p'misses before granted bargained Sold and Released with their and every of their Appurtenances and every part and parcell thereof unto the said Joseph Weeks his heires and assignes against him the said Jonathan Mendum his heires and assignes And against y'e the heires of Robert Mendum the Grand father as afores'd shall and will warrant and for ever Defend by these p'sence In witness whereof the said Jonathan Mendum hath hereunto set his hand and seale y'e day & year afors'd Annoq Domini 1702.

       Jonathan Mendum (his seal)
       Sarah Mendum (her seal)

Sealed and Delivered in the p'sence of
 Tho: Packer
 Richard Bryar
 Cha: Story

York ss/ Kittery March y'e 1st 17¾

 The within named Jonathan Mendum personally Appearing before me y'e subscrib'r one of her Maj'ts Justices of y'e peace within s'd County Acknowledged y'e within Instrum't to be his Act & Deed

        W'm Pepperrell Js pes

 A true Copie of the originall Transcribed and Compared March 1st 1703/   p Jos: Hamond Regist'r

---

 To all people to whome this p'sent Deed of Sale shall come George Munjoy of Casco Als ffalm'o in New England Gent Sendeth Greeting in our Lord God Everlasting Know

Book VI, Fol. 164.

Yee that I yᵉ sᵈ George Munjoy for and in consideration of the sum of Eeighty pounds of Lawfull money of New England to me in hand at and before yᵉ Ensealeing and delivery of these pʳsence by John Farnum of Boston in New England aforesaid Miller, well and truly paid the receipt whereof I doe hereby Acknowledge and my self therewith fully satisfied and contented And thereof and of every part thereof doe Acquit and Discharge yᵉ sᵈ John Farnum his heires Executʳˢ Admʳˢ and assignes for ever by these pʳsence Have given granted bargained sold Alened Enfeoffed & confirmed and by these pʳsenceˢ doe fully Clearly and Absolutely Give grant bargain sell Alien Enfeffe and confirm unto yᵉ sᵈ John Fernum his heires Executʳˢ Admʳˢ & ass forever all that my piece or parcell of land Lying and being in the Township of Kittery on Piscataq̄ River containing one hundred and one Acre, And is One Moitie or halfe part of that Tract of Land which was Delivered unto me yᵉ sᵈ George Munjoy by vertue of an Execution granted to me upon or against the Estate of ffrancis Small being butted and bounded Southerly by yᵉ River that leads towards Brod butt Harbour, Westerly; partly by the Land of Mʳ Simon Lynde & partly by comon land Northerly by yᵉ wilderness or comon land & Easterly the land of me yᵉ sᵈ George Munjoy Together with all profits priviledges and Appurtenances to yᵉ same belonging or in any wise Appurtaining And alsoe all the Estate Right title Interest Use possession Claime and demand whatsoever which I yᵉ sᵈ George Munjoy now have or which I my heires Executʳˢ or Admʳˢ in time to come, can, may might should or in any wise ought to have of in and to yᵉ above granted pʳmisses or any part thereof To have and to hold yᵉ sᵈ parcell of Land butted and bounded as aforesᵈ with all other yᵉ above granted pʳmisses And all woods waters water Courses fishings comodities and Appurtenances thereunto belonging, unto yᵉ said John

Munjoy
to
ffarnum

Farnum his heires Execut'rs Adm'rs and assignes and to his and their own sole and proper use benefit and behoof for ever And I y'e s'd George Munjoy for me my heires Execut'rs Adm'rs Doe covenant promise and grant by these p'sence that at y'e time of the ensealeing hereof I am y'e true sole and Lawfull owner of all the afore bargained p'misses and am Lawfully Seized of and in the same and every part thereof in my own proper Right And that I have in my self full power good Right and Lawfull Authority to grant sell convey and assure y'e same unto the s'd John Farnum his heires Execut'rs Adm'rs and assignes as a good perfect & absolute Estate of Inheritance in Fee Simple without any condition reservation or Limitation whatsoever soe as to alter change defeat or make voyd the same And that y'e said John Farnum his heires Execut'rs Adm'rs & ass'ns shall and may by force and vertue of these p'sence from time to time & at all times for ever hereafter Lawfully peaceably and quietly have hold use ocupie possess and enjoy y'e above granted p'misses with their Appur'ces free and clear and clearly Acquitted and Discharged of and from all and all manner of former and other Gifts grants bargains sales Leases Mortgages Jontures Dowers titles of Dowers Judgm'ts Executions entayles forfeitures And of and from all other titles troubles & encumbrances whatsoever/ And alsoe that I y'e said George Munjoy my heires Execut'rs and Adm'rs shall and will from time to time and at all times for ever hereafter Warrant and Defend the above granted p'misses with their Appurtenances and every part thereof unto y'e s'd John Farnum his heires Execut'rs Adm'rs and assignes against and all manner of person and persons whatsoever any ways Lawfully Claiming or demanding y'e same or any part thereof And Lastly that I y'e s'd George Munjoy shall and will give unto y'e s'd John Farnum his heires Execut'rs Adm'rs and assignes such further & ample assureance of all y'e afore bargained p'misses as in Law or Equity can be desier or required/ In witness whereof I the said George Munjoy have [165] hereunto set my hand and seal the seventeenth day of June in the year of o^r Lord one thousand six hundred seventy and five,.

George Munjoy (and a seal)

Signed Sealed and Delivered in the p^{r}sence of us
   Thomas Paddy.
   John Hayward scr

This Instrument was acknowledged by Mr George Munjoy as his act and deed: June ye 18th 1675 before me:

                    Edward Tynge Assistant:

Recorded according to ye orig^{ll} acknowledgment July ye 26 : 1723   p Abra^m Preble Reg^r

Know all men by these p^{r}sence that I Mary Munjoy wife of the within named George Munjoy doe hereby for me my heires Execut^n & Adm^n Remise release and for ever quit Claime unto ye within named John Farnum his heires Execut^n and assignes All and all manner of Right title Dower power of thirds Interest and Demand whatsoever, which I ye s^d Mary had have should or in any wise ought to have in or to ye within mentioned parcell of Land and all other ye within Mentioned p^{r}misses But from all Dower Interest power of thirds shall be ever Debarred by these p^{r}sence As witness my hand the eighteenth day of June Anno Dom 1675.

   Witness/ John Lowle   Mary Munjoy
     p Isaac V^r Gouss

The above written Mary Munjoy Acknowledged these lines to be her Act and Deed June 18th 1675. Before me
                              Edward Tyng

Recorded in the Secretarys office for his Ma^{tys} Teritory & Dominion of New England att Boston the 21st day of Apr^{ll} 1688.   John West D Sec̃ry

   A true Copie of the originall Transcribed and compared May 13th 1703   p Jos Ham̃ond Reg^r

Book VI, Fol. 165.

Know all men by these p'sence that I Nathan Littlefield of Wells in the Province of Mayn doe for Divers good causes and considerations me thereunto moveing and more Especially in consideration of two thousand foot of Merchantable pine boards received by me of William Taylor of the s^d Town and Province, wherewith I am fully paid contented and satisfied. And by these p'sence doe give, grant, assign enfeoffe and confirm unto ye s^d Will Taylor, And hereby have given and granted, sold assigned, Enfeoffed and confirmed the full quantity of one hundred Acres of Upland, from me my heires Administrat^{rs} and assignes unto ye s^d William Taylor his heires Adm^{rs} and assignes for ever, which land aforementioned is a certain tract of upland near Kenebunck falls next to Nicholas Coles land, which I the s^d Littlefield had given me by the Town of Wells, To have and to hold ye s^d tract of land as above bounded, with all the profit and priviledges, liberties advantages and Appurtenances, thereunto belonging or in any wise thereunto Appertaining wth every part and parcell thereof as above Expressed unto ye s^d William Taylor his heires Excu^{rs} adm^{rs} or assignes for ever, for his and their proper use and benefit And I the said Nathan Littlefield doe further covenant and promise to and with ye s^d William Taylor that ye s^d Littlefield have Lawfull rite title and power to dispose of ye Land afores^d by a grant from ye town of Wells, which grant ye s^d William Taylor is to fulfill Viz^t to build upon ye s^d land and to make improvem^t by tilling and fenceing as ye town grant makes mention of, or else ye s^d Taylor to loose ye land And further I ye s^d Nathan Littlefield doe engage that ye same and every part thereof is free from all other & former bargains gifts, grants sales titles and Incumbrances whatsoever And that I will Warrant and defend ye same against all persons whatsoever from by or under me or by my means or pro-

*Littlefield
to
Taylor*

Book VI, Fol. 165.

curem^t In Testimony whereof I have affixed my hand and seal this 9th of June 1684.

Signed Sealed and delivered   Nathan Littlefield (and a seal)
  in p^{r}sence of us
  Sam^{ll} Wheelwright
  John Wheelwright

Nathan Littlefield acknowledged this Instrum^t to be his Act and Deed ye 9th of June 1684

        Before me Sam^{ll} Wheelwright Jus. Peace

A true Copie of the originall Transcribed & compared the 3^d of June : 1703.   p Jos : Hammond Reg^r

---

This Indenture made the twenty Ninth day of Septemb^r in ye sixth year of the Reign of our Soveraign Lord William ye third by the grace of God of England Scotland ffrance and Ireland King &c/ Between Andrew Brown Senr in the Province of Mayn, Yeoman of ye one party and Robert Eliot of the Province of New Hampshiere of the other part Merchant, whereas the said Andrew Brown by one bond or Obligation bearing Date with these p^{r}sence is hold and firmly bound unto the s^d Robert Eliot in the penall sum of sixty pounds with condition there under written for ye true paym^t of thirty pounds with Lawfull Interest for ye same the s^d Recited bond or Obligation with ye condition relation being thereunto had may more fully and largely appear/ Now this Indenture Witnesseth that the s^d Andrew Brown Senr for ye further and better security and secureing of ye s^d sum of

Brown
to
Eliot

thirty pounds with Interest for ye forbearance thereof untill it shall be paid as in ye condition of ye s^d recited bond or Obligation and for other Divers good causes and considerations him hereunto moveing Hath Demised granted bargained and sold and by these p^{r}sence doth Demise grant bargain and sell unto ye s^d Robert

Eliot his Executors Adm[rs] and assignes All that Tract of Land and Marsh upon y[e] Easterd side of Black point river Called Andrew Browns Neck Scituate Lying and being in Scarbro' in y[e] Province of Mayn in New England, together with all the houses woods under woods water or water Courses, ways paths passages profits comodities Advantages and Appurtenances whatsoever to y[e] s[d] Marsh land or Medows belonging or in any ways appertaining or to or what y[e] same now or at any time hereafter comonly held used Ocupied possessed or enjoyed Accepted reputed taken or known to be parcel or member thereof And y[e] reversion and reversions remainder & remainders of all and singular y[e] s[d] Premisses, and. all y[e] Estate, right title Interest Claime property Challenge and Demand whatsoever of him said Andrew Brown sen[r] his heires Execut[rs] or Administrat[rs] of in or to y[e] p[r]misses or any part or parcell thereof, To have and to hold y[e] s[d] houses and Lands Marshes & Meadowes and wood and underwood warter and water courses, and all and singular other the p[r]misses aboves[d] by these presence Demised granted bargained or sold or menc̃oned so to be, with their and every of their Appurtenances and every part and parcell thereof [166] unto the said Rob[t] Eliot his Execut[rs] Adm[rs] and assignes for ever As Witness my hand and seal the day and year above written being y[e] twenty nineth day of September in y[e] year of our Lord One thousand six hundred ninety four

Signed Sealed and Delivered   mark of
   in presence of
   Tho: Packer   Andrew ⚡ Brown (his seal)
   Nicho: Heskins   sen[r]

Andrew Brown Appeared before me and Acknowledged the above Instrum[t] to be his Act and deed.

29 7[br] 1694/   Tho: Packer Jus[t] Ps

A true Copie of the originall Transcribed and compared Ap[ll] 3[d] 1703   p Jos Ham̃ond Reg[r]

BOOK VI, FOL. 166.

The Land & pmisses mentioned in this fore going Deed passed over by y® above Named Robert Elliot Esqr to Sam^ll Penhallow Esqr as appears on Record in Lib^r VIII Fol : 2nd Att^st. J. Hamond Reg^r

Be it known unto all men by these p^rsence that I William Hilton of Exet^r in the Province of New Hampshiere in New England send greeting know Ye that I the s^d William Hilton for good consideration hereunto moveing have given granted assigned and made over and confirmed And by these p^rsence doe give grant assigne make over and confirm unto my trusty and welbeloved son Richard Hilton of Exeter afores^d All that my Messuage or Tenem^t scituate lying and being in Kittery in ye Province of Mayn in ye s^d New England butting upon ye River comonly called the long Reach with all and singular ye Upland Excepting as hereafter Accepted, as it was formerly possessed and enjoyed by my father in Law John Simons being bounded on the Northwest side with Mary Bachellors high way and on the Southeast side with Daniel Pauls high way and soe between those two high ways to run from ye River aforesaid Northeast and by East till it comes to a runing brook that is ye head of it, only I ye s^d William Hilton doe Except reserve and keep to my self three Acres of ye said land begining at ye ffront of the same towards ye River afores^d and next to Daniel Pauls high way, eight Rod in breadth till ye s^d three Acres be compleated and made up, Also I the s^d William Hilton, Doe give grant, assigne and make over unto my s^d son Richard Hilton a certain piece of fresh Marsh lying from ye s^d Messuage or Tenem^t afores^d about one Mile & half by Estimation ten Acres be it more or less. To have and to hold ye said Messuage or Tenem^t, Barns, Stables out houses, fresh Marsh upland as

*Wm Hilton
to
his son Richard*

before expressed, with the wood trees Timber and underwood with all and singular ye Appurtenances in any wise Appertaining or belonging to ye p^{r}misses afores^d, To him ye s^d Richard Hilton his heires and assignes for ever And Alsoe I ye s^d William Hilton doe coven^t promis and engage to and with my said son Richard Hilton that ye p^{r}misses afore said with all and Singular the Appurtenances thereunto belonging, were free and clear And freely and clearly Exonerated Acquitted and discharged of and from All and all manner of former bargaines sales gifts grants titles Mortgages Suites Dowries And all other Incumbrances whatsoev^r from by or under me, from ye begining of the world unto ye sealing and delivery hereof.

And further I the s^d William Hilton doe coven^t promise and engage to and with my s^d son Richard Hilton, All and Singular ye Appurtenances, with ye premisses thereunto belonging excepting as before excepted to Warrant Accquit and Defend for ever ag^t all persons whatsoever Claiming any Legall Right title or Interest of or into y^e same from by or under me y^e s^d William Hilton And in Testimony hereof I the s^d William Hilton Have hereunto set my hand and seale this fourth of May of ____ Anno Dom̅ 1684° Annoq̅ Regni Caroli Regis Sc̅di XXXVI°

Signed Sealed and Delivered William Hilton W his mark (and seal)
   in the presence of
Sam : Hilton :   Rebecka Hilton her R mark
Edward Hilton   John Hilton his I mark

This Deed was Accknowledged before me this 6th day of May 1684, to be ye Act and Deed of William Hilton to his son Richard/

                        Walter Barfoote Judge
  A true Copie of the originall Transcribed and Compared June 15th 1703/   p Jos : Ham̅ond Reg^r

BOOK VI, FOL. 167.

Know all men by these p'sence that Hugh Crocket of Kittery in the County of York Marrin' for a Valluable consideration to me in hand paid by John fford of the same place Yeoman, the receipt thereof I doe confess and my self therewith fully paid/ Have given granted bargined and sold And doe by these presence give grant bargain and sell unto Jn° Ford the one half part of my grant of fiftie Acres of Land granted unto me by y* town of Kittery May y* 10th

Crocket
to
fford

1703. together with all y* priviledges thereunto belonging or in any wise Appurtaining, To have & to hold all y* above's^d half grant of land unto y* only use benefit and behoof of him y* s^d John fford his heires or assignes for ever against me the s^d Hugh Crocket or my heires or any other person under me, The peaceable possession thereof to warrant and for ever defend against all persons whatsoever from by or under me In witness whereof I have hereunto set my hand and seale this: 17th day of June. 1703.   the signe of
Signed Sealed and Delivered   Hugh H Crocket (his seal)
In presence of us.
Thomas Cox.
W^llm Godsoe
    The 17th June : 1703.
Then Hugh Crocket personally Appeared before me and Acknowledged this Instrum^t to be his free Act and Deed,
                        William Pepperrell
                                    Js pes
A true Copie of the originall Transcribed & compared the: 22^d June, 1703.   Jos: Hamond Regist^r

[167] Know all men by these p'sence that I Hugh Crocket of Kittery in y* County of York for a Valluable consideration to me in hand paid by Christopher Mitchell of

the same place shipwright the receit thereof I doe confess and my self therewith fully paid Have given granted bargained and sold And doe by these p'sence freely & Absolutely Give grant bargain and sell unto ye s^d Christopher Mitchell and heirs for ever the one half part of my fifty acre grant of land granted unto me by ye Town of Kittery May ye 10th 1703. together with all the priviledges thereunto belonging or in any wise Appertaining to him and his heires for ever To have and to hold the aboves^d half part of grant of land unto ye only and sole use of him ye s^d Christopher Mitchell his heires or assignes for ever against me ye said Hugh Crocket or my heires or any other person under me ye s^d Crocket The peaceable and quiet possession thereof to warrant and Defend against all persons laying Claime thereunto from by or und^r me. In witness whereof I have hereunto set my hand and seal the 17th day of June, 1703.

Crocket to Mitchell

Signed Sealed and Delivered   the sign of
In the presence of   Hugh *H* Crocket (and seal)
John Cox
W^{llm} Godsoe

The 17th of June 1703.

Then Hugh Crocket personally Appeared and Acknowledged this Instrument to be his free Act and Deed Before me   Wm Pepperrell Js pes

A true Copie of the originall Transcribed and compared June : 22^d 1703.   p Jos : Hamond Reg^r

---

To all Christian People to whome these presence shall come/ I ffrancis Littlefield send greeting Know Yee that I ye aboves^d ffrancis Littlefield of Ipswich in ye County of Essex Province of the Massachusets Bay in New England Inholder ffor and in consideration of the Naturall love and affection that I have for my Cousin Moses Littlefield of Wells in the County of York Province aboves[d] Planter And for divers other good & Lawfull causes and considerations me thereunto moveing Have granted and given And doe by these p'sence fully clearly & absolutely Give grant Enfeoffe

ffr: Littlefield to his Cousin Moses

confirm and make over unto my Cousin Moses Littlefield aboves[d] a certain piece of upland and salt Marsh Lying & being in y[e] Township of Wells viz[t] a twenty pole lott which was granted to me y[e] aboves[d] ffrancis Littlefield by S[r] ffardinando Gorges K[t] bounded Southerly by land which was my father Edmund Littlefields and Westerly by the Towns Comons Northerly by y[e] high way and Esterly upon the sea it being twenty pole wide, and the length as y[e] other Lotts adjoyning to it are To have and to hold peaceably and quietly to him the aboves[d] Moses Littlefield his heires Executors Administrators or assignes as a free & clear Estate in Fee Simple for ever, And I y[e] aboves[d] ffrancis Littlefield Doe for myself my heires Execut[rs] Administrat[rs] coven[t] and promise to and with y[e] aboves[d] Moses Littlefield his heires Execut[rs] Adm[rs] or ass[ns] that I am y[e] true & Rightfull owner of the above granted p'misses and that I have full power good right and Lawfull Authority To sell and dispose of y[e] same and doe also coven[t] and engage that it is free And clearly & fully clearly & absolutely Acquitted and Discharged of and from all other & former gifts grants bargains sales Dowers Mortgages Enfeoffm[ts] Intrusion rights and Incumbrances whatsoever and that I warrantise and Defend y[e] same from all or any person or persons whatsoever in by from or under me my heires Execut[rs] or Adm[rs] laying any Legall claim thereunto, To y[e] true and faithfull performance of all & singular the above granted p'misses I doe hereby bind my self my heires Execut[rs] Administrat[rs] In witness whereof I have hereunto set my hand and seal this second day of May one thousand seven hundred, And in y[e] twelfth year of the

Book VI, Fol. 167.

Reign of our Soveraign Lord William the third by y⁰ grace of God, of England Scotland ffrance and Ireland King ffidei Deff &c. 1700./

Signed Sealed and delivered   The word (seven) interlined
  In the presence of us   was before y⁰ sealing hereof
  Samuel Emery   ffr : Littlefield (his seal)
  Elizabeth Hamond

ffrancis Littlefield appeared & acknowledged this above written Instrum^t to be his voluntary Act & Deed.
                        Before me, May y⁰ 8th 1700.
                            Saml Wheelwright Jus Peace

  A true Copie of the originall Transcribed and compared July : 7th 1703.   p Jos : Hamond Reg^r

To all Christian People unto whome these p^{r}sence shall come Moses Littlefield of Wells sends greeting/ Now Know Yee that I y⁰ aboves^d Moses Littlefield of Wells in y⁰ County of York, Province of the Massachusets Bay in New England planter with Martha my wife for and in consideration of forty five pounds in Currant money of New England by bill obligatory secured to be paid to us by Samuel Emery of Wells County and Province aboves^d Clerk, bearing Equall Date with these p^{r}sence And for other good causes & considerations us thereunto Moveing Have given and granted, and doe by these p^{r}sence fully clearly and absolutely Give grant bargain sell Alien enfeoffe confirm and make over unto

Littlefield to Emery   Sam^{ll} Emery of Wells County & Province abovesaid a certain piece or parcel of Land and Salt Marsh containing by Estimation twenty five Acres be it more or less bounded Southwesterly by land in y⁰ possession of Mr Ezekiel Knights, formerly possessed by my father Thomas Littlefield. Southeasterly by Webhant River Norwesterly by y⁰ Town Comon/ It lyeth in Wells, being land confirmed to me by Deed under hand and seale of my uncle ffrancis Littlefield and was formerly y[e] place of our habitation, Alsoe four rod of Land upon y[e] Northeast side thereof from y[e] high way to y[e] Marsh and also a parcell of fresh Meadow lying at y[e] Marshes comonly called Merryland Marshes of about three Acres be it more or less being y[e] one half of a five Acre lot of Marsh lying undivided between me and my mother in Law M[rs] Sarah Knights the which pieces and parcels of land & Marsh bounded & Estimated as aboves[d] & every part & parcel of them we doe by these p[r]sence grant as aboves[d] unto Samuel Emery afores[d] with all and singular y[e] profits priviledges fences right of comonage or any appurtenances thereto belonging or in any ways appertaining To have and to hold to him y[e] aboves[d] Samuel Emery his heires Execut[rs] Adm[rs] or assignes as a free and clear Estate in Fee simple for ever, provided that if what I have sold formerly to John Buckland Jun[r] be not four Acres, that he is to have it made up four Acres on y[e] North side of y[e] river, And the aboves[d] Moses Littlefield with Martha his wife doe for themselves heires Execut[rs] Adm[rs] coven[t] and promise to and with y[e] aboves[d] Sam[l] Emery his heires Executors [168] administrat[rs] and assignes that they are y[e] true and Rightfull owners of y[e] above granted premisses And that they have full power good right and Lawfull Authority to sell and dispose of the same And doe by these p[r]sence affirm & promise it and every part thereof to be free and clear & fully and clerely acquitted and Discharged of and from all other and former gifts grants bargains sales Dowryes rights and incumbrances whatsoever And that they will warrant and defend y[e] same from all persons or person whatsoever, in by from or under them their heires Execut[rs] Adm[rs] or from any whatsoever laying any Legall Claim thereunto Lord propriet[rs] Excepted In witness to and for confirmation of y[e] above written p[r]misses, the above named Moses Littlefield with Martha his wife have hereto set their hands and seals this thirtieth day of March one thousand seven hundred & two And in y® fourteenth year of y® Reign of our Soveraign Ld William the third of England &c King Defend^r of y® faith

Signed Sealed and delivered   Moses Ɱ Littlefield (his seal)
   in presence of us   his mark
     Jonathan Hamond Junr   Martha ᴍ Littlefield (her seal)
     Joseph Littlefield.   her mark

York ss/ Moses Littlefield and Martha his wife Appeared before me one of her Ma^ts Justice of y® peace and Acknowledged this above written Instrum^t to be their Volluntary Act and Deed this ninth day of June 1703

                 John Wheelwright Jus^te Peace

A true Copie of the originall Transcribed & compared July 7th 1703   p Jos : Hamond Reg^r

Lewis to Mitchell

This Indenture made the Second Day of Octob^r in the year of our Lord God one thousand Six hundred Eighty & three between Peter Lewis and Grace his wife late of Smutynose Island one of y® Islands of y® Isles of Shoales but now of y® town of Kittery in the Prouince of Maine in New England planter and William Mitchell of y® Isles of Shoales in New England ffisherman on the other part/ Witnesseth that the s^d Peter Lewis and Grace his wife for and in Consideration of y® sum of forty two pounds to be paid According to Bills taken und^r his hand for the same haue and by these p^rsents doe Demise giue grant bargaine & sell Alien Enfeoffe & Confirm unto the s^d Wm Mitchell his heirs and Assigns foreuer, All the land with two dwelling houses on it next Adjoyning to y® house of Thomas Snell with y® garden belonging to y® s^d Two houses And the well Adjoyning wth the fflacke Room and lying Room, thereunto belonging lying and being between y® s^d houses And the house of Roger Grant & the house of William Oliuer & Michiael Endles and the halfe a stage Room the other halfe being Walter Mathews and the one third of a Moreing wth Wm Sealy one End of the Moreing fast to Mallago the other end fast to Smuttynose Sweeping a great Rock on that s^d Island Together with all wayes waters water courses easem^{ts} profits Priuiledges Aduantages and appur^{ces} to ye same or any part thereof belonging or Appertaining And free Ingress egress & Regress into or out of any part of the Demised p^{r}misses and all ye estate Right Title & Interest of them ye s^d Peter Lewis and Grace his wife or Either of them of in or to the same or any part thereof To Haue & To Hold all and singular ye aboue bargained and sold p^{r}misses with ye Appurtenances to the s^d Wm Mitchell his heirs and Assignes foreuer And they the s^d Peter Lewis and Grace his wife haue full Power good right and Lafull Authority to grant sell and conuey ye s^d houses and land wth ye p^{r}misses and Appurtenances to the s^d Mitchell his heirs and Assignes foreuer and that free and Clear from all man^r of former gifts bargains Sales Mortgages & Incumbrances whatseuer the same shall be remaine and continue unto ye s^d Wm Mitchell his heirs & Assignes foreuer and also they ye s^d Peter Lewis and Grace his wife their heirs Execut^{rs} Adm^{rs} all and singular ye aboues^d p^{r}misses shall and will foreuer warrant and Defend to ye s^d Wm Mitchell his heirs & Assignes foreuer from any p^{r}son or p^{r}sons whatsoeuer Lawfully Claiming right Title or Interest to ye same or any part thereof from by or und^r us/ In Withereof ye s^d p^{r}ties to these p^{r}sents haue put their hands & Seals the day and year first aboue written.

Signed Sealed and Deliuered   Peter Lewis Senr (his seal)

  In ye p^{r}sence of us   The mark of
    the mark of
  Peter Lewis Junr Grace Lewis Senr (her seal)
    the mark of
  Lucye Lewis
  ffrancis Tucker

Book VI, Fol. 168.

Pro: New: Hampshier/ Peter Lewis Acknowledged this aboue Instrum^t to be his & his wifes act & deed this 15th Aug^st 1702 before me

                     Theodore Attkinson J: Peace

A true Coppie of ye original Trainscribed & compared June ye 4th 1703.   p Jos: Hamond Reg^r

To All Christian People to whom this may or shall come Know yee that: I Wm Mitchel and Hono^r my Wife for and in Consideration of ye Sum of Eight pounds Cura^t mony of New England to me in hand paid before ye Signing Sealing and Deliuery hereof haue Bargained & sold Assigned and made ouer for me my heirs Execut^rs & Adm^rs foreuer to Phillip Carpenter of the Isles of Shoals ffisherman and to him his heirs Execut^rs Adm^rs & Assignes foreuer All my right Title Claime & Interest of or unto the houses lands gardens well flake room lying room stage room and moreing place in the w^thin Deed mentioned wth the Appurtenances thereunto belonging to the s^d Phillip Carpenter to him his heirs Adm^rs & Assignes foreuer to and for their onely proper vse bennefit & behoofe foreuer/ In Witness hereof wee hereunto haue put o^r hands & Seales this Thirty first day of octob^r one thousand Seauen hundred & Two/ 1702

Mitchell to Carpenter

Witness   the mark of
   Richard Hales   William Mitchell (seal)
   George Trundey   the mark of
   Francis Tucker   Honor Mitchell (seal)

Prouince of New Hampsh^r
    Octob^r 31st 1702

Wm Mitchell and Hon^r his wife came and acknowledged the aboue written Assignm^t of ye w^thin deed to be their act & deed.

                      Nath ffryer Jus Peace

A true Coppie of ye original Transcribed & Compared June ye 4th 1703.   p Jos: Hamond Reg^r

[169] To All Christian People to whom this p'sent wrighting shall come Greeting Know Yee that wee Nathaniel ffryer Esq' & Robert Jordan both Propriet'" of Cape Elizabeth within the Township of falmouth in y° Prouince of Maine in New England for and in Consideration of seauen pounds to us in hand paid well and Truely at y° Ensealing hereof by Phillip Carpenter now of Cape Elizabeth ffisherman in y° Prouince aboues^d y° Rec^t whereof wee doe hereby Acknowledge and therewth to be fully content & satisfied and thereof and Euery part thereof wee doe fully clearly and absolutely acquit and Discharge y° s^d Phillip Carpenter his heirs Execut'" & Adm'" foreuer by these p'sents haue giuen granted bargained sold Enfeoffed and confirmed and doe by these p'sents giue grant Bargaine sell Allien Enfeoffe and confirm unto him y° s^d Phillip Carpenter his heirs Execut'" Adm'" and Assignes Twenty Acres of upland lying and being on Cape Elizabeth aboues^d and Next Adjoyning to Sarah Sweat Bounded from y° Sea to runn up in the woods Sixty six pole square and then is bounded wth s^d Fryer and Jordans land againe To have & To hold Enjoy Possess & Improue all y° s^d land Timb^r Priuiledges of y° afores^d Twenty Acres wth all y° Profits and Priuiledges there-

ffryer and Jordan to Carpenter

unto belonging or in Right or in any wise Appertaining to y° s^d Phillip Carpenter his heirs Execut'" Adm'" & Assigns foreuer And further wee Nathaniell Fryer and Robert Jordan doe for o^r selues heirs Execut'" Adm'" and Assignes Promiss that y° s^d Phillip Carpenter his heirs Execut'" or Assignes shall Quietly Peaceably Enjoy y° s^d lands as aboue written from any by or und^r us with all the Profits Priuilidges and Imunityes thereto belonging or in any wise Appertaining without any let Sute Trouble Mollestation or Interruption of or from us or from any person or persons laying any claime thereto and that wee are the proper own'" of y° same at y° sealing of this Deed and that s^d land is free from all former gifts grants bargains sales Mortgages Attachm^{ts} Judgm^{ts} Executions wills Joyntures Dowryes thirds or any Incumbrances whatsoeuer and further that the s^d Carpenter shall haue highwayes to his land According to all highways vseuall, and According to the true Intent hereof and the Laws of this Prouince In Witness to all and Singular ye aboue Mentioned premisses wee ye s^d Nathaniel Fryer and Robert Jordan haue hereunto set our hands and Seals this Twentyeth day of June 1688, and in ye fifth year of ye Reign of o^r Soueraign Lord James the Second of England Scotland france and Ireland King Defend^r of ye faith &c.

Signed Sealed & Deliuered   Nathaniel Fryer (seal)
  In presence of us.   Robert Jordan (seal)
the words raced out in ye fifth
and sixth lines were raced out
before ye Sealing and Deliuery
  of this Instrum^t.
  Andrew Cranch
  John Clark
  Henry Harwood
      Pro New Hampsh^r

Nath^{ll} Fryer Esqr & Mr Robert Jordan Personally Appearing before me Acknowledged the aboue Instrum^t to be their Act & deed ye 18th of Novemb^r 1701
                 p Theodore Atkinson J Peace

A true Coppie of ye original Transcribed & Compared June ye 4th 1703   p Jos Hamond Reg^r

This Indenture made this Tenth day of February in the Eighth year of ye Reign of o^r Soveraign Lord William, by ye grace of god of England Scotland France and Ireland

BOOK VI, FOL. 169.

King Defend^r of ye faith &c Anno Dom: 169¾ between Thomas More of ye Town of York in ye Province of Main in New England Yeoman on ye one part and Nathaniel Raynes of ye same place Gent on ye other part Witnesseth that the s^d Thomas More for and in consideration of ye sum of fiue pounds curant Mony of New England to him in hand already payd by ye s^d Nathaniel Raines ye Rec^t w^rof he doth by these p^rsents Acknowledge and himselfe therew^th to be fully satisfied hath granted bargained and sold and by these presents, doth grant bargain and sell unto ye s^d Nathaniel Raynes his heirs Execut^rs Adm^rs & Assignes foreuer a Certaine piece of upland being in ye Township of York on ye wester side of York riuer being Twenty Acres or thereabouts/ Butted and bounded as followeth Viz^t Joyning on ye west side to ye land formerly Mrs Godfryes and Butted to a pond and the other side against ye Beach and so up in ye woods to a Marked Tree as may Appear by a Town grant to James Wiggins Senr of whome Francis Hooke Esqr late of Kittery Purchased s^d Twenty Acres of upland and by s^d Hooke was Conueyed to Wm Moor dec^d and by him was giuen unto ye s^d Thomas More with all ye Priuilidges and Appurtenances thereunto belonging with all Euidences wrightings or Minum^ts of or concerning s^d p^rmisses To Haue & To Hold ye s^d Twenty Acres of upland unto ye s^d Nathaniel Rayns his heirs and Assignes foreuer hereby waranting ye s^d Premisses from any person from by or under him ye s^d Thomas More or any person or persons Else whatsoeuer unto ye onely use and behoofe of him ye s^d Nathaniel Raynes his heirs Execut^rs Adm^rs and Assignes In Witness whereof he ye s^d Thomas

Moore
to
Raines

Moor with Hannah his wife haue hereunto set their hands and seales the day and year aboue written. Anno 169¾
Signed Sealed and Possession giuen of   Thomas More (seal)
   the aboue premisses in presence of us   Hannah More (seal)

John (his mark) Brawn

John (his mark) More

Jonathan Tyler

Thomas More and Hannah his wife came and Acknowledged this Instrum^t to be their act and deed this 17th day of Feb^{ry} 169¾ before me   Sam^{ll} Donnel Justice Peace

A true Coppie of ye Original Transcribed and compared Aprill ye 6th 1703.   p Jos Hamond Reg^r

[170] This Indenture or Form of agreem^t made this third day of August Anno Dom one thousand seven hundred and two Between Thomas Greely of ye one party Tanner And Timothy Waymouth on behalf of his father and himself of the other party All of Barwick in the County of York in ye Province of ye Massachusets Bay in New England Witnesseth, That inasmuch as the lands of the s^d Greely (formerly James Treworgies) and of s^d Waymouth are adjoyning to, and bounded by one another and by reason of some uncertainty of the true line of Devision between them, certain controvesies have arose between s^d Waymouth and Greely and his predecess^r about the same Therefore for a finall Issue of all contests for a certainty of their Possessions and preserving of future Amity and good

Neighbourhood among themselves and their successors on s^d Estates for ever the s^d parties have setled and by these presence doe freely and unchangeably in behalf of themselves their heires Execut^rs Adm^rs and assignes for ever Establish own confirm and settle as a Divideing line between their lands for ever/ A line that runs over from an Elm tree that stands near Thomas Greelys fence at ye Southwest corner near to the brook that runs into Mast cove And so to run strait over to William Earles land;

Greely
and
Waymouth

And a Pine standing near Mast-cove highway is ye next tree in the line And ye line is to run athwart ye whole land according to it course from s^d Elm to s^d Pine tree. And Timothy in behalf of his father himself, his heires Execut^rs Adm^rs and assignes doth for ever quit Claime unto all the land on ye Northeast side of and Joyning unto s^d line, unto ye s^d Thomas his heires and assignes for ever And s^d Thomas in behalf of himself his heires Execut^rs Adm^rs and assignes Doth for ever quit Claim unto all that land on the southwest side of and Joyning unto said line, unto s^d Timothy his heires & assignes for ever, And for an uncontrouleable settlem^t and assurance of the aboves^d bounds the s^d parties do bind themselves their heires Execut^rs Adm^rs or other Success^rs to their respective lands, in ye sum of twenty pounds, for ever to Acquiesce with this agreem^t which twenty pounds is to be paid, and shall without controversie be paid by either of these parties his heires Execut^rs Adm^rs or successors on ye p^rmisses, if by Trespass Lawsuit or otherwise he or they be found endeavouring to alter ye above stated line or make voyd this Indenture, together with all Damages Evidently ariseing from such a designe, To ye other party his heires Execut^rs adm^rs successour or successours for ever/ In witness whereof ye s^d Thomas Greely and Timothy Waymouth (after the Interlining ye words/ near to ye brook that runs into y" Mast cove) Have set to their hands and seales according to y" Date above sᵈ.

Signed Sealed and delivered
  In presence of us.
  John Gowen
  Jos Hamond Junʳ

              his
Thomas ⚹ Greely (his seale)
              mark
Timothy Waymouth (his seal)

York ss/ March 1ˢᵗ 170⅔.

The within named Thomas Greely & Timothy Waymouth personally Appearing before me the subscriber one of her Maᵗˢ Justices of yᵉ Peace in sᵈ County Acknowledged this Instrumᵗ to be their Act and deed/

                                    Jos Hamond

A true Copie of yᵉ originall Transcribed & compared March 1ˢᵗ 170⅔.   p Jos Hamond Registʳ

To all Christian People to whome this shall come Greeting/ Know Yee that I Edward Waymouth of yᵉ Town of Kittery in the County of York in yᵉ Province of the Massachusets Bay in New England, for and in consideration of yᵉ Naturall love and affection I bear to my son Timothy Waymouth Have freely and Absolutely given And do by these pʳsence for my self my heires Executʳˢ and Administratʳˢ freely and Absolutely give grant Alien Infeoffe pass over and confirm unto my aforesᵈ son Timothy Waymouth a certain parcel of land scituate and lying in the town of Kittery aforesᵈ containing ten Acres more or less as it is bounded, begining at a bridge called Nasons bridge lying over a brook that runs into Mast cove and from thence upon a North point of yᵉ Compass to yᵉ North side of my house lot And from thence upon a strait line Eastward as my lot runs And on yᵉ East bounded with James Treworgies land And on yᵉ South by a brook of water runing into Mast Cove and is partly upland and partly swamp To have and to hold the afores⁴ tract of land, together with all and singular y⁰ Appurtenances, priviledges and comodities of wood timber trees underwood, waters water Courses to him y⁰ s⁴ Timothy Waymouth his heires and assignes for ever, without let Interuption or Molestation of me the s⁴ Edward Waymouth or any other person or persons by from or under me my heires or assignes, only I reserve to my self firewood or fencen for my one use my life and my wife Esters life time And for confirmation of y⁰ premisses I y⁰ s⁴ Edward Waymouth hereunto set my hand and seale this seventeenth day of ffebruary Anno Dom one thousand seven hundred and one in y⁰ tenth year of his Maties Reign of England Scotland ffrance and Ireland Defender of y⁰ ffaith &c.

Edward Waymo to his son Timothy

his mark
Signed Sealed & delivered Edward 🅥 Waymouth (his seale)
  in p'sence of us   her mark
    William ⱮⱮ Rogers Ester 🅔 Waymouth (her seal)
      his mark

Witnes Jemima ⁊ ffost
      her mark
Daniel Emery

York ss. May 20th 1703.

The within named Edward Waymouth personally appearing before me y⁰ subscrib' one of her Ma^tys Justices of the Peace within y⁰ County of York Acknowledged this Instrum' to be his Act & deed

                        Jos. Hamond.

A true Copie of the originall Transcribed and Compared May 20th 1703.   p Jos: Hamond Reg'

Know all men by these p'sence that we Henry Snow and Job Emery do acknowledge that we have rec⁴ in full of our mother in Law Sarah Nason, our wifes. portions according to y⁰ distribution and proportion made and set and allowed them of their fathers Estate as Witness our hands.

Witness us/ Nicholas Gowen   Henry Snow.
         Daniel Emery   Job Emery.

Know all men by these p'sence that I Jonathan Nason do acknowledge that I have received in full of my Mother Sarah Nason, my portion According to y⁰ distribution & proportion set & allowed me of my fathers Estate As witness

Witness us/ Nicholas Gowen   Jonathan Nason
         Daniel Emery.

York ss : Barwick May 24th 1703 :/ Henry Snow, Job Emery Jonathan Nason personally appeared before me one of her Ma^{ts} Justices of y⁰ Peace in s^d County & acknowledged y⁰ above Instrum^t to be their Act & deed   before me
                               Ichabod Plaisted

A true Copie of y⁰ originall Transcribed & compared May 24th 1703/   p Jos : Hamond Regester

[171] Kittery Octob^r y⁰ s^d 1702/ Then Measured and bounded out to Henry Snow thirteen Acr⁰ of land or thereabouts by y⁰ request of Sarah Nason Widow Relict & Administratrix to the Estate of her Deceased husband Jonathan Nason it being in full of his wifes part and portion of her Deceased fathers Estate, the bounds of s^d land is as followeth, begining at y⁰ brook side before Edward Waymouths dore a little below y⁰ usuall foot path that goes to s^d Waymouths house And from thence on our East and be south half south line the full Extent of seventy six poles And from that extent on a square line to y⁰ brook that parts be-

Book VI, Fol. 171.

tween Edwd Waymouths land and ye aboves^d Nasons land As may Appear by severall marked trees/

Nicholas Gowen Surv^r

The land above written is rec^d p me Henry Snow ye day above written. As Witness my hand.
Witness/ Nicholas Gowen   Henry Snow
    James Emery.
York ss May 20th 1703.

The within named Sarah Nason psonally Appearing before me ye Subscrib^r one of her Ma^{ts} Justices of the peace Acknowledged the within written to be her Act and deed/

Jos : Hamond

A true Copie of the originall Transcribed and Compared
June 16th 1703   p Jos Hamond Reg^r

To all Christian people to home these p^{r}sence may concern Know Yee that I Sarah Nason of Kittery in the County of York in ye province of the Massachusets in New England Have given granted bargained sold Alienated Infeoffed & confirmed And doe for my self my heires Execut^{rs} and assignes freely and absolutely give grant bargain sell Alienate Infeoffe pass over & confirm unto my son in Law and Daughter Henry and Sarah Snow in consideration of a portion I was to pay to her of her fathers Estate it being in full her part thereof thirteen Acres of Land lying in Kittery aboves^d bouned by a brook on ye North side which devides Edward Waymouths and my Land And on ye other two sides with

Nason to Snow   my Land And it begins at s^d brook before Edwd Waymouths Dore, And from thence on an East and by south half south line ye full Extent of Seventy six poles & from thence on a square line to the brook above mentioned/ All that land with them bounds to them their heires and assignes for ever To have

Book VI, Fol. 171.

and to hold the afores^d tract of Land together with all and singular ye Appurtenances priviledges and comodities of woods timber trees under woods water water Courses &c' to them ye s^d Henry and Sarah Snow their heires and assignes for ever without let Interuption or Molestation of me the said Sarah Nason or any other person or persons by from or under me my heires or assignes and unto their own proper use benefit and behoof of ye s^d Henry Snow and Sarah Snow their heires Execut^rs or assignes for ever And ye s^d Sarah Nason her heires and assignes to and with every of them by these p'sence for ever freely Acquit, and them quietly and peaceably enjoy without any manner of Challenge Claim or demand of me ye s^d Sarah Nason my heires Execut^rs Adm^rs or assignes or any other person whatsoever in my name by my cauesment or procureing in Witness hereof I have set my hand and seal this forteenth day of June in ye year of our Lord one thousand seven hundred and three In ye second year of ye Reign of her Matie Ann by ye grace of God, of England Scotland ffrance and Ireland Queen Defend^r of ye ffaith &c

Signed Sealed & delivered   her
 in ye p'sence of us   Sarah S Nason (her Seale)
  Jonathan Nason   mark

     her
Mehetable M Stacie
     mark

Daniel Emery

York ss/ Kittery June 15th 1703.

Sarah Nason personally appeared before me on of her Ma^ts Justices of peace in s^d County and Acknowledged ye above Instrum^t to be her act & deed

          Ichabod Plaisted

A true Copie of the originall transcribed & compared June 16th 1703.   p Jos: Hamond Reg^r

Book VI, Fol. 171.

Know all men by these p^rsence that we Joseph Abbot and John Abbot doe acknowledge that we have received in full of our mother in Law Sarah Nason our wifes portions according to the Distributions and proportion made and set and allowed them of their fathers Estate as Witness our hands this second of Octob^r 1702.

James Emery } witnesses   Joseph Abbott
James Warren }   John Abbott

York ss. Barwick May 24: 1703.

Joseph Abbot and John Abbot personally appeared before me ye Subscrib^r one of her Ma^ts Justices in s^d County and Acknowledged the within Instrument to be their Act and deed.

Ichabod Plaisted

A true Copie of ye originall Transcribed and compared June 16: 1703.   p Jos: Hamond Reg^r

Articles of agreement made and concluded between Nich Gowen and John Gowen, Testifie that we the said Nich and John Gowen have Mutually agreed and Divided that tract of land formerly Trustrum Harrinsons out Lott of fiftie Acres as appears on Record in Kittery Town Book, it being in length two hundred and forty rods East and West & in breadth thirty four rods North and South, we have Divided it North and South in the Middle And John Gowen is to have ye Westermost part of s^d Land, and Nicholas is to have the Eastermost part, In witness whereof we have hereunto set our hands and seales this nineteenth day of Jan^ry 170¾.

Nichs and Jno Gowen

Signed & Sealed   Nicholas Gowen (and a seale)
  in the p^rsence of   John Gowen   (and a seale)
Daniel Emery
Lemuel Gowen

Book VI, Fol. 171.

York ss

Nicholas Gowen and John Gowen appeared before me this 20th May 1703. and Acknowledged this above agreem^t to their Act & deed.   Jos: Hamond J. Peace

Know all men by these p'sence that I James Tobey of Kittery in the County of York in New England for and in consideration of a valluable sum of ten shillings currant money to me in hand already paid by Stephen Tobey of Kittery in ye County afores^d by which payment I Acknowledge my self fully satisfied before ye signing and sealeing of this writeing Have bargained and sold And by these presence doe fully clearly and Absolutely bargain and sell unto ye s^d Stephen Tobey in plain and open manner without fraud and deceit, the one half of a grant of twenty Acres of Land

James Toby to his son Stephen

granted unto ye s^d James Tobey May the sixteenth day, in the year One thousand Six hundred Ninety four it being ten Acres To have and to hold the s^d ten Acres or half of the twenty Acre grant unto him ye s^d Stephen Tobey his heires Execut^{rs} Adm^{rs} and assigns for ever and to their proper use and behoof And I ye s^d James Tobey my heires Execut^{rs} and Adm^{rs} and every of us the s^d grant according to Law shall and will warrant acquit and Defend by these presence against all persons. In witness whereof I James Tobey have hereunto set my hand and seal this second day of June in the year of our Lord one thousand Seven hundred & two

Signed sealed & delivered   his
 in p'sence of us   James ⌣ Toby (and seal)
 Jacob Remich.   mark
 Joshua Remich

York ss/ Kittery Apr^l 15th 1703

The above named James Tobey Appeared before and acknowledged this Instrument to be his Act and deed/
                    Jos Hamond J. Peace

Book VI, Fol. 172.

A true Copie of ye originall Transcribed & compared Apr^{ll} 15th 1703/   p Jos Hamond Reg^r

[172] Know all men by these p'sence that I Christian Remich of Kittery in ye County of York in the Province of ye Massachusets Bay in New England planter with ye consent of Hannah my wife Have Demised Granted and to Farm Letten unto my beloved son Josha Remich my homestall of dwelling house, barn, Orchard, garden, planting land, pasture & Meadow, Lying on the Neck of land by the boyling rock in Kittery afores^d, together with ten Acres of land in ye woods Lying at ye head of Peter Dixons land And fifteen Acres of land more lying in ye place called Simmons his Marsh on the south side of Stephen Pauls land To have hold and faithfully to Improve as a Tenant upon ye termes following Dureing the whole Terme of my naturall life and ye life of ye s^d Hannah my wife And after my Decease and ye Decease of my s^d wife his mother. To have and to hold the s^d homestall of dwelling house, barn, Orchard, garden planting land pasture and Meadow, together wth the ten Acres of land and ye fifteen Acres of land before mentioned with all ye Appurtenances and priviledges thereto belonging To him ye said Joshua Remich & his heires for ever And also I have lett unto my said son two oxen of seven years old, five cows and a bull of three years old And two steeres of two years old And two heifers of two years old and twenty Ewes — for ye Terme of ye Naturall lives of me and my wife afores^d And for and in consideration of ye premisses the afores^d Joshua Remich shall allow & pay unto me his s^d

Chr: Remich
to
his son Joshua

father yearly And to his s^d mother if she outlive me the one half of the Increase and profits of all ye fores^d lands, as English or Indian corn Orchard and garden fruits/ And also the one half y^e of

Book VI, Fol. 172.

Increase of the Neat Cattle, to be devided once in three yeares, And y® butter and Cheese with y® Lambs and wooll to be devided in Equall halves once every year And to allow to me and to his s^d mother y® use of the one half of y® fores^d dwelling house Dureing y® whole Terme of our naturall lives, And for y® true performance hereof and every part of it the fores^d Joshua Remich doth hereby bind himself, his heires Execut^rs and Administrat^rs to his said father & Mother and his or her assignes, he y® s^d Joshua to deliver y® fores^d stock of Neat Cattle & sheep within six moneths after y® Decease of his s^d father and mother to whomesoever they or the longest liver of them shall have disposed them unto in their lives time. And for confirmation of all y® above written Premisses both parties to these presence have hereunto set their hands and seales the one and thirtieth day of April in the second year of the Reign of our Soveraign Lady Anne by the grace of God of England Scotland France and Ireland Queen Defend^r of y® ffaith &c/ And in the year of our Lord one thousand seven hundred and three — 1703.

Signed Sealed and Delivered   Christian Remich (his seal)
  In the presence of us.   her
           her   Hannah X Remich (her seale)
  Katharine K Hamond   mark
       mark   Joshua Remich (his seal)
        his
  Moses ᛖ Hunscomb
      mark
  Jos Hamond

York ss : Apr^ll 30th 1703

The above named Christian Remich, Hannah Remich and Joshua Remich personally Appearing before me the Subscrib^r one of the members of her Maties Council of y® Province of the Massachusetts Bay and Justice of Peace within the same/ Acknowledged this Instrum^t to be his Act and deed/
                                  Jos Hamond.

Book VI, Fol. 172.

A true Copie of the originall Transcribed and compared April 31st 1703   p Jos Hamond Registr

Thomas
to
Hutchins

Know all men by these p'sence that I Roger Thomas of Kittery in ye County of York in New England, for a valluable consideration to me in hand paid by Benjamin Hutchins of the same place Have given granted bargained and sold/ All my twenty Acre grant of land granted unto me by the town of Kittery May 16. 1694. And all my grant of ten Acres of land granted unto me by the town of Kittery May 24th 1699. the whole containing thirty Acres of land together with all ye priviledges Rights and title and Interst I have in the same or might any wise Acrew to me/ thereby, to him ye sd Benjamin Hutchins his heires or assignes for ever/ To have and to hold, all the above thirty Acres of land herein mentioned unto ye said Benjamin Hutchins his heires or assigns for ever the quiet and peaceable possession thereof to warrant and for ever Defend against all persons laying a Legall Claime thereunto In witness whereof I have set to my hand and seal this sixth of March one thousand seven hundred & two three 1702/3 —

Signed Sealed and delivered
   In the presence of us.   Roger Thomas (his seal)
Rowland Williams
      the sign of
Samll Hutchins
Wllm Godsoe.

York ss Kittery Augst 18th 1703

The above named Roger Thomas personally appearing before me ye subscribr one of her Mats Justices of ye peace in sd County Acknowledged this Instrumt to be his Act and deed/   Jos Hamond

BOOK VI, FOL. 172.

A true Copie of the originall Transcribed and Compared
Augst 18th 1703   p Jos Hamond Reg^r

Know all men by these p^{r}sence that I Benjamin Hutchins of Kittery in ye County of York yeoman for a valuable consideration to me in hand paid by Roger Thomas of the same place Labourer Have given granted bargained and sold to ye s^d Roger Thomas ten Acres of land lying in Kittery between Spruce Creek and York line, and is bounded by William Landalls land on ye Northwest side, Eighty one pole, And on ye south west fifty pole by my own land and my brother Sam^{lls} land, runing North west and Southeast, And on ye Southeast side by a Northeast line sixty six pole and lies in form of a Triangle and is part of that thirty Acres of land that was granted unto me by the town of Kittery May ye 24 : 1699 and laid out by W^{llm} Godsoe and Nich^o Gowen Septemb^r 8th 1699. together with all the wood and underwoods and Appurtenances thereunto belonging or in any wise appertaining to him ye s^d Roger Thomas his heires and assignes for ever To have and to hold All the aboves^d ten. Acres of land unto ye sole use of him ye s^d Roger Thomas his heires or assignes for ever, the Peaceable and quiet possession thereof to warrant and defend against all persons laying Claime thereunto, In witness hereof I have set to my hand and seal, this 6th day March 170¾

Hutchins to Thomas

Signed & Sealed in p^{r}sence of us   the Sign of
    Rowland Williams   Benj. ⌇ Hutchins (his seal)
      the sign of
        Sam^{ll} ⌘ Hutchins
    W^{llm} Godsoe.

York ss. Augst 18th 1703.

BOOK VI, FOL. 173.

The above named Benjamin Hutchins personally Appearing before me the subscrib.r one of her Ma.ts Justices of Peace in s.d County Acknowledged this Instrum.t to be his Act and deed/

Jos Hamond

A true Copie of y.e originall Transcribed and compared Aug.st 18.th 1703 p Jos Hamond Reg.r

[173] To all Christian People to whome this pres.t Deed of sale shall come/ John Lee of Boston in the County of Suffolk in New England Marrin.r, but formerly of Shadwell near London in England send Greeting Know Yee that y.e s.d John Lee for and in consideration of y.e sum of fifteen pounds in currant money of New England to me in hand well and truly paid by Thomas Fowler of Boston afores.d Marrin.r, the receipt whereof I doe hereby Acknowledge, And my selfe therewith to be fully satisfied and contented, And thereof and of every part thereof, for my self my heires Execut.rs and Adm.rs doe Exonerate acquit and discharge y.e s.d Thomas ffowler his heires Ex.ers Adm.rs & assignes firmly and for ever by these p.rsence have and hereby doe fully freely cleerly and Absolutely give, grant, bargain, sell Alien Enfeoffe, convey and confirm unto y.e s.d Thomas Fowler his heires Ex.ers Adm.rs and assignes, All that my Land lying and being in Kittery in their Ma.ts Province or County of York, which land Walter Barfoot Esq.r of y.e Province of New Hampshier in New England Dec.d bought and purchased of Francis Champernown for a valuable consideration, as by Deed under y.e hand and seal of the s.d ffrancis Champernown dated y.e twenty first of January one thousand six hundred sixty and nine more at large doth appear/ And that y.e s.d Walter Barfoot Esq.r have by a Deed of gift made over the same to me the s.d John Lee which Deed bears

date ye one and twentieth day of Novemb^r one thousand six hundred eighty & seven/ All which land being upland and swamp lyeth at a place there called and known by the name of spruce creek, or by what other name or names the same is called or known, And containing two hundred and sixteen Acres, being a part of a Town grant of three hundred Acres given unto ye s^d Francis Champernown by ye Town of Kittery afores^d as by the Records of the s^d Town of Kittery will appear wch said quantity of two hundred and sixteen Acres ye s^d John Lee doth hereby promise to procure unto ye s^d Thomas Fowler ye draught of the s^d land as it was laid out, or cause the same to be anew laid out, within the term of six moneths from the date hereof together with all paths passages, trees, woods underwoods comons easments profits comodities advantages Emoluments heredittaments and Apurtenances whatsoever to s^d tract, piece or parcel of land belonging or in any wise appertaining And also all the Right titles claimes Interest use possession, Revercon, Remainder and Demands of ye s^d John Lee of in & to the s^d Premisses and of in or unto every or any part or parcel thereof To have and to hold and peaceably to be possessed of the s^d tract piece or parcel of ye upland and swamp and every part or parcel thereof, and all ways paths passages trees woods & underwoods Comons Easments profits comodities Advantages Emoluments heredittam^ts And appurtenances whatsoever, unto ye s^d Thomas Fowler his heires Ex^trs Adm^rs and assignes for ever And to ye sole and only proper use benefit and behoof of the s^d Thomas Fowler his heires and Assignes for ever and to no other intent and meaning whatsoever And ye s^d John Lee for him self his heires Ex^trs and Adm^rs Doe coven^t promise and grant to and with the said Thomas Fowler his heirs Ex^trs Adm^rs & assignes that he ye s^d John Lee is the right true and proper owner of the s^d tract of Land soe being as aforesaid and have in my self power suffi-

Lee to Fowler

cient to bargain sell and assure y° same to the s^d Thomas Fowler his heires Ex^trs Adm^rs and assignes in manner as afores^d And that y° s^d land & appurces are at y° sealing and delivery of these presence free and cleere Acquitted and Discharged of and from all former gifts grants bargains sales Leases Mortgages Joyntures decrees wills Estates titles troubles acts Alienations or incumbrances whatsoever And y° s^d land, against my self & every other person or persons Lawfully claiming any right title or Interest thereto from by or under me y° s^d John Lee unto y° s^d Thomas Fowler his heires and assignes shall warrant and for ever defend by these presence. And further the s^d Thomas Fowler doth hereby promise and Oblige himself his heires and assignes to pay unto y° s^d John Lee upon his delivering unto y° s^d ffowler his heires & assignes, a Draught of y° s^d Land as is afore expressed the sum of five pounds Currant money of New England And the s^d John Lee doth further covenant and promise to doe and perform any further act or thing that may be for the better securing and more amply sure making the premisses to y° s^d Thomas Fowler his heires Ex^rs Adm^rs and assignes And such as by men Experienced in y° same shall be adjudged to be nessessary requisite or expedient/ In witness whereof I the s^d John Lee have hereunto set my hand and seale the eighteenth day of Septemb^r Anno Dom one thousand six hundred eighty and nine/ y° words to be in the nineteenth line Interlined before signing and sealing.

Signed Sealed and delivered   John Lee (his seal)
  In presence of
  Jotham Grover
  Jn° Harb^t Coward Not^us Pub^cus

Boston 20th Septemb^r 1689.

  John Lee personally Appearing acknowledged the within written Instrum^t to be his Act and Deed.

                       Is^a Addington assist^t

Book VI, Fol. 173.

A true Copie of the originall Transcribed & compared ffeb[ry] 24th 1703   p Jos : Hamond Reg[r]

To all People unto whome these presence shall come Thomas ffowler of Boston within his Ma[ts] Province of y[e] Massachusets Bay in New England Marrin[r] for and in consideration of the naturall love good will and affection which I beare and doe bear unto Samuel Hill the son of William Hill of Boston afores[d] Waiter as also for divers other good causes and valuable considerations me hereunto especially moving Have given granted Aliened assigned conveyed and confirmed, And by these presence do fully freely clerely & absolutely, give, grant Alien assigne convey and confirm unto y[e] s[d] Sam[ll] Hill his heires and assignes for ever All that my land lying & being in Kittery in his Ma[ts] Province of Maine County of York which Land Walter Barfoot Esq[r] of the Province of New Hampshiere in New England Dec[d] bought and purchased of Frances Champernown, which

ffowler to Hill

Land the s[d] Walter Barfoot gave to John Lee of s[d] Boston Marrin[r] which the said John Lee sold to me the s[d] Thomas ffowler All which land is upland and swamp lying and being at a place called Spruce Creek or by what ever other name or names the same is called or known containing two hundred and sixteen Acres being part of a Town grant of three hundred Acres given unto y[e] s[d] ffrancis Champernown by the Town of Kittery afores[d] as by the Records of the s[d] Town may appear Together with all the timber trees woods underwoods wayes easments waters water Courses profits priviledges rights comodities hereditaments Emoluments and appurtenances whatsoever to y[e] premisses belonging or in any wayes appertaining And also all the Estate right title Interest Claim propriety and Demand whatsoever of me y[e] s[d]

Thomas ffowler of in and to y̆ᵉ same And yᵉ reverc̃on and reverc̃ons Remainder and Remainders thereof, with all Deeds Evidences and writings wᶜʰ concern the same. To have and to hold the before bargained premises with yᵉ Appurtenances unto y̆ᵉ sᵈ Samuel Hill his heires & assignes forever to his and their sole and proper use benefit [174] and behoofe for ever And I the said Thomas Fowler for my selfe my heires Execⁿ and Admⁿ doe hereby covenant promise grant and agree to and with the said Samuel Hill his heires Execⁿ and Admⁿ in manner following (that is to say that at and imediately before yᵉ ensealing and Delivery of these presence I am the true sole and Lawfull owner of all yᵉ before bargained premises & stand Lawfully Seizᵈ thereof in my own proper right in a good sure & indefeazible Estate of Inheritance in Fee simple Having in my selfe full power good right and Lawfull Authority to dispose of the same in manner aforesᵈ And that yᵉ sᵈ Samˡ Hill his heires or assignes shall and may from hence forth and for ever hereafter by force and virtue of these presence peaceably and Quietly enter into and upon, Have hold use ocupie possess and enjoy the above granted and bargained premisses with the Appur̃ces thereof Free and cleer & cleerly acquitted and Discharged of and from all and all manner of former and other gifts grants bargains sales Leases Releases Mortgages Joyntures Dowers Judgmᵗˢ Executions entailes fines & forfeitures and of and from all other titles troubles Charges & Incumbrances whatsoever And further I doe Covenant promise grant & agree bind and Oblige my self my heires Execⁿ and Admⁿ from henceforth and for ever hereafter to warrant and Defend all yᵉ above bargained premisses with the appur̃ces unto yᵉ sᵈ Samˡ Hill his heires & assignes for ever Against yᵉ Claimes and demands of all & every person & persons whatsoever, In witnesse whereof I the sᵈ Thomas Fowler have hereunto set my hand and seal this fifteenth

Book VI, Fol. 174.

day of Octob' Anno dm̃ 1699 Annoq̃ RR Dm̃ Willi 3ᵗⁱⁱ nunc Angliæ &ᶜ Vndecimo.   Thomas Fowler (his seal)
Signed Sealed and delivered
  In the presence of us.
  John Cooke
  Joseph Trazon
  Tho: Newton

Boston 17ᵗʰ Octob' 1699

The above named Thomas Fowler yᵉ granter personally Appeared before me yᵉ Subscriber one of his Maᵗˢ Justices of the Peace for the County of Suffolk in New England and Acknowledged yᵉ above written Instrumᵗ to be his Act and Deed/   Jer: Dum̃er

A true Copie of the originall Transcribed & compared Feb'y 24: 1703   p Jos: Ham̃ond Reg'

Mason to Hutchinson

This Indenture the sixteenth day of Decemb' Anno Domⁱ one thousand six hundred Eighty seven Annoq̃ RRˢ Jacobi Angliæ &ᶜ Secundi Tertio. Between Robert Tufton Mason Esq' Grandson and heir of Capᵗⁿ John Mason late of London Esq' Decᵈ on yᵉ one part and Eliakim Hutchinson of Boston within his Majᵗʸˢ Territory & Dominion of New England Merchant of the other part Witnesseth whereas our Soveraign Lᵈ King James yᵉ first by his letters Pattents under yᵉ great Seal of England Dated at Westminster the third day of Novemb' in yᵉ Eighteenth year of his Majᵗʸˢ Reign For yᵉ considerations in yᵉ Same Letters Pattents Expressed did absolutely give grant and confirm unto yᵉ Council Established at Plimouth in the County of Devon for the Planting Ruling ordering and Governing of New England in America And to their Successors and assignes for ever All the land of New England aforesᵈ Lying and being in breadth from forty

Degrees to forty eight Degrees Northerly Latitude Inclusively Together with all ffirm lands soyles grounds Havens Ports Rivers waters fishings hunting hawking fowling & all mines Mineralls &c as in and by the s^d Letters Pattents amongst Divers other things therein conteined more at large it doth and may appear And whereas the s^d Council by their Indenture under their comon seal bearing Date the two and twentieth day of April Anno one thosand six hundred thirty five made between the s^d Council by ye name of the Council Established at Plimouth in the County of Devon for ye planting ruleing ordering & Governing of New England in Americæ of the one part and Sr Fardinando Gorges of London Knight on the other part for the considerations in ye s^d Indenture Expressed Did give grant bargain sell Enfeoff and confirm unto the said S^r ffardinando Gorges his heires and assignes for ever All that part purport or portion of ye Main Land of New England afores^d begining at ye entrance of Piscataqua Harbour so to pass up ye same unto ye River of Newgewanack through the same unto the furthest head thereof And from thence Northwestwards untill sixty miles be finished, and from Piscataqua Northeastwards along the Sea Coast to Sagadahock and up the River thereof to the River of Kenebeck and throughout the same unto ye head thereof & so up into ye land Northwestwards untill Sixty Miles be finished from the mouth or entrance of Sagadahock from which period to cross over the Land to ye Sixty Miles end formerly accompted up into the Land from Piscataqua Harbour through Newgewanack River which amongst other Lands are granted unto ye s^d Sr Fardinando Gorges together with all mines Mineralls precious stones woods Marishes Rivers waters ffishing hunting fowling &c with all and Singular their appur^ces &c as by the s^d Indenture more at Large doth appear And whereas the s^d ffardinando Gorges for Divers good causes and considerations him thereunto moveing in and by a certain Indenture under his hand and seal bearing Date y® seventeenth day of Septemb^r Anno one thousand six hundred thirty five Did give, grant bargain sell Enfeoff and confirm unto Cap^tn John Mason of London Esqr his heires and assignes for ever All that part or portion of Land begining at the entrance of Newgewanack River and so upward along the s^d River and to ye furthest head thereof and to contain in breadth throughout all the Length afores^d three Miles within the land from every part of s^d River and half way over ye s^d River together with all and singular Harbour Cricks Mrrishes woods Rivers waters Lakes Mines Mineralls precious stones fishings hauking hunting and fowling &^c comodities and heredittaments whatsoever with all and singular their and either of their appur^ces to be holden of his Ma^ty his heires and successors as of his mannor of East Greenwich in the County of Kent in Free & comon soccage & not in Capite or by Knights Service Yeelding and paying unto his Ma^ty his heires and Successors the fifth part of ye ore of gold and silver y^t from time to time and at all times thereafter shall be there gotten had and obtained For all services duties and Demands as in & by the said Letters Pattents are reserved and by ye s^d recited Indenture doth more at Large appear Now this Indenture further Witnesseth that ye above named Robert Tufton Mason Esqr Grandson and heir of the s^d Cap^tn John Mason Esqr for and in consideration of ye sum [175] of sixty pounds in currant money of New-England to him in hand at and before the ensealing and Delivery of these presence well and truly paid by the aforenamed Eliakim Hutchinson in full payment & satisfaccon for all past Rents and Demands whatsoever the recipt whereof he ye s^d Robert Tufton Mason doth Acknowledge and thereof doth Exonerate acquit and Discharge the s^d Eliakim Hutchinson his heires Exec^rs Adm^rs and assignes for ever by these presence. Also in further consideration of ye yearly Rent and payments hereafter in these p^rnts expressed and reserved on the part of the s⁴ Robert Tufton Mason &ᶜ to be payd by the s⁴ Eliakim Hutchinson his heires Execⁿ Admⁿ or assignes Hath given granted released Enfeoffed and confirmed, and by these presence Doth freely fully & absolutely give grant Alien release enfeoffe and confirm unto yᵉ s⁴ Eliakim Hutchinson his heires and assignes for ever the full quantity of five hundred Acres of Land Lying Scituate on both sides the Little River of Newgewanak Alias Newichewanick within the Township of Kittery in the Province of Maine in New England afores⁴ four hundred and fourteen acres whereof was formerly surveyed and Measured by Capᵗⁿ John Wincoll (as appears by a Draught or plat thereof by him made and signed yᵉ five & twentieth day of May Anno 1681) being now in yᵉ Actuall Possession of yᵉ s⁴ Hutchinson And yᵉ remainder to compleat yᵉ s⁴ five hundred Acres to be made up out of yᵉ adjacent Lands backwards, and severall other parcels & spots of land Marish or Meadow lying upon yᵉ afores⁴ River which were formerly granted by the Town of Kittery unto Richard or George Leader or to yᵉ s⁴ Hutchinson, And all rights and grants of Timber made by yᵉ said Town of Kittery unto yᵉ s⁴ Richard or George Leader or s⁴ Hutchinson & other Timber conveinent to be brought unto yᵉ s⁴ Hutchinsons Mill standing or lying within yᵉ s⁴ Masons Right not heretofore granted (Excepting pine trees of four and twenty Inches Diameter fitting to make Masts for yᵉ Kings ships) and yᵉ sole propriety in yᵉ falls on which s⁴ Hutchinsons Mill now stands, with yᵉ stream, waters water courses, Dam̄s banks priviledges and appurᶜᵉˢ thereto belonging, Reserving yᵉ priviledge of the River and Stream for yᵉ Transportation of Timber Loggs and boards &ᶜ as is usual and hath been formerly accustomed. Together with all woods underwoods Timber and trees (Except as afores⁴) stones Mines and Mineralls whatsoever upon yᵉ aforementioned to be granted Lands or on any part or parcel thereof springs waters water courses fishing fowling hawking hunting Rights liberties priviledges accomodations profits and appur^{ces} thereto belonging, reserving unto his Maj^{ty} his heires and successors one fifth part of ye oar of gold and silver that from time to time and at all times hereafter shall be there gotten had and obtained To have and to hold ye s^d quantity or tract of Land of five hundred Acres and other ye severall parcels or spots of land Marish or Meadow above mentioned with ye wood trees Timber and grants of Timber sole propriety in ye falls and all other ye afore granted premisses with ye Rights members priviledges & appur^{ces} thereof (Excepting and reserving as is above excepted and reserved) also all the Estate right title Interest use property possession Claime Challenge & Demand whatsoever of him ye s^d Robert Tufton Mason or his heires of in and to the same and every part and parcel thereof unto ye s^d Eliakim Hutchinson his heires and assignes to his and their only proper use benefit and behoof for ever And the s^d Robert Tufton Mason for himself his heires Exec^{rs} and Adm^{rs} doth covenant promise grant and agree to and with ye s^d Eliakim Hutchinson his heires and assignes by these presents in manner following that is to say that he s^d Eliakim Hutchinson his heires or assignes shall and may from time to time and at all times for ever hereafter by force and vertue of these p^{r}sence Lawfully peaceably and quietly have hold use ocupie possess and enjoy to his and their own proper use benefit and behoof All and every of ye above granted premisses with ye rights members profits priviledges and appur^{ces} thereof free and clere and clearly acquitted Exonerated and Discharged of and from all former and other gifts grants bargains sales Leases Mortgages titles troubles Charges Incumbrances Claims and Demands whatsoever and doth further covenant promise bind & oblige himself his heires Exec^{rs} and Adm^{rs} from time to time and at all times for ever hereafter to warrant maintain and Defend all and every of ye s^d granted premisses unto the s^d Eliakim Hutchinson his heires and assignes against all and every person and persons whomsoever and at y* Cost and Charges in y* Law, of y* s^d Eliakim Hutchinson his heires or assignes upon request or demand thereof to do, make seal execute acknowledge and suffer such other and further Deeds Instrum^ts writings act or acts devise or devises in the Law for y* more sure making and confirmation of y* s^d bargained premisses with y* memb^rs & appur^ces thereof unto the s^d Eliakim Hutchinson his heires and assignes for ever as his or their Council learned in y* Law shall devise advise or require And y* s^d Eliakim Hutchinson doth by these presence covenant promise grant and agree for himself his heires Execut^rs Adm^rs and assignes well and truly to pay or cause to be paid unto y* s^d Robert Tufton Mason his heires Exec^rs adm^rs or assignes y* full and Just Sum or quit Rent of forty shillings in currant money of New England p annum for y* s^d five hundred Acres of Land to be paid upon y* five and Twentieth day of Decemb^r yearly and in every year successively from y* five and twentieth of Decemb^r An^o one thousand six hundred Eighty and eight thence forth for ever if Demanded and in like proportion for so many Acres as y* s^d other parcels or spots of Land Marish or Meadow shall appear to contain upon survey and Measure thereof to be made and for y* grants and priviledges of Timber for the use of y* s^d Saw Mill y* full and Just Quantity of three thousand foot of boards for every hundred thousand foot which from time to time and at all times for ever hereafter shall be there sawn So alwayes that y* afores^d payments for the above granted premisses and every of them whatsoever and to whomsoever Except the fifth part of y* oar of gold and silver afore reserved to be paid to his Ma^ty his heires or Successors In witness whereof the s^d parties to these presence have interchangeably set their hands and seales the day and year first above written Also there is further granted unto y* s^d Eliakim Hutchinson his heires &^c a strip of Land of about one Acre more or Less Lying upon ye side of ye River commonly called pipestave point, formerly bought of Richard Nason.

E^m (his seal) Hutchinson

Signed Sealed and Delivered
  After interling ye words p annu
  In the presence of us.
  Nicho Paige
  Will Ardell
  Is^a Addington

A true Copie of ye originall Transcribed and Compared March 170¾   p Jos. Hamond Reg^r

To all Christian People unto whome these p^rsence shall come Elizabeth Rones sole daughter, Child and heiress of William and Mary Rones late of York and in ye County of York, within the Massachusets Bay in New England Deceased now in Boston in New England afores^d Spinster Sendeth Greeting Know Yee that the said Elizabeth Rones for and in consideration of the sum of eight pounds Currant money of New England to me in hand paid at and before ye Ensealing and delivery of these p^rsence, the receit whereof I hereby Acknowledge & myself [176] therewith full satisfied, by Samuel Came of York afores^d Yeoman Have granted bargained sold Enfeoffed and confirmed And by these p^rsence Doe give grant bargain sell Alien Enfeoff and confirm unto him ye s^d Samuel Came his heires Exec^{trs} Adm^{rs} and assignes, All that parcel of Land lying and being for ten Acres more or less, scituate lying and being within the Township of York aboves^d whereof s^d William Rones died possessed and seized butted and bounded on the North side by the Land of James ffrethy late of York afores^d Dec^d, on the East

Rones to Came

side by ẙ Country Rode way, on the south side by the Land of Arthur Bragginton, on ẙ west side by ẙ Land granted by ẙ town unto ẙ s^d William Rones and James ffreethy together with ẙ s^d piece of Land lying in partnership betwixt me and ẙ heire or heires of s^d ffreethy To have and to hold ẙ s^d ten Acres of Land more or less with all its Comodities rights members priviledges and Appurtenances whatever with all my right title Interest property Claim and Demand of in & to the premisses, And ẙ afores^d town grant unto my father afores^d & James ffreethy afores^d unto ẙ s^d Samuel Came his heires Execut^{rs} Adm^{rs} and assignes for ever And I ẙ said Elizabeth Rones Doe covenant to and with the said Samuel Came that I ẙ s^d Elizabeth Rones am the sole heiress of the afores^d granted premisses And have in my self full power good right and Lawfull authority to sell and convey in manner afores^d the s^d Premisses & untill these premisses be sealed and executed I have a good and free Inheritance of ẙ same Voyd of all former grants whatsoever, And ẙ s^d p^{r}misses and Appurtenances unto ẙ s^d Samuel Came his heires and assignes against my self ẙ s^d Elizabeth Rones her heires and assignes or any other Claimes by from or under me the same will warrant and for ever Defend by vertue of these presence. In witness whereof I ẙ s^d Elizabeth Rones unto these presence have hereunto set my hand and seal this nineteenth day of Novemb^r Anno Domini One thousand six hundrd and Ninety five Annoq Regni Regis Gulielmi Tetij Septimo Angliæ &c

The mark of

Signed Sealed and delivered

Elizabeth Rones (her seal)

   In presence of us.
   Joseph Harris
   Robert Eliot
   Edward Mills

Book VI, Fol. 176.

Suffolk ss/ Boston 19th Novembr 1695

Mrs Elizabeth Rones personally appearing before before me ye Subscribr one of his Mats Justices for ye County aforesd Acknowledged this Instrumt to be her Act and deed/
Jer : Dumer

A true Copie of the originall Transcribed and compared April 3d 1703   p Jos Hamond Regr

Memorand Boston N. E. Novembr the 19th one thousand six hundred & Ninety five then Recd of Samuel Came within Mentioned ye within mentioned sum of Eight pounds money in full I say p me   The mark of
Elizabeth Rones

A true Copie of ye originall receipt Transcribed and compared Aprill 3d 1703/   p Jos Hamond Regr

To all Christian People whome these p'sence may concern Daniel Simpson and ffrances his wife, of York in the County of York in the Province of the Massachusets bay in New England send Greeting Know Yee that ye sd Daniel & ffrances for and in consideration of a certain sum of money to them in hand and otherwise at ye signing of this Instrumt satisfactoraly secured by Samuel Came of the Town and County and Country aforesd Have given granted bargained Alienated Enfeofed and confirmed And doe by these presence give grant bargaine sell alenate Enfeoffe and confirm and fully freely and absolutely make over unto ye sd Samuel Came a certain piece or parcel of Salt Marsh containing by Estimation four Acres be it more or less scituate Lying and being within the township or precinct of York being formerly in ye possession of abovesd Daniels father Ensign Henry Simpson and known by the name of his four Acre Marsh Lying and being upon ye Northwest branch of York River a little above ye parting of sd River And is bounded

Book VI, Fol. 176.

on the west and North by the branch of s^d River, And on ye Eastward and Southward by ye Marsh of Goodman Jun-
<small>Simpson to Came</small> kins, together with all the rights benefits Emolum^ts and advantages on, appertaining unto or any ways at any time redowning from ye same or any part or parcel thereof To haue and to hold and quietly and peaceably to ocupie possess and enjoy the s^d Marish and appur^ces as a sure Estate in Fee Simple, to him ye s^d Samuel his héires Execut^rs Adm^rs and assignes for ever, moreover ye s^d Daniel and ffrancis for themselves their heires Execut^rs Adm^rs to and with the s^d Samuel his heires Execut^rs Adm^rs and assignes Doe Enden Covenat engage and promise the premisses with all their priviledges and Appur^ces from all former grants gifts sales Rents Rates Dowerys Demands and Incumbrances whatsoever as also from all future Claimes Suits or Interuptions to be had or comenced by them their heires Exec^trs Adm^rs or assignes or any person or persons whatsoever upon grounds proceeding ye Date of this Instrum^t, for ever to warrant and Defend by these presence, In witness whereof the above s^d Daniel Simpson and ffrances his wife hath hereunto set their hands and seales this twenty sixt day of Decemb^r in ye year of our Lord One thousand seven hundred and one and in the thirteenth year of the Reign of our Soveraign Ld William the third King of great Brittain, &c.

Signed Sealed and delivered   Daniel Simpson (his seal)
  In presence of us.   ffrances Simpson (her seal)
  Abrã : Preble
  Matthew Austin

Daniel Simpson and ffrances Simpson his wife came before me ye Subscrib^r and Acknowledged the above writted Deed of Sale to be their Act and deed, this 27th of April 1702.
                  Before me Abrã Preble Justice Peace

A true Copie of the originall Transcribed and compared Apr^ll 3^d 1703   Jos Hamond Reg^r

Book VI, Fol. 177.

To all People unto whome these pʳsents shall come Joseph Hamond, Junʳ, of Kittery in yᵉ County of York in yᵉ Province of yᵉ Massachusets Bay in New England sendeth Greeting Know Yee that I yᵉ sᵈ Joseph Hamond for and in consideration of five pounds Currant Money in New England to me in hand [177] paid or secured in yᵉ Law to be paid at and before yᵉ ensealing and Delivery of these pʳsents, by Thomas Rhodes of Kittery in yᵉ County aforesᵈ Joyner Have given granted bargained sold released Enfeoffed and confirmed And by these pʳsents Doe freely fully and absolutely Give grant bargain sell release assign Enfeoffe convey and confirm unto the sᵈ Thomas Rhodes his heires and assignes for ever a certain Grant of thirty Acres of land granted to me by yᵉ sᵈ town of Kittery on yᵉ twenty fourth day of May one thousand six hundred Ninety and nine according as yᵉ same was granted to me by sᵈ town of Kittery as p yᵉ grant in Kittery town book may more amply and at large appear, with all and singular yᵉ profits priviledges and appurtenances thereunto belonging or in any wise appertaining with all Right title Interest Claim and Demand of me yᵉ sᵈ Joseph Hamond my heires Executʳˢ Admʳˢ or assigns of in and to yᵉ same or any part thereof To have and to hold the sᵈ grant of Land and all and singular yᵉ pʳmisses and appurtenances herein before granted bargained and sold unto yᵉ sᵈ Thomas Rhodes his heires and assignes to his & their only proper use benefit and behoof for ever And I yᵉ sᵈ Joseph Hamond for my self my heires Executʳˢ and Admʳˢ Doe hereby covenᵗ grant and agree to and with yᵉ sᵈ Thomas Rhodes his heires and assignes that at and untill the ensealing and Delivery of these pʳsents I am yᵉ true & Lawfull owner of the sᵈ grant of thirty Acres of Land and pʳmisses herein before granted and that yᵉ same are free and clear and clearly acquitted and Discharged of and from all former and other conveyances and Incumbrances whatsoever And that I have in my self good right full power and Lawfull Authority yᵉ same to

Convey as afores^d unto him ye s^d Thomas Rhodes his heires &c for evermore And further that I ye s^d Joseph Hamond my heires Execut^{rs} or adm^{rs} shall and will warrant and for ever Defend the s^d Grant of thirty Acres of Land & p'misses herein before bargained and sold unto him ye s^d Thomas Rhodes his heires & assignes against ye Lawfull Claimes and Demands of all and every person & persons whatsoever from by or under me or by my procurem^t In Witness wereof I have hereunto set my hand and Seale the Eleventh day of ffebruary in the first Year of the Reign of our Soveraign Lady Anne over England &^{c} Queen Annoq, Dom one thousand seven hundred & two or three. 170⅔

Signed Sealed and Delivered   Jos Hamond Junr (his seal)
   In p'sents of us.
   Willm Stacie
   Jos : Hamond

York ss/ Kittery ye 15th ffebruary 170⅔

The above named Joseph Hamond Junr personally appearing before me ye Subscrib^r one of her Ma^{tys} Justices of the Peace within s^d County Acknowledged this Instrum^t to be his Act and Deed.

                                    Jos : Hamond

A true Copie of the originall Transcribed & compared ffeb : 23^d 1702   p Jos : Hamond Reg^r

INDEX OF

Date.	Grantor.	Grantee.	Instrument.
	ABBOTT, John, see Joseph Abbott		
1703, Oct. 2	ABBOTT, Joseph and John Abbott	Est. of Jonathan Nason and Sarah Nason, adm'x	Receipts
1699, Mar. 25	ABBOT, Thomas	Joshua Downing John Leighton	Deed
1699, Mar. 25	ABBOT, Thomas	Joshua Downing John Leighton	Deed
1700, Mar. 27	ABBOT, Thomas, senior et ux.	John Abbott	Deed
1638, Mar. 13	AGAMENTICUS, Colony of, by William Hooke, governor	Henry Simpson	Grant
1670, Aug. 6	ALCOCK, Job	Edward Cock	Deed
1700, Jan. 1	ALCOCK, Job	Samuel Pray	Deed
1687, Nov. 3	ALCOCK, John	Shubael Dummer	Deed
1700, Sept. 6	ALLEN, Robert	John Newmarch	Deed
1700, Apr. 20	ALLOWELL (Elwell), Hezekiah	Wm. Pepperrell	Deed
1687, July 20	ATWATER, Joshua	Humphrey Scammon	Deed

GRANTORS.

Folio.	Description.
171	In full for their wives' portions.
54	Quitclaim to the premises more fully described below.
54	40 acres upland near Sturgeon creek, with 10 acres marsh in the Great Marsh adjoining, in [*Berwick*] *Kittery*.
67	25 acres west of the top of Rocky Hill in [*Berwick*] *Kittery*.
74	Tract on north side of Agamenticus river and on west side of Bass creek, and a parcel of meadow in common with others near the head of the river, in *York*.
40	Land on the Westermost creek, between lands of Bragdon and Card, in *York*.
85	50 acre town grant, adjoining Livingstone's land and Maxfield's marsh, in *York*.
81	58 acres, being the half of Farmer Alcock's neck, at the river's mouth; also 4 acres marsh on the western branch of York river, in *York*.
114	30 acre town grant by and in *Kittery*.
138	30 acre town grant by and in *Kittery*.
79	Saw-mill, site and appurtenances, timber grant, 50 acres upland adjoining the falls, and meadow below the mill, at Dunstan falls in *Scarborough*.

Index of Grantors.

Date.	Grantor.	Grantee.	Instrument.
1684, Oct. 6	Ashleigh, William et ux.	Jona. Littlefield	Deed
1694, Dec. 10	Austin, Matthew et ux.	Micum Maccantier	Deed
1697, Apr. 7	Bamfield, Christopher et ux.	Richard Rogers	Deed
1702, May 26	Bamfield, Christopher et ux.	John Rogers	Deed
	Banks, Elizabeth, see estate of Richard Banks		
1696, Apr. 22	Banks, Richard, est.of,by Joseph Banks, adm'r, and Elizabeth Banks, John Banks	John Banks Joseph Banks	Division
1687, Nov. 21	Barfoot, Walter	John Lee	Deed
1700, Feb. 3	Bartlet, Nicholas	John Higginson junior	Deed
	Bass, Jonathan, see Peter Bass' estate		
1702, June 26	Bass, Peter, estate of, and Jonathan Bass	Samuel Johnson	Release
1700, Jan. 22	Batson, John and Samuel Hill, Joseph Storer	Each other	Partn'ship agreement
1687, Aug. 24	Bernard, Benjamin et ux.	Joseph Bernard	Deed
Acknowledged 1700, Sept. 5	Black, Daniel	James Gooch	Mortgage
1702, Oct. 9	Blackdon, Joan and Grace Tucker et ux.	Sylvanus Tripe	Deed
1686, Mar. 9	Blakeman, Benjamin	Sampson Sheafe	Deed

INDEX OF GRANTORS. 5

Folio.	Description.
107	140 acres, with buildings, 27 poles wide upon the highway next Mr. Wheelwright's; also marsh at the neck of land on the sea-wall; also 6 acres more of marsh; all in *Wells*.
51	10 acres at Goose cove, running 20 poles along the river, in *York*.
154	10 acres on the river between Grantee's and Peter Staple's lands in *Kittery*.
154	Quit-claim to all additions belonging to above lot.
123	Of said intestate's estate in *York*, securing provision for the widow and release of dower by her.
159	216 acres at Spruce creek in *Kittery*, purchased of Francis Champernown.
139	100 acres between lands of George Cleave and Michael Mitten, 100 poles along the water front and back 160 poles into the woods [on *Falmouth Neck*].
111	Of all obligations by Grantee's warrantor, George Parker of *York*. [See III. 122].
50	Relating to building and operating a saw-mill on the river at *Cape Porpoise*.
29	50 acres bought of Grantee between the river, the commons and lands of Tozier and Price in *Berwick*.
90	3 acres and buildings (excepting half-acre house-lot of John Pennel) on highway and Meeting-house creek, in *York*.
146	10 acres, fronting 20 poles on the water-side at Crooked Lane, in *Kittery*.
13	One-third of the tract on east side of Saco river, part of Lewis and Bonighton's patent, with one-third of saw-mill on Saco river falls, containing 6000 acres, with timber grant of adjoining tract, in *Saco*.

Index of Grantors.

Date.	Grantor.	Grantee.	Instrument.
1701, June —	Bodge, Henry.	Wm. Vaughan	Levy on Execution
	Bond, *alias* Simpson, Jane, see Jane Simpson		
1679, Sept. 30	Brackett, Anthony, jun.	Abraham Drake, senior	Trust Deed
1696, Apr. 8	Bracy, John	Jeremiah Mo[u]lton	Deed
1686, Feb. 14	Bragdon, Arthur, senior	James Grant, by Alex. Maxell, attorney	Deed
1701, Dec. 25	Bragdon, Arthur, senior, et ux.	Samuel Bragdon, junior	Deed
1700, Aug. 30	Bragdon, Arthur, junior, et ux.	Peter Nowell	Deed
1700, Nov. 14	Bragdon, Arthur, junior, and Abraham Preble, Peter Nowell	Each other	Partn'ship Agreement
1700, Nov. 28	Bragdon, Arthur, junior, et ux.	Lewis Bane and Job Curtis	Deed
1695, Oct. 27	Brawn, John et ux.	Wm. Pepperrell	Deed
1701, Sept. 24	Braun, John	Peter Nowell	Deed
1699, Feb. 20	Breaden, William	Nicholas Moorey	Deed
1700, Nov. 7	Bredeen, James	Peter Lewis	Deed
1699, Oct. 13	Briar, Richard et ux.	John Frink	Deed
	Broughton, Mary, see Rachel Rew		
	Broughton, Rebecca, see Rachel Rew		
1694, Sept. 29	Brown, Andrew, senior	Robert Eliot	Mortgage

Folio.	Description.
120	Two tracts, one of 8 acres on north side of Spruce creek; the other of 20 acres in the woods, in *Kittery*.
37	Marriage settlement for benefit of Susanna [Drake] his wife, of half his realty in *Casco Bay*.
88	All real estate of Grantor's in *York*.
14	40 acres upon which the buildings of Grantee stood in *York*.
128	45 acres, fronting 36 poles on the southwest side of York river, opposite the house of Samuel Bragdon, sen., in *York*.
125	3 acres salt marsh and thatch bed on west side of the southwest branch, in *York*.
126	Relating to building and operating a saw-mill at *York* Bridge.
109	50 acres, being one-fourth undivided of town grant known as Scituate plains and marsh in *York*.
138	Half an acre on the highway adjoining Grantee's land in *Kittery*.
126	2 acres salt marsh on southwest branch of the river, in *York*.
48	300 acres in *Wells* devised to Grantor by Joseph Cross.
117	30 acre town grant by and in *Kittery*.
153	50 acres near Spruce creek, devised by Francis Champernown, in *Kittery*.
165	All his land and marsh on east side of Black Point river [in *Scarborough*].

Index of Grantors.

Date.	Grantor.	Grantee.	Instrument.
1699, Nov. 22	Brown, Andrew	Wm. Vaughan	Deed
1685, July 8	Buckland, John et ux.	William Taller	Deed
1687, Apr. 14	Buckland, John et ux.	James Littlefield	Deed
1687, Nov. 1	Burregh [Burrage], William	Joshua Scottow	Release
	Burrell, John et ux., see John Prichett		
1682, Mar. 23	Carle, Richard et ux.	Samuel Spinney	Deed
1663, Apr. 12	Chadborn, Humphrey	Francis Champernown	Trust Deed
1669, Jan. 21	Champernown, Francis	Walter Barfoot	Deed
1700, Aug. 20	Champernown, Mary	Richard Cutt	Deed
	Cheeke, Richard, see Nicholas Turbet		
1701, Sept. 3	Clark, John	Thos. Abbot, sen.	Deed
	Clark, Patience et ux., see John Wells		
1671, Apr. 6	Clarke, Thomas	Roger Plaisted and John Hull	Deed
1651, Dec. 26	Cleave, George	Nicholas Bartlet	Deed
1658, May 1	Cleave, George	Michael Mitten	Deed
1658, May 20	Cleave, George	Nathaniel Mitten	Deed
1699, Sept. 5	Cock (Cox), Edward	Agnes Kelley	Power att'y

Folio.	Description.
72	100 acres upland and 50 acres salt marsh adjoining, being the neck of land formerly Henry Watts' at Black Point, in *Scarborough*.
28	All his marsh on west side Kennebunk river, in *Wells*.
24	600 acres between Kennebunk river and the Second Sands, in *Wells*.
87	From an agreement by Grantee to convey marsh land in *Scarborough* and quitclaiming the land.
23	3 acres on the north side of the Great cove in *Kittery*.
18	Land and marsh about Sturgeon creek in [*Berwick*] *Kittery*, in trust for his wife, Lucy Chadborn.
158	216 acres at Spruce creek, part of a town grant by and in *Kittery*.
81	One-half of Champernown's Island in *Kittery*.
121	One-sixth in common of land, falls and mills at Quamphegan Falls in *Berwick*.
21	The Salmon Fall grant on Great Newichewannock river, with two mills, buildings and appurtenances in *Berwick*.
139	100 acres between lands of Grantor and Michael Mitten, 100 poles along the the water front and back into the woods [on *Falmouth* Neck].
8	Tract fronting Casco river from dwelling-house of Grantee to land of Richard Tucker, thence across to Back cove [on *Falmouth* neck].
8	50 acres, fronting 50 poles on Back cove and back 160 poles into the woods [in *Falmouth*].
40	General power of attorney.

INDEX OF GRANTORS.

Date.	Grantor.	Grantee.	Instrument.
1693, July 26	Cock, William, senior	John Higginson, junior	Deed
1699, Nov. 7	Cooper, Philip	Sarah Wright	Power att'y
1699, Jan. 6	Cooper, Philip, by Sarah Wright, attorney	Lewis Bane and Andrew Brown	Deed
1701, Nov. 13	Croad, John et ux.	Samuel Ruck	Deed
1678, Feb. 10	Crocket, Ephraim	Richard White	Deed
1702, June 18	Crocket, Hugh	Wm. Pepperrell	Deed
1703, June 17	Crocket, Hugh	John Ford	Deed
1703, June 17	Crocket, Hugh	Christopher Mitchell	Deed
1701, June 27	Crocket, Joseph	Wm. Pepperrell	Deed
1700, Oct. 5	Curtis, Dodevah	Lewis Bane and Job Curtis	Deed
1702, Apr. —	Curtis, Dodevah et ux. and Thomas Daniel's estate by Samuel Keais and Samuel Penhallow executors of Bridget Graffort, his executrix	Each other	Division
1700, July 16	Cutt, Richard	Robert Cutt	Deed
1700, Aug. 22	Cutt, Richard et ux.	Tobias Fernald	Deed
1684, Dec. 27	Danforth, Thomas, for self and partners not named	Jeremiah Moulton	Deed
1695, Feb. 27	Davis, Emmanuel et ux.	Samuel Hill	Deed
1686, Dec. 22	Davis, Isaac et ux.	Sylvanus Davis	Deed

INDEX OF GRANTORS.

Folio.	Description.
140	1300 acres upland, meadow and salt marsh on west side of Sagadahoc river near its mouth, purchased of Thomas Atkins.
108	General power, with revocation of a former one to his brother Joseph Cooper.
109	11¾ acres on the country road and a road to York river in *York*.
136	309 acres, farm at Broad cove, Casco Bay [*Yarmouth*], also 6 acres at South field, Salem
8	50 acres at head of Brave-boat harbor 50 rods wide and adjoining York bounds, in *Kittery*.
129	Town grant of 30 acres by and in *Kittery*.
166	25 acres, one-half of a town grant of 50 acres by and in *Kittery*.
167	25 acres, one-half of a town grant of 50 acres by and in *Kittery*.
139	Town grant of 30 acres by and in *Kittery*.
108	50 acres, being one-fourth of a town grant known as Scituate plains and marsh in *York*.
149	Establishing line between parties on Withers' island in Piscataqua river in *Kittery*.
57	Town grant of 50 acres by and in *Kittery*.
86	85 acres upon Broad cove and Crooked lane in *Kittery*.
26	Land on Gorges' Point in *York*.
76	40 acres adjoining Little River falls in *Cape Porpoise*.
1	10 acres marsh in Nonesuch marshes in *Scarborough*.

Index of Grantors.

Date.	Grantor.	Grantee.	Instrument.
1699, Apr. 13	DEAMENT, John, estate of, by Nathaniel Rayns and John Woodman, administrators	Nicholas Walden	Deed
1701, June 14	DENNETT, Alexander	John Gelding	Deed
1700, July 16	DENIVER, Walter	Robert Cutt	Deed
1688, Mar. 14	DERING, Henry	William Hooke	Power att'y
1699, Aug. 7	DILL, Daniel, senior	Andrew Grover	Deed
1701, May 15	DILL, Daniel, sen. et ux.	John Dill	Conditional Deed
1699, Jan. 23	DOWNING, John et ux.	Joseph Hill	Deed
1687, June 13	ELLET (Elliot), Robert et ux.	Emmanuel Davis et ux.	Deed
	ELWELL, see Allowell.		
1662, Dec. 20	EMERY, James et ux.	Charles Frost	Deed
1686, May 26	EMERY, James, sen., et ux.	Edward Waymouth	Deed
1694, Jan. 2	EMERY, James, senior	James Emery, junior	Deed
1703, Mar. 23	EMERY, Job	Gabriel Hambleton	Deed
	EMERY, Job, see Henry Snow		
1702, May 23	ENDICOT, Gilbert, by James Gooch, attorney	Lewis Bane	Deed
1695, Sept. 14	ENDLE, Richard	Samuel Penhallow	Deed
	FERNALD, Nathaniel, see est. of Samuel Fernald		

Folio.	Description.
90	40 acres with buildings at Crooked Lane in *Kittery*.
114	20 acre town grant by and in *Kittery*.
56	10 acre town grant by and in *Kittery*.
84	General power of attorney.
124	20 acres upland and swamp on northwest branch of York river in *York*.
135	All his estate in *York*, conditioned for his own and wife's support and charging certain gifts upon the estate.
91	Homestead on the Long Reach in Piscataqua river (excepting 3 acres) 10 acres of marsh; and a town grant of 40 acres (part laid out) in *Kittery*.
76	40 acres; also 60 acres upland adjoining; 7 acres marsh at Prince's rock and 7 acres marsh; all in *Cape Porpoise*.
44	2 acres called the Barren marsh on north side of Sturgeon creek in *Kittery*, [*Berwick*].
83	30 acres upland and meadow at the head of Mast creek near Piscataqua river in *Berwick*.
160	20 acres on Stony brook in *Berwick*; also half an acre where Grantee's house stood, reserving a right of way.
160	20 acre town grant by and in *Kittery*, [*Berwick*].
145	80 acres, with messuage, fronting 15 poles on the highway to the corn-mill in *York*.
127	Two adjoining lots of 20 acres each near the mast-ways on west side of Spruce creek in *Kittery*.

Date.	Grantor.	Grantee.	Instrument.
1700, July 16	FERNALD, Samuel	Robert Cutt	Deed
	FERNALD, Samuel, see Katherine Paul		
1701, June 25	FERNALD, Samuel, estate of, by Hannah Fernald, exec'x, and Nathaniel Fernald	Thomas Spinney	Deed
1691, June 8	FLETCHER, Pendleton	Richard Pope	Deed
1702, Dec. 8	FOGG, Daniel et ux.	James Staple	Deed
	FOGG, Daniel, see Joseph Hammond		
1689, June 27	FOLSHAM, Peter et ux.	William Sawyer	Deed
1699, Oct. 15	FOWLER, Thomas	Samuel Hill	Deed
1685, Sept. 9	FROST, William et ux.	Lewis Allen	Deed
1692, Oct. 12	FRY, Adrian et ux.	William Fry	Conditional Deed
1688, June 20	FRYER, Nathaniel and Robert Jordan	Philip Carpenter	Deed
1700, Aug. 20	FRYER, Nathaniel	Robert Elliot	Deed
1694, June 11	FULLER, Nathaniel	Peter Tappin	Deed
1686, Apr. 25	GILLMAN, Edward, and Stephen Paul et ux.	Joseph Hill	Deed
1702, Apr. 4	GILLMAN, Maverick	Samuel Hill and Joseph Hill William Fry	Deed
	GODSOE, William, see John Shapleigh	Joshua Downing	
1700, Nov. 28	GOOCH, Benjamin	John Wheelwright	Deed

Index of Grantors. 15

Folio.	Description.
57	30 acre town grant by and in *Kittery*.
99	7 acres, the homestead of Samuel Fernald at the entrance of Pulpit Reach, at *Kittery* Point.
58	60 to 80 acres called the Middle Neck, between Scadlock's river and Whale cove in *Winter Harbor*, [now *Biddeford*].
155	40 acres, 16 poles along the highway, part of a tract purchased with others from the heirs of Thomas Clarke.
148	One-half of the farm originally John Wadleigh's in *Wells*.
173	216 acres at Spruce creek in *Kittery*, purchased of John Lee.
5	100 acres with dwelling-house, at Little river; also one-third of a saw-mill and appurtenances and of 110 acres as per town grants by and in *Wells*.
87	9 acres at Sturgeon creek's mouth and 27 acres at Horsidown Hill in *Kittery*, conditioned for support and maintenance, and reserving one acre.
169	20 acres on the seashore adjoining Sarah Sweat's land and other lands of Grantors, in *Cape Elizabeth*.
94	Champernown's Island, excepting 80 acres, in *Kittery*.
92	200 acres in the first division in *Coxhall*, [now *Lyman*].
27	40 acres adjoining land of Samuel Hill in *Kittery*.
162	All the land formerly his father, Edward Gilman's, between Piscataqua river and Sturgeon creek; also a town grant to his grandfather, Antipas Maverick, by and in *Kittery*.
114	8 acres of marsh in several pieces on Little river near Birch Point, in *Wells*.

Index of Grantors.

Date.	Grantor.	Grantee.	Instrument.
1697, Mar. 19	Gooding (Goodwin), Daniel et ux.	William Gooding (Goodwin) and Moses Gooding (Goodwin)	Deed
1698, May 17	Gooding (Goodwin), Daniel, sen., et ux.	Jonathan Stone	Deed
1701, Aug. 21	Goodwin, Daniel, senior	Daniel Goodwin, junior	Deed
1700, Nov. 6	Goodwin, Moses et ux.	Abraham Lord	Deed
1703, Mar. 23	Goodwin, Moses	Gabriel Hambleton	Deed
1697, Mar. 19	Goodin (Goodwin), William et ux.	Moses Gooding (Goodwin)	Deed
1699, Apr. 4	Goodridge, Isaac	Margaret Adams	Deed
1640, May 28	Gorges, Sir Ferdinando, by Richard Vines, steward-general	Henry Simpson	Grant
	Gowen, John, see Nicholas Gowen		
1702, Nov. 14	Gowen, Lemuel	John Gowen	Receipt
1703, Jan. 19	Gowen, Nicholas, and John Gowen	Each other	Division
1700, Mar. 14	Gowen, *alias* Smith, James	John Gowen	Receipt
1696, Dec. 5	Gowen, *alias* Smith, John et ux.	Black Will	Deed
	Gowen, *alias* Smith, John, see Nicholas Gowen, *alias* Smith.		
1700, July 10 1700, Sept. 9	Gowen, *alias* Smith, Nicholas and John Gowen, *alias* Smith	Each other	Submission and award.

Index of Grantors. 17

Folio.	Description.
67	All the remainder of a town grant by Kittery, adjoining land formerly conveyed to his son Daniel Goodwin in *Berwick*.
67	6 acres marsh on north side of Humphrey's pond, and 50 acres upland adjoining, in *Berwick*.
147	6 acres in Slut's corner marshes in *Berwick*.
84	20 acre town grant by Kittery [in *Berwick?*].
160	30 acre town grant by Kittery [in *Berwick?*].
68	Quitclaim of his half of the tract conveyed by their father, Daniel Goodwin, senior, in *Berwick*.
39	Land and house bought of Samuel King in *Kittery*.
150	10 acres of marsh on the south side of Agamenticus river, opposite William Hooke's farm in *York*.
88	In full for his proportion of his father William Gowen's estate.
171	Of 50 acres formerly Trustrum Harrinson's [Harris] in *Kittery*, [*Berwick*].
117	In full for his proportion of his father William Gowen's (*alias* Smith) estate.
43	50 acre town grant to Grantor; also 50 acre town grant to his brother William Gowen, by and in *Kittery*.
70	Of their father William Gowen's estate and charging their mother's dower and brethren's portions on said estate; also of Trustrum Harris' estate; and fixing a division line [in *Berwick*].

INDEX OF GRANTORS.

Date.	Grantor.	Grantee.	Instrument.
1702, Aug. 3	GREELY, Thomas, and Timothy Waymouth [Edward] Waymouth, by Timothy Waymouth, attorney	Each other	Division
1700, Mar. 28	GREEN, Daniel	Joseph Hill	Deed
1693, Nov. 1	GUNNISON, Elihu	Wm. Pepperrell	Deed
1699, Aug. 23	GUNNISON, Elihu	Samuel Prey	Deed
1701, Dec. 17	GUNNISON, Elihu	Richard Endle	Deed
1702, May 29	GUNNISON, Elihu et ux.	George Frink	Deed
1701, Mar. 21	HAMMOND, Joseph, and Matthew Libby Stephen Tobey David Libby Daniel Fogg	Each other	Division
1700[1], Mar. 21	HAMMOND, Joseph, and Stephen Tobey David Libby Matthew Libby Daniel Fogg	Each other	Agreement
1703, Feb. 11	HAMMOND, Joseph, junior	Thomas Rhodes	Deed
1682, Aug. 28	HARRIS, George et ux.	Thomas Fernald	Deed
1696, Mar. 31	HARRIS, John	Jacob Tappin	Deed
1701, Apr. 26	HATCH, Samuel	Josiah Littlefield	Deed
	HEARD, James, estate of, see John Heard		

Index of Grantors. 19

Folio.	Description.
170	Fixing division line between their lands at the brook running into the Mast cove, in *Berwick*.
56	30 acre town grant by and in *Kittery*.
58	250 acres, being one-half in common of a tract of 500 acres called Buckland's neck on Damariscotta river in *Jamestown*; also half in common of 50 acres meadow opposite Bread and Cheese island.
60	1½ acres, with dwelling-house, fronting 12 poles on Crooked lane, in *Kittery*.
154	60 acres at Bryan's Point in Spruce creek; also land on south side of the creek adjacent; also 30 feet square for a burying-ground, reserving the mill-privilege and a landing, in *Kittery*.
153	35 acres with dwelling-house between the highway and Spruce creek, adjoining Ingersoll's lane, in *Kittery*.
89	Of the tract of land purchased of the heirs of Thomas Clarke, between Watts' Fort and Frank's Fort, in *Kittery*.
91	Regulating the several proportions each should pay of a bond of £200 to the Clarke heirs in part payment for the above premises.
176	30 acre town grant by and in *Kittery*.
20	Quitclaiming ¼ acre and house in *Kittery*.
98	200 acres in common with other Coxhall proprietors, in what is now *Lyman*.
116	100 acres on northerly side of Ogunquet river in *Wells*.

Index of Grantors.

Date.	Grantor.	Grantee.	Instrument.
1676, Nov. 1	HEARD, John, and James Heard's estate, by Shuah Heard	John Neal	Bond
1700, Apr. 19	HEARD, John	John Newmarch	Deed
	HELLSON, Ephraim, see estate of John Hellson		
1686, July 28	HELLSON, John, estate of, by Joanna Hellson, executrix, and Ephraim Hellson Samuel Hellson	William Dicer	Deed
	HELLSON, Samuel, see estate of John Hellson		
1699, Feb. 7	HILL, John	John Plaisted	Mortgage
1702, May 2	HILL, Joseph, and Peter Staple	Each other	Division
1671, Dec. 26	HILL, Roger et ux.	John Hellson, senior	Deed
	HILL, Samuel, see John Batson		
1686, Oct. 27	HILTON, John	Francis Mercer	Bond
1681, Aug. 2	HILTON, William et ux.	Francis Mercer	Deed
1684, May 4	HILTON, William et ux.	Richard Hilton	Deed
1699, Nov. 16	HINCKSON, Peter	Peter Hinckson, [junior] et ux.	Deed

Folio.	Description.
100	Conditioned to secure possession of the half of a town grant on Piscataqua river in *Kittery*, sold by James Heard in his lifetime to Obligee, but not formally conveyed.
60	50 acres on the road from Spruce creek to Sturgeon creek, in *Kittery*.
7	100 acres on the west side of the Saco river, up to the head of tide-water, excepting one house lot, in *Saco*.
105	One-third in common and undivided of 600 acres lying in six parcels, on both sides Little Newichewannock river, at Bonnibissie pond, at Totnock, at Broughton's marsh, at White's marsh and Pipe-staff point (excepting 33¼ acres), also the mill privilege at Assabumbedoc falls, all in *Berwick*.
133	Establishing division line between their premises at the Long Reach, in *Kittery*.
6	100 acres on the west side of Saco river, up to the head of tide-water, excepting Grantor's house lot, in *Saco*.
158	Covenanting to warrant the possession of the 3 acres conveyed by Obligor's father, William Hilton, next below.
157	3 acres on Piscataqua river between Nelson and Simpson in *Kittery*, excepted from the following conveyance.
166	All his messuage (except 3 acres above) at the Long Reach between Mary Bachellor's and Daniel Paul's highways, in *Kittery*, also 10 acres marsh.
64	23 acres upland; also 10 acres marsh; also 56 acres upland and marsh on Nonesuch river at Black Point, in *Scarborough*.

Date.	Grantor.	Grantee.	Instrument.
1699, Nov. 17	HODSDEN, Benoni et ux.	Joseph Hodsden	Deed
1703, Apr. 25	HODSDEN, Benoni et ux.	Philip Hubbord	Deed
1703, Apr. 25	HODSDEN, Benoni et ux.	Nathan Lord	Deed
1687, June 2	HODSDEN, Joseph	Sylvanus Davis	Deed
1675, May 4	HOLE, John	George Harris	Lease
1690, May 2	HOLE, John, by Elizabeth Hole, attorney	Estate of John Gaskin	Deed
1698, Mar. 5	HOOPER, Thomas et ux.	Henry Barter	Deed
1698, Mar. 5	HOOPER, Thomas	Henry Barter	Bond
1700, May 3	HOOPER, Thomas	Robert Cutt	Deed
1703, Mar. 6	HUTCHINS, Benjamin	Roger Thomas	Deed
1699, Oct. 26	HUTCHINS, Enoch	James Johnson	Deed
1699, Jan. 10	HUTCHINSON, Eliakim et ux.	John Plaisted	Deed
	HUTCHINSON, Elisha et ux. see Mehitable Warren		
	INGERSOLL, George et ux. see John Ingersoll		
1684, Mar. 13	INGERSOLL, John et ux. and George Ingersoll et ux.	John Phillips and Sylvanus Davis James English John Endicott	Deed
1694, June 15	INGOLLS, Samuel, senior	William Titcomb	Deed
1694, Sept. 1	JEFFRY, Digory et ux.	Roger Dearing	De d

Folio.	Description.
70	Two adjoining tracts of 20 acres and 42 acres upon the country road and town commons in *Berwick*.
160	40 acres on the highway from the landing place near Grantor's house to Birchen Point brook, in *Berwick*.
161	12 acres adjoining Grantee's land on Birchen Point brook, in *Berwick*.
35	120 acres on Nonesuch Point in *Falmouth*, with obligation for release of dower by his wife Tabitha.
20	House and ¼ acre on south side Fernald's island in *Kittery*.
150	10 acres, 40 poles square, off the northeast end of Grantor's plantation in *Kittery*.
42	A triangular piece containing 27¾ acres and 26 poles on Spruce creek, in *Kittery*.
43	In £52 to observe the covenants in foregoing deed.
56	20 acre town grant by and in *Kittery*.
172	10 acres in a triangle, part of a town grant of 30 acres, between York line and Spruce creek, in *Kittery*.
44	20 acres near York road in *Kittery*.
102	600 acres (excepting 33¼ acres) lying in six parcels on both sides Little Newichewannock river, at Bonnibissie pond, at Totnock, at Broughton's marsh, at White's marsh and at Pipe-staff point; also the mill privilege at Assabumbedoc falls, all in *Berwick*.
1	One-half in common of saw mill and appurtenances, land and timber grants on the Mill river, in *Falmouth*.
92	100 acres in common with the Coxhall Proprietors, in what is now *Lyman*.
60	100 acres with dwelling-house, at the Stepping-stones in *Kittery*.

Index of Grantors.

Date.	Grantor.	Grantee.	Instrument.
1696, Dec. 30	JOHNSON, Samuel	Andrew Neal	Deed
1700, Oct. 28	JOHNSON, Samuel et ux.	Alex. Junkins	Deed
	JOHNSON, Sarah, see Rachel Rew		
	JORDAN, Robert, see Nathaniel Fryer		
1686, Nov. 10	JORDAN, Sarah	John Hincks	Deed
1700, Nov. 4	KING, Richard et ux.	John Dennet	Deed
1694, May 16	KITTERY, Town of	Walter Deniver	Grant
1694, May 16	KITTERY, Town of	Moses Goodwin	Grant
1694, May 16	KITTERY, Town of	Joseph Weeks	Grant
1694, May 16	KITTERY, Town of	Alex. Dennet	Grant
1699, May 16	KITTERY, Town of	Thomas Hooper	Grant
1699, May 24	KITTERY, Town of	Daniel Green	Grant
1699, May 24	KITTERY, Town of	John Morgrage	Grant
1699, May 24	KITTERY, Town of	John Thomson	Grant
1699, May 24	KITTERY, Town of	Samuel Fernald	Grant
1699, May 24	KITTERY, Town of	Richard Cutt	Grant
1699, May 24	KITTERY, Town of	Jacob Smith	Grant
1699, May 24	KITTERY, Town of	Nicholas Weeks	Grant
1699, May 24	KITTERY, Town of	Robert Allen	Grant
1699, May 24	KITTERY, Town of	Hezekiah Elwell	Grant
1699, May 24	KITTERY, Town of	William Roberts	Grant
1699, May 24	KITTERY, Town of	Hugh Crockett	Grant
1699, May 24	KITTERY, Town of	Joseph Crockett, junior	Grant

Index of Grantors.

Folio.	Description.
51	2 acres salt marsh on south side the river, in *York*.
77	10 acres upon a brook between Jeremiah Moulton and Constant Rankin, in *York*.
78	One-half of the 1000 acres (excepting 100 acres upland and 29 acres marsh conveyed) at Nonesuch [in *Cape Elizabeth*].
71	20 acre town grant by and in *Kittery*.
56	10 acres; proviso to be improved within one year.
84	20 acres; proviso to be improved within one year.
98	Number of acres not specified.
114	20 acres; proviso to be improved within one year.
56	20 acres; proviso to be improved within one year.
56	30 acres, to be clear of other grants.
56	10 acres, to be clear of other grants.
57	30 acres, to be clear of other grants.
57	30 acres, to be clear of other grants.
57	30 acres, to be clear of other grants.
57	30 acres, to be clear of other grants.
98	30 acres, to be clear of other grants.
114	30 acres, to be clear of other grants.
138	30 acres, to be clear of other grants.
139	40 acres, to be clear of other grants.
139	30 acres, to be clear of other grants.
139	30 acres, to be clear of other grants.

Index of Grantors.

Date.	Grantor.	Grantee.	Instrument.
1699, May 24	KITTERY, Town of	Nicholas Morrell	Grant
1699, May 24	KITTERY, Town of	Moses Goodwin	Grant
1699, May 24	KITTERY, Town of	Job Emery	Grant
1686, Aug. 24	KNIGHT, Samuel	Samuel Spinney	Deed
1689, Sept. 18	LEE, John	Thomas Fowler	Deed
1683, Oct. 2	LEWIS, Peter, sen., et ux.	William Mitchell	Deed
1702, Jan. 4	LIBBY, David et ux.	John Cotten	Deed
	LIBBY, David, see Joseph Hammond		
1702, Dec. 8	LIBBY, Matthew et ux.	James Staple	Deed
	LIBBY, Matthew, see Joseph Hammond		
1683, Mar. 20	LITTLEFIELD, Francis, senior	James Littlefield	Deed
1700, May 2	LITTLEFIELD, Francis, senior	Moses Littlefield	Deed
1696, Aug. 8	LITTLEFIELD, John et ux.	Josiah Littlefield	Deed
1699, Oct. 4	LITTLEFIELD, Jonathan	Samuel Wheelwright and John Wheelwright	Bond
1702, Mar. 30	LITTLEFIELD, Moses et ux.	Samuel Emery	Deed
1684, June 9	LITTLEFIELD, Nathan	William Taylor	Deed

INDEX OF GRANTORS. 27

Folio.	Description.
149	25 acres, to be clear of other grants.
160	30 acres, to be clear of other grants.
160	20 acres, to be clear of other grants.
22	6 acres on the Great cove, in *Kittery*.
173	216 acres at Spruce creek in *Kittery*, conveyed by Walter Barfoot.
168	Two houses and lots and the flake-room between, and half a stage-room on Smuttynose island; also one-third of moorings between that island and Malaga island, *Isles of Shoals*.
151	30 acres, part of my purchase with others, of the heirs of Thomas Clarke, in *Kittery*.
156	20 acres, part of my purchase with others, of the heirs of Thomas Clarke, in *Kittery*.
141	House and land bought of William Frost, on west side of Webhannet river, and enough in addition from my farm to make it equal thereto; also 100 acres on Merryland plain with 7 acres marsh and a neck of upland; also an island on the sea-wall and 4 acres marsh; also 200 acres upland and 10 acres meadow at Merryland; also Thatch island, all in *Wells*.
167	20 acres upland and salt marsh 20 poles along the seashore, granted by Gorges, in *Wells*.
116	Marsh and thatch beds between Ogunquit river and Sandy point, in *Wells*.
41	Conditioned to maintain a fence on division line, in *Wells*.
167	25 acres on northwest side of Webhannet river; also 4 rods on the highway to the marsh; also 3 acres in common in Merryland marshes, in *Wells*.
165	100 acres as per town grant, near Kennebunk falls, in *Wells*

Date.	Grantor.	Grantee.	Instrument.
1695, May 11	LORD, Abraham et ux.	Abbot, Thos., and est. of Jonathan Nason, by Sarah Nason, adm'x	Deed
1703, Apr. 25	LORD, Nathan et ux.	Benoni Hodsden	Deed
——, Oct. 24 Recorded 1702, May 2	LUGG (Lugh), Gilbert	Charles Nelson	Receipt
Recorded 1702, May 2	LUGG, Gilbert	Charles Nelson	Receipt
1701, Aug. 12	MARCH, James et ux.	John Pickerin, junior	Deed
1687, Dec. 16	MASON, Robert Tufton	Eliakim Hutchinson	Grant
1685, May 27 1686, Apr. 6	MASSACHUSETTS, General Court of	Joshua Scottow	Grant and Survey
1685, June 26	MASSACHUSETTS COLONY, Governor and Company of, by Thomas Danforth, President of Maine	Francis Champernown	Grant
1686, May 12	MASSACHUSETTS, General Court of	Joshua Scottow	Grant
1681, June 10	MAXELL, Alexander et ux.	James Grant	Deed
1686, Feb. 14	MAXELL, Alexander	James Grant	Deed
1672, Mar. 2	MENDUM, Jonathan et ux.	John Fennick	Deed
1702, May 20	MENDUM, Jonathan et ux.	Joseph Weeks	Deed

Index of Grantors.   29

Folio.	Description.
53	Ratifying (after coming of age) conveyance of 40 acres and 10 acres marsh, excepting 3 acres sold Peter Wittum, at Sturgeon creek, *Kittery*, made by Grantor's father during his minority.
161	In exchange, 7 acres on Birch Point brook, where John Morrill formerly dwelt, in *Kittery*.
133	For 18 quintals of merchantable fish and five barrels of mackerel.
133	For £21 in full payment of house and land on Piscataqua river, in *Kittery*, between Symonds and Paul, bought in common with Waymouth Lissen.
152	22 acres at Bald Head, in *York*.
174	500 acres upon both sides Little Newichewannock river, with other parcels of marsh and meadow; also timber grants and a mill privilege, all in *Berwick*.
9	500 acres on Merriconeag neck [in *Harpswell*].
78	400 acres, being the neck of land between Piscataqua river mouth and Brave-boat harbor, and 500 acres northeast of Brave-boat harbor, in *Kittery* and *York*.
37	500 acres additional to the former grant in same place [*Harpswell*].
15	5 acres marsh and ½ acre upland on which Grantee's barn stood near head of northwest branch of the river, in *York*.
15	Quitclaiming 40 acres in *York* bought, as attorney for Grantee, of Arthur Bragdon.
21	12 acres, fronting 16 poles on the water side on the north of Spruce creek, in *Kittery*.
163	25 acres at Turkey Point, on east side of Spruce creek, in *Kittery*.

Index of Grantors.

Date.	Grantor.	Grantee.	Instrument.
1702, Oct. 31	MITCHELL, William et ux.	Philip Carpenter	Deed
1701, Dec. 15	MONSON, Richard	John Monson et ux.	Deed
1697, Feb. 10	Mo[o]RE, Thomas et ux.	Nathan'l Raynes	Deed
1701, Nov. 28	MOORE, Thomas et ux.	John Morrell	Deed
1702, Mar. 16	Mo[o]RE, Thomas et ux.	Daniel Black	Deed
1694, Mar. 17	Mo[o]RE, William, estate of, by Thos. Mo[o]re, Adm'r	Daniel Dill	Deed
1699, Feb. 24	MOOREY, Nicholas	Joseph Hill	Deed
1700, Nov. 22	MOOREY, Nicholas	Joseph Bayley	Deed
1701, Oct. 2	MOOREY, Nicholas	Joseph Storer and Samuel Hill John Batson	Deed
1686, Dec. 7	MOROUGH, Dennis et ux.	James Frees	Deed
1700, July 16	MORGRAGE, John	Robert Cutt	Deed
1700, Dec. 22	MORRELL, John, senior et ux,	John Fernald, senior	Deed
1702, Dec. 18	MORRELL, Nicholas	John Morrell	Deed
1675, June 17	MUNJOY, George et ux.	John Farnum	Deed
1702, July 2	NASON, John	Jonathan Nason	Deed

INDEX OF GRANTORS. 31

Folio.	Description.
168	Two house lots and the flake-room between, and half a stage-room on Smuttynose island; also one-third of moorings between that island and Malaga island, *Isles of Shoals*.
118	32 acres upland and marsh at Ox Point, on the south side of Spruce creek, in *Kittery*.
169	20 acres on the seabeach west of the river adjoining land formerly Mrs. Godfrey's, in *York*.
119	40 acres on Hull's creek, in *York*.
142	2 acres marsh on the west branch of the river at Dummer's cove, in *York*.
45	20 acres on the highway at Scotland, in *York*.
48	Land on Cross' creek, and marsh adjoining it to Webbhannet river and 6 acres marsh at the Neck of Land, in *Wells*.
111	150 acres, [100, formerly Griffin Mortgague's; 50, the neck formerly Morgan Howell's] bought of Samuel Snow [executor] in *Cape Porpoise*.
116	60 acres at Long creek, or Mast cove, on east side of Kennebunk river, bought of John Rennals; also town grant of 100 acres on same river, in *Cape Porpoise*.
8	30 acres on the south side of Casco river, reserving right of way to the falls for water to Thaddeus Clark, in *Falmouth*.
56	10 acre town grant by and in *Kittery*.
84	60 acres between the Great cove and the head of Spruce creek, in *Kittery*.
149	5 acres, part of town grant of 25 acres, by and in *Kittery*.
164	101 acres, being half the tract taken on execution *vs.* Francis Small, northerly of the river that leads into Brave-boat harbor in *Kittery*.
144	His half in common with Grantee in town grant of 100 acres at Mast cove, in *Kittery*.

Index of Grantors.

Date.	Grantor.	Grantee.	Instrument.
1699, Feb. 29	NASON, Jonathan, est. of, by Sarah Nason, adm'x	Joshua Downing John Leighton	Deed
1702, Oct. 2	NASON, Jonathan, est. of, by Sarah Nason, adm'x	Henry Snow et ux.	Survey
1703, June 14	NASON, Jonathan, est. of, by Sarah Nason, adm'x	Henry Snow et ux.	Deed
Acknowledged 1703, May 24	NASON, Jonathan, [jun.]	Jonathan Nason, est. of, by Sarah Nason, Adm'x	Receipt
1694, Dec. 4	NEALE, John et ux.	Andrew Neale	Deed
1694, Dec. 5	NEALE, John et ux.	Andrew Neale	Condition'l Deed
1687, Feb. 29	NEW ENGLAND, Territory and Dominion of, by Sir Edmund Andros, Governor	John Hincks	Grant
	NOWELL, Peter, see Arthur Bragdon, junior		
1686, Oct. 25	PARKES, Thomas	Henry Child	Condition'l Deed
1701, June 28	PARTRIDGE, John et ux.	Daniel Simpson	Deed
	PAUL, Daniel, see Katherine Paul		
	PAUL, John, see Katherine Paul		
1702, Feb. 24	PAUL, Katharine, and John Paul, Daniel Paul, Moses Paul, John Tomson, Samuel Fernald, and Abigail, wife of one of the Pauls	Samuel Hill and Joseph Hill, William Fry Joshua Downing	Deed
	PAUL, Moses, see Katherine Paul		

Index of Grantors.

Folio.	Description.
55	One-half in common of 40 acres upland and 10 acres marsh on the south side of Sturgeon creek, in *Kittery*.
171	Of the 13 acres next below conveyed.
171	13 acres on the brook [at Mast cove in Sturgeon creek] in *Kittery*.
170	In full for his portion of his father's estate, in *Kittery*.
101	One-half of 50 acres between the river and Ferguson's bridge, in *Berwick*.
101	Of the other half of the above premises; conditioned for support of Grantee and wife.
73	1200 acres, part of Nonesuch neck on the river of that name, in *Scarborough*.
4	40 acres at Post Wigwam on Newichewannock river, in *Berwick*. Conditioned for support of Grantor.
110	House and land on the main river, bought of Hughes, between Rishworth and Penwill, in *York*.
162	As widow and surviving heirs of Stephen Paul, all the grant remaining unsold, to Antipas Maverick, between Piscataqua river and Sturgeon creek, in *Kittery*.

Date.	Grantor.	Grantee.	Instrument.
	PAUL, Stephen et ux, see Edward Gillman		
1700, Jan. 23	PENDLETON, James	Moorey, Nicholas	Deed
1699, Aug. 28	PENHALLOW, Samuel	John Dennet, junior	Deed
1700, Sept. 25	PENHALLOW, Samuel	Peter Dixon	Deed
1708, Mar. 8	PEPPERRELL, William	Nicholas Tucker	Discharge
1700, Nov. 22	PHARES, Aaron	John Newmarch	Deed
1700, Sept. 26	PICKERIN, John et ux.	John Pickerin, [junior] et ux.	Deed
1702, Aug. 8	PICKERIN, John et ux.	Wm. Pepperrell	Deed
1700, May 24	PLAISTED, James	John Pickerin	Deed
1702, May 19	PLAISTED, James	Ichabod Plaisted	Deed
1698, Dec. 2	PLAISTED, John	Benoni Hodsden	Deed
1699, Jan. 11	PLAISTED, John	Eliakim Hutchinson	Mortgage
1699, Feb. 6 1699, Feb. 6	PLAISTED, John et ux.	John Hill	Indenture Bipartite
1720, Apr. 23	PLAISTED, John	John Hill	Discharge
1694, Sept. 1	POPE, Richard, estate of, by Sarah Pope, Adm'x	Wm. Pepperrell	Deed

Folio.	Description.
50	600 acres on the west side of Saco river, described in conveyances [II., ff. 94 & 140] by William Phillips to Bryan Pendleton, in *Saco*.
39	30 acres on Spinney's cove, granted by town to Gabriel Tetherly, in *Kittery*.
128	Two adjoining lots of 20 acres each near the mast-ways on west side of Spruce creek, in *Kittery*, conveyed Grantor by Richard Endle.
163	Of mortgage recorded same folio.
114	20 acre town grant by and in *Kittery*.
151	Corn and saw mill and the land adjoining as far as Galloping Hill, and half a neck of land adjoining, in *York*.
138	One-half the single saw mill and appurtenances on Fall Mill brook, in *York*.
151	One-fourth in common with Grantee of the corn and saw mill in *York*, near where Henry Sayword's mills formerly stood.
186	10 acres known as the Fort field at Salmon Falls in *Berwick*.
156	80 acres including town grants to John Wincoll and Roger Plaisted, in *Kittery* [*Berwick*].
46	Of the 600 acres in *Berwick* conveyed by Mortgagee by folio 102.
129 104	One third in common and undivided of 600 acres [excepting 33¼ acres] lying in six parcels on both sides Little Newichewannock river, at Bonnibissie pond at Totnock, at Broughton's marsh, at White's marsh and at Pipe-staff point; also of the mill-privilege at Assabumbedoc Falls, all in *Berwick*.
106	Of the mortgage recorded folio 106.
59	80 acres at Whale cove on west of Scadlock's river in Winter harbor, [now *Biddeford*].

Date.	Grantor.	Grantee.	Instrument.
1686, Nov. 10	PRICHETT, John, and John Burrell et ux.	Henry Emms	Deed
	PREBLE, Abraham, see Arthur Bragdon, junior		
1701, Aug. 26	PREBLE, Abraham, junior	Peter Nowell	Deed
1703, Mar. 8	RAYNES, Francis, senior	John Woodman	Deed
1700, June 12	REMICH, Christian	Samuel Spinney	Deed
1700, June 12	REMICH, Christian	Samuel Spinney	Bond
1703, Apr. 31	REMICH, Christian et ux.	Joshua Remich	Conditional Deed
1687, Jan. 2	RENNALS, John	Nicholas Moorey	Deed
1701, Oct. 6	REW, Rachel et ux., and Mary Broughton, Sarah Johnson, Rebecca Broughton	John Rogers	Deed
1702, June 18	ROBERTS, William	Wm. Pepperrell	Deed
1695, Nov. 19	RONES, Elizabeth	Samuel Came	Deed
1691, Apr. 15	SANDERS, William et ux.	John Gelding	Deed
1691, June 19	SCOTTOW, Joshua et ux.	Samuel Checkley	Deed
1694, Oct. 23	SCOTTOW, Thomas	Samuel Checkley	Mortgage
1701, May 1	SEWALL, Samuel et ux.	Ichabod Plaisted	Deed

Folio.	Description.
16	All their land at the Mill Pool on Small Point side of Sagadahoc river, bought of Thomas Atkins.
126	4 acres marsh on Hull's creek and the southwest branch of the river, in *York*.
158	300 acres on the east side of Brave-boat harbor, adjoining Mrs. Godfrey, in *York*.
66	15½ acres with a frame and privilege of highway, adjoining Richard Kerle, Thomas Spinney, senior, the Grantee and John Dennet, senior, in *Kittery*.
66	In £100 conditioned not to sue Obligee, nor to molest him in the possession of the above premises.
172	Homestead opposite the Boiling Rock, 10 acres woodland and 15 acres in Simmon's marsh, in *Kittery*, conditioned for support of Grantor and his wife.
49	[60 acres] on east of Kennebunk river at Long creek, on Mast cove, opposite Gillum's point, in *Cape Porpoise*.
113	All rights as heirs of George Broughton in Salmon falls, on Great Newichewannock river in *Berwick*, with the mills and appurtenances.
139	40 acre town grant by and in *Kittery*.
175	10 acres, the homestead of William Rones, deceased, also one-half of a town grant to said Rones and James Freethy, in *York*.
80	30 acres near Sturgeon creek as per town grant by and in *Kittery*.
131	The farm bought of Abraham Joslin with the marsh bought of Andrew Brown, except 12 acres marsh sold William Burrage, at Black Point, *Scarborough*.
132	100 acres upland on Moore's brook and 40 acres meadow on Pigsgut river, in *Scarborough*.
112	All their interest derived from John Hull in and to Salmon falls, its timber and appurtenances, in *Berwick*.

Index of Grantors.

Date.	Grantor.	Grantee.	Instrument.
1699, July 3	SHAPLEIGH, John	Nathaniel Keen	Deed
1700, Feb. 13	SHAPLEIGH, John	Black Will	Manumission
1700, June 25	SHAPLEIGH, John, and William Godsoe	James Johnson	Deed
1700, Dec. 26	SHAPLEIGH, John	Walter Deniver	Deed
1700, Dec. 26	SHAPLEIGH, John	Walter Deniver	Deed
1663, Apr. 11	SHAPLEIGH, Nicholas et ux.	Humphrey Chadborne	Deed
1685, Feb. 1	SHARP, John	John Morrell, sen.	Deed
1687, Mar. 26	SHEAFE, Sampson	Samuel Walker	Deed
1701, July 2	SIMPSON, Daniel et ux.	John Partridge	Deed
1701, Aug. 1	SIMPSON, Daniel et ux.	Jeremiah Mo[u]lton	Deed
1701, Dec. 26	SIMPSON, Daniel et ux.	Samuel Came	Deed
1688, June 16	SIMPSON, *alias* Bond, Jane	Henry Simpson	Condition'l Deed
1700, July 30	SMITH, Jacob	Robert Cutt	Deed
1701, Jan. 12	SMITH, Jacob et ux.	John Cotten	Deed
1700, Mar. 16	SMITH, Sarah	John Gowen	Receipt
1702, Nov. 19	SMITH, William et ux.	John Gowen	Receipts
	SMITH, *alias* Gowen, see Gowen		

Index of Grantors. 39

Folio.	Description.
52	100 acres at the lower falls in the Western creek, in *Kittery*.
88	Of a negro slave, so named.
78	62 acres at the head of Spruce creek, in *Kittery*.
85	13¼ acres on the cross-road to the Point between Crooked lane and Spruce creek, in *Kittery*.
93	(A re-record of the above).
87	Tract on North side of Sturgeon creek between Nicholas Frost and John Heard; also in a town grant adjoining, in *Kittery*.
72	40 acre town grant by and in *Kittery*.
11	One-third in common of the tract on east side of Saco river, part of Lewis and Bonighton's patent, with one-third of the saw-mill on Saco river falls, containing 6000 acres, with timber grant of adjoining tract, in *Saco*.
120	All claim to the estate of our grandfather, Roger Plaisted [in *Berwick*].
123	5 acres between the main river and Meeting-house creek, in *York*.
176	4 acres salt marsh on the northwest branch of the river, in *York*.
74	All estate derived from Grantor's father, Walter Norton, in *York*.
57	30 acre town grant by and in *Kittery*.
118	Land in common with others purchased of Thomas Clarke's heirs in *Kittery* by Stephen Tobey and by him conveyed to Grantor.
117	For part of her portion of her father William Gowen's estate.
45	In full for his wife Sarah's portion.

Date.	Grantor.	Grantee.	Instrument.
Acknowledged 1703, May 24	SNOW, Henry, and Job Emery	Jonathan Nason's estate, by Sarah Nason, Adm'x	Receipt
1701, Sept. 17	SOUTHERINE, Thomas et ux.	Walter Burks	Deed
1700, Sept. 16	SPENCER, Humphrey	John Wade	Deed
1701, June 17	SPENCER, Humphrey et ux.	Thomas Gooding (Goodwin)	Deed
1702, Dec. 19	SPINNEY, James	John Spinney	Deed
1699, Nov. 25	SPINNEY, Samuel et ux.	John Spinney	Deed
1700, Dec. 24	SPINNEY, Samuel	Thomas Spinney	Deed
1689, Sept. 27	SPINNEY, Thomas et ux.	James Spinney	Deed
1700, Dec. 28	SPINNEY, Thomas	Samuel Spinney	Deed
1701, June 25	SPINNEY, Thomas	Samuel Fernald's estate, by Hannah Fernald, exec'x, and Nathaniel Fernald	Deed
1701, July 6	SPINNEY, Thomas	Thomas Worster	Deed
1702, Apr. 10	SPINNEY, Thomas et ux.	James Fernald	Deed
1702, June 8	SPINNEY, Thomas et ux.	John Staple	Deed
1699, Nov. 22	STAGPOLL, James	John Wade	Deed
1701, June 18	STAPLE, Peter	John Staple	Deed
1702, Apr. 15	STAPLE, Peter et ux.	John Staple	Deed

Folio.	Description.
170	In full for their wives' portions.
75	One-half in common of marsh on the west branch of the river, between John Brown's and John Parker's, in *York*.
70	85 perches in a triangle between the country road and the way toward the Great Works, in *Berwick*.
122	30 acres at Newichewannock, in *Berwick*, as per town grant of Kittery to Grantor's grandfather, Thomas Spencer.
157	1 acre on Piscataqua river between John Spinney and Thomas Fernald, in *Kittery*.
65	40 acres between Great cove and Spruce creek, as per town grant by and in *Kittery*.
98	8 acres adjoining Grantee's old lot, behind Alcock, in *Kittery*.
121	20 acres between Piscataqua river and Spruce creek, whereon Grantee's house stood in the lower part of *Kittery*.
98	8 acres near Great cove, whereon Grantee's house stood, in *Kittery*.
99	In exchange, 15¼ acres lying at the head of Alcock's lot, in *Kittery*.
99	5 acres, part of town grant of 15 acres between Great cove and Spruce creek, in *Kittery*.
134	11½ acres between Grantor's dwelling-house and land of Thomas Worster, in *Kittery*.
147	12 acres near the mast-ways in *Kittery*.
61	3¼ acres near the meeting-house on the way from the Great Works to the river in *Berwick*.
97	30 acres adjoining Remick, Spinney and Tetherly, in *Kittery*.
133	30 acres in *Kittery* [either the same land as the above, or an adjoining parcel].

Index of Grantors.

Date.	Grantor.	Grantee.	Instrument.
	STAPLE, Peter, see Joseph Hill		
1685, Feb. 25	START, John	Thomas Scottow	Deed
	STORER, Joseph, see John Batson		
Acknowledged 1685, Aug. 6	STORER, Samuel	Lewis Allen	Bill of Sale
1670, Oct. 4	SYMONDS, Harlakinden	Wm. Symonds	Deed
1684, Feb. 4	SYMONDS, Harlakinden et ux.	Robert Greenough	Deed
1693, Oct. 26	SYMONDS, Harlakinden et ux.	John Emerson, junior	Deed
1700, July 2	TAYLOR, Martha	William Goodwin	Condition'l Deed
1695, Apr. 16	TETHERLY, Gabriel et ux.	Samuel Penhallow	Deed
1703, Mar. 6	THOMAS, Roger	Benj. Hutchins	Deed
1700, Apr. 13	TOMSON, John	Robert Cutt	Deed
	TOMSON, John, see Katherine Paul		
1694, Dec. 3	THOMPSON, Miles et ux.	Thos. Thompson	Condition'l Deed
1702, Dec. 5	THOMPSON, Thomas	Thomas Roads	Deed
1689, Nov. 15	THURSTUN, Thomas et ux.	Wm. Pepperrell	Deed
1700, June 4	TINNY, John et ux.	Humphrey Scammon	Deed
1702, June 2	TOBEY, James	Stephen Tobey	Deed
1701, May 16	TOBEY, Stephen et ux.	Jacob Smith	Deed

Index of Grantors. 43

Folio.	Description.
10	30 acres marsh on the north of Pigsgut river in *Scarborough*.
6	One-half of the brigantine "Indeavour" of *Wells*, her apparel, tackle and furniture.
112	400 acres in Coxhall, [now *Lyman*].
95	100 acres to be chosen by Grantee in Coxhall, [now *Lyman*].
135	600 acres, next the lands sold Baker and Dorman, 6 miles long by 60 poles broad in Coxhall, [now *Lyman*].
68	The homestead of her late husband John Taylor in *Berwick*, conditioned for partial support and legacies.
38	30 acres on Spinney cove, town grant by and in *Kittery*.
172	Two town grants of 20 acres and 10 acres by and in *Kittery*.
57	30 acre town grant by and in *Kittery*.
45	80 acres homestead between the river and the commons and personal property, in *Berwick*, conditioned to pay Grantors part of the produce yearly.
149	15¼ acre town grant by and in *Kittery*.
137	[About 3¾ acres] between Piscataqua river and Crocket's creek, in *Kittery*.
79	400 acres between Saco river and Goose-fair river along the sea, in *Saco*.
171	10 acres, half a town grant of 20 acres by and in *Kittery*.
96	One-half of Grantor's share of the tract bought of heirs of Thomas Clarke, in *Kittery*.

Date.	Grantor.	Grantee.	Instrument.
	TOBEY, Stephen, see Joseph Hammond		
1698, Nov. 3	TOZIAR, Richard et ux.	Lewis Bane	Deed
1701, Nov. 18	TREWORTHY, James	Thomas Greeley	Deed
	TUCKER, Grace et ux., see Joan Blackdon		
1701, Dec. 8	TUCKER, Nicholas	Wm. Pepperrell	Mortgage
1698, Jan. 4	TURBET, Nicholas et ux., and Richard Cheeke	Daniel Goodwin, junior	Deed
1699, Aug. 8	TURFREY, George	Francis Foxcroft	Mortgage
1694, Oct. 31	TURNER, Ephraim	Benjamin Gillam	Lease
1698, Dec. 12	TURNER, Ephraim	Benjamin Gillam	Lease
1694, Nov. 1	TURNER, Ephraim	Benjamin Gillam	Deed
1698, Dec. 13	TURNER, Ephraim	Benjamin Gillam	Deed
1702, Oct. 27	VODEN, Moses et ux.	Samuel Johnson	Deed
1701, Oct. 28	WADLEIGH, Robert, sen.	John Wadleigh	Deed
1701, Jan. 2	WALDEN (Waldron), Nicholas	John Woodman	Deed
1701, Mar. 25	WARREN, James, senior	Gilbert Warren	Condition'l Deed
1699, Dec. 18	WARREN, Mehitable, and Elisha Hutchinson et ux., in her right	Jos. Hammond and David Libby Matthew Libby Daniel Fogg Stephen Tobey	Deed
1701, Feb. 17	WAYMOUTH, Edward et ux.	Timothy Waymouth	Deed

Index of Grantors.

Folio.	Description.
41	25 acres on both sides the road to the New Mill creek, in *York*.
115	50 acres with dwelling-house and 11 acres addition, adjoining Edward Waymouth's land, near Mast cove in *Kittery*.
163	Homestead and stock at Spruce creek, in *Kittery*.
68	15 acres, part of 100 acre town grant and one-fifth of one-half of the further marsh formerly Thomas Spencer's in *Kittery*.
47	One-half in common with Mortgagee of a saw-mill and appurtenances on Saco river, in *Saco*.
61	500 acres on the southwest side of Saco river and one-eighth of a mine above *Saco*, for term of one year.
62	400 acres adjoining the above premises in *Saco*, for term of one year.
63	Of the 500 acres above described.
64	Of the 400 acres above described.
150	30 acres on the north side of Sturgeon creek, as by town grant by and in *Kittery*.
134	Quitclaiming all rights to lands in *Wells* or *Kittery*.
100	Land and house at Crooked lane opposite Withers' Island, in *Kittery*.
97	40 acres on the east side of the river at York Bridge in *York*, charged with annual payment of 30 shillings.
88	870 acres (except 30 acres) at the Long Reach in Piscataqua river between Watts' Fort and Frank's Fort, known as the Knowles [Indian] purchase, formerly Thomas Clarke's, in *Kittery*.
170	10 acres at Nason's bridge over the brook running into Mast cove, in *Kittery*.

Date.	Grantor.	Grantee.	Instrument.
	WAYMOUTH, Edward, see Thomas Greeley		
	WAYMOUTH, Timothy, see Thomas Greeley		
1698, Nov. 9	WEARE, Joseph	Peter Nowell	Deed
1700, Sept. 11	WEBBER, Joseph	Thomas Sturges	Deed
1700, July 16	WEBBER, Mary	Joseph Webber	Deed
1700, Dec. 24	WEEKES, Joseph	Elihu Gunnison	Deed
1700, Dec. 24	WEEKES, Nicholas	Elihu Gunnison	Deed
1702, Apr. 3	WELLS, John, and Thomas Wells, Patience Clark et ux., Sarah Libby	Each other	Division
	WELLS, Thomas, see John Wells		
	WHEELWRIGHT, John et ux., see Samuel Wheelwright		
1699, Oct. 4	WHEELWRIGHT, Samuel et ux., John Wheelwright et ux.	Jonathan Littlefield	Deed
1700, Aug. 20	WHETHERICK, Richard, by Elizabeth Whetherick, attorney	Richard Cutt	Deed
1688, June 25	WHITE, Richard	Henry Dering	Mortgage

Folio.	Description.
124	20 acres upland adjoining Major Davis' marsh and lands of Daniel Dill and Daniel Livingstone, in *York*.
143	One-seventh in common of a tract four miles along the west side of Kennebec river and between it and Winnegance river and land of William Baker on the north; also the whole of three lots in *Fulmouth ;* 60 acres at the head of Long creek; 2 acres on Queen street; 6 acres between Samuel York and Richard Pierce; also all his interest in Parker's Neck, in *Saco*.
143	One-seventh in common of a tract four miles along the west side of Kennebec river and between it and Winnegance river and land of William Baker on the north.
98	Town grant (number of acres not specified) by and in *Kittery*.
98	30 acre town grant by and in *Kittery*.
145	Of the estate of their father, John Wells, in *Wells*.
40	19¾ acres between the highway and the marsh near Grantee's dwelling-house, in *Wells*.
81	One-half of Champernown's Island in *Kittery*.
82	Dwelling-house and land; also 90 acres upland at the head of Brave-boat harbor; also all the marsh in two parcels at the bridge and above it, in *Kittery*.

Index of Grantors.

Date.	Grantor.	Grantee.	Instrument.
1699, Apr. 5	WINCOLL, John et ux.	William Hearle	Deed
1691, Feb. 10	WINFORD, John	John Preble	Deed
1698, Sept. 24	WISE, Thomas et ux.	Daniel Black	Deed
1690, Mar. 14	WITHERS, Jane	Elizabeth Berry	Deed
1691, Apr. 1	WITHERS, Jane	Elizabeth Berry	Deed
1701, Apr. 3	WOODEN, John	Benjamin Curtis	Deed
1699, Aug. 10	WRIGHT, Henry et ux.	Andrew Brown	Deed
1699, Aug. 10	WRIGHT, Henry et ux.	Samuel Bragdon	Deed
1700, Sept. 7	WRIGHT, Mary	Elizabeth Southerine	Deed
1697, Dec. 19	YORK, Town of	John Pickerin and Jas. Plaisted	Grant
1700, June 5	YORK, Town of	James March	Survey
1702, Dec. 27	YORK, Town of	Mary Hooke	Survey
1680, June 3	YOUNG, Rowland, senior, et ux.	Rowland Young, junior	Deed

Index of Grantors.

Folio.	Description.
69	24 acres in the parish of Unity [*Berwick*] adjoining Nason, Spencer, Goodwin and Humphreys.
145	5 acres adjoining Grantee's land on one side and on the three others to Grantor's land in *York*.
75	11 acres at the Burnt Plain in *York*.
95	Land between Edmund Haman's and Peter Lewis' and the marshes between Haman's and Mr. Fernald's, on both sides the Eastern creek; also lands at Eagle Point in *Kittery;* reserving life estate.
96	Quitclaiming all claims to above premises.
95	80 acres on Little river and a town grant of 10 acres by and in *Wells*.
110	17½ acres on the northeast side of York river, in *York*.
128	2½ acres marsh on the southwest side of the northwest branch of the river in *York*.
75	Quitclaiming marsh on the west branch of York river between John Brown's and John Parker's, in *York*.
83	Mill privilege and land, timber grant and meadow on the creek where Ellingham, Gail and Saywood formerly built mills.
152	2½ acres at Bald Head by the seaside.
137	Of 72 acres on southwest side of the river at the town line between *York* and *Kittery*.
25	10 acres formerly part of Robert Knight's farm, in *York*.

INDEX OF

Date.	Grantee.	Grantor.	Instrument.
1700, Mar. 27	ABBOTT, John	Thomas Abbot, senior, et ux.	Deed
1695, May 11	ABBOT, Thomas, and estate of Jonathan Nason, by Sarah Nason, Adm'x	Abraham Lord et ux.	Deed
1701, Sept. 3	ABBOTT, Thomas, senior	John Clark	Deed
1699, Apr. 4	ADAMS, Margaret	Isaac Goodridge	Deed
1685, Sept. 9	ALLEN, Lewis	Wm. Frost et ux.	Deed
Acknowledged 1685, Aug. 6	ALLEN, LEWIS,	Samuel Storer	Bill of Sale
1699, May 24	ALLEN, Robert	Town of Kittery	Grant
1698, Nov. 3	BANE, Lewis	Richard Toziar et ux.	Deed
1699, Jan. 6	BANE, Lewis, and Andrew Brown	Philip Cooper, by Sarah Wright, attorney	Deed
1700, Oct. 5	BANE, Lewis, and Job Curtis	Dodevah Curtis	Deed
1700, Nov. 28	BANE, Lewis, and Job Curtis	Arthur Bragdon, junior, et ux.	Deed
1702, May 23	BANE, Lewis	Gilbert Endicot, by Jas. Gooch, attorney	Deed

GRANTEES.

Folio.	Description.
67	25 acres west of the top of Rocky Hill in [*Berwick*] *Kittery*.
53	Ratifying (after coming of age) conveyance of 40 acres and 10 acres marsh, excepting 3 acres sold Peter Wittum, at Sturgeon creek, *Kittery*, made by Grantor's father during his minority.
121	One-sixth in common of land, falls and mills at Quamphegan Falls in *Berwick*.
39	Land and house bought of Samuel King in *Kittery*.
5	100 acres with dwelling-house, at Little river; also one-third of a saw-mill and appurtenances and of 110 acres as per town grants by and in *Wells*.
6	One-half of the brigantine "Indeavour" of *Wells*, her apparel, tackle and furniture.
114	30 acres, to be clear of other grants.
41	25 acres on both sides the road to the New Mill creek, in *York*.
109	11¾ acres on the country road and a road to York river in *York*.
108	50 acres, being one-fourth of a town grant known as Scituate plains and marsh in *York*.
109	50 acres, being one-fourth undivided of town grant known as Scituate plains and marsh in *York*.
145	30 acres, with messuage, fronting 15 poles on the highway to the corn-mill in *York*.

Index of Grantees.

Date.	Grantee.	Grantor.	Instrument.
1696, Apr. 22	BANKS, John, and Joseph Banks	Est. of Richard Banks, by Jos. Banks, Adm'r, and Elizabeth Banks, John Banks	Division
	BANKS, Joseph, see John Banks		
1669, Jan. 21	BARFOOT, Walter	Francis Champernown	Deed
1698, Mar. 5	BARTER, Henry	Thomas Hooper et ux.	Deed
1698, Mar. 5	BARTER, Henry	Thomas Hooper	Bond
1651, Dec. 26	BARTLET, Nicholas	George Cleave	Deed
1700, Jan. 22	BATSON, John, and Samuel Hill Joseph Storer	Each other	Partn'ship Agreement
	BATSON, John, see Joseph Storer		
1700, Nov. 22	BAYLEY, Joseph	Nicholas Moorey	Deed
1687, Aug. 24	BERNARD, Joseph	Benjamin Bernard et ux.	Deed
1690, Mar. 14	BERRY, Elizabeth	Jane Withers	Deed
1691, Apr. 1	BERRY, Elizabeth	Jane Withers	Deed
1696, Dec. 5	BLACK WILL	John Gowen, *alias* Smith, et ux.	Deed
1700, Feb. 13	BLACK WILL	John Shapleigh	Manumission

Index of Grantees. 53

Folio.	Description.
123	Of said intestate's estate in *York*, securing provision for the widow and release of dower by her.
158	216 acres at Spruce creek, part of a town grant by and in *Kittery*.
42	A triangular piece containing 27¾ acres and 26 poles on Spruce creek, in *Kittery*.
43	In £52 to observe the covenants in foregoing deed.
139	100 acres between lands of Grantor and Michael Mitten, 100 poles along the water front and back into the woods [on *Falmouth* Neck].
50	Relating to building and operating a saw-mill on the river at *Cape Porpoise*.
111	150 acres, [100, formerly Griffin Mortgague's; 50, the neck formerly Morgan Howell's] bought of Samuel Snow [executor] in *Cape Porpoise*.
29	50 acres bought of Grantee between the river, the commons and lands of Tozier and Price in *Berwick*.
95	Land between Edmund Haman's and Peter Lewis' and the marshes between Haman's and Mr. Fernald's, on both sides the Eastern creek; also lands at Eagle point in *Kittery*. reserving life estate.
96	Quitclaiming all claims to above premises.
43	50 acre town grant to Grantor; also 50 acre town grant to his brother William Gowen, by and in *Kittery*.
88	Of a negro slave, so named.

INDEX OF GRANTEES.

Date.	Grantee.	Grantor.	Instrument.
1698, Sept. 24	BLACK, Daniel	Thomas Wise et ux.	Deed
1702, Mar. 16	BLACK, Daniel	Thomas Mo[o]re et ux.	Deed
1700, Nov. 14	BRAGDON, Arthur, junior, and Abram Preble, Peter Nowel	Each other	Partn'ship Agreement
1699, Aug. 10	BRAGDON, Samuel	Henry Wright et ux.	Deed
1701, Dec. 25	BRAGDON, Samuel, junior	Arthur Bragdon, senior et ux.	Deed
1699, Aug. 10	BROWN, Andrew	Henry Wright et ux.	Deed
	BROWN, Andrew, see Lewis Bane		
1701, Sept. 17	BURKS, Walter	Thomas Southerine et ux.	Deed
1695, Nov. 19	CAME, Samuel	Elizabeth Rones	Deed
1701, Dec. 26	CAME, Samuel	Daniel Simpson et ux.	Deed
1688, June 20	CARPENTER, Philip	Nathaniel Fryer Robert Jordan	Deed
1702, Oct. 81	CARPENTER, Philip	William Mitchell et ux.	Deed
1668, Apr. 11	CHADBORNE, Humphrey	Nicholas Shapleigh et ux.	Deed
1668, Apr. 12	CHAMPERNOWN, Francis	Humphrey Chadborn	Trust Deed

Folio.	Description.
75	11 acres at the Burnt Plain in *York*.
142	2 acres marsh on the west branch of the river at Dummer's cove, in *York*.
126	Relating to building and operating a saw-mill at *York* Bridge.
128	2½ acres marsh on the southwest side of the northwest branch of the river in *York*.
128	45 acres, fronting 36 poles on the southwest side of York river, opposite the house of Samuel Bragdon, sen., in *York*.
110	17½ acres on the northeast side of York river, in *York*.
75	One-half in common of marsh on the west branch of the river, between John Brown's and John Parker's, in *York*.
175	10 acres, the homestead of William Rones, deceased, also one-half of a town grant to said Rones and James Freethy, in *York*.
176	4 acres salt marsh on the northwest branch of the river, in *York*.
169	20 acres on the seashore adjoining Sarah Sweat's land and other lands of Grantors, in *Cape Elizabeth*.
168	Two house lots and the flake-room between, and half a stage-room on Smuttynose island; also one-third of moorings between that island and Malaga island, *Isles of Shoals*.
87	Tract on North side of Sturgeon creek between Nicholas Frost and John Heard; also in a town grant adjoining, in *Kittery*.
18	Land and marsh about Sturgeon creek in [*Berwick*] *Kittery*, in trust for his wife, Lucy Chadborn.

INDEX OF GRANTEES.

Date.	Grantee.	Grantor.	Instrument.
1685, June 26	CHAMPERNOWN, Francis	Governor and Company of Massachusets Colony, by Thomas Danforth, President of Maine.	Grant
1691, June 19	CHECKLEY, Samuel	Joshua Scottow et ux.	Deed
1694, Oct. 23	CHECKLEY, Samuel	Thomas Scottow	Mortgage
1686, Oct. 25	CHILD, Henry	Thomas Parkes	Condition'l Deed
	CLARK, Patience et ux., see John Wells		
1670, Aug. 6	COCK, Edward	Job Alcock	Deed
1701, Jan. 12	COTTEN, John	Jacob Smith et ux.	Deed
1702, Jan. 4	COTTEN, John	David Libby et ux.	Deed
1699, May 24	CROCKETT, Hugh	Town of Kittery	Grant
1699, May 24	CROCKETT, Joseph, junior	Town of Kittery	Grant
1701, Apr. 3	CURTIS, Benjamin	John Wooden	Deed
1702, Apr. —	CURTIS, Dodevah et ux. and Thomas Daniel's estate by Samuel Keais and Samuel Penhallow executors of Bridget Graffort, his executrix	Each other	Division
	CURTIS, Job, see Lewis Bane		
1699, May 24	CUTT, Richard	Town of Kittery	Grant

INDEX OF GRANTEES. 57

Folio.	Description.
78	400 acres, being the neck of land between Piscataqua river mouth and Brave-boat harbor, and 500 acres northeast of Brave-boat harbor, in *Kittery* and *York*.
131	The farm bought of Abraham Joslin with the marsh bought of Andrew Brown, except 12 acres marsh sold William Burrage, at Black Point, *Scarborough*.
132	100 acres upland on Moore's brook and 40 acres meadow on Pigsgut river, in *Scarborough*.
4	40 acres at Post Wigwam on Newichewannock river, in *Berwick*. Conditioned for support of Grantor.
40	Land on the Westermost creek, between lands of Bragdon and Card, in *York*.
118	Land in common with others purchased of Thomas Clarke's heirs in *Kittery* by Stephen Tobey and by him conveyed to Grantor.
151	30 acres, part of my purchase with others, of the heirs of Thomas Clarke, in *Kittery*.
139	30 acres, to be clear of other grants.
139	30 acres, to be clear of other grants.
95	80 acres on Little river and a town grant of 10 acres by and in *Wells*.
149	Establishing line between parties on Withers' island in Piscataqua river in *Kittery*.
57	30 acres, to be clear of other grants.

Index of Grantees.

Date.	Grantee.	Grantor.	Instrument.
1700, Aug. 20	Cutt, Richard	Mary Champernown	Deed
1700, Aug. 20	Cutt, Richard	Richard Whetherick, by Elizabeth Whetherick, Attorney	Deed
1700, Apr. 13	Cutt, Robert	John Tomson	Deed
1700, May 3	Cutt, Robert	Thomas Hooper	Deed
1700, July 16	Cutt, Robert	Richard Cutt	Deed
1700, July 16	Cutt, Robert	Walter Deniver	Deed
1700, July 16	Cutt, Robert	Samuel Fernald	Deed
1700, July 16	Cutt, Robert	John Morgrage	Deed
1700, July 80	Cutt, Robert	Jacob Smith	Deed
	Daniel, Thomas' estate, see Dodevah Curtis		
1687, June 13	Davis, Emmanuel et ux.	Robert Ellet (Elliot) et ux.	Deed
1686, Dec. 22	Davis, Sylvanus	Isaac Davis et ux.	Deed
1687, June 2	Davis, Sylvanus	Joseph Hodsden	Deed
	Davis, Sylvanus, see John Phillips		
1688, June 25	Dering, Henry	Richard White	Mortgage
1694, Sept. 1	Dearing, Roger	Digory Jeffry et ux.	Deed
1694, May 16	Deniver, Walter	Town of Kittery	Grant
1700, Dec. 26	Deniver, Walter	John Shapleigh	Deed
1700, Dec. 26	Deniver, Walter	John Shapleigh	Deed

Index of Grantees. 59

Folio.	Description.
81	One-half of Champernown's Island in *Kittery*.
81	One-half of Champernown's Island in *Kittery*.
57	30 acre town grant by and in *Kittery*.
56	20 acre town grant by and in *Kittery*.
57	Town grant of 50 acres by and in *Kittery*.
56	10 acre town grant by and in *Kittery*.
57	30 acre town grant by and in *Kittery*.
56	10 acre town grant by and in *Kittery*.
57	30 acre town grant by and in *Kittery*.
76	40 acres; also 60 acres upland adjoining; 7 acres marsh at Prince's rock and 7 acres marsh; all in *Cape Porpoise*.
1	10 acres marsh in Nonesuch marshes in *Scarborough*.
35	120 acres on Nonesuch Point in *Falmouth*, with obligation for release of dower by his wife Tabitha.
82	Dwelling-house and land; also 90 acres upland at the head of Brave-boat harbor; also all the marsh in two parcels at the bridge and above it, in *Kittery*.
60	100 acres with dwelling-house, at the Stepping-stones in *Kittery*.
56	10 acres; proviso to be improved within one year.
85	13¼ acres on the cross-road to the Point between Crooked lane and Spruce creek, in *Kittery*.
93	(A re-record of the above).

Index of Grantees.

Date.	Grantee.	Grantor.	Instrument.
1694, May 16	Dennet, Alex	Town of Kittery	Grant
1700, Nov. 4	Dennet, John	Richard King et ux.	Deed
1699, Aug. 28	Dennet, John, junior	Samuel Penhallow	Deed
1686, July 28	Dicer, William	Estate of John Hellson, by Joanna Hellson, executrix, and Ephraim Hellson Samuel Hellson	Deed
1694, Mar. 17	Dill, Daniel	Estate of William Mo[o]re, by Thos. Mo[o]re, Adm'r	Deed
1701, May 15	Dill, John	Daniel Dill, senior, et ux.	Conditional Deed
1700, Sept. 25	Dixon, Peter	Samuel Penhallow	Deed
1699, Feb. 29	Downing, Joshua, and John Leighton	Est. of Jonathan Nason, by Sarah Nason, Adm'x	Deed
1699, Mar. 25	Downing, Joshua, and John Leighton	Thomas Abbot	Deed
1699, Mar. 25	Downing, Joshua, and John Leighton	Thomas Abbot	Deed
	Downing, Joshua, see Samuel Hill		
1679, Sept. 30	Drake, Abraham, senior	Anthony Brackett, junior	Trust Deed
1687, Nov. 3	Dummer, Shubael	John Alcock	Deed
1694, Sept. 29	Eliot, Robert	Andrew Brown, senior	Mortgage

INDEX OF GRANTEES. 61

Folio.	Description.
114	20 acres; proviso to be improved within one year.
71	20 acre town grant by and in *Kittery*.
39	30 acres on Spinney's cove, granted by town to Gabriel Tetherly, in *Kittery*.
7	100 acres on the west side of the Saco river, up to the head of tide-water, excepting one house lot, in *Saco*.
45	20 acres on the highway at Scotland, in *York*.
135	All his estate in *York*, conditioned for his own and wife's support and charging certain gifts upon the estate.
128	Two adjoining lots of 20 acres each near the mast-ways on west side of Spruce creek, in *Kittery*, conveyed Grantor by Richard Endle.
55	One-half in common of 40 acres upland and 10 acres marsh on the south side of Sturgeon creek, in *Kittery*.
54	Quitclaim to the premises more fully described below.
54	40 acres upland near Sturgeon creek, with 10 acres marsh in the Great Marsh adjoining, in [*Berwick*] *Kittery*.
87	Marriage settlement for benefit of Susanna [Drake] his wife, of half his realty in *Casco Bay*.
81	58 acres, being the half of Farmer Alcock's neck, at the river's mouth; also 4 acres marsh on the western branch of York river, in *York*.
165	All his land and marsh on east side of Black Point river [in *Scarborough*].

Index of Grantees.

Date.	Grantee.	Grantor.	Instrument.
1700, Aug. 20	ELLIOT, Robert	Nathaniel Fryer	Deed
1699, May 24	ELWELL, Hezekiah	Town of Kittery	Grant
1693, Oct. 26	EMERSON, John, junior	Harlakinden Symonds et ux.	Deed
1694, Jan. 2	EMERY, James, junior	James Emery, senior	Deed
1699, May 24	EMERY, Job	Town of Kittery	Grant
1702, Mar. 30	EMERY, Samuel	Moses Littlefield et ux.	Deed
1686, Nov. 10	EMMS Henry	John Pritchett and John Burrell et ux.	Deed
	ENDICOTT, John, see John Phillips		
1701, Dec. 17	ENDLE, Richard	Elihu Gunnison	Deed
	ENGLISH, James, see John Phillips		
1675, June 17	FARNUM, John	George Munjoy et ux.	Deed
1672, Mar. 2	FENNICK, John	Jonathan Mendum et ux.	Deed
1702, Apr. 10	FERNALD, James	Spinney, Thomas et ux.	Deed
1700, Dec. 22	FERNALD, John, senior	John Morrell, senior, et ux.	Deed
	FERNALD, Nathaniel, see Samuel Fernald's estate		
1699, May 24	FERNALD, Samuel	Town of Kittery	Grant

Index of Grantees.

Folio.	Description.
94	Champernown's Island, excepting 80 acres, in *Kittery*.
138	30 acres, to be clear of other grants.
135	600 acres, next the lands sold Baker and Dorman, 6 miles long by 60 poles broad in Coxhall, [now *Lyman*].
160	20 acres on Stony brook in *Berwick*; also half an acre where Grantee's house stood, reserving a right of way.
160	20 acres, to be clear of other grants.
167	25 acres on northwest side of Webhannet river; also 4 rods on the highway to the marsh; also 3 acres in common in Merryland marshes, in *Wells*.
16	All their land at the Mill Pool on Small Point side of Sagadahoc river, bought of Thomas Atkins.
154	60 acres at Bryan's Point in Spruce creek; also land on south side of the creek adjacent; also 30 feet square for a burying-ground, reserving the mill-privilege and a landing, in *Kittery*.
164	101 acres, being half the tract taken on execution *vs.* Francis Small, northerly of the river that leads into Brave-boat harbor in *Kittery*.
21	12 acres, fronting 16 poles on the water side on the north of Spruce creek, in *Kittery*.
134	11½ acres between Grantor's dwelling-house and land of Thomas Worster, in *Kittery*.
84	60 acres between the Great cove and the head of Spruce creek, in *Kittery*.
57	30 acres, to be clear of other grants.

Index of Grantees.

Date.	Grantee.	Grantor.	Instrument.
1701, June 25	FERNALD, Samuel, estate by Hannah Fernald, exec'x and Nathaniel Fernald	Thomas Spinney	Deed
1682, Aug. 28	FERNALD, Thomas	George Harris et ux.	Deed
1700, Aug. 22	FERNALD, Tobias	Richard Cutt et ux.	Deed
	FOGG, Daniel, see Joseph Hammond		
1703, June 17	FORD, John	Hugh Crocket	Deed
1689, Sept. 18	FOWLER, Thomas	John Lee	Deed
1699, Aug. 8	FOXCROFT, Francis	George Turfrey	Mortgage
1686, Dec. 7	FREES, James	Dennis Morough et ux.	Deed
1702, May 29	FRINK, George	Elihu Gunnison et ux.	Deed
1699, Oct. 13	FRINK, John	Richard Briar et ux.	Deed
1662, Dec. 20	FROST, Charles	James Emery et ux.	Deed
1692, Oct. 12	FRY, William	Adrian Fry et ux.	Conditional Deed
	FRY, William, see Samuel Hill		
1690, May 2	GASKIN, John, estate of	John Hole, by Elizabeth Hole, attorney	Deed
1701, June 14	GELDING, John	Alexander Dennett	Deed
1691, Apr. 15	GELDING, John	William Sanders, et ux.	Deed

INDEX OF GRANTEES. 65

Folio.	Description.
99	In exchange, 15½ acres lying at the head of Alcock's lot, in *Kittery*.
20	Quitclaiming ¼ acre and house in *Kittery*.
86	85 acres upon Broad cove and Crooked lane in *Kittery*.
166	25 acres, one-half of a town grant of 50 acres by and in *Kittery*.
173	216 acres at Spruce creek in *Kittery*, conveyed by Walter Barfoot.
47	One-half in common with Mortgagee of a saw-mill and appurtenances on Saco river, in *Saco*.
3	30 acres on the south side of Casco river, reserving right of way to the falls for water to Thaddeus Clark, in *Falmouth*.
153	35 acres with dwelling-house between the highway and Spruce creek, adjoining Ingersoll's lane, in *Kittery*.
153	50 acres near Spruce creek, devised by Francis Champernown, in *Kittery*.
44	2 acres called the Barren marsh on north side of Sturgeon creek in *Kittery*, [*Berwick*].
87	9 acres at Sturgeon creek's mouth and 27 acres at Horsidown Hill in *Kittery*, conditioned for support and maintenance, and reserving one acre.
150	10 acres, 40 poles square, off the northeast end of Grantor's plantation in *Kittery*.
114	20 acre town grant by and in *Kittery*.
80	30 acres near Sturgeon creek as per town grant by and in *Kittery*.

Date.	Grantee.	Grantor.	Instrument.
1694, Oct. 31	GILLAM, Benjamin	Ephraim Turner	Lease
1698, Dec. 12	GILLAM, Benjamin	Ephraim Turner	Lease
1694, Nov. 1	GILLAM, Benjamin	Ephraim Turner	Deed
1698, Dec. 13	GILLAM, Benjamin	Ephraim Turner	Deed
Acknowledged 1700, Sept. 5	GOOCH, James	Daniel Black	Mortgage
1698, Jan. 4	GOODWIN, Daniel, junior	Nicholas Tarbet et ux., and Richard Clarke	Deed
1701, Aug. 21	GOODWIN, Daniel, junior	Daniel Goodwin, senior	Deed
1694, May 16	GOODWIN, Moses	Town of Kittery	Grant
1697, Mar. 19	GOODING (Goodwin) Moses	William Goodin (Goodwin), et ux.	Deed
1699, May 24	GOODWIN, Moses	Town of Kittery	Grant
	GOODING, Moses, see William Goodwin		
1701, June 17	GOODING (Goodwin), Thomas	Humphrey Spencer, et ux.	Deed
1697, Mar. 19	GOODING (Goodwin), William, and Moses Gooding (Goodwin)	Daniel Gooding (Goodwin), et ux.	Deed
1700, July 2	GOODWIN, William	Martha Taylor	Condition'l Deed
1700, Mar. 14	GOWEN, John	James Gowen, *alias* Smith	Receipt
1700, Mar. 16	GOWEN, John	Sarah Smith	Receipt
1702, Nov. 14	GOWEN, John	Lemuel Gowen	Receipt

Index of Grantees.

Folio.	Description.
61	500 acres on the southwest side of Saco river and one-eighth of a mine above *Saco*, for term of one year.
62	400 acres adjoining the above premises in *Saco*, for term of one year.
63	Of the 500 acres above described.
64	Of the 400 acres above described.
90	3 acres and buildings (excepting half-acre house-lot of John Pennel) on highway and Meeting-house creek, in *York*.
68	15 acres, part of 100 acre town grant and one-fifth of one-half of the further marsh formerly Thomas Spencer's in *Kittery*.
147	6 acres in Slut's corner marshes in *Berwick*.
84	20 acres; proviso to be improved within one year.
68	Quitclaim of his half of the tract conveyed by their father, Daniel Goodwin, senior, in *Berwick*.
160	30 acres, to be clear of other grants.
122	30 acres at Newichewannock, in *Berwick*, as per town grant of Kittery to Grantor's grandfather, Thomas Spencer.
67	All the remainder of a town grant by Kittery, adjoining land formerly conveyed to his son Daniel Goodwin in *Berwick*.
98	The homestead of her late husband John Taylor in *Berwick*, conditioned for partial support and legacies.
117	In full for his proportion of his father William Gowens' (*alias* Smith) estate.
117	For part of her portion of her father William Gowen's estate.
88	In full for his proportion of his father William Gowen's estate.

Index of Grantees.

Date.	Grantee.	Grantor.	Instrument.
1702, Nov. 19	GOWEN, John	William Smith et ux.	Receipts
	GOWEN, John, see Nicholas Gowen		
1703, Jan. 19	GOWEN, Nicholas, and John Gowen	Each other	Division
1700, July 10 1700, Sept. 9	GOWEN, *alias* Smith, Nicholas and John Gowen, *alias* Smith	Each other	Submission and Award
1681, June 10	GRANT, James	Alex. Maxell et ux.	Deed
1686, Feb. 14	GRANT, James, by Alex. Maxell, attorney	Arthur Bragdon, senior	Deed
1686, Feb. 14	GRANT, James	Alex. Maxell	Deed
1702, Aug. 3	GREELY, Thomas, and Timothy Waymouth [Edward] Waymouth, by Timothy Waymouth, attorney	Each other	Division
1701, Nov. 18	GREELEY, Thomas	Jas. Treworthy	Deed
1699, May 24	GREEN, Daniel	Town of Kittery	Grant
1684, Feb. 4	GREENOUGH, Robert	Harlakinden Symonds et ux.	Deed
1699, Aug. 7	GROVER, Andrew	Daniel Dill, sen.	Deed
1700, Dec. 24	GUNNISON, Elihu	Joseph Weekes	Deed
1700, Dec. 24	GUNNISON, Elihu	Nicholas Weekes	Deed
1703, Mar. 23	HAMBLETON, Gabriel	Job Emery	Deed
1703, Mar. 23	HAMBLETON, Gabriel	Moses Goodwin	Deed

INDEX OF GRANTEES. 69

Folio.	Description.
45	In full for his wife Sarah's portion.
171	Of 50 acres formerly Trustrum Harrinson's [Harris] in *Kittery*, [*Berwick*].
70	Of their father William Gowen's estate and charging their mother's dower and brethren's portions on said estate; also of Trustrum Harris' estate; and fixing a division line [in *Berwick*].
15	5 acres marsh and ¼ acre upland on which Grantee's barn stood near head of northwest branch of the river, in *York*.
14	40 acres upon which the buildings of Grantee stood in *York*.
15	Quitclaiming 40 acres in *York* bought, as attorney for Grantee, of Arthur Bragdon.
170	Fixing division line between their lands at the brook running into the Mast cove, in *Berwick*.
115	50 acres with dwelling-house and 11 acres addition, adjoining Edward Waymouth's land, near Mast cove in *Kittery*.
56	80 acres, to be clear of other grants.
95	100 acres to be chosen by Grantee in Coxhall, [now *Lyman*].
124	20 acres upland and swamp on northwest branch of York river in *York*.
98	Town grant (number of acres not specified) by and in *Kittery*.
98	30 acre town grant by and in *Kittery*.
160	20 acre town grant by and in *Kittery*, [*Berwick*].
160	30 acre town grant by Kittery [in *Berwick?*].

Index of Grantees.

Date.	Grantee.	Grantor.	Instrument.
1699, Dec. 18	Hammond, Joseph, and David Libby, Matthew Libby, Daniel Fogg, Stephen Tobey	Mehitable Warren, and Elisha Hutchinson et ux., in her right	Deed
1700[1], Mar. 21	Hammond, Joseph, and Stephen Tobey David Libby Matthew Libby Daniel Fogg	Each other	Agreement
1701, Mar. 21	Hammond, Joseph, and Matthew Libby Stephen Tobey David Libby Daniel Fogg	Each other	Division
1675, May 4	Harris, George	John Hole	Lease
1699, Apr. 5	Hearle, William	John Wincoll et ux.	Deed
1671, Dec. 26	Hellson, John, senior	Roger Hill et ux.	Deed
1693, July 26	Higginson, John, junior	William Cock, senior	Deed
1700, Feb. 3	Higginson, John, junior	Nicholas Bartlet	Deed
1699, Feb. 6	Hill, John	John Plaisted et ux.	Indenture
1699, Feb. 6			Bipartite
1720, Apr. 23	Hill, John	John Plaisted	Discharge
1686, Apr. 25	Hill, Joseph	Edw. Gilman and Stephen Paul et ux.	Deed

Index of Grantees.

Folio.	Description.
88	870 acres (except 30 acres) at the Long Reach in Piscataqua river between Watts' Fort and Frank's Fort, known as the Knowles [Indian] purchase, formerly Thomas Clarke's, in *Kittery*.
91	Regulating the several proportions each should pay of a bond of £200 to the Clarke heirs in part payment for the above premises.
89	Of the tract of land purchased of the heirs of Thomas Clarke, between Watts' Fort and Frank's Fort, in *Kittery*.
20	House and ¼ acre on south side Fernald's island in *Kittery*.
69	24 acres in the parish of Unity [*Berwick*] adjoining Nason, Spencer, Goodwin and Humphreys.
6	100 acres on the west side of Saco river, up to the head of tide-water, excepting Grantor's house lot, in *Saco*.
140	1300 acres upland, meadow and salt marsh on west side of Sagadahoc river near its mouth, purchased of Thomas Atkins.
139	100 acres between lands of George Cleave and Michael Mitten, 100 poles along the water front and back 160 poles into the woods [on *Falmouth Neck*].
129 104	One third in common and undivided of 600 acres [excepting 33¼ acres] lying in six parcels on both sides Little Newichewannock river, at Bonnibissie pond, at Totnock, at Broughton's marsh, at White's marsh and at Pipe-staff point; also of the mill-privilege at Assabumbedoc Falls, all in *Berwick*.
106	Of the mortgage recorded folio 106.
27	40 acres adjoining land of Samuel Hill in *Kittery*.

Index of Grantees.

Date.	Grantee.	Grantor.	Instrument.
1699, Feb. 24	Hill Joseph	Nicholas Moorey	Deed
1700, Mar. 28	Hill, Joseph	Daniel Green	Deed
1702, May 2	Hill, Joseph, and Peter Staple	Each other	Division
	Hill, Joseph, see Samuel Hill		
1695, Feb. 27	Hill, Samuel	Emmanuel Davis et ux.	Deed
1699, Oct. 15	Hill, Samuel	Thomas Fowler	Deed
1702, Feb. 24	Hill, Samuel, and Joseph Hill William Fry Joshua Downing	Katharine Paul John Paul Daniel Paul Moses Paul John Tomson Samuel Fernald Abigail, wife of one of the Pauls	Deed
1702, Apr. 4	Hill, Samuel, and Joseph Hill William Fry Joshua Downing	Maverick Gilman	Deed
	Hill, Samuel, see John Batson		
	Hill, Samuel, see Joseph Storer		
1684, May 4	Hilton, Richard	William Hilton et ux.	Deed
1686, Nov. 10	Hincks, John	Sarah Jordan	Deed
1687, Feb. 29	Hincks, John	Territory and Dominion of New England, by Sir Edmund Andros, Gov.	Grant

INDEX OF GRANTEES.

Folio.	Description.
48	Land on Cross' creek, and marsh adjoining it to Webhannet river and 6 acres marsh at the Neck of Land, in *Wells*.
56	30 acre town grant by and in *Kittery*.
133	Establishing division line between their premises at the Long Reach, in *Kittery*.
76	40 acres adjoining Little River falls in *Cape Porpoise*.
173	216 acres at Spruce creek in *Kittery*, purchased of John Lee.
162	As widow and surviving heirs of Stephen Paul, all the grant, remaining unsold, to Antipas Maverick, between Piscataqua river and Sturgeon creek, in *Kittery*.
162	All the land formerly his father, Edward Gilman's, between Piscataqua river and Sturgeon creek; also a town grant to his grandfather, Antipas Maverick, by and in *Kittery*.
166	All his messuage (except 8 acres) at the Long Reach between Mary Bachellor's and Daniel Paul's highways, in *Kittery*, also 10 acres marsh.
78	One-half of the 1000 acres (excepting 100 acres upland and 29 acres marsh conveyed) at Nonesuch [in *Cape Elizabeth*].
78	1200 acres, part of Nonesuch neck on the river of that name, in *Scarborough*.

Index of Grantees.

Date.	Grantee.	Grantor.	Instrument.
1699, Nov. 16	HINCKSON, Peter, [junior], et ux.	Peter Hinckson	Deed
1698, Dec. 2	HODSDEN, Benoni	John Plaisted	Deed
1703, Apr. 25	HODSDEN, Benoni	Nathan Lord et ux.	Deed
1699, Nov. 17	HODSDEN, Joseph	Benoni Hodsden et ux	Deed
1702, Dec. 27	HOOKE, Mary	Town of York	Survey
1688, Mar. 14	HOOKE, William	Henry Dering	Power att'y
1699, May 16	HOOPER, Thomas	Town of Kittery	Grant
1703, Apr. 25	HUBBORD, Philip	Benoni Hodsden et ux.	Deed
	HULL, John, see Roger Plaisted		
1703, Mar. 6	HUTCHINS, Benjamin	Roger Thomas	Deed
1687, Dec. 16	HUTCHINSON, Eliakim	Robert Tufton Mason	Grant
1699, Jan. 11	HUTCHINSON, Eliakim	John Plaisted	Mortgage
1699, Oct. 26	JOHNSON, James	Enoch Hutchins	Deed
1700, June 25	JOHNSON, James	John Shapleigh Wm. Godsoe	Deed
1702, June 26	JOHNSON, Samuel	Peter Bass est. of, Jonathan Bass	Release
1702, Oct. 27	JOHNSON, Samuel	Moses Voden et ux.	Deed
1700, Oct. 28	JUNKINS, Alex.	Samuel Johnson et ux.	Deed

Index of Grantees.

Folio.	Description.
64	23 acres upland; also 10 acres marsh; also 56 acres upland and marsh on Nonesuch river at Black Point, in *Scarborough*.
156	80 acres including town grants to John Wincoll and Roger Plaisted, in *Kittery* [*Berwick*].
161	In exchange, 7 acres on Birch Point brook, where John Morrill formerly dwelt, in *Kittery*.
70	Two adjoining tracts of 20 acres and 42 acres upon the country road and town commons in *Berwick*.
137	Of 72 acres on southwest side of the river at the town line between *York* and *Kittery*.
34	General power of attorney.
56	20 acres; proviso to be improved within one year.
160	40 acres on the highway from the landing place near Grantor's house to Birchen Point brook, in *Berwick*.
172	Two town grants of 20 acres and 10 acres by and in *Kittery*.
174	500 acres upon both sides Little Newichewannock river, with other parcels of marsh and meadow; also timber grants and a mill-privilege, all in *Berwick*.
46	Of the 600 acres in *Berwick* conveyed by Mortgagee by folio 102.
44	20 acres near York road in *Kittery*.
78	62 acres at the head of Spruce creek, in *Kittery*.
111	Of all obligations by Grantee's warrantor, George Parker of *York*. [See III. 122].
150	80 acres on the north side of Sturgeon creek, as by town grant by and in *Kittery*.
77	10 acres upon a brook between Jeremiah Moulton and Constant Rankin, in *York*.

Index of Grantees.

Date.	Grantee.	Grantor.	Instrument.
1699, July 3	KEEN Nathaniel	John Shapleigh	Deed
1699, Sept. 5	KELLEY, Agnes	Edw. Cock (Cox)	Power att'y
1687, Nov. 21	LEE, John	Walter Barfoot	Deed
	LEIGHTON, John, see Joshua Downing		
1700, Nov. 7	LEWIS, Peter	James Bredeen	Deed
	LIBBY, David, see Joseph Hammond		
	LIBBY, Moses, see Joseph Hammond		
	LIBBY, Sarah, see John Wells		
1683, Mar. 20	LITTLEFIELD, James	Francis Littlefield, senior	Deed
1687, Apr. 14	LITTLEFIELD, James	John Buckland et ux.	Deed
1684, Oct. 6	LITTLEFIELD, Jonathan	Wm. Ashleigh et ux.	Deed
1699, Oct. 4	LITTLEFIELD, Jonathan	Samuel Wheelwright et ux. John Wheelwright et ux.	Deed
1696, Aug. 8	LITTLEFIELD, Josiah	John Littlefield et ux.	Deed
1701, Apr. 26	LITTLEFIELD, Josiah	Samuel Hatch	Deed
1700, May 2	LITTLEFIELD, Moses	Francis Littlefield, senior	Deed

INDEX OF GRANTEES. 77

Folio.	Description.
52	100 acres at the lower falls in the Western creek, in *Kittery*.
40	General power of attorney.
159	216 acres at Spruce creek in *Kittery*, purchased of Francis Champernown.
117	30 acre town grant by and in *Kittery*.
141	House and land bought of William Frost, on west side of Webhannet river, and enough in addition from my farm to make it equal thereto; also 100 acres on Merryland plain with 7 acres marsh and a neck of upland; also an island on the sea-wall and 4 acres marsh; also 200 acres upland and 10 acres meadow at Merryland; also Thatch island, all in *Wells*.
24	600 acres between Kennebunk river and the Second Sands, in *Wells*.
107	140 acres, with buildings, 27 poles wide upon the highway next Mr. Wheelwright's; also marsh at the neck of land on the sea-wall; also 6 acres more of marsh; all in *Wells*.
40	19¾ acres between the highway and the marsh near Grantee's dwelling-house, in *Wells*.
116	Marsh and thatch beds between Ogunquit river and Sandy point, in *Wells*.
116	100 acres on northerly side of Ogunquit river in *Wells*.
167	20 acres upland and salt marsh 20 poles along the seashore, granted by Gorges, in *Wells*.

Index of Grantees.

Date.	Grantee.	Grantor.	Instrument.
1700, Nov. 6	LORD, Abraham	Moses Goodwin et ux.	Deed
1703, Apr. 25	LORD, Nathan	Benoni Hodsden et ux.	Deed
1694, Dec. 10	MACCANTIER, Micum	Matthew Austin et ux.	Deed
1700, June 5	MARCH, James	Town of York	Survey
1681, Aug. 2	MERCER, Francis	Wm. Hilton et ux.	Deed
1686, Oct. 27	MERCER, Francis	John Hilton	Bond
1703, June 17	MITCHELL, Christopher	Hugh Crocket	Deed
1683, Oct. 2	MITCHELL, William	Peter Lewis, senior, et ux.	Deed
1658, May 1	MITTEN, Michael	George Cleave	Deed
1658, May 20	MITTEN, Nathaniel	George Cleave	Deed
1701, Dec. 15	MONSON, John, et ux.	Richard Monson	Deed
1687, Jan. 2	MOOREY, Nicholas	John Rennals	Deed
1699, Feb. 20	MOOREY, Nicholas	Wm. Breaden	Deed
1700, Jan. 23	MOOREY, Nicholas	James Pendleton	Deed
1699, May 24	MORGRAGE, John	Town of Kittery	Grant
1685, Feb. 1	MORRELL, John, senior	John Sharp	Deed
1701, Nov. 28	MORRELL, John	Thomas Moore et ux.	Deed

INDEX OF GRANTEES. 79

Folio.	Description.
84	20 acre town grant by Kittery [in *Berwick?*].
161	12 acres adjoining Grantee's land on Birchen Point brook, in *Berwick*.
51	10 acres at Goose cove, running 20 poles along the river, in *York*.
152	2½ acres at Bald Head by the seaside.
157	3 acres on Piscataqua river between Nelson and Simpson in *Kittery*, excepted from the conveyance to Richard Hilton.
158	Covenanting to warrant the possession of the 3 acres conveyed by Obligor's father, William Hilton, above.
167	25 acres, one-half of a town grant of 50 acres by and in *Kittery*.
168	Two houses and lots and the flake-room between, and half a stage-room on Smuttynose island; also one-third of moorings between that island and Malaga island, *Isles of Shoals*.
8	Tract fronting Casco river from dwelling-house of Grantee to land of Richard Tucker, thence across to Back cove [on *Falmouth* neck].
8	50 acres, fronting 50 poles on Back cove and back 160 poles into the woods [in *Falmouth*].
118	32 acres upland and marsh at Ox Point, on the south side of Spruce creek, in *Kittery*.
49	[60 acres] on east of Kennebunk river at Long creek, on Mast cove, opposite Gillum's point, in *Cape Porpoise*.
48	300 acres in *Wells* devised to Grantor by Joseph Cross.
50	600 acres on the west side of Saco river, described in conveyances [II., ff. 94 & 140] by William Phillips to Bryan Pendleton, in *Saco*.
56	10 acres, to be clear of other grants.
72	40 acre town grant by and in *Kittery*.
119	40 acres on Hull's creek, in *York*.

Index of Grantees.

Date.	Grantee.	Grantor.	Instrument.
1699, May 24	Morrell, Nicholas	Town of Kittery	Grant
1684, Dec. 27	Moulton, Jeremiah	Thos. Danforth, for self and partners not named	Deed
1696, Apr. 8	Mo[u]lton, Jeremiah	John Bracy	Deed
1701, Aug. 1	Mo[u]lton, Jeremiah	Daniel Simpson et ux.	Deed
1702, July 2	Nason, Jonathan	John Nason	Deed
Acknowledged 1703, May 24	Nason, Jonathan, est. of, by Sarah Nason, adm'x	Henry Snow and Job Emery	Receipt
Acknowledged 1703, May 24	Nason, Jonathan, est. of, by Sarah Nason, adm'x	Jonathan Nason, [junior].	Receipt
1703, Oct. 2	Nason, Jonathan, estate of, and Sarah Nason, adm'x	Joseph Abbott John Abbott	Receipts
	Nason, Jonathan's estate, by Sarah Nason, Adm'x, see Thomas Abbott		
1694, Dec. 4	Neale, Andrew	John Neale et ux.	Deed
1694, Dec. 5	Neale, Andrew	John Neale et ux.	Condition'l Deed
1696, Dec. 30	Neal, Andrew	Samuel Johnson	Deed
1676, Nov. 1	Neal, John	John Heard and James Heard's est., by Shuah Heard	Bond
———, Oct. 24 Recorded 1702, May 2	Nelson, Charles	Gilbert Lugg (Lugh)	Receipt
Recorded 1702, May 2	Nelson, Charles	Gilbert Lugg	Receipt

Index of Grantees.

Folio.	Description.
149	25 acres, to be clear of other grants.
26	Land on Gorges' Point in *York*.
88	All real estate of Grantor's in *York*.
123	5 acres between the main river and Meeting-house creek, in *York*.
144	His half in common with Grantee in town grant of 100 acres at Mast cove, in *Kittery*.
170	In full for their wives' portions.
170	In full for his portion of his father's estate, in *Kittery*.
171	In full for their wives' portions.
101	One-half of 50 acres between the river and Ferguson's bridge, in *Berwick*.
101	Of the other half of the above premises; conditioned for support of Grantee and wife.
51	2 acres salt marsh on south side the river, in *York*.
100	Conditioned to secure possession of the half of a town grant on Piscataqua river in *Kittery*, sold by James Heard in his lifetime to Obligee, but not formally conveyed.
133	For 18 quintals of merchantable fish and five barrels of mackerel.
133	For £21 in full payment of house and land on Piscataqua river, in *Kittery*, between Symonds and Paul, bought in common with Waymouth Lissen.

Index of Grantees.

Date.	Grantee.	Grantor.	Instrument.
1700, Apr. 19	NEWMARCH, John	John Heard	Deed
1700, Sept. 6	NEWMARCH, John	Robert Allen	Deed
1700, Nov. 22	NEWMARCH, John	Aaron Phares	Deed
1698, Nov. 9	NOWELL, Peter	Joseph Weare	Deed
1700, Aug. 30	NOWELL, Peter	Arthur Bragdon, junior, et ux.	Deed
1701, Aug. 26	NOWELL, Peter	Abraham Preble, junior	Deed
1701, Sept. 24	NOWELL, Peter	John Braun	Deed
	NOWELL, Peter, see Arthur Bragdon, junior		
1701, July 2	PARTRIDGE, John	Daniel Simpson et ux.	Deed
1695, Apr. 16	PENHALLOW, Samuel	Gabriel Tetherly et ux.	Deed
1695, Sept. 14	PENHALLOW, Samuel	Richard Endle	Deed
1689, Nov. 15	PEPPERRELL, William	Thos. Thurstun et ux.	Deed
1693, Nov. 1	PEPPERRELL, William	Elihu Gunnison	Deed
1694, Sept. 1	PEPPERRELL, William	Richard Pope, est. of, by Sarah Pope, Adm'x	Deed
1695, Oct. 27	PEPPERRELL, William	John Brawn et ux.	Deed
1700, Apr. 20	PEPPERRELL, William	Hezekiah Allowell (Elwell)	Deed

Index of Grantees. 83

Folio.	Description.
60	50 acres on the road from Spruce creek to Sturgeon creek, in *Kittery*.
114	30 acre town grant by and in *Kittery*.
114	20 acre town grant by and in *Kittery*.
124	20 acres upland adjoining Major Davis' marsh and lands of Daniel Dill and Daniel Livingstone, in *York*.
125	3 acres salt marsh and thatch bed on west side of the southwest branch, in *York*.
126	4 acres marsh on Hull's creek and the southwest branch of the river, in *York*.
126	2 acres salt marsh on southwest branch of the river, in *York*.
120	All claim to the estate of our grandfather, Roger Plaisted [in *Berwick*].
38	30 acres on Spinney cove, town grant by and in *Kittery*.
127	Two adjoining lots of 20 acres each near the mast-ways on west side of Spruce creek in *Kittery*.
137	[About 3¾ acres] between Piscataqua river and Crocket's creek, in *Kittery*.
58	250 acres, being one-half in common of a tract of 500 acres called Buckland's neck on Damariscotta river in *Jamestown*; also half in common of 50 acres meadow opposite Bread and Cheese island.
59	80 acres at Whale cove on west of Scadlock's river in Winter harbor, [now *Biddeford*].
138	Half an acre on the highway adjoining Grantee's land in *Kittery*.
138	30 acre town grant by and in *Kittery*.

Index of Grantees.

Date.	Grantee.	Grantor.	Instrument.
1701, June 27	PEPPERRELL, William	Joseph Crockett	Deed
1701, Dec. 8	PEPPERRELL, William	Nicholas Tucker	Mortgage
1702, June 18	PEPPERRELL, William	Hugh Crockett	Deed
1702, June 18	PEPPERRELL, William	Wm. Roberts	Deed
1702, Aug. 8	PEPPERRELL, William	John Pickerin et ux.	Deed
1684, Mar. 13	PHILLIPS, John, and Sylvanus Davis James English John Endicott	John Ingersoll et ux. and Geo. Ingersoll et ux.	Deed
1697, Dec. 19	PICKERIN, John, and James Plaisted	Town of York	Grant
1700, May 24	PICKERIN, John	James Plaisted	Deed
1701, Aug. 12	PICKERIN, John, junior	Jas. March et ux.	Deed
1700, Sept. 26	PICKERIN, John, junior et ux.	John Pickerin et ux.	Deed
1701, May 1	PLAISTED, Ichabod	Samuel Sewall et ux.	Deed
1702, May 19	PLAISTED, Ichabod	James Plaisted	Deed
	PLAISTED, James, see John Pickerin		
1699, Jan. 10	PLAISTED, John	Eliakim Hutchinson, et ux.	Deed
1699, Feb. 7	PLAISTED, John	John Hill	Mortgage

INDEX OF GRANTEES. 85

Folio.	Description.
139	Town grant of 30 acres by and in *Kittery*.
168	Homestead and stock at Spruce creek, in *Kittery*.
129	Town grant of 30 acres by and in *Kittery*.
139	40 acre town grant by and in *Kittery*.
188	One-half the single saw-mill and appurtenances on Fall Mill brook, in *York*.
1	One-half in common of saw-mill and appurtenances, land and timber grants on the Mill river, in *Fulmouth*.
88	Mill-privilege and land, timber grant and meadow on the creek where Ellingham, Gail and Saywood formerly built mills.
151	One-fourth in common with Grantee of the corn and saw-mill in *York*, near where Henry Sayword's mills formerly stood.
152	22 acres at Bald Head, in *York*.
151	Corn and saw-mill and the land adjoining as far as Galloping Hill, and half a neck of land adjoining, in *York*.
112	All their interest derived from John Hull in and to Salmon falls, its timber and appurtenances, in *Berwick*.
136	10 acres known as the Fort field at Salmon Falls in *Berwick*.
102	600 acres (excepting 33¼ acres) lying in six parcels on both sides Little Newichewannock river, at Bonnibissie pond, at Totnock, at Broughton's marsh, at White's marsh and at Pipe-staff point; also the mill-privilege at Assabumbedoc falls, all in *Berwick*.
105	One-third in common and undivided of 600 acres lying in six parcels, on both sides Little Newichewannock river, at Bonnibissie pond, at Totnock, at Broughton's marsh, at White's marsh and Pipe-staff point (excepting 33¼ acres), also the mill privilege at Assabumbedoc falls, all in *Berwick*.

Index of Grantees.

Date.	Grantee.	Grantor.	Instrument.
1671, Apr. 6	PLAISTED, Roger, and John Hull	Thomas Clarke	Deed
1691, June 8	POPE, Richard	Pendleton Fletcher	Deed
1699, Aug. 23	PREY, Samuel	Elihu Gunnison	Deed
1700, Jan. 1	PRAY, Samuel	Job Alcock	Deed
	PREBLE, Abraham, see Arthur Bragdon, jun.		
1691, Feb. 10	PREBLE, John	John Winford	Deed
1697, Feb. 10	RAYNES, Nathaniel	Thomas Mo[o]re et ux.	Deed
1703, Apr. 31	REMICH, Joshua	Christian Remich et ux.	Condition'l Deed
1702, Dec. 5	ROADS, Thomas	Thos. Thompson	Deed
1703, Feb. 11	RHODES, Thomas	Joseph Hammond, junior	Deed
1699, May 24	ROBERTS, William	Town of Kittery	Grant
1701, Oct. 6	ROGERS, John	Rachel Rew et ux., and Mary Broughton Sarah Johnson, Rebecca Broughton	Deed
1702, May 26	ROGERS, John	Christopher Bamfield et ux.	Deed
1697, Apr. 7	ROGERS, Richard	Christopher Bamfield et ux.	Deed
1701, Nov. 13	RUCK, Samuel	John Croad et ux.	Deed

INDEX OF GRANTEES. 87

Folio.	Description.
21	The Salmon Fall grant on Great Newichewannock river, with two mills, buildings and appurtenances in *Berwick*.
58	60 to 80 acres called the Middle Neck, between Scadlock's river and Whale cove in *Winter Harbor*, [now *Biddeford*].
60	1½ acres, with dwelling-house, fronting 12 poles on Crooked lane, in *Kittery*.
85	50 acre town grant, adjoining Livingstone's land and Maxfield's marsh, in *York*.
145	5 acres adjoining Grantee's land on one side and on the three others to Grantor's land in *York*.
169	20 acres on the seabeach west of the river adjoining land formerly Mrs. Godfrey's, in *York*.
172	Homestead opposite the Boiling Rock, 10 acres woodland and 15 acres in Simmon's marsh, in *Kittery*, conditioned for support of Grantor and his wife.
149	15¼ acre town grant by and in *Kittery*.
176	30 acre town grant by and in *Kittery*.
139	40 acres, to be clear of other grants.
113	All rights as heirs of George Broughton in Salmon falls, on Great Newichewannock river in *Berwick*, with the mills and appurtenances.
154	Quitclaim to all additions belonging to lot below.
154	10 acres on the river between Grantee's and Peter Staple's lands in *Kittery*.
136	309 acres, farm at Broad cove, Casco Bay [*Yarmouth*], also 6 acres at South field, Salem

Index of Grantees.

Date.	Grantee.	Grantor.	Instrument.
1689, June 27	Sawyer, William	Peter Folsham et ux.	Deed
1687, July 20	Scammon, Humphrey	Joshua Atwater	Deed
1700, June 4	Scammon, Humphrey	John Tinny et ux.	Deed
1685, May 27 1686, Apr. 6	Scottow, Joshua	General Court of Massachusetts	Grant and Survey
1686, May 12	Scottow, Joshua	General Court of Massachusetts	Grant
1687, Nov. 1	Scottow, Joshua	Wm. Burregh [Burrage]	Release
1685, Feb. 25	Scottow, Thomas	John Start	Deed
1686, Mar. 9	Sheafe, Sampson	Benj. Blakeman	Deed
1701, June 28	Simpson, Daniel	John Partridge et ux.	Deed
1638, Mar. 13	Simpson, Henry	Colony of Agamenticus, by Wm. Hooke, Governor	Grant
1640, May 28	Simpson, Henry	Sir Ferdinando Gorges by Richard Vines, steward general	Grant
1688, June 16	Simpson, Henry	Jane Simpson, *alias* Bond	Conditional Deed
1699, May 24	Smith, Jacob	Town of Kittery	Grant
1701, May 16	Smith, Jacob	Stephen Tobey et ux.	Deed
	Smith, *alias* Gowen, see Gowen		

INDEX OF GRANTEES. 89

Folio.	Description.
148	One-half of the farm originally John Wadleigh's in *Wells*.
79	Saw-mill, site and appurtenances, timber grant, 50 acres upland adjoining the falls, and meadow below the mill, at Dunstan falls in *Scarborough*.
79	400 acres between Saco river and Goose-fair river along the sea, in *Saco*.
9	500 acres on Merriconeag neck [in *Harpswell*].
37	500 acres additional to the former grant in same place [*Harpswell*].
37	From an agreement by Grantee to convey marsh land in *Scarborough* and quitclaiming the land.
10	80 acres marsh on the north of Pigsgut river in *Scarborough*.
13.	One-third of the tract on east side of Saco river, part of Lewis and Bonighton's patent, with one-third of saw-mill on Saco river falls, containing 6000 acres, with timber grant of adjoining tract, in *Saco*.
110	House and land on the main river, bought of Hughes, between Rishworth and Penwill, in *York*.
74	Tract on north side of Agamenticus river and on west side of Bass creek, and a parcel of meadow in common with others near the head of the river, in *York*.
150	10 acres of marsh on the south side of Agamenticus river, opposite William Hooke's farm in *York*.
74	All estate derived from Grantor's father, Walter Norton, in *York*.
57	80 acres, to be clear of other grants.
96	One-half of Grantor's share of the tract bought of heirs of Thomas Clarke, in *Kittery*.

INDEX OF GRANTEES.

Date.	Grantee.	Grantor.	Instrument.
1702, Oct. 2	SNOW, Henry et ux.	Jonathan Nason's estate, by Sarah Nason, Adm'x	Survey
1703, June 14	SNOW, Henry et ux.	Jonathan Nason's estate, by Sarah Nason, Adm'x	Deed
1700, Sept. 7	SOUTHERINE, Elizabeth	Mary Wright	Deed
1689, Sept. 27	SPINNEY, James	Thomas Spinney et ux.	Deed
1699, Nov. 25	SPINNEY, John	Samuel Spinney et ux.	Deed
1702, Dec. 19	SPINNEY, John	James Spinney	Deed
1682, Mar. 23	SPINNEY, Samuel	Richard Carle et ux.	Deed
1686, Aug. 24	SPINNEY, Samuel	Samuel Knight	Deed
1700, June 12	SPINNEY, Samuel	Christian Remich	Deed
1700, June 12	SPINNEY, Samuel	Christian Remich	Bond
1700, Dec. 23	SPINNEY, Samuel	Thomas Spinney	Deed
1701, June 25	SPINNEY, Thomas	Samuel Fernald's estate, by Hannah Fernald, exec'x, and Nathaniel Fernald	Deed
1700, Dec. 24	SPINNEY, Thomas	Samuel Spinney	Deed
1702, Dec. 8	STAPLE, James	Daniel Fogg et ux.	Deed
1702, Dec. 8	STAPLE, James	Matthew Libby et ux.	Deed

Index of Grantees.

Folio.	Description.
171	Of the 13 acres next below conveyed.
171	18 acres on the brook [at Mast cove in Sturgeon creek] in *Kittery*.
75	Quitclaiming marsh on the west branch of York river between John Brown's and John Parker's, in *York*.
121	20 acres between Piscataqua river and Spruce creek, whereon Grantee's house stood in the lower part of *Kittery*.
65	40 acres between Great cove and Spruce creek, as per town grant by and in *Kittery*.
157	1 acre on Piscataqua river between John Spinney and Thomas Fernald, in *Kittery*.
23	3 acres on the north side of the Great cove in *Kittery*.
22	6 acres on the Great cove, in *Kittery*.
66	15½ acres with a frame and privilege of highway, adjoining Richard Kerle, Thomas Spinney, senior, the Grantee and John Dennet, senior, in *Kittery*.
66	In £100 conditioned not to sue Obligee, nor to molest him in the possession of the above premises.
98	8 acres near Great cove, whereon Grantee's house stood, in *Kittery*.
99	7 acres, the homestead of Samuel Fernald at the entrance of Pulpit Reach, at *Kittery* Point.
98	8 acres adjoining Grantee's old lot, behind Alcock, in *Kittery*.
155	40 acres, 16 poles along the highway, part of a tract purchased with others from the heirs of Thomas Clarke.
156	20 acres, part of my purchase with others, of the heirs of Thomas Clarke, in *Kittery*.

Index of Grantees.

Date.	Grantee.	Grantor.	Instrument.
1701, June 18	STAPLE, John	Peter Staple	Deed
1702, Apr. 15	STAPLE, John	Peter Staple et ux.	Deed
1702, June 8	STAPLE, John	Thomas Spinney et ux.	Deed
	STAPLE, Peter, see Joseph Hill		
1698, May 17	STONE, Jonathan	Daniel Gooding, (Goodwin) sen. et ux.	Deed
1701, Oct. 2	STORER, Joseph, and Samuel Hill John Batson	Nicholas Moorey	Deed
	STORER, Joseph, see John Batson		
1700, Sept. 11	STURGES, Thomas	Joseph Webber	Deed
1670, Oct. 4	SYMONDS, William	Harlakinden Symonds et ux.	Deed
1685, July 8	TALLER, William	John Buckland et ux.	Deed
	TALLER, see Taylor		
1696, Mar. 31	TAPPIN, Jacob	John Harris	Deed
1694, June 11	TAPPIN, Peter	Nathaniel Fuller	Deed
1684, June 9	TAYLOR, William	Nathan Littlefield	Deed
	TAYLOR, William, see Taller		
1703, Mar. 6	THOMAS, Roger	Benj. Hutchins	Deed

INDEX OF GRANTEES. 93

Folio.	Description.
97	30 acres adjoining Remick, Spinney and Tetherly, in *Kittery*.
133	30 acres in *Kittery* [either the same land as the above, or an adjoining parcel].
147	12 acres near the mast-ways in *Kittery*.
67	6 acres marsh on north side of Humphrey's pond, and 50 acres upland adjoining, in *Berwick*.
116	60 acres at Long creek, or Mast cove, on east side of Kennebunk river, bought of John Rennals; also town grant of 100 acres on same river, in *Cape Porpoise*.
143	One-seventh in common of a tract four miles along the west side of Kennebec river and between it and Winnegance river and land of William Baker on the north; also the whole of three lots in *Fulmouth ;* 60 acres at the head of Long creek; 2 acres on Queen street; 6 acres between Samuel York and Richard Pierce; also all his interest in Parker's Neck, in *Saco*.
112	400 acres in Coxhall, [now *Lyman*].
28	All his marsh on west side Kennebunk river, in *Wells*.
98	200 acres in common with other Coxhall proprietors, in what is now *Lyman*.
92	200 acres in the first division in *Coxhall*, [now *Lyman*].
165	100 acres as per town grant, near Kennebunk falls, in *Wells*.
172	10 acres in a triangle, part of a town grant of 30 acres, between York line and Spruce creek, in *Kittery*.

Index of Grantees.

Date.	Grantee.	Grantor.	Instrument.
1699, May 24	THOMSON, John	Town of Kittery	Grant
1694, Dec. 3	THOMPSON, Thomas	Miles Thompson et ux.	Condition'l Deed
1694, June 15	TITCOMB, William	Samuel Ingolls, senior	Deed
1702, June 2	TOBEY, Stephen	James Tobey	Deed
	TOBEY, Stephen, see Joseph Hammond		
1702, Oct. 9	TRIPE, Sylvanus	Joan Blackdon Grace Tucker et ux.	Deed
1708, Mar. 8	TUCKER, Nicholas	Wm. Pepperrell	Discharge
1699, Nov. 22	VAUGHAN, William	Andrew Brown	Deed
1701, June —	VAUGHAN, William	Henry Bodge	Levy on Execution
1699, Nov. 22	WADE, John	James Stagpoll	Deed
1700, Sept. 16	WADE, John	Humphrey Spencer	Deed
1701, Oct. 28	WADLEIGH, John	Robert Wadleigh senior	Deed
1699, Apr. 13	WALDEN, Nicholas	John Deament est. of, by Nathaniel Rayns John Woodman, admin'rs	Deed
1687, Mar. 26	WALKER, Samuel	Samson Sheafe	Deed

Index of Grantees.

Folio.	Description.
57	30 acres, to be clear of other grants.
45	80 acres homestead between the river and the commons and personal property, in *Berwick*, conditioned to pay Grantors part of the produce yearly.
92	100 acres in common with the Coxhall Proprietors, in what is now *Lyman*.
171	10 acres, half a town grant of 20 acres by and in *Kittery*.
146	10 acres, fronting 20 poles on the water-side at Crooked Lane, in *Kittery*.
163	Of mortgage recorded same folio.
72	100 acres upland and 50 acres salt marsh adjoining, being the neck of land formerly Henry Watts' at Black Point, in *Scarborough*.
120	Two tracts, one of 8 acres on north side of Spruce creek; the other of 20 acres in the woods, in *Kittery*.
61	$3\frac{1}{4}$ acres near the meeting-house on the way from the Great Works to the river in *Berwick*.
70	85 perches in a triangle between the country road and the way toward the Great Works, in *Berwick*.
134	Quitclaiming all rights to lands in *Wells* or *Kittery*.
90	40 acres with buildings at Crooked Lane in *Kittery*.
11	One-third in common of the tract on east side of Saco river, part of Lewis and Bonighton's patent, with one-third of the saw-mill on Saco river falls, containing 6000 acres, with timber grant of adjoining tract, in *Saco*.

Index of Grantees.

Date.	Grantee.	Grantor.	Instrument.
1701, Mar. 25	WARREN, Gilbert	James Warren, senior	Condition'l Deed
1686, May 26	WAYMOUTH, Edward	James Emery, senior, et ux.	Deed
	WAYMOUTH, Edward, see Thomas Greely		
1701, Feb. 17	WAYMOUTH, Timothy	Edward Waymouth et ux.	Deed
	WAYMOUTH, Timothy, see Thomas Greely		
1700, July 16	WEBBER, Joseph	Mary Webber	Deed
1694, May 16	WEEKS, Joseph	Town of Kittery	Grant
1702, May 20	WEEKS, Joseph	Jonathan Mendum et ux	Deed
1699, May 24	WEEKS, Nicholas	Town of Kittery	Grant
1702, Apr. 3	WELLS, John, and Thomas Wells, Patience Clark et ux., Sarah Libby	Each other	Division
	WELLS, Thomas, see John Wells		
1700, Nov. 28	WHEELWRIGHT, John	Benj. Gooch	Deed
	WHEELWRIGHT, John, see Samuel Wheelwright		
1699, Oct. 4	WHEELWRIGHT, Samuel, and John Wheelwright	Jonathan Littlefield	Bond
1678, Feb. 10	WHITE, Richard	Ephraim Crocket	Deed
1701, Jan. 2	WOODMAN, John	Nicholas Walden (Waldron)	Deed

Index of Grantees. 97

Folio.	Description.
97	40 acres on the east side of the river at York Bridge in *York*, charged with annual payment of 30 shillings.
83	30 acres upland and meadow at the head of Mast creek near Piscataqua river in *Berwick*.
170	10 acres at Nason's bridge over the brook running into Mast cove, in *Kittery*.
143	One-seventh in common of a tract four miles along the west side of Kennebec river and between it and Winnegance river and land of William Baker on the north.
98	Number of acres not specified.
163	25 acres at Turkey Point, on east side of Spruce creek, in *Kittery*.
98	30 acres, to be clear of other grants.
145	Of the estate of their father, John Wells, in *Wells*.
114	8 acres of marsh in several pieces on Little river near Birch Point, in *Wells*.
41	Conditioned to maintain a fence on division line, in *Wells*.
8	50 acres at head of Brave-boat harbor 50 rods wide and adjoining York bounds, in *Kittery*.
100	Land and house at Crooked lane opposite Withers' island, in *Kittery*.

Index of Grantees.

Date.	Grantee.	Grantor.	Instrument.
1703, Mar. 8	Woodman, John	Francis Raynes, senior	Deed
1701, July 6	Worster, Thomas	Thomas Spinney	Deed
1699, Nov. 7	Wright, Sarah	Philip Cooper	Power att'y
1680, June 3	Young, Rowland, junior	Rowland Young, senior, et ux.	Deed
1699, Jan. 23	Hill, Joseph	John Downing et ux.	Deed
1702, Dec. 18	Morrell, John	Nicholas Morrell	Deed

Folio.	Description.
158	300 acres on the east side of Brave-boat harbor, adjoining Mrs. Godfrey, in *York*.
99	5 acres, part of town grant of 15 acres between Great cove and Spruce creek, in *Kittery*.
108	General power, with revocation of a former one to his brother Joseph Cooper.
25	10 acres formerly part of Robert Knight's farm, in *York*.
91	Homestead on the Long Reach in Piscataqua river (excepting 3 acres) 10 acres of marsh; and a town grant of 40 acres (part laid out), in *Kittery*.
149 .	5 acres, part of town grant of 25 acres, by and in *Kittery*.

INDEX OF OTHER PERSONS.

Abbet, Abbot,
  John, 54, 55.
  Thomas, 55.
Adams, 98.
  Elizabeth, 142.
  George, 11.
  John, 39.
  Margaret, 99.
  Philip, 41.
  Samuel, 143.
  Thomas, 137.
Addington, Isaac, 32, 47, 103, 132, 173, 175.
Alcock, 98, 99.
  Job, 88, 128, 156.
  John, 31.
  Joseph, 31.
Alexander, Joseph, 72, 157, 158.
Alford, Benjamin, 89.
Allen,
  Benjamin, 136.
  Robert, 87.
Alline, Hope, 139.
Ameredith, John, 86.
Andros, Sir Edmund, 74, 131.
Appleton,
  John, 75.
  Samuel, 93.
Ardell, William, 175.
Ashby, Benjamin, 7.
Atkins, Thomas, 17, 140, 141.
Atkinson, Theodore, 35, 94, 128, 168, 169.
Austin, Matthew, 75, 83, 138, 176.
Averil, Averell,
  Paul, 160.
  Thomas, 142.

Bachellor, Mary, 166.
Baker,
  Sarah, 1.
  Thomas, 135.
  William, 143, 144.
Ballentine, John, 132.

Bane, Lewis, 97.
Banfield, Christopher, 55.
Banks,
  Joseph, 109.
  Richard, 108, 109.
Barfoot, Walter, 166, 173.
Barkwell, William, 77.
Barnard, Joseph, 4.
Barter,
  Henry, 34, 114.
  Sarah, 114.
Barton, James, 12.
Batting, William, 65.
Beal, Edward, 51, 138.
Beckham, Mary, 53.
Belcher, John, 122.
Berry, Joseph, 96.
Billing,
  John, 32.
  Joseph, 132.
Blachford, Francis, 43, 80.
Black,
  Daniel, 109, 152.
  Josiah, 126.
Blackey, Benjamin, 79.
Blackman, Blakeman, Benjamin, 11, 12, 79.
Blanne, John, 96.
Blasdall, Henry, 36.
Bodge, Elizabeth, 117.
Bolls, Mr., 116.
Bonighton, John, 11, 13.
Brackett, Anthony, 1.
Bradstreet, Simon, 22, 27.
Bragdon,
  Arthur, 15, 26, 74, 128.
  Arthur, junior, 51, 135.
  Arthur, senior, 51, 82.
  Samuel, 110.
  Samuel, senior, 128.
  Samuel, junior, 137.
Bragginton (Bragdon),
  Arthur, 83, 176.
  Goodman, 40.

INDEX OF OTHER PERSONS. 101

Bran, Ann, 42.
Brasey, William, 152.
Braun, Brawn, John, 90, 169.
Bray, John, 137.
Breaden, Willam, 48.
Bready, John, 115.
Broad, William, 61.
Brook, Peter, 115.
Broughton,
    George, 4, 22, 30, 136.
    Thomas, 21, 84, 121.
Brown,
    Andrew, 128, 131, 132.
    Bartholomew, 140.
    Benjamin, 140, 141.
    John, 48, 75.
    Nathaniel (?) 135.
    Susanna, 135.
    William, 141.
Bryar, Briar,
    Richard, 85, 94, 149, 164.
    William, 86, 153.
Buckland, John, junior, 167.
Burkis, Walter, 126.
Burnum,
    Nathaniel, 135.
    Samuel, 53.
Burrage, William, 2, 131, 132.
Bush, John, 112, 135.
Butler, Thomas, 53.

Came, 98.
Card, Goodman, 40.
Carle, see Kirle.
Carr, William, 48.
Carter, Richard, 23.
Carthero, John, 112.
Cash, William, 136.
Chadborn, Humphrey, 121.
Chamberlain, R., 157.
Champernoun, Champernowne,
    Francis, 42, 88, 94, 153, 159, 173.
    Mary, 42, 56, 57.
Clark, 82, 83.
    Elizabeth, 35.
    John, 169.
    Jonathan, 2.
    Nathaniel, 114.
    Thaddeus, 3.
    Thomas, 63, 88.
Clearb, error for Clarke, 35.

Cleeves, George, 139, 140.
Clements, Richard, 131.
Cock, Cox,
    Edward, 40.
    John, 141, 167.
    Thomas, 141, 166.
    William, 141.
Coffin, Peter, 134.
Cole, 121.
    George, 121.
    John, 121.
    Nicholas, 5, 35, 165.
    Thomas, 95.
Conly, Abraham, 53, 144.
Cooke,
    Doctor, 121.
    Elisha, 48.
    John, 174.
Cooper,
    John, 53.
    Joseph, 108.
    Philip, 108, 109.
Cornish, Richard, 150.
Corwin, Jonathan, 136.
Cotton,
    Solomon, 86.
    William, 72.
Couch, Ann, 39.
Coward, John Harb[er]t, 173.
Cox, see Cock.
Crafford, John, 121.
Cranch, Andrew, 169.
Crap, Walter, 158.
Creasie, Cresy, Crusy, Crucy,
    George, 57, 158.
    Patience, 59.
    Richard, 163.
Credifer, Rachel, 154.
Crockett,
    Ephraim, 23, 32.
    Thomas, 32.
Croker, Richard, 152.
Cross,
    Joseph, 48.
    Richard, 49.
Crosslee, Henry, 35.
Crowder, John, 163.
Curtice, Curtis, 78.
    Benjamin, 146.
    Dodevah, 90.
    Job, 124.

Index of Other Persons.

Curtice, Curtis, continued.
  Joseph, 78, 108, 120, 138.
  Thomas, 108, 109, 124.
  William, 136.
Cushing, Thomas, 182.
Cutt,
  Mr., 4, 85, 93.
  Richard, 41, 56.
  Robert, 86, 146.

Daniel, Bridget, 149.
Davenport, Additon, 62.
Davis,
  John, 40, 45, 79, 96, 125, 145.
  Major, 124, 128.
  Nicholas, 75.
  Samuel, 48.
  Sylvanus, 9, 10.
Deament, Diament.
  John, 100.
  William, 86, 146.
Dearing, Joan, 80.
Denis, Lawrence, 141.
Dennison, George, 50.
Dennett,
  John, senior, 66.
  Mehitabel, 114.
Dill,
  Daniel, 124, 135.
  Elizabeth, 135.
  Joseph, 135.
  William, 135.
Dixon, Peter, 100.
Dongan, Thomas, 58.
Donnell,
  Ali[c]e, 119.
  John, 80.
  Samuel, 51, 82, 83, 108, 119, 120, 123, 124, 125, 126, 127, 129, 145, 152, 169.
  Thomas, 128.
Dorman, Timothy, 135.
Downing,
  Joshua, 89, 146, 151, 155, 156.
  Patience, 146.
Drown, Leonard, 55.
Dummer,
  Jeremiah, 48, 62, 64, 176.
  Mr. 51.
Durram, Humphrey, 2.

Earle, see Hearle,
  John, 70.
  William, 69, 170.
Edwards, Robert, 140.
Ellingham, Ellinggam, 82, 83.
  William, 101.
Elliot, Robert, 72, 176.
Ellis, Richard, 113.
Elkins, Henry, 11, 77.
Elwell, Hezekiah, 153.
Emery,
  Daniel, 67, 70, 71, 84, 170, 171.
  James, 42, 69, 70, 160, 161, 162, 171.
  Job, 67.
  Samuel, 116, 167.
Emerson, James, 116.
Eme[r]son, John, 46, 84, 95, 102, 104, 106, 129.
Endicot,
  Gilbert, 49, 145.
  John, 139.
Endle, 154.
  Michael, 168.
  Richard, 127, 128, 138.
Epes, Daniel, junior, 95.
Esmond, Sarah, 153.
Etherinton, Thomas, 101.
Evans, John, 88.
Everet, Isaac, 41.
Eyre, John, 49.

Fairweather, Benjamin, 35.
Fenich, John, 138.
Fernald,
  Captain, 78, 84.
  Hannah, 98, 100.
  James, 84.
  John, 23, 71, 134.
  Mary, 157.
  Samuel, 41, 98.
  Thomas, 20, 83, 84, 157.
  William, 59.
  William, senior, 86.
Fletcher,
  Pendleton, 59.
  Seth, 7.
Fluellin, Indian, 135.
Fogg, Daniel, 96, 118.
Fo[o]llet, Hannah, 163.
Ford, John, 59.

INDEX OF OTHER PERSONS. 103

Forguson, Widow, 101.
Fost, Jemima, 170.
Foster, 89.
Fowler, Philip, 93.
Fox, Jabez, 22.
Freeman,
  Alice, 143.
  Nathaniel, 75, 119, 143, 145, 148.
Frethy,
  James, 176,
  Widow, 110.
Frost,
  Charles, 28, 45, 53, 67, 87, 101, 102.
  John, 44.
  Major, 43, 80, 87.
  Mary, 113.
  Nicholas, 38, 87, 113.
  William, 141.
Fryer, Nathaniel, 82, 168.
Furbish William, 101.

Gail, 82, 83.
Gard, Roger, 74.
Garland, Jabez, 160.
Geare,
  John, 147.
  Sarah, 147.
Gerrish,
  John, 62, 64.
  Timothy, 61.
Gibbens, James, 11, 13.
Gidding,
  George, 32.
  John, 32.
Gidney, Bartholomew, 7.
Gillam, Zachariah, 61, 62, 63, 64.
Gilman,
  Edward, 163.
  William, 163.
Godfrey, Mrs., 158, 169.
Godsoe,
  William, 39, 42, 44, 60, 65, 85, 90, 94, 98, 99, 100, 150, 153, 154, 162, 163, 166, 167, 172.
  William, senior, 154.
Gooch, James, 83, 116.
Gooding, Goodwin, 147.
  Daniel, senior, 46, 67, 69, 101, 102, 104, 106, 129, 147, 160.
  Daniel, junior, 67.
  James, 147.

Gooding, Goodwin, continued.
  Thomas, 61, 67, 68, 69, 147.
Goodridge,
  Isaac, 44.
  Josiah, 67.
Gorges,
  Sir Ferdinando, 27, 78, 167, 174.
  Thomas, 150.
Gowen,
  Elizabeth, 45.
  John, 160, 170.
  Lemuel, 45, 171.
  Mercy, 111.
  Nicholas, 39, 60, 170, 171, 172.
  Sarah, 45.
  William, 43, 45.
Gowen, *alias* Smith,
  Elizabeth, 117.
  William, 70, 117.
Graffort,
  Bridget, 149.
  Thomas, 149.
Grant,
  Hannah, 51.
  James, 51, 77.
  Peter, 44, 67.
  Roger, 168.
Green, John, 65, 67, 91.
Greenland, Henry, 61, 159.
Griffin, Mary, 7.
Grover, Jotham, 178.
Gunnison,
  Elizabeth, 59.
  Hugh, 154.
  Mr. 153.

Hales, Richard, 168.
Haley, Hallye, Andrew, 61, 127.
Hall, Kinsley, 69.
Hamans, Edmund, 95, 96, 120.
Hammond,
  Benjamin, 154.
  Elizabeth, 167.
  Goodman, 142.
  Hannah, 56, 60, 72, 77.
  Jonathan, 5, 25, 41, 48, 49, 50, 107.
  Jonathan, junior, 168.
  Joseph, 20, 28, 88–177.
  Joseph, junior, 43, 52, 57, 71, 81, 82, 90, 91, 92, 114, 119, 139, 151, 170.

104   INDEX OF OTHER PERSONS.

Hammond, continued.
　Katherine, 172.
　Mary, 117.
　Mercy, 81.
　Mrs., 43.
　William, 25.
Hanchinson, for Hutchinson.
Hancock, John, 51, 83, 124.
Hareis, John, 92.
Harmon, Lydia, 157.
Harper, Thomas, 108.
Harris,
　Joseph, 176.
　Thomas, 16.
Harrison, Trustrum, 70, 71, 171.
Hart, Thomas, 93.
Harwood, Henry, 169.
Hatch, Widow, 51.
Hatherly, Henry, 76.
Hathorn,
　Ebenezer, 65.
　John, 65, 95, 141.
　John, junior, 65.
Hayman, Samuel, 76, 143.
Hayward, Howard, John, 18, 27, 139, 165.
Heard,
　James, 45, 100.
　John, 38, 43, 87.
Hearle, see Earle.
　John, 70.
　William, 69.
Hellson, John, senior, 6.
Hening, Shubael, 128.
Heskins, Nicholas, 72, 94, 166.
Higgins, Beriah, 38.
Higginson, John, jun., 141.
Hill,
　Captain, 122.
　John, 50, 85.
　Joseph, 50.
　Peter, 6.
　Roger, 7.
　Samuel, 28, 39.
　William, 173.
Hillard, Ed: 136.
Hilton,
　Edward, 166.
　John, 166.
　Richard, 91.
　Samuel, 157, 166.

Hilton, continued.
　William, 34, 158.
　William, jun., 157.
Hinckes, John, 4, 23, 94, 159.
Hodsden,
　Benoni, 45.
　Israel, 115.
Holloway, Malachi, 48.
Homes, 110.
Hooke,
　Captain, 34.
　Francis, 9, 21, 23, 34, 45, 58, 59, 61, 96, 137, 169.
　Major, 60.
　Mary, 9, 58, 127.
　William, 34, 110, 128, 137, 150.
Houghton, Mr., 10.
Howell, John, 37.
Hubart, Mr., 60.
Hubord, Philip, 70, 161, 162.
Hughs,
　Arthur, 110.
　Sarah, 110.
Hull,
　John, 63, 112.
　Mr., 119.
　Phineas, 72.
Hunniwell, Richard, 72, 74.
Hunscomb,
　Moses, 172.
　Thomas, 96, 118, 151, 155, 156.
Hurry, William, 76.
Hutchinson,
　Eliakim, 104, 105, 106, 129, 130, 131.
　Elisha, 89, 91, 96, 118.
　Elizabeth, 89, 91, 96, 118.
　William, 46, 62, 63, 64, 102, 103, 104, 105, 106, 129, 130.
Hutchins, Samuel, 172.
Hutchings, David, 120.

Ingarson, see Ingersoll.
Ingersoll,
　George, 60.
　George, junior, 2.
　John, senior, 153, 154.
　John, junior, 153.

Jackson,
　Clement, 61.

Index of Other Persons.

Jackson, continued.
  Daniel, 115.
  John, 157.
Jefferies, Francis, 144.
Jinkins,
  Reinold, 44.
  Robert, 14.
Johnson,
  Andrew, 11.
  Edward, 88.
  Eliezer, 75, 109, 112, 129.
  Francis, 27.
  James, 52, 127.
  Mr., 52.
  Samuel, 78, 120, 126.
Jones,
  Daniel, 85, 94.
  Deborah, 73.
  Thomas, 88.
Jordan,
  Deborah, 78.
  Dominicus, 9.
  Jeremiah, 78.
  Robert, 8, 73.
Joslin, Abraham, 131.
Joy, Ephraim, 53, 61.
Judd, Jonathan, 47, 48.
Junkins, Goodman, 176.

Keais, Samuel, 149.
Kemble, Thomas, 19, 88.
Kennard, Edward, 94.
Kent, John, 111.
Kettle, Sarah, 143.
Key,
  Hannah, 40, 77, 91, 95, 98, 119, 133, 136, 148.
  John, 40.
King,
  Mary, 39, 162.
  Richard, 38, 162.
  Samuel, 39.
Kirle, Kerle, see Carle,
  Richard, 22, 23, 66.
Knap, Peter, 30.
Knight,
  Ezekiel, 167.
  Robert, 25, 26.
  Sarah, 167.
Knock, Sylvanus, 161, 162.
Knowles, Mr. 88.

Lake, Thomas, 21, 22, 80.
Landall, William, 172.
Lead, John, 26.
Leader,
  George, 175.
  Mr., 4.
  Richard, 122, 175.
Lee, John, 173.
Leighton, John, 43.
Leverett, John, 21.
Levitt, Samuel, 148.
Lewis,
  Andrew, 117.
  George, 8.
  Lucy, 168.
  Peter, junior, 168.
Libby,
  David, 96, 118.
  John, 65.
  Matthew, 96, 118, 155.
Lissen, Lisson, 91.
  Waymouth, 133.
Littlefield,
  Daniel, 116.
  Dependence, 155.
  Edmund, 141, 167.
  Francis, 40, 107, 167.
  Francis, junior, 141, 142.
  Joseph, 144, 168.
  Nathan, 36.
  Rebecca, 141.
  Thomas, 142, 167.
Livingstone, Daniel, 26, 85, 124.
Lockwood, 61.
Lord,
  Abraham, 4, 55.
  Martha, 53.
  Nathan, 53, 54, 55, 70, 101, 102, 144, 160, 161.
  Robert, junior, 93.
  William, 136
Lowle, John, 165.
Lurton, Robert, 142.
Lynde, Simon, 164.

Macgoune, John, 115.
Mackenny, John, 65.
Makerty, Thaddeus, 27.
Manly, William, 89.
March,
  James, 123.

106   Index of Other Persons.

March, continued.
  Mary, 123.
Markue, Timothy, 45.
Marshall, John, 77.
Marston, John, junior, 141.
Mason,
  Arthur, junior, 62, 63.
  John, 46, 103, 105, 130, 174.
  Robert Tufton, 46, 103, 104, 105, 130, 131, 147.
  Samuel, 50.
Mathews, Walter, 168.
Mattocks, Samuel, 112.
Maverick,
  Antipas, 162, 163.
  Samuel, 74.
Maxell, Alexander, 14, 15.
Maxfield, Alexander, 85.
Mendum,
  Jonathan, 90.
  Robert, 163, 164.
Middleton, Matthew, 13.
Milberry, Henry, 31.
Milborne, William, 79.
Miller, Samuel, 133.
Mills,
  Edward, 176.
  Thomas, 148.
Mitten, Mitton, Michael, 2, 139, 140.
Monson, Samuel, 118.
Moody,
  Caleb, senior, 93.
  Eliezer, 12, 108, 112, 132.
  Samuel, 90.
Moore, 45.
  Dorothy, 45.
  John, 34, 169.
  Richard, 65.
  William, 169.
Morrell, John, 87, 121, 161.
Morton, John, 37.
Moulton, Molton,
  Jeremiah, 14, 77, 152.
  Joseph, 125.
Munjoy, George, 3.

Nason,
  Jonathan, 54, 55, 171.
  Richard, 46, 67, 69, 102, 104, 106, 129, 175.

Neal, Neale,
  Amy, 55.
  Francis, 3, 8.
Negus, Isaac, 124.
Nelson,
  Charles, 91.
  Lydia, 57.
Newcomb, Simon, 140, 141.
Newmarch, John, 43, 59, 80, 81, 82.
Newton, Thomas, 174.
Nicholls, Robert, 79.
Nock see Knock.
Norton,
  Jane, 74.
  Walter, 74.
Nowell, Peter, 67.
Noyce, Cutting, 93.

Oliver, William, 168.

Packer, Thomas, 38, 77, 164, 166.
Paddy, Thomas, 165.
Paige, Nicholas, 175.
Palmer,
  George, 61.
  John, 58.
Parker,
  Abraham, 128.
  George, 111, 112.
  John, 41, 75, 143.
Parsons,
  John, 74,
  William, 48.
Paul,
  Daniel, 166.
  Stephen, 162, 172.
Pearce, Pearse, Pierce,
  Daniel, 72, 93, 111.
  John, 61.
  Leuing (Living?), 65.
  Richard, 144.
Pearson, George, 142.
Pemberton, Joseph, 50.
Pendleton,
  Brian, 7, 50, 62, 63, 64.
  Joseph, 50.
Penhallow,
  Joshua, 127.
  Samuel, 60, 66, 73, 81, 86, 88, 105, 107, 131, 149, 157, 163, 166.
Pennel, John, 90.

Penny,
　Henry, 86.
　Thomas, 38.
Penwill, John, 40, 79, 110, 145.
Pepperrell,
　Andrew, 43, 138.
　William, 42, 43, 80, 83, 90, 92, 114, 117, 120, 127, 147, 154, 158, 164, 166, 167.
Phillips,
　Bridget, 61, 62, 63, 64.
　John, 112.
　Major, 112.
　William, 50, 61, 62, 63, 64, 92, 93.
Phipps,
　Joseph, 76.
　Samuel, 76, 143.
　Thomas, 66.
Pickerin,
　John, senior, 53, 72, 78, 88, 127, 135, 156.
　John, 53, 125, 127.
　John, junior, 135.
Picket, Christopher, 65.
Pierce, see Pearce.
Pike, Robert, 148.
Plaisted,
　Elizabeth, 156.
　Ichabod, 85, 144, 160, 170, 171.
　James, 51, 82, 152.
　John, 40, 53, 55, 61, 70, 71, 85, 122, 138, 147, 158, 160.
　Olive, 113.
　Roger, 113, 120, 156.
　Roger, junior, 46, 102, 104, 106, 120, 129.
Pousland, Richard, 3.
Preble,
　Abraham, 42, 75, 82, 83, 90, 97, 108, 109, 110, 115, 125, 128, 135, 137, 143, 151, 152, 165, 176.
　Abraham, junior, 75, 109, 126, 129, 145, 151, 152.
　John, 41, 74.
　Nathaniel, 123, 126.
　Stephen, 123.
Presbury, Nathan, 49.
Price, John, 30.
Pride, John, 47, 48.
Puddenton, George, 123.

Rackliff, William, 97, 133.
Rainking, Constant, 77.
Ramich, see Remick
Randall, William, 76, 77.
Randolph, Edward, 18, 32, 37.
Rawson, Edward, 9.
Raynes,
　Nathaniel, 100, 125.
　Nathaniel, senior, 158.
Remick,
　Abraham, 147.
　Christian, 22, 23, 28.
　Isaac, 71.
　Jacob, 38, 66, 84, 90, 92, 97, 134, 155, 171.
　Joshua, 97, 121, 133, 171.
Renols, John, 117.
Rhodes, Thomas, 45.
Rice,
　Mary, 118, 149.
　Thomas, 44, 52, 118, 149.
Richards, John, 80.
Rider, Phenik, 3.
Rindge, Daniel, 59.
Rishworth, Rushworth, Edward, 15, 16, 19, 26, 29, 75, 110, 115.
Roads, Jacob, 149.
Roberts, Elizabeth, 134.
Robinson,
　Daniel, 52.
　John, senior, 141.
Rogers,
　John, 97, 111.
　Richard, 155.
　William, 38, 117, 170.
Rones,
　Mary, 175.
　William, 175, 176.
Rowles, Indian, 121.
Rushford, see Rishworth, 82, 83, 123.
Russell, Richard, 21.

Samson, John, 73.
Sanders,
　John, 135.
　William, 43.
Sargent,
　Edward, 72, 111.
　Peter, 112.
Saturly, Robert, 58.

Savery, Samuel, 61.
Sayer,
  Joseph, 145, 146.
  Sarah, 117.
  William, 5, 117.
Saywood, Sayward, 109.
  Henry, 82, 83, 151.
  John, 15.
  Mary, 15, 25.
Scamonds, Mary, 128.
Scottow,
  Joshua, 37, 65, 80.
  Thomas, 1-37, 77.
Scottoway, see Scottow.
Scriven,
  Aaron, 81, 82.
  William, 86.
Sealey,
  Richard, 6.
  William, 168.
Searle, Andrew, 101.
Sewall,
  Samuel, 62, 63, 108, 132, 135.
  Stephen, 140, 141.
Shapleigh,
  Alexander, 38.
  John, 19, 52, 108.
  Major, 61.
  Nicholas, 18, 19, 43.
Sharp, James, 41.
Shelding (Sheldon), William, 65.
Sheppard,
  John, 100.
  John, senior, 134, 150.
  John, junior, 100.
  T., 79.
Shory, Samuel, 149.
Simmons, John, 133, 157, 166.
Simpson,
  Daniel, 125.
  Henry, 74, 176.
Skillin,
  John, 2, 144.
  Samuel, 154.
Skid, James, 159.
Smaley, Samuel, 72.
Small,
  Francis, 164.
  Samuel, 45, 160.
Smith,
  Edward, 148.

Smith, continued.
  Jacob. 151.
  James, 124.
  Joseph, 90, 126.
  Mercy, 60.
  William, 117.
Smith, *alias* Gowen, see under Gowen.
Snell,
  George, 31.
  Thomas, 168.
Snow, Samuel, 111.
Sosowen, Indian, 135.
Spencer,
  Humphrey, 61, 69, 122.
  John, 152.
  Patience, 68.
  Thomas, 68, 69, 121, 122.
  William, 61.
Spinney,
  James, 65, 97, 100, 133, 147.
  John, 28, 66, 98, 100, 121, 122, 147, 148.
  Mary, 99.
  Samuel, 66, 91, 97, 99, 118, 133.
  Thomas, 28, 38, 84, 121, 157.
  Thomas, senior, 65, 66.
  Thomas, junior, 64.
Stacie,
  Mehitable, 171.
  William, 115, 136, 177.
Stackpole, Stagpole,
  James, 69, 97.
  Margaret, 69.
Staples, 65.
  John, 155, 156.
  Mary, 97.
  Peter, 91, 97, 154.
  Peter, senior, 133.
  Peter, junior, 133.
Start, Edward, 110.
Stewart, John, 92.
Stileman, Elias, 20.
Stone,
  Benjamin, 7.
  Daniel, 69, 122, 161, 162.
  Patience, 128.
Stoodleigh, James, 122.
Storer,
  Hannah, 57, 72.
  Mary, 90, 92.

INDEX OF OTHER PERSONS. 109

Story, Charles, 39, 105, 107, 131, 164.
Stoughton, William, 12, 36, 84.
Suite, Zachariah, 18.
Sweat, Sarah, 169.
Symonds,
  Harlakinden, 92, 93.
  Priscilla, 113.
  Samuel, 113.

Tappin, Jacob, 93.
Taylor,
  George, 10, 182.
  James 92.
Tetherly,
  Gabriel, 71.
  William, 97, 133.
Thacher,
  John, 144.
  Lydia, 144.
Thaurley, Thomas, 35.
Thomas, Captain, 42.
Thompson, Tompson,
  Edward, 45, 101, 102, 160.
  John, 100.
  Thomas, 70.
  William, 74.
Thwing, Benjamin, 139.
Tilton, Abraham, 142.
Tobey, Stephen, 118, 151.
Tompson, see Thompson.
Townsend, Penn, 113.
Tozer, Toziar, Richard, 80, 145.
Trazon, Joseph, 174.
Treworgy,
  James, 38, 170.
  Katherine, 101.
Trott, John, 107.
Trundey, George, 168.
Tucker,
  Francis, 147, 168.
  Jane, 127.
  Nicholas, 42, 153.
  Richard, 8.
Tufton, Robert, 159.
Turbut, Peter, 112, 135.
Turfrey, Edward, 47, 103.
Twisden,
  John, 16, 31.
  Peter, 133.
  Samuel, 108, 109.

Tyler, Jonathan, 169.
Tyng,
  Edward, 1, 2, 3, 9, 10, 11, 18, 25, 31, 35, 37, 165.
  Edward, senior, 63.
  Elizabeth, 2, 3.

Usher, John, 19, 35, 92.

Valentine, John, 62, 64.
Vaughan, William, 54, 55.
V[e]rgouss, Isaac, 165.
Vines, Richard, 78.

Waddock,
  Henry, 80.
  Jane, 80.
Wade,
  Elizabeth, 42.
  John, 42, 68, 70, 71, 97, 121, 147.
Wadleigh,
  Henry, 134.
  John, 148.
  Jonathan, 134.
  Robert, 148.
Wakefield,
  James, 115.
  Rebecca, 115.
Waldron, Richard, 100.
Walley, John, 132.
Wallis, Nathaniel, 136.
Ware, Joseph, 110, 128, see Wier.
Warren,
  Gilbert, 126.
  James, 67, 68, 69, 125, 171.
  James, junior, 67, 68.
  Mehitable, 89, 91, 96, 118, 151, 155, 156.
Watkins, Thomas, 159.
Watts, Henry, 10, 72.
Waymouth, 144.
  Edward, 115, 171.
Weare, Elias, 124.
Webb, 82, 83.
  Joseph, 62, 63.
  Thomas, 107.
Webber,
  Lydia, 58.
  Mary, 144.
  Samuel, 138, 151.

Index of Other Persons.

Weeks,
  Joseph, 149.
  Nicholas, 137.
Wells,
  John, 114, 145.
  Thomas, 114, 146.
West, John, 74, 159, 165.
Wethers, see Withers.
Wheelwright,
  John, 6, 49, 116, 117, 131, 146, 165, 168.
  Mr. 107.
  Samuel, 5, 6, 13, 29, 49, 50, 107, 116, 117, 124, 138, 142, 165, 167.
  Samuel, junior, 6.
Whidden, Michael, 56.
Whipple, Mary, 91.
White, John, 38.
Wier, Joseph, 82, 83, see Ware.
Wiggens,
  James, 32, 169.
  Thomas, 159.
Williams,
  Lewis, 45.
  Matthew, 150.
  Rowland, 120, 172.
Wilson,
  John, 21.
  Joseph, 21, 127.
Wincoll,
  Captain, 8, 55, 87, 98, 127.

Wincoll, continued.
  John, 21, 23, 38, 44, 46, 65, 69, 79, 87, 100, 101, 102, 104, 106, 113, 121, 127, 129, 156, 175.
Winthford, John, 145.
Winthrop, Wait, 8.
Withers,
  Elizabeth, 149.
  Mary, 149.
  Mr., 86.
  Thomas, 52, 85, 90, 93, 95, 96, 149.
Wittum, Peter, 52, 53, 121.
Wittup, Paul, 144.
Woodbridge, Benjamin, 137.
Woodman, John, 42, 96, 162.
Wooster, Worster, Worcester,
  Thomas, 134.
  William, 122, 135.
Wright, Hannah, 114.

York,
  Benjamin, 145.
  Samuel, 144.
Young,
  Israel, 134.
  Job, 90.
  Richard, 76, 77.
  Rowland, 152.

Surname not given,
  Edward, 111.

INDEX OF PLACES.

Agamenticus, 74, see York.
Accamenticus river, 74, 150, see York river.
Amesbury, Mass., 35.

Barbadoes island, 150.
Barnstable county, Mass., 143, 144.
Berwick, 4, 29, 38, 41, 45, 61, 67, 68, 69, 70, 83, 84, 97, 101, 121, 147, 160, 170.
   commons, 4, 45, 46, 102, 104, 106, 129.
   Assabumbedock falls, 46, 102, 104, 106, 129.
   Birch Point, 156, 161.
   Bonnibissie pond, 46, 102, 104, 106, 129.
   Broughton's swamp, 71, 102, 104, 106, 129.
   Fort field, 136.
   Ferguson's bridge, 101.
   Great works, 61, 69.
   Humphrey's pond, 67.
   Mast cove, 170.
   Mast creek, 84, 170.
   Meeting-house, 46, 61.
   Nason's bridge, 170.
   Newichewannock, 83, 109, 121, 122.
   Newichewannock river, 4, 61, 101, 104, 106, 121, 174, 175.
   Great, 21, 118.
   Little, 46, 102, 104, 129, 175.
   Pipe-stave point, 46, 102, 104, 106, 129, 175.
   Post Wigwam, 4.
   Quamphegan, 121.
   Rocky hill, 67.
   Salmon falls, 22, 136.
   Salmon falls river, 121, 136.
   Slut's corner, 147.
   Stony brook, 160.
   Totnock, 46, 102, 104.

Berwick, continued.
   Unity parish, 69.
   White's marsh, 46, 102, 104, 106, 129.
   Wilcock's pond, 68.
Beverly, Mass., 136.
Boston, Mass., 1, 3, 9, 11, 13, 16, 21, 32, 34, 35, 37, 46, 47, 48, 49, 61, 62, 63, 64, 66, 74, 78, 79, 88, 89, 91, 102, 108, 109, 110, 111, 112, 113, 128, 131, 132, 145, 159, 165, 173, 174, 175, 176.
Bristol county, Mass., 48, 50, 111, 116.

Cambridge, Mass., 26.
Cape Elizabeth, 169.
Cape Porpoise, 49, 50, 76, 77, 92, 93, 95, 111, 112, 116, 117, 139.
   river, 50.
   Gillum's point, 49.
   Little river, 76.
   Long creek or Mast cove, 49.
   Prince's rock, 76, 77.
Casco or Casco bay, 1, 2, 8, 37, 136, 139, 144, 164, see Falmouth.
   river, 2, 3, 8.
   Point of rocks, 8.
Chadwell, England, 159.
Charlestown, Mass., 1, 50, 76, 143, 144.
Connecticut, see Stratford.
Cornwall county, 58.
Coxhall, now Lyman, 92, 93, 112, 135.

Damariscotta river, 58.
Devon county, England, 174.
Dorchester, England, 121.
Dorset county, England, 121.
Dover, N. H., 29, 30, 61, 91, 158.

Index of Places.

East Greenwich, England, 175.
England, see Chadwell, Devon county, Dorchester, Dorset county, East Greenwich, Foxhall, Holbourn, Kent county, London, Middlesex county, Plymouth, Shadwell, St. Andrew, Suffolk county, Westminister.
Essex county, Mass., 64, 75, 92, 93, 95, 111, 112, 134, 135, 136, 139, 140, 141, 167.
Exeter, N. H., 27, 134, 148, 157, 158, 162, 166.

Falmouth, 1, 2, 3, 9, 35, [140], 144, 164, see Casco.
  Back cove, 2, 8.
  Long creek, 144.
  Long marsh, 2.
  Mill river, 1.
  Neck, 2.
  Nonesuch point, 35.
  Queen street, 144.
  Round marsh, 2.
Feversham, *alias* Westerly, R. I., 50.
Foxhall, England, 121.

Gloucester, Mass., 135.
Great Island, N. H., 20.

Hampton, N. H., 37.
Harpswell.
  Crooked lane or (Little river), 9.
  Merriconeag neck, 9.
  Pulpit island, 9.
  Sandy point, 9, 10.
Holbourn, England, 121.

Ipswich, Mass., 75, 92, 93, 95, 112, 135, 167.
Isles of Shoals, 146, 168.
  Malaga island, 168.
  Smutty-nose island, 168.

Jamestown, 58.
  Bread and Cheese island, 58.
  Buckland's neck, 58.
  Corbett's sound, 58.

Kennebec, 143.
Kennebec river, 141, 143, 144, 174.
Kennebunk, 24, see Wells.
  river, 24, 29, 49, 117.
  falls, 165.
  Second sands, 24.
Kent county, England, 175.
Kittery, 4, 8, 18, 19, 20, 21, 22, 23, 28, 30, 31, 32, 38, 39, 42, 43, 44, 46, 51, 52, 53, 54, 55, 56, 57, 58, 59, 60, 61, 65, 66, 67, 68, 69, 70, 71, 72, 77, 78, 79, 80, 81, 84, 85, 86, 87, 88. 89, 90, 91, 92, 93, 95, 96, 97, 98, 99, 100, 101, 102, 103, 104, 106, 108, 111, 112, 113, 114, 115, 117, 118, 119, 120, 121, 122, 127, 129, 133, 134, 136, 138, 139, 144, 146, 147, 149, 150, 151, 153, 154, 155, 156, 157, 158, 159, 160, 161, 162, 163, 164, 166, 167, 168, 169, 170, 171, 172, 173, 175, 176, 177.
  bounds, 137.
  commons, 38, 43, 60, 70, 87, 101, 115, 160, 164.
  Barren marsh, 44.
  Berry's island, 90.
  Boiling rock, 172.
  Brave-(Broad-)boat harbor, 8, 32, 78, 82, 164.
  creek, 32.
  Bryant's point, 154.
  Champernown's island, 81, 82, 94.
  Crocket's creek, 137.
  Crooked lane, 60, 85, 86, 90, 93, 146.
  Eagle point, 96.
  Fernald's island, 20.
  Frank's Fort, 89.
  Great cove, 22, 23, 38, 65, 84, 86, 98, 99, 100, 121, 149.
  Hammond's swamp, 43.
  Heard's swamp, 43.
  Mast cove, 115, 144.
  Mast-way, 147.
  Ox point, 118.
  Pulpit reach, 99.
  Spinney's cove, 38.

Index of Places. 113

Kittery, continued.
  Spruce creek, 21, 42, 52, 60, 65, 78, 84, 85, 93, 100, 118, 120, 121, 127, 153, 154, 158, 159, 163, 164, 172, 173.
    Eastern creek in 52, 95, 96.
    Little cove in 52.
    Western creek in 52.
  Stepping Stones, 61.
  Sturgeon creek, 18, 19, 38, 44, 53, 54, 55, 60, 80, 87, 150, 162, 163.
  Turkey point, 164.
  Watts' Fort, 89.
  Withers' island, 149.
  Woodman's ferry, 85, 93.
  York line, 172.
  York road, 44.

London, England, 46, 103, 105, 130, 159, 174, 175.
Lyman, see Coxhall.
Lynn, Mass, 64.

Massachusetts: see Amesbury, Barnstable county, Beverly, Boston, Bristol county, Cambridge, Charlestown, Essex county, Gloucester, Ipswich, Lynn, Middlesex county, Newbury, Newton, Norfolk county, Rumney Marsh, Salem, Salisbury, Southfield, Suffolk county, Taunton, Topsfield, Watertown, Yarmouth.
Middlesex county, England, 121.
Middlesex county, Mass., 76, 95, 143, 144.
Mousam river, 92.

Newbury, Mass., 35, 92, 93, 111, 135.
New Castle, N. H., 94.
New Hampshire, 66, 85, see Dover, Exeter, Great Island, Hampton, New Castle, Portsmouth, Strawberry Bank.
Newport, R. I., 61.
Newtown, 141.
Newto[w]n, Mass., 76.

New York, N. Y., 40.
  colony of, 58.
Norfolk county, Mass., 37.
Piscataqua harbor, 174.
Piscataqua river, 30, 33, 60, 61, 78, 88, 99, 100, 101, 121, 133, 137, 149, 154, 157, 162, 163, 164.
  Long Reach in, 88, 91, 94, 166.
Plymouth, England, 174.
Portsmouth, N. H., 38, 39, 46, 70, 71, 72, 73, 77, 82, 83, 84, 88, 89, 90, 91, 99, 100, 101, 102, 104, 105, 110, 114, 115, 118, 120, 121, 127, 128, 129, 138, 149, 151, 156, 157, 158, 159,

Rhode Island, 61, 62, 63, 64, see Feversham, Newport, Westerly.
Rumney Marsh, (Chelsea) Mass., 16.

Saco, 6, 11, 13, 47, 48, 50, 63, 80, 144.
  river, 6, 11, 13, 50, 61, 62, 63, 64, 80, 92.
  falls in, 11, 13.
  dock, 6.
  Goose-fair river, 80.
  Little river, 58, 59.
  Nichols brook, 11, 13.
  Parker's neck, 144.
  point, 6.
  Scadlock's river, 58, 59.
  West brook, 62, 63, 64.
  Whale cove, 58, 59.
  Winter harbor, 58, 59, 72.
Sagadahoc, 17, 140, 141, 174.
  river, 140.
  Long cove, 140, 141.
  Mill pool, 17.
Salem, Mass., 65, 95, 136, 139, 140, 141.
Salisbury, Mass., 134.
Scarborough, 2, 10, 11, 36, 65, 72, 73, 74, 79, 131, 132.
  Beaver-knucke river, 73.
  Black Point, 2, 37, 65, 72, 76, 131.
  river, 165.
  Dunstan falls, 79.

INDEX OF PLACES.

Scarborough, continued.
  Mill river, 72.
  Moore's brook, 132.
  neck, 73.
  Nonesuch, 73.
  Nonesuch marshes, 2.
    river, 73.
  Pine creek, 65.
  Pigsgut river, 10, 132.
  Spurwink, 73.
Shadwell, England, 173.
Small Point, 17.
Southfield, Salem, Mass., 136.
St. Andrew, Holbourn, England, 121.
Stratford, Conn., 13.
Strawberry Bank, (Portsmouth) N. H., 69, 85, 93, 149.
Suffolk county, England, 121.
Suffolk county, Mass., 16, 46, 48, 61, 62, 63, 64, 88, 89, 108, 109, 110, 112, 113, 132, 145, 174, 176.
Summertown, S. C., (?) 81.

Taunton, Mass., 48, 50, 111, 116.
Tom's island, Sagadahoc river, 140.
Topsfield, Mass., 135.

Unity Parish, 69.

Watertown, Mass., 21.
Wells, 5, 24, 25, 28, 35, 36, 40, 41, 48, 50, 92, 95, 107, 114, 115, 116, 134, 141, 145, 148, 165, 167.
  commons, 116, 167.
  Cross' creek, 48.
  Kennebunk, 24.
  Little river, 5, 95, 114, 146.
  Merryland, 142, 167.
  Orgunquit river, 116.
  Thatch island, 142.

Webhannet river, 48, 141, 167.
Westerly, R. I., 50.
Westminister, England, 174.
Winnegance, 58.
  river, 143, 144.

Yarmouth.
  Broad cove, 136.
Yarmouth, Mass., 143, 144.
York, 8, 14, 15, 16, 25, 26, 27, 31, 35, 40, 41, 42, 45, 51, 64, 72, 74, 75, 77, 82, 83, 85, 88, 90, 97, 108, 109, 110, 111, 119, 120, 123, 124, 125, 126, 127, 128, 135, 136, 137, 138, 142, 145, 151, 152, 158, 169, 175, 176.
  called Agamenticus, 74.
  bounds, 8, 137.
  bridge, 97, 127.
  river, 16, 31, 51, 75, 89, 97, 109, 124, 126, 128, 137, 142, 151, 169, 176.
  called Accamenticus river, 74, 150.
  Bald head, 152.
  Bass creek, 74.
  Brave-boat harbor, 78, 158.
  Burnt plain, 75.
  Dummer's cove, 143.
  Fall mill brook, 138.
  Farmer Alcock's neck, 81.
  Galloping hill, 151.
  Goose cove, 51.
  Gorges' point, 27.
  Hull's creek, 119, 126.
  Meeting-house creek, 90, 123.
  Mill creek, 82, 83.
  New mill creek, 41.
  Roger's cove brook, 128.
  Scituate marsh, 108, 109.
    plain, 108, 109.
  Spruce swamp, 41.

GENERAL INDEX.

Agents, 55.
Annuity, 68, 71, 97, 172.
Assistants, members of the Governor's Council:
  of Connecticut:
    Mason, Samuel, 50.
  of Massachusetts:
    Addington, Isaac, 173.
    Hathorn, John, 95.
    Pike, Robert, 148.
    Symonds, Samuel, 113.
    Tyng, Edward, 165.
Associates, Yorkshire Magistrates:
  Pendleton, Bryan, 7.
  Scottow, Joshua, 37.
  Wincoll, John, 38, 101.
Attorneys, 14, 15, 34, 40, 81, 108, 113, 145, 150, 170.

Berwick. See Index of Places.
  meeting-house, 46, 61, 102, 129.
  ministry lands, 46, 61, 102, 129.
  grants recorded, see Index of Grantors under names following:
    Abbot, Thomas, 54, 67.
    Bernard, Benjamin, 29.
    Chadborn, Humphrey, 18.
    Clark, John, 121.
    Clarke, Thomas, 21.
    Emery, James, 44, 88, 160.
    Emery, Job, 160.
    Goodwin, Daniel, 67, 67, 147.
    Goodwin, Moses, 84, 160.
    Goodwin, William, 68.
    Gowen, Nicholas, 171.
    Greely, Thomas, 170.
    Hill, John, 105.
    Hodsden, Benoni, 70, 160, 161.
    Hutchinson, Eliakim, 102.
    Mason, Robert Tufton, 174.
    Neale, John, 101, 101.
    Parkes, Thomas, 4.

Berwick—Grantors, continued.
    Plaisted, James, 136.
    Plaisted, John, 46, 104, 129.
    Rew, Rachel, 113.
    Sewall, Samuel, 112.
    Simpson, Daniel, 120.
    Spencer, Humphrey, 70, 122.
    Stagpoll, James, 61.
    Taylor, Martha, 68.
    Thompson, Miles, 45.
    Turbet, Nicholas, 68.
    Wincoll, John, 69.
  grants referred to:
    town (*i.e.*, Kittery) to George Broughton, 113.
    town (*i.e.*, Kittery) to Eliakim Hutchinson, 46, 175.
    town (*i.e.*, Kittery) to William Hutchinson, 46.
    town (*i.e.*, Kittery) to George Leader, 175.
    town (*i.e.*, Kittery) to Richard Leader, 175.
    town (*i.e.*, Kittery) to Roger Plaisted, 156.
    town (*i.e.*, Kittery) to Thomas Spencer, 121, 122.
    town (*i.e.* Kittery) to John Wincoll, 156.
    Joseph Bernard to Benjamin Bernard, 30.
    Thomas Broughton to George Cole, 121.
    Council of New England to Sir Ferdinando Gorges, 174.
    Nicholas Frost to George Broughton, 113.
    Daniel Goodwin to Daniel Goodwin junior, 67.
    Sir Ferdinando Gorges to John Mason, 174.
    Eliakim Hutchinson to John Emerson, 46.

Berwick—Grants, continued.
    Eliakim Hutchinson to Daniel Goodwin, 46.
    Eliakim Hutchinson to Berwick Ministry, 46.
    Ephraim Joy to James Stagpoll, 61.
    Robert Tufton Mason to Eliakim Hutchinson, 46.
    Sylvanus Nock to Nathan Lord, 161.
    Elizabeth Plaisted to John Plaisted, 156.
    Roger Plaisted to George Broughton, 113.
    Rowles, Indian, to Thomas Spencer, 121.
    Thomas Spencer to Thomas Broughton, 121.
    Thomas Spencer to Humphrey Spencer, 122.
    William Spencer to Ephraim Joy, 61.
    John Wincoll to Thomas Clarke, 21.
    John Wincoll to George Broughton, 113.
    John Wincoll to Roger Plaisted, 156.
Bridges, 32, 97, 101, 127, 170.
Buildings, houses, etc., 4, 14, 30, 38, 71, 73, 91, 118, 119, 133, 135, 149, 161, 163, 168.
    barns, 14, 16, 22, 24, 45, 68, 71, 86, 90, 107, 135, 172.
    dwelling-houses, 5, 6, 8, 14, 20, 22, 24, 32, 40, 60, 68, 73, 86, 87, 90, 99, 101, 107, 134, 160, 172.
    frames, 66, 119.
    out-houses, 14, 73, 119.
    stables, 22.

Cape Elizabeth. See Index of Places.
    grants recorded, see Index of Grantors under the names following:
    Fryer, Nathaniel, 169.
    Jordan, Sarah, 73.

Cape Porpoise. See Index of Places.
    grants recorded, see Index of Grantors under the names following:
    Batson, John, 50.
    Davis, Emmanuel, 76.
    Eliot, Robert, 76.
    Moorey, Nicholas, 111, 116.
    Rennals, John, 49.
    grants referred to:
    town to Nicholas Moorey, 117.
    to William Randall, 77.
    to Richard Young, 76, 77.
    Nicholas Cole to Thomas Wells, 35.
    Henry Hatherly to Richard Young, 76.
    John Renols to Nicholas Moorey, 117.
    Samuel Snow, Exe'r, to Nicholas Moorey, 111.
    Thomas Thurley to Thomas Wells, 35.
Captain General of New England:
    Andros, Sir Edmund, 73.
Clerk of Courts:
    Hammond, Joseph, 120.
    of Essex County:
    Sewall, Stephen, 135.
Commissioner of New Hampshire:
    Stileman, Elias, 20.
Compass, points of, 170.
Confirmation of previous titles to Inhabitants of Maine, authorized, 78.
Constitution, *i.e.*, of Lygonia, 3, 8.
    confirmed by supreme authority of England, 8.
Corn-mills:
    at Saco, 11.
    at York, 82, 83, 138, 145, 151, 152.
Costs of arbitration, 71.
    of court, 120.
Councillors of Massachusetts:
    Addington, Isaac, 47, 103, 132.
    Cooke, Elisha, 48.
    Hammond, Joseph, 39, 40, 41, 53, 54, 55, 59, 60, 61, 67, 68, 69, 70, 72, 82, 84, 87, 172.

General Index. 117

Councillors of Massachusetts, continued.
  Hathorn, John, 65.
  Phillips, John, 112.
  Sewall, Samuel, 62, 68, 132.
  Tyng, Edward, 2, 3.
  Walley, John, 132.
  Winthrop, Wait, 3.
Councillors of New England:
  Hincks, John, 159.
  Randolph Edward, 18, 32.
  Stoughton, William, 12, 36, 84.
  Tyng, Edward, 10, 11, 18, 25, 31, 85, 87.
  Usher, John, 35.
Councillors of New Hampshire:
  Elliot, Robert, 72.
  Hall, Kinsley, 69.
  Hincks, John, 4, 23.
  Waldron, Richard, 100.
Councillor of New York:
  Palmer, John, 58.
Courts:
  Inferior Court of Common Pleas, 120.
  Inferior Court of Common Pleas at Newbury, 135.
  Quarter Sessions held at Ipswich, 135.
  Superior, held at Boston, 66, 90.

Depositions:
  Abbot, Thomas, sen., 55.
  Allen, Robert, 87.
  Banfield, Christopher, 55.
  Beckham, Mary, 53.
  Brown, Susanna, 135.
  Burnum, Nathaniel, 135.
  Cock, John, 141.
  Cock, Thomas, 141.
  Denis, Lawrence, 141.
  Donnell, Samuel, 51.
  Emery, Daniel, 70, 71.
  Endicot, Gilbert, 49.
  Grant, Peter, 44.
  Hammond, Joseph, jun., 71.
  Hearle, John, 70.
  Heskins, Nicholas, 94.
  Johnson, James, 52.
  Jones, Deborah, 78.

Depositions, continued.
  Jones, Thomas, 38.
  Judd, Jonathan, 48.
  Kemble, Thomas, 19.
  Kennard, Edward, 94.
  Neale, Francis, 8.
  Pickerin, John, 158.
  Plaisted, James, 51.
  Pride, John, 48.
  Rice, Thomas, 52.
  Sargent, Edward, 72.
  Saywood, John, 15.
  Saywood, Mary, 15.
  Shapleigh, John, 19.
  Skid, James, 159.
  Tufton, Robert, 159.
  Tyng, Edward, 10, 11.
  Webber, Lydia, 53.
  White, John, 38.
  Wiggen, Thomas, 159.
Deputy Presidents
  of Maine:
    Davis, John, 79, 145.
  of New Hampshire:
    Stileman, Elias, 20.
Deputy Surveyor:
  Clements, Richard, 131.
Dock, 6.
Domestic animals:
  bull, 172.
  calves, 87.
  cattle, 45, 87, 135, 168.
  colt, 16.
  cows, 84, 87, 172.
  ewes, 45, 172.
  heifers, 135, 172.
  hogs, 45.
  horses, 135.
  lambs, 87, 172.
  mares, 16, 135.
  oxen, 12, 45, 47, 172.
  sheep, 45, 135, 172.
  sow, 135.
  steers, 172.
  swine, 45.
Double inheritance of the eldest son, 120.
Dower, set out, 71.

Eares, for heirs, 72.

General Index.

Falmouth. See Index of Places.
  grants recorded, see Index of Grantors under the names following:
    Bartlet, Nicholas, 139.
    Brackett, Anthony, jun., 87.
    Cleave, George, 3, 8, 139.
    Hodsden, Joseph, 85.
    Ingersoll, John, 1.
    Morough, Dennis, 3.
    Webber, Joseph, 143.
  grants referred to:
    town to Dennis Morough, 3.
    George Cleeve to Nicholas Bartlet, 140.
    George Cleeve to Michael Mitten, 3.
    Massachusetts to George and John Ingersoll, 1.
Fealty, 8.
Fees, sheriff's, 120.
Fences, 30, 40, 41, 71, 78, 87, 90, 101, 115, 118, 161, 170.
Ferry, 93.
Fish, mackerel, 133.
  merchantable, 133.
  refuse, 133.
Flake-room, 168.
Foot-path, 3, 6.
Freshets, 127.

Gardens, 68, 71, 73, 87, 172.
General Assembly of the Province, 111.
General Court of Massachusetts, 9, 37, 78, 89.
Gifts charged upon an estate, 135.
Governors:
  of Agamenticus:
    Hooke, William, 74.
  of Massachusetts:
    Andros, Sir Edmund, 73, 74, 131.
    Bradstreet, Simon, 22, 27.
    Endicott, John, 139.
  of New York:
    Dongan, Thomas, 58.
Grants referred to.
Grantors:
  Agamenticus, Proprietors, 74.
  Alcock, Joseph's estate, 31.

Grantors, continued.
  Atkins, Thomas, 17, 140, 141.
  Barfoot, Walter, 173.
  Bernard, Joseph, 30.
  Berwick, town of, 5, 95, 165.
  Blackman, Benjamin, 11.
  Bolls, Joseph, 116.
  Bragdon, Arthur, 15.
  Breaden, William, 48.
  Broughton, Thomas, 121.
  Brown, Andrew, 131.
  Bush, John, 112, 135.
  Cape Porpoise, town of, 76, 77, 117.
  Champernown, Francis, 94, 159, 173.
  Cleeve, George, 3, 140.
  Cole, Nicholas, 35.
  Council of New England, 174.
  Crocket, Ephraim, 32.
  Diament, John's estate, 100.
  Downing, Joshua, 146.
  Falmouth, town of, 3.
  Fletcher, Pendleton, 59.
  Fluellin, Indian, 135.
  Frost, Nicholas, 113.
  Frost, William, 141.
  Fryer, Nathaniel, 94.
  Goodwin, Daniel, 67.
  Gorges, Sir Ferdinando, 78, 167, 174.
  Greenland, Henry, 61.
  Hatherly, Henry, 76.
  Hellson, John, 6.
  Hilton, Richard, 91.
  Hooke, Francis, 169.
  Hughes, Arthur, 110.
  Hutchinson, Eliakin, 46.
  Jordan, Robert, 73, 73.
  Joslin, Abraham, 131.
  Joy, Ephraim, 61.
  King, Samuel, 39.
  Kittery, town of, 8, 23, 38, 43, 60, 65, 69, 71, 72, 81, 88, 91, 101, 102, 104, 106, 114, 115, 121, 127, 129, 144, 149, 150, 154, 159, 162, 163, 166, 167, 171, 172, 177.
  Knight, Robert, 26.
  Lake, Thomas, 80.
  Littlefield, James, 24.

General Index. 119

Grantors, continued.
  Lord, Abraham, 54.
  Lord, Nathan, 53, 55.
  Mason, Robert Tufton, 46, 104.
  Massachusetts, 1, 37.
  Moore, William, 169.
  New England Government, 58.
  Nock, Sylvanus, 161.
  Palmer, George, 61.
  Parker, John, 143.
  Phillips, William, 50, 61, 62, 63, 64.
  Plaisted, Elizabeth. 156.
  Plaisted, Roger, 113.
  Renols, John, 117.
  Rice, Thomas, 118, 149.
  Richards, John, 80.
  Rowles, Indian, 121.
  Sanders, John, 112, 135.
  Scarborough, town of, 79.
  Scottow, Joshua, 36, 80, 131.
  Shapleigh, Nicholas, 18.
  Skillin, John, 2.
  Small, Francis, 164.
  Smith, Jacob, 151.
  Snow, Samuel, 111.
  Spencer, Thomas, 121, 122.
  Spencer, William, 61.
  Spinney, James, 148.
  Spinney, Thomas, 98, 121, 157.
  Symonds, Harlakinden, 92, 92, 92, 135.
  Thurley, Thomas, 35.
  Tobey, Stephen, 118.
  Toziar, Richard, 145.
  Turbut, Peter, 112, 135.
  Wadleigh, John, 148.
  Wadleigh, Robert, 148.
  Wallis, Nathaniel, 136.
  Warren, Mehitable, 89, 91, 96, 118, 151, 155, 156.
  Watts, Henry, 72.
  Webber, Mary, 143, 144.
  Wells, town of, 5, 95, 165.
  Wheelwright, John, 41.
  Wheelwright, Samuel, 41.
  Wiggens, James, 169.
  Wincoll, John, 21, 55, 113, 156.
  Winthford, John, 145.
  Withers, Thomas, 52, 149.
  Woodbridge, Benjamin, 137.

Grantors, continued.
  York, town of, 14, 45, 51, 82, 83, 85, 97, 108, 109, 127, 128, 151, 169, 176.
Grantees:
  Abbot, Thomas, 53, 54, 55.
  Alcock, Job, 85.
  Austin, Matthew, 51.
  Baker, Thomas, 135.
  Baker, William, 143, 144.
  Bane, Lewis, 145.
  Banks, Richard, 108, 109.
  Barfoot, Walter, 159, 173.
  Bartlet, Nicholas, 140.
  Bernard, Benjamin, 30.
  Blackman, Benjamin, 11, 13, 79.
  Bragdon, Arthur, sen., 128.
  Bragdon, Arthur, jun., 127.
  Bready, John, 115.
  Broad, William, 61.
  Broughton, George, 113.
  Broughton, Thomas, 121.
  Buckland, John, 24.
  Burrage, William, 36, 131.
  Carle, Richard, 28.
  Chadborn, Humphrey, 18.
  Champernown, Francis, 78, 159.
  Clarke, Thomas, 21.
  Cock, William, 140, 141.
  Cole, George, 121.
  Cotten, John, 151.
  Croad, John, 136.
  Crocket, Ephraim, 8.
  Crocket, Hugh, 166, 167.
  Curtis, Thomas, 108, 109.
  Daniel, Thomas, 149.
  Davis, Isaac, 2.
  Deament, Joan, 146.
  Dorman, Timothy, 135.
  Downing, John, 91.
  Drown, Leonard, 55.
  Dummer, Shubael, 31.
  Ellingham, William, 101.
  Emerson, John, 46.
  Endicot, Gilbert, 145.
  Endle, Richard, 127.
  Folsham, Peter, 148.
  Freethy, James, 176.
  Frost, William, 5.
  Fryer, Nathaniel, 94.
  Fuller, Nathaniel, 92.

Grantees, continued.
  Gard, Roger, 74.
  Gillam, Benjamin, 61, 63.
  Goodwin, Daniel, 46.
  Goodwin, Daniel, jun., 67.
  Gorges, Sir Ferdinando, 174.
  Gowen, John, 43.
  Gowen, William, 43.
  Grant, James, 14.
  Greenland, Henry, 61.
  Gunnison, Elihu, 58.
  Gunnison, Hugh, 154.
  Harris, John, 92.
  Hatch, Samuel, 116.
  Hammond, Joseph, et als., 89, 91, 96, 118, 151, 155, 156.
  Hammond, Joseph, jun., 177.
  Heard, John, 60.
  Hill, Roger, 6.
  Hinckes. John, 94.
  Hooke, Francis, 169.
  Hutchins, Benjamin, 172.
  Hutchinson, Eliakim, 46, 102, 104, 106, 129, 175.
  Hutchinson, William, 46, 102, 104, 106, 129.
  Ingersoll, George, 1.
  Ingersoll, John, 1.
  Ingolls, Samuel, 92.
  Jefferys, Digory, 61.
  Jordan, Robert, jun., 73.
  Joy, Ephraim, 61.
  King, Richard, 71.
  Knight, Samuel, 22.
  Leader, George, 175.
  Leader, Richard, 175.
  Lee, John, 173.
  Littlefield, Francis, 141, 142, 167.
  Littlefield, Jonathan, 41.
  Littlefield, Nathan, 165.
  Lord, Nathan, 161.
  Mason, John, 174.
  Maverick, Antipas, 162, 168.
  Maverick, Samuel, 74.
  Maxell, Alexander, 15.
  Mendum, Robert, 163.
  Ministry of Berwick, 46.
  Mitten, Michael, 3.
  Monson, Richard, 118.

Grantees, continued.
  Moore, Thomas, 169.
  Moore, William, 45, 169.
  Moorey, Nicholas, 48, 111, 117.
  Morough, Dennis, 3.
  Munjoy, George, 164.
  Nason, John, 144.
  Nason, Jonathan, 144.
  Nason, Jonathan's estate, 53, 54, 55.
  Partridge, John, 110.
  Pendleton, Bryan, 50.
  Phares, Aaron, 114.
  Plaisted, James, 151.
  Plaisted, John, 156.
  Plaisted, Roger, 156.
  Pope, Richard, 59.
  Preble, Abraham, 108, 109.
  Prichett, John, 17.
  Randall, William, 77.
  Rones, William, 176.
  Samson, John, 73.
  Sanders, John, 81.
  Scottow, Joshua, 87, 131.
  Shapleigh, John, 52.
  Shapleigh, Nicholas, 88.
  Sharp, John, 72.
  Sheafe, Sampson, 11.
  Smith, Jacob, 118.
  Spencer, Humphrey, 122.
  Spencer, Thomas, 69, 121, 122.
  Spinney, James, 157.
  Spinney, Samuel, 65, 98.
  Spinney, Thomas, 100, 121, 148.
  Spinney, Thomas, jun., 121.
  Tetherly, Gabriel, 38.
  Thomas, Roger, 172.
  Thompson, Thomas, 149.
  Thurston, John, 187.
  Tinny, John, 80.
  Tobey, James, 150.
  Treworthy, Katherine, 101.
  Turner, Ephraim, 61, 62, 63, 64.
  Twisden, Samuel, 108, 109.
  Voden, Moses, 150.
  Waddock, Henry, 80.
  Waldron, Nicholas, 100.
  Warren, James, 97.
  Webber, Joseph, 144.
  Webber, Mary, 148.

GENERAL INDEX.   121

Grantees, continued.
  Wells, Thomas, 35.
  White, Richard, 32.
  Wiggens, James, 169.
  Wincoll, John, 156.
  Withers, Elizabeth, 149.
  Withers, Mary, 149.
  Wooden, John, 95.
  Young, Richard, 76, 77.
  Young, Rowland, 26.
Grinding of corn, 45.
Grist-mills, see Corn-mills.

Harpswell. See Index of Places, also, Merriconeag.
  grants recorded, see Index of Grantors, under the name following:
    Massachusetts, 9, 37.
  grants referred to:
    Massachusetts to Joshua Scottow, 37.
Highways, 4, 38, 41, 45, 60, 69, 71, 72, 87, 90, 93, 107, 141, 151, 160, 166, 167.
Household goods, supplies, wares, 101.
  movables, 45, 101.
Husbandry, appliances and products:
  tools for, 45, 71.
  butter, 172.
  cheese, 172,
  cider, 45, 87.
  corn, 135.
  grain, 45, 71, 87, 135.
  hay, 71.
  perry, 87.
  wood, 45, 67, 87, 170.
  wool, 45, 87, 172.

Improvements by tenants, 55, 87, 115, 172.
Indian purchases, 88, 121, 134, 135.
Indian War (King Phillip's), 9, 141.
  (King William's), 141.
Inrollment, registration, 3.
Interest at six per centum, 46.
  lawful, 165.
Isles of Shoals. See Index of Places.

Isles of Shoals, continued.
  grants recorded, see Index of Grantors, under the names following:
    Lewis, Peter, 168.
    Mitchell, William, 168.

Jamestown. See Index of Places.
  grant recorded, see Index of Grantors, under the name following:
    Gunnison, Elihu, 58.
  grant referred to:
    New England Government to Elihu Gunnison, 58.
Joce, joist, 127.
Joint tenancy, 1, 11, 37, 55, 67, 88, 96.
Judge of Probate:
  Wheelwright, Samuel, 124.
Judge of Courts of New Hampshire:
  Barfoote, Walter, 166.
Justices of the Peace.
  Alcock, Job, 88, 156.
  Champernown, Francis, 88.
  Donnell, Samuel, 108, 119, 123, 124, 125, 126, 127, 129, 145, 152, 169.
  Frost, Charles, 28, 45, 53, 67, 68, 87, 101, 102.
  Hammond, Joseph, 39, 40, 41, 43, 44, 52, 53, 54, 55, 56, 57, 59, 60, 61, 65, 67, 68, 69, 70, 71, 72, 77, 78, 82, 84, 85, 87, 88, 91, 95, 96, 97, 98, 99, 100, 111, 114, 115, 118, 119, 120, 121, 122, 133, 134, 136, 138, 139, 147, 148, 149, 150, 151, 153, 155, 156, 157, 161, 163, 170, 171, 172, 177.
  Hooke, Francis, 9, 21, 34, 45, 58, 59, 61, 96.
  Johnson, Edward, 88.
  Pepperrell, William, 42, 43, 80, 88, 90, 92, 114, 117, 127, 147, 154, 158, 164, 166, 167.
  Plaisted, Ichabod, 144, 160, 170, 171.
  Plaisted, John, 40, 53, 55, 138, 158, 160.

Justices of the Peace, continued.
  Preble, Abraham, 42, 75, 90, 109, 110, 115, 125, 128, 135, 143, 151, 152, 176.
  Rishworth, Edward, 15, 16, 19, 26, 29.
  Tyng, Edward, 1.
  Wheelwright,
    John, 116, 117, 146, 168.
    Samuel, 6, 13, 49, 50, 107, 116, 138, 142, 165, 167.
  Wincoll, John, 121.
Justices of the Peace, elsewhere in Massachusetts.
  Addington, Isaac, 47, 103, 132.
  Appleton, John, 75.
  Appleton, Samuel, 93.
  Brown, Benjamin, 140, 141.
  Brown, John, 48.
  Cooke, Elisha, 48.
  Corwin, Jonathan, 136.
  Dummer, Jeremiah, 48, 62, 64, 174, 176.
  Eyre, John, 49.
  Foster, John, 89.
  Hathorn, John, 65, 141.
  Hayman, Samuel, 76, 143.
  Peirce, Daniel, 72, 93, 111.
  Phillips, John, 112.
  Sargent, Peter, 112.
  Sewall, Samuel, 62, 63, 108, 132.
  Thacher, John, 144.
  Townsend, Penn, 113.
  Wade, Thomas, 92.
  Walley, John, 132.
Justices of the Peace of New Hampshire.
  Atkinson, Theodore, 94, 128, 168, 169.
  Chamberlain, R., 157.
  Coffin, Peter, 134.
  Fryer, Nathaniel, 168.
  Packer, Thomas, 38, 77, 166.
  Penhallow, Samuel, 60, 66, 73, 81, 86, 105, 107, 131, 163.
  Waldron, Richard, 100.
  Woodman, John, 162.

Kennebec region. See Index of Places.

Kennebec region, continued.
  grants recorded, see Index of Grantors under the names following:
    Webber, Joseph, 143.
    Webber, Mary, 143.
  grants referred to:
    John Parker to Mary Webber, 143.
    Mary Webber to William Baker, 143, 144.
    Mary Webber to Joseph Webber, 144.
Kittery. See Index of Places.
  meeting-house, 133.
  selectmen, 88, 144.
  town book, 43, 56, 57, 71, 85, 150, 171, 176.
  or records, 65, 114, 115, 120, 149, 158, 173.
  town clerk, 56, 57, 85, 98, 114, 138, 139, 149, 160.
  town meetings, 56, 57, 85, 98, 114, 138, 139, 149, 160.
  town grants, 56, 57, 85, 98, 114, 138, 139, 149, 160.
  other grants recorded, see Index of Grantors under the names following:
    Allen, Robert, 114.
    Allowell, Hezekiah, 138.
    Bamfield, Christopher, 154.
    Barfoot, Walter, 159.
    Blackdon, Joan, 146.
    Bodge, Henry, 120.
    Brawn, John, 138.
    Bredeen, James, 117.
    Briar, Richard, 153.
    Carle, Richard, 23.
    Champernown, Francis, 158.
    Champernown, Mary, 81.
    Crocket, Ephraim, 8.
    Crocket, Hugh, 129, 166, 167.
    Crocket, Joseph, 139.
    Curtis, Dodevah, 149.
    Deament, John's estate, 90.
    Dennett, Alexander, 114.
    Deniver, Walter, 56.
    Downing, John, 91.
    Endle, Richard, 127.
    Fernald, Samuel, 57.

Kittery—other grants, continued.
  Fernald, Samuel's estate, 99.
  Fogg, Daniel, 155.
  Fowler, Thomas, 173.
  Fry, Adrian, 87.
  Fryer, Nathaniel, 94.
  Gillman, Edward, 27.
  Gillman, Maverick, 162.
  Goodridge, Isaac, 39.
  Gowen, John, 43.
  Green, Daniel, 56.
  Gunnison, Elihu, 60, 153, 154.
  Hammond, Joseph, 89, 91.
  Hammond, Joseph, jun., 176.
  Harris, George, 20.
  Heard, John, 60, 100.
  Hill, Joseph, 133.
  Hilton, John, 158.
  Hilton, William, 157, 166.
  Hole, John, 20, 150.
  Hooper, Thomas, 42, 56.
  Hutchins, Benjamin, 172.
  Hutchins, Enoch, 44.
  Jeffry, Digory, 60.
  King, Richard, 71.
  Knight, Samuel, 22.
  Lee, John, 173.
  Libby, David, 151.
  Libby, Matthew, 156.
  Lord, Abraham, 53.
  Lord, Nathan, 161.
  Massachusetts, 78.
  Mendum, Jonathan, 12, 163.
  Monson, Richard, 118.
  Morgrage, John, 56.
  Morrell, John, 84.
  Morrell, Nicholas, 149.
  Munjoy, George, 164.
  Nason, John, 144.
  Nason, Jonathan's estate, 55, 171.
  Paul, Katherine, 162.
  Penhallow, Samuel, 39, 128.
  Phares, Aaron, 114.
  Remich, Christian, 66, 172.
  Roberts, William, 139.
  Sanders, William, 80.
  Shapleigh, John, 52, 78, 85, 88, 93.
  Shapleigh, Nicholas, 87.
  Sharp, John, 72.

Kittery—other grants, continued.
  Smith, Jacob, 57, 118.
  Spinney, James, 157.
  Spinney, Samuel, 65, 98.
  Spinney, Thomas, 98, 99, 99, 121, 134, 147.
  Staple, Peter, 97, 133.
  Tetherly, Gabriel, 38.
  Thomas, Roger, 172.
  Thompson, Thomas, 149.
  Thurston, Thomas, 137.
  Tobey, James, 171.
  Tobey, Stephen, 96.
  Tomson, John, 57.
  Treworthy, James, 115.
  Tucker, Nicholas, 163.
  Turbet, Nicholas, 68.
  Voden, Moses, 150.
  Wadleigh, Robert, 134.
  Walden, Nicholas, 100.
  Warren, Mehitable, 88.
  Waymouth, Edward, 170.
  Weekes, Joseph, 98.
  Weekes, Nicholas, 98.
  Whetherick, Richard, 81.
  White, Richard, 32.
  Withers, Jane, 95, 96.
grants referred to:
  town to John Bready, 115.
    Richard Carle, 23.
    Francis Champernown, 159.
    Ephraim Crocket, 8.
    John Downing, 91.
    William Ellingham, 101.
    Richard Endle, 127.
    John Gowen, 43.
    William Gowen, 43.
    Hugh Gunnison, 154.
    Joseph Hammond, jun., 177.
    John Heard, 60.
    Benjamin Hutchins, 172.
    Eliakim Hutchinson, 102, 104, 106, 129.
    William Hutchinson, 102, 104, 106, 129.
    Richard King, 71.
    Antipas Maverick, 162, 163.
    Robert Mendum, 163.
    John Nason, 144.
    Jonathan Nason, 144.
    John Sanders, 81.

Kittery—grants referred to, continued.
   town to Nicholas Shapleigh, 88.
   Thomas Spencer, 69.
   Samuel Spinney, 65.
   Thomas Spinney, 100, 121.
   Roger Thomas, 172.
   Thomas Thompson, 149.
   James Tobey, 171.
   Moses Voden, 150.
  Walter Barfoot to John Lee, 173.
  William Broad to Digory Jefferys, 61.
  Richard Carle to Samuel Knight, 22.
  Francis Champernown to Walter Barfoot, 159, 173.
  Francis Champernown to Nathaniel Fryer, 94.
  Ephraim Crocket to Richard White, 32.
  John Diament's estate to Nicholas Waldron, 100.
  Joshua Downing to Joan Deament, 146.
  Nathaniel Fryer to John Hinckes, 94.
  Sir Ferdinando Gorges to Francis Champernown, 78.
  Henry Greenland to William Broad, 61.
  Richard Hilton to John Downing, 91.
  Samuel King to Isaac Goodridge, 39.
  Abraham Lord to Thomas Abbot, and Jonathan Nason's estate, 54.
  Nathan Lord to Thomas Abbot and Jonathan Nason's estate, 53, 55.
  Robert Tufton Mason to Eliakim Hutchinson, 104.
  George Palmer to Henry Greenland, 61.
  Thomas Rice to Thomas Daniel, 149.
  Nicholas Shapleigh to Humphrey, Chadborne, 18.

Kittery—grants referred to, continued.
  Francis Small to George Munjoy, 164.
  Jacob Smith to John Cotten, 151.
  James Spinney to Thomas Spinney, 148.
  Thomas Spinney to James Spinney, 157.
  Thomas Spinney to Samuel Spinney, 98.
  Thomas Spinney to Thomas Spinney, jun., 121.
  Stephen Tobey to Jacob Smith, 118.
  Mehitable Warren et als. to Joseph Hammond et als. 89, 91, 96, 118, 151, 155, 156.
  John Wincoll to Leonard Drown, 55.
  Thomas Withers to John Shapleigh, 52.
  Thomas Withers to Elizabeth and Mary Withers, 149.
  Benjamin Woodbridge to John Thurston, 137.

Laws of the Province cited, 51, 64, 71.
Letter.
  John Pickerin to town of York, 82.
Life estate, created, 19.
  reserved, 19, 61, 68, 87, 170, 172.
Limited warranty, 1, 22.
Livery of seizin, 34.
  by turf and twig, 23, 49, 79, 147.
Lord Proprietor of the Province, 8, 27, 84.
  Sir Ferdinando Gorges, 27, 78, 150.
  Massachusetts Bay Company, 78.
  in case one should appear, 91.
Low water mark, 86.
Lyman. See Index of Places; also Coxhall.
  grants recorded, see Index of Grantors under the names following:
   Fuller, Nathaniel, 92.

General Index. 125

Lyman—grants rec'd, continued.
  Harris, John, 93.
  Ingolls, Samuel, 92.
  Symonds, Harlakinden, 95, 112, 135.
  grants referred to:
    Fluellin, Indian, to Harlakinden Symonds, 135.
    John Bush, Peter Turbut, and John Sanders to Harlakinden Symonds, 112, 135.
    Harlakinden Symonds to Thomas Baker and Timothy Dorman, 135.
    Harlakinden Symonds to Nathaniel Fuller, 92.
    Harlakinden Symonds to John Harris, 92.
    Harlakinden Symonds to Samuel Ingolls, 92.
Maine.
  See under Associates; Clerk of Courts; Courts; Deputy Presidents; Deputy Surveyor; General Assembly; Governors; Judge of Probate; Justices of the Peace; Laws of the Province; Lord Proprietor; President; Recorder; Registers of Deeds; Sheriff; Steward General; York County records.
Manumission of a negro slave, 88.
Marked trees, 1, 8, 9, 25, 52, 61, 118, 134, 142, 158, 160, 162.
Market, 85, 93.
Marriage portion, 74, 170, 171.
  settlement, 37, 124.
Massachusetts Bay, Governor and Company of, 9, 78.
  called Lord Proprietor of Maine, 78.
  authorize confirmation of previous titles to inhabitants of Maine, 78.
  grants by, 9, 87, 78.
  See also under Assistants; Clerk of Courts; Councillors; Courts; Deputy Presidents; General Court; Governors; Justices of the Peace; Laws

Massachusetts Bay, continued.
  of the Province; Lord Proprietor; Notaries Public; Registers of Deeds; Secretaries.
Mast-ways, 91, 127, 147.
Meeting-house at Berwick, 46, 61, 102, 129.
Meeting-house at Kittery, 133.
Michaelmas, 3.
Mill-pool, 17.
Mill implements, appurtenances and products.
  boards, 46, 47, 52, 127.
  dams, 22, 46, 72, 82, 83, 138.
  flumes, 22, 138.
  gears, 22, 47.
  iron work, 138.
  joist, 127.
  landing place, 52, 154.
  logs, 46, 52.
  plank, 47, 127.
  timber, 46, 47, 127.
  toll for grinding corn, 82, 83.
Mines, 61, 63.
Ministry, land for support of in Berwick, 46, 61, 102, 129.
Minority, 58, 99.
Moorings, 168.

Negro, 43, 88.
New England, manner of, for selling land in plain and open market, 85, 93, 163.
New England, Dominion and Territory of.
New England, grant by the government of, 78.
  see also under Captain General; Councillors; Deputy Surveyor; Secretaries.
New Hampshire. See under Commissioner; Councillors; Deputy President; Judge; Justices of the Peace; Secretaries.
New York. See under Councillors; Governors.
Notaries Public.
  Howard, Robert, 139.
  Valentine, John, 64.

Ore, gold and silver, the fifth reserved to the king, 46, 174.
Occupations.
 baker, 17.
 blacksmith, 54, 124, 137.
 brazier, 61, 62, 63, 64.
 bricklayer, 84.
 carpenter, 97, 111, 128, 147, 153, 157, 158.
 chirurgeon, surgeon, 158.
 clerk, *i.e.*, minister, 31, 73, 167.
 cordwainer, 5, 110, 121, 123, 134, 147, 163.
 doctor, 61, 121.
 ferryman, 10.
 fisherman, 6, 25, 49, 75, 79, 114, 128, 139, 168, 169.
 goldsmith, 21.
 house-carpenter, 71, 95.
 husbandman, 26, 61, 64, 76, 91, 95, 100, 108, 109, 145.
 inn-holder, 136, 167.
 joiner, 149.
 laborer, 172.
 locksmith, 93.
 mariner, 5, 11, 16, 42, 43, 48, 58, 60, 61, 62, 63, 64, 69, 76, 85, 132, 137, 159, 166, 173.
 mercer, 79.
 merchant, 11, 13, 21, 32, 34, 46, 47, 87, 88, 90, 91, 102, 104, 112, 121, 129, 131, 132, 136, 139, 140, 150, 165, 174.
 millwright, 44, 116, 134.
 minister, 31, 35, 61, 69, 70.
 planter, 6, 15, 17, 23, 24, 66, 69, 72, 87, 114, 116, 127, 148, 167, 168, 172.
 plasterer, 119.
 preacher, 135.
 saddler, 152.
 sailor, 124.
 seaman, 108, 109.
 shipwright, 3, 20, 38, 56, 57, 58, 60, 71, 85, 86, 93, 128, 136, 153, 154, 162, 163, 167.
 shopkeeper, 38, 127.
 surveyor, 38, 44, 60, 127, 131, 152.
 tailor, 88, 100.
 tanner, 115, 170.

Occupations, continued.
 turner, 91.
 vintner, 69, 110.
 waiter, 173.
 weaver, 75, 90, 92.
 yeoman, 3, 20, 21, 29, 31, 39, 42, 43, 44, 50, 52, 54, 60, 65, 79, 81, 84, 86, 93, 98, 99, 107, 111, 114, 121, 123, 134, 141, 143, 149, 153, 154, 157, 161, 162, 163, 165, 166, 169, 172.
Orchards, 45, 68, 71, 87, 118, 172.

Partnerships, 26, 47, 50, 55, 96, 109, 118, 126, 138, 156.
Patent of Agamenticus, 74.
 to the Council of New England, 174.
 to Sir Ferdinando Gorges, 174.
Pay:
 balance of accounts, 151.
 beef, 68.
 bill or note, 35, 116, 167, 168.
 cider, 68.
 colt, 16.
 current, 14, 20, 100, 135, 138.
  lawful, 158.
 current money, 10, 17, 29, 35, 39, 46, 47, 48, 51, 52, 54, 55, 63, 64, 66, 67, 72, 79, 84, 85, 86, 88, 90, 93, 94, 95, 102, 106, 109, 116, 122, 129, 132, 137, 143, 155, 156, 160, 168, 171, 175, 176.
 equivalent to money, 90, 125, 151.
 fish, 20.
 goods, 20, 110.
 headings, 83.
 hides, 138.
 Indian corn, 68.
 land in exchange, 24, 98, 99, 161.
 mare, 16, 72, 95.
 Mexico pillars, 46.
 money, 8, 19, 22, 26, 28, 39, 41, 43, 49, 51, 56, 61, 68, 69, 73, 75, 80, 84, 90, 92, 95, 99, 107, 109, 110, 114, 118, 121, 125, 127, 128, 135, 139, 142, 145, 147, 149, 150, 153, 154, 158, 162.

Pay, continued.
  pieces of eight, 46.
  pine boards, 79.
  pork, 68.
  provisions, 23, 68.
  secured, 7, 13, 28, 68, 107, 116, 119, 126, 128, 145, 148, 176.
  Seville pillars, 46.
  staves, 83, 84.
Pieces of eight, equal six shillings, and to contain 17 dwt. Troy, 46.
Pine trees reserved for masts for the King's ships, 46, 102, 104, 106, 129, 175.
Plans, surveyors, 46, 70, 89, 102, 129, 131.
President of Maine, 1.
  Danforth, Thomas, 78, 79.
Price:
  money price, 83.
  pieces of eight, 46.
  vessel of 45 tons, 5.

Recorder of the Province, Rishworth, Edward, 115.
Referees, 71, 87.
Registers of Deeds:
  Hammond, Joseph, sen., 38-57.
  Hammond, Joseph, jun., 57-177.
  Preble Abraham, 165.
  Scottow, Thomas, deputy register, 1-37.
  of Essex County:
    Sewall, Stephen, 140, 141.
  of Suffolk County:
    Davenport, Additon, 62.
    Webb, Joseph, 62, 63.
Rent, arrears of, 82, 83.
  one farthing per acre, 8.
  one pepper corn, 62.
  quit rents, 46, 58, 103, 105, 106, 131, 150, 175.
  service, 3, 74, 78, 130, 139.
  winter wheat, 74.
Reservations, 53, 67, 78, 87, 91, 135, 154, 156.
Reversions, 65, 97, 152.
Rights of way, 38, 72, 86, 150.
  for water, 8.

Saco. See Index of Places.
  grants recorded, see Index of Grantors under the names following:
    Blakeman, Benjamin, 13.
    Fletcher, Pendleton, 58.
    Hellson, John's estate, 7.
    Hill, Roger, 6.
    Pendleton, James, 50.
    Pope, Richard's estate, 59.
    Sheafe, Sampson, 11.
    Tinny, John, 79.
    Turfrey, George, 47.
    Turner, Ephraim, 61, 62, 63, 64.
    Webber, Joseph, 143.
  grants referred to:
    Benjamin Blackman to Sampson Sheafe, 11.
    Pendleton Fletcher to Richard Pope, 59.
    James Gibbens and John Bonighton to Benjamin Blackman, 11, 13.
    John Hellson to Roger Hill, 6.
    William Phillips to Bryan Pendleton, 50.
    William Phillips to Ephraim Turner and Benjamin Gillam, 61, 63.
    William Phillips to Ephraim Turner, 62, 64.
    John Richards, Thomas Lake and Joshua Scottow to Henry Waddock, 80.
    Henry Waddock's estate to John Tinny, 80.
Sagadahoc region.
  grants recorded, see Index of Grantors under the names following:
    Cock, William, 140.
    Prichett, John, 16.
  grants referred to:
    Thomas Atkins to John Prichett, 17.
    Thomas Atkins to William Cock, 140, 141.
Saw-mills.
  at Berwick, 21, 22, 47, 102, 104, 106, 121, 129, 175.

Saw-mills, continued.
  at Cape Porpoise, 50.
  at Falmouth, 1.
  at Kittery, 52, 154.
  at Saco, 11, 13, 47.
  at Salem, 136.
  at Scarborough, 72, 74.
  at Wells, 5.
  at York, 127, 138, 151, 152.
Scarborough, see Index of Places.
  grants recorded, see Index of Grantors under the names following:
    Atwater, Joshua, 79.
    Brown, Andrew, 72, 165.
    Burregh, William, 37.
    Davis, Isaac, 1.
    Hinckson, Peter, 64.
    New England Government, 73.
    Scottow, Joshua, 131.
    Scottow, Thomas, 132.
    Start, John, 10.
  grants referred to:
    Town to Benjamin Blackman, 79.
    Andrew Brown to Joshua Scottow, 131.
    Robert Jordan to Robert Jordan, jun., 73.
    Robert Jordan to John Samson, 73.
    Abraham Joslin to Joshua Scottow, 131.
    Joshua Scottow to William Burrage, 36.
    John Skillin to Isaac Davis, 2.
    Henry Watts to John Pickerin, 72.
Secretaries:
  of Massachusetts,
    Rawson, Edward, 9, 37.
  of New England,
    West, John, deputy secretary, 74, 159, 165.
  of New Hampshire,
    Chamberlain, R., 157.
Sheriff of the County:
  Curtis, Joseph, 120.
St. Michael's Day, 62.
Stage-room, 168.
Statute of Uses, cited, 62.

Stepping stones, 17, 61.
Support and maintenance, 4, 26, 45, 68, 74, 87, 97, 101, 123, 135.
Tenancy in common, 5, 11, 13, 58, 67, 96, 104, 121.
Timber grants, 11, 22, 46, 50, 79, 82, 112, 127, 175.
Titles.
  captain, 9, 21, 38, 40, 42, 44, 46, 50, 55, 65, 72, 73, 74, 83, 84, 94, 98, 100, 102, 103, 104, 105, 106, 116, 122, 125, 126, 127, 128, 129, 130, 132, 136, 137, 153, 156, 158, 174, 175.
  captain-general, 74.
  colonel, 58.
  ensign, 67, 176.
  esquire, 27, 41, 46, 58, 73, 78, 79, 88, 89, 91, 92, 94, 102, 106, 112, 120, 128, 130, 138, 139, 149, 150, 158, 159, 163, 166, 169, 173, 174.
  gentleman, 2, 8, 40, 52, 78, 85, 93, 94, 95, 104, 105, 112, 113, 139, 157, 158, 164, 169.
  gentlewoman, 150.
  goodman, 40, 176.
  lieutenant, 78, 82, 98, 120.
  lieutenant-colonel, 74.
  madam, 149.
  major, 18, 21, 43, 50, 60, 61, 62, 63, 64, 80, 88, 90, 92, 93, 112, 124, 125.
  Mr., 3, 4, 9, 10, 12, 13, 19, 20, 21, 22, 38, 41, 44, 51, 52, 58, 59, 60, 61, 62, 63, 69, 70, 71, 72, 75, 77, 78, 82, 83, 84, 85, 86, 88, 90, 92, 93, 95, 96, 98, 99, 100, 107, 110, 114, 116, 117, 119, 121, 122, 123, 135, 137, 138, 139, 145, 146, 149, 152, 153, 154, 159, 162, 163, 164, 165, 167, 169.
  Mrs., 39, 41, 42, 43, 73, 81, 82, 89, 91, 95, 96, 101, 118, 137, 151, 155, 156, 158, 163, 167, 176.
  spinster, 108, 109, 175.
  steward-general, 78, 150.
  widow, 25, 51, 81, 88, 95, 143, 144.

Toll for grinding corn, 82.
Trustees, 19, 37.

Vessels:
  boats, 6.
  brigantine, 5, 6.

Wading-place, 80.
Wages, 82.
Watercourses, 46.
Wells, see Index of Places.
  town-book, 95.
  grants recorded, see Index of Grantors under names following:
    Ashleigh, William, 107.
    Breaden, William. 48.
    Buckland, John, 24, 28.
    Folsham, Peter, 148.
    Frost, William, 5.
    Gooch, Benjamin, 114.
    Hatch, Samuel, 116.
    Littlefield, Francis, 141, 167.
    Littlefield, John, 116.
    Littlefield, Moses, 167.
    Littlefield, Nathan, 165.
    Moorey, Nicholas, 48.
    Wadleigh, Robert, 134.
    Wells, John, 145.
    Wheelwright, Samuel, 40.
    Wooden, John, 95.
  grants referred to:
    town to William Frost, 5.
      to Nathan Littlefield, 165.
      to John Wooden, 95.
    Thomas Averil to Francis Littlefield, 142.
    Joseph Bolls to Samuel Hatch, 116.
    William Breaden to Nicholas Moorey, 48.
    William Frost to Francis Littlefield, 141.
    Sir Ferdinando Gorges to Francis Littlefield, 167.
    James Littlefield to John Buckland, 24.
    John and Robert Wadleigh to Peter Folsham, 148.
    John and Samuel Wheelwright to Jonathan Littlefield, 41.

Wills referred to:
  Francis Champernown, 42, 153.
  George Cole, 121.
  Abraham Conley, 58.
  Joseph Cross, 48.
  Samuel Fernald, 99.
  James Grant, 51, 77.
  John Hellson, 7.
  Robert Mendum, 164.
  Bryan Pendleton, 50.
  John Taylor, 68.

Yarmouth, see Index of Places.
  grant recorded, see Index of Grantors under the name following:
    Croad, John, 136.
  grant referred to:
    Nathaniel Wallis to John Croad, 136.
Yeares, for heirs, 40.
York. See Index of Places.
  selectmen, 82, 83, 85, 97, 128, 152.
  stipulations for grinding town's corn, 83.
  town clerk, 82, 152.
  town meeting, 82, 127.
  town records, 51, 82, 85, 108, 145, 132.
  votes by, 82, 83.
  town grants, 83, 137, 152.
  other grants recorded, see Index of Grantors under the names following:
    Agamenticus Colony, 74.
    Alcock, Job, 40, 85.
    Alcock, John, 81.
    Austin, Matthew, 51.
    Banks, Richard's estate, 123.
    Bass, Peter's estate, 111.
    Black, Daniel, 90.
    Bracy, John, 88.
    Bragdon, Arthur, sen., 14, 128.
    Bragdon, Arthur, jun., 109, 125, 126.
    Braun, John, 126.
    Cooper, Philip, 108.
    Curtis, Dodevah, 108, 149.
    Cutt, Richard, 57.
    Danforth, Thomas, 26.

York—other grants, continued.
  Dill, Daniel, 124, 135.
  Endicot, Gilbert, 145.
  Gorges, Sir Ferdinando, 150.
  Johnson, Samuel, 51, 77.
  March, James, 152.
  Massachusetts, 78.
  Maxell, Alexander, 15, 15.
  Moore, Thomas, 119, 142, 169.
  Moore, William's estate, 45.
  Partridge, John, 110.
  Pickerin, John, 138, 151.
  Plaisted, James, 151.
  Preble, Abraham, jun., 126.
  Raynes, Francis, 158.
  Rones, Elizabeth, 175.
  Simpson, Daniel, 123, 176.
  Simpson, Jane, 74.
  Southerine, Thomas, 75.
  Toziar, Richard, 41.
  Warren, James, 97.
  Weare, Joseph, 124.
  Winford, John, 145.
  Wise, Thomas, 75.
  Wright, Henry, 110, 128.
  Wright, Mary, 75.
  Young, Rowland, 25.
  grants referred to:
    town to Job Alcock, 85.
      to Matthew Austin, 51.
      to Richard Banks, Thomas Curtis, Samuel Twisden and Abraham Preble, 108, 109.
      to Arthur Bragdon, sen., 128.
      to Arthur Bragdon, jun., 127.

York—grants referred to, continued.
  town to James Freethy, 176.
    to James Grant, 14.
    to William Moore, 45.
    to John Pickerin and James Plaisted, 151.
    to William Rones, 176
    to James Warren, 97.
    to Webb, Clark, Sayward, Gail & Ellingham, 82, 83.
  Agamenticus Proprietors to Roger Gard, 74.
  Agamenticus Proprietors to Samuel Maverick, 74.
  Joseph Alcock's estate to Shubael Dummer, 31.
  Arthur Bragdon to Alexander Maxell, 15.
  Francis Hooke to William Moore, 169.
  Arthur Hughes to John Partridge, 110.
  Robert Knight to Rowland Young, 26.
  William Moore to Thomas Moore, 169.
  Richard Toziar to Lewis Bane, 145.
  James Wiggens to Francis Hooke, 169.
  John Winthford to Gilbert Endicot, 145.
York County. See under Maine.
  records, 92, 115, 119, 151.

7

CPSIA information can be obtained
at www.ICGtesting.com
Printed in the USA
LVHW081013100521
686793LV00049B/82